D1233303

MATERNAL JUSTICE

MATERNAL JUSTICE

Miriam Van Waters and the
Female Reform Tradition

Estelle B. Freedman

The University of Chicago Press
Chicago and London

ESTELLE B. FREEDMAN is professor of history at Stanford University. She is the author of *Their Sisters Keepers*, co-author with John D'Emilio of *Intimate Matters*, and editor of *The Lesbian Issue: Essays from Signs*, published by the University of Chicago Press.

The University of Chicago Press, Chicago 60637
The University of Chicago Press, Ltd., London
© 1996 by Estelle B. Freedman
All rights reserved. Published 1996
05 04 03 02 01 00 99 98 97 96   1 2 3 4 5
ISBN 0-226-26149-2 (cloth)

Library of Congress Cataloging-in-Publication Data

Freedman, Estelle B., 1947–
    Maternal justice : Miriam Van Waters and the female reform
tradition / Estelle B. Freedman.
        p.   cm.
    Includes bibliographical references and index.
    1. Van Waters, Miriam.   2. Prison reformers—United States—
Biography.   3. Women correctional personnel—United States—
Biography.   4. Women social reformers—United States—Biog-
raphy.   5. Female offenders—Rehabilitation—United
States—History.
I. Title.
HV8978.V35F74   1996
365′.43′0973—dc20   95-49171
                                                          CIP

⊗This book is printed on acid-free paper.

For my mother, Martha H. Freedman,
and to the memories of
Annette Kar Baxter
and
Michelle Zimbalist Rosaldo

CONTENTS

Contents

PROLOGUE

In 1973, when I was a graduate student studying the origins of separate women's prisons in America, I first visited the Massachusetts Correctional Institution at Framingham. I was looking for historical documents about the founding of this nineteenth-century women's prison and the so-called fallen women who had been incarcerated there. The staff sent me to the librarian, Anne Gladding, a warm and charming white-haired woman in her sixties who had been working at Framingham for forty years. Miss Gladding put herself at my service, locating annual reports and mentioning some dusty old ledger books in the basement that turned out to be a gold mine of inmate records. I spent days poring over these sources, fairly oblivious to the prison world around me.

One day, when I reentered the library, Miss Gladding called me aside as if to show me a special find. "I don't know if you've read about Dr. Van Waters and her work at Framingham," she said, "but she is still living in this area, and if you'd like to meet her, I could possibly arrange an introduction." The name Van Waters rang a bell. It appeared on lists of prominent women reformers in the field of penology but had not come up in my current research. "When was Dr. Van Waters here?" I asked somewhat skeptically. Miss Gladding answered with gleaming eyes and a tinge of pride: "She came as superintendent in the 1930s, just before I arrived." I stood there in conflict for a moment, not wanting to disappoint the librarian, but determined that my dissertation research would not reach beyond 1920 if I was ever to get through graduate school. And so I refused her offer, explaining that I was interested in the period from 1870 to 1920, and I would leave the modern era for another project.

A year later, in 1974, Miriam Van Waters died at the age of eighty-seven. Since her retirement in 1957 she had been living in an apartment in Framingham with two women, then in their sixties, who had once served time at the prison and then became trusted staff members. Reporting on her death, the *Boston Globe* recalled the days when Van Waters' name had made daily headlines in the area. A friend of mine sent the obituary, thinking it might be of interest to me. I filed it away, and for years I forgot about Miriam Van Waters. When I finished *Their Sisters' Keepers,* my book on the origins of women's prisons, I vowed never to do research on such a depressing topic again. Women's prison reform, I had concluded, could never live up to the ideals of its founders, who sought better, more feminine care for women inmates. Even the most progressive "reformatory" institutions, I felt, remained prisons at heart.

Eventually, almost unwillingly, my research would bring me back to women's prisons and to Miriam Van Waters. Studying early inmate records had made me curious about the differential labeling of women's crimes, which were largely sexual offenses, such as prostitution. In teaching women's history and thinking about the regulation of female sexuality, I wondered what happened to the category of crimes against chastity after the so-called sexual revolution of the early twentieth century. If the boundary of proper female behavior shifted to allow, even encourage, heterosexual activity, were there new boundaries forming? If so, what happened to prostitution, and when did a new taboo emerge concerning female homosexuality? These kinds of questions led to a larger study, *Intimate Matters: A History of Sexuality in America,* which preoccupied me during the 1980s.

In the meantime, the papers Miriam Van Waters had donated to the Schlesinger Library at Radcliffe College had been carefully cataloged. Once, while I was at the library, I thought about browsing through some of Van Waters' files for information on women's crime in the twentieth century. Among dozens of boxes of personal and professional papers, I discovered psychiatric reports on inmates. They appeared to be collated as a defense of prison policy during the late 1940s, when Van Waters fought dismissal from her job as superintendent of the Framingham reformatory. I wasn't sure what to make of the sources, but I knew there was a story behind them. Perhaps it would be worth learning more about Miriam Van Waters after all.[1]

By the time of my next research trip to the library, in 1983, I was fighting for my own job. For over a year I had been embroiled in a devastating tenure case that was undermining my ability to do historical work. My fate was then in the hands of a university official who was investigating my grievance that sex discrimination had influenced the administration to reverse my department's recommendation of tenure. Local and national newspapers had covered the case as a fight over the legitimacy of feminist scholarship, leaving me feeling exposed and highly vulnerable. When I left for a research trip to the Schlesinger Library, I had just spent months preparing the grievance with my lawyer. I had exhausted my financial and emotional resources, surviving through the critical support of friends and loyal colleagues. This research trip was like a vacation from hell, a chance to immerse myself in the past and try to recover my intellectual grounding.

As soon as I got to the East Coast I went to the library to make a quick foray into those psychiatric records in the papers of Miriam Van Waters. But what I found drew me into surrounding files, and then more deeply into the Van Waters case. In 1949, a new commissioner of corrections had dismissed Van Waters from the superintendency of the Massachusetts Reformatory for Women. She did not go quietly. Van Waters appealed all the way to the governor, defending her administration from charges that she overstepped her authority, hired known criminals, condoned homosexuality among inmates, and allowed women to work for wages outside the institution. Day after day I read the documents of the case, including her correspondence with her lawyer, the fund-raising appeals and letters from her supporters, the news clippings on the investigation, and accounts of the public hearings at which Van Waters stood up for her record. I felt as if I were reading my own files back home, except here the distance of time and space made them tolerable. I read empathetically, eager to learn the outcome of the case, and I felt triumphant at Van Waters' reinstatement by the governor. The Van Waters case provided an emotional catharsis I had deeply needed. In a sense, my own tenure victory, a few weeks after I returned from the library, felt anticlimactic.

Empathy and identification drew me to the Van Waters case, and so I wrote a conference paper that used her ordeal to examine attitudes toward women's authority and homosexuality in the period after World War II. I thought I would stop there and leave Miriam Van Waters for good. But some historical instinct, some desire for the "whole story," made me go back yet again to look further into the vast sources preserved at the archives. I knew that Van Waters had left diaries that were closed to readers during the lifetime of her youngest brother, Ralph. I called him and asked for permission to read the diaries, and he granted it. Once I began to read these documents of Van Waters' internal life, to recognize the disparity between the confident, buoyant public persona and the agonized private soul, it became hard to turn back. For several years, as I wrote the sexuality book, working my way through the Van Waters papers became an avocation, what I did for "fun" in an effort to comprehend this public saint and savior of the imprisoned. I told myself that I was not writing a biography, but over the years I reluctantly admitted that I wanted to write about Miriam Van Waters' life.

My reluctance as a biographer had something to do with my training as a social historian. I entered the profession at a time when the new social history exulted the study of the masses of people, especially marginal groups and women. Writing a biography, the study of just one life, and that of an elite, white woman, seemed almost frivolous. Yet the personal draw remained strong, though no longer through identification, for I had come to see little in common between me and this spiritually devout Episcopalian reformer who did not even call herself a feminist. Rather, a quest for historical understanding had taken hold, in part because Van Waters seemed to contradict everything I had earlier concluded about women's prison reform. She had entered the field after 1920, when I thought reform had all but disappeared, and she reinvigorated it during the 1930s and 1940s. Her worldview defied the distinctions typically drawn between reformers who favored equal rights and those who emphasized female difference rooted in maternalism. The clear evidence throughout her career of the role women's networks played in fostering reform revised my older interpretation of the postsuffrage era.[2] And the discovery that Van Waters had a deeply romantic relationship with one of her benefactors, Geraldine Thompson, but did not identify as a lesbian, forced me to think about the limits of the sexual categories that have been read onto the past.

The path toward biography was thus encouraged by my recognition that Miriam Van Waters' life allowed me to write about a much larger and still neglected historical subject: women's persistent quest for social justice during the twentieth century, which drew upon both maternal roles and women's separate institutions. Miriam Van Waters, I learned, revealed a great deal about the fate of a reform tradition that had originated in the nineteenth-century female voluntary organizations that provided social services to poor women and children. Although dominated by white, Protestant, middle-class women, this tradition was extensive within the black, Jewish, and Catholic middle-classes, as well. Despite the centrality of class relations in these efforts to ameliorate the impact of industrialism, most reformers spoke a language of gender, rather than class. Even among minority groups that also combated racial and religious discrimination, female reformers drew upon a rhetoric of maternalism, emphasizing women's public roles as mothers. By the twentieth century, historians have argued, maternalism had helped expand women's public authority within their communities and, especially for the white Protestant majority, within the larger political culture.[3]

Miriam Van Waters' career illuminates what happened to this female reform tradition in the twentieth century. Highly educated, socially conscious, and professional "new women" like Van Waters, often aided by older women patrons, applied their professional training to modern movements for social change. In the process they continued to rely on the domestic-based rhetoric of maternalism and the voluntarist tradition. Against the trend of professionalized social work, Van Waters and her colleagues kept alive not only personalized social service but also the religious values that had influenced reform movements since at least the 1820s. Often dispersed within local rather than national campaigns, these reformers survived the waning of progressivism. Through churches, charities, and even prison reform, they delivered social services to women and children who were left untouched by the nascent American welfare system. After 1932, both the New Deal and a class-based leftist politics seemed to displace middle-class women's national prominence as reformers. But locally, women like Van Waters combined the earlier voluntarist model with the limited political authority women had gained with suffrage. They also combined maternalist with equal-rights rhetoric, recognizing implicitly the interdependence of these strategies.[4] The Van Waters case of 1949 illustrates the vulnerability of this female reform tradition in the wake of both the resurgent domesticity and the political and sexual conformism fostered by postwar anticommunism.

Miriam Van Waters championed maternal justice, or personal salvation through maternal love, instead of punishment, for women accused of crime. Her career began in the juvenile justice movement of the Progressive Era. She played a central role in the Los Angeles Juvenile Court, both as a referee—the term for a female judge—and as the founder of a nationally known alternative school for delinquent girls. During the 1920s her widely read works, including *Youth in Conflict* and *Parents on Probation,* popularized a new psychological explanation of delinquency. She then served as president of the National Conference on Social Work, as a member of private and governmental commissions on crime, and as an officer of the American League to Abolish Capital Punishment. Like other women who gained administrative authority after suffrage, she learned painful lessons about the limits of reform under conservative political administrations.

By the time she accepted the superintendency of the Massachusetts Reformatory for Women at Framingham, in 1931, Van Waters had achieved national prominence. In an era of supposed quiescence in the women's movement, she established an experiment in social reform in Massachusetts, linked politically to the women of the New Deal through the friendship between her patron, Geraldine Thompson, and Eleanor Roosevelt. For twenty-five years Van Waters applied progressive educational principles to prison administration in an effort to redeem the inmates she called "students" through her unique "Christian penology." A "child-centered institution" that encouraged mother-child ties, she believed, could save even the most hardened woman criminal. When women's community groups provided critical support for these efforts, they kept alive an older voluntarist female reform tradition.

A charismatic figure, Miriam Van Waters touched the lives of thousands of people, from Boston Brahmins to desperate criminals. Her protégés called her a "beacon of light" who "kindled a spark" that inspired their careers in social work and public service. A former inmate recalled her as "a friend, adviser, and mother." Political opponents, however, accused her of having "utter disregard for law," for which they temporarily ousted her from office in 1949. In a revealing diary entry, Van Waters did place herself above the law, explaining that while politicians dwelled within the legal code, "I try to dwell within the Law of the Kingdom of God on earth—and laws of health, medicine, psychology and social work."[5] Understanding this unusual reformer, a saint to many and a villain to others, illuminates not only her complex character but also a missing chapter in the history of women and social reform in modern America.

Once I had embraced the project of writing about Miriam Van Waters, I tried to rectify a youthful mistake. Although it was too late to meet Van Waters herself, I decided to track down Anne Gladding, who might still be alive and able to share her memories. In 1988 I located her recent address and wrote to the former librarian. In response, I received a letter from Margaret van Wagenen. "I am replying to your letter to Miss Gladding because she is no longer able to do so," van Wagenen wrote. "She has had Alzheimer's Disease for several years and comprehension and communication are woefully impaired. She can be of no help to you. Nothing would have given her greater joy than to be of service to someone working on a biography of Dr. Van Waters."

A few months later I visited Miss Gladding and Miss van Wagenen (Anne and Van, as they were known) in the modest home near Framingham that they had shared for thirty years. Van graciously provided hours of memories of Van Waters and of Framingham, along with the names and addresses of other former staff members I might interview. Anne watched us talk through the same sparkling eyes that had once tried to alert me to the powerful legacy of Miriam Van Waters.

Anne Gladding died in 1992, just as I was beginning to write this biography of her "beloved teacher," Miriam Van Waters. Although I was never able to talk with her about my subject, Gladding's sense of history profoundly affected this project. A year later, as Margaret van Wagenen prepared to move from their home, she wrote to tell me of an attic full of boxes containing material related to Van Waters. Gladding had saved everything "Doctor" had ever written—letters, notes, plays for inmates to perform, as well as cartons of missing family papers, pictures, and correspondence with friends and colleagues. For days I worked in Anne Gladding's room, sorting this precious legacy for deposit in historical archives. It was there I learned of the deep spiritual bond between Gladding and Van Waters, located family pictures, discovered romantic correspondence from Van Waters' intimates, and confirmed many of the impressions I had formed about her personal and professional life. The preservation of these papers by Anne Gladding testifies, I think, to the charismatic power Miriam Van Waters held for her loyal followers, who insured that her history would survive.

I cannot express deeply enough my gratitude to Margaret van Wagenen for granting me access to this material as well as providing personal recollections and introductions to former staff and students from Framingham who agreed to be interviewed. I am thankful to Anne Gladding for first alerting me to the importance of Miriam Van Waters and, twenty years later, providing me with yet another historian's gold mine.

I also want to acknowledge my debt to the many institutions, colleagues, and friends who helped make this book possible. Grants from the Stanford University Institute for Research on Women and Gender and The Schlesinger Library, Radcliffe College, facilitated my research, while fellowships from the National Endowment for the Humanities and the American Council of Learned Societies allowed me to devote an uninterrupted year to drafting the manuscript. Librarians and archivists around the country helped me locate sources. Stanford reference librarian Jim Knox made my research easier in myriad ways. I thank the staff of the Schlesinger Library, especially Diane Hamer, Eva S. Moseley, and Susan von Salis, as well as the following archivists: Roland Baumann, Oberlin College Archives; Lynn Ekfelt, St. Lawrence University;

Kathleen Gilday, Commonwealth of Massachusetts Archives; the Rev. Chandler C. Jackson, Diocesan Archivist, the Episcopal Church in Western Oregon; Victoria Jones, University Archives, and Keith Richards, Special Collections, University of Oregon; William Koelsch and Dorothy Mosakowski, Clark University Archives; Ruth S. Leonard, Society of the Companions of the Holy Cross; Linda Long, Stanford University Special Collections; Waverly Lowell, National Archives and Records, Pacific-Sierra Branch; Judith W. Mellins, Harvard Law School Library; the Right Reverend William B. Spofford, Assistant Episcopal Bishop of Washington, retired; and Jeanne M. Vloyanetes, Media Specialist at Brookdale Community College Learning Resources Center.

Both scholars and prison reformers generously shared sources with me. Cynthia Eckert, Barbara Melosh, Mary Odem, and Joan M. Sakalas each sent material from their unpublished research. Blanche Cook directed me to William Preston, who graciously sent Thompson family photographs and aided my search for sources. Kathleen Dennehy located invaluable transcripts stored at the Framingham reformatory; Nancy Rubackin facilitated interviews; Katherine Gabel, Mary Q. Hawkes, and Howard P. Kellett each sent copies of primary sources in their possession and allowed me to interview them. I am grateful as well for interviews granted by other relatives and colleagues of Miriam Van Waters: Geraldine Boone, Raymond Gilbert, Harriet Gunning, Richard J. Hildebrandt, Mary Marcin, Margaret McLeod, Lois McWilliams, Pauline Orsi, Cynthia Thomas, Margaret van Wagenen, Ralph Van Waters, and the Rev. William Wiltenburg.

I could not have completed this project without the aid of the dependable research assistants who worked with me over the years: Alida Black, Todd Benson, Susan Christopher, Cynthia Eckert, Diane Glass, Amy Hanson, Leslie Harris, Sandy LaRoe, Sue Lynn, Martha Mabie, Elaine Morales, Kevin Mumford, Dan Perlstein, Julie Smith, and Wendy Wall. Pete Holloran offered critical technical advice at the beginning of my research. I am especially indebted to Rita Abraldes, who with patience, competence, and good humor tracked down sources, carefully entered my notes into a text data base, and managed all bibliographical references. At the University of Chicago Press, Doug Mitchell shared my excitement about this project; he and Matt Howard facilitated each step toward publication.

Many colleagues offered helpful comments on early drafts of this book. I thank all of the members of the Stanford Biographers Seminar, especially Barbara Babcock, Mary Felstiner, and Nancy Ungar. Allan Berube, Emily Honig, and Ilene Levitt offered encouraging comments as I

Prologue

began to write, and Jane Collier, Margo Horn, and Julie Reuben each pointed me to useful secondary literature. I benefited enormously from detailed comments on the first draft of the manuscript from Elaine Tyler May, Diane Middlebrook, Peggy Pascoe, Elizabeth Hafkin Pleck, Leila Rupp, and Nancy Stoller, each of whom I thank deeply. John D'Emilio read several versions of this book and, as always, helped me to refine my thinking. Kathryn Kish Sklar provided both a model of feminist biography and a brilliant reading of the final draft.

In addition to these colleagues, I want to thank those closest to me who helped sustain me as I wrote. Ricki Boden has given me a wealth of insight into myself and my subject. In Boston, my sister, Mickey Zemon, and my niece, Jenna Moskowitz, not only housed me during research trips but also provided an appreciative audience for my archival stories. At home in San Francisco, Susan Krieger has offered both enthusiastic support and perceptive interpretations ever since the inception of this project. She has provided the most valuable companionship and intellectual inspiration that I can imagine.

I dedicate this book to three women who have deeply influenced my work: to my mother, Martha Freedman, whose commitment to writing I eventually acquired, and to the memories of Annette Baxter, who first encouraged me to study women's history as an undergraduate, and Shelly Rosaldo, whose appreciation of complexity so enriched my own thinking and the field of feminist scholarship.

PART I

1887–1917

The Family Legacy

I n the stories she told as an adult, Miriam Van Waters often invoked her childhood in a close-knit, loving, middle-class family to explain the seeds of her life's work. "I am the most fortunate of mortals," she once wrote to her parents, George and Maud Van Waters, "for my Home was the great constructive force of my life." During childhood, her father's Portland, Oregon, church provided a stimulating library and fascinating visitors. Oregon's beaches and woods became her summer playground and inspired a lifelong appreciation of nature. At home, she learned "tolerance and understanding," as well as the "principle of universal love—by experiencing full parental love in childhood." In 1928, when she published her second book, *Parents on Probation,* Miriam Van Waters dedicated it "To my Father and Mother to whose understanding and sturdy acceptance of the role of parents in the modern world this book owes its being."[1]

Along with dedication to service, a love of the outdoors, and a commitment to the life of the mind, young Miriam also took from the Van Waters' home less cherished legacies. The private journal she kept at midlife referred to a "childhood misery" of "dragging nameless shadows and yearnings." As if to minimize this confession, she immediately added that "all children must know this." Yet Miriam Van Waters had her own particular miseries—longings for maternal comfort during her own mother's absences, heavy responsibility for domestic and child care duties, deep needs for parental approval, and unspecified childhood fears. For reasons never clearly stated, a dread of returning "to the black pit of childhood" haunted her adult dreams, and an undercurrent of depression threatened to immobilize her at times.[2] To fight these shadows she often drew upon the positive, spiritual values of her family. Returning from a particularly moving church service in 1936, for example, Van Waters recalled how "the sonorous melody, the caressing rhythm opened the flood gates of tenderness and memory, clarifying the bitter cup of youth, throwing a dusty beam of sunlight into the dark church of my childhood."[3] Both the grateful accounts of her loving family and the nameless fears evoked by childhood memories would coexist in the complex inner world of Miriam Van Waters.

Beyond the immediate setting of her childhood, Van Waters grew up in an era, and a region, that created unique opportunities for a woman of her background. In the 1890s, a "new woman" appeared in America. Whether a working-class factory operative or a middle-class college graduate, this new woman transcended the imaginary, yet influential, line that in the nineteenth century divided a female domestic sphere and a male public world. In contrast to her mother's generation, the new woman spent fewer years at home bearing and raising children, and she spent more time earning and spending money or participating in political and cultural life. In the early twentieth century, Miriam Van Waters would become one sort of new woman—the highly educated, professional, and politically active career woman who devoted her life to social service.

The opportunities created by the women's movement converged with the legacy of her family to shape the contours of Miriam Van Waters' career. She was born in 1887—the year that graduates of women's colleges opened the first American settlement house in New York, and two years before Jane Addams established Hull House to serve Chicago's immigrant community. She came of age in the western United States, where women early had access to public higher education and waged the first successful campaigns for state suffrage. As a child, of course, Miriam was unaware of these historical opportunities. But the young girl raised in the rectory of her father's evangelical Episcopal church clearly learned about social justice and sexual equality. She absorbed rudiments of the Social Gospel, which obligated Christians to rectify the inequalities around them, and which would infuse her life's work of ministering to prisoners. As the oldest surviving child in her family, she helped raise four younger siblings and witnessed the physical toll that domestic life took on her mother. As an adult, Miriam Van Waters championed the cause of incarcerated children and women. In her family and in the world, she dedicated herself to saving others.

Maud and George Van Waters passed on to their daughter their own historical and familial legacies. Raised in the decades surrounding the Civil War, each of her parents came from solidly middle-class families with Dutch ancestry. Genealogy, and the status that lineage could provide, mattered to such Protestant, middle-class families at the turn of the century, when waves of new immigrants, many of them Catholics and Jews, changed the social landscape of American communities.

Maud Ophelia Vosburg Van Waters cared enough about her genealogy to apply for membership in the Daughters of the American Revolution—her mother's ancestors had arrived in Boston in 1640, and several of them fought in the Revolutionary War. Maud's paternal grandmother traced her "pedigree" to an early New England family. Her father, who came from an upstate New York Dutch family, had migrated to western Pennsylvania in the early nineteenth century.[4]

Maud Van Waters instilled in her daughter Miriam both pride in family heritage and admiration for "aristocratic" bearing. Born in Williamsport, Pennsylvania, in 1866, the only girl among Ophelia Robinson Vosburg and George Vosburg's six children, Maud led a relatively privileged life. Her father had worked as an express agent for the Pennsylvania Railroad before becoming superintendent of a lumber mill, first in Williamsport and then in the small company town of DuBois, Pennsylvania. He prospered enough to purchase land in Oregon and become a director of the DuBois Board of Trade. In her youth, Maud Vosburg went driving in the countryside with her girlfriends, looked forward to sleigh-riding parties, and at some point ceased her studies because of an eye injury. Her comfortable status would change markedly, however, after marriage. When a newly ordained clergyman arrived in DuBois to form the town's first Episcopal congregation, George Vosburg offered to house the young Reverend George Browne Van Waters. On July 15, 1884, Reverend Van Waters married Maud Ophelia Vosburg. She was eighteen and he was twenty-seven years old.[5]

George Browne Van Waters kept no genealogical records, reflecting his lesser concern with social standing, but his family appears to have been solidly middle class. The Van Waters resided in the small village of Rensselaer Falls, New York, not far from the St. Lawrence River. George's father, Cornelius Orin Van Waters, married Sarah Ann Browne, an educated woman descended from a Canadian member of parliament. They had two children: Charles, born in 1854, and George, born in 1857.[6]

In 1872, George accompanied his older brother to Oberlin College, where Charlie spent his freshman year and George enrolled in the preparatory department. Over two hundred students, mostly "gentlemen" but with fourteen "ladies" as well, attended the Oberlin Preparatory Department. As important as the classes he took, at Oberlin George Van Waters encountered a liberal strain of evangelical American Protestantism. The earliest coeducational and racially integrated college, Oberlin had been a seedbed of antebellum reform, including women's rights and abolitionism.[7] During the 1870s, when he studied at Oberlin, the college remained closely tied to the tradition of its former president, the revivalist and abolitionist Charles Grandison Finney, who had retired in 1866. The new administration continued to stress the development of Christian service among its students. Along with biblical study and prayer meetings, the college offered strong encouragement to missionary good works.[8]

At Oberlin, George Browne Van Waters acquired his lifelong passion for social justice and an interest in studying theology. A few years after completing the preparatory course, he moved to the small town of Gambier, Ohio, and enrolled in Bexley Hall, the Episcopal seminary affiliated with Kenyon College. Bexley Hall represented the evangelical, as opposed to High Church, Episcopal tradition. Along with an emphasis on spiritual regeneration and justification by faith, Bexley Hall embodied low-church suspicion of ritual and encouragement for revivalism. A required course on Christian missions, for example, would serve George Van Waters well in his later years. In seminary he became a "broad term churchman," interested in scholarship and society as much as theology.[9]

According to one of his sons, when George Van Waters received his divinity degree in 1883, "he wanted to spend his life as a teacher, but he was in love with my mother, a young girl."[10] Instead of pursuing a doctorate, Van Waters entered both the clergy and a fifty-year devoted marriage with Maud Ophelia Vosburg. In letters to his wife, written during frequent separations, he expressed a deep and caring love, as well as "great pleasure" in knowing that "my love is fully returned."[11] Maud wrote in the self-deprecating style typical of the period. During courtship, for example, she confessed her faults to Reverend Van Waters: "I sometimes say things which will lead people to suppose I was very good, but in reality I am wicked," she wrote. "I often do things more for woman's 'glory,' than for our makers." Whether her choice of words—"woman's glory," rather than the generic "man's glory"— indicated a self-consciousness about gender is uncertain. But Maud's desire to triumph over "earthly will," while formulaic, nonetheless seemed sincere.[12] Becoming a minister's wife would give her ample opportunity to do so.

In 1885, George and Maud Van Waters celebrated the birth of their first child, Rachel. The growing family moved to George's second pulpit, in nearby Greensburg, Pennsylvania. Maud was soon pregnant again, but a month before her delivery, two-year-old Rachel, only recently "well and hearty," died. For years, George Van Waters carried with him her bronzed baby shoe; fifty years later, Maud still recalled a premonition of Rachel's death. The precariousness of infant life must have weighed heavily on George and Maud when, on October 4, 1887, Miriam Van Waters was born. "A perfect baby from head to toe," George assured his father. "Is plump and has a vigorous appetite, lungs *good*. Head made for the classics."[13]

As his scholarly prediction suggested, the family placed high expectations upon Miriam Van Waters at her birth. Her father, particularly, focused attention upon her, perhaps to ease the sorrow of his recent loss, perhaps to relieve her grieving mother from responsibility. From his bishop came a letter of congratulations, tinged with messianic expectations: "Much joy to you, my dear brother, in the coming of a messenger of peace and love from heaven." As Reverend Van Waters well knew, Miriam's namesake, the sister of Moses, was one of the few female prophets in the Bible. Looking back, near the end of his life, he recalled pleasant daydreams he had about Miriam's future at her birth, confessing that they seemed "paltry" compared to the actual accomplishments of her "great life."[14]

The early years of Miriam Van Waters' childhood in Pennsylvania are not well documented. At times, her mother, presumably with Miriam, returned to the Vosburg home in DuBois, Pennsylvania, while George boarded with a family in Greensburg. But the lack of correspondence suggests that the family of three remained together much of the time. Miriam later recalled spending time with her father, who taught her the names of birds when she was just three years old. She also remembered going along with her grandfather, George Vosburg, when he visited the jails in Williamsport, Pennsylvania, to bring food and Bibles to inmates.[15]

In 1891, when Miriam was four years old, the Van Waters moved to Portland, Oregon. Her father became the rector at St. David's Episcopal Church, a position he held for the next seventeen years. In addition to answering the call of his bishop to help build a missionary church in the Pacific Northwest, Reverend Van Waters may have decided to move his family because his father-in-law had economic interests in the region. From her father, Maud soon received several parcels of real estate in Portland and on the Oregon coast; the prospect of rental income supplementing a meager preacher's salary could have appealed to the growing family. In addition, Maud's brothers George and Lonnie Vosburg soon moved to Oregon to work in the lumber industry.[16]

Logging provided one stimulus for the growth of Portland. A commercial economy, based on shipping and railroad expansion, had boomed in the 1880s. The village originally founded in 1851 had grown to a population of seventy-five thousand by the 1890s. Despite the nationwide economic depression that began in 1893, Portland continued to attract migrants, tripling its population by 1915. The lumber industry brought workers to the area, and rebuilding parts of the city after a major flood in 1894 gave jobs to the unemployed. More importantly, the Alaska gold rush of 1897 created a boom in mining and transportation industries. Although workers suffered from unemployment, and later the militant Wobblies would flourish in the region, a middle-class community prospered. Miriam later recalled that the locals called Portland "the Boston of the West," citing its library, hospitals, and other philanthropic activities. Still, the city retained a frontier atmosphere during her childhood, with wood-planked sidewalks by the waterfront and a wood-burning street railroad running past St. David's. There the Van Waters family settled into a newly built, simple wood frame rectory, which Maud dreamed of furnishing "neatly and aristically [*sic*]."[17]

The move to Portland separated Maud Van Waters from her parents, to whom she now wrote regularly about family life. Her letters often described Miriam's childhood, providing clues about the role her eldest daughter would play within the family. Maud took great pride in her daughter's precocity, delighting in signs of intelligence. "She sees farther than some children," she wrote of five year-old Miriam, "for she knows how to explain everything."[18] On another occasion, when Miriam was six, her mother recounted the child's insights to her parents. "Miriam is such a busybody," Maud wrote in 1893. "I don't know what to do with her sometimes. I was correcting her the other day when she commenced laughing and when I asked her the cause of her merriment (when it was right in the middle of a lecturing) she replied, 'Oh, I was wondering what you would do if you had four or five as bad as I?'"[19]

Young Miriam could not have known how prophetic was her quip. Over the next five years, the births of three siblings—Ruth, Rebekah, and George—would transform the Van Waters household and Miriam's role within it. Above all, the treasured child could no longer depend on her mother's constant attention. Aside from the demands of caring for these infants, Maud Van Waters' health suffered from her repeated pregnancies. She lived with a constant fear of miscarriage, and with each successful birth, her child-rearing and domestic tasks threatened to overwhelm her stamina. At times her nerves prevented her from coping with the household—a classic condition among middle-class women in the nineteenth century, who were often diagnosed as neurasthenic.[20]

No medical records exist to establish whether underlying physical conditions accounted for Maud's fragile health, but the death of her own mother in 1894 may have contributed to her nervous exhaustion. The sheer labor of housework and child care, when she could not afford to hire domestic help, also debilitated her. Raised in relative comfort, Maud Van Waters reluctantly surrendered her class aspirations, while she struggled to maintain her household. Her eldest daughter Miriam must have felt the disappointment and associated it with her own loss of maternal care. She later recalled how her mother waged a "sturdy protest against 'nastiness'" in her surroundings. Maud's "terse speech"—a phrase suggesting practicality—would rise above her "burning longing, the desire for happiness." Young Miriam early determined to do her own part to lift her mother's sorrows.[21]

Reverend Van Waters also felt keenly the pressure on his wife. More children, and the need for household help to relieve Maud, placed greater financial stress on his family. At the same time his congregation was struggling to finance a new church building. During the depression of the 1890s, George Van Waters repeatedly, and unsuccessfully, sought greater income. His loving letters to his wife when he traveled spoke frequently of the quest for money and for an easier existence for Maud. In 1895, for instance, he sent his "Beloved Wife" three dollars with apologies that "it is all I can spare just now. It will help you a little and you may expect to receive something more within a week." A few years later George sought a job as a general missionary in the South because, as he explained to Maud, "It is so hard on you to do the work in Portland. You have so much responsibility in that big house. . . . I shall not suffer you to work so hard." In "a nice aristocratic town" in the South, he wrote, Maud could "get good colored help" at low wages, and everything would be "much cheaper than in Portland." Clearly responding to his wife's concerns about social status, he assured her that "society would be very congenial" there. The job, however, never materialized, and Reverend Van Waters continued to worry about money, and about Maud's health.[22]

In response to these family strains, oldest daughter Miriam assumed increasing responsibility, caring for the babies and helping with housework, especially when her mother sought rest away from the family. Although it was not unusual in the nineteenth century for an oldest daughter to serve as her mother's helper, Miriam filled a much larger familial role, one that carried great emotional weight. From a precocious object of attention in early childhood, during adolescence Miriam became, in her father's later words, "the mother of us all." She labored vigorously to relieve and to please Maud, as a Sunday morning in 1895 illustrates. Miriam, her mother, and baby sister Ruth were staying in coastal Newport, Oregon. Reverend Van Waters hoped that the sea air would cure Maud of nervousness and calm her during her fourth pregnancy. Despite the fact that eight-year-old Miriam herself was not well, she dutifully went to Sunday School with her offering and then came home to take care of sister Ruth so that her mother could go to church. Because responsibility for others so pleased Maud, Miriam developed a pattern of self-sacrifice, priding herself on fulfilling her family duties without complaint. At the same time, she formed her own deep longing to be close to Maud, whose health problems increasingly took her away from the family for extended visits to her parental home in Pennsylvania. The "nameless shadows and yearnings" she later recalled could well have referred to young Miriam's tireless efforts to relieve, and thus regain, her mother.[23]

More difficult for Miriam were separations from her family. Sent to the Oregon coast one spring to stay with her Uncle Lonnie Vosburg, she missed her parents terribly. In her letters home, however, nine-year-old Miriam adopted a tone of cheerful resignation that would recur throughout her family correspondence. She assured her parents that she knew it was best that her mother remain in Portland.[24] For years, Miriam's letters during separations from her mother spoke of her longing, but they always placed her mother's health above her desire to see her. "Darling, though I long to see you . . . do not come home till you are rested," she wrote at age fifteen. "I am quite content to know that by staying here I am helping a slight degree to your welfare. But oh how I miss you." To justify this separation, Miriam vowed to remember that the trip "is adding years to your life." The submersion of her pain would emotionally haunt her. Years later, she would still recognize "a little Miriam" when she watched a child who longed for her mother exert a "strong will" to control her anguish, noting empathetically how the child's "eyes filled with tears she did not shed."[25]

During Maud's absences, Miriam took charge of the Portland rectory or a coastal summer cottage, managing the household and her three younger siblings. In 1901, for example, fourteen-year-old Miriam toiled alongside a domestic worker to get the washing done and clean the house. When Maud arrived, Miriam outdid herself, rising early to make a big breakfast before her mother woke up. And when Maud returned home from church, Miriam had dinner ready. "Miriam is a perfect treasure," Maud wrote to her husband, "she tries to save me all she can."[26] Her phrase could have referred merely to a saving of time and energy, but it also suggests a desire by Miriam to rescue her mother, perhaps in order to preserve her for herself.

The most difficult period for Miriam was the spring of 1902, when Maud, troubled by ill health, returned to her parents' home in DuBois, Pennsylvania, for several months. It was not unusual for a woman to visit her family to get assistance with child care and, separated from her husband, reduce the risk of pregnancy. In Maud's case, the distance between Oregon and Pennsylvania necessitated a lengthy trip. She brought her youngest child, George, and her husband joined her for part of the visit. Fifteen year-old Miriam held down the rectory. "I exerted myself" while entertaining visitors, she wrote her mother, repeating the word "exerted" twice. Reverend Van Waters assured his wife that Miriam "bears her honor and responsibilities gracefully with no disposition whatever to be overbearing." [27] Miriam herself took special pride in her child-rearing abilities. She washed, dressed, and fed her sisters Rebekah (Beckie) and Ruth, then seven and nine years old. She managed to get them to school on time and claimed to be a strict disciplinarian. When her father departed as well, Miriam packed her sisters off to the coast to stay with their Uncle Lonnie. She missed the children very much, and she dreamed of holding her baby brother George in her arms. When she woke for a "solitary breakfast" with another uncle, George Vosburg, Miriam felt "forlorn." How she wished to be with her mother, father, and little George in Pennsylvania, she wrote to them, but "perish the thought—for it can never be." [28]

Throughout this separation, Miriam was clearly resentful about being left behind. As much as she professed her resignation, she also communicated her desire and disappointment. "When you travel and have father and a baby to kiss you can't imagine how I miss you alone all the time," Miriam wrote to her "precious dearest" mother. A girl named Dorothy Moore was staying with Miriam, and when Mrs. Moore came and "took Dorothy's face in her hands and kissed—a great longing came over me," Miriam wrote. "I wish I had the courage to ask her to kiss me," she added, reiterating her longing for maternal affection. But the voice of triumph over disappointment repeated itself, as it would throughout her life: "I too have a mother—the dearest, truest, noblest in the world. But she has been taken away from me for a time. We will value each other more and more when again we are together." In another letter, Miriam attempted to justify the separation by spiritualizing her desire. Drawing on the language of romantic love that characterized contemporary girls' fiction, she wrote to her mother: "What is the material part of love? The greater part, perhaps, but the love which needs no eyes or fingers or voices only the soul and the heart is the sweetest most enduring kind." [29]

On at least one occasion Miriam mildly acted out her anger toward her absent mother and then wrote to her confessionally, perhaps in a veiled complaint about being left. After three days with "not a soul in the house," she wrote, "I got desperate and of all dreadful things I *smoked half* a cigarette. I am awfully sorry and I won't do it again but I felt easier if you knew about it." More typically, however, Miriam turned to fantasies of saving her mother's life by freeing her from physical and financial worries. It was during this long separation that she first contemplated becoming a writer in order to earn her fortune. Her career goals rested firmly upon a sense of responsibility to others. For one, she later recalled, "the little Miriam did not let dreams of writing a 'great book' interfere with the housework and the care of children." In addition, she assured her mother that "The first cent I make I will lay humbly at your feet and you can buy soda pop with it." More seriously, she imagined that once she began making money, her mother would be able to rest and travel.[30] Her sense of mission, and of martyrdom, recurred a few weeks later, when she dreamed about Ben Hur and the Roman prosecutor, "whom I beat in a race," and of her mother. As she explained to Maud, "only you didn't love me much because I persisted in riding races with the Roman whom you hated." In Miriam's mind, even heroics tinged with martyrdom could not necessarily win her mother's love, but they were worth a try.[31]

The early Christian context of these dreams suggests the kind of imagery that appealed to young Miriam Van Waters. Growing up in the rectory of St. David's Episcopal Church, she read not only the Bible but also the literature of Christian heroes. Biblical themes would recur in her writing throughout her career, as would the lives of saints and the writings of theologians and philosophers. Indeed, the sermon provided a literary format for much of Miriam Van Waters' later writing. Years later she recalled the importance of her father's books for her development. The redwood-paneled rectory library had been a warm, inviting space in her childhood home. Light from the fireplace threw shadows on the books that lined the walls from floor to ceiling. "While the Oregon rain poured down," Miriam later recalled, "I read my father's library from left to right, up and down and to without discrimination." Once, when Maud Van Waters confiscated a book—"a Balzac, a Whitman, a Byron, I forget which," Miriam wrote—her father overruled his wife.

"Never interfere with a child's reading," he said. "The important thing is that they read. Taste will come later." Her mother acquiesced, and Miriam became a voracious reader throughout her life.[32]

Even more than his library, the personal model of the Reverend George Browne Van Waters shaped his daughter's spiritual, social, and intellectual values. His gentle, bearded face framed by white clerical collar and dark hair, Reverend Van Waters emanated Christian charity. For Miriam he represented a "struggle for righteousness . . . courage, loyalty, steadfastness and compassion against the odds." Always immensely responsive to the needs of others, he would drop everything "the instant a child or parishioner was in need." A model of generosity and open-mindedness, his most abiding message was respect and tolerance for all people. "In all his long ministry on earth," Miriam wrote after her father's death in the 1930s, "only one sort of misery (as far as I know) ever clouded the brightness of those eyes"; this was when "some one of his brood" disregarded the rights of others. "'You don't get his view point,' he would say." Miriam tried to emulate his tolerance throughout her life. She also turned to her father's memory at times of crisis or self-doubt, invoking his spirit to restore her own. When she felt no "will to live," Miriam found "one thread to hold to. My father believed in me and rejoiced in me — with a boundless joy." Nonetheless, his model of Christian morality offered a very high standard of achievement. Indeed, a child like Miriam, so intent on doing good, could be left with feelings of inadequacy, and as an adult, she did suffer grave doubts about her ability to live up to her father's ideals.[33]

Aside from the influence of his personality, the social thought and religious practice of George Browne Van Waters provide important clues to the later career of his eldest daughter. In many ways, Reverend Van Waters embodied the Social Gospel movement, which fostered liberal ideas and social service within American Protestant churches at the turn of the twentieth century. Drawing on older concepts of Christian nurture, including a belief in innate human goodness, Social Gospel emphasized both individual and cultural regeneration through good works. Theologically, Social Gospel clergy proclaimed God's presence within humanity; socially they called on Christians to respond to the glaring inequalities wrought by industrialism. In the aftermath of violent labor conflict and rising urban poverty at the end of the nineteenth century, some middle-class Protestants began to seek class reconciliation through social service to immigrants and workers. Whether their intent was to preserve or to reform the social order, Social Gospelers initiated both evangelical and philanthropic work among the poor.[34]

Within this movement, the Episcopal Church took a leading role in addressing issues of labor relations, social justice, Christian unity, and race relations. Richard T. Ely, author of a major Social Gospel text, *The Social Aspects of Christianity* (1889), worked through the Christian Social Union to pressure the Episcopal Church to establish a social service commission. The settlement house movement included a strong contingent of Episcopal women, including Hull House cofounder Ellen Gates Starr and Wellesley professor Vida Scudder, who spearheaded Boston's Denison House settlement. Many of these women belonged to the Society for the Companions of the Holy Cross, a lay organization of select Episcopal women devoted to working for social justice.[35]

Even within this liberal movement, George Browne Van Waters stood out as a unique churchman. For one, he was extremely ecumenical, a legacy his daughter would later draw on to advantage. As a minister Van Waters gladly cooperated with other denominations, and he even showed an interest in Eastern religions. In later years, when he became a full-time missionary riding the eastern Oregon circuit, he addressed "people of all creeds and no creeds," in any church, lodge hall, or hotel he could find.[36] Drawn to scholarship, in 1901 he received an honorary doctor of divinity degree from a progressive theological seminary. He read not only theology but also the emerging social science literature on labor conditions. Reverend Van Waters' missionary efforts resembled lay seminars as much as religious services, for he often lectured on the psychology of religion, comparative religion, and even on hypnosis and psychotherapy. One reporter claimed that anyone "who heard Dr. Van Waters will long remember" his addresses. Personally, he acted on his principles, refusing to invest in the stock of railroads, whose corporate practices he deplored. In addition, he called on the church to change the world. As he explained in a sermon, "The hope of both State and Church lies in its reformers, without them . . . things would be static."[37]

Above all, Reverend Van Waters was a committed individualist who found himself at odds with the church hierarchy and had little tolerance for traditionalism. In the 1920s, when conservative forces contested the Social Gospel, he spoke of a "lurking passion for medievalism" in the church and wanted to write a book titled *Against Traditionalism in the Churches.*[38] The "Episcopal officialism," he stated in a sermon, had a "fondness for authority which tends to interfere with others' initiative." Interestingly, his case in point was the experience of women in the church: "The men would take the honors and have the women do the work," despite the fact that the "Woman's Auxiliary beats any of our organizations." Why, then, he argued, should women not have equal authority, within the church hierarchy and within society?[39]

George Van Waters' individualist, antiauthoritarian social views, along with his own strong will, made a lasting impression on his children. From him Miriam inherited not only a faith in the Social Gospel but also an interest in social science and a commitment to social change. She long recalled her father standing in the rectory library as he read out loud or expounded his religious and social ideas. "Sin," he used to say, leaning in toward the children, "is a Hebrew word for mistake. Sin is a mistake like missing the target." The concept of redemption loomed large in her household. "My father's philosophy and that of his era was buoyant and optimistic," Miriam recalled. "It was the age of liberalism. It was the age of faith in social action." Sometimes he would read aloud from the British social Darwinist Herbert Spencer. "'Man is only in an early stage of his evolution' he would say. 'His progress is inevitable.'" But the men and women she met at family dinners, Miriam recalled, "had no mind to let this progress take its course without their aid or violent protest." While visitors to the rectory also included conservative pillars of the church—such as bishops who stayed there en route to missionary outposts in Alaska, the Philippines, or China—Reverend Van Waters liked to entertain theological students, vagrants, and "people of every race and color." Whoever joined the family circle, he always tried to bring conversations back to the common man, "how he fared and what he felt." Long after his death, Reverend Van Waters' children remembered their father's "Violent Championship of Evolution in Nature, and Liberalism in Education." They also recalled his personal magnetism, the way he "greeted each person he met with warm delight" and "established intimacy immediately, and usually told them all about his family as if they had known his children for years."[40]

A variety of people had occasion to hear the Reverend George Browne Van Waters. His St. David's congregants, on Portland's east side, were predominantly white and middle class (Trinity Episcopal Church, on the southwest side, served the upper class). An "aggressive missionary," he established Episcopal churches in three small communities on the outskirts of Portland. But George Van Waters also introduced young Miriam to a broader population.[41] Some of the men and women who stopped in Portland on their way to the Alaska gold rush sought his help, among them miners, gamblers, and prostitutes. Sitting in the rectory study, he explained his perspective on them: "You must seek to get the view of these individuals. When you know their view point you can understand them and begin to help." Other workers arrived in town with the rise of the salmon canneries, among them Chinese immigrants. To reach out to these newcomers, Reverend Van Waters held services at a downtown mission, where he taught both literacy and Christianity. As in other urban missions established around the country, classes met in the evening, when workers could attend. As a young woman, Miriam taught English at the Chinese mission, claiming with pride that she made "many converts to Christianity."[42]

St. David's also hosted theological students from the East who either lived at the rectory or visited regularly. "My father instructed them in theology and philosophy," Miriam recalled, "and they taught me Greek and Latin." In hindsight she compared the atmosphere to "living in a Settlement House where everyone was welcome, and no one was ever turned away empty." Amid their "free and frank" discussions of current events, literature, and philosophy, Miriam began to define her own politics, often in response to visitors who introduced her to the problems of machine politics and business corruption.[43]

Miriam Van Waters' warm memories of the rectory—as a settlement house, a refuge for stray animals as well as people, and a place of humor and goodwill—may well have idealized her father's world. In her eyes, Reverend Van Waters had no faults. Though later she became aware of his financial struggles, she always valued his philosophy rather than his practical abilities to support the family. She made no connection between the constant stream of rectory visitors and her mother's domestic burdens. Nonetheless, along with her glowing memories of home, Miriam carried darker, though well-submerged, images. In midlife, when she routinely recorded her dreams, the rectory or a familiar old house often contained hidden dangers, lurking figures, and threatening mobs. Not long after her mother's death, when Miriam was over fifty years old, she dreamt "of sobbing bitterly in old House—Mother young and well downstairs—I am looking for clean linen for beds for many guests. I cry because of despair and lon[e]liness (like a child for attention ignored)." Home thus represented not only nurture but also the labor of domesticity, fear of abandonment, and longing for attention.[44]

However idealized in retrospect, her family life clearly left a strong mark on Miriam Van Waters' career. She would long invoke the rectory spirit of vigorous yet tolerant, good-humored discussions as a path toward individual renewal and social reconciliation. In the penal institutions she later administered, she tried to reproduce that atmosphere, combining the roles of maternal nurturer and spiritual father. Toward the end of her life she explained that "It was in the Rectory and the Church that I learned that each person born into the world is a Child of God and capable of redemption." This belief would guide her, for better and for worse, throughout her life.

While her father provided her with a spiritual mooring, and her mother remained the object of her deepest emotional longing, Miriam Van Waters came of age within a region and a generation that also shaped her values. At the turn of the twentieth century, western Oregon still resembled small-town or rural American cultures of the past. In eastern cities, immigrants and workers were forging a heterosocial youth culture that included new practices, such as dating, and centered around new commercial pleasures, such as movies and amusement parks. But in Miriam's middle-class, religious, West Coast milieu, separate spheres for boys and girls persisted into adulthood. Strong female bonds, not only between mothers and daughters but also among close friends, helped shape her adult identity. Some newer cultural models for female behavior also influenced Miriam, as did the rustic environment around her. The increasingly popular image of a robust, athletic new woman who took part in sports and the outdoors well described her youth. Horseback riding, rowing, and swimming provided some of her greatest joys. Throughout her life she recalled gratefully "the heritage of wholesome out-of-doors life" of her childhood.[45]

Her family's property on the Oregon coast allowed Miriam unusual opportunity to explore nature. When her mother was well enough to take the family on camping excursions to the coast, Miriam would "disappear in the forests," much to the distress of her father, "whose love of nature," she later recalled, "was Wordsworthian and did not embrace briars, bugs, nettings, bugs, bruises and dangers to life and limb." Maud defended her daughter's wandering spirit, allowing her to explore to her content among the Douglas firs and Oregon spruce in the still uncut timber regions. When her mother's health faltered or she traveled back east, Miriam sometimes stayed with Uncle Lonnie Vosburg, who had settled on one of his father's coastal land parcels. Sent to visit, with or without her younger siblings, Miriam roamed the coast freely. "I rode the black stallion, Billy, and caused a lot of excitement and censure," Miriam recalled, but Uncle Lonnie "only smiled." Once she followed him out cougar hunting in the middle of the night, and "he didn't scold me." Walking on the beach by herself, she wrote to her mother in Pennsylvania, was one of her best times. In adulthood, as well, the outdoors would provide her with both a keen sense of her own competence and solace during times of despair.[46]

Being female rarely interfered with Miriam's explorations of the world around her. In fact, she seemed to take particular pride in her abilities as a young woman. Even at age eleven she wrote home that she never had to ask the boys to go rowing, because she could go out on the boat all by herself. She could swim all day long, and once she swam across the Willamette River at Oregon City, at a time, she recalled, "when girls *never* did." At age thirteen Miriam proudly told her mother that she could unhitch and hitch up a wagon "to suit a king," so that she could drive herself to church when she was staying at the coast.[47]

Like other young women of her background, Miriam Van Waters formed fiercely passionate attachments to her female friends. Several relationships began during periods when she was separated from her mother. At thirteen, for example, Miriam wrote to Maud about Mattie, a sweet fourteen-year-old girl whom she wanted to bring home from the coast for a long visit: "She wouldn't make you any trouble at all," Miriam assured her mother. "I want her awfully—for I've fallen in love with her. . . . It would make me very happy if you would love her too." A more lasting friendship formed the next year, during Maud Van Waters' long absence, with a young woman named Genevieve, a soul mate and the first girl Miriam had "to love." Separations from her new friend made her very unhappy, in part because they merged with her longing for her mother. In both cases, Miriam resigned herself to accepting spiritual love in the absence of her beloved: "When Genevieve is far away, do I stop loving her? No, a thousand times no. And if I love Genevieve with enduring love, how much more will I love my mother," she wrote to Maud.[48]

Miriam's close ties to women, as well as her sense of female competence, found reinforcement through her formal schooling. After an epidemic closed her primary school, she had been tutored at the rectory by a parishioner, curates, or visiting theological students. For secondary education she enrolled in St. Helen's Hall, an Episcopal girls' school located three miles across town, "in an aristocratic part of Portland." Because she often pocketed her trolley fare to save for the price of a moving-picture show, Miriam's walks across town allowed her to observe the working-class districts of Portland. Here she discovered not only the Chinese quarter, but also a red-light district where sailors roamed the cobblestone streets in search of drink and sex. Prostitutes worked out of small "cribs," although as a child Miriam did not under-stand what the women were peddling. She did preserve a strong mem-ory of the aromas of the waterfront district as reeking of "tar, rope, pitch, beer, whiskey, perfume and incense."[49]

When she arrived at St. Helen's, however, propriety ruled. Estab-lished in 1869, St. Helen's Hall (named for the nearby volcano) was one of several girls' schools the Episcopal Church established in western U.S. cities. Like the pioneering female seminaries of the mid–nine-teenth century, St. Helen's Hall emphasized academics alongside tradi-tional female accomplishments. Although Miriam could have enrolled in a coeducational public high school or the private Portland Academy, her father's position in the church insured her attendance at St. Helen's. Fees were high for boarding students, but Miriam, as well as her younger sisters, attended by day much more cheaply.[50]

St. Helen's offered abundant models of female achievement. Twenty women staff members served a total student body of about 150. In the late 1890s, when Miriam was in the intermediate depart-ment, both the principal and the Latin and Greek instructor held doc-torates from the University of Pennsylvania. Graduates of elite women's colleges—including Vassar, Mills, Wellesley, and Smith—offered in-struction in languages, mathematics, science, and history, and the resi-dent physician had graduated from the Woman's Medical College of Philadelphia. Other staff provided courses in music and "physical cul-ture." All but two faculty members were single women, and the student publication, *The Spinster,* reflected the school's emphasis on female in-dependence.[51] "Though nothing was said about this," Miriam later remi-nisced, "the school impressed one with the importance of women in the world which was to become modern."[52]

St. Helen's Hall was clearly more than a finishing school. Although all students took music, elocution, and art (and "special attention was given to manners"), it had a rigorous academic curriculum. Latin classes began in the intermediate grades, with French, German, Greek, Bible, science, and mathematics available for older girls. Here, Miriam recalled, she felt "enjoyment of using the mind" and learned a "respect for scholarship." The school also encouraged outdoor exercise, includ-ing "calisthenics, walking, tennis, basketball, bicycling (under proper escort), and riding." Far from a cloistered environment, St. Helen's Hall brought the outside world to its students. At Wednesday evening parlor lectures, for example, local professors, lawyers, and judges met with the students and faculty.[53] Not surprisingly, some graduates pursued academic careers themselves. Luella Clay Carson, class of 1877, became a professor of rhetoric at the University of Oregon, and, from 1909 to 1913, the president of Mills College for women in California.[54]

School provided Miriam with further evidence of her abilities as well as a means to please her parents. Perhaps because Maud had been forced to give up her own studies, and George aspired to a scholarly life himself, the Van Waters valued education very highly. Miriam, their first surviving child, more than fulfilled their expectations. In her earliest letter to her "dear papa," when she was seven, Miriam reported proudly that she got 100 in all her studies that day. Later report cards confirm her "excellent" performance.[55] At times, however, she overextended herself. At one point during high school Maud had to remove Miriam from St. Helen's Hall because, in her uncle's words, "She has been studying too hard and had broken down." Maud took her daughter to the seaside for a month of peace and quiet, a respite that must have soothed Miriam both physically and emotionally.[56]

Other serious health problems plagued Miriam, for her later journals recall bouts with serious illness and childhood memories of "the taste of digitalis" in her mouth. Her parents monitored her weight with an eye to health, while the adolescent Miriam—just over five feet tall—worried about becoming too "fat."[57] A photograph taken when she was thirteen shows an apparently healthy, attractive young woman with dark, wide, penetrating eyes, her dark hair pulled back loosely and wisping around her face. Above all, she looked strikingly serious.

Whether for reasons of health or family circumstances, when Miriam did graduate in 1904 she remained at St. Helen's as one of two "Post Graduate Students," completing the equivalent of her first year of college. Perhaps she chose to delay her departure from Portland because that year Maud Van Waters unexpectedly found herself pregnant. Just before Miriam left for the University of Oregon at Eugene in 1905, Maud gave birth to her last child, Ralph. For much of his life, Miriam would serve as a second mother to Ralph Van Waters. Thus, even as she prepared to leave her childhood home, her family ties strengthened.

Childhood at St. David's and on the Oregon coast had provided Miriam Van Waters with a wealth of happy memories and a deep gratitude to her parents. Her mother, Miriam wrote, was the ideal "of all Christian beautiful living . . . an inspiration and a saint," while her father modeled both intellect and compassion.[58] Throughout her life she would draw on the positive legacy of her childhood to overcome its harsher memories—of ill health, the toll of domestic responsibilities, her deep longing for her mother's happiness and affection, and her need for her parents' approval. The church, spirituality, music, nature, children, ideas, intimate friends—all these would sustain her when she faced internal despair and external challenges. As she entered adult life, leaving her family for college, Miriam Van Waters was already becoming a unique kind of "new woman." Steeped in both the nurturing roles of motherhood and the intellectual life of the rectory and St. Helen's, she sought to combine the best of each throughout her long career.

2

An Educated Woman

When Miriam Van Waters arrived at the University of Oregon in the fall of 1905, both her familial caretaking role and her liberal Protestantism were already well established. Each would deepen during her years of higher education, even as she found new intellectual and political avenues for exploring these commitments. At the university her intellectual confidence strengthened, and she gained a clearer sense of the political world around her. By the time she left Oregon in 1910, she had begun to envision an academic career as one route toward social justice and personal service.

The pioneering efforts of an earlier generation of college women created the educational opportunities Miriam Van Waters enjoyed. In the late nineteenth century, the Association of Collegiate Alumnae had begun to disprove conservative claims that intellectual work destroyed women's reproductive capacities. Increasing numbers of women now pursued higher education, not only in the elite, private women's colleges that served the wealthy, but also in public, coeducational institutions, like state universities, that made college affordable for the middle classes. Twentieth-century female college graduates also enjoyed more varied career choices than in the past. In addition to training as public-school teachers, they sought new jobs as social workers, librarians, and journalists, and some pursued graduate studies with the goal of academic careers. Others joined the ranks of Progressive Era reformers, whether in settlement houses, civic organizations, or the woman suffrage movement.[1]

These newly educated women, Miriam Van Waters among them, did not necessarily reject older gender roles. Rather, as one historian has explained, "Under the aegis of progressivism, women college students balanced Victorian ideals with newly emerging beliefs and behavior."[2] They carved out a female sphere within the university, and after graduation, they applied the maternalist values of their mothers' private world within new professional careers. At the same time, coeducation did transform the lives of many second-generation college women. They married much more frequently than had their predecessors, and they struggled to be accepted as equals with men, even as they relied on women's separate communities for support.[3]

Miriam Van Waters' educational experiences, first at the University of Oregon (1905-10) and then at Clark University in Massachusetts (1910-13), provide both a case study in the formation of female consciousness during the Progressive Era and a clue to the future reformer's character. Over the course of her undergraduate years at a coeducational, western state university, she took full advantage of extracurricular and academic opportunities to develop her skills. While she drew on traditional forms of female community, both within her family and among a close circle of friends, she gradually adopted new goals for herself and for women. Transcending the limitations on her mother's educational opportunities, she was able to pursue the life of the mind first nurtured in her father's rectory.

The University of Oregon was the obvious choice for Miriam Van Waters' higher education, given the proximity of Eugene, just 150 miles south of Portland, and the strains on Reverend Van Waters' finances. With total costs of around two hundred dollars a year, even the daughters of clergymen could attend. More egalitarian than the elite women's schools, the university nonetheless resembled a liberal arts college. A student body of under five hundred and a small, verdant campus provided an attractive educational setting. Like other state universities, Oregon encouraged women's attendance, and during Miriam's college years women's enrollment increased by 38 percent, compared to a 20 percent increase for men. By hiring a few female faculty, appointing a dean of women, and establishing extracurricular activities that paralleled men's organizations—such as women's literary and debating societies—Oregon combined the virtues of women's separate group activities with the intellectual opportunities of coeducational classrooms.[4]

Dual goals of women's higher education—for womanhood and for work—were clearly articulated by Oregon's dean of women, Professor of Rhetoric Luella Clay Carson, a St. Helen's Hall graduate. Dean Carson offered a reassuring message to female high-school graduates that education, public service, and true womanhood were not incompatible. She cited Florence Nightingale to illustrate "the tender ministry of woman, and, even more, the transforming power of woman as a scholar and a thinker and a benefactor." Like Nightingale, the educated American woman could aspire to "become wise, loving, helpful, and strong in . . . [a]ny honorable work that she is able to do well without hurt to her sense of womanhood."[5]

Dean Carson's affirmation of women's traditional nurturing skills fit well with eighteen-year-old Miriam Van Waters' sense of herself as she entered college, still deeply immersed in her familial role as the mother of us all. During the course of her undergraduate years, Miriam's social world would expand well beyond this base, yet her family continued to define her identity in powerful ways. Even as she arrived in Eugene, for example, she volunteered to return home because her ailing mother was "lots more important than college." Although she stayed in school, her letters to her parents complained of severe homesickness. When she didn't hear from her mother regularly enough, Miriam tended to panic. Once, for example, she sent a worried telegram, later apologizing that she knew her mother was too busy to write all the time. Although she begged her mother to visit, she was still delighted when Reverend Van Waters, without his wife, brought her baby brother, Ralph, to Eugene.[6]

A measure of Miriam's continuing attachment to her family appeared in a letter written shortly before her first visit home from college. Concerned about her mother's health while nursing Ralph, Miriam vowed that "at Christmastime" she herself would "wean that infant and then perhaps you will be stronger."[7] Although she could not provide long-distance care for the baby, she did take responsibility for her younger sister Ruth, who moved to Eugene to attend high school. During Miriam's last years at the university the sisters set up housekeeping together, renting the Eugene home of the western writer Joaquin Miller, about a mile from the university. There they cooked their meals, raised chickens, and kept a horse for Miriam to ride. When Ruth's grades faltered, Miriam tutored her an hour a day, and when her sister faced continued academic and personal problems, Miriam assured their parents she did "everything to make her happy constantly. At her slightest word I throw up my work to help her in any way." While her parents appreciated these efforts, a cousin, responding to Maud's proud stories about her oldest daughter, captured well the quality of Miriam's life. "The great trouble with her," he wrote, "is that she is likely to overdo." Close friends and relatives would repeat this observation throughout her life.[8]

Although Miriam continued to reenact her caretaking role, once she adjusted to college her tone toward her family shifted in subtle ways. Sometimes, she confessed, she could "scarcely endure" the separation from her "precious mother," as when she wrote that "an inexplicable longing came over me to fly home and see with my own eyes you're all well."[9] As her own social world expanded, though, she adopted a bearing of greater emotional distance. The old expressions of noble resignation now supplanted the more blatant longings of her adolescence. A letter Miriam wrote to her mother when a senior professed a calm acceptance that "your burdens are so heavy dearest that I shall not expect any letters from you." A few months later she complimented her sisters' growing responsibility for household matters: "More and more completely are they filling the eldest daughter's place. I am proud of them." Writing to her father, she took the perspective of an outside observer when she characterized her mother. "She is like a rose, too much frost and cold, of spirit I mean, hurts her." Throughout her life, Miriam would invoke such emotional distance in order to accept disappointment, even when she continued to suffer inside.[10]

At college, Miriam found new relationships that continued the close female bonds of her adolescence. Much of her early social life in Eugene revolved around women students with whom she boarded (there were no dormitories, and she did not join the recently established sororities). Recreation included taking long walks with her friends Ruth and Eve to admire the changing seasons, going riding together, and entertaining other women students. "Our little dinners are becoming famous," Miriam wrote her mother during senior year. "We live so much together" she wrote of her roommates; several of her friends were even menstruating at the same time, she once noted, using her code word "Belinda" to refer to her menstrual period.[11]

Belinda had plagued Miriam for years, making her "miserable" during days of heavy, painful bleeding. She often confided to her mother about her discomfort and rejoiced when she avoided it. "Belinda flowed constantly and took all vitality," excused a brief gap in her letters home. On the return from a vacation, she revealed, "My friend and lover Belinda joined me at Oregon City and continued during the journey . . . she has been unusually mild and thoughtful." When Belinda sent her home from the university early, Miriam sometimes bundled up before "a roaring fire with a hot toddy and the army blanket," sleeping through the day. Her women friends tried to ease her physical distress at these times. During two sleepless nights of migraine and cramps, for example, Eve and Ruth took care of Miriam. Eve later took her driving out-of-doors while she regained her strength. On another occasion, her friend Alice nursed a feverish Miriam, who was "forlorn" when left alone.[12]

Miriam derived emotional as well as physical nurture from her circle of women friends. She had not forsaken her girlhood love, Genevieve Parke, whom she begged to come visit her at college. By her senior year, however, a woman named Rachel had become her "dearest friend." One letter from Rachel left Miriam "too full of emotion to talk about it." She sent the letter to her mother for safekeeping with the comment, "There are certain kinds of people whose friendship is sweeter than life." Two years later Miriam still thought enough of Rachel to send her a box of wildflowers, so that her friend could have a "breath of the woodsy spring."[13] The romantic quality of her writing about Rachel set this relationship apart from those with Ruth, Eve, Alice, or with a young English instructor, Elizabeth (Bess) Woods, who would become Miriam's lifelong friend. Her willingness to share Rachel's letter, and her own feelings, with her mother testify to the innocence that still attached to college women's crushes and romantic friendships in the early twentieth century.[14]

Alongside the female community that so nourished Miriam during college was a coeducational campus culture that introduced her to the rituals of dating. Although the raucous pranks and hazing so prevalent on nineteenth-century campuses had declined with coeducation, a buoyant new heterosocial student culture now emerged. Miriam's letters home suggested that she remained aloof from the collegiate men and women who partied and played sports more than they studied. Rather, she engaged in a fairly active social life with both male and female students who formed what has been called an "outsider" culture. This set attracted the more intellectual and political students on American campuses, including Miriam Van Waters.[15]

A comparison with one of Miriam's classmates highlights the divergent, though sometimes intersecting, paths available to "coeds" in this period. Louise Bryant, later famous for her political radicalism and her relationship with journalist John Reed, arrived in Eugene a year after Miriam, a junior transfer from the University of Nevada. Along with four other women, Bryant founded a sorority chapter and served as its first president. Known for her "floaty" look, she created a scandal when she wore rouge on campus at a time when makeup still connoted fallen womanhood. According to Miriam, Louise Bryant "openly flaunted drinking, smoking and flashy dressing, in cafes in the town and neighboring towns," in blatant disregard of Dean Luella Clay Carson's strict rules for female-student conduct. "I know the dean was deeply hurt," Miriam later recalled. Unlike Bryant, Van Waters concentrated on her studies (earning A's and B's to Bryant's D's), took an interest in the "social issues" that Bryant then ignored, and dressed conservatively. Miriam's graduation picture, for example, exuded the fresh, natural look of a country girl, holding an open book on her lap. Her yearbook photo showed her with hair pulled back simply, rather than piled high, and seated in a businesslike pose that masked her diminutive, five-foot, three-inch stature. Despite their different styles, on the small Eugene campus Miriam and Louise often crossed paths. Bryant drew illustrations for Van Waters' short stories in the student literary magazine, and in the senior-class production of Sheridan's *The Rivals,* the future penologist played Mrs. Malaprop to the future radical's Lydia Languish.[16]

If Bryant epitomized an extreme form of the "college woman," Van Waters stood clearly in the outsider camp. During her first month of college, for instance, Miriam dismissed the "wretched" fraternity teas that "bother us dreadfully" and professed little interest in the football games that were so central to campus culture.[17] Despite her aloofness from certain aspects of college social life, Miriam reported excitedly about the attentions of glee club boys and of an engineering student, and she wrote home with evident pride when a suitor gave her a well-bound edition of the letters the eighteenth-century writer Lady Mary Wortley Montagu. She also enjoyed the prospect of parties, and her major expenses during her first year in Eugene seemed to be for party clothes, which she described to her mother in loving detail.[18] Throughout her life she would write home of her favorite outfits, revealing a taste for well-made, stylish, and flattering public attire.

Fashions aside, Miriam often made light of dates and male attention. Her comment on getting her friend Genevieve to come for a party—"I hope she will for I have succeeded in procuring a male for her"—contained a hint of sarcasm about the value women placed on male companionship.[19] So did Miriam's description of an instructor who invited her to a debate. A "clean-shaven, smug young man of about thirty," he was not very attractive, but, Miriam explained, "he is a human biped wearing trousers which after all is the main point."[20] In fact, for Miriam Van Waters, the main point was scholarship rather than social life, as she began to form an identity as an intellectual woman.

Her early comments on university women could not have predicted Van Waters' later interest in an academic life. She joked about the inability of her own "feminine mind" to grasp economics, and she referred to a course she took on railroad problems as "a queer one for a female."[21] She also showed little sense of identification with the few women on the faculty. Despite her initial appreciation of "the 'eminently' adorable English teacher," Miss Bidgelow, Miriam soon turned against the instructor for wrongly suspecting her of talking with a friend during an exam. Even Luella Clay Carson aggravated her by attempting to censor student publications. Miriam seemed far more generous in her evaluations of male instructors, whose attentions she appreciated.[22]

Gradually, however, a new concern about women appeared in her private and public writings. Personal experiences as a student may have influenced this shift, but another inspiration could have been the recurrent political controversies over woman suffrage in Oregon. Since the 1890s, suffrage crusader Abigail Scott Duniway had been lobbying the Oregon state legislature for the vote. The opposition of the *Portland Oregonian*—edited by her own brother, Harvey Scott—had thwarted Duniway's efforts. While Miriam Van Waters was in college, however, growing support from the women's club movement and a newly enacted referendum law revitalized the Oregon suffrage campaign. In the suffrage referenda of 1906 and 1908, prohibitionists battled the liquor dealers, who feared that women voters would outlaw alcohol. Miriam wrote home to ask her father how he planned to vote on the question, no doubt confident of his support. Although the Oregon state woman suffrage campaign would not succeed until 1912, Duniway and the growing women's movement kept the cause alive while Miriam Van Waters was a student.[23]

At the same time, college students were likely to be exposed to a new consciousness about women's issues through their literary and social studies. Miriam found the plays of Henrik Ibsen important enough to share with her mother. Both of them appreciated *The Doll's House,* with its message of female self-emancipation. Her comments on Ibsen's treatment of venereal disease revealed a new awareness of sexual injustice. "*Ghosts* isn't pretty I admit," she wrote her mother, but it taught "a necessary social lesson. If *that wife* had left her husband, at once, instead of tolerating his vices for the sake of convention and 'duty,' there would have been no terrible heritage left for the son." From Ibsen she learned to question whether "the wife should endure everything from the husband."[24] Her new concern echoed that of nineteenth-century social-purity activists, whose belief in woman's right to say no to sex remained influential for women of Van Waters' generation, even as modern ideas about female sexual emancipation gained popularity in America.

When Miriam Van Waters thought about women's emancipation, it usually involved not sex but a release from the home. For years she had brooded over her mother's heavy burden of child care and housework. Now she related her personal concern to the larger political agenda of women's movement into public life. Recounting her own domestic chores in Eugene, for example, Miriam joked to her mother that

"Woman really cannot 'emancipate' herself as long as that innate tendency of spring housecleaning inbred from generations assails her once a year." When Maud Van Waters reported on her new volunteer work in a local charity, Miriam commented proudly: "Now that my mother is so emancipated as to serve on public committees and attend clubs I am beginning to feel quite important and set up."[25] Life beyond housework appealed to both of them.

At the university, Miriam herself was serving on committees and participating in clubs, and gaining a sense of her own powers. As a member of the select Eutaxian Society, she participated on the women's debate team. She also became the literary editor and later editor-in-chief of the *Oregon Monthly,* a campus magazine whose associate editors included Louise Bryant.[26] Editing the magazine preoccupied Miriam for hours a day, forcing her studies into the background. It also provided her first lesson in weathering a political crisis. When Dean Carson insisted on reading the proofs of the *Monthly,* Miriam refused, despite the "strong partisanship" students expressed against her decision. "Instead of feeling hurt," she wrote home, "deep down in the Dutch currents of my being—I glory in the fights." Somewhat prophetically she reassured her mother that "As for resignation my darling . . . No Van Waters resigns—especially under difficulties."[27]

Miriam's editorials in the *Monthly* provide the clearest evidence of her evolving conception of women's political roles. For the most part she called for full equality for women, but she despaired at women's own lack of interest in politics. In her editorial, "Co-eds and the Franchise," she prodded women to participate in upcoming elections at the University of Oregon, citing events at the University of California at Berkeley, where male students unsuccessfully attempted to exclude women from participation in student government.[28] Although she blamed college women for their "inertia" when they failed to support Oregon's Eutaxian Society, the deeper problem, Miriam charged, was that the university valued men's organizations more than women's, as evidenced by its funding of intercollegiate competition for men only. By offering women "no opportunities" to compete with other schools, Oregon "consciously, and unconsciously, destroys their initiative." Aware of the way that inequality subtly undermined women's confidence, she called for an equal-rights solution—soon to be labeled feminism—namely, the extension of intercollegiate and interstate contests to women. But she recognized that equality required political mobilization as well as individual achievement, and so she again urged women to exert a "collective force in student body activities."[29]

During her years in Eugene, Miriam deepened her views not only on the woman question but also on contemporary social issues first raised in her father's rectory. At the turn of the century, social critics launched an assault on the excesses of industrial capitalism and the corruption of American government. Ranging from voluntary reformers who tried to ameliorate the plight of the urban poor to coalitions of government and business leaders who tried to regulate economic competition, the "progressives" varied greatly in background and politics. As a whole, however, they experimented with new forms of social welfare and governmental response to economic change.[30] Like the Social Gospel in which she was reared, progressivism spoke to Miriam Van Waters' concerns about social inequality and the responsibility of the community to improve health and welfare. Whether in the writings of muckraking journalists or of socially conscious academics, college students like her absorbed these criticisms of older political structures.

Courses offered at the university exposed Miriam Van Waters to the intellectual underpinnings of progressivism. The newly instituted elective system permitted her to choose courses of interest, including "Railroad Problems Considered Sociologically and Politically." The class convinced her that "the men who are approaching modern problems in sociology are most narrow." She gained an appreciation of public-health efforts through lectures on the movement to prevent tuberculosis within the public schools.[31] The service orientation of the state universities like Oregon encouraged these applications of social science to the solution of social problems. Unlike most private universities, which tended to value research for its own sake, state schools emphasized a combination of scholarship and public service.[32] In this way, college education deepened her early training in the Social Gospel and dovetailed with her missionary role in the family and community. The topic of her senior thesis, "The Relation of Philosophical Materialism to Social Radicalism," suggested that Miriam Van Waters hoped to apply abstract ideas to the transformation of society.

Aside from deepening her commitment to social service, during her college years Miriam explored the religious controversies that dominated American Protestantism. At a time when evolutionary thought was weakening the hold of traditional faith for many students, she stood firmly in the Darwinian camp, with a strong social Darwinist twist. Her father had exposed her to the writings of Herbert Spencer, and she now elaborated the evolutionary view of social change. In her 1908 commencement oration, for example, she discussed the Darwinian principle of variation, arguing that individuality, as well as social tolerance of individual difference, were requisite for social progress. Reflecting her father's insistence on getting the other person's point of view, Miriam heralded an educational policy that aspired "not to make everyone alike, but to make everyone different." This strong commitment to individualism, tempered by her belief in social responsibility, endured throughout her life.[33]

During her senior year, Miriam's political education spilled outside of the classroom and into the community, providing lessons that she would later use to her advantage. In 1907, Oregon's governor, under pressure from rural voters, vetoed a $125,000 legislative appropriation bill that would have allowed the construction of new buildings, laboratories, and libraries at the university. Opposition to the faculty's modern educational values had been fueled when one professor published an archaeological paper supportive of the theory of evolution. In response, as Miriam later recalled, local Baptist farmers were "up in arms." Supporters of the appropriations bill included the Portland women's clubs and the students at the university, who mobilized a letter-writing campaign and made speeches throughout the state. Sixty teams of students, each accompanied by a professor, went to speak to the local Grange chapters to ask their support for funding higher education. Miriam felt "tremendously excited" about the effort and volunteered "to tour the State holding meetings to prove we were not Godless." The students won their case, and the appropriation passed in the June 1908 referendum. Her report on the victory for the *Portland Oregonian* used rhetoric that would recur in Van Waters' later political struggles. The campaign, she wrote, was "the fight of the forces of progression against the blind and prejudiced forces of the Leviathan. . . . a struggle against ignorance and intellectual death."[34] In it she learned not only the drama of political battle but also the value of mobilizing loyal volunteers to gain public support for a controversial cause.

These extracurricular activities seemed to feed, rather than compete, with Van Waters' emerging academic commitments. Other than a few rough spots during her first year and the B she earned for her senior thesis, she received A's in her courses on literature, social history, economics, and psychology. A young professor of philosophy and education, Henry D. Sheldon, especially fostered her scholarly aspirations. In courses ranging from "Hindoo Philosophy" and "The Philosophy of Kant" to "Evolutionary Philosophy" and "Genetic Psychology," Sheldon taught her "that facts were meant to support ideas and ideas supported conclusions [and] conclusions must lead to decisions."[35] Scholarship, in short, could provide a powerful tool for action.

Professor Sheldon discovered that Miriam Van Waters was capable of "turning out large quantities of good work in a short time," and he soon made excellent use of these talents. At the beginning of her second (junior) year, when Sheldon needed to attend a conference, he asked Miriam to take over his class to discuss Darwin's *Origin of Species*. The prospect both daunted and delighted her. As she wrote home, "Fancy such an absurdity as Mayo [her family nickname] giving notes before a philosophy class! Dr. S. seems to have confidence in me, but I feel my anatomy dissolving. He will be gone four meetings of the class."[36] The teaching went well, however, better than she had expected. Again, just before her senior year, Sheldon asked her to cover his classes and manage the freshmen at the opening of school. Sitting in his office, setting up courses, taking roll, and holding his office hours, Miriam felt "most 'proffesorial [*sic*].'" After graduation, she stayed to complete a master's degree, serving as Sheldon's teaching assistant. More confident now, and aware of his dependence on her, she negotiated a better stipend. For three hundred dollars a year, she taught a daily class filled, as she later put it, with "theological students and college seniors who had flunked the year before." When she wasn't teaching, she worked on her master's thesis, expanding on the subject of philosophical materialism as a basis for social progress. She also began to make inquiries about doctoral programs in the East.[37]

It was probably at Sheldon's suggestion that she applied to Clark University, in Worcester, Massachusetts, where he had received his doctorate. Under the presidency of G. Stanley Hall, Clark had established nationally renowned graduate programs in psychology and pedagogy. Hall had been an important stimulus for the child study movement in the 1890s, and his 1904 book on *Adolescence* had both coined the term and set the research agenda on youth for the next generation. He also published studies of pedagogy and education. An experimental psychologist, Hall became interested in new psychoanalytic theories, as well. In 1909 he succeeded in bringing both Sigmund Freud and Carl Jung to speak at a conference held at Clark, bolstering the school's prestige after a period of declining reputation.[38]

Miriam Van Waters had majored in philosophy, not psychology, but her choice for graduate study made sense on several counts. Academic psychology had emerged in the nineteenth century from the broader discipline of philosophy, and at some universities, such as Clark and Harvard, the two continued to be taught within the same department.

At Clark, the psychology department encompassed courses on anthropology, philosophy, and education. Miriam Van Waters had also taken several laboratory courses in psychology, and she may have had an interest in pedagogy from her early teaching experiences. Clark was also a likely choice for graduate study because it had very recently joined the handful of private research universities that admitted women graduate students.

Whether Miriam Van Waters would be one of those accepted to Clark depended solely on the letters of recommendation to G. Stanley Hall from her Oregon professors. All of them rated her highly, but alongside their strong praise, their letters contained hints about the expectations that awaited a woman graduate student. University of Oregon president P. A. Campbell, for example, attested to Van Waters' "unusually brilliant" record, but alluded as well to her "attractive personality which wins friends and holds them." Such evaluations of personality, rather than intellect, appeared less frequently in recommendations for male students. Similarly, her sociology professor commented on Van Waters' "pleasing personality" and made significant gender distinctions: "In mental virility she is considered . . . to stand first among the young women who have come to us in recent years." Implicit in his language was the belief that male students, by definition, excelled further in "mental virility." [39]

Henry Sheldon's recommendation was even more revealing of faculty attitudes toward women interested in academic careers. Most of the letter to Hall, his old adviser, concerned Sheldon's own interest in a job in Kansas. He added, though, that a woman student in his department, well read in philosophy, ethics, and psychology, was highly capable, as well as "young and rather adaptable." Interestingly, Sheldon claimed that Miriam wanted to teach in a women's college, a goal she never articulated herself, but one that might have made her seem less threatening as a future colleague. Perhaps Sheldon thought his comment would help her chances, but if so, he immediately undermined her case when he asked, "Would there be any possibility for her in the way of scholarship or fellowship, or do you prefer men? I have a man who is good material, but he won't be ready for another year." Luckily for Miriam, Hall accepted her rather than wait for the male candidate. Beginning in fall 1910, she would hold a Junior University Fellowship at Clark to study psychology with G. Stanley Hall. [40]

Miriam Van Waters was not the only Oregon graduate to pursue doctoral work. Between 1902 and 1917, of the forty-seven students who earned master's degrees at Oregon, fifteen went on to eastern graduate schools for further study. Of these, almost half were women, including Miriam and her friend Elizabeth Woods, a literature major who also enrolled in the psychology department at Clark.[41] It is hard to know what motivated so many Oregon women to seek doctorates. Perhaps Luella Clay Carson and Miss Bidgelow had a more positive influence than Miriam's letters suggested. Or perhaps the widening currents of the women's movement encouraged these western coeds to seek careers in formerly male professions. In the case of Miriam Van Waters, there were personal considerations, as well. As she wrote to her mother after learning of her acceptance and fellowship, "dearest whatever of worth there may be in my work I want you to know that it is done in hope you and father will enjoy it and approve it."[42] Earning a doctorate was another step in fulfilling her parents' dreams, but one that would take Miriam beyond the Oregon boundary and further from her family base.

A Graduate Degree in Life

When Miriam Van Waters set out for Massachusetts in September 1910, at the age of twenty-two, she gradually left her West Coast childhood home to enter a bustling new world of academic inquiry and cultural difference. During the next three years, Clark University provided lessons that Van Waters would draw upon throughout her life. Although she absorbed the language of social science, her graduate experiences also led in unexpected directions. Increasingly conscious of gender and of women's movements for social change, she became critical of the limits of academic inquiry. By the time she left Clark in 1913, Van Waters had rejected many of the values she encountered there and was determined to find a way to combine her familial commitment to caring with the pursuit of an intellectual life.

From the beginning of her journey, it was clear that Miriam would not leave her past entirely behind. She made the cross-country railway trip with her friend Bess Woods, who also enrolled at Clark. Together they marveled at the western landscapes en route. "Maxfield Parrish gilded the sky and molded the contours of this *Arabian Nights* country," she wrote her mother. Reverend Van Waters met the young women in the East and took Miriam to visit his upstate New York hometown and meet her grandmother, Sarah Ann Van Waters. Once they reached Worcester, her father remained nearby for several weeks, sending home detailed accounts of the town, the university, and Professor G. Stanley Hall.[1]

George Browne Van Waters quickly bestowed his blessings on his daughter's new surroundings. Worcester, he declared, was "a fine healthy town to live in," and he assured his wife that Miriam would have no trouble meeting "the most prominent people of the city." Above all, he felt that she had been "most cordially received" at the university, where she met her new mentor, Clark University president G. Stanley Hall. "It is doubtful if I can have ever met his equal," Reverend Van Waters wrote of the sixty-six-year-old eminent psychologist. Hall spoke to him "in praiseworthy terms of Miriam" and of her training, professing a special interest "because of the fewness of her sex in this university and such institutions."[2]

Hall's statement about women students is suspect, given the history of coeducation at Clark University and Hall's own attitudes. The university's founder, local self-made businessman Jonas Clark, had wanted to endow an undergraduate college for men. His choice for president, G. Stanley Hall, insisted on creating a graduate research institution modeled on the German universities, with undergraduates to be added later. When Clark opened in 1889, the faculty and students were entirely male. Indeed, when Jonas Clark discovered that the chemist Helen Michael had full access to her husband's laboratory on the campus, the founder insisted that she be prohibited from entry, and Hall enforced the edict.[3]

The exclusion of women from graduate study at Clark in the 1890s contrasted with several other elite research universities. The University of Chicago, Stanford, Columbia, and Brown had each opened their doors to women graduate students, sometimes after campaigns by college-educated women pressured them to do so. As a result of new educational opportunities, the number of women earning doctorates increased dramatically, from 1 percent of all Ph.D.'s in 1890 to 11 percent in 1910.[4] At several schools, sympathetic male scholars had begun to foster social science research by women. Pioneering new work on the psychology and sociology of gender resulted from the tutelage of professors James Angell and George Herbert Mead at Chicago, for example. But G. Stanley Hall remained ambivalent, at best, about women students. He held conservative views about the innate differences between the sexes and claimed that college women lost the ability to nurture children. His fear that the influx of women into teaching endangered the manliness of boys was labeled, even at the time, as "reactionary."[5]

Hall's outlook would greatly affect Miriam Van Waters' life at Clark. In principle, he thoroughly supported the exclusion of women. "I am strongly opposed to giving women the slightest foot-hold in the college, even if we could do so under the Founders will," he wrote privately in 1909; "I feel they would crowd out the best men a little later." In practice, however, Hall reasoned that admitting a few women to the Ph.D. program "would save us a good deal of pounding by feminists" by staving off demands for undergraduate coeducation. His strategy followed that of Yale University, where women's admission to graduate study had been linked to the continuation of an all-male undergraduate college. Hall further argued that by depriving women of graduate education "we would needlessly shut off possible bequests." He was no doubt aware of the bargain struck at Johns Hopkins University in the 1890s, when wealthy women promised to donate significant sums to the medical school only if female students would be admitted. President Hall seemed especially concerned about keeping the women's movement from politicizing the issue at Clark. "A too drastic policy of exclusion," he feared, "would bring a reaction in favor of the women." Responding to his concerns, the Clark trustees compromised in 1910, ruling that courses in Clark College would be reserved exclusively for men, but that women could attend public lectures, and "those few women of marked ability and real promise" could enroll in the graduate programs. The stated purpose, however, was to keep the institution— which Hall ran almost single-handedly—"in the strictest sense an institution for young men only."[6]

G. Stanley Hall had envisioned "an average of one [woman] in ten years" completing a doctorate at Clark, but quite a few more, like Miriam Van Waters and Bess Woods, persevered. In 1911, over a fifth (seven out of thirty-one) of the graduate students in psychology were women, and a third (four out of eleven) of the psychology Ph.D.'s awarded in 1913 went to women. By 1916, however, the proportion of female graduate students in psychology had dropped to around an eighth (two out of fifteen), suggesting a weakening of support for women at the university.[7] When Miriam Van Waters enrolled at Clark in 1910, she thus took advantage of what turned out to be a small window of opportunity for her gender. Her experiences there would attest to the obstacles facing women.

At first Van Waters shared her father's enthusiasm about her new mentor, G. Stanley Hall. He seemed "very strong, and big and courteous," and a few months later she characterized him well as "that clear-thinking, logical man of science." Miriam liked both his practice of allowing students to drop by his study in the evenings to talk informally about their ideas and the Monday evening seminar he held at his home, just across the street from campus. These lively seminars lasted from seven o'clock until after midnight, with up to thirty students participating. At each seminar, two students, or sometimes a visitor, would present formal papers about their work. Heated debate followed, and the evenings concluded with Hall's erudite summations. During the break between papers, Florence Smith Hall would serve refreshments. Miriam's accounts of these evenings frequently commented on Mrs. Hall, an unpretentious former high-school teacher who made the insecure western emigrant feel more welcome.[8]

Miriam was having a difficult time adjusting to the social climate of New England. In Worcester, an industrial elite ruled over a large, ethnically mixed working class, imposing their standards of decorum whenever possible. The population, she felt, consisted largely of "polite, courteous people with frightful hats and ill-fitting clothes" who "make no noise." They were so polite and quiet that Miriam wanted to go out and stomp her feet. "I am perfectly satisfied with the University," she assured her mother, "but never, never—shall I love the East. I could never accustom myself throughly [*sic*] to the climate and the people are just the same!" Amid the coldness she identified with Easterners, she felt terribly homesick. Her letters frequently referred to the superiority of western states and their people. "My heart is not in Worcester," Miriam confessed. Only the friendship of Bess Woods eased the transition. "I love her dearly," she wrote of Bess, "and were it not for her I think I could not endure the longing."[9]

Miriam treasured the "adorable little flat" she shared with Bess. They rented the middle level of a three-decker family home from a French-speaking family. Its fully equipped kitchen and proximity to the university and city streetcar lines made her feel very fortunate. She and Bess shared the bedroom and used the other room for study and dining. The flat became a domestic refuge from the cold New Englanders of Worcester and the stresses of the university. When a particularly painful Belinda forced Miriam to bed for the day, her dear friend Bess nursed her there "with every care and tenderness," bringing her coffee and helping her dress.[10]

Despite her homesickness and a lingering western provincialism, Miriam was exulting in her exposure to new ideas and new people. She attended as many lectures as possible, especially when visitors came to Clark or the community. She had read with pleasure the books of Harvard philosopher George Santayana, and she eagerly anticipated his Worcester lecture in 1911. Disappointed by his talk, Miriam now judged his views "hazy and indefinite and mystic." More to her liking was John Spargo, who spoke before the Clark Socialist Society. She praised the muckraking socialist who supported the International Workers of the World, as "a poet and thinker and . . . a doer." This distinction between mystic and doer would recur as her intellectual and political views developed in graduate school. Along with Bess Woods she became active in the campus socialist group, a branch of a then-popular political movement on the left of the progressive political spectrum. With another friend she went to Boston to listen to Eugene Debs, the Socialist presidential candidate, in 1912. Miriam called the meeting "a high water mark in community enthusiasm." Although radicals had congregated in her hometown of Portland, only now did she begin to identify with their views.[11]

In graduate school Miriam Van Waters encountered not only more radical political ideas but also more diverse cultures than she had known in Oregon. Her undergraduate campus had consisted almost entirely of young, white, Protestant, middle-class Westerners. Clark included people of other religions, races, and cultures who fascinated Miriam. Her initial impression of the university noted its variety: "Many Europeans, one negro, one Japanese are enrolled," she wrote home, adding that some students were as old as her parents.

Her encounters with foreign cultures challenged some of Miriam's earlier views. During her first semester, for example, Clark hosted an international history conference at which she met George Washington Ellis, an African American lawyer and former U.S. diplomat in Liberia who had begun a second career as a student of West African cultures. Dr. Ellis called on Miriam and Bess several times, bringing native artifacts as gifts and sharing parts of his forthcoming book. "I never met a more polite, learned, dignified man in my life," Miriam commented. Given the portrayal of Africans in the missionary appeals she heard as a child, Ellis' theories about African contributions to world civilization must have taken her by surprise. At the same time, the former convertor of Chinese immigrants to Christianity heard G. Stanley Hall lecture that missionaries should "*conserve* the national and racial religions of foreign people" rather than destroy them. Similarly, an anthropologist speaking on South American tribal cultures challenged her belief in missionary uplift of the heathen. A more romanticized notion of the noble "savage"—a term she retained—entered Miriam Van Waters' thinking. "I learn here that we have had the wrong idea of savages," she wrote her mother. "People who *live* among them have decided they do not fight, murder, or commit as many sex crimes as we do . . . savages are gentle and human." In these exchanges she began to absorb the new theories of cultural relativism that would later influence both her dissertation and her approach to reform.[12]

Miriam also discovered racial concerns closer to home. At one of Hall's evening seminars, "a fiery discussion" followed a paper by a black doctoral candidate who was studying the American race problem. "Our Southern students were most biased," she concluded. Suddenly conscious of race herself, Miriam now took note whenever she met a Black or a Jew, describing them in terms meant to convey liberal acceptance. Even with her liberal Christian upbringing, she had been taught that

Jews needed to be converted. In Boston, however, she now attended a Jewish religious service and judged the rabbi to be "excellent, full of father's views." When she met Jessie Sampter, "a fascinating little Jewess" who had published a book endorsed by Harvard philosopher Josiah Royce, she wrote home several times about the woman's accomplishments. The routine exclusion of Jews and Blacks from elite universities at this time accounts in part for her curiosity about a Jewish author and an African American professor. Yet in pointing out these minorities, Miriam sometimes perpetuated racial stereotypes by her emphasis on their exceptionalism. For years, even as she reached out professionally to both Blacks and Jews, her language belied old attitudes, as if it were necessary, for example, to distinguish "fine Jewish women" from some other sort. Compared to the discriminatory culture in which she lived, however, her liberal tolerance and concern for racial justice were exceptional.[13]

During her years at Clark, Miriam Van Waters also viewed a wider world of possibilities for women. Previously, her primary models had been her mother, an overburdened minister's wife, and her female teachers at St. Helen's and in Eugene, who had taught but not necessarily inspired her. Now Miriam noticed a variety of women's roles, writing home in detail about the faculty wife, the faculty woman, and the activist. For all of her fascination with what she called the "'big man' work" at the university, she observed carefully the world of women who quietly facilitated academic life, usually without recognition.

Miriam gained a faculty wife's perspective on the university when Mrs. Hall invited her to help serve guests during receptions at their home. Florence Hall provided the hospitality to make her husband's students more comfortable, with special outreach to the women of the university. She regularly entertained the wives of students and faculty and asked Miriam and Bess to help her serve coffee for this group. It was "not a very august gathering but we enjoyed meeting them," Miriam remarked, suggesting her identification with faculty, not their wives. But she and Bess felt very appreciative of Mrs. Hall's efforts, and when Dr. Hall was away, they invited his wife to dinner. Florence Hall reciprocated, introducing the young women to her personal friends. Miriam soon began to pity her professor's wife because of the duties that went with her position, astutely observing how the social tasks expected of faculty wives could take a heavy personal toll. In contrast to her husband's vitality, Mrs. Hall looked ill and sad. In fact, she was later diagnosed with a deteriorative illness, but only after her husband had her committed to a mental institution.[14]

In contrast to faculty wives, the "women of the university"—graduate students and postdoctoral fellows—impressed Miriam greatly. Some of them were married yet pursuing academic life, a rare enough phenomenon to warrant her comment. All seemed to her "most cordial." What especially inspired her was the ability of women to succeed within the academic world. One German woman had won an academic prize shortly after women gained university admission. She even met women who were "really *paid* for writing books—apart from the book sale which will be theirs too."[15] The vision of a career as a woman scholar was becoming more concrete.

Miriam also noticed the differential treatment of academic women. Dr. Theodate Smith—a Yale Ph.D. whom she called "Dr. Hall's memory and general information bureau"—told the women students a "hair-raising" story about Wellesley psychology professor Mary Calkins. Harvard University refused to grant Calkins a Ph.D., even though she had completed her doctoral work there. They offered her a Radcliffe degree, but she refused, Miriam recounted, "saying she had never put her foot in Radcliffe; with her it was to be Harvard or nothing." Miriam recognized discrimination at Clark, as well. When Theodate Smith walked into a lecture, "twenty men jumped up and offered her twenty chairs and it was the most embarrassing moment of her life." Chivalry, she was learning, often masked disrespect for women's intellectual accomplishments.[16]

In response to a hostile climate, university women banded together, sharing both horror stories and moments of triumph. On several occasions Hall's weekly seminar motivated such gatherings. The male students usually "excluded" the women, but on one occasion, the men "sat perfectly dumb" because two of the female participants— Bess Woods and Caroline Fisher—dominated a discussion. Later that night the excited women students gathered in Miriam's flat and sat up talking until 2:00 A.M., reassuring Fisher that she had not "made a fool of herself." After they "comforted our tall and lanky psychologist," Miriam "rolled up on the couch," while Fisher "went to sleep with B[ess]." The next fall, when a German scholar, Dr. Hersh-Ernst, appeared at G. Stanley Hall's seminar, Miriam reported that her professor "was inclined to sneer because she is a woman. So he called her Fraulein instead of Doctor." Hersh-Ernst had the last word. "She said before all, 'But Dr. Hall, as you are not Mr. so I am not Fraulein. And besides I am not a single woman'!" Miriam loved the retort and invited Hersh-Ernst to dinner. Other women students stopped by, and they stayed up until midnight arguing about politics in Germany and America.[17]

As Miriam became conscious of discrimination within the university, she showed increasing interest in the women's movement. Though less successful than in Oregon, the suffrage movement had recently revived in Massachusetts, animated by the new public, militant strategies of the British suffragists and by an influx of younger American members. Just before Miriam arrived in Worcester, Massachusetts suffragists had traveled by trolley from Springfield to Boston, staging outdoor rallies along the way. Alongside the older state and regional suffrage associations, activist groups recently formed at Wellesley, Smith, and Mt. Holyoke Colleges.[18] Meanwhile, women social reformers in Boston were organizing to help working women and children. As in other parts of the country, Boston women targeted the low wages paid female laborers and the problems working-class families faced, including poverty and crime.

Hearing about these social and political activists inspired Miriam. Just a few weeks after she came to Clark she met a "splendid" young woman Ph.D. who had been "engaging in the suffragist movement" in England. Her sympathies for activists recurred alongside a critique of more conservative women, such as two sisters who represented "Boston ultra-society." "I suppose each one of them per year consumes enough to keep five families alive," Miriam complained, "and yet they are loud in denunciation of those 'frights in flat-heeled shoes, who carry men's handkerchiefs and lead shirt-waist girls' strikes and eat and sleep nothing but woman suffrage!'"[19]

Other Boston women were more appealing to her than these society types. Over Thanksgiving, when Miriam and Bess visited Boston, they lunched at "a truly wonderful place," the Women's Educational and Industrial Union. The WEIU, founded in 1877, was a cross-class women's exchange through which volunteers offered lectures, skill training, a job registry, a lunchroom, and legal aid for the city's working women. When Miriam joked about Boston philanthropists helping "truly respectable working girls to acquire an accent," she revealed her distrust of condescending uplift efforts. At the WEIU, however, she found much to admire. "It is like a great arts and crafts display," she wrote, "filled with the skill of clever women." Here women from diverse class, religious, and ethnic backgrounds truly cooperated to provide economic and intellectual opportunities for women workers. The vision appealed to Miriam Van Waters.

She felt less comfortable around Boston's more Bohemian crowd, which congregated at the English Tea Room. Her reaction to this set revealed conventional notions of gender and attire. "Some women wore sleeves rolled to the elbow and were manish [*sic*] in the extreme," she wrote, and "all had a 'look'" that told her that she was out of her element.[20] Whether or not she had already read Havelock Ellis' new theories of sexual inversion, which linked mannish attire to homosexuality, her own tastes ran to more feminine, though tailored, styles. Her politics, too, remained more conventional than this Bohemian set, despite her attraction to socialism. The emerging feminist movement, with its goal of equal citizenship for women, had greater appeal for her. She eagerly anticipated spending Christmas vacation in Boston because, she wrote home, there were "some famous suffragette meetings that week and we will surely go." Caught up in the gathering wave of women's politics, she also expressed pride when a huge suffrage parade—"the best parade in [the] political history of New York!"—took place in New York City in 1911.[21]

Even more influential than suffrage militants, indeed the most important influence on Miriam's developing social consciousness, was Jane Addams. A model of maternalistic leadership in social reform, Addams had cofounded the Hull House settlement in Chicago and campaigned to improve work, housing, and recreation for urban families. Miriam first learned about Addams' accomplishments at Clark, both during a lecture on recreation for working men and women and from Dr. Ellis, who had worked at Hull House. Together Miriam and Bess read out loud Addams' "splendid books," *The Spirit of Youth and the City Streets* (1909) and *Twenty Years at Hull House* (1910). Miriam found these books inspirational because they showed her that "even in a dingy, saddened world one energetic loving, clever woman can work miracles." This description could have become her own life creed, for it captures well the public role she would assume through much of her career. Deeply impressed by what she read, Miriam aspired to meet Jane Addams and wrote to her about possibly visiting Hull House, a goal she would achieve repeatedly in later life.[22]

The books that so inspired Miriam Van Waters in 1911 summarized Addams' approach to social reform through community services. Like many other progressives, Jane Addams identified urban, working-class youth as the innocent casualties of industrialization. With the decline of traditional social life, based in families and communities, youth lacked guidance and faced the temptations of the city streets. Whether crusading against child labor or against the seduction of working girls into prostitution, Addams decried a society that exploited the labor, or the sexuality, of youth. Like G. Stanley Hall, she targeted the transition from childhood to adulthood as a critical period in the formation of morality, but in contrast to Hall, Addams offered an interventionist rather than academic approach to the problems of wayward youth. Reading her books introduced Miriam to the movements for parks, playgrounds, and legitimate theater that could "provide for the insatiable desire for play" and counteract the streets or commercial dance halls. Here, too, she read about the juvenile court, an experiment in judicial social work first established in Chicago in 1899 through the efforts of Hull House reformers and middle-class women's clubs. Indeed, *The Spirit of Youth and the City Streets* contained the seeds of most of Miriam Van Waters' later interest in juvenile delinquency, imprisoned women, progressive education, and alternative forms of recreation.[23]

Addams' books so impressed Miriam that she recommended them to her mother and anticipated their reading them together over the summer. Their subsequent mother-daughter talks provided an opportunity for Maud to express her anxiety about Miriam's future. Ever since her daughter had gone to Clark, Maud Van Waters had worried about the effect of graduate school. Reading Miriam's accounts of famous scholars and her "great ambition" to be like them, Maud may well have detected a growing intellectual snobbery. She also feared that Clark University was driving a wedge between mother and daughter. Maud did not want Miriam's education to unfit her for the "companionship of ordinary intellects," such as members of the Van Waters family. In response, Miriam had reassured Maud that deeper learning about "the secrets of life" would allow her to love all of mankind, not only "the specialists and scientists" but also "the people who stay at home and make the world go round." Succeeding at Clark could lead to her goal of accomplishing "something definite" in life, but it would not, she promised, make her feel superior to her parents and siblings.[24]

Maud Van Waters' concerns about the usefulness of education made her daughter more conscious of the limitations of the scholarly life around her. Some students "shrink up under knowledge," Miriam observed, but for others knowledge was "merely a tool in the hand for service, or better understanding of life." She assured her mother that she hoped to become like the latter, never "too learned" to serve others. The exchange no doubt touched a deep-seated desire to be of help to her mother, who now seemed to direct that instinct, whether intentionally or not, toward social service. Both talking with her mother and reading Jane Addams eased Miriam Van Waters' eventual transition "away from 'teaching,' and into real living—contact with women and men." Increasingly committed to an ideal of knowledge as service, she wrote home that "had I not known two great women—my Mother and Jane Addams—I would not have the insight into this."[25]

Miriam Van Waters' appreciation of the women's movement, and her interest in putting knowledge into service for others, gathered strength alongside her growing disillusionment with graduate school. Self-doubts about her abilities to succeed at Clark had plagued her from the outset, but serious questions about the value of academic training soon emerged. Her high hopes about becoming an accomplished university woman gave way to apprehension about remaining at Clark, especially in the light of growing disenchantment with G. Stanley Hall. She did persist, but only by redesigning her academic program entirely and shifting her allegiance to a new mentor.

The autonomy she enjoyed at Clark had in fact fed Miriam's doubts about her own abilities. "The flow of work is wholly personal," she explained. "You go to any, or all lectures without restraint—or you stay away and work." The graduate students also met at a weekly Journal Club to review current literature, and they attended Hall's Monday evening seminar. But the only measures of their performance would be the oral examination, taken at any time from one to three years after entrance, and the all-important doctoral thesis. Miriam soon learned that not everyone passed these tests. At the end of her first year at Clark, for example, she and Bess consoled a fellow student whose thesis Hall had rejected.[26]

The pressure to win Hall's approval began to undermine her confidence further. Usually quite verbal, Miriam remained silent at the Monday evening seminars during her entire first semester at Clark. Then, in January 1911, fortified by "a fresh shirt-waist, a new tie, well-brushed clothes, shoes, and a very stiff collar," she gave her first public presentation at the seminar. Despite her professional attire, the evening was a "great strain," and she suffered from a nervous headache the next day. "But," she proclaimed, "I shall never feel so timid again; the ice is broken." By the end of the year she ventured a critique of Hall's views at the seminar, parrying the attacks of his students until Hall—whom she now described as "the clever old Sulten [*sic*] himself"—came to their aid. Then Miriam once again "crawled down and out."[27]

If Miriam Van Waters had expected Hall's seminars to resemble her father's comfortable rectory chats, her confrontation with a truly autocratic academic must have been personally devastating. Yet she struggled for another year trying to find a way to appease Hall without acceding to his demands for intellectual conformity. The blind loyalty of Hall's students, not only in the seminar but also in their academic work, dismayed her. She realized fairly quickly how Hall's demands for allegiance served his ends. "He uses his tractable students to collect data of all kinds, which later he combines," she explained to her mother. Although she tried to interest him in her own ideas during their meetings, Miriam felt that unless she tackled "one of *Dr. Hall's* problems—one got nothing out of him." His posture during these sessions—eyes half-closed, legs crossed at the knees—made Miriam feel that he was sailing off by himself as she spoke. As much as she wanted Hall's attention, Miriam resisted undertaking one of his projects, for they seemed to her to produce such "minute results."[28]

One irreconcilable difference between mentor and student arose from Miriam's academic training in philosophy, which inclined her to raise broad questions about human behavior that were unanswerable through experimental psychology. G. Stanley Hall had been inspired by philosophy himself. As a student of William James in the 1870s, he had written about Hegel; he continued to try to synthesize philosophy, psychology, and Darwinian biology in his grand theories of "genetic psychology." But early on Hall had embraced the new scientific psychology, and he encouraged his students to undertake rigorous laboratory and survey research that elaborated on his notions of the evolutionary inheritance of mental capacity.[29]

For some time this new experimental method had been replacing the older, nineteenth-century philosophical approach, creating a social science that emphasized objectivity rather than humanitarian reform. Miriam mourned the passing of "the old scientific, philosophical, literary school," with its broader humanistic approach. She told Hall that she valued applied philosophy as an "important humanizing and socializing influence" that could guide individual moral conduct. Citing the American reformer Lester Frank Ward, author of *Applied Sociology* (1906), Miriam stressed the relationship between "philosophical ideas and social progress." She proposed an ambitious dissertation on the impact of German idealists upon "the normal thousands who found their philosophy congenial." But Hall did not value this kind of project. As she wrote to her parents early in her graduate career, "It is born in upon me yet a trained psychologist measuring heartbeats in a laboratory experiment in attention, memory, fatigue etc. is rated higher in the modern academic world than the most oracular of living philosophers." For her, however, writing a dissertation in psychology depended too much "on one's ability to dissect thoroughly one inch of reality." She hesitated to "harness" herself "to some sort of mental peanut, and by much straining and groaning—lift it from the ground."[30]

Her disillusionment with Hall extended to his theories as well as his methods. Hall promulgated the "recapitulation" theory, by which individual human development followed the evolutionary progress of "the race." Thus children's behavior could be explained by reference to primitive cultures, while adults recapitulated advanced civilization. Primitive peoples represented development arrested at the stage of childhood or adolescence. Although he was, for his time, generally tolerant about racial difference, Hall did place great weight on the biological determinants of behavior and culture. In Miriam's words, "Dr. Hall is interested only in *Genetic* methods, tracing of origins of the racial stock of knowledge, feeling etc.; and in brilliant expositions of theories I cannot possibly accept."[31]

Despite these differences, she repeatedly tried to find some way to please Hall with a thesis topic acceptable to both of them. She refused his suggestion that she edit his lectures, presented her own ideas about Schopenhauer, and contemplated leaving Clark. Eventually Miriam recognized what many of Hall's colleagues and students already knew— how little room there was for disagreement with the method, and the theories, of positivistic social science, or with the psychology and personality of G. Stanley Hall. Even one of Clark's prize students, Lewis M. Terman, who later popularized the IQ test, acknowledged that "to go into anything at Clark without the backing of Dr. Hall, makes unpleasant business."[32] Clark had in fact deteriorated under Hall's autocratic leadership, and bright scholars repeatedly refused to work under him. In Miriam's words, "mediocrity and *agreement* go better here than originality and one's own opinions." Even when she tried working in philosophy, she found that "Dr. Hall insists on edging in his own problems. And his edging in is like the camel's nose in the tent: once in— and the whole game is up."[33]

Although her struggles with Hall lasted for two years, a marked change in outlook characterized Miriam after spending the summer of 1911 with her family in Oregon. Talking with her mother about Jane Addams helped Miriam redefine her values, while the comforts of home helped her recuperate from the struggles with Hall. When she and Bess returned in September 1911, Worcester didn't seem "quite so ugly" as before, and, she wrote home, the "abruptness of the people doesn't hurt as it used." Decorating their new flat gave her endless pleasure, as did her landlord's family, the Carrs, for they were not New Englanders.[34]

Miriam started the school year with a symbolic declaration of independence from her mentor. She began to organize women graduate students to demand that Hall grant them access to the college gymnasium. After circulating a petition to the president, with her signature at the top of the list, she met with him to argue the women's case. She also became active in the Intercollegiate Socialist Society, contributing to the wave of support that gave the Socialist Party its peak electoral popularity. In a further break from the values of pure scholarship, she even planned to attend an Ivy League football game, something she had disdained in college. And in contrast to her earlier reaction to the styles of mannish women in Boston, she now wrote home about a boy's coat she had purchased for herself at a men's clothing store, emphasizing its lower price as her motive.[35] Miriam Van Waters, age twenty-three, seemed determined to carve her own path.

Having relinquished her vision of a philosophical thesis, she still tried to find a research project that would be acceptable to Hall but broad enough to have social implications beyond the laboratory. Reading Jane Addams and visiting Boston had piqued her interest in urban reform, particularly the Progressive Era movement to understand juvenile delinquency. Settlement workers had been instrumental in establishing the first specialized juvenile courts in major cities, and several women social scientists, concerned about poverty and crime, were investigating the backgrounds of female offenders. In his book *Adolescence,* G. Stanley Hall had argued that juvenile crime was increasing and called for the scientific study of "criminaloid youth."[36] A dissertation on some aspect of female criminality might combine Miriam's interests in social reform with Hall's requisite psychological methods.

At the time Miriam Van Waters attended graduate school, social scientists heatedly debated the hereditary theories of crime popularized by the nineteenth-century Italian criminologist Cesar Lombroso. Several women scholars who were curious about the origins of prostitution argued that economic discrimination and alienating work conditions led women to become prostitutes. Like these critics, Miriam wondered whether women's low wages had more to do with their delinquency than did their family backgrounds. In 1911 she decided that she could make a substantial contribution through a scientific study of these questions.[37] Using one of Hall's favorite methods, she designed a questionnaire. Entitled "Psychology of Adolescence," it

would "divide the environmental cases of delinquency from the hereditary" for a group of local "defective children."

Her proposed survey previewed the topics Van Waters would write
about during the next two decades, when she became a leading national authority on juvenile delinquency. It also raised questions that
she would ponder in her own life, as she faced the changing possibilities for women's social and sexual roles. Intended to be distributed to
two thousand girls, the survey inquired into their family and social life,
as well as their personal values. It sought qualitative answers to questions about girls' initial sex education; gender identity ("did you wish
to be a boy?"); sexual development (was your first "love for some one
you knew closely, or for some distant person . . . or for some older
woman or girl friend?"); career plans ("Which would you prefer, a domestic life, or a public life in any of the above careers?"); marriage and
childbearing plans; and political interests ("Have you ever longed for
philanthropic service; . . . Have you any interest in politics? Woman
Suffrage? Socialism?"). A separate questionnaire for teachers also asked
about group behavior and leadership patterns among girls, the value of
coeducational versus single-sex schools, and the nature of "crushes"
between girls (are they "based on mutuality of interest and inclination;
or are they more likely to exist between 'masculine,' and excessively
'feminine' types?").[38]

It is not clear whether Miriam ever collected the data for this project. She printed up the questionnaire, but she never wrote the study,
for the inevitable parting of the ways soon took place. Although they
maintained polite relations in their correspondence for some time, G.
Stanley Hall ceased to advise Miriam Van Waters. By the spring of 1912,
her second year at Clark, she had switched fields. As she wrote home,
Alexander Chamberlain, "under whose sympathetic and wonderfully
scientific advice I am now working," would direct her dissertation in
anthropology.[39]

While G. Stanley Hall represented an old guard resistant to academic women, Alexander Chamberlain held out a vision of an egalitarian and politically engaged university. Miriam had first heard of Chamberlain at one of Mrs. Hall's teas, where she met his wife, Isabel
Cushman Chamberlain, who was a suffragist. Miriam and Bess soon
dined with the Chamberlains and their ten-year-old daughter, a free-
spirited tomboy being educated at home. Miriam marveled at the way
the three "live together like chums in charming disorder and freedom."
During her first year at Clark, the Chamberlains took Bess and Miriam

under their wing, winning their hearts and providing an alternative perspective on academics and politics. In Miriam's view, Alexander Chamberlain was, like Hall, a great scholar, yet he also struck her as tender and simple as a child. She recognized the human quirks of this "very erratic man," whom she called "quite adorable and always different." Chamberlain allowed her intellectual independence and seeming unconditional support. An unconventional academic, possibly reminiscent of her unconventional clergyman father, he proved to be a much more suitable mentor for her than had G. Stanley Hall.[40]

Alexander Francis Chamberlain was a maverick in the university. His refusal to wear a cap and gown for Founder's Day exercises symbolized his irreverent stance. A Canadian born in England, he had originally come to Clark to work under Franz Boas, the pioneer in ethnographic fieldwork methods and theories of cultural relativism. Chamberlain earned the first doctorate in anthropology offered by an American university. In 1892, when Boas, along with other disgruntled professors, left Clark, Chamberlain succeeded his mentor as a professor. He remained a loyal faculty member until his death, at age forty-nine, in 1914. An expert on folklore, childhood, and Native American peoples, Chamberlain coedited the *Journal of Religious Psychology* with Hall. His cross-cultural study, *The Child* (1900), enjoyed considerable popularity. While Hall emphasized inheritance, Chamberlain, like Boas, turned to learning experiences to explain racial differences. Chamberlain argued that most gender differences resulted not from biology but from the "subjection of woman by man."[41] He also provided a model of a politically engaged academic. He chaired the Worcester Democratic City Committee and served as alderman-at-large in 1905. A popular lecturer, Chamberlain frequently addressed local groups in support of labor unions, prohibition, and woman suffrage. The outspoken professor railed against the liquor trust, criticized Worcester's school system, and urged a packed crowd at a Congregational church to support equal suffrage and the "end of the servitude of the sex."[42]

Alexander Chamberlain was a perfect solution to Miriam Van Waters' academic dilemma. Here was a professor who combined joy in scholarly research, advanced social views, and political engagement. For almost two years she had struggled to please G. Stanley Hall and to justify a narrow thesis in the light of her awakening consciousness about economic and sexual inequality. As the problems of the real world increasingly intrigued her, she looked to reformers like Chamberlain and Jane Addams, who placed research in the service of social progress.

The Chamberlains also provided Miriam with a link to the world of social service. Isabel Chamberlain's brother, Roy Cushman, worked as a probation officer at the Boston Juvenile Court. Over dinner at her professor's house, Miriam heard Cushman describe the court's efforts to prevent juvenile delinquents from going to jail. The court had been established in 1906, under the supervision of Judge Harvey Baker. When Miriam and Bess visited Boston, Cushman's sightseeing tour included a visit there. The experience was eye-opening for Miriam. She learned that thousands of boys were brought to court every year for offenses such as stealing food or playing ball in the street or on Sunday. Her reaction echoed the child-saving efforts of urban reformers. "Really," she wrote, "their elders ought to be busy building playgrounds instead of locking them up." On another visit Cushman introduced her to Judge Baker, who allowed her to sit in on his relatively informal juvenile court hearings. The importance of Baker's court left her "profoundly thrilled."[43] Something in the court, perhaps the authority of the earnest Judge Baker and his efforts to save children's lives, touched a deep chord in Miriam Van Waters, who would one day sit in judgment in her own court.

While talking with social workers at the Boston Juvenile Court, Miriam discovered their common outlook on the social, rather than hereditary, causes of crime. "These capable women," she wrote, "helped strengthen my own beforehand conviction that there is no 'juvenile vice.' There are no 'wicked' boys and girls—only bad homes—rich and poor—and bad health and bad civic life and no adequate work for eager hands to do." A society that spent more for jails and gallows than for preventive services had wrong priorities, in her view. Similarly, she criticized American courts for protecting the economic privileges enjoyed by Standard Oil, the railroads, and other corporations, which were then the objects of muckraking journalistic exposés. Reflecting Progressive Era rhetoric, with its critique of laissez-faire capitalism, she blamed social problems on the selfish interests that impeded America's general welfare. Like progressive educational reformers, she linked child welfare with the reform of social values. Thus, she concluded, "the only remedy" for selfishness was to teach children to care for the common good, "not by instruction—but by real and true simplicity in living." This phrase contained the germ of her future quest for alternative, educational responses to delinquency.[44]

The juvenile court inspired Miriam Van Waters to contemplate new career possibilities. Through the university she worked on a project that sent her to inspect girls' reformatories and industrial schools in

Massachusetts. Her travels showed her that "some of the cleverest and highly organized women in Massachusetts" were involved in the administration of these schools. Still looking for a thesis topic, she envisioned making a scientific study of them. She also interviewed for a paid position in a Boston social welfare agency, but Alexander Chamberlain advised her to concentrate on a thesis before taking a job. They agreed that Miriam should spend one last year at Clark, 1912–13, to work on a thesis exploring "the anthropology, psychology etc. of the adolescent girl . . . past and present." The topic combined Chamberlain's interest in cross-cultural studies of childhood with her new concerns about juvenile delinquency.[45]

During the summer of 1912 Miriam collected data on delinquent girls at the Portland Municipal Court, once again looking for physical and social determinants of criminality. When she returned to Worcester she mined the available ethnographies of "primitive" cultures, especially the work of Franz Boas, Alice Fletcher, and P. E. Goddard. From dozens of studies she culled lists of puberty rituals, tabulating their frequency and the extent of gender overlap or difference. She also read general works on social theory, childhood, and sexuality, including Sigmund Freud and sexologists Havelock Ellis and Richard Krafft-Ebing. In winter 1913, she submitted a draft of her thesis to Chamberlain and was elated when he found it satisfactory. After completing the final dissertation, she produced a fifty-page condensation for publication in the *Journal of Religious Psychology.*[46]

Miriam Van Waters' doctoral thesis, titled "The Adolescent Girl among Primitive People," reveals her intellectual grounding in contemporary psychology and anthropology. She introduced it by criticizing Hall's recapitulation theory and rejecting Freud's views of infantile sexuality, stressing instead (as did G. Stanley Hall), the importance of adolescence in sexual development. Aside from these opening comments, the study was largely descriptive, as were most anthropology dissertations written to elaborate on the cultural theories of Franz Boas. One underlying theme that emerged in the thesis was the social function of puberty rituals, which, she pointed out, often served to maintain group cohesion, male control, or social status. In this approach Van Waters anticipated the functionalist anthropology that would soon succeed the evolutionary school.[47] The thesis also emphasized the need for greater sexual freedom for adolescent girls, which meant not promiscuity but access to sexual information.

Like Chamberlain's work, her thesis tended to romanticize native cultures, especially American Indians, citing, for example, their egalitarian treatment of women and acceptance of out-of-wedlock births. Implicitly or explicitly she drew contrasts highlighting the superiority of native tolerance over modern sexual repression. In discussing homosexuality, for example, she described institutionalized gender-crossing among North American Indians and then concluded: "Among primitive peoples, a useful and appropriate life-role is commonly furnished the inverted individual. It is quite possible that modern policy could profitably go to school to the primitive in this regard."[48]

The final section of her published thesis, subtitled "Some Suggestions as to Modern Application," reported on the cases of three hundred women brought to the Portland Municipal Court between 1908 and 1911, along with twenty-five recent cases Van Waters investigated herself. It seemed oddly out of place, as if tagged on to her anthropological review, but it suggested the direction of her future work. In this section she reiterated her earlier view that there was no correlation between physical defect and delinquency. In the past, however, she had been sympathetic to eugenic calls for the sterilization of the "feebleminded" to prevent criminality.[49] Her research now showed that only 2 percent of the delinquent girls she tested had extremely low intelligence scores. Along with illustrating her faith in scientific measurement, the discussion pointed toward Van Waters' sociological approach to criminology.

In an effort to use the methods of anthropological research to displace both an older Lombrosian criminology and the "race psychology" of Hall, Van Waters detailed two intriguing case studies that anticipated her later approach to women prisoners. The first involved "H. A.," a young woman arrested for vagrancy and accused of being a "white slaver" because she brought girls to her rooms at night. She was, in fact, a cross-dresser who had adopted men's clothing and housed girls to protect them from becoming prostitutes. According to Van Waters, since H. A. lacked the privilege of labor "accorded to men and boys," her criminality resulted from discrimination: "She steadfastly refuses to wear woman's clothes, declaring that it is impossible for her to earn an honest and adequate living while dressed as a woman." Reluctant to label H. A. a "true homosexual," Van Waters argued that sympathy for women of the underworld rather than sexual proclivities accounted for her approaches to girls. The second case also emphasized economic and social forces. A woman who had been raped at age sixteen and later abandoned by her fiancé was struggling to earn a living, first as a dance hall girl and then as a factory operative. Economically desperate, she hustled a "cad"—a man on the prowl—who died in her room during a struggle with her boyfriend. This case, too, pointed toward Van Waters' overall conclusion that crime resulted from "the operation of social environment and the lack of adequate safeguard and outlet at the period of puberty."

Echoing the theories of both G. Stanley Hall and Jane Addams, Miriam Van Waters used her case studies to show that delinquent women often exhibited normal adolescent traits of "energy, activity, independence," which needed to find "outlet and expression." Among primitive peoples, she explained, these instincts would have been channeled into appropriate rituals or roles, such as institutionalized cross-dressing among Native Americans. In modern society, however, these young women became criminals for lack of appropriate social and economic outlets. In other words, as labeling theorists would later propose, society created the delinquent girl by stigmatizing certain behaviors that, in other cultures, would be considered normal and necessary stages of development.[50]

Miriam Van Waters' doctoral dissertation did not intend to break new scholarly ground. As she wrote home, "I dare not hope to be an authority; I shall be content to become a judge of authorities." The final product, though, is significant on several counts. For one, her thesis detailed without moralism a variety of sexual practices at a time when sexuality was still not a respectable subject for academic research. Even G. Stanley Hall had been severely criticized for too explicit a discussion of sexuality in one of his recent books. In addition, Van Waters' study represented an early application of Boas' cultural anthropology to the study of gender, well before the pioneering fieldwork of Margaret Mead. Years later, Mead wrote to Van Waters that "The Adolescent Girl among Primitive Peoples" had been "the only existing material in the field when I started my work," for which Mead had "always been grateful." Finally, the detailed case studies included at the end of the published version of the thesis anticipated the individual-case method associated with Dr. William Healy, whose book, *The Individual Delinquent* (1915), would soon transform research methods in criminology.[51] Above all, "The Adolescent Girl" revealed Miriam Van Waters' effort to combine theory, research, and practical applications of knowledge. A decade later she would achieve success with this formula in popular rather than scholarly publications on juvenile delinquency.

Miriam Van Waters deposited her dissertation and on Friday, June 13, 1913—a date she would never forget—she faced the "great ordeal" of her dissertation defense. President Hall, Dr. Chamberlain, and two other faculty members examined her from 3:00 until 6:00 P.M. When she reentered the room after their deliberation, she later recalled, "I looked into Dr. Chamberlain's eyes and found his joy in victory." Her own joy in passing the defense no doubt mingled with great relief.[52]

As she prepared to leave Worcester, Miriam anticipated with glee the date of what she called "the great emancipation." Clark had been a trying experience, yet it had taught, as well as reinforced, many lessons. She learned that she could stand up to authority, hold her ground, and survive, especially with the support of women friends and progressive men. Other women students who experienced discrimination at Clark had not challenged G. Stanley Hall, but Miriam Van Waters was already an individualist when she arrived, and she insisted on following her own path, despite formidable obstacles.[53] In the process she both strengthened her determination and became more sensitive to the sufferings of others. Newly conscious of racial hierarchies and sexual discrimination, she sympathized with the underdog—whether woman, Jew, Black, or criminal—and she supported movements for social change. She also discovered a field of research, criminology, that would fascinate her for the rest of her life. Above all, she had learned that social service rather than social science would be the most satisfying career for her.

Rejecting the tutelage of G. Stanley Hall and the life of the research university, Miriam Van Waters drew upon the maternal advice of Maud Van Waters, the social service model of Jane Addams, and the political instincts of Alexander and Isabel Chamberlain throughout her long career. She did not, however, entirely reject academic values, for like other women of her generation, she would combine social scientific research and social service. As much as she would emulate Hull House in the institutions she later directed, she also tried to reproduce a modified version of G. Stanley Hall's academic seminars to stimulate inquiry among her staff. And like Alexander Chamberlain, she would serve as a humane mentor to a series of younger protégés.

An incident during her last year in Worcester highlighted the lessons Miriam had learned and the direction her life would take. For over a year she and Bess had been renting a flat from Lil Carr and her husband, Gus, a fireman. Miriam idealized this working-class couple for their simple, kind-hearted hospitality. While she was writing her thesis, however, she discovered that Gus had been addicted to morphine for over twenty years. One day, in the throes of withdrawal, he became delirious and Lil hysterical. When neither their hostile New England neighbors nor his well-to-do but "proud and heartless" family would

help, Miriam and Bess took Gus to the hospital, nursed him, and comforted his wife and child. Ever the family savior, Miriam then took
charge, contacting doctors and arranging child care with relatives to
enable Lil to earn a living. If they had not stepped in, Miriam believed,
Gus would have died.

Writing home about the crisis, she felt "glad for this experience
personally," for it would make her "more able to cope with human difficulties another time." But she also felt deeply disturbed by the "hard-
ness of heart" of neighbors and relatives who withheld their assistance.
The entire episode reinforced her commitment to service rather than
research. "I have seen many kinds of pain and misery—but I guess this
is a sort of graduate school diploma," she wrote of the incident. Although "laboratory work is a good thing," she concluded, life offered
the opportunities to test academic knowledge. Summarizing the political and intellectual journey she had made since leaving Oregon, she
concluded that "Socialists have all too few chances to air their theory
and I fancy any theory that lies in a trunk gets musty."[54] Miriam Van
Waters would excel at service, rather than at theory, through a long
career devoted to lifesaving.

A New Career

I n the early twentieth century, highly educated and socially conscious women like Miriam Van Waters had the opportunity to pursue new careers in the expanding field of social work. This emerging profession rested upon a long tradition of voluntary female benevolence in which middle-class women assumed social responsibility for
the welfare of poor, sick, or delinquent women and children. Since the
1840s, for example, the Women's Prison Association of New York had
been aiding women released from jail; during the Civil War women
spearheaded relief efforts for soldiers and their families; after the 1890s,
settlement houses, staffed predominantly by women, provided medical
and child care services for immigrant families.

By the Progressive Era, women's roles in social welfare reform had
moved beyond earlier voluntary efforts. The excitement that fueled the
suffrage movement inspired some educated women to form consumer
leagues and to organize workers. Others, especially those who needed
a self-supporting income, often employed their new training as paid
public servants working in the expanding arena of social welfare administration. Increasingly, women professionals played a critical role in
the movement to ease the harsh impact of industrialism on workers
and the poor, while they enthusiastically joined campaigns to rational-
ize government through electoral reform and new bureaucratic structures.

In some states, women had already begun to serve on unpaid
boards of "charities and corrections" in the late nineteenth century.
During the Progressive Era, the new public-welfare agencies that proliferated to confront urban social problems began to employ college graduates with expertise about poverty, disease, and crime. Women who
had been schooled in social science and were committed to social service now staffed housing or health departments. The growth of public
health services provides one example of how women entered government jobs with responsibility for care once provided by families or
private charities. In some instances, traditional women's voluntary
groups led campaigns that established new state agencies, which in

turn hired younger professional women. Thus women's clubs and settlement houses played a key role in the founding of specialized juvenile courts, which then hired women as probation officers and even as judges. Educated women like Katharine Bement Davis, Molly Dewson, and Miriam Van Waters found jobs within the criminal-justice institutions established by women reformers.[1]

Between 1913 and 1917, Miriam Van Waters sought to establish herself as an administrator within the expanding system of juvenile justice. Ultimately she succeeded in obtaining a civil service position at the Los Angeles County Juvenile Hall, which served as the base for her rise to national prominence during the 1920s. The path to this appointment, however, included several false starts, years of ill health, and dreams of an alternative profession as a writer. Against the backdrop of her parents' deepening economic problems, she struggled to find a satisfying career as a professional reformer. By 1917 she would succeed, becoming a symbolic mother not only for her own kin but also within an institution full of troubled children.

As a graduate student, Miriam Van Waters had been impressed by the work of the Boston Juvenile Court. Part of the national response to concerns about poor and immigrant urban youth, juvenile courts removed children, usually under age sixteen, from criminal prosecution and offered less formal, and less punitive, procedures. Youths brought to the juvenile court were to be treated as social welfare, not merely legal, cases. The first juvenile court opened in Illinois in 1899; by the 1930s, almost every state had at least one. The central legal precept justifying the court, *parens patriae*—the parenthood of the state—dictated an expansive jurisdiction. As one reformer explained, the juvenile court placed the state in a "relationship as the parent to every child within its borders." Not only youths who committed crimes, but also dependent and neglected children and their families, came under its authority. The courts had broad powers to determine the best interests of children brought before their judges, who often assumed a paternal role. Denver Juvenile Court judge Ben Lindsey, for example, popularized the image of the judge as a pal of the delinquent boy. At the same time however, the informal proceedings of the juvenile courts came under criticism for expanding state authority over children without guaranteeing due-process rights.[2]

For the most part, juvenile courts preferred probation, which meant a suspended sentence under court supervision, rather than incarceration. Probation officers, like social workers, investigated home conditions and then supervised the child's progress. When the home or the child failed to meet its standards, the juvenile court did sentence children to specialized detention homes and reformatories. In addition to providing sympathetic judges and probation officers, the juvenile courts often sponsored social investigations of the children under their care. Several courts established psychological clinics to help diagnose behavioral problems and recommend treatment during probation. The women Miriam Van Waters had met in Boston in 1912 were part of this national movement to apply scientific studies of delinquency to the disposition of juvenile cases. Only by understanding the causes of delinquency, progressive reformers believed, could offenders be rehabilitated and crime prevented.[3]

Given her training in social science and her curiosity about female delinquency, it is not surprising that Miriam Van Waters looked for a job in the field of juvenile reform. Her first position, with the Boston Children's Aid Society (BCAS), brought her into contact with the Boston Juvenile Court she had so admired. A traditional voluntary organization founded in 1863, Boston Children's Aid, like its counterparts in other cities, had coordinated efforts by nineteenth-century Protestant reformers to salvage neglected, abandoned, or delinquent children. In contrast to an earlier movement to place these youths within regimented "houses of refuge," children's aid societies emphasized placement within families, particularly in rural environments. The Boston society had also pioneered in the use of juvenile probation officers. By the twentieth century, BCAS cooperated with the newly founded juvenile courts in a quasi-official capacity, caring for children who awaited trial or sentencing and providing special services for girls sentenced to the court.

Although girls appeared in only a tenth of the cases brought to the Boston Juvenile Court, they represented half of the neglect cases and the large majority of those charged with immorality or running away from home. The personal, and especially sexual, contexts for their hearings made these cases especially sensitive. Just as they advocated separate courts and prisons staffed by and for women, reformers preferred to have female juvenile cases handled by female staff. The official probation officers provided by the court, however, were all men. To remedy this problem, the Catholic Charities Bureau furnished its own female agent to handle probation for Catholic girls. Following their lead, the BCAS decided to provide its own woman probation officer to handle cases of Protestant girls sent to juvenile court. In 1913 they offered this job to Miriam Van Waters, who had just completed her doctorate at Clark.[4]

BCAS executive secretary Prentice Murphy had been eager to have social science methods applied to the study of delinquent children. A sensitive man, Van Waters recalled, he had "rigid professional standards and a sorrowful compassion for the children of Boston slums." Murphy had been impressed when G. Stanley Hall brought Freud and Jung to lecture at Clark, and Miriam's association with the university, as well as her friendship with Roy Cushman, may have helped land her the job. One of four "visitors" within the Department of Advice, Assistance, and Probation, she was assigned as "Special Agent" handling research, diagnosis, and recommendations in cases of girls brought to the Boston Juvenile Court. Years later she still recalled the setting in the basement of the Pemberton Square Court House. Along one hallway children, parents, policemen, and an occasional lawyer waited for their hearings. Off to the left, Roy Cushman, chief probation officer, had a "tiny begrimed office." Judge Baker's chamber, to the right, was "a kind of cell used for all the court hearings."

In these inauspicious surroundings, Miriam Van Waters faced the task of understanding delinquent girls. "The air was electric with newly discovered complexes which were going to account for all problem children," she remembered. Several juvenile courts had begun investigations of the mental and emotional problems of children. Although her training in psychology fit well with this growing interest in individual, rather than social, influences on delinquency, Van Waters, like other Progressive Era social workers, looked for broader causes of crime. As she later explained, "Trained as an anthropologist to observe individuals in their natural habitat and culture pattern[,] the elaborate theories of the Freudians did not seem necessary to explain the sexual habits of the children of Boston slums." In her job she investigated family and school conditions—as the agency declared, "without *unnecessary* intrusion on self-respecting privacy"—and then recommended treatment.[5]

Historians have offered mixed evaluations of the motives and efficacy of Progressive Era juvenile reformers. Most writers credit the specialized juvenile courts for looking beyond incarceration as a response to crime, but some interpretations emphasize how the courts expanded state surveillance over the behavior of their largely working-class clients. By drawing into their jurisdiction school truants or sexually active girls, for example, the courts stigmatized these youths as criminals. Probation officers who monitored cases represented a form of state intrusion into the private affairs of families. Although the BCAS insisted on parental responsibility, the visitors could, and did, remove children from homes that endangered their morals. At the same time, some immigrant and working-class families welcomed this intervention, calling on the court and probation officers to help with difficult behavior problems or in family conflicts. Other families, especially those steeped in traditional patriarchal authority, no doubt resented the power of middle-class, often Protestant, women to dictate behavioral norms.[6]

Over the years, Miriam Van Waters would articulate her own views in favor of the *parens patriae* doctrine, but she left few records of her early reaction to the Boston Juvenile Court. In her notebooks she recorded brief observations of social workers, favoring those who seemed humane and "approachable." But her once prolific letters home dwindled, in part because of the fatigue that began to haunt her soon after she took up residence on Beacon Hill and began her job at BCAS. Added to exhaustion and recurrent illness, between January and April 1914, Miriam watched as her beloved teacher, Alexander Chamberlain, slowly died of gangretic diabetes. The first year of her new career was not an auspicious one.[7]

Whatever she thought of the court and her job, she clearly did not want to remain in Boston, far from her family. Since Miriam had left Oregon, Reverend Van Waters had suffered serious financial losses. A brass works in which he invested the family savings failed in 1912, and her parents could barely pay the taxes to maintain ownership of the Oregon properties Maud had inherited. As bank notes came due, the Van Waters gradually relinquished title on most of their deeds in order to pay the huge business debt of the Van Waters–Cook Manufacturing Company.[8] As always, Miriam felt responsible for comforting, if not financially supporting, her family. Meanwhile, her two youngest siblings, George and Ralph, were growing up without having known their oldest sister.

Not long after she began working at BCAS, Miriam learned that Oregon might establish a state industrial school for delinquent girls in Portland. The legislature had in fact approved an institution that would supplant private charitable homes for unwed mothers and accept girls convicted of prostitution. Like other communities, Portland had recently established a vice commission to expose the once-tolerated red-light districts. Several states, such as New York, also established specialized courts and reformatories as part of their crusades to abolish "the social evil." Learning that Oregon might establish its own school for delinquent girls, Miriam imagined that under her supervision, the institution could develop into a major research center, such as the well-known women's reformatory in Bedford Hills, New York, which was directed by progressive criminologist Katharine Bement Davis.[9]

Van Waters wanted the Oregon job badly enough to write to G. Stanley Hall for a letter of recommendation. Playing rather blatantly to Hall's ego, she included a deferential request for a picture of her former mentor. The strategy succeeded, for Hall's letter to the governor recommended Miriam not only for her competence, experience, and "attractive person" but also for her "personal tact, and *savior faire* in getting on with other people." Privately, though, Hall tried to discourage his former student's interest in the job. "You are too good for it," he wrote, warning her more generally of the prejudice she would encounter in working "with this class of girls." She thanked him for his letter, responding with her characteristic tact: "You yourself have taught me that one should follow one's science wherever it may lead." Despite Hall's support, the job never materialized, for neither the state school nor a planned detention home for "unfortunate women" was established in Portland.[10]

In 1914, however, another career opportunity arose, in large part due to the efforts of Oregon's women reformers. The Portland Juvenile Court had been founded in 1905, at the urging of the Federation of Women's Clubs, and with the model of the pioneering Chicago Juvenile Court in mind. When it opened, the court sent children detained for trial to reside at the home of a volunteer probation officer. Because Judge Arthur L. Frazer increasingly relied on long-term detention, the state legislature authorized construction of a permanent home, which opened in 1908. Intended for boys only, by 1911 almost a third of the twenty-six residents were girls. Although the Frazer Detention Home included a school, it emphasized discipline, not education, and its methods soon attracted widespread public criticism. Building deterioration, mixed use for temporary and long-term commitments, and insufficient funding led to a grand jury investigation in 1913 and community mobilization for reform.[11]

Portland women played an important role in efforts to improve conditions at the Frazer Home. Newly enfranchised in 1912, Oregon women were beginning to have an effect on local and state government. In 1913, for example, after a militant strike by Portland cannery workers, the Oregon Consumer's League and the Catholic Women's League successfully lobbied for an Industrial Welfare Commission that regulated working women's hours and wages. In Portland, women police officers began to criticize the juvenile court's treatment of pregnant girls as criminals. In 1913, the newly formed Oregon Congress of Mothers targeted the Frazer Detention Home, which they felt had the "taint of the repressive spirit of a jail." The congress placed several of its members on a newly appointed citizens' advisory committee to oversee the home. The women then worked for passage of the Juvenile Court Act in 1913, which increased funds for probation as well as for improved detention facilities. With the support of this advisory committee, the home hired its first woman superintendent, Dr. Miriam Van Waters.[12]

In the spring of 1914, Miriam returned to Portland and threw herself into the work of reforming the Frazer Home. Located on four acres of land in northeast Portland, the institution consisted of a large building containing two dormitories plus areas for officers, dining, and recreation. The inmates, all under age eighteen, had been declared "incorrigible" by the juvenile court because of truancy, running away from home, or other offenses too minor to warrant commitment to the state reform school. Before she took over, Miriam later recalled, the home had been "run with the lash." In addition to harsh treatment, problem children wreaked havoc whenever possible. Boys beat each other up and attempted to set fires. Schooling was inadequate and individual treatment nonexistent.[13]

The new superintendent, supported by the community group that helped hire her, set out to overhaul the institution. She eliminated corporal punishment, improved the diet, and attempted to prevent infection by isolating incoming children and hospitalizing the ill. When she went to visit her parents, Superintendent Van Waters would bring five or six delinquent boys with her to spend the night at the rectory of her father's new church, Grace Memorial. Reverend Van Waters, she recalled, instantly had children peeling apples, reading books, and making a fire in the fireplace. Echoing the Social Gospel's faith in the innate goodness of children, she also invested unusual trust in her charges. With minimal staff and free railroad passes, she transported the boys and girls to her family's summer camp on the Oregon coast for an exercise in outdoor living. At the detention home she tried to instill pride by giving the children responsibility for maintaining the garden and much of the institution itself.[14]

Reflecting her social science training and her political instincts, Van Waters mobilized the community to support her goal of creating a social laboratory to study delinquents. Reed College had recently opened in Portland, so she invited psychologists on the faculty to become involved at the home. With the help of the board of education and volunteers from the college, she reorganized the educational system at Frazer, sending some children out of the home to school. She convinced her old friend Bess Woods to spend her vacation working with the children and asked G. Stanley Hall to recommend a man who was "alert, athletic, [and] sympathetic" to work with the boys. The juvenile court cooperated with her reforms by sending children to the home for detention and care before trial, rather than for long-term punishment.[15]

This promising start to Miriam Van Waters' career as a juvenile reformer came to a premature end during the winter of 1914–15. For over a year she had been feeling physically exhausted. By December 1914, after months of intense activity at the Frazer Home, she could not ignore the signs of illness. Her doctor insisted that she enter Good Samaritan Hospital for rest and recuperation. An acting superintendent took over her duties, but from her sickbed Van Waters continued to direct policy. As her illness lingered, the county commission eventually refused to pay her salary. At the end of February 1915, she reluctantly resigned for reasons of health.[16] Even had she remained in office, her reforms might well have been doomed. By summer 1915, fiscal conservatives in the state legislature transferred jurisdiction for the juvenile court from the state circuit judiciary to a Multnomah County judge who hoped to close the detention home. Although the Frazer Home remained open, under a reappointed former superintendent it reverted to its older patterns, periodically provoking grand jury and editorial critiques.[17]

The illness that had been plaguing Miriam Van Waters turned out to be tuberculosis. Although she would recover after three years, the disease would have a profound effect on her life for over a decade, and its memory would haunt her long after. To be diagnosed with tuberculosis in the early twentieth century meant to live with a stigma of contagion, to be feared and discriminated against, and to confront mortality. Then in her midtwenties, a time when she might have been establishing both a career and a personal life, Van Waters faced at the worst a possible death sentence and at the best an indeterminate period of immobilization.

Once called consumption, tuberculosis had been the most common cause of death in nineteenth-century America. At the beginning of the twentieth century, it accounted for 11 percent of annual mortality in the United States, exceeded only by heart disease and influenza as the major cause of death. Although associated with poor ventilation and epidemic in urban tenement neighborhoods, TB could strike anyone, especially those under twenty-five or in old age. Van Waters probably contracted the disease years earlier. The tubercle bacteria, carried through the air, could lie dormant in the lungs for some time, encased in protective scar tissue. But when they escaped their encasement, the bacilli began to infect body tissue, and the tubercular lesions would gradually break away from the lung passages, destroying a person's breathing capacity. The debility, breathlessness, and fever that had slowed her for over a year were typical symptoms of tuberculosis, along with appetite loss, coughing of blood or phlegm, and night sweats.

Although the bacteria that causes tuberculosis had been identified in 1882, effective drugs had not been discovered by the time of Van Waters' diagnosis in 1914. If detected early enough, and treated with rest, exposure to fresh air, good food, and sunlight (which killed the tubercle bacilli), TB no longer meant a death sentence. The only real cure was to nourish the patient, encouraging a stronger immune system that might destroy the invasive disease on its own. This process usually meant a long recovery, often spent in isolation in order to protect others from infection.[18]

In late 1914 the Van Waters remained hopeful that a month or more of rest would restore their daughter. At first Miriam recuperated at Portland's Good Samaritan Hospital, which was run for the Episcopal diocese by a staff of laywomen. George and Maud Van Waters had long supported the charitable work of Good Samaritan, which offered "several endowed beds . . . to provide for the care of Free Patients." Now their daughter was a paying patient, and at a time when none of the Van Waters could easily afford the fee of ten to thirty-five dollars a week for private rooms. Perhaps because of the cost, but more likely because she needed rest rather than intensive care, Miriam left the hospital to recuperate near the fresh sea air of coastal Oregon.[19]

During the summer of 1915 Miriam returned to the beaches she had roamed as a child. Although her father's financial setbacks had forced the sale of several of their coast properties, her parents deeded to her their land at Cannon Beach. This summer resort community, about twenty miles south of the Columbia River, overlooked breathtaking expanses of beach. In the forest Miriam set up camp in a large, wood-floored tent, cared for by Abby Whiteside, an aspiring pianist and close family friend who nursed Miriam that summer. Abby would get their supplies, gather wood, and take her patient walking on the beach.

Sister Beckie and ten- year-old Ralph Van Waters came to visit them. In a reversal of her childhood pattern, Miriam's health, not her mother's, now required separation from the family and a calm atmosphere, free of excitement. She kept in touch with her parents with brief cards, even when she did not have the energy to write fully. In August, when Dr. Mary MacLachlan visited Cannon Beach, she expressed satisfaction with the improvements Miriam had gained by rest and moderate exercise.[20]

Just as her women friends had nursed her through the worst of Belinda when she was in college, a supportive female community now helped Miriam survive serious illness and financial insecurity. Abby Whiteside faced the formidable task of trying to keep her patient from overexerting herself. As she wrote to Maud Van Waters, "We have a bit of the same struggle with Miriam as of old. Try as I will I am not quite equal to the job of curbing her." Abby also offered to pay the taxes on the Cannon Beach property so that Miriam could keep it. Appreciative of Abby's efforts and loyalty, Miriam felt "proud to have her love."[21]

Another stalwart supporter was childhood friend Genevieve Parke. The two women had remained in touch during the years when each had lived on the East Coast. When Miriam finished the first draft of her thesis, she had celebrated by visiting Genevieve in her Greenwich Village apartment. Now Genevieve sent money to tide Miriam over during her illness, and she offered to take her on expense-paid trips to Montana or Arizona to recuperate. Bess Woods also pitched in, nursing Miriam despite recent surgery of her own, and Caroline Fisher stopped to visit on her way to a new job teaching in Los Angeles. These powerful bonds of friendship alleviated the isolation and fear of illness.[22]

Aside from being sick, Miriam loved living at Cannon Beach. "The sea air and sea beauty make one whole," she wrote to her family. As she recuperated, she imagined spending the rest of her life near the beach with her parents, living cheaply, growing food in their own garden. But with four children still at home, it was most impractical for the Van Waters to think about living by the sea. In June 1915, Reverend Van Waters had given up his position as rector of Grace Memorial Church. In October he transferred to the Diocese of Eastern Oregon to become its archdeacon, in charge of missionary work. Based in Portland, he now spent much of his time on the road ministering in numerous small towns. Nonetheless, Miriam clung to her hope that the family could all be together at the coast, at least during the next summer.[23] Meanwhile, she would rely on the care of friends.

At the end of the summer of 1915, Miriam Van Waters left Cannon

Beach. Still suffering from tuberculosis, she entered the Pottenger Sanatorium, just west of Pasadena, California. The institution had been established in 1903 by local antituberculosis crusader Dr. Marion Pottenger. It resembled others throughout southern California and the southwest, where dry, sunny climates had attracted TB patients since the 1880s. The sanitariums that proliferated throughout the country in the early twentieth century ranged from charitable public to elite private institutions. Enterprising doctors modeled their treatment on European health resorts, providing nursing care, food, moderate exercise, and a tightly controlled schedule. Those who could afford to go to a sanatorium might also be subject to greater medical intervention. Years later, Miriam declared "a song of Thanksgiving" that she had been "poor" when she had tuberculosis, and thus avoided any "surgical interference."

Although the best of the institutions may have resembled mountain resorts, a sanatorium stay was no vacation. As one historian has summarized the environment, it "could be a lonely, depressing, even disgusting place. It meant living with other sick people, being exposed to the sights and sounds of illness, and losing one's privacy." Or, as another scholar put it, inmates "living in the shadow of death" placed their fate in the hands of all-powerful physicians, who could offer only rest and exercise as treatment. At Pottenger, the regimen consisted largely of keeping patients "isolated, protected, and controlled." Not surprisingly, sanatorium inmates sometimes compared their plight to that of prisoners, their rooms described as cells. For Miriam Van Waters, the constraint was intolerable. Whether because of her discomfort or the costs, she did not remain an inmate for long. Indeed, her one experience as an institutional resident left a strongly negative impression, convincing her of the efficacy of the speedy release of prisoners. Within just a few months she "ran away" from Pottenger to the apartment of her friend Caroline (Sara) Fisher in Los Angeles, although she continued to be an outpatient at the sanatorium.[24]

Sara Fisher provided physical and emotional support for Miriam, as well as economic aid. After a day of teaching psychology to college students, Fisher would return to their apartment, make light conversation, have dinner with her convalescent friend, and turn to her research. She insisted on hiring a maid and forbid Miriam from lifting a finger. Although she felt protected by these efforts, Miriam noticed that her dependency left her emotionally aloof. During their meals, she consciously withheld the feelings of despair that plagued her and tried not to speak of her fears about her future. How would she support herself, given how easily she still became fatigued? What kind of work could she do, and what kind of personal life could she expect to build? As late as summer 1915, Miriam had not given up hopes of returning to the Frazer Home, for she asked her father to check the political winds at the court. They did not blow in her favor, nor did she have the stamina to return to that demanding position. By fall, however, she did have enough energy to go on outings in Los Angeles and to resume a more regular correspondence with her parents. The Pottenger Sanatorium approved of a trip to Carmel, and she took off with her old friend Genevieve. Back in Los Angeles, much to her relief, Miriam soon reported that she could "take a deep, full breath without the slightest pain." [25]

As soon as she had the energy, Miriam began to set aside two hours a day for writing. She began by drafting an article about social workers, and working on it suggested a solution to the career dilemma posed by her health. She confided to her parents that she had "resolved to do nothing but write to try to forget my longing for active work with the world's children and the unfortunate." Only after she had succeeded, she explained somewhat apologetically, could she rejoin the family. Perhaps she realized that her role in the Van Waters household would require greater stamina than she had regained, and she knew that establishing herself as a writer required "absolute retirement." The decision to remain near her friends in Los Angeles may also have represented an important step toward weaning herself away from the Van Waters family. Although she remained a more than dutiful daughter, Miriam never again lived near her parents. She had determined to make her own way, with the help of her women friends. [26]

Miriam Van Waters' goal of a new, literary career had its origin in her childhood fantasies. During her mother's long absence from home in 1902 she had first devised a scheme to help support the family as a fiction writer. At the time she would invite her friend Genevieve to tea, read her "latest production" out loud, and then the two girls would cry in sympathy with what must have been romantic or tragic tales. At college, Miriam had edited the campus literary magazine, which published several of her short stories. Unlike most fiction by college women of the era, her work had avoided campus romance and explored instead moral dilemmas placed within exotic settings. "A Box of Jade" invoked a mysterious Asian backdrop for a tragic tale of ill-fated lovers, while "Eagle Hearted" sketched a backwoods individualist from Alaska whose rejection of civilization raised questions about the meaning of success. [27]

After she entered graduate school, Miriam seemed to forgo her literary ambitions. Once, during Alexander Chamberlain's illness, she produced a long verse to this "Stern champion of the human race, of man as human / Scorner of the petty pride of creed and skin and strength." A sentimental tribute to Chamberlain's cultural egalitarianism, the poem appeared in the memorial published after his death in the *American Anthropologist.*[28] The encounter with tuberculosis now revived her old literary dreams. So many artists and writers of the previous century had suffered from tuberculosis that some considered the disease to be a kind of muse. For Miriam, the enforced leisure, along with the satisfaction she had long gained from mastery of language, combined to encourage a serious effort to craft prose and poetry.

Van Waters' writing offers clues to her physical and spiritual struggles with tuberculosis. At least three themes recurred in her unpublished stories and poems: the stigma her disease carried, its implications for love and sexuality, and the healing powers of nature. A character in one short story, racked by "violent coughing that would shake her as a dog shakes a rat," suffered as well from social hostility toward "lungers" like herself, who could not find jobs or housing if their coughs revealed the disease. While the world feared contagion, the woman herself feared that her kiss could bring death to a young male admirer. He, however, desired her kisses even more because of their mortal danger. Similarly, in notes for a verse she imagined a diseased young man who longed for human kisses but had to avoid the "kiss of death." Eventually he turned to the earth, which was "his to kiss—to drink greedily." Her explorations of sexual desire reflected a cultural tradition that associated TB with passion. In response to desire, though, Van Waters called for a kind of sublimation, repeatedly invoking the erotic qualities of nature when the physical kiss of a lover seemed too dangerous. In one fragment the sun became a mythic lover. In "California Love Song," she exalted in drinking the fragrance of the desert. In "Nature Love Song," written on the Oregon coast, she offered herself as the mountains opened to the sea, declaring that "acres of me crave to be drowned by you." These images of sensual longing and of conscious sublimation recall some of the romantic passages in her adolescent letters. Now, however, she incorporated a sexual awareness that reflected her own maturity as well as her exposure to contemporary psychological and literary depictions of the erotic.[29]

Writing itself provided a means of channeling her longings during this enforced leisure. A draft of the poem "Illness," alternately titled "Energy," likened her days to a "Fragile, delicately cut" bottle offered to the sun each morning and reclaimed "Eagerly, with rough haste" each evening, when she counted within it her work: "My precious drops / My sparks of fire / My glowing, marvellous wine of life!" Another poem, "Art Is Born," began with images of balloons and kites vanishing into the air, like the hours that passed while she recuperated. At some point, though, her "leisure" allowed her to possess time and hurl her light — her art — "into the heart of my enemy / The *stillness* who lurks there in the depths of the dark."[30] The dark depths of stillness portrayed in these poems contrast strongly with Miriam's earlier hyperactivity. They also reveal a painful emotional state that she rarely revealed in letters. To combat the depression that surfaced during her illness, she turned to writing, a disciplined form of expression that she would come to rely on throughout her life.

In addition to composing poetry and children's stories, Miriam worked on several nonfiction articles related to her abandoned social work career. She sent to the *New Republic* an essay critical of the execution of a "feeble-minded boy" accused of murder. In response to the debates over U.S. entry into World War I, she began an article titled "Some Ancient Peace Movement," influenced by the pacifist views of her father and Jane Addams. She also envisioned writing a book depicting a cross section of American life and manners through prose sketches of the "personalities and conditions found anywhere by average social workers." Her goal of making "a fresh contribution to American literature" with this book may have been overly ambitious, but it sustained her in the absence of acceptances of her writing. When journals rejected her manuscripts, it felt to her like the worst calamity she could endure. Even more devastating, though, was the humiliation she experienced upon the publication of her first poem.[31]

Miriam had submitted "Art Is Born" to a free-verse contest sponsored by the *Little Review.* Edited by the cultural Bohemian Margaret Anderson, this avant-garde journal championed modernism and sexual nonconformity. When it later serialized James Joyce's novel *Ulysses,* the editors would be convicted of obscenity. Miriam's interest in publishing in the *Little Review* implies an affinity with the Greenwich Village radicals of the pre–World War I era. She had adopted the style of the new woman when she bobbed her hair in 1916. Politically she claimed that "the only paper that tells the truth is the *Masses*," the radical journal edited by Max Eastman, and she would become sympathetic to the Russian Revolution. Nonetheless, Anderson's literary magazine seemed like an unlikely venue for Van Waters' fairly conventional poetry.[32]

When the April 1917 issue appeared, one of the dozen poems published was by Miriam Van Waters. Someone told her that she had won the prize, and she proudly wrote home the good news, sure that "Father will be pleased over the success of his ugly duckling." A few days later, however, having read the April issue of the *Little Review,* a crestfallen Miriam felt ashamed for that "disgraceful bit of conceit." For one, Margaret Anderson's introduction to the published verses claimed that no contest "could boast so many really bad poems." The editor then cited a "pompously anachronistic" line from "Art Is Born" as an example of the poor quality of the entries. Softening Anderson's harsh judgment, one of the three judges, Helen Hoyt, had nominated Miriam's poem for the verse prize, along with a poem by the western feminist writer Sarah Bard Field. Neither of the other two judges, Eunice Tietjens and William Carlos Williams, had agreed. Yet Anderson published all entries that received at least one vote, introducing them with caustic editorial comments. The poems by Van Waters and Fields, she proclaimed, were "pretty awful." Given the pride she took in her writing, and her ambitions for a literary career, this public humiliation must have been devastating. If she took any comfort in the fact that her poem had won some recognition, and that the two unanimous winners turned out to be the accomplished poets H. D. (Hilda Doolittle) and Maxwell Bodenheim, she did not record the feeling.[33]

After this defeat, her visions of literary greatness painfully disappeared. In a prose fragment entitled "Abortion," written after a manuscript rejection, Miriam had bitterly cited "things slain—more precious than lives," like the songs "slain in the hearts of poets." Comparing the loss of artistic vision to the abortion of an unborn child revealed the depths of the pain she experienced upon rejection. It also suggests a deeper source of her anguish, given her association of motherhood and literary creativity. Like other tuberculosis patients, she had no doubt been warned that pregnancy could be debilitating if not fatal. Some women with TB had been sterilized to protect their health. Whether or not she had planned to bear children, Miriam had certainly embraced the maternalist values of women reformers through a career of child saving. Deprived of either possibility for mothering, she had turned to another kind of creativity, publicly announcing that "Art Is Born." Privately, however, she despaired: "How pale, born still—it lies."[34]

In the months between writing "Art Is Born" and learning of its fate, Miriam had turned her attention to her family in Oregon, reviving one of her maternal roles. Short of spending a summer at Cannon Beach with all of the Van Waters, she devised a plan to set up camp with her younger brothers, George and Ralph. She would attend to her own writing in the mornings and tutor the boys in the afternoons. They would all share the housework and entertain their parents on visits. To entice eleven-year-old Ralph, Miriam assured him that their mutual compact to work hard was "not a brother-sister one, but a strictly pal affair and I expect real results."

The arrangement she proposed served each family member in some way. Miriam herself was still a semiconvalescent in need of fresh air and a calm environment, and she may have wanted to give her friend Sara Fisher a respite from caring for her. The beach had been a place of solace for her, and in this period of emotional stress, it may have appealed as a self-nurturing retreat. Moreover, taking the boys off to the beach freed Maud Van Waters from responsibility. Just as Miriam had once spent months raising her younger sisters, now she took charge of the two youngest Van Waters children. Both boys needed the academic work. They had been educated largely at home and lacked discipline. George was about to apply to the University of Oregon (Bess Woods had offered to loan Miriam the money to pay half of his tuition), and Miriam had high hopes for Ralph. She wrote to her youngest brother about the long-term possibilities for law or graduate studies at an Ivy League university if he succeeded in high school and the University of Oregon.[35]

Miriam relished the sea air and woodland trails during that summer of 1916, but sharing camp with her adolescent brothers turned out to be far from idyllic. George proved remiss in household duties, and tutoring both boys took more strength than she had realized. When Bess Woods came to visit, Miriam thought longingly of returning to southern California, where Bess had been hired as a school psychologist for the city of Pasadena. But Miriam felt that she had made a commitment to her mother to remain for nine months, and so she did. Her justifications for continuing the pedagogical experiment echoed the resigned tones of her adolescent letters. "Since my own profession has been smashed I am more than ever eager to serve youth—whose chances are good, and whose success—at least—a hopeful thing." Whatever came of her own writing, by giving George a start she could "accomplish something for you and Father and that would be my great happiness." Her request that her mother destroy this letter suggests that admitting defeat came hard for her.[36]

In other ways, besides serving youth, Miriam Van Waters sought to live vicariously through her family during the trying years while she recuperated from tuberculosis. She took greater interest in her father's career during this period. In the past, when she had written to her parents, her letters were usually addressed to her mother, sometimes called "mumsie," with the expectation that her father would read them, as well. During her convalescence, which coincided with Reverend Van Waters' new missionary work, she more frequently addressed him directly, writing about literature, religion, and politics. Her tone treated Reverend Van Waters like a colleague who needed encouragement, but the letters also served to give Miriam an outlet for her own ideas and a thread of connection to the professional world. Father and daughter corresponded about an imminent spiritual and social revolution in America, on how to translate ethics into everyday behavior, and about what books to read. She recommended Franz Boas and James George Frazer on primitive religions, and they compared notes on the novels of George Eliot. Politically the two Van Waters found common ground both as pacifists and as supporters of the birth control movement, which had just emerged as a radical crusade. When its founder, Margaret Sanger, spoke in Portland in 1916, both George and Miriam Van Waters met with the woman who had recently coined the term *birth control*.[37]

Reverend Van Waters undoubtedly appreciated his daughter's support for his increasingly unpopular views. No longer a parish minister, his itinerant preaching in eastern Oregon had come to resemble Chautauqua circuit lectures rather than sermons. Drawing on the kinds of books Miriam recommended, Reverend Van Waters spoke on modern literary interpretations of the Bible, the anthropology of religion, and hypnosis and psychotherapy. His new bishop, the liberal reformer Robert Paddock, shared Van Waters' preference for preaching in ecumenical settings rather than building the institutional church. When Bishop Paddock was recuperating from nervous strain, Archdeacon Van Waters took over his superior's work, and Paddock hoped that Van Waters would succeed him. The church hierarchy, however, passed over the aging archdeacon, despite strong local support. As a result, Miriam's father had to relocate. The sixty-five-year-old Reverend George Browne Van Waters would take up his final pulpit in Wellsboro, Pennsylvania, in 1922.[38]

In the meantime, Miriam Van Waters had to reevaluate her own career choices. Over two years of rest and fresh air had strengthened her system, nearly eliminating her tuberculosis. Though the threat of recurrence would hover for years, she could begin to think of a new stage in her life. She needed to support herself; she had not succeeded as a writer; and she missed the social service work she had once chosen as a career. "My impatience to return to work is very acute," she wrote her parents from Pasadena, where she went to stay with Bess Woods after completing her tutoring duties in Oregon at the beginning of 1917.

In May 1917, the same month that the *Little Review* published her poem, Miriam Van Waters took a civil service examination in Los Angeles, gaining a top-priority listing. Still resting several hours a day, she prepared for an oral examination for a job as superintendent of the Los Angeles Juvenile Hall. She did not enjoy the interview. Aside from suffering from a sore back, she felt annoyed by the sense of being judged for "the way you walk and do your back hair," which she had, in fact, arranged specially for the occasion. If she succeeded, though, the job would place her in control of the detention center for youths awaiting trial or sentencing at the Los Angeles Juvenile Court, and the position would revive her dormant social service career. Despite the auspices of the civil service, Miriam found herself "engrossed with politics" related to the $1,500 a year position. She told her parents that she still hoped "to land something in Oregon after I get a little boost here," but neither she nor they were "rich enough" for her to turn down a job with that salary.[39]

The appointment came through in late June, to begin in August 1917. No doubt greatly relieved to have her career back on track, she spent a month vacationing with her family in Oregon. She stopped in San Francisco on the way south to visit its juvenile court and detention hall and to see her sister Beckie, who was attending nursing school there. On August 1, 1917, she took over as superintendent at the Los Angeles County Juvenile Hall. Two weeks later she wrote to her father: "Eleven days I have been on duty, and the waters have not subsided, or the dove returned." At the helm of this ark full of delinquent children, Miriam Van Waters began a successful yet politically turbulent career in Los Angeles juvenile reform.[40]

PART II

1917–1932

Surrogate Mother

I n August 1917, Miriam Van Waters resumed the work that had so engaged her in Portland, becoming part of a national network of women reformers in the juvenile justice system. Her new job resembled the earlier one in several ways. As in Portland, women reformers in Los Angeles had been influential in the founding of the juvenile court (1903) and juvenile hall (1911). With their support, Van Waters once again attempted to make sweeping reforms in the treatment of the youths under her charge. This time, unhampered by illness, she threw herself into the task thoroughly, gaining both an important sense of personal accomplishment and a growing reputation as an influential reformer. As superintendent of juvenile hall from 1917 to 1920, referee at juvenile court from 1920 to 1930, and founder of the El Retiro School for Girls, Miriam Van Waters combined maternal concern and firm authority in her treatment of the "so-called delinquent."[1]

Los Angeles provided a receptive setting for the juvenile reform movement that promoted Van Waters' early career. Since the late nineteenth century, midwestern migrants had poured into the young city, making it the fastest growing urban area in America. After the completion of the aqueduct in 1913 insured a source of water to the desert community, the area boomed demographically and economically. The native-born, Protestant settlers who dominated Los Angeles attempted to recreate their values of hard work and family stability. They elected progressive politicians with greater ease than did their eastern counterparts, who had to battle the long-entrenched urban political machines. Within California, efforts to wipe out gambling and prostitution proved more successful in Los Angeles than in San Francisco. Even though the statewide progressive movement faltered after World War I, during the 1920s Los Angeles citizens elected a reform mayor and sustained both temperance and antivice crusades.[2]

Middle-class women contributed to the quest for a moral and efficient Los Angeles through a vibrant club movement committed to civic improvement and the advancement of youth. The two largest women's organizations, the Friday Morning Club and the Ebell Club, had been founded in the 1890s. By 1920 their combined rolls included over three thousand women. Club members served on a variety of state commissions that regulated wages, housing, and charities and corrections, exercising the maternalist politics that fueled progressivism nationally. Through their public-affairs committees, the L.A. clubs aided local philanthropic and civic reforms. In 1903 the women's clubs supported the College Settlement House campaign to establish a juvenile court in Los Angeles. Settlement, temperance, and club women then formed a juvenile court committee to monitor the new institution. They paid the salary of the first probation officer, encouraged the hiring of women for this job, and later called for the appointment of a woman referee to hear cases of girls brought to the court.[3]

When the juvenile court opened, children awaited their hearings in a building adjacent to the county jail. At the urging of the women's groups, the county authorized the construction of a separate juvenile hall, which was to be "as nearly like a home as possible." The building opened in 1911, run by a male superintendent. In the wake of a 1914 sex scandal that involved an assistant superintendent and a female inmate, the reformers demanded that a woman become the next superintendent of juvenile hall. When the job became open in 1917, Miriam Van Waters ranked first in the civil service exam and won the position.[4] Once again, local, voluntary reformers drew on the tradition of maternalism to place a professional woman in a position of political authority.

Like the Frazer Home in Portland, juvenile hall in Los Angeles housed both girls and boys detained by the juvenile court. The total number of youths varied from under one hundred to over two hundred. Their backgrounds reflected the population structure and social hierarchy of Los Angeles: slightly over half came from the white, native-born families that dominated the area, while a fifth were Mexican American, a group that constituted under 10 percent of the population. Only a handful of Asian and African American youths appeared in the records.[5] Most boys had been charged with criminal offenses, such as theft, begging, or assault; the large majority of the girls had been detained for status offenses, especially sexual immorality. Of the boys brought to court, only 16 percent were detained at juvenile hall, but almost half of the girls initially sentenced had to remain there, often because they were being treated for venereal infection.[6]

Detentions at juvenile hall reflected local concerns about the morality of youth during a period of rapid population and economic growth. During the first decades of the century, Los Angeles experienced booms in oil and real estate, while the motion picture industry attracted young women seeking stardom to the area. Although the reform politicians who dominated the city waged periodic crusades against prostitution and gambling, the rise of legitimate, commercial amusements outpaced their efforts. Beachside concessions in the neighboring towns of Venice and Long Beach, along with access to automobiles, allowed a sexually charged youth culture to flourish. To their parents' generation, the Jazz Age emphasis on pleasure seeking threatened family authority and social stability.[7]

Some towns passed strict morals laws to regulate the new public expressions of sexuality. In 1914, the Los Angeles Police Department established a City Mothers' Bureau to offer advice to parents of wayward youth. During World War I, arrests of teenage girls thought to be sexually delinquent increased as part of a nationwide campaign to protect soldiers from venereal disease. Even during the 1920s, when Hollywood marketed images of flappers and flaming youth, Los Angeles authorities attempted to enforce traditional morality among local adolescents. Policewomen patrolled the beaches and dance halls, arresting girls they believed to be either sexually active or sexually vulnerable. When public surveillance and family authority proved inadequate, the juvenile court stepped in, often at the request of parents who could not control their teenage daughters. Juvenile hall detained the youths before, and often after, their hearings.[8]

When Miriam Van Waters took over the administration of juvenile hall, she found "many things to settle" in her new job. As in Portland, she envisioned an institution run by professionals who would provide social services and humane treatment, rather than simply detain inmates. She found, however, that many of the sixteen staff members employed solitary confinement and corporal punishment to enforce their rule. The hall had provided hospital treatment for venereally infected inmates since 1915, but it offered few other medical or social services. Despite these challenges, Van Waters felt that she had "reasonable chances of success" as she turned to the task of reorganizing the institution.[9]

To achieve her goals, the new superintendent began by making sweeping changes in the staff. Although a few of the employees befriended her, among others she encountered some "disloyalty and deceit." Ever confident of her own judgment, she explained to her parents that "the hostile ones are also poor workers and will be removed in time." In their place Van Waters sought to hire "experts" in child welfare and more "honest" workers. Her friend Sara Fisher joined the staff as a psychological examiner, and later Hebe Mack, a college-educated

African American woman, conducted "expert child study work." Van Waters' Sunday night training sessions for officers and volunteers evolved into a popular university extension course. To insure that educated, socially committed workers could join her staff, the superintendent individually prepared seven young women to take the civil service exam. Continuing the medical and psychological care she had offered in Portland, Van Waters hired a full-time nurse and a woman psychologist, established dental services, and laid plans for a "mental clinic."[10]

Along with providing health care, Van Waters wanted to improve morale among the youths detained at the hall. Shortly after she took over, several boys had escaped, and within a few months she faced a potential riot among the hospital girls. "I talked Dutch" to the leaders, she wrote, proud to have avoided both a riot and another escape attempt. In reaction to the children's clear expressions of discontent, the superintendent abolished solitary, improved the diet, and instituted morning assemblies with a focus on current events. She started a club to interest the older boys in self-government, a move that resulted in one runaway returning voluntarily rather than double-cross his peers in the club.[11]

Echoing the language of Progressive Era politicians, Van Waters claimed that the children responded well to her "square deal." After two months on the job she wrote with relief, and irony, "This morning they were absolutely orderly for fifteen minutes." Less than a year later she proudly told her parents that they "would probably like to see my 65 or 70 boys march in, sing patriotic songs, and tell what they know of current events each morning. They are ready to tell whether they know or not." Study assemblies had produced "a marked change in discipline" for boys, but female inmates showed less interest in self-government and politics. To help them feel personally involved in current events, Van Waters employed the participatory methods of progressive educators. As the Russian Revolution unfolded, for example, she told the weekly girls' club all about a regiment of Russian women, then played the mazurka and got them singing. With her encouragement, the hospitalized girls wrote a play and performed it for guests.

The new superintendent also emphasized outdoor activity. On holidays she organized special ball games for both boys and girls, and in 1919 she opened a new playground, celebrating its completion with a day of festivities capped by an ice cream party. The event reinforced her faith in the redeeming power of recreation. Although the participants included "rough, untrained, and undisciplined youngsters of all races," she wrote, "there was not a hitch." Apart from these special events, structuring each day around study, work, and play, along with creating a homelike environment, helped her maintain discipline within her "household of 140."[12]

Writing home about her long days at juvenile hall, Miriam sounded buoyant, engaged, and, as she put it, "very happy in the job." In contrast to the enforced leisure of her convalescence, she now threw herself into the task of establishing her professional base. To make her office "more homelike" she decorated it with paintings by a local woman artist and filled the shelves with books. At the same time, perhaps to reinforce her authority, she added a portrait, writing sarcastically to her parents that "Stanley Hall's wonderful face looks down from the office wall." Now, however, Superintendent Van Waters, rather than President Hall, was the powerful figure. By 1919 she administered a budget of over one hundred thousand dollars and had become a popular community lecturer. The sunken spirits of only a few years ago had risen along with her authority and sense of efficacy.

The job did involve challenges, and they often tried her patience. Only occasionally did her generally optimistic accounts acknowledge the stresses. "My own job has sufficient downward tendencies to keep me from getting self-satisfied," Van Waters explained in the spring of 1918. "In fact earthquakes are so common with the detention home — that I hardly noticed the real one we had last Sunday." The minor trials included children who arrived lice-ridden, a "colored mother" who tried to get opium to her son at the hall, and a steady stream of visitors who demanded a thorough two-hour tour. "Constant vigilance, eternal conferences, infinite series of emergencies are one's weekly lot," she explained, not so much complaining as exulting in her vigorous routine.[13]

From the beginning, Superintendent Van Waters provoked controversy, whether by firing staff members, spending county money for health care, or challenging parents. In her first month on the job, she survived a poisoning attempt by disgruntled employees. Within six months of her appointment her efforts to turn juvenile hall into a medical and psychological laboratory had already led to "two nasty fights with politicians." But her reforms also attracted positive community attention. Under the heading of "Feminism," the *Los Angeles Times* reported on the "young, buoyant, delightful" Van Waters. *Good Housekeeping* praised her "unfailing courtesy, chivalry, and consideration" toward inmates. In addition, women's clubs invited Van Waters to speak to them about her work, while University of California students volunteered to entertain hospitalized inmates.[14]

A major test of Van Waters' authority took the form of a lawsuit by parents who objected to the pelvic exams that were routinely performed on girls admitted to juvenile hall. The case exemplified a conflict that recurs throughout the history of juvenile reform, pitting the rights of parents against the responsibility of the state to protect children. In Los Angeles, juvenile hall doctors screened both boys and girls for venereal infection as part of their admission procedures, but only girls found to have syphilis or gonorrhea were isolated in the hospital. Since all girls, whether sexually active or not, had to have pelvic exams, some parents objected to having their daughters treated as if they might have a sexually contracted disease. In addition, the exams categorized girls according to whether or not they had intact hymens, thus creating a moral divide among inmates.[15]

The lawsuit, however, did not arise from a routine examination. Rather, it concerned an atypical case in which five girls, aged seven to fourteen, had been sexually abused by the leader of a sun-worshipping religious cult to which the girls' families belonged. The pelvic exams could provide evidence in his trial. The parents of the girls, devoted followers of the cult, sued both Van Waters and the woman physician she had hired for not requiring parental consent before conducting the pelvic exams. In April 1919, the court ruled in favor of the juvenile hall practice of routine, compulsory pelvic exams. The superintendent considered the decision a great victory in favor of state responsibility and against parental exploitation of children. The Los Angeles County Board of Supervisors, however, passed a resolution opposing pelvic exams without parental consent and exempting girls from "moral homes" from undergoing them. Whether their order was carried out or not, it illustrated the way that class, and probably race, determined whether parents or the state had the right to determine the treatment of children, for the term "moral home" may well have exempted white, middle-class families from having their daughters examined.[16]

The lawsuit also illustrated a recurrent theme in Van Waters' approach to delinquent and dependent girls. Parents, she often felt, could present an obstacle to her reforms. "No child ever came before the Juvenile Court," she told the Friday Morning Club, "save through the neglect, depravity, or the omissions of some adult." She especially disliked religiously zealous parents, who could be found in abundance in the cults that flourished in southern California. Her letters home ridiculed both a Pentacostalist mother for claiming that "the lord healed her of constipation" and a washerwoman who "does not believe in medicine."[17] An air of class superiority permeated these comments, as did a faith in the power of science, rather than religion. Later in her life, when she returned to the spiritual moorings of her childhood, Van Waters would elevate religion to an equal status with science in her theories of reform. But she would always have a harsh word for Christian Scientists and other spiritual movements that stood outside the mainstream of modern American religion.

Once the maternal figure in her own family, at juvenile hall Miriam Van Waters assumed the role of a wise, compassionate, yet professional mother. "You see my little family is as troublesome as other families— occasionally," she told her parents. When Maud Van Waters visited her daughter in 1919, she was pleased to report that Miriam's children were "adopting me as the 'grandmother.'" In a reversal of their earlier relationship, when Miriam had tried to relieve her mother's burdens, Maud now wanted to make her daughter's job easier. During her visit, she wrote, some of the girls "come to me to tell some little secret or else something that troubles them. If I weren't here, it would be Miriam that would have to listen." [18] More often than not, however, it was her daughter who listened, directed, and cared, and who, in the process, derived great satisfaction from her public maternal role.

When she first arrived at juvenile hall in August 1917, Miriam Van Waters had been greeted by juvenile court referee Orfa Jean Shontz, who would soon play an important role in her life. Shontz had migrated to Los Angeles in 1909 from Iowa, where she graduated from Ames College. A progressive Republican with political ambitions, she first worked as a probation officer and then became secretary to the probate court. Meanwhile she earned a law degree at the University of Southern California and became active in professional women's clubs. In 1915, juvenile court judge Sidney Reeve appointed the thirty-nine-year-old Shontz as the first judicial "referee" for girls' cases, a position created at the urging of women's clubs and women lawyers. The rationale was to assure that girls involved in sex cases would have a private hearing, free from the presence of male authorities. As the *Women Lawyers' Journal* had argued, "a girl will express herself more fully in the presence of three women who want to help her than in a big courtroom half full of men." Shontz heeded their charge, creating a homelike courtroom complete with curtained windows, flowers, and an all-female staff. She earned a reputation for bringing "the mother instinct" to the problems of city youth. [19]

When she met Miriam Van Waters, "Judge" Shontz recognized a kindred spirit and quickly began to groom her new colleague for higher office. Having set her own sites on election to the judiciary, Shontz believed that Van Waters could someday succeed her as juvenile court referee. She urged the superintendent to study law, offered her support during the trying early days of her job, and earned Miriam's enthusiastic political and personal loyalty. In 1918, for example, when Shontz ran for superior court justice, Van Waters felt that the election was important enough to postpone a vacation with her family. "Politics are seething," she explained to them. "The whole future of my work in California seems to depend on these next few weeks." She called the Shontz campaign "an historic step in the woman movement," and even though her civil service appointment precluded any public role, she labored behind the scenes by writing speeches and publicity releases.[20]

Though unsuccessful, the Shontz campaign represented an important effort by professional women to take advantage of the political momentum created by the national suffrage movement. In January 1918, the House of Representatives finally passed the woman suffrage amendment. Throughout the country women campaigned to elect pro-suffrage politicians to the Senate and to state legislatures, which still had to approve the amendment. At the same time, women like Shontz aspired to local office. In December 1920 — just four months after ratification of the federal suffrage amendment — L.A. mayor Meredith Snyder fulfilled an election pledge to give women equal representation in his administration by appointing Shontz to the influential position of city clerk. The first woman in the country to hold this office, she directed five male deputies and had oversight of city election boards. Although the mayor's action alienated several city council members, local women's clubs held a joint celebration of the appointment. With suffrage in hand, these voluntary reformers looked to women officials like Shontz to effect their progressive reforms. The newly appointed clerk pledged to do her best to prove that "women can make good as administrative officials in city government."[21]

Shontz's political appointment paved the way for Judge Reeve to appoint Miriam Van Waters as the next woman referee. Less than a decade earlier, Miriam had first visited juvenile court in Boston and admired Judge Harvey Baker as he presided over children's cases. Now, at age thirty-two, she would begin to sit in judgment herself. To prepare for her new job, she studied law at night. Although she never took the bar, in 1920 she passed a series of civil service examinations that qualified her for the job of court referee. The procedure included an oral interview that tried her patience and hinted at future obstacles. "I've been through a good deal in this county," Miriam wrote to her parents, "but I was never so badly insulted—as by this same Judge Jackson. I got through it alright—his chief objection seemed to be that I would think I was as good as the judges." Although such opposition to women's political authority persisted, it did not prevent her from taking office.[22]

When she began work as referee in April 1920, Miriam Van Waters continued in the spirit established by Orfa Jean Shontz. She presided in informal chambers where judge, clerk, reporter, and bailiff were all women. Three days a week these officials sat around a table at juvenile hall, rather than at the Hall of Justice, making recommendations on the cases of all girls and of boys under age twelve brought to court. Following the practice of other juvenile court officers, like Ben Lindsey of Denver, Van Waters tried to play down the judicial nature of these hearings. She treated them more like family counseling sessions, with an emphasis on mediation and diagnosis, rather than judgment. In her view, the child's offense was "merely an incident as the cough of the patient in the clinic is regarded as incidental to the whole group of symptoms of ill health."

In keeping with this medical model of delinquency, the referee was quite willing to reject standard legal protection for the accused. "The court is one of guardianship, not a penal court," Van Waters wrote. Because its focus was child welfare, not punishment, rules of evidence could be suspended. Thus the early personal history of the "defendant," far from being excluded, became critical to gaining insight into adolescent rebellion. In juvenile court, families rarely hired attorneys, either because they could not afford them or because they did not know they were entitled to legal representation. Van Waters did, however, support the safeguards enacted in many states that forbid the use of evidence gathered in juvenile court in any other legal proceedings. Otherwise, she feared, parents would not speak freely about family problems. Her goal was to encourage families to cooperate with her rulings, even as she impressed upon them the authority of the court.[23]

As she had at juvenile hall, Van Waters tried to make the juvenile court a diagnostic and treatment center for family problems. She sought skilled social workers and psychiatrists to investigate cases and provide community services. Through her connections with the women's clubs, she succeeded in hiring new staff members to help in this effort. In 1922, for example, she addressed the Los Angeles Council of Jewish Women, who soon provided her with "a full-time paid, trained worker" for Jewish girls. Similarly, the referee reached out to black and Mexican groups to provide social services for girls. Establishing ties to women's national reform networks, she felt gratified when Judge Mary Bartelme of Chicago sent two juvenile court workers from England to study her methods. U.S. Children's Bureau director Julia Lathrop sent Dr. Hans Weiss, a Swiss social worker, who soon became Miriam's intimate friend. Throughout the 1920s, Van Waters served as a mentor not only to Weiss but especially to younger professional women, who in turn adopted her maternal approach to justice. Both Edna Mahan and Alma Holzschuh, for example, first sat at Van Waters' feet and later applied her principles as the superintendents of women's reformatories.[24]

Much of the work of the juvenile court concerned female sexual delinquency. Fear of innocent girls' becoming prostitutes loomed large in American culture, but most sex cases at juvenile court did not involve commercialized prostitution. Rather, the "girl problem" consisted of young women who sought sexual adventures for pleasure, not pay. An earlier generation of working-class women, whose low wages permitted few consumer luxuries, had earned the label of "charity girls" when they traded dates or sexual favors for dinners and gifts of clothing. By the 1920s, however, youthful sexual experimentation had crossed class lines, and even among working-class girls it no longer implied economic need. The L. A. Juvenile Court cases revealed rebellion against families more often than economic need. Both middle- and working-class girls appeared in court when their families could not accept their new sexual ethos, but working-class cases predominated. Psychiatrists sometimes labeled these sexually active young women "hypersexual" or "psychopathic" and portrayed them as predators who seduced young men. Some social workers also condemned these girls as a social threat because they spread venereal disease. Others worried more about the personal impact of pregnancy and venereal disease on the adolescent girls themselves. Both groups of social workers, however, frequently blamed lax or broken families for allowing girls to "go wrong." Many sought to substitute state "protection" of girls through court-supervised probation or reformatory sentences.[25]

Miriam Van Waters' approach to the girl problem neither condemned nor celebrated young women's new sexual enterprise, although she did emphasize the risks involved and faulted families for not protecting their daughters. In some ways, her views echoed an earlier generation of sexual reformers who wanted to shift responsibility to the young men involved in sex cases. In the nineteenth century, a coalition that included temperance advocates, suffragists, socialists, and radical advocates of free love had rejected the sexual double standard and called for equal penalties for male and female sexual misconduct. Now, as women like Van Waters gained public authority, they had the power to implement this reform agenda.

A story she told years later about a juvenile court case represents Van Waters' public version of her judicial strategy. A fifteen-year-old Mexican girl, whose mother had died and whose father was disabled, became pregnant after having sexual relations with a number of local firemen. Van Waters held a private meeting with the firemen, explaining the potential criminal penalties she could extract from them for contributing to the delinquency of a minor. She stressed that her goal was not to punish the men but rather to provide for the support of the mother and child at a Salvation Army home. Either one or all of the firemen, she suggested, could contribute a weekly donation for their care. "Every Saturday morning that money came," Van Waters recounted, and at Christmas "they all wanted to go up and see the baby, and they all did, and took as their project the painting of toys and furnishing of Christmas cheer for others in the home." After a year the young mother married a man who adopted her child, and the firemen were relieved of responsibility. Van Waters felt "quite sure that no one of those individuals in the fire department repeated that with any girl under marriageable age." She hoped that seeing "the good women in the maternity home taking care of this child and other illegitimate children" had taught them some responsibility and thus prevented future unwed pregnancies.[26]

Van Waters' recollection of this case idealized her procedures, but it nonetheless illustrated some of the realities of her courtroom. The case was typical in several respects: most girls who came into the juvenile court were between fourteen and seventeen years old, from working-class families in which one or both parents had died, and most had been charged with sexual or moral offenses. Although girls with steady boyfriends were sometimes arrested for their premarital sexual relations, having multiple partners or becoming pregnant elicited stronger responses from families and from the court. Approximately 25 percent of the girls brought to court were pregnant. In most of the cases Van Waters heard, consensual rather than commercial sex was at issue. Although most girls were placed on probation or sentenced to juvenile hall, those who were pregnant were more likely to be sent to institutions such as the House of Good Shepherd, the Florence Crittenton Home, and the Salvation Army Home.[27]

In other ways, however, the story of the firemen portrayed Van Waters as a more benevolent judge than she often appeared in court. For one, she vigorously pursued statutory rape charges against young men who impregnated their casual sexual partners. The referee would practically browbeat young women who were reluctant to name their lovers or seducers, threatening them with detention until they revealed who had possibly impregnated them. "We can control you without beating you," Van Waters told a girl who would not name the men she went out with, "and if you don't behave we will have to keep you locked up some place." In another case, she refused to believe a respectable fourteen-year-old girl's story that a casual date had impregnated her. "Who are you trying to shield, Maureen?"* she asked, sending the girl off by herself to think about the question. Eventually Maureen admitted that she had been raped by her brother, who then confessed. Van Waters also called men to task for their actions. When a young woman was arrested for spending the night with a sailor, Van Waters had a policewoman arrest the man, whom she reprimanded severely in court. In another case she sternly lectured a man who had no interest in the woman he had impregnated, insisting that he pay costs for the maternity home. "I would suggest to you, young man," she explained, "if you don't want to have some more financial responsibility, to let girls alone." Van Waters also had a young Mexican man arrested when he did not keep his promise to marry the fifteen-year-old girl whom he had seduced.[28]

Van Waters did not, however, assume that young women were innocent victims. Rather, she insisted that they too take responsibility for their sexual behavior. "You are not a fool[,] Ruth," she told a fifteen-year-old who contracted venereal disease through casual sex. "You know perfectly well if you go into a man's room at that hour of night, a man to whom you are not married this sort of thing is going to happen." She asked another girl, arrested in a hotel room with several sailors, to consider whether she found "anything wonderful" about her adventures, to which the girl admitted, "If there is no more sensation than this about it, what is the use of trying it." In other cases the referee urged girls to think about their futures rather than temporary pleasures.[29]

Although the court gave Van Waters the authority to enact her judgments, she still had to navigate the tricky waters of family relations to do so. In the sentimental tale of the firemen, she easily acted in loco parentis because the impregnated girl had no guardians. At other times, family members or guardians eagerly turned to the court for help, referring half of the girls brought there. Thus when a single mother asked

---

*All names found in court or reformatory records have been changed.

the juvenile court to help enforce control of her eighteen-year-old daughter, Referee Van Waters threatened the young woman with detention at juvenile hall unless she promised to obey her mother. Placed on probation, and supervised by an officer from Catholic Charities, the young woman enrolled in business courses and within a year had "obtained a good office position." Similarly, Mexican American parents often sought help in maintaining their strict moral codes, and according to Van Waters, "Mexican girls accustomed to the benign authority of their homes" tended to have faith in "the good intentions of the court." Van Waters gladly complied when a mother wanted her daughter placed in a reformatory to protect the girl from her father's abusive behavior, as she did when a father did not want his venereally infected daughter returned home because of the bad example she set for her younger siblings.[30]

Other families were not so cooperative, and from Van Waters' perspective, those parents who contested her rulings were failing to protect young girls from the risks of pregnancy, venereal disease, and lost reputations. Some parents, for instance, tolerated child abuse in the home, as did a mother who had witnessed a daughter's repeated molestation by her stepfather and did nothing about it. When another family hesitated to press statutory rape charges to avoid public scandal, Van Waters bemoaned their decision because the young man might feel free to impregnate other girls irresponsibly. At times she lectured parents as severely as she did delinquents. The referee chastised a divorced father for allowing his sixteen-year-old daughter, Mae Tanner, to work at one of the seaside amusement parks, which the court blamed for encouraging casual sexual relationships. "It would have been better for you to leave well enough alone and leave your daughter in the east with her mother," she told Mr. Tanner. The Tanner case illustrated, however, that not all family members shared the court's dislike for the "cheap amusements" that so attracted youths. Mae had written openly to her mother back east that she had "done no worse than millions of others." Far from cooperating with the court, the mother helped Mae escape from probation.[31] Even parents who initially turned to the court later resisted the imposition of reformatory sentences if they relied on the wages earned by daughters in stores, factories, or offices.

Given the contrasting class backgrounds of the professionals who worked at the court and the families who appeared before them, it is not surprising that historians have often interpreted the juvenile court as an effort to impose middle-class morality on the working class. The conflict could take complex forms, however. Thus Van Waters also opposed parents who imposed traditional moral values on their daughters. When "unassimilated foreign parents" refused to accept the "modern standards of an adolescent girl of Los Angeles," Van Waters blamed parental overprotection for sexual delinquency. In one case, she even championed a fifteen-year-old girl who lied about her age in order to elope with "a rich young Mexican" because the girl's home life was "so wretched."[32]

In these court rulings, Referee Van Waters favored a modern form of child rearing that combined the goals of internalized control and personal autonomy. Like other sexual liberals of the era, she accepted heterosexual pleasure as a positive goal, but one that should be deferred until marriage. Van Waters placed no moral stigma on girls who became pregnant. "By all means," she wrote, "let us let go of the concept of the moral judgment and seek as patiently as social physicians must, the causes that underlie behavior." Those causes included both overprotective parents and those who exposed their daughters to the risks of pregnancy, venereal disease, or the loss of standing in their communities. As the consumer economy fostered by both Hollywood films and advertising increasingly relied on the sexual allure of young women to sell products, Van Waters argued that families had to take a firm stand against female sexual exploitation. When families failed to provide protection and to promote what she considered healthy amusements—plays, films, and outdoor recreation—Van Waters believed that the court should do so. So firmly did she believe in the "parenthood of the state" that she proclaimed "to our critics who say the court has been too parental, we say boldly: the thing is impossible; we have not been parental enough."[33]

Alongside her critique of inadequate familial care, Miriam Van Waters envisioned an alternative model for nourishing delinquent girls. In 1919 she founded El Retiro, an experimental school for girls who had been sent to juvenile court. El Retiro provided a semirural retreat where residents learned self-government and self-esteem. For over eight years, Miriam Van Waters served as its unofficial godmother. During this period, El Retiro, more than any other project, fulfilled her quest to find creative, child-saving work. In later years she would refer to the school as her "first born child." In it she recreated the positive foundations of her own childhood: the warm spirit of her father's rectory, her mother's love of the outdoors. But the school would also provide some of her harshest political lessons.[34]

Since the mid-nineteenth century, children's aid societies had recommended placing urban delinquents in rural settings, and in the early twentieth century, a few states established farm schools for delinquent girls, sometimes incorporating self-government. El Retiro adapted these earlier models. Set amid ten acres of olive trees in the San Fernando Valley, twenty-three miles from downtown Los Angeles, it had been built as a tuberculosis sanitarium. During World War I, the county of Los Angeles acquired the site, most likely as part of the wartime effort to detain prostitutes. But local residents had objected to this use, and in 1919 the county allocated twenty-five thousand dollars to remodel it as an industrial school for girls.

Sometimes called the Opportunity School for Girls, El Retiro provided an alternative to the Ventura State School for Girls, which had opened in 1916 as the girl's division of the Whittier State School. At Ventura, 150 girls, most housed in dormitories, remained for an average of two years each. At El Retiro, the court referee "placed" rather than sentenced selected girls, aged fourteen to nineteen, who were of "normal, or borderline mentality" and free from venereal disease. At the open, unlocked institution, between 25 and 60 girls lived in tented cottages for average stays of six months, or until "graduation." Those who proved unresponsive, however, might be sent to Ventura.[35]

During the 1920s, transforming El Retiro into a model alternative school became Miriam Van Waters' pet project. Although she directed the institution only at the outset, she took an ongoing interest in its operation, visiting at least weekly and establishing close, maternal relationships with many students. Driving out to see the site in the summer of 1919, she had thrilled at the homelike atmosphere and recreational possibilities. The buildings, which included reception and living areas, had semiprivate rooms with baths and porches. Converting the sanitarium must have appealed especially to the former TB patient. On the grounds she would build a swimming pool and tennis courts to provide "wholesome exercise." She would also emphasize the dignity of labor, whether through tilling the land or in dressmaking and millinery classes. According to Beckie Van Waters, who was visiting during El Retiro's founding, her sister was creating this "Honor Suburban Girls School" to have an influence on selected girls who "can see a future." Miriam preferred to think of the school as a place for particularly rebellious girls who seemed beyond help, or those from "unfit" or broken homes. Neither race nor psychological problems, she determined, would prevent a girl's admission. Beckie hated to see her sister take on the responsibility of running El Retiro in addition to juvenile hall, but, she told their parents, Miriam was "crazy about the idea so there is no stopping her."[36]

The spirit of El Retiro reflected Van Waters' youthful love of the outdoors and her growing faith in empowering girls to run their own affairs. She had been impressed by the work of Martha Falconer, who established self-government at Sleighton Farms, the Pennsylvania girls' reformatory. Similarly, the heart of the El Retiro experiment was an elaborate club system by which the residents made rules and enforced them. The El Retiro Student Association wrote its own constitution, voted on whether a student could remain at the school, held initiation ceremonies for acceptable members, punished wrongdoing, and, for a time, published its own newspaper. Van Waters met weekly with student leaders to insure that the system worked. On at least one occasion, when girls ran away from the school, she even allowed student officers to offer informal opinions in the case at juvenile court.[37]

Self-government served both as training for democratic citizenship and as an effective means of behavioral control. As Maud Van Waters commented on the students when she visited El Retiro, "it is funny how they discipline. They really are more intolerant with one another than [are] their teachers." She was observing one of her daughter's central principles: that internalized control was more effective than externally imposed rules. As Van Waters explained in a discussion of state farms for girls, open institutions run by their students resulted in better discipline and "less perversion." Because strict rules, like strict families, stifled creativity, they forced emotional needs underground. The result could be either rebellion or the "crushes" that "infected everyone, even the officers" at many women's institutions. In contrast, she argued, El Retiro would free "the energies of the girl delinquent into the channels of creative work."[38]

In her doctoral thesis Van Waters had echoed Jane Addams' concern that modern civilization lacked appropriate channels for healthy youthful impulses. As a remedy, El Retiro attempted to provide an environment where adolescent girls could find self-expression in legitimate, rather than delinquent, activities. The results seemed to confirm her theories. Few El Retiro students tried to escape, caused serious trouble, or returned to court. Van Waters felt vindicated in her efforts when, in 1921, a riot broke out at the Ventura State School for Girls, while in contrast, El Retiro remained calm. Many of the riotous inmates had been at juvenile hall without trouble, but at Ventura, she believed, the girls had been "goaded into rebellion by the ancient repressions of an evil system!"[39]

To establish legitimate channels of creativity, Van Waters filled the days of El Retiro students with recreation, education, and work. Students planted fruit trees and bulbs on the institution grounds, and they learned to harvest the olives that grew around them. The residents themselves performed most staff functions, directing the kitchen, poultry department, sewing room, and library. Student "heads of departments" were placed on the county payroll and encouraged to accumulate bank accounts. Others helped build the swimming pool and the cabins in the mountains, where they went hiking. Students could play tennis, baseball, basketball, and volleyball. Drawing on her college dramatic experience, Van Waters helped the students rehearse plays, which they sometimes performed for the members of the local women's club. Along with other staff members she brought students and graduates of El Retiro to Los Angeles to see plays, films, and the circus. She often entertained groups of El Retiro graduates at her home and even experimented with having the El Retiro students hold parties at the school, inviting their own friends as guests. In 1922, the students rewarded her efforts in kind by throwing a surprise birthday party for the thirty-five-year-old reformer, complete with decorations, cake, and poems.[40]

The educational program at El Retiro included a grammar school and the first two years of high school, but Van Waters wanted the students to complete high school in the community. Despite strong opposition, the San Fernando Board of Education agreed to admit El Retiro girls to the local high school, and eventually the grammar school became an annex to the junior high. Van Waters' victory, however, left a trail of political resentment that would later contribute to opposition to the school. In the meantime, students could take either commercial or academic courses at both schools, and several honor students went on to college. Although El Retiro did offer a Bible class, religion did not play a major role at the school. Students could attend church in the community, a practice that created a crisis when a local church refused to admit the black students. Another church took all of the students, black and white, "and that required education," Van Waters later recalled.[41]

El Retiro reflected Miriam Van Waters' values not only in its training programs but also in its diagnostic approach. Regular staff conferences, initiated by Van Waters as a "round table discussion," drew on psychiatrist William Healy's casework conference method. At these sessions, which were attended by "chosen El Retiro girls," Van Waters presented a court history, the physician provided a medical history, Sara Fisher discussed the results of psychological tests, a social worker reported on the family background, and a teacher provided a school evaluation. A psychiatrist, privately funded by Chicago philanthropist Ethel Sturges Dummer, also commented. The conference group then discussed the case and the student's experiences at El Retiro and recommended medical, psychological, and vocational goals.[42]

The records of these conferences illustrate how Van Waters implemented ideas she first developed in her dissertation. The case of Harriet Bailey, a fifteen-year-old white girl, represented a success story. Her record showed that Harriet had stayed out all night, had sexual relations with three different boys, and did poorly in school. Reflecting the El Retiro philosophy, the staff concluded: "Has seemed a problem of energy misdirected. Is overflowing with life." Indeed, Harriet had so much energy that at first she seemed "almost beyond management," disgusting the other girls with her lewd dancing. Gradually, however, through peer pressure, sports, and recognition for her kitchen work, she transformed into a good student. "She is still boisterous and loud," the staff reported, "but this is just the exuberance of good health." The theme of finding healthy outlets for youthful energy appeared in more problematic cases, as well. A fourteen-year-old leader of a group of girls known as the "Death Gang" had been caught stealing; her stepfather was in San Quentin prison, and she had "no existing home." Echoing Van Waters' views of troubled youth, the El Retiro psychiatrist concluded in this case that "There is a very strong sense of self that never has been able to express itself in healthy forms. This may be the thing that prompts her stealing . . . her desire for tough company . . . may simply be a desire for excitement of a legitimate enough sort." The treatment included more individual attention and rewards for taking responsibility.[43]

At El Retiro, as in court, Van Waters often had to balance her desire to subvert problematic familial influences with her beliefs in maintaining strong family and cultural ties. She attributed the "illicit sex relations" of a fourteen-year-old girl to a "broken home" and her Mexican family's difficulty in adapting to customs in the "American neighborhood" in which they lived. The El Retiro staff wanted to instruct the mother that "the child cannot be shut up entirely—she must have normal companionship." Recognizing the importance of the Catholic

Church and the need "not to break down their traditions too quickly," they recommended healthy recreation guided by a Big Sister from the Catholic Welfare Bureau. The case of Nora Madden, an African American student "who kept late hours, had inferior parental control and poor companions," also illustrates the El Retiro approach to cultural difference. Nora's mother, a domestic worker, had been born in the South, where, according to Van Waters, she was "thoroughly saturated" with habits of deference to Whites. Nora's lack of racial pride presented the central problem discussed at the conference. She spent hours "trying to get the kink out of her hair" and used creams to whiten her skin. Van Waters wanted to channel Nora's interest in race in positive directions: "If she were to continue school and learn to teach and help her race, especially the children of her race, I think that gradually the race inferiority feeling would disappear." Staff suggested introducing Nora to "fine colored people" and giving her a copy of *The New Negro,* an anthology that reflected the race pride of the Harlem Renaissance.[44]

Reflecting Van Waters' own views, the El Retiro case conference reports pointed to the psychological impact of the family more than to any other explanation of delinquency. In public talks, Van Waters claimed that "Research now points to the genesis of delinquency in the emotional responses of little children to the human relationships that surround them, particularly that of father and mother and teacher." Her growing emphasis on the family both echoed and helped shape the Freudian direction of social work in the 1920s, when many practitioners, such as those involved in the child guidance movement, turned away from a broader attack on social inequality and emphasized the family as the source of delinquency. At El Retiro, staff still collected data on heredity and used IQ tests to screen students. Above all, however, they now employed the language of family dynamics, individual complexes, and the costs of repressing sexual drives.[45]

The discussion of fifteen-year-old Vivian Leroy shows not only this Freudian influence but also Van Waters' sexual liberalism, and its limits. Vivian had been sexually active with several boys and an older man, but at El Retiro she developed intense crushes on female students and teachers. The social worker did not attribute Vivian's homosexual tendencies to heredity or mental defect, as did contemporary sexologists. Rather, she related Vivian's behavior to "the death of her father and her adoration for him," explaining female homosexuality as "a wish to take the place of the father in the home." Because she believed that silence about sexuality bred perversion, Van Waters recommended that the staff openly discuss the problem of Vivian's "homo-sexual tendency" with the students who had been affected. At the same time, she held firmly that Vivian should leave El Retiro because of the crushes.[46]

The psychological emphasis at El Retiro revealed an important shift within Miriam Van Waters' reform outlook. Increasingly she rejected not only Lombrosian theories of inherited crime but also either environmental accounts or radical critiques of the impact of poverty on delinquency. Now she considered these interpretations too deterministic, identifying instead the child's role within the family. As treatment she increasingly relied upon a kind of individual redemption, a response to which she was both intellectually and temperamentally drawn. At a time when other reformers, such as those who administered the Children's Bureau, placed their hopes in new social policies, Miriam Van Waters was beginning to forge a different role as a charismatic counselor whose psychological insights could help uplift lost souls.

The El Retiro conference reports reveal a great deal about Van Waters' attitudes toward delinquency, such as a sense of superiority toward many families from which students came and a desire to foster self-esteem among youth. The reports tell little, however, about how students themselves felt about the school. A set of over twenty letters that El Retiro students wrote in 1926 does provide a glimpse of their perspective. Van Waters solicited the letters to find out how El Retiro students would improve the treatment of juvenile delinquents. Although it is hard to know how much their answers intended to please her, the letters do reveal strong opinions about the juvenile justice system. The students most frequently complained that the court separated children from their families. As one girl wrote, "it is absolutely unfair to any child to take them away from their own home and put amongst strangers." Another writer pointed out astutely that social workers often turned a "critical eye" to the homes of parents who were not wealthy and could not afford better housing. As a result, their children might be taken away, even though "it isn't always a wise thing to take a child away from its mother." Students realized that both poor families and single mothers were at greater risk of having their children removed from the home. As one El Retiro resident wrote dramatically, "My own mother suffered *hell* and no doubt many others have. On account of courts, always courts. I think that if America is a *free* country lets have more *Liberty absolutely.*"[47]

Being sent to juvenile hall or El Retiro clearly represented a traumatic event for the girls who wrote these complaints. Their pain at separation, and their sense of injustice, may well have created strong resistance to Van Waters' efforts to create an atmosphere of cooperative learning at the school. In fact, only one letter writer specifically stated a preference for remaining at El Retiro rather than going home. At the same time, however, most of the respondents criticized their parents in ways that reflected the training they were getting at the school. Having a taste of self-government and an atmosphere of constant activity contrasted sharply with many of their family backgrounds. Thus the letter writers often called for more trust at home, particularly when girls went out with their friends, and they repeatedly spoke of a longing for companionship from parents. Students wished, as one explained, that "their parents would join in the fun." Another, possibly reflecting Van Waters' views, called on parents to provide sex education, rather than leaving the children to "go and find out for themselves."[48]

Taken together, the El Retiro conference reports and the student letters illustrate a series of conflicts involving reformers like Van Waters, the families of delinquent girls, and the girls themselves. Reformers criticized families for providing either too little supervision or too much protection. Their ideal was a child-centered family in which parents fostered both self-esteem and self-control in their adolescent daughters. It drew upon the model of the middle-class "companionate family" of the 1920s, which fostered democratic as opposed to patriarchal relations between husbands, wives, and children. Many immigrant and working-class parents preferred family governance in which daughters respected their parents, whether their rule was strict or lax. The daughters sent to El Retiro seemed to internalize both models, creating conflicts with parents and with reformers. El Retiro students longed for child-centered families and personal autonomy, but above all they longed to be reunited with kin. In most cases, Van Waters and the El Retiro staff confirmed the importance of family reunion, but sometimes they did so with obvious regret that not all families resembled their middle-class ideal.[49]

Despite their desires for family reunion, not all El Retiro graduates could go home again. Some feared either abuse or overprotection, and others wanted to be self-supporting. To provide a transitional residence for these young women, Van Waters helped establish a home for El Retiro graduates in downtown Los Angeles. The female reform tradition had long included homes for released women prisoners, beginning in New York City in the 1840s. The modern concept of an urban club house for delinquent girls had originated in Chicago in 1914, when

Mary Bartelme, then assistant to the judge of the juvenile court, began to establish halfway houses with the support of local women's clubs. In February 1921, Van Waters had met Bartelme when both women dined at Hull House as the guests of Jane Addams. A few months later Van Waters turned to Chicago philanthropist Ethel Sturges Dummer to help establish a clubhouse in Los Angeles. Dummer provided the first few months' rent for "a beautiful old home of 10 rooms and a garden," which opened in downtown L. A. in 1921. It would house up to twenty El Retiro graduates at a time. As Van Waters described the enterprise to Dummer, "One girl will live there and manage the El Retiro Shop. Another will receive a scholarship in a business college. The rest will work in stores, factories and offices."[50]

During the 1920s, several hundred El Retiro graduates lived in private rooms at the clubhouse, each staying for approximately four months. In at least one case, a young single mother resided with her child after giving birth. The clubhouse provided both a residence and a social world while these young women looked for work. In contrast to some of the stricter homes, such as those of Italian and Mexican immigrants, the clubhouse allowed young women to entertain boyfriends, hold "dancing parties," and have a place to receive friends. The suppression of these social interests, Van Waters believed, often led to delinquency. Therefore residents could have visitors on weekend evenings; on Saturdays they could stay out until 10:30 P.M. The residents would have liked even later hours, but the club provided a compromise between strict homes and some autonomy for youths.[51]

As at El Retiro, a Girls Council enforced the curfews and discussed "such group problems as borrowing, smoking and membership requirements." Residents, however, clearly defied the club's values in many respects. The director reported that "'petting' on visitors' night was sometimes a problem," and the staff required "Constant watchfulness to keep the girls from getting behind in paying their board." Although the director tried to encourage the kind of recreation Van Waters favored—tickets to the Philharmonic and Hollywood Bowl concerts, picnics, and swimming at the YWCA—the residents often made their own choices. While they enjoyed the official roller skating parties, they preferred to swim at a crowded pool where they could meet boys, and they often stayed in town after work "to have a date." Not surprisingly, when a woman who conducted a "Charm School" at the YWCA spoke at the club, she "left little impression" on the residents.[52]

Like El Retiro, the clubhouse provided a surrogate family for young women, one that fostered the values of professional reformers like Miriam Van Waters. These values included both self-support and respectable marriage, as illustrated by a probation officer's pride in one eighteen-year-old: she supported herself by earning seventy-five dollars a month as a "messenger girl" at the American Canning Company, and she was planning to be married within six months. Similarly, when Van Waters entertained El Retiro graduates at her home, she welcomed the "twelve happy healthy babies on our cradle roll, their mothers all married and 'respectable.'" Despite this emphasis on traditional women's roles, as many recent El Retiro graduates worked for wages, either in private homes or offices, as married. A sporadic newsletter published at the club, called the Business Girl, included articles on ways to hold a job and manage a budget.[53]

The goals for residents of the clubhouse mirrored the economic outlook for young women in the 1920s, when independent wage earning usually preceded marriage and motherhood. At the same time, a significant minority of American women—like Miriam Van Waters—began to identify primarily either as workers or professionals. During World War I, white-collar workers formed the Business and Professional Women's Clubs (BPW) to advance women's economic opportunities. A local BPW branch, the Woman's Business Club, became an important source of financial and moral support for the El Retiro Club House. The business women used the space for their headquarters, and once a month the young residents served dinner when the older women's club members met there. The residence became known as the Los Angeles Business Girls Club, and its residents could graduate into the Business Woman's Club. This process, Van Waters felt, "gives the girls unlimited chances of self-respect and a new start." She also enlisted the aid of the Junior League, which raised two thousand dollars for a scholarship for a club member. Van Waters hoped to organize "a club for colored girls, with a clubhouse," suggesting that the original Business Girls Club was limited to white women. In 1922, with the support of the Colored Women's Club, she helped found the East Side Mother's Club for African American girls sent to juvenile hall or El Retiro.[54] For residents of each club, older women active in community life offered a model of the new woman as worker, rather than as flapper.

At juvenile hall, juvenile court, and El Retiro, Miriam Van Waters alternately listened, cajoled, threatened, nurtured, entertained, and directed. Her maternal approach to juvenile justice integrated a modified version of domesticity—one that accepted women's independent wage earning as well as motherhood—along with progressive educational techniques and new psychological theories. To these Van Waters added her own brand of redemptive love through self-empowerment, a method that would become her trademark. These efforts had mixed effects. She could not always provide sufficient excitement or autonomy for young women raised in a modern urban environment. Thus many residents of the clubhouse and El Retiro preferred the sexually charged youth culture around them. Other residents, however, welcomed her reforms as a healing respite from troubled families. Some even adopted the goals of the surrogate mothers who helped create these alternative homes. As one woman wrote to Van Waters in 1970, "I often think back to El Retiro [as] the truly happiest days in my life . . . and you made it all possible—not only for me but many, many other girls."[55]

Throughout her career in Los Angeles, Miriam Van Waters incorporated several distinct strains within the female reform tradition. She utilized the local women's clubs as allies, thus drawing on an older, voluntarist network. At the same time, she participated in a more modern world of professional women, such as Orfa Jean Shontz and Chicago's Mary Bartelme, who cooperated in their efforts to modify state bureaucracies by providing community-based responses to juvenile delinquency. Finally, Van Waters' powerful personal appeal and her ability to command a loyal following resembled the model of individual, charismatic leadership, best represented at the time by militant suffragist Alice Paul. Above all, however, it was the persistence of women's reform networks in the 1920s that allowed Miriam Van Waters to expand her familial caretaking role and to become a successful, public, maternal authority.

A Colony of Reformers

M iriam Van Waters' life had changed markedly since 1917, when she accepted the superintendency of juvenile hall. Cured of disease and lifted from depression, she now filled her days with activity. During one week in November 1924, for instance, she gave her weekly lecture for the university extension course, handled Juvenile court cases, made her regular trip to El Retiro, visited the Business Girls Club, taught two classes, booked several lectures, and completed her job as chair of the Woman's Committee to reelect the juvenile court judge. That week, too, Ethel Sturges Dummer asked Van Waters to give the keynote address at the twenty-fifth-anniversary celebration of the founding of the Chicago Juvenile Court.[1] The invitation signaled her rise to national prominence as an authority on juvenile justice.

The communities that supported Van Waters' professional life in the 1920s raise questions about historical notions that progressive social movements, including feminism, withered away in the decade after World War I.[2] To a degree, right-wing attacks, business-dominated politics, and pleasure-oriented consumerism diminished the power of women's public culture in the 1920s, compared to the height of progressive political influence before the war. Nonetheless, many women around the country, like Van Waters, felt empowered by the passage of suffrage and optimistic about their role in creating social change. Despite the growing conservatism, they looked ahead to achieving greater public authority through recently established political institutions like the juvenile courts, state regulatory agencies, and the federal Women's and Children's Bureaus. As women began to dominate social work and gain appointment or election to public office, many thought they were on the verge of implementing their particular visions of social justice.

To be sure, women reformers, like women professionals, faced serious obstacles during the 1920s, including the dilemma of combining marriage and career. In addition, ideological conflicts undermined women's solidarity after the National Woman's Party introduced the Equal Rights Amendment, which threatened to undermine the gender-based social policies favored by a majority of reformers.[3] For black women, largely disenfranchised by race, woman suffrage had little impact. At the same time, however, in both black and white communities, crusades for peace, health care, and child welfare persisted, strongly grounded in close personal ties that insured women's loyalties. While a younger cohort of white, middle-class women who came of age in the 1920s may have felt the lures of homemaking in suburban cottages or sexual emancipation within companionate marriages, a significant number from Van Waters' generation had already made a firm commitment to social service and professional life. They ranged from women like Lugenia Burns Hope, who organized Atlanta's black women to provide community services, to Lena Madesin Phillips, who expanded the predominantly white business and professional women's clubs internationally. Sometimes against serious odds, and often with the support of powerful female patrons, these women sustained reform traditions throughout the interwar decades.[4]

The continuing strength of both local and national women's reform networks contributed to Miriam Van Waters' career during the 1920s. In Los Angeles, Van Waters learned to cultivate support from a variety of organizations, including the Friday Morning Club, the largest women's club on the West Coast. She frequently lectured to them about child welfare, and nearly two thousand people attended one of her Friday morning talks. Van Waters also reached out to professional women's groups, speaking to the Professional Woman's Club and fostering their ties to the Business Girls Club. She worked with African American women's clubs, as well. The East Side Mother's Club, part of the Colored Women's Federation, elected her an honorary member after she spoke to them about establishing a training school for "colored girls." With her help the BPWs provided Christmas gifts for these young women. In the racially segregated 1920s, even this minor cooperation between black and white club women represented a significant break with the past.[5]

Van Waters reached beyond the club movement, as well. Her 1921 newspaper series in the *Evening Herald* explained the work of the juvenile court to the public. She also made what she called some "rather trying" speeches to local civic organizations in the towns surrounding Los Angeles. To the Daughters of the American Revolution she explained why women should enter the profession of social work; at a conference on civic problems she argued for the establishment of public playgrounds; at the California state social workers' convention she discussed the consequences of World War I for social agencies. Parent-teacher groups, women's clubs, and church welfare associations competed for her time as a public speaker.[6]

Mobilizing community support was politically strategic, a lesson Van Waters had first learned in college and saw clearly in Los Angeles. In 1917, when her friend Bess Woods lost her job in Pasadena through a "political tangle on the school board," the network of women friends that had come to Van Waters' aid over the years went into high gear. Sara Fisher "put her bank account" at their disposal, and the old friends "called or telegraphed every social agency, organization, important club, or prominent person in the county and some from every state." They circulated a petition, met with members of parent-teacher associations, and presented "a monster opposition." When the school board met, Bess Woods' friends "carried the day," and she returned to her job.[7]

As a progressive reformer at juvenile hall, Van Waters needed all the support she could get. During the 1920s, progressive and machine administrations battled over corruption in the L.A. police department and for control of the city council.[8] Local women's clubs were an important pressure group, monitoring juvenile justice. In addition, the State Federation of Women's Clubs, which represented seventy-five thousand California women voters, lobbied for selected social welfare bills. Therefore, when she traveled to conferences throughout the state, Van Waters spoke to locals of the federation about her work in Los Angeles. Like most club members, she did not call herself a feminist, a term then used by younger, professional women, such as those in the National Woman's Party.[9]

Although Van Waters shared the women's club emphasis on maternal roles as a basis for reform and special legislation, and she appreciated the clubs as a source of political support, she was not an active participant. Most club members were the wives of business and professional men whose politics were more conservative than her own, and by the late 1920s, many clubs departed from their earlier commitment to social welfare. At one point Van Waters bemoaned "the conservative element" in the Friday Morning Club for seeking punishment rather than rehabilitation. Her personal attitude toward women's clubs sometimes bordered on the arrogant. About to give a speech to one in a neighboring town, she asked her mother if she could "imagine a beach so disgusting as to have a woman's club," contrasting the image of a stuffy organization with her familial love of the beach as a place of play. Van Waters did, however, join the Women's Athletic Club in downtown Los Angeles. Founded in 1921 as a middle-class alternative to the YWCA, its rapid growth—over one thousand members in a year—hints

at the larger world of professional women seeking recreation and cama-
raderie outside the traditional clubs. At the athletic club's spacious
downtown building, she used the swimming pool and sometimes took
El Retiro graduates to lunch.[10]

Aside from the elaborate organizational network of the clubs, a less
formal women's community provided personal sustenance for Van Waters' reform career. Building on the female friendships she had made in
college and graduate school, she created an alternative domestic life
that overlapped with her public work world. She consciously chose to
live within this female world, rather than enter a conventional marriage. Just after Van Waters began working at juvenile hall, she told
a serious suitor that she would not marry him. The young lawyer
was "sensitive and a very fine-spirited man," but, Miriam explained to
her parents, "I cannot care enough for him to run the risk." Given her
history of tuberculosis, she might have meant the health risks of
pregnancy, especially since she had witnessed the debilitating effect of
childbearing on her mother. She might also have worried about the
pressure to give up her career if she married, or simply the risk of not
being able to return her suitor's love. Equally important, however, she
felt no compunction to marry, for she had already established secure
friendships and a fulfilling social life through her unique female household at the Colony.[11]

In 1917, Van Waters moved into the Colony, a group of redwood
residences located in a quiet neighborhood between Los Angeles and
Pasadena. She rented a shared house, joining Sara Fisher and her friend
Emily Reynolds. Nicknamed Pole because of her tall, lean appearance,
Fisher continued to teach psychology at UCLA, enlisting her students
to visit the juvenile hall inmates and serving as a consultant at El Retiro.
Miriam's other close friend from Clark University, Bess Woods, visited
the Colony whenever she returned to Los Angeles from a new job as
state director of special education in Wisconsin. In 1925, when Woods
established an educational-research department for the Los Angeles
Board of Education, she too moved into the Colony. In the meantime,
Orfa Jean Shontz had become a central resident of the household.
Miriam adored both Bess and Orfa. The harmonious, loving relations
among her friends is clear from her joy when she introduced Shontz
and Woods in 1919. "She and the Judge had quite a case on each other,"
Miriam told her parents. "It was entirely mutual and they had great
times."[12]

The Colony was more than a shared residence; it was a kind of
community center where family, friends, and colleagues of Miriam,

Pole, Bess, and Orfa regularly visited. In 1920, when Maud Van Waters stayed there, she felt surrounded by Miriam's friends, who entertained her and introduced her to the household's beloved Persian cats. Orfa's relatives sometimes celebrated Christmas at the Colony, where Miriam joined them after gatherings at juvenile hall and El Retiro. Beckie Van Waters also lived at the Colony for awhile, and when she became engaged in 1922, the housemates threw a shower that typified their social spirit. As Miriam described the scene: "We finished the evening with a mock wedding and charades, all dressing up. Pole was the groom, I the bride, and Orfa, the priest. I guess we were a sight. We danced and played games til 1 A.M.—a really good time."[13]

Although Miriam lived at the Colony and worked at juvenile hall, her personal and professional life frequently overlapped, resembling the spirit if not the structure of the settlement houses. When her old friend Abby Whiteside came to town to give a concert, Miriam invited not only her coworkers but also some El Retiro graduates to a reception for the pianist. Each year she held a special party for former El Retiro students, entertaining up to sixty young women, along with their children. A "cozy dinner" she organized in 1919 provides a good example of both Van Waters' efforts to draw diverse networks together and the limitations she faced. To honor the lawyer who had defended her in the sun-worshiper's suit, she invited doctors and psychologists from juvenile hall to join Fisher, Reynolds, Shontz, and Beckie Van Waters. She then hired as caterer Mrs. Jules Slaughter, the vice president of the Federation of Colored Women's Clubs, whom she had recently met when she addressed the group. She also hired Hattie James, a black student from El Retiro, to wash dishes at the house that night, with the goal of convincing the Colored Women's Clubs to finance Hattie's nurse's training. "She and the club vice president had a fine long evening together," Miriam reported. "My attention was about equally divided between kitchen and living room," an image that captured well the racially segregated world within which she operated.[14]

The Colony also became a way station for visiting reformers, such as Chicago philanthropist Ethel Sturges Dummer, who frequently stayed there. Hull House residents who came to see juvenile court and El Retiro often dined and slept at the Colony, while Miriam Van Waters began to make Hull House a regular stop when she traveled across the country. Grace and Edith Abbott and Sophonisba Breckinridge, who helped make the University of Chicago a center for social welfare research, visited the Colony on a trip to Los Angeles. So did European child welfare and court workers. Men involved in child psychology and prison reform visited as well, including Adolf Meyer, a leading psychiatrist in the mental-hygiene movement, and George Kirchwey, prison reformer and former dean of the Columbia University Law School.[15]

Besides entertaining at home, Colony residents loved to go hiking, and sometimes they traveled together. The outdoors continued to nourish Miriam. During one summer vacation, she went camping in the High Sierra with Bess, Abby, Orfa, and other friends. Miriam and Orfa liked to go driving to the beach or in the mountains on a day off. On one such outing they took Bess and a group of probation officers with them to the Sierra Madre. Miriam also delighted in going bareback riding with Bess and digging in the garden with Pole.[16]

In June 1927, while the housemates were at the beach, a fire swept through the Colony, destroying the buildings, cats, and most of Van Waters' possessions. Ethel Sturges Dummer sent a generous gift to help her resettle, and the residents quickly regrouped. Within a month they had rented a cobblestone home in suburban Glendale that was "big enough for parties," and soon held an El Retiro gathering there. They called it Stone House. "It is a nest, a shelter for body and spirit," Van Waters wrote to Dummer. Miriam, Bess, and Orfa made up the core residents, but Fisher remained in touch after she moved closer to UCLA. Visitors continued to arrive for El Retiro reunions, salonlike teas, and extended stays.[17]

At the Colony and Stone House, Orfa Jean Shontz became an especially influential colleague and the first of Van Waters' patrons. Eleven years older than Miriam, Orfa had a striking, serious face. According to one woman reporter, she was "rather slightly built, fair-haired and gray-eyed, quiet in manner and speech, to a marked degree womanly." At first meeting Miriam had been suspicious of her, but the two women soon formed a lasting friendship. In October 1917, Orfa drove them to a conference in Santa Barbara, and during the five-hour ride she proposed that her younger colleague prepare to succeed her at court. Writing to her parents of her new mentor, Miriam now declared that "Judge Shontz is so wonderful so splendid [a] person to work with!"[18]

Over the next few years Miriam and Orfa cooperated at juvenile court in a number of ways. They planned to coauthor a handbook on children's law, with Orfa writing the legal parts and Miriam the social and anthropological. Although that project never materialized, the two continually supported each other's reforms. Orfa recommended girls for El Retiro in her reports to the judge, and she also looked out for Miriam's interest at court. Together they helped defeat legislation introduced in 1921 that would have sent juvenile offenders to criminal court. When Orfa established a private legal practice, Miriam expressed great admiration for her friend's ability to handle clients and judges.[19]

These two professional women enjoyed the cultural and political life of Los Angeles during the 1920s. Orfa took Miriam to the theater, chauffeured their household guests to restaurants, and planned symphony outings. They lunched regularly with other professional women, such as Mabel Walker Willebrandt—who would soon become the first woman appointed U.S. assistant attorney general—and with women doctors, educators, and journalists. In 1921, when Kate Richards O'Hare came to Los Angeles, Orfa and Miriam dined with the notorious socialist, who had just spent a year in federal prison, and they then attended O'Hare's "courageous talk at the Labor Temple." Sometimes the two friends went off for a weekend alone, camping out at Laguna Beach or exploring California's deserts.[20]

The emotional texture of the relationship between Orfa Jean Shontz and Miriam Van Waters resembled the romantic friendships of nineteenth-century middle-class women. In letters written after Miriam left California, Orfa addressed her as "My Precious" or "Dearheart" and easily expressed her affection. "I love you beloved," she exclaimed, "and am so glad you are enjoying your work." This language also echoed the earlier correspondence between Miriam and Maud Van Waters, and some observers felt that Orfa had become a "second mother" to Miriam. She kept after her friend to preserve her health, while her terms of endearment—addressing her "little Brown Bear" and signing "Your grizzly loves you always"—evoked an older woman's affection for a child. While Orfa did act maternally, the two women shared a more romantic attachment, as well, one that Miriam seemed intent on limiting. Orfa may have envisioned a traditional "Boston marriage," in which two career women shared their household for life. Many single women reformers formed such partnerships in the early twentieth century. By the time Miriam left California, Orfa would settle down with a woman named Eve, with whom she worked and traveled. It is also possible that Orfa was more comfortable than Miriam with adding eroticism to their companionship. A new admirer who recognized Orfa's importance waited to learn if Miriam would go to Orfa "on her conditions," while an entry in Miriam's journal stated simply "Orfa spends the night. 'Try Me,' she says."[21]

By the 1920s, some women friends had accepted a sexual component to their close relationships, despite the medical and social stigma that had begun to attach to homosexuality at the turn of the century.

Several lesbian couples became central to reform circles in New York, such as those surrounding Eleanor Roosevelt, and in some cities lesbians began to form social networks. Unlike an earlier generation of women reformers, many of whom remained ignorant of the erotic implications of same-sex love, Miriam Van Waters was well aware of homosexuality from her reading in sexology and psychology.[22] Although her own writing revealed a strong tolerance for gender nonconformity—whether in careers, manners, or clothing styles—she considered homosexuality a form of psychopathology. Her view that homosexuality resulted from unresolved childhood conflicts reflected the influence of Sigmund Freud more than that of the biological determinist Havelock Ellis. Above all, she believed that deeply rooted same-sex desires could be channeled, or sublimated, especially into social service.

Van Waters' comments on Radclyffe Hall's lesbian novel of 1928, *The Well of Loneliness,* provide a clue to her thinking about homosexuality. She and Orfa both read the controversial book, and in her journal Miriam disagreed with Hall's position—drawn from Havelock Ellis—that the mannish female protagonist, Stephen Gordon, was "biologically conditioned" to be a tragic figure. Had her parents been more loving, Miriam mused, Stephen could have "run a girls camp," become a high-school counselor, supervised a juvenile protective agency, or even had children.[23] Significantly, the alternatives she recommended closely reflected Miriam's own work, while her insistence that loving parents prevented homosexuality exempted her from being at risk. Over the years, she would struggle to understand her own attachments to women, but at this point in her life she was unlikely to accept homosexual passion, whether or not Orfa offered it. Their loyal and caring friendship remained eminently respectable, a passionate collaboration between reformers that helped root Miriam in California.

Through her determination to protect Miriam's health and career, Orfa Shontz paved the way for another female patron, Ethel Sturges Dummer. Orfa privately wrote to the Chicago philanthropist to let her know when Miriam needed help, and Dummer provided personal and material support. An Episcopalian and both the daughter and wife of successful bankers, Dummer had been born in 1866, the year of Maud Vosburg Van Waters' birth. She acquired her strong sense of noblesse oblige in part from her teacher, Ellen Gates Starr, who cofounded the Hull House settlement. Like other reform-minded women of her class, Dummer used her considerable wealth to support investigations of social problems, particularly the welfare of urban children. She not only gave money but also took an active interest in the reformers whose careers she advanced. In 1909 Dummer had funded the Chicago Juvenile Psychopathic Institute, where William Healy and Augusta Bronner pioneered a psychological interpretation of delinquency. During World War I, Dummer became increasingly concerned about the discriminatory treatment of both prostitutes and unwed mothers. While at her vacation home in southern California, she learned of Miriam Van Waters' work with female delinquents in Los Angeles. In 1920 Dummer visited the L. A. juvenile court, where Van Waters had recently begun to serve as referee.[24]

Ethel Dummer was so impressed by what she saw at the juvenile court hearings that she accepted Miriam Van Waters' invitation to come home with her to the Colony. A long-standing and intensely productive friendship originated during that visit. The two women corresponded for decades. The older philanthropist introduced her younger protege to a national community of reformers concerned with the psychological dimensions of delinquency. Through Dummer, Van Waters also gained entrée into the Chicago-based networks that emanated outward from Hull House and influenced federal policy through the national Children's Bureau in Washington. In Los Angeles, Dummer became a frequent visitor to the Colony, Stone House, and El Retiro. She especially loved Van Waters' use of dramatics and recreation at the school. Dummer helped pay the rent for the Business Girls Club and funded its field secretary. A firm believer in psychoanalysis, she also provided funds for a psychiatrist to participate in the El Retiro case conferences. Equally important, through her correspondence Dummer offered constant inspiration and occasional solace to Miriam Van Waters.[25]

Orfa Shontz initially facilitated Dummer's patronage of Van Waters. In 1920, concerned about the state of her friend's health, Orfa wrote to the philanthropist explaining that although Miriam was doing "beautifully" at court, the work was "*killing* her." The problem seemed more emotional than physical. According to Orfa, Miriam felt sensitive about not being an attorney, and other lawyers felt jealous of her position. Moreover, as in her family, Miriam's sense of responsibility for others bordered on self-denial, even self-destruction. Rather than see her "crucified as she is every day," Orfa wanted to lighten her dear friend's burden by granting her a sabbatical year to write and rest. Since Miriam would never accept such a gift from her, Orfa wanted to conspire with Mrs. Dummer, who would act as her agent. "[W]ould you please, *please* for me as well as for her write and tell her you have set aside a sum for a Foundation or anything you want to and ask her to write other articles or a book," she pleaded, offering to send $150 per month that Dummer could then pay Van Waters.[26]

Dummer agreed, insisting, however, that she provide the funds herself—as Shontz may well have anticipated—and that Van Waters work on a specific project. With an initial grant of two thousand dollars, Dummer recommended a six-month survey of the institutions that housed approximately twelve thousand girls and young women around the country. Aside from relieving Miriam from overwork, a goal that remained unstated, the survey was supposed to expose the horrors of punitive methods and to proselytize the El Retiro model nationally. Miriam explained the arrangement to her parents as part of Mrs. Dummer's "missionary" ideal. "When she found the way the girls lived and worked and studied at El Retiro, their freedom and democracy—she became convinced that it is a new idea," she wrote, adding that "of course it is old—as old as the spirit of revolution." Van Waters applied for a leave from the civil service commission and began her national tour at the end of 1920, leaving Orfa Shontz as substitute referee.[27]

From November 1920 through March 1921, Miriam Van Waters traveled throughout the United States, investigating twenty-four reformatories and industrial schools, meeting superintendents and social scientists, and establishing a personal network made up of reformers and social-policy makers. With introductions from Ethel Sturges Dummer, she had easy entrée into the overlapping worlds of men and women who tried to apply social science to social problems. On this trip she first met Adolf Meyer, whose pioneering clinical studies of the childhood origins of mental illness Dummer had funded. Van Waters described the Johns Hopkins medical-school professor as the "wisest psychologist in America" and responded to his "book-filled home" much as she had once thrilled to the Chamberlain residence in Worcester. In Boston, she consulted the "stimulating" Dr. William Healy, since 1917 director of the Judge Baker Foundation, which provided psychiatric evaluations for the Boston Juvenile Court. In Philadelphia, she interviewed psychologist Jessie Taft, who had once worked under Katharine Bement Davis at the Bedford Hills, New York, reformatory for women, and who now directed a mental-hygiene clinic for troubled youths. In Washington she encountered "a real power," Janie Porter Barrett, a Hampton Institute graduate and settlement house founder who had been president of the Virginia State Federation of Colored Women's Clubs. Later, on a beautiful moonlit night, the "intelligent, vivid, forceful" Barrett drove Van Waters by mule-drawn surrey through the Vir-

Rev. George B. Van Waters passed on to his daughter Miriam a deep commitment to the Social Gospel of liberal Protestantism. At times of stress Miriam Van Waters found sustenance in the knowledge that "My father believed in me and rejoiced in me— with a boundless joy." *(Courtesy Margaret van Wagenen and Anne Gladding)*

Maud Vosburg Van Waters bore six children, five of whom survived. Standing in front of St. David's Episcopal Church (*above,* c.1900), she holds her son George and is surrounded by daughters Ruth and Rebekah. Her youngest son, Ralph, was born five years later. Despite recurrent ill health, Maud Van Waters managed the rectory where the family lived, with the help of eldest daughter Miriam (*right,* c.1900). At age thirteen, Miriam Van Waters had the wholesome look of a country girl. *(Courtesy Margaret van Wagenen and Anne Gladding)*

Throughout her life, Miriam Van Waters enjoyed two distinct kinds of apparel. A photo taken in 1904, when she was seventeen, showed her dressed as a cowboy, illustrating her tomboy side. She loved to play out of doors, swim, hike, and ride horseback in the woods or at her family camp at Cannon Beach, Oregon. In contrast, her 1908 graduation picture from the University of Oregon showed Van Waters' taste for soft and elegant attire. *(Left, courtesy The Schlesinger Library, Radcliffe College; above, courtesy Margaret van Wagenen and Anne Gladding)*

After earning her B.A. and M.A. degrees in philosophy at Oregon, Miriam Van Waters won a graduate fellowship at Clark University in Worcester, Massachusetts. She planned to study with the eminent psychologist and university president G. Stanley Hall *(left)*. After two years of intense struggle with her adviser, she switched to anthropology and earned her doctorate under the direction of Professor Alexander Chamberlain *(right)*, a political maverick who supported women's rights and progressive reform. *(Courtesy Clark University Archives, Worcester, MA)*

In college, graduate school, and during her early career in Los Angeles, Miriam Van Waters lived among close women friends and colleagues. Van Waters and Elizabeth (Bess) Woods *(left)* met at the University of Oregon, shared a flat while they attended Clark University, and joined in two cooperative female households near Los Angeles—the Colony and Stone House. They remained friends throughout their lives. Orfa Jean Shontz *(right)* preceded Van Waters as referee at the Los Angeles Juvenile Court. An older mentor as well as an intimate friend, Shontz also lived at the Colony and Stone House in the 1920s. *(Courtesy Margaret van Wagenen and Anne Gladding)*

Miriam Van Waters loved the outdoors throughout
her life. In the 1920s, she and her women friends
often camped and hiked in California and Mexico.
(Courtesy Margaret van Wagenen and Anne Gladding)

In 1920, after serving three years as superintendent of Los Angeles Juvenile Hall, Miriam Van Waters succeeded Orfa Jean Shontz as woman referee in the Los Angeles Juvenile Court. Here she is presiding over an informal hearing in the case of an adolescent girl. Family members and teachers often participated in these hearings. *(Courtesy Margaret van Wagenen and Anne Gladding)*

Chicago philanthropist Ethel Sturges
Dummer *(left)* became Miriam
Van Waters' first patron, providing funds
for her research on juvenile detention
facilities for girls and her travel to
professional conferences. Van Waters
inscribed this picture *(below)* to Dummer,
whose emotional and financial support
made possible Van Waters' first book, *Youth
in Conflict,* published in 1925. *(Courtesy
The Schlesinger Library, Radcliffe College)*

Geraldine Morgan Thompson *(right)* met Miriam Van Waters in the mid-1920s, several years after this picture was taken at Brookdale, Thompson's 800-acre estate in Red Bank, New Jersey. After 1930, Thompson became Van Waters' patron and her lifelong romantic partner. The main entrance to Brookdale *(below)* suggests its elegance.
(Courtesy William Preston)

Miriam Van Waters remained close to her parents throughout their lives. She and her father (*below,* c. 1930) shared liberal views on religion, literature, and women's rights. After his death in 1934, Miriam increasingly returned to her Episcopalian roots and tried to fill his place as head of the family. Her mother, Maud (*left,* 1938), came to live with Miriam in Massachusetts after Rev. Van Water's death. *(Below, courtesy Richard J. Hildebrandt; left, courtesy Margaret van Wagenen and Anne Gladding)*

In 1929, Miriam Van Waters fell in love
with a seven-year-old ward of the juvenile
court, whom she invited to live with her
at Stone House. She renamed the girl
Sarah Ann Van Waters and eventually
adopted her. In this studio portrait, Sarah
was nine or ten years old. *(Courtesy
Richard J. Hildebrandt)*

ginia woods so that they could visit the Industrial School for Colored Girls near Richmond, an El Retiro–like school that operated on an honor system.[28]

Chicago, however, provided the densest hub connecting Van Waters to powerful women in the world of child welfare. As a guest of Jane Addams at Hull House, she first met Judge Mary Bartelme, who had originated the urban clubhouse for girls; resident Edith Abbott, who with Sophonisba Breckinridge had written *The Delinquent Child and the Home* (1912); and Jessie Binford, who had directed the Juvenile Protective Association. In Washington, she met former Hull House resident Julia Lathrop, who directed the U.S. Children's Bureau, an agency that represented the expansion of Hull House residents into national social welfare administration.[29]

Aside from making contact with movers and shakers in the world of child welfare, Van Waters threw herself into the job of studying girls' reformatories. She encountered a few hopeful institutions that measured up to her El Retiro standard. The premier institution, Pennsylvania's Sleighton Farms, had been established in 1906 by former settlement house worker Martha Falconer, who had helped Lathrop found the Chicago Juvenile Court. The self-government and the cottage system of family-like dwellings Falconer had instituted remained in effect when Van Waters spent a week there during her tour. A few other institutions also impressed her. "I had a most interesting time at Clinton Farms, New Jersey, and at Niantic, Connecticut, where they have very progressive farm-schools for woman offenders," she wrote to Dummer. "Nowhere is really scientific analysis and adjustment being done," she added, "but there are germs of the new day everywhere apparent." It was her task to spread the good word, much like a missionary in the field. As she wrote to her benefactor, "I feel that much of our service will be best rendered by pointing out these new elements, stressing them, interpreting them, so that harassed superintendents and timid boards of directors may take courage."[30]

Van Waters visited many institutions that sorely needed these new elements. The Maryland School for Girls, for example, was "terrible beyond words," a "factory system" whose "horrors" she would not even describe. Girls were horsewhipped at the Delaware institution, and the "school at Chillicothe, Missouri is appalling," she told Dummer. "I could hardly write you the things they do to the girls there, by way of punishment for sex offenses. They are herded in tiny rooms, four in two beds, one bath for 75 girls, and that 3 flights below." At other institutions guards beat the female inmates. In Massachusetts, Van Waters heard about "the frightful Woman's reformatory" at Framingham. Around the country, she feared, formerly progressive allies had become more sympathetic to punitive measures. "My beloved Mrs. Dummer," she cautioned, "a wave of disbelief in parole and probation is sweeping over people's minds." Even the Juvenile Protective Association, she worried, "is wondering about longer terms being wise." Her observation accurately assessed the trend during the 1920s, when despite an emphasis on probation, juvenile reformatory commitments actually increased nationally by one-fifth.[31]

As Van Waters traveled, Dummer periodically sent checks to support her work, referring to herself as "a silent partner" in the survey. Occasionally, though, she suggested ways that Miriam could represent their shared views. "Could you put the spiritual side of all this, or rather the spiritual factor in rehabilitation in terms which scientists would recognize?" she asked in a letter about the treatment of prostitutes. Dummer and Van Waters also shared an assumption that women had unique insight into the need for restoring, rather than punishing, children. As Miriam wrote shortly after her trip, "Dr. Meyer and the others, after two years are beginning to get the idea. Fertilization of the male mind *does* take time." To spread the word about the El Retiro method of rehabilitation, Dummer urged Van Waters to give talks. At the Chicago City Club, the Illinois League of Women Voters, the "deeply conservative" Woman's City Club of Boston, and elsewhere, Van Waters promoted the three central tenets of progressive penology: parole, probation, and the indeterminate sentence.[32]

Dummer expected her protege to write up the results of her survey and the El Retiro experiment, possibly as a book that would "prove the very point so in my mind and heart for the last three years." To encourage her, Dummer worked behind the scenes to help set up professional talks. But as of August 1921, five months after her return from the trip, Van Waters had not yet written anything. When news reached Chicago that Miriam had taken ill, Dummer sent a sympathetic, maternal letter of support, suggesting cautiously that Miriam might have bitten off more than she could chew. Which came more easily, speaking or writing? she asked, strongly hinting that Miriam should choose either conference presentations or a written report on her survey. "Dear child," Dummer wrote, "do rest now, and if it is the survey which is bothering, put it aside. . . . [P]lease rest in the knowledge that not until you are ready, not until it comes spontaneously, do I desire your report."[33]

Dummer was not the first to observe that Miriam Van Waters had a tendency to overcommit herself. Her relatives had noticed how hard she pushed herself as a student; Bess Woods and Abby Whiteside had trouble keeping their patient from overexerting herself while she recuperated from tuberculosis; and Orfa Shontz continued to worry about her friend's burdensome responsibilities. Miriam, however, had trouble accepting her own limitations, and repeatedly friends intervened to relieve her. In order to allow time to write, Dummer ultimately offered a salary that would allow Miriam to take periodic leaves from juvenile court, either for travel or writing. Thus she was able to pursue her role as a national reformer even as she held her local court position.[34]

For several years, thanks to the support of Ethel Sturges Dummer, Miriam Van Waters served two constituencies, her local community and a national professional world. In fall 1921, for example, she went to Florida to present talks on female delinquents at meetings of the National Probation Association and the American Prison Association. Dummer financed the trip, and Miriam expressed her gratitude in terms that let her benefactor know how much she was needed: "In this field, more than any other we need the courage of mutual support. To find that *you* believed in my ideas has given me a driving force I could never have obtained otherwise." Describing the conferences, she bemoaned the outdated attitudes of conservative members but took heart at signs of change. "The prevalence and power of the women this year, they say is marked," she reported, so much so that old-timers complained because the program included substantial material on women and children. In January 1922, Van Waters traveled to New Orleans, where she visited the juvenile court; to Pittsburgh, where Dummer chaired a roundtable discussion with her, Jessie Taft, and Emma Lundberg of the Children's Bureau; and to Chicago, where Miriam again met with Jane Addams. In Wisconsin she visited Bess Woods and declined an invitation to direct a new state bureau on juvenile delinquency. While visiting at Hull House, she finally began to write up her survey.[35]

By spring 1922, Van Waters had completed her report. With Dummer's financial support, the article appeared in a special supplement to *The Survey,* the premier social service journal. Accompanied by over twenty photographs, it arrived just before the annual meeting of the National Conference of Social Work. "Where Girls Go Right: Some Dynamic Aspects of State Correctional Schools for Girls and Young Women" took its title in part from an earlier essay by Jane Addams, "Where Girls Go Wrong." The article further established Van Waters' national reputation. In it she explained that her survey "was neither statistical, nor 'investigatory,'" nor did she compare the "efficiency" of the institutions she visited. Rather, her suggestive account—as she called it, "a voyage in search of dynamic ideas" — emphasized the central theme of her career: the importance of "freeing the energies of the girl delinquent into the channels of creative work."[36]

Interspersing her report with lively vignettes about individual girls and with praise for college-educated, professional staff, Van Waters outlined what, in her opinion, worked to transform troubled girls. She celebrated women-run institutions that offered diagnostic services, self-government, vocational training, and a healthy dose of outdoor labor and recreation. In the Sauk Center, Minnesota, institution, for example, she praised girl teamsters, farmers, plumbers, carpenters, painters, electricians, and landscape gardeners. Lest her readers worry about a potential subversion of gender roles, she added that the graduates also learned to make their own dresses out of dainty material. Sleighton Farms, Clinton Farms, and the urban clubhouses earned Van Waters' praise, while she condemned the still prevalent punishments of flogging, solitary isolation, limited diet, head shaving, and fire-hosing at other schools. Although she concluded with the belief that institutional life "is not a desirable thing," Van Waters accepted the probability that correctional institutions would not soon be supplanted by preventive and community work. In the meantime, "constructive programs filled with the spirit of scientific humanism" would best help girls "go right."[37]

With Ethel Sturges Dummer sending reprints of the article around the country, Van Waters began to receive fan mail. "A superintendent of a jail in Philadelphia writes to know if these methods can be applied to drug addicts and street walkers," she proudly reported to her patron. Dummer continued to provide financial support for Van Waters' travels, including payments to reimburse the city of Los Angeles for days of missed work, and Van Waters published a series of articles in *The Survey* based on her further experiences. Of her financial support, Dummer explained, "It is my great pleasure to cooperate in this way with all of you brilliant young professional women, carrying your vision as far as I can." When Dummer failed to interest the *New Republic* in publishing an article by Van Waters, the philanthropist assumed responsibility, apologizing that she "did not sparkle sufficiently" at lunch with the editor.[38]

Dummer's comment about faulty social graces no doubt intended to ease the rejection, but it also revealed an important dynamic between the two women. Like other philanthropists, Ethel Sturges Dummer consciously used her wealth and personal contacts to provide a form of patronage for younger professionals like Miriam Van Waters. In return she earned gratitude, loyalty, even love, as well as evidence that she was accomplishing a social mission. Although she was extremely well informed and articulate, Dummer felt self-conscious about her lack of a college education. She appreciated Van Waters' ability to get a professional hearing. As she put it, the two of them made "a good working team," stimulating each other's ideas.

To some extent, Miriam Van Waters and other protégés may have played to Dummer's maternal identity to win her patronage. At the same time, Van Waters authentically needed Dummer's unconditional support and financial security, each of which had eluded her since childhood. Her expression of disappointment when Dummer visited California without coming to the Colony closely resembled the letters she had once sent to her own absent mother: "I feel . . . as if the only one who could give me light and strength at this time had gone. I know spiritually you are here, your influence is here, yet the actual practical word, the contact of your wisdom is needed." As a child, Miriam had rationalized her mother's absences and assumed a parental role herself. Now, as an adult, she politely demanded the maternal attention for which she longed.[39]

From 1920 to 1930, Ethel Sturges Dummer absorbed some of the emotional intensity that had once characterized Van Waters' relationship with her mother. Miriam continued to express her love and longing for her own mother, who remained "dearest in the world" to her. "I love you so much and I need you so much, darling, that words fail," she wrote to Maud in 1919. Increasingly, however, she apologized that the press of business at juvenile hall or El Retiro kept her from writing. "I feel always the *need* of telling my mother my troubles," she explained, but the "rush has been so great that I could have conveyed only wrong impressions." Maud felt the change and complained when she did not hear from Miriam. Even so, almost weekly letters kept her parents informed, while Maud's visit to the Colony in 1920 affirmed their bond. After her parents moved to Wellsboro, Pennsylvania, in 1922, Miriam frequently sent clippings and references on topics such as "Negro Intellectuals," which Maud incorporated into her talks to the local Friday club. Ethel Dummer's financial support allowed Miriam to visit her parents new home en route to professional meetings. After one such trip she confided her feelings to Dummer. "For the eighth time my mother has moved everything and made herself a home," she explained. "O dear Friend—the brave pathos, the sublimity of Mothers is all I can think of, just now."[40]

Since Dummer strongly advocated psychoanalytic theories, she may well have been aware of the role of transference in the relationship with her protégé. Whether consciously or not, she provided a sympathetic, steady maternal figure on whom Miriam could depend. At the same time, Dummer recognized the dangers of patronage. In 1924, for example, when Orfa Shontz made another confidential request for financial support for Miriam, Dummer quoted a new lesson she had learned: "Never try to take the burden from a friend. Draw out in him that which will enable him to carry it." In her own family, Dummer explained, she had learned that allowing someone to struggle helped them to "gain rapidly in power. We see this very decidedly in Miriam, do we not?". Dummer would only offer money if Miriam gave her a sign that she needed help, which she would not do. "It was not unwillingness to help," Dummer wrote, "but my inability to find a way before Miriam's quiet courage. She gave me no glimpse of any discouragement or depression, which she may show to those of you who are with her more constantly." Perhaps only Orfa knew the extent of Miriam's need. To the rest of the world, especially to her parents and to Ethel Dummer, she maintained her "quiet courage."[41]

In Los Angeles, a social world of professional women facilitated Miriam Van Waters' reforms, as they did for other women of her generation. In her case, though, the personal ties seemed especially strong. Miriam's wit, energy, and graciousness created a powerful magnetism that allowed her to command a highly loyal following. Over the years, older friends, like Abby Whiteside and Orfa Jean Shontz, continued to profess their devotion to their "dearheart" Miriam, and each tried to mother her at times of stress or ill health. New acquaintances, especially younger protégés, also felt the strength of her personal appeal. For some, like Edna Mahan, she became a maternal figure—"mother Miriam"—while to others she became an object of romantic longing. Thus when a young German student of penology left the country, she wrote sorrowfully to Miriam of "the faint—faint possibility of seeing you again—oh, Beloved I can't tell you what it already means to me."[42]

Alongside these maternal and romantic female bonds, Miriam Van Waters established one important intimacy with a man, the Swiss social worker Hans Weiss. Perhaps because their friendship did not fit easily within her female social world, or perhaps because he was younger and less professionally established, she rarely spoke or wrote about their relationship. Yet she later acknowledged Weiss as the one man she seriously considered marrying. They became colleagues when he came to Los Angeles to study the juvenile court on the recommendation of Julia

Lathrop, whom Van Waters admired greatly. But she later remembered her first encounter with him. It was at a conference where she was giving a talk, and Weiss, speaking in his broken English, rose to challenge her. As Miriam later wrote to Ethel Dummer, "In his challenge I felt as if an angel had appeared to demand who there was, in the company of the 'wisest and best' who really *cared* for the child." Weiss felt to her like both an intellectual equal and a kindred spirit. "His social conscience is acute where so many of us are lulled," she once wrote of him. "More than anyone I have met for a long time," she told Ethel Dummer, "he understands the spiritual nature of what we social workers are attempting."[43]

Hans Weiss must have been an unusual young man for Miriam Van Waters to encourage his affections as she did. Although she maintained her distance, both publicly and emotionally, she undoubtedly came to care deeply for him. Eight years younger than her, Weiss was fair haired, small framed, and emotionally intense. During the Swiss general strike in 1918, he had opposed student scab laborers, earning him the animosity of his peers. In his view, he had been blacklisted from jobs in "public social work" because of his opposition to the government during the strike. Thus when he came to the United States in 1921, at the age of twenty-seven, he sought work as well as further education.

Hans Weiss had an extremely sensitive streak in his character, sensitive both to the injustices perpetrated on children and to any slights to himself. His own conflicted family background, which Miriam learned of only later in the decade, helped shaped these traits. Like her own, his father was a minister, and like her, he grew up exploring the outdoors in his beloved mountain home. But in place of the aspirations and adoration she had experienced in her family, he had been abused physically and demeaned emotionally by his parents. At the University of Zurich, where he received a doctorate, a male teacher who offered platonic love had become a healing spiritual guide. Deeply romantic, sensual, and quite self-absorbed, Hans Weiss longed for both love and justice with a passion that matched Miriam's own. In his commitment to child welfare, his aestheticism, and his spirituality, he resembled many of her female friends.[44]

Like her other admirers, Hans felt strongly attracted by Miriam's charismatic qualities, or what he later called the "magic power [that] flows out from you." He recalled first seeing her in the courtroom. Aside from the bond of devotion to child welfare, he felt an immediate romantic attraction. It was at the court, he recalled, "Where I first enjoyed your deep laughter—where you first passed to me the mystic word

'Tonight'—where your love for children was so beautifully revealed to me—where you knew first that we loved each other."[45] An important professional comradeship had, for him, quickly developed into a romantic attachment.

As much as Miriam enjoyed Hans' company and his attentions, she seemed conflicted about the relationship. In 1923, for example, when she spent her thirty-sixth birthday with him, she picked Hans up a few blocks away from juvenile hall before driving to the Colony, where, he later reminded her, "we did not dare go into your own little house." Instead they visited privately in the adjacent quarters. Since Hans was not only a coworker but her subordinate at the court, she may have felt uncomfortable about being seen with him. She did not, however, discourage his courtship, and she expressed deep affection for him. As Hans put it, they had shared the "sudden experience of seeing the inmost [of] another."[46]

During his stay in Los Angeles, Miriam and Hans attended church services, swam together at Laguna Beach, and visited San Juan Capistrano. She gave him a cross for his office, and he gave her "a little red cross" that she still treasured years later. When Hans moved to Massachusetts in 1924, she presented a more personal gift, a silk shirt. Wearing it reminded him of her, he wrote in a letter: "It caresses my body as thy white hands would gently caress me." His grammar left unclear if the caress was in memory or only in fantasy. Hans wrote that he longed to be near his "wonderful comrade" and pour out to her the frustrations of his work as a probation officer at the Boston Juvenile Court. He also clearly wished to be her lover.[47]

Weiss' letters gave the impression that despite their spiritual union, Miriam Van Waters continued to withhold from him a degree of love, commitment, or public acknowledgment that he desperately wanted. He recognized that he had no claims upon her, yet he felt comfortable calling her "my woman," telling her that "I long for my woman," and confiding that "every night a sweet dream of our being together soon sings me into sleep." Whether Miriam shared his dreams is not clear. "Is it the same with thee—my Love?" Hans wrote to her. He wondered if he could hear "the hymn of a silent prayer whispered by the sweet lips of a longing woman?" When Miriam sent Hans some leaves as a memento of a trip to the desert, he pressed them to his lips and later imagined covering her body with kisses. In one letter he closed by recalling their closeness in California: "I am holding the redfingered leave that you sent me as I held the warmth of thy loving lips . . . after those nights at the Colony. I am thine—completely—Thy Hans." For years he continued to write in the familiar language of a lover, while longing for the "Sister of my Soul." When he shopped for a Japanese robe to send for her birthday, for example, Weiss described how he trembled with excitement at the thought of her "exquisite body," imagining "the caressing softness of this garment on your so beloved flesh that is far more spirit than flesh."[48]

Since only his side of their correspondence has survived, it is difficult to know just how Miriam responded to these longings for intimacy. During their initial involvement, she did not mention Hans in her newsy letters to her parents, an omission that could mark his significance, or her discomfort with her feelings for him, as much as a lack of interest. Later she wrote of him in quite formal terms as a colleague. To other friends, Miriam referred to Hans as a protégé, one of the several "children" whose careers in juvenile reform she hoped to shape. But her private journal contained rare allusions to an unidentified young Beloved with whom she had experienced both a spiritual epiphany and a "yielding to love." In one of these entries, the erotic images of her earlier poetry recurred. She remembered a candlelit scene in which her "hands were flung up by a strong clasp of young hands on my wrists—and with another soul—I plunged down a glittering waterfall immeasurably high, and sunk at last—into a pool—where two floated in weariness and content."[49]

As in her relationship with Orfa Shontz, Miriam placed clear limits on this intimacy. "As a lover I yield to no one in sustained worship," she wrote in her journal. While she denied that she was intentionally avoiding love, she repeatedly elevated spiritual and universal forms of love over more personal intimacy. To Hans, as well, she insisted that their spiritual union transcended the need for physical proximity. She even suggested that unrequited love could yield the "deepest spiritual gain." Those who were strong, she believed, knew "that life must be lived alone." Repeatedly, when Hans requested more time with her, Miriam insisted that even one moment could suffice to sustain true love.[50]

For complex reasons, Miriam refused to marry Hans. Aside from the emotional distance she kept, the formal obstacle to their marriage was his "tremendous longing for a home and for children." Hans accepted "the cruel reality" that he could not have this with Miriam, for like many professional women, she had chosen career over marriage. Although some women reformers did try to combine the two, having a job and children would be too physically taxing for her and, given her history of tuberculosis, possibly fatal. They faced, in his words, "a physical, scientifically established reality we have to admit." To Miriam he later wrote that the thought of her bearing their child was a "glorious, heavenly, proud feeling of joy," but a "tremendous anxiety seems to shake all this sacred joy to death—and that makes the outcome tragic. If anything happened—both our lives would be destroyed. Mine may not count—but yours could never be replaced. And this age needs you more than anything else."[51] As self-sacrificing as he seemed, Hans never considered the possibility of marriage without children, nor did Miriam raise the possibility.

Moreover, just before Hans left for Europe to visit his family at the end of 1927, Miriam wrote to him about another, unidentified, attraction she had developed. They had previously agreed to reveal their other love interests, and Miriam believed strongly, as she once wrote to Edna Mahan, that "Frankness is the main thing" in an egalitarian relationship. Hans struggled to accept the news. After spending three hard days "facing the Devil" of his pain, he let her know that "whatever you do is all right in every way . . . do not deny anything that life offers you." He believed that no matter what happened, their love would always be "sacrosanct." After all, he wrote, "we have reached bedrock in our relationship."[52]

Weiss resigned himself to exquisite suffering, claiming to feel "no disappointment" with the memories of their union and his visions of "the contours of thy delicate sweet body." Yet inklings of discontent soon appeared in his love letters, which increasingly concerned his attractions to other women. Soon Miriam became a confidante in Hans' quest to find a suitable wife. Each time he met a potential mate, he described her in detail, asked for Miriam's advice and approval, and then recounted the sagas of his courtships, some replete with descriptions of women's amorous advances toward him. Miriam did not seem to mind these highly narcissistic letters. She encouraged most of his romantic interests, cautioned him occasionally, and drew the line when Hans announced that he would tell his future wife about her. To her caveat about revealing their relationship he conceded, "I have no right to say anything unless you agree." Although he courted eagerly, his devotion to Miriam remained strong. "You are my wife—Beloved One—in every sense except in the eye of the law and of society. When I call you that—my blood quickens and my soul begins to sing. I know of no more beautiful name for you than this." Not surprisingly, his other romantic quests usually ended in disappointment.[53]

Once again, Miriam maintained an ardent admirer at arm's length. Whatever limits she placed on their relationship, however, she did think of Hans as a soul mate, a loving, spiritual partner in their respective efforts to improve child welfare through the juvenile courts. In this sense, her romantic friendship with Hans resembled those she had with women. Yet Miriam found it difficult, and at times impossible, to integrate this heterosexual bond into her female social world. In the 1920s, despite growing suspicions about the homosexual potential of female friendships, professional women could still live together, travel together, and cooperate on work projects. Their friendships enhanced, rather than threatened, their careers. A male suitor, however, raised the dilemma of choosing between work and family, since most women left the workforce after marriage. Hans and Miriam had agreed that her career and her health took priority, and that she would not marry him. In the respectable middle-class culture in which they operated, it was unthinkable to conduct an open love affair. And so their union remained shrouded in secrecy, maintained largely through correspondence and during rare visits. Still, Miriam knew that at moments of self-doubt, she could turn to Hans and enjoy his lavish professions of unconditional love.

During the 1920s, as she established her reputation in juvenile reform, Miriam Van Waters drew heavily upon local and national communities of women. Even as the power of women's national organizations diminished from the prewar decade, a female reform network—fueled in part by significant patrons—continued to support the careers of women like Van Waters. Women's clubs contributed to her local efforts; the Colony and Stone House served to connect her intersecting personal and professional worlds; and Ethel Sturges Dummer helped elevate Van Waters' national prestige. In her intimate life, colleagues at the court became spiritual and romantic partners. In all of these relationships, however, Van Waters maintained a safe emotional distance, allowing herself to be adored but remaining self-protective. Fiercely independent, she granted to Orfa Jean Shontz and Hans Weiss dear but circumscribed places in her heart. Limited commitments also left her less constrained in her quest for public recognition. As she traveled throughout the country and endured political challenges in Los Angeles, Miriam Van Waters could be confident that a colony of reformers stood ready to sustain her.

In Conflict

During the 1920s, the shifting American political climate posed serious challenges to the female reform tradition. For one, liberal and conservative political forces clashed throughout the decade, as dramatized by the courtroom battle between fundamentalists and evolutionists in the Scopes trial. In the wake of the Russian Revolution, a Red Scare fueled attacks on progressive policies, including those cherished by women reformers, such as maternal health care programs. But conservative opposition was not the only challenge facing women like Miriam Van Waters. According to some historians, the very success of maternalist politics may have undermined women's authority, since government agencies increasingly assumed responsibility for social welfare functions that had once "belonged to the woman's sphere." Although women themselves often gained authority as public officials who dispensed social services, they also experienced greater political vulnerability than in the past. An earlier generation of reformers, such as Jane Addams, had once enjoyed a measure of political immunity because they operated from a voluntary base. With the professionalization of social work and its centralization within state agencies, a younger generation of reformers, including Van Waters, entered administrative hierarchies, usually headed by men, under the watchful eyes of municipal or state legislators.[1] Thus, women's growing public authority could be accompanied by a loss of administrative autonomy.

From the time she first applied for her job at juvenile hall, Miriam Van Waters knew that politicians strongly influenced the pursuit of reform in Los Angeles. Even as she established a national reputation as a popular writer on juvenile delinquency and the family, Van Waters repeatedly had to fight conservative forces and corrupt politicians on her home turf. Like so many other Progressive Era reformers, by the end of the 1920s she would be forced to compromise some of her ideals. Her conflicts in Los Angeles, however, taught Van Waters important political lessons that would strongly influence her later reform career.

Miriam Van Waters' local struggles had their roots in the structure of the juvenile court, which depended upon a larger political system for its leadership and funding. The selection of judges presented one set of problems, for the judge who presided at juvenile court did not necessarily seek this job. All judicial candidates in Los Angeles County ran in a general election, and those elected then picked their courtrooms on the basis of seniority. As Miriam once wrote to her father, "No one wants the Juvenile Court because the judge cannot get into the newspapers, so it is a department used to punish those judges whom their colleagues do not like." In addition, the judge did not have the authority to appoint the court's probation officers, who were key figures in implementing the reform agenda. That power fell to the probation committee, a seven-member, unpaid board appointed by the Los Angeles County supervisors. The probation committee also controlled funds for juvenile court and El Retiro. Although the early probation committee supported Van Waters, when political winds changed on the board of supervisors, hostile probation committee members impeded her work.[2]

By necessity, then, Van Waters threw herself into the political machinations of the court. When the supportive Judge Sidney Reeve planned to resign at the end of 1920, she worked for a judicial candidate who "if elected—we may count on [as] a good friend for social legislation." When her man did not win, Van Waters feared for her job. "Our enemies are very busy," she wrote to her mother. A grand jury wanted to abolish the position of woman referee, and she felt a need to "build defenses against earthquakes—political earthquakes." Fortunately, the new appointee proved to be sympathetic, but when he lost the next election, Van Waters complained to Ethel Dummer that "Affairs political here are bad." She campaigned "silently and quietly" to persuade Edwin Hahn, an elected judge whom she respected, to accept the juvenile court appointment. Commiserating with her father, who had just been overlooked as a candidate to lead the Archdiocese of Eastern Oregon, she wrote: "Judges are as bishops, so you can see that my days and nights are not spent in peace." Her behind-the-scenes strategy proved more successful than her father's, for Hahn became the next judge at juvenile court.[3]

Tensions among religious groups soon began to contribute to Van Waters' political anxiety. Relations between the Catholic Charities Bureau and the court had been quite cordial during the first few years that she served as referee. In fact, Van Waters had antagonized some probation committee members by allowing Catholic children to have Catholic social workers. Lately, however, she had been embroiled in "a fight with the Church of Rome." In her view, the Catholics wanted to get a judge of their own faith, and to that end, she claimed, "one of their workers" had been interfering with her work. To complicate matters further, she worried about whether Judge Hahn could win reelection because he was a "non-Orthodox Jew, hence not acceptable to Jew, Catholic, or church federation."[4]

Hahn did survive the next election and served through 1923. The next year Van Waters chaired the Woman's Committee that helped elect a sympathetic successor, Judge Harry Archbald, who remained at the court until 1927. He worked with her to recommend an alternative school for boys on the model of El Retiro, and she socialized with the Archbalds even after he left the court. But during his term, a new board of supervisors took office in Los Angeles and discharged the relatively supportive probation committee. In its place they installed a more hostile group of overseers for the court and El Retiro. One probation committee member, Mrs. Elizabeth McManus, would soon become Van Waters' nemesis.[5]

Political conflicts had surfaced even earlier, when Van Waters struggled to maintain control of El Retiro after she gave up the superintendency to become court referee in 1920. If she could have run the school single-handedly, Van Waters might have been satisfied, but short of complete control, she wanted to influence her successors. She worried, for example, that Superintendent Ianthe Densmore dealt too harshly with the students. Other staff members did not meet Van Waters' standards, either because they were not highly educated or did not appreciate the reform methods she so valued. Learning that one of the matrons "was in fact using *blows!*" was "one of the most crushing experiences in my life," she wrote. When the civil service commission not only agreed to reinstate this matron but also charged that Van Waters had interfered with the management of the school by having her fired, the ruling shook her thoroughly. "If they deny that right they must prove that I do not possess it. They must challenge it!" she wrote to Ethel Dummer.[6]

Now more clearly aware of the limitations on her authority at the school, Van Waters confided that for the first time "I realize that the present El Retiro may go smash." Always a fighter, and eager to retain control of the school, she met with the probation committee to ask them to confirm her policies. Van Waters emerged victorious in this round, but the incident foreshadowed later conflicts in which her demands for total authority alienated supervisory agencies. Her immediate success, though, helped inspire Van Waters to begin to write a book that she would call *Youth in Conflict.* "I am filled with new hope," she wrote to Ethel Dummer. "Suddenly, I have gained a buoyant courage and belief. I too have faced a conflict."[7]

In this book, Van Waters hoped to popularize the lessons of her work in Los Angeles to a national audience. The writing, however, proved extremely painful for her. She felt insecure about taking time to write when the court seemed to be in political jeopardy, and she worried about the quality of her early drafts. Ethel Dummer offered advice and personal encouragement. Acknowledging the writing struggle, Dummer suggested that Miriam "turn this psychic pregnancy from a period of pain and worry into one of great joy and health." Schools and courts needed this book, Dummer explained, using an argument that fit both of their identities as women who should serve others.[8]

Service, however, could conflict with writing, especially as Van Waters took on even greater public responsibility. In 1923 she became the founding president of the Southern California Society for Mental Hygiene, a branch of a national movement to establish local child guidance clinics to help prevent delinquency. During the 1920s, private philanthropies began to fund these experimental child welfare programs, and the Los Angeles group headed by Van Waters was one of thirty nationally to receive funds from the Commonwealth Foundation to open a model child guidance clinic. "It is a glorious movement," Van Waters wrote Dummer, describing their goal of "an independent organization for bring[ing] knowledge about mental health to the community." Still working on her manuscript, she now added regular mental-hygiene meetings to her already busy schedule of court hearings and El Retiro conferences.[9]

In order to complete her book, Van Waters requested a three-month leave of absence from the juvenile court, once again relying on Orfa Jean Shontz as her substitute. She promised to put local politics out of mind and concentrate only on the book and the weekly lectures she gave at the University of California. Each month Dummer sent a $250 check, equivalent to the referee's salary, and she later sent funds to pay Shontz when the court would not do so. Beginning in January 1924, Van Waters concentrated long enough to establish a rhythm for her writing. "I have a peculiar feeling that it is inevitable," she wrote Dummer. "Sometimes it does not come very fast, but when I write it flows easily and simply. . . . The truth is that this book is the very core and expression of my whole work. I am happy doing it."[10]

As she completed chapters, Van Waters sent them to Dummer for comment. She also asked her opinion—perhaps by way of requesting permission—to dedicate the book to "two women pioneers" who worked with delinquent girls but were too shy to seek public recognition: Orfa Jean Shontz and Martha B. Falconer. Dummer liked the idea, and did not seem to expect that her patronage would be rewarded by a formal dedication. She continued to work behind the scenes, negotiating a contract for the book with the publishers of the *New Republic*. Dummer also wrote the introduction for *Youth in Conflict*, which appeared in 1925.[11]

Van Waters' influential first book combined a popularized version of her doctoral dissertation with vivid case studies from the Los Angeles Juvenile Court. In an accessible, dramatic style she took the side of the children termed delinquent and blamed their parents and the society around them for the conflicts facing youth. In the opening chapter, for example, she sketched a dozen cases of children brought to court, emphasizing in each one either parental overprotection or inadequate attention to youth. Old World families, she argued, often exerted too much discipline, stifling the "savage spirit of creation" in their children. Midwestern American parents who led an adult-centered life drove youth beyond the family to find outlets for their cravings. Girls who failed to get approval at home sought it on the streets. More cruelly, immoral parents forced children into prostitution or to run away from home. As in the courtroom, Van Waters judged these parents unworthy of their rights and declared the state the protector of child welfare.

A psychological interpretation of delinquency dominated *Youth in Conflict*, although recurrent themes of social disorganization reflected the urban sociology associated with the University of Chicago. Van Waters assumed a closed psychic-energy system in which youthful impulses inevitably sought release, whether healthy or delinquent, thus reflecting the Freudian ideas incorporated by both G. Stanley Hall and Ethel Sturges Dummer. As her patron summarized the theme in the introduction, "Delinquency is a more simple healthy reaction to emotional stress than is mental regression." Like William I. Thomas, whose study *The Unadjusted Girl* had appeared the previous year, Van Waters preferred a romanticized past in which families and communities eased the transition to adulthood. When the peasant family had worked the land together, she argued, the child's "primitive outburst of energy" had found natural expression through labor and play. In the modern urban world, however, that "volcanic jet of elemental forces" remained buried under a "crust of intolerable dullness, barrenness and meanness" in everyday life. In reaction, youth stole, took joyrides, and defied adult authority.[12]

For girls, Van Waters explained, sex usually provided the alternative creative outlet, in part because of inadequate sex education in the home, and in part because the culture around them both encouraged and profited from young women's sexuality. She did not condemn adolescent sexuality, as did more conservative observers, nor did she label these girls hypersexual, as did some psychiatrists. As she wrote of teenage girls who smoked, drank, and went on all-night joyrides: "Sex is not sacred to them, or terrifying; it is merely fun. While their attitude may be less harmful than that of some of their critics, it is still dangerous, inadequate and abnormal, running swiftly into perversions." In most cases, though, the girl could be redeemed by channeling youthful impulses toward some alternative kind of fulfillment, and ultimately toward marriage.[13]

At times an economic critique broke through Van Waters' psychological gloss, revealing the long-standing influence of Jane Addams' *The Spirit of Youth and the City Streets*. In a chapter titled "Conflict in Industry," Van Waters lashed into motion pictures and other consumer industries for their ill effects on youth, especially girls. The use of child actors, the premium placed on youth in advertising and film, even the emphasis on speed rather than skill in factories all exploited young people without giving them a sense of creativity and responsibility. Especially troubling were "industrial enterprises which derive profit from gratification of pleasure-cravings of youth." Dance halls, theaters, hotels, eating places, and amusement parks all exposed, even trapped, youth into selling their sexuality in some form. The problems of youth, then, could not be solved without rebuilding "our economic civilization." Writing in terms that echoed both the Social Gospel of her childhood and the utopian socialism of her student years, Van Waters argued that to prevent delinquency, the "profit-economy would have to be replaced by a system based on respect for human life."[14]

In her economic critique, however, Van Waters stressed the psychological impact of consumerism rather than economic exploitation and deprivation per se. Although she rejected censorship of movies or books, she decried the popular images that exposed "the youngest children" to cheap versions of "relations of the sexes." As an alternative model she invoked her vision of "primitive" cultures, in which religion, art, and even science filled youth's need for "an enlarged, creative power." In contrast, modern youth turned to idols and fetishes because neither the church nor art nor science provided for their needs.[15]

Delinquents, then, were the creation of adults, not the product of bad heredity, low mentality, or an impoverished environment. Adults failed to provide adequate outlets for creativity; then some group of powerful adults profited by channeling youth into the consumer culture, exploiting their sexuality, and, in the process, undermining their self-esteem. Then other adults labeled youth in conflict as juvenile delinquents, creating an antisocial identity. Van Waters' psychological solution to this cycle was to restore the individuality of each young person. Again drawing from Freudian psychology, and probably directly influenced by Adolf Meyer and William Healy, she proposed that the "therapeutic function of consciousness" could make children aware of the sources of their conflicts. With the problem clearly addressed, adults could foster some form of transference of a child's longings for parental approval to a substitute love-object, such as a sympathetic social worker, teacher, relative, or even a pet. If the social worker avoided selfish or dependent relationships, such transference could help build a strong internal sense of self, the key to Van Waters' response to youth in conflict.[16]

Miriam Van Waters, like her father, had great faith in the salvation of individuals. Just as the physically sick could recover, she wrote, so too can delinquents reform. Even a girl "who has given herself to many lovers, has suffered disease, abandonment and rough handling" could become a "healthy, charming woman, devoted to children and husband," if she could lose her delinquent identity. To illustrate her point, Van Waters provided success stories of such girls—one abused within her family and seduced by a movie director at age fourteen; one the daughter of an insane mother and brutal father; another formerly disorderly person who had become a "girl architect" by age twenty-three. Girls who "make good" did not always marry, she explained; some became self-supporting businesswomen. Along with this faith in individual salvation, however, Van Waters also called on the state—in the form of juvenile courts, schools, and reformatories—to help children adjust and provide child welfare services in communities. Whether through child-centered families or redemptive public agencies, she insisted, when adults accept emotional responsibility for youth "we shall see the burden of delinquency lifted from the shoulders of the children."[17]

The spate of books on the problems of modern youth that appeared at mid-decade provided a context and an audience for *Youth in Conflict,* but Van Waters struck a particularly responsive chord. Social workers, teachers, and psychiatrists who sought to combine older spiritual values with newer psychological theories especially appreciated her message. William Alanson White, the influential superintendent of St. Elizabeth's Hospital, declared the opening section of the book "the most brilliantly presented material that I have seen." In his review, the politically progressive psychiatrist Ira Wile praised "the humanity of the author, her vision of justice, her sense of scientific evaluation." More conservative readers, such as social-hygiene activists, also admired the "simplicity and directness" of the book and its message of parental responsibility for delinquency. A particularly astute critic, former Bedford Hills, New York, women's reformatory superintendent Katharine Bement Davis, called attention to the religious moorings of the book's psychology. Davis noted that with "little change of wording," Van Waters' call for an "inner change of motive . . . to produce lasting changes in human behavior" could have been "text for a sermon by an orthodox clergyman at any time during the last three centuries," although the clergyman "probably would have called the change 'conversion.'" [18]

Whatever the label, Miriam Van Waters' optimistic accounts of soul saving appealed to a wide audience in the field of social welfare. Even eight years after the book appeared, the British sexologist Havelock Ellis declared it required reading for all juvenile court judges and "a wise and beautiful book." Sales of *Youth in Conflict* pleased both her editor, who requested another book to head their next publication list, and Van Waters, who made over one thousand dollars in royalties within a year. She asked Hans Weiss to translate the book into German, and within a few years translations also appeared in Dutch, French, and Turkish. New American editions came out in 1926 and 1928, and the book stayed in print for almost twenty years. Van Waters remained mindful of the source of her fame. To Ethel Sturges Dummer she wrote: "Oh, My Dear! Such a strange wonderful thing has happened to me. And remember it is all because of *you*. You gave me freedom to write the book and many ideas and inspirations to put into it and you believed in me." [19]

As a result of the success of *Youth in Conflict*, Van Waters enjoyed new opportunities. An officer at the Laura Spelman Rockefeller Fund read the book and decided to supply fellowships to researchers who would work with Van Waters in Los Angles. The Rockefeller Foundation also paid her expenses to travel to New York, where, she felt, her book had an even better reception than in California. Schools and community groups invited her to speak, and in Portland, where she had once defended Margaret Sanger, Van Waters now lectured civic groups on birth control and sex education. Not yet forty years old, Miriam Van

Waters returned triumphant to both her hometown and her alma mater, an authority on child saving and, at last, a published author.[20]

The national popularity of her liberal views may have allowed Van Waters to underestimate the staying power of punitive responses to delinquency. Yet back home, conservatives kept their eye on El Retiro, and with Van Waters traveling around the country, her local reforms became more vulnerable to attack. In the years after the publication of *Youth in Conflict,* Van Waters' already hectic schedule became even more pressed. As new opportunities presented themselves, she rarely refused an invitation or an added responsibility. She accepted speaking engagements around the country, continued serving as referee at juvenile court, reported at case conferences and student meetings at El Retiro, attended mental-hygiene meetings, directed the Laura Spelman fellows, served as mentor to other professional women, began writing a new book, organized conferences, and continued to host an expanding stream of visitors to the Colony and later Stone House. "Sometimes I think I do too many things—and none of them well," Miriam confided to her parents that fall. "But," she wrote in justification of her choices, "some of us are meant to be pioneers—in several fields—a sort of surveyor's job and others can come along and settle up the country." Those who knew her well continued to worry about the extent to which she threw herself into project after project. As Ethel Dummer wrote to her protégé, "Are you learning to work without the nervous strain of feeling personally responsible for it all? I hope so. Otherwise, I must not make many demands upon you."[21]

Unmindful of the hints about her near compulsive sense of responsibility, soon Van Waters also accepted a demanding national position that would increasingly draw her to the East Coast. Harvard Law School professor Felix Frankfurter, a liberal supporter of protective labor legislation and child welfare policies, was then directing the Harvard Crime Survey, and he was looking for an investigator to study juvenile justice. His wife, Marion, had recommended *Youth in Conflict* to him, and in 1926 Frankfurter invited Van Waters to direct the juvenile delinquency section of the survey.[22]

The Harvard Crime Survey resembled other social scientific investigations launched in the early twentieth century to address America's social problems, beginning in 1907 with the comprehensive Pittsburgh Survey. Almost three thousand other social surveys were completed over the next twenty years. Crime surveys became more popular in the 1920s, probably in response to both Prohibition-era concerns about the criminal underworld and the conservative call for law and order that emerged during the postwar Red Scare. In 1921, Felix Frankfurter and Roscoe Pound had directed the first community survey of crime in Cleveland, Ohio; other cities followed suit during the decade. Although quantitative and survey research methods couched these studies within a framework of scientific objectivity, the goals of the early social surveys often resembled those of muckraking journalism that exposed the evils of entrenched institutions. The Pittsburgh Survey, for example, had revealed the primitive standards of workers' housing and sanitation, while Miriam Van Waters' own reformatory survey had publicized the physical mistreatment of incarcerated juveniles.[23]

In formulating the Harvard survey, Felix Frankfurter and his law school colleague Sheldon Glueck had a definite social critique in mind. "We want to show that the present system of handling crime under present court proceedings—whether against adults or juveniles—is a complete failure," an internal memo explained. One goal of the survey was to emphasize crime as a symptom of "a diseased individual." Frankfurter believed that juvenile case materials from Boston could show that criminal tendencies "begin at a very early age," so that crime prevention required greater attention to juvenile behavior problems. Sheldon Glueck felt that telling the dramatic case histories of juvenile delinquents would appeal to public concerns about preventing the "infection" of crime. Once they had aroused these sentiments, the surveys' authors would recommend that social, and not merely legal, experts had to intervene with delinquent children. The entire enterprise—the disease model, dramatic storytelling, and social rather than legal reforms—fit perfectly with Miriam Van Waters' methods.[24]

Accepting this position would require frequent trips to Boston to survey institutions and meet with other researchers, and it would clearly complicate Van Waters' already busy life. Orfa Shontz recognized that the survey presented a wonderful opportunity, but, she wrote confidentially to Ethel Dummer, "Miriam isn't very well—she has just been carrying too much." In addition, Judge Archbald came up for reelection, and Miriam needed to be in Los Angeles to "protect the situation" if a new judge was assigned to juvenile court. After visiting the East Coast, even Miriam found herself praying "that I will not have to drink this Boston cup: I do not feel as if it were really 'on my path,'" although, she added, "were I free from other obligations I would gladly do it."[25]

Why, then, did Van Waters accept the job? Her growing admiration for Frankfurter may have influenced her decision, as did a reverence for Harvard. It is also possible that the presence of Hans Weiss in Cambridge made traveling there more attractive. The Harvard survey also appealed as part of a life plan that had recently begun to take shape in her mind. Since the publication of *Youth in Conflict,* Van Waters viewed herself as a national reformer and set her sights on higher office than the increasingly troubled Los Angeles Juvenile Court. As she explained to her parents in 1926, "some day—I may move from here—and go to New York or Washington—but not for five years. There is no plan yet, nothing definite, but if I should be offered the children's bureau, I should take it." To do so she would need to become more centrally located within the national social work network, which was based in Chicago, New York, and Washington. The East Coast connections she would make through the Harvard survey could advance her goal of national office while easing her immediate distress. "My life here is made up of routine—so that I must work from 9-11:00 P. M. almost everyday," Miriam wrote. The survey promised at least a temporary change of pace.[26]

In Los Angeles, Van Waters' days had become even more overburdened because of local politics. Serious conflicts at El Retiro pitted her model of internalized control against a more traditional form of externally imposed discipline. For example, when an El Retiro superintendent punished the students with silence and segregation, Van Waters succeeded in having the probation committee dismiss the woman. But the new probation committee, which had taken over in 1924, provided less support for her approach. Van Waters feared that politically motivated members would remove El Retiro girls from the public high school and that a new superintendent, less to her liking, would be appointed.[27]

Committee member Elizabeth McManus seemed determined to wrest control of the school from Van Waters and her protégés. When McManus solicited recommendations from the staff, the results revealed simmering tensions over methods of control. At one extreme some staff members called for greater discipline by teachers, backed up by punishments and long terms. As one woman wrote, the school needed a "superintendent who stands as the last word in control and discipline of the girls." In contrast, a social worker stressed contact between students and their families and "the atmosphere of home life" at El Retiro, achieved through events such as dainty afternoon teas and reading aloud of novels. Similarly, an El Retiro teacher who recommended "Rule by Love not Fear" reminded McManus that "Self control and love," rather than punishment, provide the foundation for obedience.[28]

Miriam Van Waters much preferred the latter style of discipline, and she supported the hiring of staff members who agreed with her. She had heartily approved of the appointment of superintendent Alma Holzschuh in fall 1924. A highly educated social worker, Holzschuh represented the kind of socially conscious professional woman whose career Van Waters had begun to promote. Above all, the new superintendent met her standard of uncompromising loyalty to the "principle of friendly rehabilitation of delinquent girls." When Holzschuh arrived at El Retiro, she reorganized a demoralized staff and instituted a merit system that elaborated upon Van Waters' concept of internalized control. Students who earned gold stars—about half of the forty girls in residence—enjoyed the privileges of overnight hikes, trips to concerts in Los Angeles, and weekend visits home.[29]

With Alma Holzschuh as superintendent, Miriam Van Waters felt assured that her reform tradition would prevail at El Retiro. Over the next few years Holzschuh's reports portrayed an "increasingly good spirit" on the part of the students, as well as improvements in the physical plant. The conference group continued to meet to evaluate and plan for students, with Van Waters attending whenever she was not traveling. During her absences, just as she turned her court duties over to Orfa Jean Shontz, Van Waters left El Retiro in the hands of Alma Holzschuh.[30]

Even in the East, Van Waters remained conscious that some members of the board of supervisors remained hostile to the juvenile court and considered Holzschuh too idealistic. The probation office, a critical link between the court and El Retiro, seemed to her like "an evil dream." Van Waters also had to contend with her own enemies. Antagonistic supervisors and probation committee members refused to raise her salary, even when Minnesota tried to hire her for much more than she earned in L.A. Her national travels may have caused resentment back home. "I have some trouble with politics," she had written to her father at the end of 1925. "Someone started the old rumor, 'Dr. VW only works part-time' and asked for a grand jury investigation! I'm not worrying," she assured him, though she probably knew that there was much cause for worry.[31]

To help maintain the balancing act between the juvenile court in Los Angeles and the Harvard Crime Survey in Boston, Van Waters hired Edna Mahan, a Berkeley graduate and one of her Los Angeles protégés, who had been serving as superintendent of juvenile hall. In 1927 Mahan told the county that she was taking a sick leave, but she moved to Cambridge to serve as Van Waters' "personal representative throughout the survey." Mahan evaluated female juvenile delinquency in Boston, freeing Van Waters to return to Los Angeles. In the summer of 1928, however, Mahan would become superintendent of the Clinton Farms reformatory in New Jersey, requiring Van Waters' return to the East. By then, local politics in Los Angeles had reached a nadir.[32]

In August 1927, while she was on a trip to the East Coast to work on the crime survey, Van Waters' worst nightmare about El Retiro came to pass. The probation committee summarily dismissed Alma Holzschuh on the grounds that the superintendent had not complied with either their policies or their requests for information. They further charged lack of discipline, disregard for county property, lack of diplomacy and tact, and failure to cooperate with the probation committee. Holzschuh asked for more specific charges and a hearing by the civil service commission. Despite protests from both the local chapter of the American Association of Social Workers and the PTA, the commission denied her request. According to probation committee chair Charles Lusby, the problem was "too much freedom without thought of necessary discipline to make for the success of the undertaking." He helped install a more punitive superintendent, and policemen soon appeared at the school to control the students.[33]

Van Waters was devastated by the news of "the sacking of El Retiro," as she called the dismissal of Holzschuh and the appearance of male guards. The school, she wrote to Ethel Sturges Dummer, had been "wiped out" while "everyone, including the Judge, was out of town." For a moment, Miriam felt hopeless. Just two months earlier, fire had engulfed the Colony, destroying among her possessions several draft chapters of her new book. The weight of depression from that trauma had only recently lifted. Now her dream of an alternative school had been demolished, and she fully expected that her job as referee would be the next target of the probation committee. "Against entrenched political power, we can do nothing," she lamented. And yet, her very next thought was to take command: she began to imagine the construction of "a private El Retiro" to replace the school she had lost.[34]

When her emotions cooled, Van Waters assessed the politics of the episode. Elizabeth McManus, she felt sure, had engineered the destruction of El Retiro to serve the interest of a vengeful former probation office employee who wanted the board of education to get control of the juvenile court. But Van Waters recognized that deeper political currents ran beneath this power play. During the 1920s, not only in Los Angeles but throughout the country, social welfare measures that had been introduced by progressive reformers—including limitations on child labor and public funding for maternal and infant health programs—were falling victim to the laissez-faire spirit of the decade. In the case of El Retiro, she wrote, "The real reason for the smash is the move of Retrenchment of service and money—in our county—for children, aged, poor, and sick, made necessary by the expansion of building, and high salaries for executives." In this atmosphere, it was not surprising that Van Waters encountered conservative supervisors who objected to El Retiro's expenditures to take delinquent girls to concerts and movies, as well as to the rehabilitative principles that these outings represented.[35]

Determined to resist these conservative forces, Van Waters decided not to resign from the court "till I am fired—maybe not then." She would keep fighting the probation committee from her position at the court, and she would mobilize community support for her cause. Members of thirty women's organizations, including the League of Women Voters and parent-teacher groups, rallied to her side. Perhaps because of their pressure, the male guards left El Retiro, and a new superintendent, more to Van Waters' liking, soon took over.[36] El Retiro, however, had already slipped from its founder's control. The probation committee still authorized placements for the school, but by the spring of 1928 they had reduced the number of girls sent there by over half. Students no longer attended the local public schools, and the committee began to design new, cell-like residences, with high windows covered with "slits like bars." Van Waters protested the architectural changes, but to no avail. In the meantime, she proceeded with her plan to establish a private alternative school to replace El Retiro. With the support of the Episcopal Bishops Committee and community groups, a "new little school" opened at a beachside camp early in 1928. Twelve girls attended, under the direction of Alma Holzschuh, for a six-month experimental program. The probation committee failed to block the effort, but without sufficient private funds to continue it, the camp ended that summer. By then, Van Waters had given up hope of rebuilding El Retiro. The school, she realized, "is dead. . . . The wonder is that it endured so long without political interference."[37]

During the trying months after she lost control of El Retiro, Miriam Van Waters faced "days when I came dangerously near—blindness and despair." For inspiration she thought of the students who had been most affected by the change in administration. "The girls set me the example," she wrote to Dummer. For years Van Waters recalled the story of the mass walkout of El Retiro students in the wake of the firing of Alma Holzschuh and the arrival of male guards. At the end of a week, all but seven of the girls "set out on foot, walking 18 miles in the hot California sun, with blistered feet. Policemen rode in cars behind them, refusing to let them ride, and threatening them with the county jail." Later, the remaining students repeated the walk, voluntarily returning to juvenile hall "rather than live in a school which threatened to be an 'institution.'" According to Van Waters, "some of the county officials said the girls were likely to become bolsheviks if they were allowed to walk out," but Orfa Shontz, acting as substitute referee, placed the girls in the custody of their original probation officers rather than return them to El Retiro.[38]

Possibly to document the case against the new administration at El Retiro, Shontz held hearings with the students who walked out. Their comments reflected both fears about their future treatment and support for Van Waters' reforms. Several students explained that they left because they thought they might be sent to a convent or to the Ventura School for Girls. "Yes I liked it, it was a wonderful school," one student reported; "I want to go back home and when Miss Holzschuh gets back, I want to go back to El Retiro," answered another. Some feared the new superintendent, while other students had clearly internalized the message of the school and adopted its goals as their own. As one young woman explained: "I expected to stay there until I was a lady to go out and be a nurse, that is what I was going to be."[39]

El Retiro continued to operate, and Van Waters continued to participate in case conferences, but the school had ceased to embody her reforms. As one supporter wrote in 1928, "Due to politics the school as dreamed of and carried out by Miriam Van Waters has vanished. Only the buildings and name remains. A school started in idealism cannot function properly if soiled by the filthy hand of politics." Even Orfa Shontz called for the school to close because it had already ended the mission for which it had been founded, and "there are enough penal schools for girls now." For Miriam Van Waters the blow felt like the loss of a child. The school she had created as a model for national juvenile reform had been destroyed; her reputation, and her ego, felt shattered. Almost a year later she continued to mourn, writing in her journal that "El Retiro child and dream—yields up its soul to the night: murdered yet ascendant—Gone—yet unreally present[—]Gone—How—Where—by whose hands—to what purpose . . . Gone—Forever—forever-forever."[40]

To recover from her defeat, Van Waters threw herself into projects that would strengthen her national position. She took a month's sick leave to reconstruct the lost chapters of her book manuscript, which flowed more easily than her earlier writing. "In a borrowed house, with a borrowed fountain pen, in a borrowed smock," she tried to coax it "to rise from the ashes." Just a month after the fire she had completed over six chapters of *Parents on Probation;* in September 1927, recovering from the loss of El Retiro, she wrote in her journal that the manuscript was "a seven months child" that was with her "constantly during the bitterest hours of my life." The book appeared in early 1928 to less acclaim than *Youth in Conflict.* Though quickly written and repetitive, it earned respectable reviews and decent royalties, going through three editions in its first five years in print. Once again, Van Waters' plainspoken, anecdotal style appealed to readers. One reviewer proclaimed that parents who might never open another sociological work would actually read this "'how-to-do-it' book rich in cultural values."[41]

Parents on Probation reiterated many of the themes of Van Waters' earlier work. Historical shifts in family life had deprived modern youth of both clear models and adequate attention. Emotional, rather than eugenic or economic, factors bred delinquency. To prevent sexual delinquency, parents needed healthier attitudes toward sex. They should not blame children for crimes perpetrated against them by adults, such as incest and rape. At the same time, adults should not assume that "illicit sexual experience is harmless for children." Above all, Van Waters emphasized the overriding need for steady parental love and respect for children. Drawing on studies conducted in juvenile courts and child guidance clinics, she argued that unsatisfactory family relations, especially a child's sense of being unwanted, led teenage girls to seek sexual approval. The prognosis for both delinquent children and their parents, however, was good. Each could be redeemed through "perpetual mutual adjustment" of the parent-child relationship. As if to confirm the possibility of healthy parenthood, Van Waters dedicated the book "To my Father and Mother to whose understanding and sturdy acceptance of the role of parents in the modern world this book owes its being."[42]

Along with her new book, the Harvard Crime Survey offered Van Waters a chance to heal from her political reversals and deepen her national connections. She spent the fall of 1928 based in Cambridge while visiting state institutions. With the help of a hardworking staff, including Alma Holzschuh, she tabulated accounts of inmates and conditions at the schools. Working under Felix Frankfurter's expert leadership provided "one of the compensations for seeing seven years of work crushed under heel" at El Retiro. In Cambridge Van Waters also enjoyed the companionship of Hans Weiss, to whom she had increasingly turned for support over the past year. Hans felt privileged that Miriam "longed to lean on me—to rest [her] head on my breast and seek comfort." During the fall they dined together, went to the symphony, and talked of his childhood, the juvenile court, the insanity defense, and the injustice of capital punishment.[43]

Despite their closeness, Van Waters continued to minimize Weiss' importance, while he began to protest her limits. When she asked Edna Mahan to stay with her in Cambridge, Hans felt enraged because he would have to maintain the pretense of being a mere colleague in Edna's presence. In a rare expression of misery, he chastised Miriam for assuming that he would understand. "I have tried my best—but I don't," he complained. "All this suffering is so wholly unnecessary—that I don't understand why you take this attitude. . . . I cannot possibly make my heart see why *I* should always be the one who has to step aside. We have had very little time to ourselves—I have accepted it all—but it is harder than I can tell." Although his romantic soul seemed to thrive upon his agony, he now expressed his pain more plaintively. "I long with all my heart to comfort you, as I know how tired you are—but I am not even permitted to do it when you are here," he wrote.[44]

After Miriam left Cambridge, Hans became more resigned to the limits she placed on their love, as well as more desperate in his search for a mate. His detailed discussions of other romantic interests may have been intended to make her jealous, but Miriam always seemed to encourage his ventures rather than compete with them. He continued to invoke sensual memories of her and to long for more time together, even as he wondered if his wish were too bold. Although he tried to accept her dictum that "the sharing of time together does not matter in the end if we share love," he wanted "a more natural, a more carnal, a more simple and freer way of meeting." They would have one last romantic visit in California the next summer, when Hans spent the "most beautiful" night of his life, nestling the sleeping Miriam in his arms as if he were a protective mother. Even as he expressed his wish "to watch you sleeping for the rest of our lives and ever thereafter," Hans knew that his dream was impossible. Thus he prayed for the power to be "your mate spiritually—in our service to others."[45]

In the meantime, Miriam Van Waters' social world expanded beyond her private relationship with Hans Weiss and the California colony of reformers. Living in Cambridge in 1928, socializing with the Harvard elite, and speaking to local civic groups, she gradually discarded her earlier distaste for the East. Given her concern about status, Maud Van Waters must have been delighted when her daughter wrote that Miss Fanny Curtiss, "an ancient Bostonian" and president of the City Women's Club, invited Miriam to dinner along with Judge Frederick Cabot, Felix Frankfurter, and Lady Astor, an American divorcée who had married into the British peerage. "Felix and she talk politics knowing everyone[,] it would appear[,] all over Europe by their first names," Miriam reported, explaining that Lady Astor had been kind to her because she had been staying at Brookdale, the estate of Geraldine Thompson, a New Jersey philanthropist who greatly admired *Youth in Conflict*. Miriam herself had just returned from Brookdale, where she and Thompson had deepened their friendship during horseback rides and evening talks by the fire.[46]

Although drawn to social elites, Van Waters aligned herself with liberal patricians rather than defenders of the status quo. In the 1928 presidential election, for instance, many of her colleagues were supporting Al Smith, the Democratic Party candidate who hoped to end Prohibition and become the first Catholic elected president. "Harvard Law school is strong for Al," she noted, as were several women she came to admire. These included Dorothy Kirchwey Brown, the daughter of George Kirchwey, whose sister, journalist Freda Kirchwey, later became editor of the *Nation,* and Jessie Wilson Sayre, the daughter of Woodrow Wilson, whose husband Franklin taught at the Law School. "I am sure the Van Waters family goes solid for Hoover," Miriam wrote, but breaking with family tradition, she now commented that when she met Smith supporters, "Naturally I'm pleased."[47] By the end of 1928, these new personal and political ties increasingly drew Miriam Van Waters toward the East Coast, to which she would return shortly.

Back in California in 1929, Van Waters confronted her declining local political fortunes. Despite her relief at the ouster of the "dreadful chief of police," Al "Two-Gun" Davis, conservatives still dominated Los Angeles. The newly elected judge at juvenile court, Robert H. Scott, was barely cordial to her, and she felt hostility from the probation committee and two members of the board of supervisors. Letters to confidantes like Hans Weiss and Edna Mahan revealed her ·"sadness and silent despair." To Mahan she confided that "Politics are simply hell," complaining in an uncharacteristic use of profanity about "those darn bastards" who maligned her in the press. The monthly meetings at El Retiro, she told her parents, were "the hardest thing I do." Her health also suffered. Recurrent colds had been diagnosed as pleurisy, a painful inflammation of lung membranes that could indicate a recurrence of tuberculosis. Despite weight loss and anemia, she did not have TB, but she was physically debilitated.[48]

Van Waters' personal distress became quite tangible in an account she wrote to her parents of a workday soon after she returned to L. A. After hearing "120 cases in court," she "had the disagreeable task of going to the Juvenile Hall Opening—½ million dollars worth of new buildings." Aside from the graft that she suspected contributed to the high cost, the new structure symbolized the reaction against her brand of reform. "The place looks exactly like a detention home. . . . There is an 18 foot *cement wall* around the place." In one of her rare expressions of explicit indignation, she revealed how offended she felt during the ceremony by the lack of recognition for her efforts. "I hope I am beyond infantile pique and jealousy," she began, "but I must say—I was pretty mad. For 25 years social work in California has gone on slowly building—Orfa has labored 20 years and I 12—and there was no credit given." Although she acknowledged that the court "has taught me almost all I know," she prepared herself that "when the time comes I shall give it up." Recalling a nightmare in which "a fat deputy sheriff" led her away, she wrote that "I would depart this life with faith & fear: This political life—this court—this Petty-petty little Hotbed."[49]

It was up to Van Waters to decide on the timing of her resignation. For over a year she hesitated to leave. For one, she needed to find another job. In addition, just as she had persisted in struggle with G. Stanley Hall, she seemed loathe to abandon a fight without first reestablishing her sense of self-worth. In March 1929, she wrote to her parents that she was still thinking about resigning from the court, but she wanted to wait until after the annual meeting of the National Conference on Social Work (NCSW) in San Francisco in June 1929, thinking she might be nominated to become its next president. In 1928, when Edith Abbott had suggested that she run for the office, Van Waters refused to imagine the possibility. "It is too soon to talk about it, I certainly do not WANT it, and there would be a good deal of opposition, so probably I could not get it," she wrote to her parents. But the following year she began to think seriously about winning.[50]

The strategy of waiting for the NCSW election before resigning from the court had both practical and symbolic advantages. If she won, the national position would enhance both Van Waters' leverage in Los Angeles and her chances of finding a better job. At the same time, being recognized as the leader of American social workers, an office previously held by Jane Addams, could ease her pain over her local defeats. Close friends who knew of Miriam's tendency to overcommit herself worried about the effect the job would have on her health and her local career. As Hans Weiss wrote to her, given the poor health Miriam had recently experienced and the fact that the job carried no salary, there seemed "no earthly reason" why she should accept such a "tremendous obligation at this time." To her, however, the honor seemed irresistible.[51]

By late June 1929, when Bess Woods and she drove up to San Francisco for the social work conference, Miriam felt confident about the election. She had been officially nominated to run against a man who was not well known, and "Fortunately," she believed, "I have no national enemies." To present her best face, she had purchased striking outfits—a fashionable suit, a black lace evening gown, a silk dress, a stylish hat. "I am *not* going to look like a social worker!" she promised her parents. The conference was filled with old and new friends. Ethel Dummer, Hans Weiss, Grace Abbott, and Sophonisba Breckinridge all admired her work; Paul Kellogg had frequently published her articles in *The Survey;* Eleanor and Sheldon Glueck, as well as George Kirchwey, knew her through the Harvard survey. Other delegates learned of Van Waters' views through a series of talks she gave at the conference, in which she covered as many political bases as possible.[52]

Van Waters' account of the San Francisco meeting portrayed her as a brave crusader challenging the status quo. Her first speech, she told her parents, outraged the Traveller's Aid Society by urging its members to stay in their own field rather than attempt to do casework. Her second speech, she claimed, offended the Boston group because "I told of conditions in their courts: a real show-down." A third talk to a girl's council went smoothly, but her fourth speech, she felt, "got me friends and LOTs [of] enemies. I talked about negroes and capital punishment." In it Van Waters chided social workers for outmoded racial views and argued that there was "no biological, no cultural reason why the Negro should not share life on equal terms with those colored white, yellow, red, or brown." She even discussed the "advantages of race-mingling," a highly unpopular topic that might explain why her talk "outraged a large number" of delegates. Lest the conference mistake her for anything but a liberal social worker, Van Waters proudly "talked against breaking up homes by court action[,] against the smugness of social workers, against sterilization as a remedy, against capital punishment," and against the jailing of local socialist Tom Mooney and the executions of Massachusetts anarchists Sacco and Vanzetti. Although she feared that she "must have lost 25 votes by that speech" alone, she won the presidential election by one vote, 167 to 166.[53]

Van Waters may have portrayed herself as an unpopular liberal in order to explain this narrow margin of victory, but however close the election, it represented a major triumph. Since its founding in 1874, only a handful of women had held the presidency of the NCSW, among them Jane Addams, Julia Lathrop, and Grace Abbott. Despite the numerical dominance of women in the profession, men continued to occupy the majority of high-level administrative positions, a common pattern for professions that underwent "feminization" in nineteenth- and twentieth-century America. For Van Waters to have won this election, as a woman and a self-professed liberal, she must have attained a significant national reputation. Her books, *Youth in Conflict* and *Parents on Probation,* along with her *Survey* articles, had introduced her to a wide audience in her field. Extensive public speaking throughout the decade also enhanced her prestige. As Bess Woods once described her friend's lecture style, "Miriam's directness, mastery and grace took them all." The same personal charisma that attracted the loyalty of El Retiro girls no doubt affected professional colleagues, as well.

Once in office, Miriam Van Waters appointed women to NCSW committees and pursued the issues that had won her both friends and enemies in San Francisco. Following through on her comments about race, she created a Committee on the American Indian, to which she appointed Edith Abbott, Franz Boas, and Indian reformer John Collier. Her presidential talk on the new morality and the social worker appeared in *Opportunity: A Journal of Negro Life.* She also promoted her interest in abolishing capital punishment. The presidency of the NCSW bolstered Van Waters' career, despite her local setbacks. In addition to providing the comfort of professional approval, the new office, she believed, would keep her "free from serious political interference in Los Angeles—for at least a year." That year would buy the time to redirect her life, which would gradually depart from both the juvenile court and Los Angeles.[54]

By the time she had been elected to the presidency of the NCSW, Van Waters had already begun to think about relocating. Her dear friend Sara Fisher had been "ousted" from the court in May 1929, and while Miriam felt relieved that her own "personal work is not molested," she knew she could not remain there long. Her friends had begun to make inquiries into a possible teaching or administrative appointment. A letter-writing campaign to establish a social work professorship for her at UCLA did not succeed, even with the support of lawyers such as Harry Archbald and Felix Frankfurter and philanthropists such as Ethel Sturges Dummer and Geraldine Thompson. "She is one of the few leaders in social welfare who could develop programs and attract a following of both professional students, and the general public, on a basis of philosophic understanding and scientific technique," Thompson had written in her recommendation for Van Waters. But in the late 1920s, social welfare programs did not command abundant political resources.[55]

It is tempting to speculate whether a man with Van Waters' credentials would have had the same difficulties finding a suitable job. He might have been elected to public office, appointed to head a government bureau, or become a major professor at a university. The options for Miriam Van Waters, however, were limited, both by her gender and by a political climate unfriendly to social welfare reform. Even when gender was an advantage, in agencies concerned with the social welfare of women and children, Van Waters' West Coast base made her less likely to be considered. In the federal government, for example, the Children's Bureau drew most of its high-ranking officials from the women's reform network that emanated out from Chicago's Hull House community. Private foundations that hired professional women often turned to this network, as well, or to East Coast reformers. For all of these reasons, options for public service did not readily appear.[56]

For a moment Van Waters determined to quit her job at the court even without a new position. In September 1929—just a month before the stock market crash that helped trigger the Great Depression—she declared to her parents that she would strike out on her own in October. "It is high time for change," she explained to her parents. "I shall have faith in my money making capacity, work hard, and trust in capital Providence, also take private cases." Perhaps, she speculated, she would direct a progressive school in Hollywood the next year. Officially she would cite the responsibilities of the Harvard survey and her presidency of the NCSW, but her "personal reason" for leaving amounted to despair over the politics of the juvenile court. "No scientific work can be done in this court. Everyone who amounts to anything is sooner or later put out. They never put me out, but gradually my work will become more isolated, our judge is hopeless." Hans Weiss applauded her decision. He offered to help pay her rent when she returned to Boston and commiserated with her over the demise of their dreams about juvenile reform. "The spirit of it is gone," he lamented. "Hypocrisy, selfishness, crookedness and cold hearted cruelty" had driven "the best of us" from the judicial experiment. No single crisis had forced her decision, Miriam explained to her family, but one day, "Just as St. Paul saw the light on the road to Antioch—if that is where he did—so I have seen it. Congratulate me please."[57]

When she wrote of her epiphany, Van Waters knew, in fact, that she had prospects for a better job, thanks to the efforts of her East Coast supporters. In June, Felix Frankfurter had telegraphed to let her know that she was likely to be appointed to the commission on law enforcement established by President Herbert Hoover. Frankfurter urged Van Waters to accept the position if offered, and she did not think she could refuse. Geraldine Thompson also counseled acceptance. A former Republican national committeewoman, Thompson probably influenced Hoover's nominations for the commission, but Miriam believed that it was "being very orchestrated" by Frankfurter. His plan was for Hoover to ask Van Waters to take a one- or two-year leave from the L. A. juvenile court so that she could direct the juvenile delinquency division of the commission.

The job appealed to Van Waters as a national platform for her theories. She wanted to seize the opportunity, she explained, "to take the nation to school [to] SEE the problem of delinquency in children is not a matter of better courts and fewer policemen (nor more laws)—but a spiritual architecture for the whole land. Reform is not through buildings, but a change in viewpoint." In November 1929, she accepted the position as director of the juvenile crime survey for the National Commission on Law Observance and Enforcement, chaired by former attorney general George Wickersham.[58]

Miriam Van Waters faced a great deal of unfinished business at the time she accepted her appointment. She still had to write up her section of the Harvard Crime Survey, a task that generated panic when she turned to it. She also had to preserve her job at court in case she had no other position when the Wickersham commission disbanded. As Ethel Dummer wrote to her, taking on this new survey without getting a leave from the court would be like "going into unchartered sea." When Judge Robert Scott insisted that she resign, Van Waters displayed a rare outburst of temper, and he quickly retreated. The civil service commission granted her a year-long leave of absence from the court.[59]

At the end of 1929, Miriam Van Waters held her last session as referee of juvenile court. She talked to the probation officers about her new job and appealed to them to carry on the high standards of the past. "It was sad and gay," she told her parents, "for they cried and I made them laugh a little by reminding them of their fine deeds in court." The next day she would "start work full tilt." She planned to tackle the Harvard survey, sit for a portrait, and "try to learn the new role of a Free Woman."[60]

Van Waters' account of her departure from the court resembled her graduation from Clark University sixteen years earlier. In both cases she had become embattled against a powerful force that both frustrated her goals and animated her will to succeed. At the end of each struggle, she viewed herself as an emancipated woman, set loose to make her way in the world, armed with the lessons of her struggle. As a graduate student she had learned tact and the importance of strategic retreat. Now, evaluating her years in Los Angeles, she wrote, "I am grateful for my long training in politics—one develops the epidermis of a horned toad, the lethargy of a opossum, the patience of a donkey." Just as Clark had disappointed her expectations of the university, Los Angeles had been disillusioning in terms of her high hopes for juvenile reform. As she told the Friday Morning Club, "The idea of the Juvenile Court has not been tried in any city of the United States over a long period of time. We have the laws and all the machinery necessary to make it a success, but we have not sufficient recognition on the part of the public, only a meager supply of probation officers and inadequate education." Institutional reform, she had learned, relied on a broader public opinion and on political resources.[61]

In some ways, Miriam Van Waters seemed to retreat from her progressive goals at the end of the 1920s, disappointed by reformers as well as politicians. The women's clubs had become more conservative, and probation committee members like Elizabeth McManus held a very different notion of juvenile reform than did Van Waters. In her presidential address to the NCSW in 1930, she greatly toned down the crusading politics of just a year earlier, emphasizing individual rehabilitation rather than social programs. "Social work has realized that a program cannot make men moral, religious, or happy," she explained. "The strength of a program depends upon the morality and the religion and the happiness of those who build and execute it." Denouncing "the uselessness of programs, particularly those dependent upon state action, or force," she sounded an individualist creed. Reformers, she now stated, "have commonly a low opinion of mankind. . . . [T]he reformer would like you to believe he knows what is best for you to do, better than you know yourself." In contrast she held up the ideal of a modern social worker who recognized that "the true springs of action" resided in the internal nature of the individual. Her statement not only relied on psychological theory but, in a sense, it rejected the concept of social control in favor of self-empowerment, a persistent theme in her approach to reform.[62]

The seeds of her belief in individual regeneration had been planted during Van Waters' childhood exposure to the Social Gospel, with its faith in innate human goodness. Her liberal Christianity, however, had been tempered by both her training in psychology and her political conflicts in Los Angeles. Instead of inspiring Van Waters to become a radical critic of economic and social injustice, the painful experience of failed reform propelled her away from a systemic analysis of social problems and further toward a narrower psychological, and eventually deeply spiritual, approach to her work. As the nation entered the Great Depression, she defended both the classical liberal distrust of the state and the emphasis on individual salvage that lay at the foundation of professional social work. Unlike those reformers who entered the arena of social policy and legislative politics, Van Waters remained committed to voluntary efforts to ameliorate social problems. Although she drew upon state resources in her professional life, and she had learned much about political engagement, she flourished in the charitable, voluntarist tradition of social work. The aid of powerful patrons like Ethel Sturges Dummer facilitated her approach, substituting individual support for that of a social movement.

Van Waters did remain connected to a variety of reformist groups, ranging from radical to liberal to fairly conservative ones. In addition to her involvement with the NCSW, by 1930 she sat on the boards of the American League to Abolish Capital Punishment, the National Probation Association, the National Society of Penal Information, the American Social Hygiene Association, and the National Commission for the Study of Social Values in Motion Pictures. She also served as vice president of the International Association of Children's Magistrates, based in Brussels; as an international council member of the Howard League for Penal Reform in London; and as director of the program committee for the upcoming International Conference for Social Work. Still uncertain of her future career in California, with her broad connections and national reputation, she had good reason to expect that something suitable would come her way at the conclusion of her tenure on the Wickersham commission. At midlife, Miriam Van Waters confidently faced an unchartered professional sea and embarked on the reconstitution of her personal life.[63]

In Love with a Child

A s she faced the crisis in her career, Miriam Van Waters entered midlife. She had celebrated her fortieth birthday in October 1927, just two months after the "sacking of El Retiro." These convergent events prompted her to take stock of the past and contemplate changes in her future. She had already formed a five-year plan for reviving her professional life, preferably in response to a call to national office. The Wickersham commission provided at least a temporary step toward that end, although her long-term career remained in limbo. Meanwhile, as she waited for suitable professional opportunities, Van Waters continued to rethink her personal world. As she confided to Ethel Sturges Dummer, "Sometimes it is incredible to me that I am not mated, have no children, yet have lost El Retiro which I so passionately loved. The pain of that separation grows ever more constant." In response to her loss, the troubled reformer began to reconstruct what she later called her "house of life," the network of close relationships that brought personal meaning to her.[1] Building on her long-standing familial role, she continued to assume responsibility for her siblings, especially her youngest brother, Ralph. In 1929, she also chose to become a parent herself.

Although Miriam Van Waters separated from her parental home when she moved to Los Angeles, she continued to act as a surrogate mother to all of her family members. During the 1920s, her father's financial difficulties, combined with her own success and sense of responsibility, kept her active as the keystone in the family structure. Financially unable to retire, at the age of sixty-five Reverend Van Waters and his wife had relocated to a new pulpit in Wellsboro, Pennsylvania. Miriam comforted her father during the ordeal, praising his impact on "social reform" and his "breadth of vision." She even entertained a fantasy of family reunion in which her father would be called to preach at a nearby California church, and she made several inquiries to this end. As late as 1930 she imagined her father taking over the Glendale church near Stone House.[2]

By this time, however, Reverend Van Waters was ready to retire, and Miriam herself was contemplating a move to the East. In the meantime, she did as much as she could to provide moral support. In cheerful notes she recommended books and articles—George Bernard Shaw's *Back to Methusala* on aging, Harry Emerson Fosdick on Christian ethics—and she sent gift subscriptions to liberal magazines. By the late 1920s she also sent frequent checks for Mother's Day and Father's Day or to help with medical expenses. When her father required surgery, Miriam paid the bill and accompanied him to Johns Hopkins for the operation, reporting on his progress to an appreciative family. "Miriam is splendid to send us word every day—she is a wonderful daughter and sister and friend," Maud wrote to her hospitalized husband. When the couple retired to Syracuse, New York, in 1932, Miriam sent monthly checks to supplement their meager pension. To raise the money, she sold the property they had given her at Cannon Beach, Oregon, severing her last ties to her favorite childhood haunt.[3]

Perhaps to ease her parents' burdens, but also because of her traditional role in the family, Miriam took an active part in directing the lives of her younger siblings. By 1920 her sister Ruth had married and established her own home, but Miriam supervised the young adulthoods of Beckie, George, and Ralph Van Waters.[4] Just after World War I, for example, she determined to steer George into a career in social service. She convinced him to take classes at Columbia University while living downtown at the Greenwich House settlement. Her plan backfired, however, for George wrote that he was "disgusted with the slum life in New York" and asked for money to get back to Portland after his exams. He poured his feelings out to his sister, explaining that he had only come east because of her, then realized that his nature just did not fit with social work. George had his heart set on going into business back in Portland. By starting at the bottom and studying business law, he believed he could get his own "higher education;" he would then repay all the money Miriam had invested in him and help support their parents. His letter suggested the need for both a strong will and persuasive self-justification for a member of the Van Waters family to choose business over the church or social service. George knew his mind, though, and with a friend he established a prosperous cleaning and chemical supply business in Seattle that allowed him to help support his parents during their retirement.[5]

Both Beckie and Ralph responded more willingly to Miriam's parental overtures. In 1919, when Beckie was in her early twenties and Ralph was in high school, they stayed with their older sister in Los Angeles. Each one had entered a "period of adjustment" that Maud and

George Van Waters could not handle on their own. When Beckie was wounded in love and thwarted in her efforts to get a nursing degree, Miriam counseled her mother to let Beckie recover and grow. Elaborating on the personal philosophy that informed both her work and her family relations, she explained that "What she needs most now is the utmost assurance of love and trust. . . . Just blind, overwhelming, trusting love — in an individual — right or wrong — is the only force than can hold, or change — a human being." Miriam offered love, but along with it came heavy-handed advice for self-improvement and an extensive sense of responsibility. As Ethel Dummer once wrote pointedly to Miriam, "The worry of relatives is a psychic drain upon an individual."[6]

Miriam Van Waters never absorbed this lesson, as evidenced by her lifelong concern about her youngest brother, with whom she had the closest and most emotionally entangled relationship within the family. She had always thought of Ralph as her child as much as her brother, and by the late 1920s, she had almost completely taken over responsibility for his transition to adulthood. Ralph Van Waters had a very hard time establishing himself, in part because of his personality and in part because of the historical moment in which he came of age. His childhood had differed from his older siblings in important ways. Miriam, Ruth, Beckie, and George had grown up in the child-filled St. David's rectory, enjoying the benefits of a domestically stable, though financially strapped, home. By the time Ralph was born in 1905, his siblings were no longer children, and, according to Miriam's letters from college, Maud felt depleted by the care of yet another infant. In addition, during Ralph's childhood the Van Waters home became much less stable, for Reverend Van Waters both traveled extensively as an itinerant missionary in eastern Oregon and failed miserably in the brass business.

George and Maud Van Waters did not know quite how to handle Ralph as he entered adolescence. A moody, reserved young man, he presented a stark contrast to Miriam, with her spirited and cheerful external demeanor. Ralph's reputation in the family can be gleaned from a letter Maud sent to Beckie in 1919, when fourteen-year-old Ralph remained at home with his sister. "If Ralph is as nice as he knows how to be, it will be less burdensome," Maud wrote. The subjunctive "if" told worlds. Admonitions to Ralph to shape up recurred in the family correspondence, suggesting the pressure he must have felt to meet parental expectations. In a postscript to Maud, for example, Reverend Van Waters wrote, "Tell Ralph I much enjoyed his letter and look forward to seeing him on Saturday. It is not enough to barely pass. He can stand in the front row if he will."[7]

To improve his academic performance Ralph came to Los Angeles in 1922, where he could finish high school under Miriam's strict supervision. She had her own plans for his future. First, he should go to the University of Oregon and then apply to transfer to Harvard or Yale; she would share the expenses with her father. Recognizing the obstacles to Ralph's achieving these goals, she admitted that he had "no self-starter as yet but runs well when cranked." She would provide his starter engine. Each week Miriam made out a list of his failings, among them lack of neatness and poor motivation. To correct these faults she set firm hours for study and play, hired him to drive her car for social workers on Saturdays, and tried to develop his intellectual interests. According to Miriam, he was "remarkably happy and contented" with her regime. Ralph later recalled himself as "a prideful young man."[8]

Thanks in part to her efforts, Ralph did enroll at the University of Oregon for his freshman year of college, but Miriam urged him to take classes at the University of Southern California, perhaps in order to supervise his progress. During this time, his admiration for Miriam's work at juvenile hall directed Ralph toward psychological studies. He returned to complete a B.A. and M.A. at Oregon and then, again at his sister's suggestion, he enrolled in a doctoral program in psychology at the University of Chicago. Miriam provided a fifty-dollar monthly allowance to support his studies and had high hopes of his future academic career in the field she had once abandoned. Ralph did not flourish at Chicago, however. Despite his scientific curiosity about the psychology of perception, he had a hard time overcoming the challenges posed by a demanding graduate program. His continuing economic dependence on his parents and sister seemed to undermine his confidence, yet he needed their support. As he tried to explain in 1926, his problem was not so much financial as it was the "individual development" he needed to have "courage and confidence." For Ralph, a job represented "independence," which he defined as "a thing which I have been fighting for all of my life . . . financial independence so that I might be a burden to no one — ego independence so that I might obtain the mere satisfaction to myself of being able to function as an individual and as a unit."[9]

The following year Ralph expected to achieve these goals. He prepared for his doctoral exams, defined a research problem, and gained access to a well-equipped laboratory to pursue his thesis. His letters home assumed an extremely condescending tone, as if he were in training to become an academic snob. His cockiness, which probably masked self-doubt, did not serve Ralph well. He did not pass his exams the first time, nor when he tried again in 1931, and after many years of effort, he never completed his degree. The failure haunted him throughout his life. It also left Ralph adrift in his early twenties at an inopportune historical moment, just after prospects for employment crashed along with the stock market.[10]

During his troubled years as a graduate student, as Ralph withdrew from his parents, Miriam extended her traditional helping hand. As during her father's crisis, she made job inquiries, drawing on her connections in Chicago and within academic psychology. No doubt her influence helped Ralph find a salaried position working at the Institute for Juvenile Research in Illinois. Miriam tried to reassure her parents, telling them not to worry and minimizing her own role: "He is finding his way and must do so unaided I know he will succeed." She cautioned them not to send him money while he struggled with his thesis, which she hoped would be published someday. But when she contemplated holding back part of his monthly allowance, Miriam confessed: "I talk big, but when I look into [his] merry, sad, intelligent brown eyes, I could no more deprive him of a little money, provided that I could find any, than I could my [cat] Aramus of cream and liver." Whether in response to his need, or to spare her parents further worry, Miriam assumed the role of Ralph's economic safety net and the one family member who continued to profess high hopes for his future. Her dual, and perhaps contradictory, efforts to get Ralph established professionally and to maintain him financially would continue into the 1940s.[11]

Although Ralph's economic future looked bleak at the outset of the depression, his personal fortunes improved when he met Bert Green, a nurse, in Chicago. Bert would later become an important colleague for Miriam, as well as her sister-in-law. Bert adored Ralph and had great faith in his abilities. "She thinks Ralph is a genius. And her lifestation is to serve him," Miriam explained to her parents. "Some women are fools," she continued, but "Bert is the kind of fool that St. Francis of Assisi wrote about[.] R is *in luck*." Miriam approved heartily of Ralph's choice, in contrast to her parents, who may have been troubled by Bert's German immigrant family and lack of Episcopalian credentials. The prospect of Ralph marrying anyone, given his financial insecurity, must also have disturbed them. But Miriam ran interference for the couple. "Dearest do not worry about Ralph & Miss Green, whom we all call Bert," she wrote after they visited. "I would welcome her as a sister, and she would make an ideal wife for Ralph." To her brother she confided her own second thoughts about refusing to marry Hans Weiss, encouraging him not to place practical concerns above his desire to wed. To her parents, though, she provided an unusually candid assessment of her brother. She acknowledged that Ralph was "Darling, simple and unspoiled, full of love and affection, doubting his own powers, and somehow pathetically young, and unable to cope with life's problems, smart as he is in his work." As much as he distressed them all, she concluded, they needed to "have faith and love and trust."[12]

After Ralph married in 1931, Miriam tried to ease Bert's entry into the family. She looked for the best angle on which to report on the newlyweds to her parents. Bert worked as a nurse and Ralph stayed home and did the cooking, so Miriam wrote home that "Modern matrimony has great advantages," since the arrangement allowed Ralph to continue his studies. She also continued to contribute money for his support. During long years of his dependence on her, Ralph sometimes represented the kind of "psychic drain" that Ethel Dummer had warned Miriam about. At the same time, however, he came to serve as her valued confidante and the closest member of her original family circle.[13]

By the time Ralph married, Miriam Van Waters had already taken steps to establish her own family. For years her work with children, especially at El Retiro, had satisfied the maternal longings she had articulated during her convalescence. Now, however, Van Waters' disillusionment with the court and loss of control over El Retiro left a void in her personal life. Although she showed no inclination to reconsider her refusal to marry, she did take steps to become a single parent.

In June 1929, shortly before her election to the presidency of the NCSW, Van Waters encountered a seven-year-old ward of the juvenile court, Margaret Mary Butler. The girl's foster parents, who had renamed her Betty Jean Martin, had not provided adequate care, so she now lived in a boarding home used by the court. Referee Van Waters noticed Betty Jean's ill-fitting sandals and the uncut nails on her "restless little hands," but she also observed a quick intelligence and a deep need for affection. "She's a superior child, very quiet and good, and utterly friendless—I never saw in all my work such a thoroughbred," she wrote to her parents. Taken to lunch at the Women's Athletic Club, Betty Jean showed "beautiful table manners," and although she spoke little, her smile and the glow in her eyes struck Miriam like "a streak of sunlight in the gray sea-line." When she learned of the child's deprived background—she had no dolls, shoes, or new dresses—Miriam took Betty Jean on a shopping spree. At the end of the day, after teaching her to say "Aunt Miriam," Van Waters wrote in her journal that "I am in love, in love with a child."[14]

By the end of July, Betty Jean had come to live at Stone House. An elflike, underweight, and solemn child, she had large hazel eyes and straight fine brown hair. Miriam marveled at her "breeding," her inquisitiveness, and the way she had preserved her manners despite having "lived in the worst places." To her parents she wrote that "Perfect manners, English—poise, consideration of others, and refinement, absolute obedience mark this child." Already Miriam was forming dreams for the future. "Her IQ is about 170%—she will be a leading figure when she is 25–30." To nurture her abilities, and to compensate for her neglect, Miriam determined to open the world to the child. She showered her with presents, took her for a pony ride, and began swimming lessons. As if recreating the best features of her own Oregon childhood, she promised "all the books you want—all the outdoors you want." To the child's astute observation that Aunt Abby, Aunt Bess, and Aunt Miriam seemed to go away all the time, she offered reassurance:

> "Betty when I go away—either I take you with me—or Aunt Bess stays here: see:["]
> —a deep sigh: a hand stuffed in mine—the dawn of confidence
> "Then when you go away Aunt Bess is here, and when Aunt Bess goes away you are here"
> ["]Yes child—or I take you with me. Forever you are my little girl.["][15]

As juvenile court referee, Miriam Van Waters had seen hundreds of neglected or abused young children placed in new families, but she had never before contemplated inviting one of them to share her own home. For a single, professional woman to adopt a child was quite unusual, although a few models existed. In the nineteenth century, pioneer woman physician Elizabeth Blackwell had adopted a poor orphan as her daughter, while her sister also adopted two children. Closer to Miriam's experience, Assistant United States Attorney General Mabel Walker Willebrandt, who had lived in Los Angeles and helped found the Women's Athletic Club, adopted a daughter in 1925; a divorced woman, she shared child care with two other professional women with whom she lived. Psychologist Jessie Taft, whom Miriam had met during her survey of reformatories, adopted two children with her life partner, Virginia Robinson, during the 1920s. Other women who had chosen not to marry and could afford to do so also sought to adopt.[16]

At first, however, Miriam assured her parents that she would not adopt this child. She gave no explicit reason for her decision to become only a legal guardian. Given her political conflicts in Los Angeles, she may have worried about the publicity that could ensue if she chose to adopt a ward of the juvenile court. Would her enemies raise objections, or accuse her of misusing her office? Would reporters sensationalize the child's background? Although California law did allow adoption by a single person, it also required more home investigation than did other states. Once she moved to Massachusetts, which required less scrutiny and thus less publicity, Van Waters did proceed with legal adoption. In the meantime, within six months of meeting the child, Miriam became her legal guardian. As she reported to her parents, "My new little girl— Betty—now to be called Sarah Ann came to live with me."[17]

In renaming Betty Jean Martin as Sarah Ann Van Waters, Miriam not only honored her "old dutch grandmother" but also sought a rebirth for the child whose background caseworkers had deemed "too undesirable for adoption." As she wrote to her parents, "I would not like to put in a letter her heredity: for I have *destroyed everything,* obliterated her old name, and she has mine now (tho I shall not adopt her)—she calls me Mother." Just what Van Waters found so disturbing in Sarah's past is not clear. All that the historical record reveals is the child's birth in a midwestern county hospital to a white, eighteen-year-old, unmarried housemaid, who had one other child living with her. The nineteen-year old father, also white, was a glassworker.[18] The baby was taken from her mother, either at birth or soon after, partially raised by a grandmother, and eventually moved to California. According to Van Waters, Sarah had been "a victim of social work," but now she would redeem her. As she reflected years later, "It was I who reached out to my child, made her Sarah Ann Van Waters—this wistful and powerful little atom— Sarah—this child of God—to 'save' her—from a life of neglect & disorder." That life included guardians who had slapped her, left her to play with several "defective" children, and were arrested for making bootleg whiskey. They also took her to worship at the Angelus Temple, where the charismatic evangelist Aimee Semple McPherson represented the antithesis of Van Waters' religious ideal. From the Martins, Betty Jean had learned "all the bad words," which she now refrained from using. "I wish I had not lived there," Sarah Ann told her new mother.[19]

Aside from saving Sarah, Miriam articulated a range of personal motives for her decision to become a mother. For one, she thought that raising Sarah in enriched, loving surroundings would prove that environment was more important than heredity, although her insistence that she chose Sarah because she detected a strong native intelligence qualified this argument. More importantly, Miriam felt a strong need to have a child of her own at this moment in her life. Asking for her own parents' "blessing and approval," she explained that "Ruth, George and Beckie have their children, and I need one of my own to raise as I think best." Even though her parents quickly accepted her decision, Miriam continued to defend it. "I don't suppose you approve much of it," she wrote, knowing that her mother worried about the "extra work" involved. In one telling passage, she invoked a rarely expressed sense of entitlement. Although she had always loved caring for her siblings and delighted in her nieces and nephews, she explained that it was "not the same as having a child every day and every night under my own roof." Asking again for her mother's blessing, she insisted that she did not "act rashly (or long ago I would have married some body and had my own seven children)."[20]

Van Waters' job also justified her decision, she argued, giving her both the judgment with which to choose a child and the right to have one. "The 12 years labor in the court with all its sorrows, is richly compensated—like Jacob when he finally got Rachel," she told her parents. In her private journal she enjoyed the irony of deriving such happiness from her troubled workplace. "Court—Juvenile Court Detention House laughter of children in jail—hours of invisible anguish—you have given me Betty." Sarah clearly represented a salve for Miriam's political defeats. Whatever the added responsibilities, she wrote home, "this child compensates to me—for the loss of El Retiro." Above all, Sarah offered a kind of personal affirmation that neither work nor family nor friends had previously supplied for Miriam. "I love this child—not as I love other children—but with the intense feeling that she belongs to me—and hence to us all. It has been a strange experience but one of the deepest in my life."[21]

In her detailed accounts of Sarah's manners and intelligence, Miriam assured her parents that they had an exceptional grandchild. "This morning she said—'O I am so happy to be in a family where they make black-berry jam,'" the proud mother reported. After Sarah's first party, an outing that included the children of several professors, Miriam wrote proudly that "My child was radiantly happy and very much better and quicker in all her responses to the situation than the University children her age." Sarah's intelligence heightened Miriam's expectations for the child's future. "Someday—in the field of letters or science she will be among our greatest—our very greatest—and so my life will count to the race—even tho I have no children of my own." Miriam knew that she sounded "like other parents, and [I] talk too much about her. But all my life I have listened to other people talking about their children. Now it is my turn."[22]

Adding the responsibility of child rearing to her already busy life did not seem to perturb Miriam in the least. She proceeded as if Sarah's unusual capacities, combined with her improved environment, would insure the child a healthy upbringing. Indeed, her casualness about the new domestic arrangement suggests that she initially underestimated the physical and emotional labor involved in raising a young child. Aside from giving up her weekly evening class, Miriam hired a young El Retiro graduate to look after Sarah while she was at court. The Stone House residents would help, but they could not provide constant companionship. Orfa Jean Shontz had recently opened a swimming camp in the country, where she often stayed, and Sara Fisher had moved closer to UCLA. Bess Woods could be counted on, and she often took over when Miriam left town or was ill.[23]

Even when Miriam was at home, she needed to concentrate on the Harvard survey and her other obligations. To get her work done, she explained to Sarah that she was going into her study and did not want to be disturbed for three hours. According to Miriam, Sarah simply went about her business. The conversation she recounted suggested otherwise: "But why do you work so hard?" Sarah asked; "To write articles—to make money," Miriam explained. "Then you shouldn't buy me so many dresses—for you get too tired." To Miriam, the request showed that "There was never a more appreciative child."[24] For Sarah, however, it may well have been a call for more attention, even if it meant fewer presents.

Although Miriam Van Waters tried to incorporate Sarah into her household with a minimum of adjustments, having a child forced her to rethink some fundamental patterns in her own life. For years, she had been the most token of Episcopalians, citing her busy schedule when she apologized to her mother for not observing church holidays. For all of her efforts to find a nearby pulpit for her father, she did not really have a local church of her own. But soon after Sarah moved in, Miriam registered her daughter at St. Marks Church and its Sunday school. When Sarah professed that she loved to go to church, Miriam promised, "I shall take you every Sunday" and later offered to teach the Sunday school class herself. "For years I have not thought I had time to go to church," she wrote home, "But as soon as I have a child of my own to be responsible for—I want her to have the best—and the best—is still the church. It has profoundly influenced me in ways that are not always conscious."[25]

Along with religious training, Miriam sought the best opportunities for her daughter, revealing her own ambitions for class mobility. She took pride in having Sarah play with the children of doctors, lawyers, and professors, and she planned to take her to a summer camp run for "well to do girls." Miriam proudly reported to her mother when Sarah said that the Presbyterian church looked "more like a dance hall" than a church, adding that "you see instinctively this little one is an aristocrat." To add refinement to Sarah's education, Miriam bought a piano and hired a private music teacher; later she enrolled Sarah in a school where she could begin studying French. At the same time, she sought to instill liberal social views. Confronting her daughter's fear of black people and of being called a "nigger," she insisted that "God made us all brothers. . . . We are all alike." When Sarah wondered if she was herself "a nigger," instead of denying the possibility, Miriam replied, "Well—maybe we are all niggers." Similarly, when Orfa Shontz included a Chinese boy in an outing, and Sarah wondered if that made Orfa "a Chinaman," Orfa responded "Well—I am if he is." Although their responses may have confused Sarah about her own racial identity, they intended to preach the common humanity of all people.[26]

Miriam Van Waters attempted to apply to her own child the advice she had offered to other parents in her books, but the task sometimes proved formidable. However well-mannered, smart, and promising she seemed, Sarah had already led a hard life. She must have harbored bitterness, and she consciously experienced sadness and often reacted to her pain. Commenting on the importance of her first day of school, for example, Sarah declared that she was "making a radical change" in her life, promising that she would not be mean anymore. "I feel dark inside, now I feel light." The dark feelings recurred, however, erupting at times into rage. As an adult, Sarah told her mother that she remembered living in a "House full of experts," yet crying her self to sleep "many a night." Like most children, she feared the dark and being left alone. When her mother comforted her, though, she remained afraid until she "got over it" herself. In nightmares Sarah returned to her foster home, where "the Juvenile came to get me."[27]

Learning of this image of the court as "a monster hand in the dark," Van Waters worried that "I am the Juvenile." She contemplated how much it would take to "free children from fear." Her own approach when Sarah became fearful, moody, obstinate, or disobedient was to rule "by adult approval, not disapproval." Rather than punish, she withdrew her affection. According to Van Waters, the policy was effective; Sarah soon vowed that she would not do anything wrong again "because when you are tired or mad you don't smile and your hair doesn't dance." Yet Sarah could not always control her feelings in order to maintain her mother's affection. Consequently, she developed a withdrawn moodiness that occasionally took the form of angry rebellion. She tested the El Retiro graduate who cared for her, for example, and caused a "scene" at Sunday school.[28]

During her first few months as a parent, in the late summer of 1929, Miriam seemed confident that her daughter would triumph over her past and adjust easily to her new life. So sure was she of Sarah's maturity and adaptability that when she had to travel to Boston that fall she left Sarah with her parents in Pennsylvania for several weeks. Aside from the convenience of child care, the trip was supposed to give the Van Waters a chance to get acquainted with their new granddaughter. The visit turned out poorly for Sarah, who behaved as might be expected of an abandoned eight-year-old, far from her new home and longing for her new mother. She apparently wreaked havoc in the Van Waters household. Even Miriam acknowledged that "the best of children are troublesome sometimes, and Sara is not easy to manage." Miriam picked her daughter up in Pennsylvania on her way home, and when they stopped in Chicago, she left her at Hull House in the care of Jessie Binford, with no ill effect. But after the trip, Miriam decided not to take Sarah out of school again when she traveled. How ironic— or perhaps predictable—that Miriam, who in childhood so longed for Maud, could not perceive the ways in which she now became an absent mother.[29]

Back in Los Angeles, Van Waters realized that she had to make better child-care arrangements. She admitted that Sarah was not "an easy person." Her daughter had an "imperious will" and a hard edge that could make enemies for her. She began to make lists of Sarah's faults as well as her strengths: Though a "good conversationalist," she tended to "monopolize it"; she did not trust adults; she tended to violent passion without tenderness. But Miriam was "much in love" with Sarah and confident that the child's imagination and energy would carry her through. To help rear her, she hired a recent Pomona College graduate, Elizabeth Bode, as a part-time secretary and housekeeper, with special responsibility for Sarah. Bode—who was always referred to by her last name—had been working at the Business Girls Club, and she hoped to become "a great juvenile court leader." Because of the contacts she would make, she was willing to live in the summer cottage at Stone

House and serve as Sarah's caretaker. Sarah quickly accepted her as a kind of teacher, and she seemed willing to obey her. Pleased that Bode helped out "just like Bess or Edna Mahan," Miriam wrote home, "I feel blessed to have her." Now when she traveled, Sarah remained at home, with Bess Woods as surrogate mother and Bode as mother's helper. That Christmas, for example, it was Bess who reported to Maud Van Waters how happy her granddaughter was, and how much she missed her "mother." While Van Waters traveled, Bode sent accounts of Sarah's tantrums and her good days. In the summers, Sarah went to camp for six weeks, which allowed her mother to travel in the East. Despite her written prescriptions for parental involvement and her fond memories of seaside family gatherings, Miriam admitted regretfully, "I cannot take six weeks off to take her camping, and I welcome the 'canned' camping experience."[30]

Her first two years of parenthood coincided with Miriam Van Waters' gradual withdrawal from the juvenile court and her search for a new job. The traveling required for the Harvard and Wickersham surveys kept her away from Stone House more frequently than she or Sarah desired. In the fall of 1931, while she was on leave from the juvenile court, Miriam decided to shift part of her domestic base to Cambridge. She was not sure she would settle there, but for the time being, the move would solve the logistical problems of balancing work and parenting. Besides, she liked the social life in Cambridge, where she still saw Hans Weiss and enjoyed well-connected neighbors like Felix Frankfurter and Radcliffe College president Ada Comstock.

In September 1931, Van Waters rented a furnished house in Cambridge and moved in with Sarah and Bode. En route they visited her parents in Pennsylvania and then Edna Mahan at Clinton Farms, New Jersey, where Geraldine Thompson came to take Miriam off to her estate in Red Bank, leaving Sarah with Edna and Bode. In Cambridge, their household expanded to include Alma Holzschuh, who was working on the Harvard survey, as well as a puppy for Sarah and a cat for Miriam. Bode began a job at Boston Children's Aid. Miriam enrolled Sarah in the progressive Shady Hill School, directed by Katherine Taylor, the daughter of Chicago Commons settlement house founder Graham Taylor. At home, Miriam's study provided a sanctuary where no one was to bother her while she worked.

The prospects for domestic happiness looked good. "The Cambridge portion of my family is cozily settled in an old house on a quiet street within walking distance of the Law School and Shady Hill School. Sarah rejoices in her school, showing in every posture and attitude a

new zest of living," Miriam reported to Ethel Dummer. "I believe I am
receiving more assistance with my child than I ever have before. Day
by day Sarah improves in health and happiness." Her daughter provided
"a great comfort." When Miriam could no longer stand writing and research without "some human daily life," Sarah kept her "from getting
too dry and selfish and mean."[31]

In the late 1920s, as she entered her forties, Miriam Van Waters
had reconfigured her family life significantly. Although she had lost her
symbolic children in the demise of El Retiro, she found new ways to
express her maternal longings. In her family, she continued to mother
her youngest sibling, Ralph. While avoiding the physical and emotional
risks of marriage, she had become a parent by bringing Sarah into her
home. Even as she loosened her ties to the colony of reformers in
southern California, she had begun to recreate a female household in
Cambridge, where a staff of young protégés enabled her to pursue her
career while she rebuilt her house of life. When Miriam stopped for
dinner at Hull House during a trip to Chicago, she must have felt unusually fulfilled by the vision before her: her daughter Sarah Ann sitting at
the right hand of Jane Addams, and her brother Ralph next to her.[32]

9

Most Precious Possession

I n the late 1920s, along with welcoming a daughter into her life,
Miriam Van Waters formed her most important intimate relationship, with New Jersey philanthropist Geraldine Livingston Thompson. Soon after the two women met, Thompson decided to bestow her
kindness, and her abundant resources, upon the younger reformer. At
first, Miriam was not fully aware of the depth of her new benefactor's
feelings for her. Only later did she learn that Thompson had written a
legacy into her will so that Miriam would not have to worry about the
future. Geraldine Thompson seemed to be replacing Ethel Dummer as
patron, but this newer bond evolved into an even more intimate personal relationship. By 1930, Geraldine and Miriam had pledged to "belong to each other in love and friendship." That year, in a correspondence resembling the romantic courtship letters written by Victorian
couples, Geraldine expressed not only her intense "longing to *do* something" for Miriam but also her wish "to kneel down and worship your
loveliness and goodness." Although Miriam placed limits on the relationship, as she had with others, she gradually accepted the largesse of
this remarkable woman, returning her devoted love.[1]

The woman who won Miriam's trust and heart had already lived an
extremely full life, one that was characterized by both class privilege
and social activism. Geraldine Livingston Morgan had been born in
1872, fifteen years before Miriam's birth, into a well-established New
York City family. The female reform tradition ran deep on her mother's
side. Her maternal grandmother, Geraldine Livingston Hoyt, typified an
earlier generation of bountiful matrons who aided the poor and imprisoned. In the early nineteenth century she had visited city asylums, urging specialized treatment for the sick, insane, and criminal, and she
helped found the social service department at New York's Bellevue
Hospital. Geraldine's mother, Angelica Livingston Hoyt Morgan, helped
establish the first nursing school at Bellevue. The heir to their tradition,
Geraldine Morgan, would grow up to become known as the "First Lady
of New Jersey" because of her strong influence on social service and
philanthropy in that state.[2]

As a child Geraldine Livingston Morgan spent summers at the family residence near Staatsburg, New York, where she first encountered members of the Roosevelt family of nearby Hyde Park. She and her sisters, Margaret and Ruth, had private tutors near their Washington Square home in New York City. After her father died in 1886, Geraldine attended a convent school in France. In 1896 she married Lewis Steenrod Thompson, a graduate of the Massachusetts Institute of Technology and heir to a much larger fortune than the Morgan family's more modest wealth. Lewis Thompson's father had profited abundantly from the expansion of industrial capitalism in post–Civil War America. A former Confederate colonel and a lawyer, William Payne Thompson had founded the National Lead Company, which merged with John D. Rockefeller's Standard Oil, of which Colonel Thompson became treasurer. When his son Lewis contracted tuberculosis, doctors recommended a strenuous outdoor life as a cure. Thanks to Colonel Thompson's fortune, Lewis S. Thompson—Geraldine's future husband—was able to devote his entire life to the pursuit of fishing, hunting, and horse racing. His wealth also supported the philanthropic and political career of Geraldine Livingston Thompson.[3]

Geraldine Thompson had been a striking bride. A friend described the slender, five-foot, four-inch young woman as having "the most amazing eyes" and "a very strong chin." Despite an early battle with tuberculosis, which had brought her to the Colorado resort where she met the ailing Lewis Thompson, Geraldine exhibited a fierce physical stamina. She was a championship tennis player, a very good shot, an avid baseball fan, and a nature enthusiast. Relatives recalled her remarkable physical stamina and love of vigorous exercise. Aside from her strength, a large domestic staff at Brookdale—the Thompson estate in Red Bank, New Jersey—enabled her to raise nine children. Between 1896 and 1904, she bore four children of her own, and the couple took in five orphaned relatives as well.[4]

Lewis and Geraldine Thompson lived in two relatively separate social spheres. Although the family spent part of each summer together at an Adirondack mountain lake, "Colonel" Thompson left for his seasonal fishing and hunting haunts, spending half the year at Sunny Hill, a plantation he bought in southern Georgia, just north of the Florida border. Geraldine visited him there during winter vacations but lived in New York City and at Brookdale with the children for most of the year. She directed the household at the sprawling, eight-hundred-acre estate, where she entertained guests from the political and social elites of her time, including "every New Jersey Governor, the State Senators, Legislators, U.S. Congressmen & Senators, [and] Commissioners of Corrections," as well as assorted Morgans, Reids, Roosevelts, and Payne Whitneys. Children did not join in the adult activities; their huge playing grounds included farms, barns, and the stables where the prizewinning Payne Whitney horses were kept.[5]

While her children were growing up, Geraldine Thompson increasingly directed her energies toward the establishment of social service institutions in New Jersey. Her wealth, and her commanding personality, allowed her to shape a variety of quasi-public agencies. In 1912, she helped found a State Charities Aid and Prison Reform Association, in part to provide public-health nurses in the county. The agency, over which she presided for almost forty years, developed into the Monmouth County Organization for Social Services (MCOSS). Deeply concerned about the prevention of tuberculosis, Thompson lobbied vigorously to get the state to establish the Allenwood Sanitarium, of which she served as president from its opening in 1920 until 1950. In 1918, she was the first woman appointed by the governor of New Jersey to serve on the State Board of Control, which oversaw charitable and correctional institutions, including the Clinton Farms women's reformatory. As an active member of the Board of Control until 1957, she pressed for health education, probation services, and child study programs. Through the MCOSS Thompson also helped establish a child guidance clinic, county nursery schools, free ambulance service, and home nursing care. From 1923 to 1949, the organization also assumed responsibility for parole work for the state's reformatories and mental hospitals.[6]

Geraldine Thompson bridged the eras of the lady bountiful and the woman politician. Unlike some New Jersey women's club members, she had supported female suffrage, although she was less active in the women's movement than were her sisters, Margaret Morgan Norrie, a strong suffragist, and Ruth Morgan, a feminist active in the League of Women Voters and the women's peace movement. Like her grandmother and mother, Geraldine specialized in charitable works, but she also entered politics and encouraged other women to do so. A lifelong Republican, in 1923 she became the first woman elected to the Republican National Committee from New Jersey. After four years she resigned, citing both her grief over the death of her sister Margaret and her distaste for the "hypocrisy" of politics. "Politics is a fine adventure," Thompson wrote in 1927, "The best women must go into it. They will have to choose, however, between power that comes easily through patronage[,] and fighting for the higher stands of political philosophy which will bring about the greatest ultimate success."[7]

Despite her disillusionment, Geraldine Thompson remained active in the party, serving as a state committeewoman and a delegate to each Republican national convention between 1920 and 1962. Her lobbying efforts for improving social services were quite bipartisan, at both state and national levels. After the election of Franklin Roosevelt as president, Geraldine became a close colleague and personal confidant of Eleanor Roosevelt. For the rest of their lives the two patrician reformers pooled their resources to respond to pleas for charitable aid, with the First Lady sending New Jersey requests to Thompson for action and Thompson in turn calling on Roosevelt to intervene politically whenever one of her reforms needed a boost.[8]

Among the state institutions Geraldine Thompson oversaw were jails and prisons. She became particularly concerned about the women and children detained within their walls. Like Ethel Sturges Dummer and Miriam Van Waters, Thompson preferred rehabilitation to punishment and wanted to provide both recreation and psychological counseling to troubled youth. She had urged the creation of the Clinton Farms reformatory for women, which opened in 1913, and helped oversee it from her position on the State Board of Control. In 1928, when a new superintendent was being hired, Thompson consulted with Miriam Van Waters, who recommended her protégé Edna Mahan for the job. Mahan's appointment at Clinton Farms made Van Waters happier than she had been in a long time. For one, an advocate of reform had won the job, but she may also have been pleased because Thompson had accepted her advice.[9]

Miriam Van Waters and Geraldine Thompson first crossed paths in 1925 or 1926, probably at a prison association or social work conference, or at Clinton Farms. Thompson had been greatly impressed by *Youth in Conflict,* and the two women had been corresponding at the time of the Colony fire. "Dearest Mrs. Thompson," Miriam wrote in July, 1927 — the earliest surviving letter between them — "How many times I have thought of you! The letter you were to have was lying on my desk 5 weeks ago — when our house burned down." She told her "Dear Friend" about her plans to reconstruct *Parents on Probation,* asked to see her in October when she returned to the East Coast, and sent love and a blessing in closing. They did meet that autumn, and Geraldine asked to see Miriam once again before she returned to California.

"Dearest Miriam," Thompson wrote from Brookdale, "If you are possibly through N.J. on your way west . . . I would be most grateful for a chance to see you again. But don't have me on your mind (providing you keep me closely in your heart). . . . I would love to try to arrange for another glimpse of you." It was soon after this trip that Miriam told Hans Weiss of a new attraction in her life.[10]

Although the relationship remained formal, their early letters revealed Thompson's deep admiration for Van Waters. Explaining her feelings of concern for Miriam, she referred to "a sense that human beings are precious and the greater the lover the wider the range of the capacity to feel it." Like Christ and St. Francis, she wrote, Miriam had a broad capacity to love humankind, especially through service to children. Like other "lovely saints," however, she did not always take good enough care of herself. Thompson knew of Van Waters' bout with tuberculosis, and of the pleurisy that had troubled her more recently. Like Miriam's other intimates, she wanted to protect her friend. "I wish I could take care of you in some wise way myself," Thompson wrote, adding that "I don't believe you particularly want to be precious to me, but you are very necessary for my sense of reassurance."[11]

By 1928, the fifty-six-year-old Thompson was finding ways to ease the way for Van Waters, who was then forty-one years old. She recommended her for jobs, invited her to spend time at Brookdale, and offered gifts. In describing this new friendship to her parents, Miriam portrayed herself as the reluctant recipient of Thompson's benevolence. When the philanthropist sent a check to enable her new friend to travel in a private railroad compartment from Chicago to Los Angeles, Miriam wrote, "It seems a waste of money, yet I have a great deal to do." She accepted the gift and enjoyed the trip "in peace, quiet and comfort." Two years later, in 1930, when Geraldine sent her two dresses from New York, Miriam wrote home that she did not know what to think or say. Mrs. Dummer had contributed large amounts of money to her professional career, but a personal gift of clothing signified a different kind of relationship. As Miriam told her mother, "Save for the family, I don't like to receive gifts of this kind. She says they are inexpensive, and I guess that is so." She liked the dresses, though—attractive clothing had always pleased her—and she thought she could wear one of them. And so Miriam finally decided to accept the gift. Whether she needed to convince herself, or her mother, of the propriety of her acceptance, she did so by explaining that Thompson "is a dear friend and I ought to take it in good heart. She said she was buying clothes for her daughter and thought I could make good use of these."[12]

In many ways, Geraldine Thompson's outreach to Miriam Van Waters mirrored the earlier patronage of Ethel Sturges Dummer. An older, wealthier, married woman advanced the reform career of a younger, single, professionally trained woman. But the Thompson–Van Waters collaboration had a deeper emotional undercurrent, resembling instead a model in which patronage merged with romantic friendship to form a life partnership. This kind of relationship surfaced frequently in the history of women's reform. Thus temperance leader Frances Willard enjoyed the love and financial support of the British Lady Somerset. In the United States, the wealthy Mary Garrett supplied funds for her beloved M. Carey Thomas, president of Bryn Mawr College, and the two women ultimately lived together at the college deanery. Polly Porter's family wealth supported the reform career of her partner, Molly Dewson. Suffrage and peace activist Emily Greene Balch received financial as well as personal sustenance from her lifelong friend, Helen Cheever. Like these couples, Thompson and Van Waters' public collaboration rested upon a private, romantic foundation.[13]

Van Waters' sense of privacy, if not secrecy, about her relationship with Thompson set this friendship apart from her earlier attachments to women. The fact that she would later destroy most of Thompson's correspondence, in contrast to the careful preservation of the Dummer letters, suggests the different meanings of each partnership. So does the depth of affection expressed within the surviving letters. Correspondence to Miriam from her mother, Orfa Shontz, or Ethel Dummer often included terms of endearment, but none matched Geraldine's expressions of love. "I love you so much, old sweet," she wrote in 1930; "God bless you, Darling, all this day long. I send all my dearest and best love. I am your friend, your none too worthy lamb, but one you are to keep. My own dear, blessed precious sweet my dearest love, your Geraldine," she closed a letter in 1939. Even twenty years after their first meeting, Miriam remained the darling lamb and "dearest heart" for Geraldine. Unfortunately, only fragments of Van Waters' letters to her "Dearest Love my Geraldine" have survived, but her private journal — cryptic as it often was — still revealed the emotional importance of the relationship. As she wrote in 1934, after arriving at Brookdale, "I am deeply at peace, cherished and blessed beyond words by Geraldine's love and care."[14]

Surviving letters and journals permit a reconstruction of the formation of this remarkably productive lifelong partnership. The shift from professional acquaintances to loving friends occurred during years of personal crisis. Van Waters had lost El Retiro and increasingly found her workplace intolerable; Thompson's sister had recently died, and she reevaluated her political commitments. During the years when Van Waters worked on the Harvard Crime Survey, the two women began to spend time together, either at Brookdale or at Thompson's New York City townhouse. They talked during long drives on country roads, and Miriam began to meet Geraldine's family members. By the time of the NCSW conference in 1929, Geraldine had begun to promote her friend's career with an eye to bringing her back east. She no doubt helped secure the Wickersham commission appointment, and later she introduced Van Waters to other liberal reformers. In response to Miriam's political troubles, Geraldine expressed her wish "to exorcise some of that evil, so that there would be a clearer road for your fine purposes."[15]

Thompson had wanted to attend the NCSW conference in San Francisco when Van Waters was nominated as president. She asked if Miriam would then "let me live near you for ten days or two weeks and then travel east with me?" That way she could see Miriam at her work, then take her to the mountains for rest and rehabilitation. Van Waters, however, had already promised Hans Weiss that they could have one last California holiday together after the conference, a commitment she honored. That summer she brought Sarah into her life, and in the fall she worked on the crime survey, staying with Thompson at Brookdale for awhile. It would not be until the following spring, in 1930, that Geraldine entered Miriam's world at Stone House.

In the meantime, Thompson expressed concerns long articulated by those close to Van Waters. "Sometimes I think that one should limit the extent of one's projects to a size where the quality can be protected," she wrote tactfully of Van Waters' extensive commitments. "I don't suppose this can often be done, but on the other hand one often deliberately gives hostages to fortune to a point beyond all safety lines." She worried not only for Miriam, but also for those who cared about her. "When your vulnerability is tied up with other human beings," she explained rather abstractly, health risks could be "too painful to bear" for those who cared about her. In another message Thompson stated her feelings in more personal terms: "I don't believe you realize how quickly my desire for happiness is harnessed to any plan that brings you within reach."[16]

Thompson's long-awaited visit to California finally occurred in March 1930, signaling Van Waters' willingness to incorporate this new relationship into her existing colony of reformers. Writing to her parents, Miriam minimized the importance of the event. "Geraldine Thompson arrives today or tomorrow evening to spend the weekend," she told her parents. "As this is her first (probably only) visit to me, I must give her a good time. I am not having anyone in for dinners, but I shall drive her to the institutions she wants to see. Of course—what she did want to see most was the court." Although they did go to juvenile hall, the two friends also took walks in the parks, went to church together, and visited sites of Miriam's past glory—an El Retiro campground and the former Colony. "Geraldine said she was like a squirrel storing nuts for the winter," Miriam wrote in her journal. Thompson charmed the Stone House crowd. To Bode, Orfa, Bess, Sarah, and each luncheon guest, "she had the right thing to say—to bring out their interests." Miriam seemed to appreciate that Geraldine had thought to leave the maid who usually traveled with her at her hotel when she stayed at Stone House. The class difference between them, and the conspicuousness of Geraldine's wealth, could have made Miriam uncomfortable in front of her friends. Afterward, she told her parents that it was "happiness" to be with her "dear friend"; in her journal she wrote that "her charm, her presence still linger."[17]

In letters they exchanged that year, Miriam and Geraldine began an extended process of interpreting the meaning of their friendship. The conversation continued after Miriam arrived at Brookdale in September 1930. She had left Sarah in Bode's care and used the Red Bank estate as her home base while she attended meetings in Boston, New York, and Washington. The two friends went to the local Episcopal church together—Geraldine was an "ardent churchwoman" and a longtime Sunday school teacher—and Miriam worked on speeches and reports. To her friends, Miriam emphasized only the practicality of the visit. She told Edna Mahan that Geraldine was "a miracle of understanding and consideration; I got heaps of work done and had a good time." To her parents she wrote descriptions of the old church they attended.

In the privacy of their country drives, walks, and talks, however, and later in long-distance telephone conversations, the friendship between Geraldine Thompson and Miriam Van Waters was deepening into love. Driving around in "*our* car," the two women shared "complete joy." They pictured themselves as fellow travelers on a path toward a higher spiritual plane. Would their friendship take them "above timberline," beyond the mere foothills of life? they wondered. Along with contemplating how they might encourage their spiritual quest, they consciously addressed the romantic nature of their bond. Geraldine carefully explained how strongly attracted she was to images of "the Justice of the Peace and church bells," terms that became code words in their letters for the commitment they were making to each other. In her journal, Miriam seemed to be coming to terms with the unusual bond that was forming. "The object which arouses love—cannot be foreseen or controlled," she wrote obscurely. "All we know is—that same force which engulfs us, and makes us ready for service to husband and children—some times—to some persons—flows out to a man, woman, child, animal, 'cause,' idea."[18]

Familial bonds soon marked their deepening personal commitment. Miriam established a friendly relationship with "The Boss," Lewis Thompson, while Geraldine took steps to win the acceptance of Orfa Shontz, Abby Whiteside, Elizabeth Bode, and the Van Waters family. During the summer of 1930, when Miriam's mother was in New York, Geraldine called on her, then sent a telegram to Stone House to report that Maud, who had recently been in an automobile accident, looked exceedingly well. In October the two women visited Wellsboro together to see Miriam's parents. Preparing her mother for the event, Miriam directed that everything should be as simple as possible: no meals, no fuss; Mrs. Thompson should have the big room, and Miriam would take the one across the hall; they would attend her father's church on Sunday and then depart. The carefully orchestrated visit was a great success. In a gracious thank-you letter Geraldine told Maud: "Naturally you must realize how devotedly I love Miriam and prize her friendship and these last few days have brought me the greatest joy and satisfaction." It was after this visit that Geraldine revealed to Miriam the legacy she had written into her will five years earlier.[19]

Between their visit to Wellsboro in October and their reunion in Washington, D.C., in January 1931, Miriam and Geraldine corresponded daily and spoke frequently on the telephone. Even though Van Waters eventually destroyed most of the correspondence from their forty-year friendship, for this one period she carefully preserved Geraldine's letters, keeping them apart from the public record of her life. They provide a rare and extraordinarily intimate record of the courtship between two highly independent women who sought to build a lasting, loving comradeship. Like new lovers, they eagerly anticipated their reunion, imagining church bells and justices of the peace. At the same time, they struggled to define the meaning of their commitment, dwelling especially on the problem of how to give oneself to another without losing a sense of independence. Integrating their love into existing personal ties also posed challenges. How would Miriam relate to Hans, or to Orfa, when Geraldine became primary in her heart? What could Geraldine tell her husband Lew about this new love?

The soul-searching letters began to arrive even as Miriam traveled back to California. Finding herself in "unchartered seas," Geraldine asked for Miriam's help in making decisions about her future, decisions that "will always keep us together vitally, and closely." Once Miriam arrived at Stone House, Geraldine called often to hear her voice or clarify issues in their letters. "You are a fine telephoner," she explained in one letter, "but the better you are the more thwarted I feel not to be able to see and touch you."[20] Geraldine needed to maintain a close connection as she sorted through the meaning of her new love. She read and reread Miriam's letters, which she kept in her safe, "for their wisdom" and for "the warmth of their affection." As she once explained, "They are an event in my life and one so full of value to me that I shall have to hold myself down to earth while at the same time not understate my gratitude (the blood of love and gratitude) that I feel for you." She eagerly awaited each delivery, making frequent visits to the front door to check for the mail. If the presence of relatives or servants prevented her reading the letters at once, Geraldine felt thwarted. Sometimes she read them on the subway or train, for privacy. "I have had your last three letters tucked in my purse," she wrote, "so I could get the comfort just the sight of them brings me." On a day without letters she lacked her "daily bread." Her own letters sometimes began in the morning, with later entries in the afternoon and again at night. As one ended, "it's hard to stop to loosen up hold even for a moment. I love you. Geraldine."[21]

At night Geraldine often telephoned, carefully scheduling her call after she had left her own family circle and Miriam had put Sarah to bed. She often wrote in her next letter about the loveliness of Miriam's voice on the phone, but a poor connection could disturb her peace of mind. When Geraldine left for Christmas with Lew at Sunny Hill, where she would not be able to call in privacy or receive letters, she dreaded the insecurity of not knowing where Miriam was daily. "You have spoiled me," she explained, "and I don't like anything that breaks into our sense of consecutive and constant contact."[22]

In her letters, Thompson exulted in the joy of knowing Miriam Van Waters. "Something in me responds to you, to your philosophy, something to your actions, to your own self," she tried to explain. "I see this quite radiant and beautiful and there is some real understanding and almost complete acceptance on my part in what you say of yourself, your sense of values about living, your techniques, your faith and strengths." Like others who had been drawn to Miriam's charismatic appeal, Geraldine felt an almost magical pull. "Do you think you are something of a fairy?" she once asked, citing Miriam's "almost dangerous powers of bewitchment: powers that emanate . . . almost unconsciously." Gratified that Miriam was in fact "some sort of human being," though an exceptional one, she explained her attraction in a romantic, yet uncommonly precise, description of Van Water's complex persona: "sheer beauty with strength of tragedy making deep shadows against a bewildering radiance." To Geraldine, Miriam opened "new visions of beauty" and showed "new interpretations of old thinking," giving her "a chance in a thousand."[23]

Geraldine's professions of love both paralleled and differed from those of Miriam's male suitor, Hans Weiss. Both wrote of the spiritual power of their beloved, and each expressed concern about her welfare. Just as Hans spoke of his spiritual marriage to Miriam, Geraldine invoked the image of church bells. In contrast to Hans' great need of Miriam, and the demanding tone of his letters, Geraldine always aspired to be of service to, rather than fulfilled by, her love. Thus she longed to be a daily "serviceable accepted part" of Miriam's life. "My great privilege and adventure might be to find some way, with you, to fulfill your vision of beauty by being absorbed into the rhythm of your spiritual life—avoiding desires and hunger that might make me try to draw these great currents into my personal life, *for* my personal life and need," she wrote.

While Hans sent expansive descriptions of his sensual desires, Geraldine never wrote of carnal lust. She limited her expressions to romantic and spiritual longings. In her journal, Miriam suggested that the two women consciously controlled their erotic longings. When Geraldine expressed a desire "to 'catch your soul's breath' in kisses," Miriam questioned the impulse. "What one calls appetite—satisfaction of warmth needs—hunger needs—is not just that," she wrote. "In maturity some times in some circumstances—to feed hunger fully—is to lose hunger. There are other ways of quenching the fire—and all must be escaped." The goal of transcending carnal desire fit well with Miriam's own emphasis on physical self-discipline, as well as with her long-standing identification with Christian saints. It also paralleled her professional advice about channeling youthful sexual energies into service. But the particular message that desire could be maintained best by leaving it largely unfulfilled called not for complete triumph over the flesh but rather for limited erotic expression as a means of enhancing spiritual union. Miriam had often communicated this message to Hans Weiss. Now, staying at Brookdale, she alluded to it again in her journal: "The secret of life is manifested in hunger—it can't safely be quenched—neither by denial, nor complete feeding, nor running away, nor escape—but by a new way." While Miriam and Geraldine sought a new way, one that neither denied nor completely satisfied their hungers, they instinctively knew to keep their love a secret. Earlier female couples had comfortably expressed their affection, but in the modern world, a romance like theirs would have raised the specter of homosexuality and thus of psychological deviance.[24]

The most pressing concern in this courtship correspondence was not sex but rather the challenge of maintaining independent identities as they fell in love. Thompson worried at length about how to bring her beloved closer, to possess her, without losing her own bearings, while Van Waters continued to maintain her geographical distance, even as she drew emotionally closer. Over the summer, Geraldine had asked Miriam "not to possess me too completely or there wouldn't be anything of sufficient value to offer you." When Miriam in response insisted on pledging her "whole being," with all her heart, the promise frightened Geraldine. How could she "contain such a gift," she wondered, warning Miriam of the dangers of dependency. The impulse to offer oneself fully, she believed, occurred to "all true lovers when they become the object of such reckless love and adventurous desire." In response, they seek to "draw back the curtain" on their own "impulse of love, worship and adoration." For Geraldine, however, a lover could not belong to another without risking her own sense of self.

Drawing on her experience as a wife and a mother, Thompson recalled the "danger" of trying to own another being. In a passage that revealed a great deal about the survival of her marriage, she explained that "with Lew there was something of it at first—from both of us," referring to the impulse to belong to another. But, she continued, "we kept our heads and won an equality and pursued the several ways while not losing each other." To do so, Geraldine learned that she "had to get past Lew to something larger, more powerful, more world-embracing and then come back to him—belonging more to myself—without that process I am sure we would have been close to the rocks."[25]

Constructing an egalitarian marriage remained a rare feat in this era, especially given the persistent social inequalities between men and women. Geraldine's independence had been hard won, and she wanted the same, for both Miriam and herself, in their relationship. And so she warned of the dangers of dependency, framing her concerns at this point in terms of protecting Miriam. When she was "at a low ebb," Geraldine warned, instead of being a guardian angel, she might hurt her beloved's "warm vivid life." Later she provided a litany of her limitations, warning Miriam of her tendencies to nervous exhaustion. Despite these caveats, Geraldine promised that she would never "close the door" on Miriam.[26]

Given her own emotional history, Miriam Van Waters probably did not need to be told the importance of self-protection. Within her family, she had distanced herself from vulnerability for years; with Hans and Orfa she kept free of commitment. Offering advice on love to Edna Mahan, she counseled her to "Keep yourself well in hand" because "balance is the essence." Miriam struggled to balance her own desires for care and for independence. More than in the past, though, she showed a willingness to take risks. In response to the caveats about possession, Miriam insisted that she and Geraldine already belonged to each other, and she asked Geraldine to trust their love. Perhaps she felt freer to make these statements because of Geraldine's appreciation of the pitfalls of dependence. Or, at this crisis point in her life, her need may have been so great that she had to learn to be more trusting and vulnerable. Both emotionally and materially, Geraldine provided a safer, more secure haven than anyone Miriam had previously loved. Whatever her reasons, she asked Geraldine to have faith, to love freely, and to trust that when they met in person, took their long drives in the countryside, and had their private talks, "meanings would become clearer without using other words."[27]

Even so, Geraldine still felt compelled to define "belonging" and "possession." In letters that offered critical insight into her personality, as well as into female benevolence in general, she explained that ever since earliest childhood she had found "that even after the most joyful, spontaneous, dedicated giving, I somehow got myself back again! I was 'given back' I think: psychologically at least though the giver (the other party) might not have realized that the package was being 'returned' by them." Geraldine's comments on the satisfactions of giving may help explain the pleasure, and sense of mastery, she found in a lifetime of public service and philanthropy. In her personal life, however, she found it problematic to be given possession of the beloved. Perhaps she recognized her tendency toward merger from her relationships with her children, whose lives she continued to direct throughout their adult years.

Underneath her sense of satisfaction at pure giving, however, Geraldine recognized that she was responding to a deep-seated fear of losing herself, a fear that may well have haunted other women raised in the tradition of service. Giving was, in a sense, safer than receiving. "I might be bartering my freedom if I were to accept the gift of anyone else's," she explained. When her husband once spoke of his "belonging" to her, for example, she "responded instinctively . . . I wouldn't want him that way nor know what to do about him in such terms." Risking an imbalance of power if she accepted such gifts, or possessed another, Geraldine's "healthy instincts of self-preservation" indicated "that I had better fear all statements of devotion that might have been too heavy a demand on the freedom of my life as even under the guise of a mutual arrangement." Otherwise, "I as the weaker one would soon become a chattel or possession—at first instinctively to shout with joy at being a loved one's chattel!" Thus, like Miriam, Geraldine distrusted caretaking because it implied a loss of freedom. And so, when Miriam professed her complete belonging, Geraldine too was shaken by conflicting desires "to meet you with a rush of giving or to run for my life."[28]

Aside from her fears of being possessed by the one who pledged belonging, Geraldine had other reasons to be cautious in defining her relationship with Miriam. Although she claimed to be "fiercely loyal" to her husband Lew, and frequently expressed concern about his fragile health, Geraldine found it difficult to accept Miriam's other loves. She had cried when Miriam told her that she "could enjoy warm, cherishing love with more than one person." Just as Hans had to accept Miriam's other attractions, Geraldine set out to remain loyal to their greater love, in spite of the competition.

Twice, however, Thompson recalled that her heart seemed to stop beating "for pity of myself" when she had to face the reality of these relationships. Once, when Orfa Shontz seemed to be challenging Miriam to reach "above timberline" with her in California, Geraldine waited in fear of losing Miriam.[29] In a letter she hesitated to mail, but ultimately found the courage to send, Geraldine stated clearly her jealousy of Orfa, voicing her anxiety that Orfa could not provide the emotional life that Miriam sought. "Suddenly I knew you would end by going to her on her conditions," she wrote. "I would have to recognize the beautiful necessity of your act and then go on living without your warmth if I *could*." On the other occasion, when Miriam was in Boston with Hans, Geraldine hesitated to advise Miriam against marrying. Later, though, she stated her case:

> I'm sure you're looking for something radiant, strong and
> beautiful, and perhaps not looking where it might be found.

You'll find a place for me my dearest always a place I'll be willing to take in your warm circle of love. I didn't say anything like this when I felt it might be possible and still feel that there may be a real possibility for you to find with Hans the best completion of "your passionate life." Did you read it between the lines?[30]

Whether Miriam had intuited Geraldine's feelings about Hans earlier or only now, she took the advice seriously. After a long silence, she wrote to Hans and told him that she would not be able to see him when she came east in January 1931, during her reunion with Geraldine.[31] In response he wrote of his disappointment, wishing that he could feel "sexless" toward Miriam and professing a Whitmanesque sublimation of his erotic desires. Although he did not entirely abandon hope of a "real marriage" with Miriam—perhaps in a "future life"—he reiterated the importance of their "spiritual marriage." Miriam described the letter to Geraldine, who wasn't sure whether she wanted to read it or not. Thompson did know how she felt, though: "There is a total response from all my source of wisdom—from all my roots of hopes and fears—beseeching you to direct your life so that you will not be in a position where any emotion might draw you or compel you to take any more risks." Perhaps she too referred to the medical risks of marriage and childbearing; perhaps she had other risks in mind. In any case, Geraldine closed the letter with a request to help influence Miriam's decision. "Let me have a chance to talk this over with you, won't you, my darling? I truly would give you of my best my most unselfish understanding."[32]

The exchange of letters about these other relationships, along with several telephone conversations, helped clear the path for Miriam and Geraldine. For one, Hans no longer pursued a serious courtship of Miriam, and by the next summer he had met the woman he would soon marry. In addition, in the process of baring her soul, Geraldine seemed to come to terms with her fears about possession. After mailing the letter about Orfa, for example, she wondered if she wasn't "on a hot trail—psychologically speaking?" In a mood of acceptance she wrote that "We *do* belong to each other. Oh I know oh dearest and that might mean anything in the way of tender reverent understanding. Things that might have been agonizing amputation might suddenly become a complete merging of our deepest selves, something quite radiant almost a miracle for two people ever to have shared. So good night 'most precious possession.'"[33]

This concept of complete merger represented an alternative vision of love, one in which Geraldine could experience a deeper, less self-protected emotional intimacy than she had ever known. Nonetheless, Miriam would long protect their miracle by maintaining her separate life and the privacy of their precious possession. A combination of Miriam's proud independence and her intense reticence about her personal life kept the relationship highly secretive. Perhaps she feared the power of her lover's wealth and fierce determination to have her way; or, perhaps she set the limits for both of them. In correspondence, however, Geraldine seemed more willing to proclaim their love openly. She expressed an urge, not uncommon in the afterglow of love's discovery, to tell the world what her beloved meant to her. Like a convert who had triumphed over doubts to profess her faith, she wished that she could "shout about it, partly because I want all my family, those I love, to know what life through you is giving me." She had spoken to Lew about the possibility of taking a trip with Miriam, and he had written back acknowledging the importance of the friendship. Geraldine reported to Miriam that "he knew when I was off with you (this spring to our Wellsboro trip) that I didn't know the names of the places I was visiting, I was so overjoyed to be with you." She wished she could tell him "just what you do mean to me," but first Geraldine would discuss that possibility with Miriam in person. Though Miriam remained circumspect about revealing her new love to others, to Geraldine she did make it clear that "I have never felt so purely, so surely, the *goodness* of life."[34]

As Geraldine reached "a sense of security" about their "fidelity, common joy or love," she felt released "to build a house of love and friendship for your tenancy on those most beautiful supports." This new security, along with Miriam's understanding response to her explanations of the act of giving, emboldened her to make a generous, though futile, proposition. If Miriam decided to return to the East, "you will have to let me build you a bungalow (for you and family) at Brookdale." Why not "agree to consider a new place for work as of January 1, 1932," she wondered. Once Miriam completed her Wickersham report in July, she could spend six months "resting upon your oars and writing and readjusting and getting full recourse of health and strength during the last months of 1931."[35]

To bolster her case, Geraldine compared herself with Ethel Dummer and challenged Miriam to prove the primacy of their new love. "I am haunted constantly by Mrs. Dummer," she explained. "She is a symbol and a challenge (and if you're not careful) she will become an object of hate. Don't you love me *at least ten* times more than you do Mrs. Dummer? If so, then six months of leisure(?)" Dummer had previously financed six weeks of research; accepting six months of leisure would be "an acceptable way of saying 'Geraldine has a precious possession' she is 'to keep it' — warm, and safe — and happy." Intensifying the pressure, she continued that "there is no answer to this except first 'yes I agree' or second 'I truly love you.'" The next day she elaborated on the details of her plan, adding "an unobligated sum of $5,000" to support Miriam during her retreat. "This may not sound like a love letter," she emphasized, "but it is! Only it's a concept of a grown up and intimate sharing and acceptance of love's opportunities for building. Its part of the Justice of the Peace and the church bells and the house building."[36]

Miriam disliked the comparison to Mrs. Dummer, and ultimately Geraldine had to agree that "there's naturally no analogy at all." As she waited for her offer to be accepted or rejected, she tried to leave the decision to Miriam, even as she made her preferences clearly known. Miriam hesitated to accept, worrying about how the arrangement would affect their relationship. Geraldine tried to reassure her that "For me it would be a great step forward. A sense of close, warm intimacy. A sense of simple sharing. A feeling of 'living together' openly." The vision of Miriam recuperating from stress at Brookdale, and the two friends taking time to talk about their "economic faith, philosophy, plus, our demonstrations of sincerity," appealed greatly to Geraldine Thompson.[37]

Although Miriam had professed her comfort in being possessed by Geraldine, she remained skeptical about the prospect of living with and being supported by Thompson, and ultimately she refused to do so. Staying at Brookdale in 1931, she felt the tensions that inevitably arise when strong-willed intimates lived together. "My cigarettes annoy you—perhaps they symbolize waste," she wrote in her journal after a rare argument, realizing that Geraldine would "not again open the door and come in" that night. "My words seem preposterous to you— 'foolish' and then you say perhaps 'you are wise enough—so I need not do any thinking.' I told you to go ahead—do all the thinking you can[,] a solitary business thinking." In truth, Miriam insisted on thinking for herself. Even in anger, however, she recalled their evening fondly. "You let me lie to you tonight—I loved the way you did it—we know so well when the cockles of our hearts—or the heart we love are warm." Still, Miriam resisted Geraldine's desire to provide a refuge for her. "Yet you want me here—under your roof—refreshed, blessed, replenished," she wrote in her journal. "I rebel at having chain dogs for pets. There is something monstrous in this." Identifying with these creatures, Miriam recognized that on some level they would not be kept "if they didn't wish to," and she implicitly condemned herself for the "craven pitiable weakness of them in surrendering." She would not take that course, appealing as it could seem, nor would she reject Geraldine. "As a party to a human relationship I can never be a success—but I won't accept failure," she told herself.[38]

Committed to their relationship, Miriam nonetheless chose not to live with Geraldine. Articulating her life goals in 1931, she wished "To make enough money to have Sarah, and my books—to have a place for myself or as the slogan goes 'a room of one's own' *and* a fireplace . . . To keep the soul peeled of wrappings and to remain in love."[39] Within a year, she would establish her own home in the East, and during the course of her long and loving comradeship with Geraldine, she never spent more than a month at a time living at Brookdale. For decades, however, the two women would work together as reform colleagues, visit every few weeks, and spend annual vacations together. In between, letters and daily telephone calls maintained their connection. Geraldine Thompson became a guardian angel, supporting Miriam Van Waters' career both financially and through political interventions at times of trouble. To the outside world they appeared to be close friends and colleagues; in their inner lives they had achieved a romantic as well as spiritual marriage.

Like her decision to raise Sarah, Miriam's relationship with Geraldine was unconventional but not without precedent. Loving comradeship between women had deep historical roots. Middle-class women had formed romantic friendships in childhood or at female academies during the nineteenth century. Despite geographic separation by marriage or migration, these relationships often lasted over lifetimes, sustained by correspondence and visits. By the turn of the century, the "Boston marriage" had emerged, in which two highly educated, single women, usually romantic friends, set up a household together. Reformers such as Wellesley professor Vida Scudder and novelist Florence Converse; educator and feminist activist Jeannette Marks and Mt. Holyoke president Mary Wooley; and Democratic Party politician Molly Dewson and social worker Polly Porter, who had met when they both worked at a Massachusetts girls' reformatory, all lived openly together. Miriam personally knew Jessie Taft, who lived with Virginia Robinson; her dear friend Orfa Jean Shontz had set up a home with Eve after Miriam left Los Angeles. Geraldine must have known the female couples in the networks surrounding Eleanor Roosevelt, such as Esther Lape and Elizabeth Read, or Nancy Cook and Marion Dickerman.[40]

Rarely termed anything besides friendships, these woman-centered relationships ranged from the purely spiritual to the deeply passionate to the clandestinely erotic. Middle-class female couples rarely adopted a lesbian identity, which then implied either the gender inversion symbolized by "mannish" women like the fictional Stephen Gordon, or the psychosexual pathology that Van Waters decried when she encountered "perverse" crushes among reformatory residents. Many women who did consider themselves lesbians belonged to artistic, literary, or Bohemian sets, such as expatriates Gertrude Stein and Alice B. Toklas. At the other end of the social hierarchy, when working-class women had same-sex relations, medical authorities tended to categorize them as lesbians. Prostitutes and prison inmates, especially those who were black, often acquired the label as well, in part because of the assumption that these women had stronger, more masculine, sexual desires than did white, middle-class women.[41]

Because of the class- and race-specific meaning attached to lesbianism in the early twentieth century, few professional women like Miriam Van Waters consciously claimed the identity, regardless of any erotic desire they may have experienced in private. Yet many of them did recognize their homosexual capacities. In her 1929 study of female sexuality, Katherine B. Davis found that over one-fourth of unmarried women college graduates acknowledged a sexual component within their intense emotional relationships with other women. When Van Waters read an article about the Davis study, she starred the point that it represented normal, not pathological, women.[42] This scientific judgment may have been comforting for her, but it also revealed her own self-doubts. Perhaps if she had been less concerned about the possibility of being a lesbian, she would have been less secretive about her relationship with Geraldine Thompson. Or, she may have feared that public knowledge of their love would discredit their careers as reformers. In an era when lesbianism was beginning to be stigmatized by medical authorities and condemned within the broader culture, even loving friends knew to remain circumspect. Privately, however, for almost forty years Miriam Van Waters enjoyed, at the very least, professional comradeship, spiritual kinship, and deeply passionate love through her relationship with Geraldine Thompson.

Geraldine Thompson's love and patronage added another reason for Miriam Van Waters to rethink the location of her professional future. If she moved east, they could collaborate on prison reform and enjoy their intimate friendship. Miriam had told her parents that she would not make up her mind about a new job until her trip east in 1931. First she had to complete her Wickersham report, but already the personal and professional ties with Thompson pointed toward the future. Geraldine again provided a private railway car to ease Miriam's travels, strategized about how to enact her friend's Wickersham recommendations into law, and kept an eye out for career possibilities that would bring Miriam closer to her.[43]

Like so many of her enterprises, the Wickersham commission report stirred controversy for Van Waters. She enraged the director of federal prisons, Sanford Bates, when she released to the press her harsh criticisms of the national system, claiming that it treated juveniles like hardened criminals. As a job seeker, she could not risk alienating the head of the prison system, and her allies, including Grace Abbott, Adolf Meyer, and psychiatrist William A. White, rallied to support her report by writing to Wickersham of its strengths. Although Bates long harbored ill feeling toward Van Waters, the storm seemed to pass quickly. In the end, her work for the Wickersham commission earned her widespread respect. Her 175-page report, *The Child Offender in the Federal System of Justice,* filled with statistics and "illustrative case histories," culminated Van Waters' two decades of research on juvenile offenders. Her recommendations that "the Federal Government recognize the concept of juvenile delinquency," return youthful offenders to local juvenile facilities, and decline the establishment of a federal juvenile court all influenced national policy. Thanks in part to the lobbying efforts of Geraldine Thompson, New Jersey senator Warren Barbour introduced the legislation that adopted Van Waters' recommendations.[44]

Meanwhile, Thompson's family connections came into play in the search for a new position for Miriam. Geraldine's sister, Ruth Morgan, was a good friend of Cornelia Bryce Pinchot, a suffragist and Republican politician whose husband served as the Progressive governor of Pennsylvania. In July 1931, Gifford Pinchot sent a telegram to Van Waters asking her to become the "first deputy" in the Pennsylvania Department of Welfare. Although the offer pleased her, she hesitated to accept a job involving state politics, especially since she feared that Pinchot would not remain in office long. Letting this opportunity pass, especially during the depths of the economic depression, did not make obvious sense unless she had other prospects. Her own savings had been wiped out by a bank failure, and her family could not offer support. Van Waters may have known that Geraldine Thompson could cushion her economically, for the crash had not devastated her husband's wealth, as it had Ethel Dummer's. She also knew that her Cambridge friends Felix Frankfurter and Ada Comstock had been trying to find money to create a research and teaching position for her at Radcliffe or Harvard.[45]

It was at this time that Van Waters relocated to Cambridge, even though it meant giving up her ties to Stone House. She still struggled to complete the overdue Harvard Crime Survey report, which would haunt her for years. The writing did not come easily, and the surrounding signs of economic crisis disturbed her. Driving by striking dockworkers, witnessing hundreds of men, women, and children wearing rags, she wrote that she had "never seen anything like it—though Dickens writes of such scenes." When Hans Weiss visited her in Cambridge at the end of 1931, he thought that she seemed especially depressed and worried about her future, "professionally and financially." He failed to realize, however, that Miriam in fact lived comfortably. She had placed Sarah in private school, hired helpers, and was spending restorative weekends with Geraldine, either in Cambridge or at Brookdale. Moreover, the prospect for a secure job in Massachusetts promised to resolve the stalemate in her career.[46]

Weiss' expressions of concern may have told more about his own state of mind than hers. A few months earlier he had proposed to a young woman he had been courting, after sending some of her letters to Miriam for approval. Hans married in the fall of 1931, but within weeks he panicked, fearing that he had mistakenly surrendered his dream of marrying Miriam. It was in this context that he looked upon her as a maiden in distress. He loved his wife, and she loved him, he wrote to Miriam, but he realized that "my love for you is as constant as ever. What I thought one could do—spiritualize it or whatever you may call it—I cannot do—at least, not now." When he visited Miriam in Cambridge, he had seen "a task for me in your life—it was like lightening—but, I had already married! It is tragic beyond words." Hans seemed to forget Miriam's disinterest in marrying him, but he did know that she still loved him in her own way. For years he would remain a friend and comrade in reform, and he would continue to turn to her for "strength of spirit" and "power of faith."[47]

In November 1931, the prospects for Miriam Van Waters' future brightened when she learned that she was about to be offered the superintendency of the Massachusetts Reformatory for Women in Framingham. She had once described this nineteenth-century women's prison as "frightful," and on a visit in December she disliked the "cagey prison smell" and lifelessness of inmates.[48] But the job began to attract her. Thanks to the connections she had made in Massachusetts reform circles, Van Waters seemed an obvious choice to succeed Jessie Hodder, the superintendent of the reformatory since 1911, who had just died. The position would mean a shift from juvenile to adult corrections and a permanent move to Massachusetts. In charge of several hundred women and a large staff at the historic thirty-acre reformatory site, she would report to the state commissioner of corrections. Van Waters respected the current commissioner, psychiatrist Warren Stearns, whom she knew from her early work at Boston Children's Aid. Contemplating the superintendency, and well aware that few other administrative jobs had come her way, Miriam wrote to her parents. "I do not care for a desk job—or an empty title. I would rather run a 'good' prison than be president of the best women's college on earth. I would teach students—from all over U.S. and world, and have the training school I am interested in."

Having control of her own institution meant a great deal, given her loss of El Retiro, but so too did the greater status she associated with this job. "National foundations are interested. I would have connection both with Tufts Medical and Harvard Law. It is the outstanding position in penology today in America there is no question about that." Although she claimed that the income was not a factor, the equivalent of five thousand dollars a year—including salary, expenses, a house, and the use of a state car—must have looked appealing. She also let Stearns know that within a year she expected "that effort be made to fix the salary at the rate paid to superintendents of similar institutions in the state for men." Meanwhile, the reasons to accept stacked up higher. "No time clock to punch. I would be better off financially than I am now," she wrote. Ethel Dummer added her enthusiastic approval, as did Felix Frankfurter and Geraldine Thompson.[49] By the end of 1931, Miriam Van Waters envisioned a new professional path, paralleling the new love she had gained at midlife. Her future awaited her in Framingham.

PART III

1932–1949

Building the Framingham Symphony

In March 1932, when Miriam Van Waters moved into the superintendent's house at the Massachusetts Reformatory for Women, she did not know that it would remain her home for the rest of her career. Although other professional prospects would come her way, Van Waters seemed increasingly determined to cast her fate among the several hundred women inmates at Framingham. By 1934 she realized that there was no turning back. "Now in mid-age," she wrote in her journal, "I become a prison warden—conductor: conscious of the past but leaving it as background—to be drawn upon but not re-entered." Now her life's work was "building the Framingham Symphony . . . a way of life, a monastery, a prison—farm—factory—workshop—laboratory—studio—chapel—nursery—hospital—a place where books are written, pictures made, prayers said, lives are begun and ended." From 1932 until 1957, Miriam Van Waters served as conductor, as teacher, as a kind of mother superior who ruled, with love and wit, at Framingham.[1]

Van Waters' vision, an elaboration upon her earlier El Retiro experiment, would have pleased many of the founders of the reformatory. In the 1870s, they had convinced the state legislature to build a separate institution, run by and for women only, the second of its kind in the United States. Female inmates, the reformers argued, required a different kind of treatment than men either provided or received in the state's jails and prisons. Instead of the harsh condemnation of the "fallen woman" that had prevailed earlier in the nineteenth century, they offered a vision of rehabilitation through maternal uplift, in bucolic, cottage-style reformatories that offered a strong dose of domestic training.

When Framingham opened in 1877, it met only some of the original goals of women's prison reform. In spite of a massive stone edifice built in the traditional congregate, rather than cottage, style of prison architecture, the new institution did embody some rehabilitative features. Located on thirty acres of land, about thirty miles west of Boston, it achieved the pastoral setting reformers desired. Inmate quarters resembled rooms rather than cells; they were larger than men's quarters, their windows had no bars, and white linen adorned their beds. Those who earned the privilege could add individual decorative touches. The most distinguishing feature was the nursery, where infants brought with their mothers or born at the institution remained until the age of two. In addition, the administration and staff was almost entirely female. Several outstanding women ran Framingham over the years—Dr. Eliza Mosher and Clara Barton each held the office in the nineteenth century, and Jessie Hodder revitalized the reform tradition after her appointment in 1911. Hodder changed the name of the institution from "reformatory prison" to "reformatory," transformed a cell block into a gymnasium, and called the residents "women" rather than "inmates."[2]

From the time of its founding, Framingham was supposed to receive young first offenders. Many had been convicted of "crimes against chastity," including fornication, soliciting as a prostitute, or the more vague charges of "lewd and lascivious behavior" or being a "stubborn child" beyond parental control. Some of these women were simply unwed mothers or sexually active youths, not unlike the girls whom Van Waters tried to keep out of prison in Los Angeles. Over half of the women incarcerated at the reformatory in the mid–1920s had been pregnant outside of marriage at some time, and a third had children out of wedlock. As late as 1928, when the Harvard Crime Survey compiled extensive data on the inmates, 80 percent had been sentenced for "crimes against public order." Over 40 percent had been charged with lewdness, idleness (which "invariably" indicated "sex delinquency"), or stubbornness; 14 percent served time for adultery or fornication, crimes for which male partners never received penalties, and for which middle-class women would rarely be charged. As in the nineteenth century, many inmates had been committed for drunkenness.[3]

Drawing on the model of the reform school, rather than the prison, Framingham administrators hoped to rehabilitate these least-hardened, and thus most hopeful, cases. Sentences of up to two years intended ample time for character retraining, while an indenture program offered women the opportunity to earn money and learn domestic skills as dayworkers in nearby households. Even though most inmates probably emerged from custody unchanged, they had at the very least avoided the harsher conditions women faced in county jails and state prisons built for men.

At the time of Superintendent Hodder's death, in 1931, Framingham was in the midst of a transitional period in its history. During World War I the institution had become overcrowded, in part because of the nationwide increase in arrests of young women suspected of having sexual relations with soldiers. After the passage of Prohibition, the proportion of women committed to Framingham for drunkenness increased, as did the age of the reformatory population. In the nineteenth century, the majority of inmates were under age twenty-five; by 1937, over half of the inmates were over age thirty, and a third were over age forty. More served longer sentences, and fewer were first offenders. Over half had worked in mills, factories, or as domestic servants, while some drifted in and out of prostitution. The Great Depression of the 1930s further affected the population. When families and social agencies lacked resources to care for alcoholics and their children, or when poor, unwed mothers could not afford hospital care, Framingham increasingly received these homeless, rather than criminal, women. In the depths of the depression, over 90 percent of the Framingham inmates had been sentenced for crimes against public order.[4]

The depression decade was not an auspicious era for women's prison reform. For one, the organized women's movement seemed weak, compared to the Progressive Era, and despite the appointment of women to positions within the New Deal, the plight of male rather than female workers often dominated the reform agenda. At the same time, economic austerity measures in most states reduced rather than expanded resources for institutions, while conservative political forces within Massachusetts resisted any liberal "coddling" of prisoners. Even the Norfolk Prison Colony for Men, a once-promising experiment in rehabilitation, had resorted to custodial control by 1933; its reform-minded warden, Howard Gill, had become a "victim of state politics." Meanwhile, as the media sensationalized images of imprisoned gangsters and gun molls as public enemies, taxpayers measured the success of prison wardens by their ability to maintain strict discipline, sometimes through paramilitary regimes. Nationally, most women offenders served time in state prisons that were at best custodial and, especially for black women in the South, often quite punitive.[5]

Amid this conservative climate, Miriam Van Waters announced her commitment to provide social services rather than punishment. To do so she would draw upon the maternalist rhetoric of the middle-class female reform tradition, combining private philanthropy, voluntarism, and state resources. She would also stretch her own public authority well beyond its legal limits. Along with a handful of other women superintendents, such as Edna Mahan in New Jersey, Van Waters used the prison system to create a small social welfare fortress for women whose lives remained largely unaffected by New Deal programs. In contrast to her earlier efforts to prevent juvenile delinquency, she now undertook a salvage operation for already lost souls. As in the past, Van Waters assumed the posture of surrogate mother, but more than ever she drew upon the religious moorings of her childhood. To her earlier applications of social science theory and social work methods, she now added a stronger element of the Social Gospel. Increasingly, she gained a reputation as a charismatic healer.

Always an individualist, rather than the leader of a social movement, Van Waters' strategy of personal uplift may have been especially appropriate in a period when women's public culture seemed less powerful than during the heyday of progressivism and the suffrage movement. Nonetheless, she continued to draw upon, and to stimulate, a broader world of female reform. The institution she created at Framingham served as a magnet for local women's voluntarism, supplementing national efforts to relieve social problems. Van Waters also maintained her ties to national reform networks through her frequent talks at social work and educational conferences. The annual meetings of women superintendents, for example, allowed her to share information with women colleagues from around the country. At the same time, her broad service on public commissions kept her politically connected. In the 1930s, for example, Van Waters accepted appointments to the Massachusetts Liquor Law Commission, the Washington, D.C.–based American Youth Commission, and the 1939 White House Conference on Child Welfare. She actively worked with the American League to Abolish Capital Punishment, and she periodically took up other causes, such as the work of the Committee for Relief of Spanish and Chinese Children. From 1932 until 1957, however, Framingham became the microcosmic center of her quest for maternal justice.

On the eve of becoming a prison superintendent, Miriam Van Waters told the *Boston Globe* of her intentions. "The goal of the modern institution must be to have institutional life approximate outside normal life as nearly as it can," she explained. To the reporter, the "slight, gray, athletic-looking" Van Waters resembled a college president more than a prison warden. She "seemed to have spent most of her life in keeping people out of prison," but now "she was taking a job of keeping them in." To Van Waters, though, the challenge was not one of maintaining security but rather of unlocking the doors between prison and community and getting away with it. As she wrote to her parents soon after taking office, "Bars off . . . curtains in . . . Will bring the outside world in. I have to go slow *inside*. Staff thinks I'm crazy to be crazy about pictures—colors—curtains—flowers—and not Morals!" Even some reformers, such as the influential Harvard criminologists Sheldon and Eleanor Glueck, had their doubts about Van Waters' ability to succeed.[6]

Although the previous superintendent, Jessie Hodder, had been sympathetic to rehabilitative goals, the legacy of her administration dismayed Van Waters. After her first day on the job, she lay awake brooding over the pervasive symbols of imprisonment, the lack of wages for women's prison labor, the depressing physical plant. As she later recalled, "The institution struck me full on the chest, something ponderous and immovable." Lack of funds had allowed the building to deteriorate, but the most disturbing feature, she wrote, was not the "leaky roofs, rotten floor boards, intolerably cold and draughty corridors: it was the dust-encrusted red tape that had paralyzed all free motion on the part of the staff."

The Framingham Van Waters inherited did have a regimented quality to it. Each inmate had to wear a blue-and-white check dress, and no one could adorn herself or her room. "No short hair, no curls, no powder, face cream or personal soap" read the rules. Meals had to be eaten in silence, with desserts on Sundays only. No newspapers were allowed, and library use was limited. One evening each week inmates could enjoy some kind of recreation, except in the "Annex," where newcomers spent several weeks in complete isolation.[7] As one visitor recalled the old regime,

> I saw drab, expressionless, discouraged inmates in their daily life. They did not speak in the corridors or look up as they met an officer. Some of them turned and faced the walls when visitors passed by. Older prisoners put their hands behind their backs when speaking to an officer. No conversation was allowed at meals: women were punished for smiling or waving hands to one another.[8]

The critic surely exaggerated the old order—as one former officer explained, "No unnecessary talking was allowed; but unless the conversation got too bawdy, I turned a deaf ear." Nonetheless, the critical account captured a spirit of resignation at Framingham that others noted as well.[9]

In the opening chapter of an uncompleted memoir, Van Waters used a telling biblical reference to describe her initiation at Framingham: "The Evening and the Morning Were the First Day, March 1932." The title proclaimed not only her intention to create a new order but also her assumption of near divine power, a posture that would later fuel the resentment of those who disagreed with her. During her first week in office, though, Van Waters easily seized the authority to reframe institutional life. She called an assembly, appointed one of the few black inmates as its chair, and enlarged the self-government system that Hodder had established. Addressing the gathering from the pulpit of the reformatory chapel, the new superintendent made a "vow to bring our neighbors into our planning, to have the community flow into us, and our institution into the community." She also "vowed to save the trees and birds and brooks and the wild-life" that surrounded the institution. "I shall break down the wall," she promised herself.[10]

"Before the first week ended," Van Waters proudly recalled, "I had talked in my office to four hundred girls and to each staff member." She learned that most of the inmates were short-term "social offenders"; only 20 percent served longer terms, from five years to life, for offenses that "ranged from abortion, robbery, forgery, drug peddling to murder." Over the years Van Waters often repeated these figures to support her emphasis on social services rather than punishment. "More than half the people here should not have been sent here," she told a reporter in 1935. "There are the chronic alcoholics. To send them to prison is absurd. Likewise prostitutes. Prostitution is a social problem, not a criminal offense." Law enforcement, she later argued, "should be directed against organized business of prostitution and corruption."[11]

Of all the inequities she discovered, none disturbed Van Waters more than the prison sentences of up to five years meted out to single mothers "merely for pursuing the fathers of their unborn babies." She referred to the fact that a woman who acknowledged an illegitimate birth by seeking paternal support could be charged for lewdness or fornication. Once branded as criminals, these innocent women had a difficult time reentering society after their release. In one case, for example, a woman's common-law husband demeaned her because she had served a prison sentence for having borne their child; he had received only six months probation.[12]

Although the courts had not been just to many of the women sent to Framingham, Van Waters resolved to take advantage of their incarceration by providing social and medical services that most of them needed. Many inmates came from the poorest backgrounds in the state. Some had entered the textile mills as children and had never received health care. A rare middle-class inmate had taken to drink and narcotics after the depression had financially devastated her family. Even women convicted of offenses against property, such as forgers and thieves, had often acted while drunk or in need of drugs.[13] As in the past, Van Waters instituted a "program for each individual," but now in command of her own institution, her impact was even stronger.

At that first assembly, facing almost four hundred inmates in the prison chapel, Van Waters hesitated before speaking, wondering what to call her charges. Looking out over the group, she recalled, her eyes focused on two figures, "their faces like children." *Women,* the term Hodder had used, did not seem appropriate for them. But *girls* would not do, either, she explained, for "old white-haired bent grandmothers and great-grandmothers, probably sixty persons faced me who were between sixty and eighty years of age." The term *inmates,* she felt, was "a herd name," as was *prisoners.* Van Waters chose the term *students,* explaining to them "what steps I had taken to call them that."[14] The term had great significance for her. "Names are important," she later wrote in her journal. "If you call those in prison—prisoners or inmates—rather than students—you have taken [the] aspect of their custody, namely the shut-in-by-force and sentenced to hard labor and loss of rank." She preferred to "attend to another aspect—namely their training and their willingness to learn—and call them students.[15]

Just as she had renamed her daughter to achieve a symbolic rebirth, Van Waters introduced the term *students* to mark the beginning of her new regime. She wanted to suggest that the institution was a school—albeit a reformatory—rather than a prison. Calling the inmates students also set the tone for her attempt to create a progressive educational environment in which she led as a teacher rather than a disciplinarian. At the same time, however, by rejecting Hodder's term, *women,* Van Waters dismissed the importance of gender, while she also leveled inmates of every age to the juvenile status of students. Within the institutional hierarchy, students were referred to by first names, staff by their last names, while both groups called Van Waters simply "Doctor." Similarly, when she organized monthly birthday parties to help restore students' lost childhoods, she simultaneously created a familial dependency upon their maternal keeper. Yet observers credited her for successfully creating a sense of community. As a psychiatric social worker described her effect, "We all felt that this was a New Deal. We felt that we were part of it—from the newest arrival in hospital quarantine to the Superintendent—'All for one. One for all.'"[16]

To effect her new regime, Van Waters instituted the kind of sweeping changes that had characterized her administrations at the Frazer Detention Home, L.A. juvenile hall, and El Retiro. She reduced the period of initial isolation to two weeks, with recreation permitted, painted the Annex in bright colors, and hung curtains throughout the reformatory. On Easter Sunday she took all the inmates on a walk through the nearby fields, woods, and pastures. The women could now choose from print dresses, decide on their own hairstyles, and decorate their rooms, although like officers, they could not wear makeup. Van Waters also allowed greater personal privileges, including free use of the library, weekly letter writing, and conversation at meals. "Talk is a safety valve," she later wrote, "and it talks itself out." Rather than silence between officers and inmates she encouraged communication and even fostered social bonds. Watching women dance together at a Halloween party for younger inmates, she delighted in "this unity of girls and staff—in order and friendship."[17]

Within a few months of Van Waters' arrival, visitors and staff marveled at Framingham's new atmosphere and the superintendent's role in creating it. According to a reporter, Van Waters brought to the reformatory "a sense of excitement—that nice things are about to happen—and of friendly expectancy." Anne Gladding, who arrived in 1932 as an intern, early recognized Van Waters' ability to inspire the students' confidence through her "strength and sincerity and understanding as a human being." It was surprising at first, Gladding wrote, that "so many of the girls talked of this almost on first acquaintance with a new interne—but it was apparent that to those girls it was of first importance—more than the new privileges they had received or hoped to receive." Other officers felt that the privileges Van Waters extended to inmates kept them from planning escapes. Even an observer who noted the bleak, long, dark hallways, the lack of comfortable furnishings and adequate baths, and the "rather wide extent of profanity" at the institution "was impressed almost most of all by the familiarity of the women with the officers" and by the freedom of movement. "I could hardly believe it was true that some of the women were sent outside, unwatched and unsupervised, to take care of the Van Waters' grounds. . . . I saw two of the girls, who work at Dr. Van Waters' house taking a walk up the road one evening, all alone."[18]

An incident that occurred just a month after these accounts were written illustrates the superintendent's reliance on student trust to achieve institutional order. A woman who had been allowed to go home for a visit failed to return to the reformatory. Van Waters called a student assembly to explain the seriousness of the offense and why the woman, who had been arrested, received an extra sentence. According to the superintendent, the students showed "a splendid demonstration of concern for honor," and as a result, their privileges remained in force.

For the next twenty-five years, Framingham students could be found working outside, walking between buildings, and conversing with officers. Despite occasional runaways, the large majority adhered to Van Waters' honor system.[19]

During the first years she ran Framingham, skeptics waited for inmates to abuse their freedoms and for Van Waters to follow in the footsteps of liberal wardens like Howard Gill. A major public test occurred in August 1934, when Van Waters faced an incipient riot. "I was confronted by a mob of 35—at the door of East Wing at 6:10 P.M.," she recounted in her journal. The recent transfer of fifty women from the Bridgewater State Hospital had overcrowded the institution, while an inmate suicide the previous week heightened tensions among the women. Faced with a "mob" demanding better conditions, Van Waters immediately called all the students into the chapel. As a security precaution, she alerted the state police, but she proceeded to calm the assembled students, in part by appointing one of the agitators "chairman of a new food committee" to handle grievances. "Perhaps democracy worked," she wrote that night, but it had been "a tense and dreadful situation." The calming of the near riot earned great respect for Van Waters' strategy of appealing personally to students and involving them in the administration of the reformatory.[20]

Along with extending privileges to students, Superintendent Van Waters consciously arranged moments of grandeur and orchestrated uplifting spiritual rituals. Like her predecessors in the nineteenth century, she would gather students and staff for inspirational viewing of the night-blooming cereus plant. In the reformatory chapel she installed stained-glass windows created by the noted craftsman Charles Connick. Two local women artists, hired through the New Deal Works Project Administration, filled the chapel walls with murals of women at work, play, and worship. In this chapel, Van Waters presided over the student assemblies. Dressed in an elegant evening gown, the striking, silver-haired superintendent would ascend to the pulpit to introduce honored guests. After student officers presented reports, the choir performed, and the visitors spoke, she closed each session by saying good night to the students, who rose and replied in unison, "Good night, Doctor Van Waters." "God bless you," she answered, and then they departed. The dramatic ritual created a kind of bond between charismatic leader and her followers, reinforcing her spiritual authority while making prison life more bearable because of these moments of transcendence.[21]

In instituting programmatic reforms, Van Waters once again drew upon the settlement house model she had emulated in Los Angeles. She brought philanthropists, psychologists, reformers, and artists into her Framingham world as often as possible. One month Felix and Marian Frankfurter, attorney Arthur Hill, and Geraldine Thompson all spoke at student assemblies, as did Ethel Dummer and Adolf Meyer on later visits. When Robert Frost read his poems at Harvard, Van Waters sent him an invitation signed by all of the students, and the poet came the next day to visit. Thanks to Geraldine Thompson, Eleanor Roosevelt also spoke to the student assembly on several occasions during the 1940s. Thompson also contributed funds, much as Dummer had done for El Retiro, enabling Van Waters to hire psychiatrists and interns who would never have been funded by the state. Ethel Dummer, Boston reformer Margaret Herrick, and a Friends of Prisoners committee all helped fund psychiatric services at Framingham.[22]

As in Los Angeles, Van Waters encouraged women's clubs to participate at the reformatory. In 1933 she invited members of the local women's federation to dinner to suggest that they start an arts-and-crafts-manufacturing project. Later, settlement workers from Boston's Denison House contacted Van Waters to set up a hand-weaving course. The Roxbury Ladies Choir came to sing, performing along with inmates. Women's clubs also raised money to supplement institutional resources. In the 1940s, they provided funds to help released inmates get reestablished at work. As a businesswoman from Boston's Altrusa Club explained, "One of our pet peeves is that men in institutions have the privilege of earning and saving money through their labors while such privileges are not given to women."[23]

The most important infusion of energy came through the internship program that Van Waters initiated. Aided by anonymous contributions from Geraldine Thompson, the superintendent annually accepted up to twelve recent college graduates as interns. As she explained to her daughter Sarah, an intern was like a novice in a monastery. In exchange for working a forty-eight-hour week, each woman received room, board, and laundry, but no salary, for a period of up to six months. Van Waters never had to advertise the opportunities, for word about them spread quickly through women's and liberal arts colleges in the Northeast. During the depths of the Great Depression, with almost a quarter of the workforce facing unemployment, educated young women interested in child care, education, or social services faced slim job prospects. An internship at Framingham provided experience, a letter of recommendation, and potential employment. Over fifty women applied for the positions each year.

The interns, many of whom lived together in the staff home across from the main reformatory building, created a special community within Framingham. While other young people underwent political radicalization during the 1930s, the type of woman who came to Framingham continued the Social Gospel tradition of service. Most came from relatively liberal, churchgoing families, and many shared Van Waters' spiritual beliefs. The superintendent felt that through their jobs the interns gained a chance at personal fulfillment. As she once mused after addressing the "society set" in Boston's Junior League, that "discouraged, over-stimulated lot" compared poorly to her interns, some of whom "come from the same type of home, yet are happy." [24]

Former interns long remembered the lure of the reformatory during the 1930s. Anne Gladding, a nursery-school-education major at Vassar, had planned to spend only the summer of 1932 working with the children of inmates. She liked to recall that "she came for tea and she didn't leave for 42 years." When a mothers' cottage opened, Gladding became its director. For years she lived in the superintendent's house as a central member of Van Waters' extended household. Margaret van Wagenen, a graduate of the home economics program at Cornell, had been employed in a state school but was out of work in 1936 when Gladding invited her to become an intern at Framingham. A half century later she still remembered the precise day she arrived—June 22— and her first impression: "Oh this is it. This is wonderful." Both she and Gladding felt that coming to Framingham "was like finding something that you had dreamed about." It was "more like a progressive school. There was no prison atmosphere whatsoever," especially in the mothers' cottage, where she worked. After returning to graduate school for her social work degree, van Wagenen rejoined the reformatory staff and remained there until her retirement. Lois Rice heard about the internship from a Framingham officer who spoke at Wheaton College, near Boston, where she was a senior. "A lot of us were wondering what we were going to do, and she spoke about Dr. Van Waters' program for interns, and I came here to talk with her further." Rice worked at Framingham from 1933 to 1938, when she left to attend social work school at the University of Chicago. She also introduced her cousin and aunt to the reformatory, where they served as volunteers. [25]

Van Waters attempted to hire older, African American, and working-class interns as well. She invited a forty-five-year-old divorced woman who needed a job to teach weaving as an intern. At least two black women held internships. One, who remained for three years, felt "unusually well received" from "the racial point of view," despite two encounters with blatant prejudice. Pauline Orsi, from a local Italian American family, was attending nearby Framingham College when a teacher tried "to get help for Dr. Van Waters." At her interview, Orsi recalled, "I met Dr. Van Waters, talked to her, and she was the one who convinced me it was the up and coming thing to do. There were no jobs." Orsi came in 1933 and stayed for thirty-eight years, eventually serving as deputy superintendent.[26] Van Waters also invited an earnest but uneducated working-class young woman with a troubled past to spend a month as a trial intern in 1934. Margaret O'Keefe stayed to become Van Waters' loyal, hardworking assistant until the superintendent retired in 1957. Her down-to-earth style nicely complemented Van Waters' dignified charm. As a former student recalled, you could hear Peg O'Keefe "from one end of the corridor to the other, her yelling at some girl that did something that she shouldn't have." Soon, though, O'Keefe would put her arm around the tearful offender and offer her a cigarette. "She was that type. She was a wonderful person," the inmate reminisced. "They could get close to her when they were afraid to get close to Doctor."[27]

For some of the middle-class staff and interns, Framingham quickly provided an education in the mores and language of the largely working-class inmate culture. "Those first few weeks I learned a great deal," staff member Harriet Gunning later recalled. When she referred to a young inmate as "a little doll," she found out that in prison the term "doll" meant a woman who had romantic or sexual relations with another woman. At the nursery, Gunning referred endearingly to some of the babies as "dear little rats." No one spoke to her for an entire weekend. Finally a black student explained to her that in prison, a rat was something quite terrible, someone who informed on another inmate.[28]

While the reformatory provided them with jobs and an unconventional education, the interns performed invaluable services. They took over when officers went on vacation, taught classes to students, provided research assistance for the medical and psychiatric staff, and in several instances designed unique educational projects. In 1932, for example, Hilda Hinkley, who had a master's degree from Columbia, visited Framingham for a weekend. Van Waters liked this "fresh wholesome girl" and hired her for a month as a library intern. Hinkley stayed for years, creating a theater program that produced over twenty plays with student actors. Another theater project evolved when a Radcliffe anthropology graduate student directed a play written and performed by the Italian American women; another Radcliffe student arranged a musical play from the Russian, Polish, and Portuguese folk songs that students taught her. Intern Amy Row, who taught art classes, arranged exhibits of student paintings in Boston and New York City museums.[29]

When she accepted the superintendency, Miriam Van Waters imagined herself at the head of a research enterprise as well as a prison. As Felix Frankfurter wrote when he congratulated her on her appointment, he envisioned Framingham "as a laboratory for the best scientific thought in penology and as a training school for young workers." Through the internship program, Van Waters assumed the role of master teacher. She invited all of the interns to the superintendent's house for a regular symposium. Like G. Stanley Hall's Clark University seminar, at each gathering one member would present her research, followed by group discussion.

Just as she recruited highly educated interns, Van Waters also sought an expert staff to serve as classroom teachers and counselors. Staff meetings at Framingham, like the case conferences at El Retiro, also resembled graduate seminars. "I'll never forget staff meetings when staff would be all sitting around a long library table," the Reverend William Wiltenburg recalled. "After everybody was seated there, smoking, rapping a bit about the day, Dr. Van Waters would come in. Everyone would stand as one and this was virtually at every staff meeting occasion. 'Please be seated' and we'd all sit." No one resented the ritual, he felt, for it "gave her the respect that was due to her." Once seated, Van Waters might clarify institutional rules or explain the chain of command; she also lectured on particular problems, such as alcoholism, homosexual liaisons, or race relations; and she listened to staff ideas and complaints, inviting feedback from interns, teachers, and officers.[30]

Van Waters treated the interns and staff members not only as their teacher but also as if she was their minister. She worried about their personal problems and their adjustments to institutional life. "*Problem*—liason [*sic*] bet[ween] internes who are scientific and sophisticated—and 'young' staff who are in thrall of what is right and proper," she wrote in her journal with the query "*How make* Progressive education *vital here*." She counseled staff to strike a happy medium between kindness and discipline, but the young, often inexperienced interns did not always have the judgment to know where the balance lay. "I find I'm a very poor policeman and disciplinarian for a group," one new staff member wrote to the superintendent, "but taking them singly, it's O.K."[31]

When officers with divergent styles came into conflict with each other, Van Waters found herself trying to mediate. She herself disagreed with some staff members, especially the deputy superintendent she inherited from the Hodder administration, who did not share her approach. Disgruntled staff sometimes complained about this deputy or about Van Waters' protégé Elizabeth Bode, who had a hard time getting along in an administrative position. Inmates also sent complaints to the superintendent, citing staff members who yelled at them, refused to accept the principle of student government, or undermined Van Waters' reforms. "You, Dr. VW, can't see everyone," one student pointed out. Van Waters felt personally responsible when staff morale was low. "There is an air of depression among the 'internes,' an indication the Boss is not lifting enough," she wrote in her journal in 1935.[32]

Drawing on the model of progressive education, in which students learn from doing, Van Waters encouraged the staff to sponsor a variety of clubs and classes. Inmates worked eight-hour days, either making flags and clothing for state use or helping to run the kitchen, hospital, farm, or poultry plant. During the rest of their time they could take advantage of unusual opportunities. The International Club offered plays and concerts; the Glee Club performed Gilbert and Sullivan musicals; the handful of black students belonged to the Merry Makers, who sang spirituals, studied "Race History," and learned about the NAACP; the Drama Club performed plays such as *Our Town;* the Literary Club produced a hand-bound poetry magazine; the Two Sides Club held debates; and the Parole Club held discussions on how to adjust to life after release. In 1937 students began publishing the *Harmony News,* which lasted for over twenty years. In the 1940s a series of clubs helped fulfill Van Waters' goal of breaking down the prison wall by sending students to explore the outdoors. The Hikers' Club admitted a dozen carefully selected students committed to preserving and beautifying the surrounding countryside. By 1945 the Rangers were clearing land and taking regular Saturday hikes in the woods surrounding the reformatory.[33]

Officers and interns offered classes attended by a majority of the inmates. For seventeen years, Van Waters herself led a literary class, in which up to forty women would gather to listen to the superintendent read to them for an hour, usually from works of contemporary fiction. She also encouraged students to write essays on prominent women for a biography class. Their subjects—including Helen Keller, Jane Addams, and Julia Lathrop—reflected the superintendent's interest in the female reform tradition. For a time an editor at the *Atlantic* taught a poetry class at the reformatory, and in the 1950s, professional women's baseball star Dottie Green directed recreational activities as a staff member. Over the years other staff and volunteers provided classes ranging from civics and psychology to folk dancing and weaving. With scholarships provided by the State Federation of Women's Clubs, several students were able to attend college after release, while others trained as practical nurses.[34]

Van Waters cherished these success stories and maintained contact with many of the former students. Sometimes she helped tide them over during hard times, paying medical bills or sending inspirational notes. On one woman's anniversary she sent orchids to lift her spirits. Not surprisingly, grateful inmates credited Van Waters for her healing powers. The superintendent and her staff "brought me to find a 'way of life,'" one woman wrote from parole. Even a hard talking "tough baby" who turned up in court again calmed down when reminded of Dr. Van Waters. The woman's "whole manner changed and a gentleness appeared . . . an almost nostalgic quality," a former staff member noted. For years grateful inmates would remember how the Doctor had given them hope.[35]

Along with spiritual uplift, the centerpiece of both education and social service at Framingham was the program for mothers and babies. One penologist called it the "vital program for nourishing mother-love," while Van Waters referred to Framingham as a "child-centered institution." Over half of the inmates had living children, and infants had long been permitted to remain with their mothers. In the past the nursery had been neglected. According to one critic, the babies were "the most pitiful inmates in 1932." Many looked pale and apathetic, dressed in nondescript garments made from remnants, and lacking toys. When Van Waters arrived, she wrote to her parents that "one thing made my breast ache—the mothers nurse their babies seated on the hard floor! I am leaving orders for chairs."[36]

Ever since she wrote her doctoral dissertation on adolescents in primitive cultures, Van Waters had been impressed by societies that integrated rather than ostracized the unwed mother. She herself was a single mother, and her child had been born to an unwed mother. In Los Angeles she had sought to prevent adolescent pregnancies and to hold the fathers responsible for impregnating young women. Now, at Framingham, Van Waters approached the problem from the perspective of caring for young, usually poor, pregnant women and new mothers who had been labeled criminal because of their pregnancies.

The creation of a model nursery, with adequate health care and maternal education, became both an end in itself and a means toward a more humane reformatory. "The program of an institution adapted to children can never be the same cut-and-dried thing that is found in some men's institutions," she wrote. "Harshness is mitigated, voices lowered, smiles are more frequent." Thus the superintendent stressed the importance of "more family contacts" and resolved "not to separate mother and child." Unlike many social workers, who considered single mothers unfit to raise children, her policy was "to treat mother and child as an inseparable relationship and to glorify motherhood." Toward this end she successfully lobbied to defeat a bill that would have prevented inmates from keeping their babies with them.[37]

Within a few days of taking office, Van Waters had organized the weekly Mothers' Club, where "each Mother is made free to talk." In addition, in order to create a homelike atmosphere and fulfill the original reformers' goal of cottage-style quarters, she applied for federal funds to build a separate residence for mothers and infants, as well as a cottage for young inmates. With support from Eleanor Roosevelt, Massachusetts did receive funds to build two cottages. Hodder Hall, for students age seventeen to twenty-one, opened in 1935, named for the former superintendent, who herself had born a child in a common-law marriage. Jessie Wilson Sayre Cottage, for mothers and babies, opened in 1936. It was named for the recently deceased daughter of Woodrow Wilson, a liberal activist in Boston whose widower, Harvard Law School professor Francis B. Sayre, had served briefly as Massachusetts commissioner of corrections.[38]

Wilson Cottage, as it was called, was located about a quarter of a mile away from the main building, with no locked doors or barred windows. The residents walked between the cottage and the main building along the public highway, sometimes unaccompanied by staff. Between twenty-five and thirty mothers and as many children lived at Wilson Cottage, along with up to ten officers and interns. In addition, a nursery in the main building took care of up to sixty children whose mothers did not live at Wilson, either for lack of space or because they were considered at risk for escape. In 1933, Van Waters hired her sister-in-law, Bertha Green Van Waters, to head the nursery and supervise the mothers' cottage. A trained nurse, Bert Green earned the respect of the reformatory staff for her skills as an administrator. Working with her were a pediatrician, several nurses and teachers, a dietitian, and a psychologist. Their child service center could only operate because of external funding from philanthropists. The Thompson Fund provided stipends for several of the nursery staff; another benefactor once turned over her Cape Cod summer house and paid two mothers to care for six children there.[39]

Many of the mothers at Framingham spent their days working with children in the nursery; other mothers visited their children during a one-hour break from other institutional jobs. Some women who did not have children also worked at the nursery, a practice that Van Waters believed could be therapeutic. As one former student who had been suicidal explained, "I was given charge over a difficult group who called me 'mother' and to them I became as a mother . . . my cure had been effected." All mothers could attend a "mothercraft" course initiated by the Framingham Woman's Club and supported in part by a local manufacturing company. During the 1930s, student teachers from Framingham State College taught the classes, despite the fact that the college students had less experience with child care than did some of the mothers. But as intern Margaret van Wagenen recalled, a spirit of cooperation prevailed, a sense that "we were all in this together, students and staff."[40]

Fostering mother-child ties continued even after women left the reformatory. Because children could not remain at the institution after age three, a staff member supervised child placement with kin or in foster families and facilitated visits by mothers; a public-health nurse followed the child's welfare after placement. For example, when Anne Gladding served as child placement officer, she sometimes drove incarcerated or paroled mothers to visit their children. Similarly, when a woman left on parole, the child placement officer monitored foster care until she could reunite the mother and child. Van Waters routinely allowed former students to return to the institution with their children for psychological counseling, even though state rules forbade the practice. According to the superintendent, released mothers had the lowest recidivism rate of any students. She herself adopted an openly maternal relationship with inmates and their children. As a reporter early noted, "Her attitude is that of a house mother in a girl's dormitory." To children of inmates, she became a kind of grandmother, or a fictive aunt. Over the years she sent birthday cards, and whenever a child born at the institution became a mother herself, the newborn received an engraved silver cup from "Aunt Miriam." For twenty-two years she held an annual "Baby Party" for mothers and children who had left the reformatory, like the reunions she had for El Retiro graduates in California. For Van Waters, maternalism provided an effective means for restoring women's self worth.[41]

Mother education worked particularly well at Framingham in part because those students with children at the institution were themselves young, in need of maternal affection, and highly motivated to behave well to earn early parole. Not all women sentenced to Framingham shared these characteristics, and the variety of clubs and classes served different functions for them. For one, they kept students occupied. "Anything to keep the girls from brooding and thinking themselves to death," Van Waters told a reporter. They also helped maintain order. In the case of the Merry Makers, Van Waters wrote privately, "the Negro girls can be the terror of Framingham or a very real asset in song, dancing, art and drama." At one point, when she detected "black-white manifestation of homosexuality," the superintendent took over the leadership of the Merry Makers from an intern, with the goal of "stressing their prestige in Dramatics, Spirituals, Orchestra." Tighter surveillance of the privileged club members allowed her to spot troublesome activities early. In addition, problem students could be drawn out through the cultural life of the institution. In 1937, for example, a young woman who had just been brought back to the reformatory after a daring escape from a third-story window pleaded to be allowed to attend an operetta that night; she was reportedly "pleased as punch" to be granted permission by a soft-hearted staff member. Just as Van Waters had once advised parents to channel youthful energy into appropriate forms of recreation, she now tried to avoid institutional conflict by providing legitimate, often educational, forms of entertainment.[42]

Although the very extent of classes and cultural productions suggested widespread participation, not every student embraced the program. As one woman wrote, "I don't intend to continue classes because I have no interest in them." Reformatory privileges, such as working outside maintaining the grounds, could actually intensify resentment over imprisonment. A seventeen-year old committed by her family as a stubborn child wrote home that "Every time I go outdoors I cry because its so nice and I have to stay 100 months in this Prison." Her letter included a glimpse into an alternative inmate culture that was less appreciative of Van Waters' reforms and more realistic about the meaning of imprisonment. The young woman reproduced the words inmates sang to the tune of "It's Only a Shanty in Old Shantytown": "Its only a *Prison* in old *Framingham.* They gave me *2 yrs.* and I don't give a darn. I've been here quite awhile and I learnt how to smile. But I wouldn't be here if I'd a file. I've only learnt *sorry* and *loneliness* here. But when I get out I'll drown them all in *beer*."[43]

Prisoners have always longed to be free, but at Framingham, the administration shared the goal of early release. As part of her effort to break down the wall between prison and community, Van Waters created opportunities to get students away from the reformatory. One reason she brought so many outside groups into Framingham was to facilitate the transition to release. Van Waters herself fostered initial, small steps outside. In her first year as superintendent she made headlines for taking members of the parole class downtown: "Women Prisoners Let Out to do Xmas Shopping," a Boston newspaper reported. In the spring, she and Geraldine Thompson took two students with them to attend the commencement ceremonies at the Shady Hill school in Cambridge, where Sarah Van Waters was a student. Staff members sometimes took students out to visit their children. The superintendent accompanied students to church services in Framingham, and she sent them to see their families for visits. In later years, staff occasionally escorted trusted students to movies or restaurants. Groups of Framingham inmates would dress up for the occasion of walking to a nearby ice cream parlor, with staff escorts, proud to have their own spending money in hand. Van Waters also allowed the reformatory chaplain to take the entire choir to Boston's Symphony Hall. Later, when state officials learned of these outings, they would be enraged at the superintendent's blatant disregard for official regulations.[44]

Most women at Framingham served indeterminate sentences, with the possibility of parole well before their release date. Those serving up to two years for drunkenness or lewdness could be paroled after eleven months; those serving up to five years for adultery could be paroled after fourteen months. Under the previous administration, however, parole had been granted sparingly. In 1928, members of the Harvard Crime Survey had speculated that no other correctional institution in the country recommended "such a small proportion of its population for release." Van Waters, in contrast, proposed parole as frequently as possible, far exceeding the willingness of the parole board to grant early release. As she recorded in her journal after one board meeting, "6 out of 45 get it. I take a beating and am wretched."[45]

Even when women did win parole, they remained subject to state supervision until their original release date. Strict rules prohibited communication between current inmates and those on parole, or among released inmates. But Van Waters believed that ongoing relationships among former students could be "constructive." Thus some students were allowed to receive letters from parolees. When women formed close friendships at Framingham, Van Waters felt that those ties could be helpful to their reentry, as "when two women have a common housekeeping arrangement, one going out to work, the other remaining to care for the home and children." Just as women's networks had been critical for her, the superintendent wanted to foster other female support systems. Women's unique status, she argued, necessitated flexibility in the parole process. Men had "a variety of positions open to them," but women parolees usually wound up as servants "in small towns and rural neighborhoods." Because "a woman's isolation is often greater," the superintendent told her staff, "she may need the support and encouragement of her friends who are making good." Once again, she broke the rules to further her vision of maternal justice.[46]

The conservative parole board often thwarted Van Waters' efforts for early release of Framingham students, but the superintendent had an alternative—indenture—that bypassed the official board. In the nineteenth century, indenture invariably meant live-in domestic service, a suitable means for retraining fallen women as respectable homemakers, as well as a source of cheap domestic labor for the neighboring community. In the early twentieth century, Superintendent Hodder had also used the system to send inmates out as hospital-ward maids, kitchen helpers, and laundresses.[47]

When Miriam Van Waters came to Framingham, she revitalized the indenture program, stretching its scope far beyond the letter of the law. With the approval of Commissioner of Corrections Arthur Lyman, she interpreted the statute as liberally as possible to allow daily excursions of Framingham students to local employers. In the 1930s, most students still worked as domestics. Each morning a bus picked up fifteen to twenty women and deposited them at local homes for daywork, returning them to the reformatory in the evening. Their weekly earnings of three to five dollars remained in a bank account until release. Some of these indentured students worked for Van Waters' colleagues and family members, including Felix Frankfurter, one of Miriam's sisters, her parents, and State Representative Allan Hodder, whose mother had once run the reformatory. During World War II, when military service drained the male labor force and American women were welcomed into war industries, Framingham students had the opportunity to take more skilled jobs. In addition to working in local industries, they made shoes at the reformatory, eventually joining a labor union that at first protested their work; they also held jobs in commercial laundries and a restaurant. After the war some women continued in these higher-paying positions.[48]

Van Waters knew that students might abuse their privileges while on indenture. Some brought contraband items, such as alcohol, back into the institution; others entreated their employers for favors or funds; a few spent their wages for extravagances once they were released. Women were sometimes returned from indenture for unsatisfactory work, staying out late at night, or stealing. Yet the superintendent felt that the advantages of approximating wage-earning life outweighed the risks. In 1939 she won the first round in an ongoing, sometimes vicious, battle against legislators and parole board members who wanted to abolish daywork. Commissioner Lyman, who officially authorized each indenture, helped Van Waters argue for the benefits of the system. He released a survey that showed that in 97 percent of the 120 indentures held between 1932 and 1935, the women had become self-supporting. Eighty percent of the employers who answered his questionnaire considered the inmates "good workers." Although she prevailed in the short run, repeated attacks on indenture haunted her administration for years.[49]

In addition to circumventing the parole board, indenture also provided a means to pay women for their work within the reformatory. Students who labored in the kitchen, laundry, farm, or hospital did not receive wages. But when Van Waters "hired" indentured students as live-in domestics in the superintendent's house, they did get paid, usually through the Thompson Fund. In the 1940s, for example, Van Waters indentured a student to serve as a nurse for the aging Maud Van Waters. Another student earned fifty dollars a month, a typical staff salary, working as a bookkeeper at the institution. Other students assumed the duties of officers through indenture; after release some of them "graduated" to internships that led to paid staff positions. Van Waters championed this unusual practice of hiring former inmates as officers because, as she often explained, only former inmates fully understood the needs of inmates. She was greatly impressed by the philosophy of Alcoholics Anonymous, which originated in the 1930s, and she drew upon its emphasis on self-treatment to justify the hiring of inmates. AA members, Van Waters wrote, "have this sense of belonging together, fighting a common enemy," not unlike members of a minority group. As she frequently repeated, "only delinquents can solve the problem of delinquents."[50]

One particular student illustrated for Van Waters how indenture and internship could circumvent the injustices that surrounded women's imprisonment. The inmate, Dr. Caroline Cook, had a long criminal record, beginning with her first conviction in 1911, at age forty-five, for performing abortions. Returned to the reformatory in 1928, after her seventh arrest, the sixty-two-year-old physician began to serve an eight-year sentence. When Van Waters arrived four years later, Dr. Cook was eligible for parole, but she had no job or home to return to, and she struggled with a drinking problem. In 1933, Van Waters sent the doctor to Syracuse, New York, on indenture to nurse her father, Reverend Van Waters, during a serious illness. "I am asking you to do service of a lonely nature for my dearest ones," the superintendent wrote to Dr. Cook, enclosing a check for fifteen dollars and an apology that she could not pay more. After this indenture, Cook returned to Framingham, where she remained for the rest of her life. Van Waters became "her Mother confessor." In 1939, the superintendent approved a temporary release so that Cook could spend a week at the New York World's Fair. In 1942, Van Waters appointed the eighty-year-old doctor as an intern, working in the reformatory office, in return for her room and board. In this case, Framingham served as an old-age home, providing, in Van Waters' words, a "happy ending" to this inmate's story.[51]

The case of Dr. Cook suggests a curious circularity within the superintendent's effort to break down the wall between prison and community. Although for the most part, she used indenture and internships to release women from Framingham, in some cases her policies actually prolonged women's dependence on the institution. Occasionally Van Waters detected within a student either the potential for service, or the need for continued group support, or a combination of the two. She then cultivated that student as a potential staff member, encouraging her to go on to help others in the process of recovery. In the 1940s, for example, Van Waters employed a former larcenist, then on parole, as the choir director at Framingham. Another inmate, indentured as a paid bookkeeper, lived and ate at the Staff Home, made visits to her family, and served as secretary of the Framingham chapter of Alcoholics Anonymous. One former student first held a series of jobs at other state institutions, but when she faltered in her resistance to drugs, she returned to Framingham to work. Not all succeeded in refraining from drink or drugs while on duty, and in one case a student paroled to the superintendent's house disappeared along with a diamond hat pin. "The blows fell fast," Van Waters wrote in her journal, even though the hat pin was restored.[52]

Former student Alice May recalled in detail how Van Waters recruited her onto the staff. In the 1930s, while still in her teens, May had served her first term at Framingham. Almost twenty years later she returned on a two-year sentence, probably for drunkenness. Just before she became eligible for parole, Van Waters called May into her office to ask her to complete her sentence rather than take early release. A devoted student, May accepted without question. As she explained to her supervisor back in the kitchen, "I don't mind, in fact, I like it here, because you are so kind, you are so good, and everybody has been wonderful to me, but I just can't understand Dr. Van Waters telling me that I should stay here. It isn't like her." A few months later, when May's sentence expired, Van Waters again called her to the superintendent's office. "What does she want with me this time?" May recalled thinking, "she can't keep me any longer." Van Waters asked May if she had been hurt about being held back from parole. "Well, I was hurt, in the beginning, but I got over that, and I felt at home, and I felt people around me that I loved and they loved me." Then Van Waters revealed her motive. As May recalled the conversation, "Doctor" explained

> "Well I'm glad you stayed back because what I want for you is you're to be an officer." And I said, "An officer?" and she said "Yes, I want you to work here." I said, "I don't know if I'd want that." And she said, "Oh well, you will, you will, everybody loves you and there is no reason for it." . . . And, so that was that, I stayed with Doctor worked with her, until she retired.[53]

Only a few women chose to remain voluntarily at Framingham after release, but their willingness to do so suggests a more widespread phenomenon—the profound attraction that Miriam Van Waters held for her students. The superintendent's charismatic personality appealed in a special, almost spiritual, way to these women who had so often been considered, and considered themselves, lost souls. To Van Waters, no student had strayed beyond the reach of what she called "Christian penology." Her ability to reach deeply into the hearts of her students, implant a germ of self-worth, and cultivate a devoted following, represented her most important and unique contribution. In an era of professionalized social work and welfare bureaucratization, her religious outreach sustained the historical link between Protestant spirituality and progressive reform. Van Waters' explicitly spiritual approach, however, transcended denominational boundaries, influencing the majority of Catholic inmates as deeply as the Protestant and Jewish minorities. Although a Catholic priest visited daily and a Lutheran minister held weekly services and regular counseling sessions, Superintendent Van Waters provided the core of Framingham's spiritual life. One local minister claimed that Framingham was the headquarters of a new religion, where everyone worshiped Miriam Van Waters. Staff chaplain William

Wiltenburg insisted in response that they worshiped "another person-ality named Jesus," but he admitted that there were "plenty of people" who got them mixed up.[54]

One simple religious precept, derived from the Protestant Social Gospel of her youth, provided the foundation for Van Waters' extraordi-nary spiritual appeal: Every child is a child of God. By convincing Fram-ingham's alcoholics, unwed mothers, forgers, and murderers—most of whose families had given up on them—that they were indeed the chil-dren of God earned Miriam Van Waters the lasting gratitude of her stu-dents. As one woman explained, "she changed my whole life. Well, I thought it was the end of the world when I went there. And it was really just the beginning for me. . . . [S]he would say no one was bad, really bad, there was good in everyone. That was one thing she always hammered down." As Margaret van Wagenen described Van Waters' ap-proach, "there was this universal esteem and this ability to pick out that thing that would be meaningful to this particular person that would make her feel important." Van Wagenen also recalled how the superintendent's behavior in staff meetings reiterated the message of unconditional love. While discussing a treatment plan Van Waters would say, "Well the important thing is that Mary is a child of God.'" If she repeated that phrase several times, however, "you could make up your mind that Mary was a hellion. You just knew." Even when her work sorely tested Van Waters' revitalized religious faith, she preached her father's creed that "You never give up on a person. You just never give up; you just keep on and on and on." What theologians have since labeled a "radical love ethic" laid the foundation for Miriam Van Waters' exceptional approach to penology, one that incorporated a strong dose of maternalism: "I mother this cold girl—kiss her resistant forehead— melt her into smiles: send her to Hodder."[55]

Miriam Van Waters' theory of redemption involved more than sim-ple faith in the innate humanity of all sinners. To this belief she added insights from her training in modern psychology, building a synthetic approach to inmate recovery that defied the professional trend toward the purely clinical.[56] In addition to convincing students that they were lovable in the eyes of God and the superintendent, she preached a gos-pel of self-redemption that incorporated both contemporary psychi-atric social work and popular self-help credos. As in Los Angles, Van Waters emphasized self-government and self-control. In assemblies, her classes, and personal conversations with students, she also stressed re-sponsibility for one's past and the importance of psychological insight.

In her career, as in her personal life, religion increasingly served a therapeutic function.

That many inmates internalized Van Waters' message is evident in both their letters and the essays many wrote entitled "I Am Here Because." As one student explained her plight, "I cannot blame my heredity, environment was always good but rather unsettled and no one who cared for me understood the psychology of childhood well enough to control my imagination." At Framingham, however, "self analysis, education, good reading, the study of psychology and the interest of a very wise superintendent" taught her that "it is because of a false sense of values that I am here." She also learned that society had a different attitude "toward the woman who has gone wrong. The man gets the better chance." Another student reiterated the importance of gender consciousness, maternalism, and Miriam Van Waters:

> I know that a man in the same set of circumstances in which
> I am placed would be accepted by society again where I
> would not be, I shall go out into the community doing the
> best I possibly can for my children's sake as well as my own;
> also because my Superintendent has that much confidence in
> me to expect me to.[57]

The effect of Van Waters' faith in students recurred in letters, notes, essays, poems, and eventually in public testimony to the personal power of the superintendent to heal troubled women. "Remember, dear students, when troubled by doubt, Go to Dr. Van Waters to work your way out," an inmate verse began. One older inmate wrote in pebbles on the lawn outside the reformatory "Dr. VW is our saver" [*sic*], a sentiment many shared.[58]

As superintendent, Miriam Van Waters kept her door open to women who needed to talk or complain; even when she detected deceit or self-justification, she maintained her authentic concern for their welfare. When students left the reformatory, she continued to correspond with them, responding to pleas for help by sending references, contacting potential employers, and not infrequently sending small sums of money from her own pocket to help tide them over during hard times. She also drew upon philanthropic accounts, such as the Thompson Fund, to help pay medical bills for former students. "How can you retain faith in one who has lost all in herself?" wrote one former inmate who was struggling to stay off narcotics. Van Waters sent comfort, cash, and a staff member, Anne Gladding, to visit the recovering addict. "I can't really tell you about the light in their eyes when they talk about you," Gladding reported back, "but I guess you have seen it." Another backslider called from Boston while she was drunk to seek the superintendent's help; she had held onto the memory of a conversation with Van Waters about the "Great Companion" and now reached out for a reminder that she was not alone.[59]

Miriam Van Waters provided both a spiritual and a maternal lifeline for students and former students. "Dearest Mom," wrote a woman who was about to leave the reformatory after having "adopted" the superintendent as a surrogate mother. She thanked Van Waters and the staff for "giving me a chance to find my footing and a goal for me to achieve and above all faith in myself, that's what I needed most of all." In Van Waters she had found "a friend, adviser, and a mother" to replace the real mother she hardly knew. Another thank-you letter came from the father of a student whom the superintendent had inspired to lead a constructive life of service to others. Another devoted former inmate became a friendly visitor at Framingham after her own release. "I owe my happiness to my stay in Framingham," she wrote gratefully. Other students dreamed of entering the field of social work, becoming true disciples to Van Waters. "Doctor," one wrote, "I can't very well put into words what knowing you has meant but the fact that I want to go into Social Science in Penology may say it for me."[60]

Not all Framingham students or staff members became loyal disciples. A few dissatisfied employees held grudges against Van Waters for her criticisms of their work, her familiarity with students, or her lenience toward criminals.[61] More frequently, inmates defied her authority, and the handful of runaways especially troubled her. Yet few students entirely escaped Van Waters' personal appeal. Of the recalcitrants, Alice May recalled, "I think that most of them, they respected her, all of them and there were some of them that loved her, I think, although they didn't always show that they did." When no one else could quiet an "unruly" student, "as soon as Doctor talked to that person, everything was all right." Even when inmates became violent, "Doctor would come over, and all she had to do was walk into their corridor, and everything was quiet. Not a sound." The secret, May concluded, was "that most people use the strong arm method, and she used kindness and love."[62]

In 1932, when Miriam Van Waters was appointed superintendent at Framingham, a reporter had asked Jack Black, a former convict turned journalist, how long it would take to make a regular warden out of the liberal Van Waters. "Never," Black had answered, "she will never fall." Over the decades, Superintendent Van Waters resisted the tendency of most prison administrators to resort to force, maintain order at any cost, or placate conservative political forces on the outside. Her one concession was to accept a few patronage appointees in order to keep local political bosses from joining forces with the opponents of indenture. Despite periodic attacks on her authority and on daywork, Van Waters usually kept her critics at bay as she built extensive community support and pursued her unique, maternal brand of Christian penology at Framingham. "Framingham shall be more durable than El Retiro, that first born child, that bright flame — dead," she vowed in 1936. To a remarkable extent she succeeded in building the Framingham Symphony, a spiritually grounded social welfare institution ministering to women who had no other safety net.[63]

Mother of Us All

During her twenty-five years at Framingham, Miriam Van Waters presided over two interconnected households. She supervised over three hundred students and staff members at the reformatory, while in the three-story, red-brick superintendent's house, connected by covered walkway to the prison, she constructed an unusual family circle. Along with Miriam, Sarah, and Bode, the house lodged several staff members, including Anne Gladding, Hilda Hinkley, and Peg O'Keefe, as well as reformatory students who lived on the third floor and worked in the kitchen and the conservatory. Sarah's Irish setter, Bulba, Miriam's beloved Persian cat, Emperor Jones, and assorted kittens prowled the grounds. In 1933, when Van Waters hired her sister-in-law to run the nursery, Ralph and Bertha Green Van Waters joined the household, as did Maud Van Waters after the death of her husband the following year. In addition, guests regularly stayed at the superintendent's house. On her frequent visits, Geraldine Thompson occupied the Blue Room, adjacent to Miriam's second-floor chamber. Interns, old friends, and assorted nieces and nephews often shared the third-floor sleeping porch that overlooked a sprawling front lawn. At frequent dinner parties, luncheons, receptions, and in daily interactions, Miriam Van Waters recreated the bustling spirit of her father's rectory.

The superintendent's house had a lived-in quality about it, comfortable and welcoming, but, as one frequent visitor recalled, "it would never have made House Beautiful." Van Waters appreciated fine silver and good food properly served, but she never fussed about decorating. Like other depression-era, middle-class dwellings, the furnishings ran to shabby at times. Nonetheless, it provided the comforts of home to Miriam and a welcome haven for visitors. Her description on returning from a trip one spring hinted at the simple pleasures she found there: "A lovely homecoming: white lilacs, a white birch log fire—Bode—Sarah—Ralph—Bert well and happy. The copper beech tree a flame of fire against the vivid green."[1]

To the members of her household, Miriam Van Waters appeared to be a woman leader of extraordinary accomplishment and personal equanimity. She rose before dawn, then started her day with exercises, a cold bath, and a vigorous horseback ride, accompanied either by Bode, Anne Gladding, or Geraldine Thompson. During the day she directed staff conferences; managed visiting politicians and parole board members; heard student complaints; eased institutional tensions; and taught classes. Outside her job, she raised a daughter; entertained company; gave frequent public talks at conferences and to community groups; served on state and national commissions; and appeared regularly at church, the symphony, and school events at Shady Hill.[2]

The quick-wittedness that characterized Van Waters' correspondence no doubt impressed those with whom she worked and lived. So did her noble demeanor—her white hair pulled back accentuating "friendly, penetrating eyes." As a visitor later described her, walking along prison halls wearing her blue Chinese silk jacket, she was "the exact opposite of one's mental picture of a jail superintendent, warm, sympathetic, beautiful, and yet at the same time she was strong, wise, and clearly in authority." Staff members marveled at all Van Waters accomplished, and with what aplomb. Doctor never seemed hurried, one woman recalled, and she always projected an aura of peacefulness, even though she was in constant motion.[3]

Behind this grand persona, however, another Miriam Van Waters dwelled. Internally, the beloved superintendent battled self-doubt and "private depression," while she longed for unconditional love. "I have a sense of lonliness [*sic*], a wicked sense of being hurt," she chided herself. "My honest desire for death—as sleep," she wrote in 1934, "my knowledge that I have every qualification for 'sturdy living,' facing *any* emergency, enduring my pain but longing to be assured—I am loved— once—as I am—not through—my masks—[.]" In their long-distance relationship, Geraldine Thompson frequently provided this assurance, but in her solitary moments, Miriam turned to her journal, and increasingly to prayer, to battle inner demons.[4]

Like other confessional diarists, Van Waters used her journal to evaluate her progress toward achieving her ideal self. "I seek to measure my shortcomings," she wrote in a typical entry; "I lived a disciplined day," she recorded in momentary triumph. "My own life is a struggle against fatigue and confused purposes," she confided. These purposes included her longings "to 'create' beauty and to affirm truth in the significant drama of human lives" and "to administer a small part of the world—out of chaos—into order." Although her "'pilgrimage' commenced with full abundant energies," she felt that she had not made good use of them. "I still see the mountain ranges where the High

Gods may be found, I feel kinship with them. I know I can achieve, yet I do not live one day under the discipline to achieve: 'next day' I say." Christian images and literary references recurred in the journal, which chronicled an almost messianic quest:

> Joy: Love: Beauty: I will ask for as the Prayer book does in the prayer for the confirmation class. a ghostly strength—a holy fear. I will seize this day, these 13 last days of May, these 7 last months of 1936, this next decade, these next 11 years before 60: I will call for my 7 League boots, my arrows of desire, my Chariot of Fire: in these dark Satanic mills, I will build the New Jerusalem.[5]

In part, this sense of spiritual embattlement reflected the daily reality of running Framingham. However confident, composed, and gracious she appeared to students and staff, Van Waters lived with constant reminders of the impossibility of creating a kingdom of God on earth. She could never fully transform either her students' lives or the social system that had brought them to her. In nightmares she imagined "evil men" taking over her pulpit, or inmates attacking her for decisions she had made. Typically, she internalized responsibility, blaming her own lack of discipline for most problems, as if renewed personal commitment would give her the power of universal healing. In one of the nightmares she detailed, for example, Miriam, Sarah, and Anne had to eject a threatening intruder from the rectory of her childhood—a recurrent code for Framingham—while an army of unemployed men battled outside their window. In the middle of the dream Van Waters noticed that "A long screw loosed in the wood showed the lock useless. I must get it repaired. I had a sense of inefficiency, helplessness and frustration." Her failures to maintain the institution, she implied, had made them vulnerable to attack. In waking life, too, she tried to ward off minor threats by vigilant control. In an entry for Labor Day, 1933, she wrote:

> The immediate task is to plan this day—from the *end* to the beginning—to avoid senseless repetition, and to capture— channels for vital conduct. . . . *Stability* and *routine* are the prerequisites of civilization—but each day must have novelty, progress toward a more exclusive order, and more spontaneity.[6]

The entries about self-discipline often coincided with notes for a book she planned to call "Vital Conduct," a phrase that referred to the significance to be found in the activities of everyday life. Vital conduct could mean producing a novel, a child, or a career, or it could simply mean completing one task with a sense of its integral place in a larger universe. Given her administrative duties, however, Van Waters rarely had the time for sustained intellectual work; she never published her Harvard Crime Survey report, nor did she complete "Vital Conduct." She did use the concept, though, as a standard to measure both her self-discipline and the worth of her daily toils. Thus she noted in her journal: "V.C.—I breakfasted alone: the management of *sleep* and *hunger* is a test." Her every act contributed to making each day "not mechanical . . . not clouded or depressed—but radiant with meaning." At the end of one day she wrote, "I lighted my own fire at 6:30," commenting,

> In writing this down I know I am a prisoner of Habit. I think there are ideas imprisoned in myself who could if the chains were loosened spring out and use their supple muscles to the service of the concepts which serve Essence. But administrator that I am or have become I seem to want to catch meaning out of the drift of daily life and so I enumerate and record. Like other prisoners I look forward to the Date of my Parole but do not seize the freedom I possess, in my own being. My prisoners do better than I do.[7]

Van Waters sought meaning not only in events but also in her dreams, which she sometimes interpreted. Often she relived scenes from her childhood, usually set at St. David's rectory or modeled on romantic tales she had read as a youth. Her father's death may have unleashed memories of those years, as did raising her own adolescent daughter and having her mother close at hand. Reading Proust's novels further stimulated her associative recollections. Even in this self-reflective writing, however, she encoded many of her personal outpourings under layers of camouflage, carefully preserving elements of the social mask she so consciously wore in public. "If this phrasing is obscure, thank God for symbols," she once wrote, hinting at the deeper significance of events she alluded to in the journal. Someday, she suspected, her daughter or one of her nephews might read these thoughts; she may have hoped that historians would mine it for insight into her life.[8] To do so, however, they would have to read between lines and beneath symbols.

Despite the intentional silences, Miriam Van Waters left an unusually revealing record of her inner life. She agonized over how to integrate her mother into Framingham, how to support her brother Ralph in the face of his continuing unemployment, how to balance love and discipline in raising Sarah. Taken together, the personal agony she experienced in these relationships contrasted starkly with the satisfaction she derived from her public maternalism. In the reformatory chapel, standing high above the assembled students, Van Waters convincingly preached her sermon of unconditional love, for there she remained at a safe personal distance from her troubled charges. For close family members, who became extensions of her own worth, unconditional love was tempered by a driving need to rescue, improve, and transform. Their weaknesses became a sign of her own failure, a cross that both she and her dependents had to bear.

In her family, Miriam Van Waters had always maintained the persona of enthusiastic, invincible crusader. Like her closest friends, her parents recognized the tensions beneath the surface. Reverend Van Waters repeatedly urged her to take vacations, rest, and "Practice moderation—a little." Even though she seemed "never troubled with depression of spirit," he warned that there was "a straining point—a breaking point—of which you should beware." Similarly, when Maud Van Waters thanked her daughter for her attentions, she gently chided as well: "You are most generous, darling, but against your own good."[9]

Despite their warnings, Miriam Van Waters' sense of familial responsibility deepened, especially after her father's death from pneumonia in 1934. Throughout that year, and long afterward, she tried to come to terms with the loss, in large part by pledging to emulate his character and enact his philosophy of unconditional Christian love. When she reiterated her vows to "be able to do 'my Father's will,'" Van Waters clearly referred to her earthly, as well as heavenly, creator. She invoked Reverend Van Waters' spirit as she ministered to students. "He who was so intrepid on the platform and so inspired in his pulpit—was at my side," she wrote after the Thanksgiving assembly that year. She purposefully held on to her "sense of loss," wanting "each old memory of him to deepen the present: and each new vision to give me more of his spirit."[10] In the years after his death, religion became increasingly important to her as a source of both personal solace and professional authority. In a later historical era, Van Waters might well have followed her father's vocation and become an Episcopal priest rather than a prison warden; among the women at Framingham, she informally assumed her father's spiritual role.

In her family life, as well, she shouldered her father's responsibilities after his death. "As I travel further into this adventure of being a sort of substitute for 'head of the house,'" she wrote, "I penetrate some of the secrets of Father's robust character." After his funeral, Miriam brought her mother back to Framingham to stay with her. For the next fifteen years, the superintendent's house served as Maud Van Waters' home and the base from which she made frequent visits to her other children's households. Miriam went to great pains to integrate her mother into both of her Framingham worlds. Maud became a much loved volunteer at the reformatory. She taught a class on the lives of famous women, took students on field trips to historic sites, and inspired the Maud Ophelia Club for older inmates. Miriam accompanied her mother to church on Sundays and regularly took her to the Boston Symphony. Before visits to see the families of Ruth Van Waters Burton, Beckie Van Waters Bartholomew, or George Van Waters, Miriam made sure that her mother had the best train reservations and a fresh orchid corsage for the trip. She remembered to send flowers on what would have been Maud's fiftieth wedding anniversary.[11]

Miriam claimed that she felt a "sense of joyousness rather than obligation" in her relationship with her mother. In a way, Maud's homecoming to Framingham fulfilled a childhood fantasy and lifelong desire for mother-daughter reunion. When Maud left on trips, Miriam continued to write to "precious Mumsie," sharing detailed accounts of her days. "Come back soon to your *Home* which needs you to give it a soul and a spirit of love and tenderness and aspiration for a better life," she wrote after one departure. Her long idealized mother offered Miriam a standard of "Christian, beautiful living . . . an inspiration and a saint." In a conscious effort to approximate her childhood home, Miriam made Maud a spiritual companion in her Framingham ministry.[12]

For all of her efforts to recreate fond childhood memories, Miriam felt conflicted over her family roles. She wondered privately whether she was doing enough to make Maud happy, and whether Framingham was too barren and hard for her mother. She also had nightmares that revealed some troubling family images. One night, for example, she had "a confused dream" in which she rescued Sarah and a niece from a rat by taking them to her "childhood Portland Rectory Room: Mother's bed." As she slept crowded next to Sarah, she recorded, "a coated shabby figure female comes in with stupid stealthy step, back bowed." Here the dream ended, because Empie the cat stirred Miriam awake.

The female figure who so resembled the wicked stepmothers and witches of fairy tales seemed the precise antithesis of the saintly Maud Van Waters. Yet this dark underside of her maternal imagery may have felt threatening to Miriam, who had in a sense usurped her mother's place, in her bed and as a maternal figure herself.

More typical of her nightmares were scenarios of child saving in which Miriam battled mobs of lower-class men. In one, Maud made a significant cameo appearance. In this "dreadful" dream Miriam and her mother were "imprisoned in a vast warehouse in the slums." They had gone to an evangelical church where costumed worshipers listened to "a curious evil speaker" and to "a dreadful choir of women, and another of small boys." They could not escape because at every "entrance there was a new figure, Negroes, longshoremen, truck drivers, and the keepers took us in charge." In the face of these symbols of the underclass, Miriam managed to rescue one child—as she had Sarah—but she soon faced "a new iron barred prison." Once again in dreams Miriam inverted a positive image from childhood—in this case, the church—into an evil world, peopled by threatening working-class men and the type of women and children she had pledged her life to redeem. Maud dropped from sight as Miriam attempted to save one child and found herself, as in life, hopelessly imprisoned.[13]

Occasionally, Van Waters' emotional underside broke through in daily life. Once, for example, she confessed sarcastically that she had committed "the unforgivable sin against the Holy Ghost"—she had wounded her mother. The episode is suggestive of Miriam's insistence on caring for others and her resistance to acknowledging, in waking life, her deep vulnerabilities. Dismayed because Geraldine Thompson had canceled a visit, Van Waters must have showed external signs of distress. Her mother asked with anxiety "Have you a headache?"—hoping, Miriam believed, for "a caressing reassuring response." Rather than reply, "why no Darling—I do feel very well but I am thinking or busy," she flared out, "Why do you ask that?: I am never ill. I *never* have a headache: have I utterly failed that *you ask* that." As a commentary on her behavior, she wrote self-deprecatingly of her "impossible: useless: cruel: coarse: indifferent sins: my defect is—I want to be let alone."

Her desire to be alone—not to be cared for, indeed, not to have her deepest feelings known—is quite meaningful. Whenever Maud tried to ease her daughter's burdens, Miriam refused. Long ago she had relinquished that childlike desire in favor of self-sufficiency. As Miriam recognized once when "Saint Anne" Gladding tried to nurture her, "because of the 'early pattern'—I turn on a protest." Not long after the headache incident, for example, Maud wrote gratefully to Miriam that "my hope in living, is to be some help to you." A few years later, when Maud invited her daughter to unburden herself, Miriam insisted that she had no cares to unburden. In fact, she did have headaches, cares, and burdens, but she continued to suppress her needs, maintaining the mask of self-sufficient authority.[14]

In one action, however, Maud Van Waters succeeded in providing lasting material comfort for Miriam. In 1940 she purchased a plot of wooded land just down the road from the reformatory, which she bequeathed to her daughter. There Miriam established a log cabin retreat that she called Hill Top. The lodge became her country refuge, a special room in her "house of life." She and Geraldine often spent their weekends in privacy at Hill Top. At other times, Miriam invited privileged students and personal friends to join her there. Guests included dozens of members of the student Rangers Club; favorite interns and staff members, such as Anne Gladding; and Maud, Ralph, and other visiting family members. At Hill Top she recreated the family camp she had so loved at Cannon Beach, Oregon, presiding over an extended family circle reminiscent not only of the rectory but also of the Colony and Stone House. With family and friends gathered around, she cooked dinners, after which Ralph played the banjo, and she led guests in campfire songs—whether or not they wanted to sing, one staff member recalled.[15]

Miriam also found personal solace in the fields and woods surrounding Hill Top. When tensions mounted at the reformatory or in the family, she would steal away in the early mornings or at the end of the day and toil on the land. Hours of physical labor—clearing poison ivy, cutting wood, pruning trees—restored her spirits. "I have a glorious time cutting wood from the Hurricane Pine," she wrote during a week of worry about her mother and her daughter. "Hill Top 6 A.M. I feel refreshed. Kind of shock treatment—that tapped Vital Energies," her journal read. Alone, in nature, and in command, she felt physically, even spiritually, fulfilled. Returning to the tensions of her job, she invoked the mood. As she wrote of a parole board meeting, "I droop and grow tense. Then God speaks—and I see the forest vistas of Hill Top, rejoice in my blessings—and . . . putting on the armor of a quiet mind I achieve an atmosphere of Understanding which changes the whole climate of the room."[16]

In addition to bringing her mother to Framingham, Miriam continued to support her youngest brother, Ralph. He and Bert had been living in

Chicago, where she worked as a nurse and he looked for a job. In 1933, Miriam invited Bert to work at Framingham, explaining to the family that she expected the couple would live with her only "while they are getting started."[17] Her father's death the following year intensified her sense of responsibility for her brother. She had already introduced him to Francis Sayre, George Kirchwey, and Felix Frankfurter in the hope that they could "help Ralph's future." When none of her contacts brought results, she wrote to Ralph's academic adviser at Chicago, explaining that her father's death had made her "more than ever mindful that my responsibility is not over." Should she urge him to return to Chicago? Miriam asked. What requirements would he have to fulfill to complete his degree? Or should she leave him to his own devices? "I have a strong feeling," she confessed, "that he is on a thin dividing line between great success (I do not mean money) and something considerably less."[18]

Over the next six years Miriam and Ralph maintained the fantasy that he was working toward his Ph.D. She set up a study and "lab" for him in her home and convinced herself that he was conducting important research for Framingham. "We shouldn't hurry Ralph," she explained to her family. "Once life gets going for Ralph he will write" and "once Ralph gets going. . .," she wrote expectantly. Occasionally Miriam invented research projects for him, working behind the scenes to fund his labors. In 1938, for example, she asked her mother to write a check for $150, which she would claim came from an anonymous donor, to hire Ralph to conduct psychological tests on students. The same year Geraldine Thompson asked him to conduct a survey of social welfare in Massachusetts; he declined, explaining that others were more qualified to do the job.[19]

Ralph Van Waters' refusal to accept what looked too blatantly like charity stemmed from his strong sense of pride. He preferred to find his own means of support, and he professed that his principles limited his opportunities. As he told Miriam a few months after their father's death, "I am an idealist, damn it I have standards (I had them always even when I was a little boy) which will not let me do certain things." He would not, for example, become a highly paid corporate personnel director, but, he continued, "I could dig a ditch at .25/hr if I had to." Miriam never mentioned his self-sufficiency to others, but during the depression Ralph joined the carpenters' union and worked on construction sites outside Boston. "Those people didn't know who I was, that was o.k.," he recalled. "I really had a good job." Ralph also made himself useful at Framingham. He chauffeured Miriam, Sarah, and his mother to appointments, and he escorted his sister to meetings and dinners. He loved to work with his hands, and at the reformatory and in the superintendent's house he repaired furniture and helped out with plumbing and painting. He also built a cabin in Maine and eventually, in the 1950s, constructed a house for his family on land adjacent to Hill Top.[20]

Maintaining his dream of finding a professional career, until 1941 Ralph still contemplated finishing his doctorate. Sometimes he chafed under the strain of living off his sister's kindness. When he signed a birthday gift to Miriam "from your poor relations," he reminded them both of the terms of his residency at Framingham. Once again he made her heart ache. To ease her own conscience, Miriam continued to seek work for him. She asked him to address the student assembly, hired him to tutor their nephew, encouraged him to write a book on scientific methodology, and promoted his fleeting plan to become a short-story writer, a goal she had once had for herself. Recreating the role she played during his adolescence, Miriam assumed responsibility for enforcing industrious work habits. One morning, after she woke him at 7:30, she commented that he looked "only fairly well" and continued, as if in explanation: "I am not sufficiently buoyant and disciplined. I give neither enough stimulus steadiness, nor structure. I begin practicing my vows today. His study is well cleaned. His awnings up in his bed room." In another entry she asked herself "What can I do to aid Ralph's quest of truth?"[21]

Miriam's material, spiritual, and emotional resources were at Ralph's disposal, and yet she felt characteristically inadequate, faulting herself for not expressing fully her love for her brother. A conversation she analyzed in her journal illustrated the pattern. "You are out of tobacco, Ralph," she observed. "No—but this is no good," he replied. Had her gift of tobacco been good enough? If so, she would get him some more. "No—don't—why should you?" Ralph replied. Miriam reflected to herself:

> Why indeed. I love you. I would "give my body to be burned
> for you"—I would—I do—even live for you—by far the
> harder task—as St. Peter learned. Why can't I tell Ralph this
> and live it so he understands: I think he really does: I think
> he knows . . . Why is love hard to communicate—when hun-
> ger, ambition, fear, anger—are all so easily expressed?[22]

In fact, Miriam had difficulty expressing many of these emotions, especially anger, which she might have harbored toward Ralph, deservedly or not, for his prolonged reliance upon her. Occasionally her less sanguine emotions would surface in dreams, though usually they were projected upon the figures of angry, unemployed men, like those who lurked threateningly on the American social landscape during the depression. Ralph, of course, was an unemployed man, and he may have been encoded into these fantasies. In her waking life, however, in place of anger Miriam tended to express guilt, often followed by feelings of inadequacy. Thus, when her sister-in-law suffered a severe depression, Miriam assumed blame because she had counseled them to marry and brought them to Framingham, then let things slide, procrastinated, or withdrew to her room in fatigue. After Bert's "miraculous recovery" and Ralph's return to the family circle, "seemingly with an enjoyment of life," Miriam recommitted herself to making their lives more comfortable and to finding a job for him.[23]

Aside from illustrating Miriam's pervasive sense of responsibility, what is most intriguing about her attachment to her brother was the way she began to idealize him as a gifted philosopher and her intellectual conscience. Soon after his arrival at Framingham, she began to formulate this image. "He was made for a philosopher's life," she told her parents. In a journal entry, in which she contemplated the "laws" that allowed the spirit to survive physical pain, she wrote: "Spinoza sets them forth, and Ralph lives them. Ralph must be set free to make discoveries." In the process, her brother would enrich Miriam's life. "Ralph is a symphony in himself—he is gathering his forces—: but he is in my symphony too," she insisted.[24]

During the summer of 1935, Miriam began to refer to Ralph in her journals as "her Abelard." The allusion tells much about her own self-perception, as well as her idealization of him. She had recently read George Moore's fictionalized account *Heloise and Abelard,* and in her dreams and fantasies she became Heloise, the twelfth-century nun, while her brother Ralph stood for the beloved priest-teacher. Framingham was like the convent; Miriam's work there rested on faith, but she longed to be a philosopher as well as an administrator. "Forever the soul seeks Abelard," she wrote, "he who will give clear reasons to her faith and will awaken her senses to unappeasable hunger." The only hunger she acknowledged was for a philosophical meaning for her daily life at Framingham; she never alluded to the lust that plagued her medieval predecessors nor associated Ralph with other than intellectual passion.[25]

Although the historical allegory did not match precisely their relationship, it allowed Miriam to elevate her brother to the role of resident intellectual. "How full and rich and mature is my relationship with my philosopher, my scientific and literary conscience, my joy and delight—my Abelard—Ralph," Miriam wrote. Soon she was deferring to his superior ideas, writing that "I must ask my Abelard" about matters of philosophy. He became "the Voice of my Ancestors: Ralph brings me to Reality. Ralph is also the Binder—for my loose and random—'works.'" She cheered when "Today my Beloved Abelard is well," and his birthday became "a holy day" for her.[26]

To suggest that Van Waters created an idealized philosophical genius to justify her support for Ralph does not diminish the definite contributions he made to his sister's life. Ralph did provide Miriam with important intellectual companionship and sometimes a useful foil. Together they read the fiction of Proust and Joyce and the philosophy of George Herbert Mead. During long walks they talked about faith, reason, and "the anatomy of despair." Ralph offered advice on how to handle students, family members, and politicians, injecting practicality and compromise. "Better shake his hand, Doctor," he wrote to her of one judge, "because you can't tell when you'll need a bullet for your little cannon."[27]

Although he supported his sister's reform agenda, Ralph Van Waters also took issue with her ideas. He criticized church dogmatism and argued for a reasoned, scientific worldview. Challenging her liberalism, he professed a more radical political analysis of the social problems that disturbed them both. "Ralph hates the rich and predatory," Miriam noted, citing especially both Republican and Episcopal aristocracies. He blamed America's capitalists for the depression, convincing even the wealthy Geraldine Thompson that the country's natural resources had been "wasted by the ruthlessly greedy." For Sarah Van Waters, her uncle's criticisms of the rich provided perspective on the reformist efforts of her mother and Mrs. Thompson.[28]

Quite apart from their lofty conversations about ideas, Ralph provided Miriam with more proletarian escapes from her daily tasks. They went camping together, cooked on an open fire, and walked through the woods; he played his banjo and entertained the family; Bert and Ralph joined a bowling league and invited an unresponsive Miriam to join them; at least once they managed to take her to a baseball game; and for years the family played bridge almost nightly. Finally, they shared a common memory of their parents. Despite the chronological gap between their births, each of them had been raised by George and

Maud Van Waters, and especially after their father's death, the siblings would reminisce, revere, and contemplate the legacy of their imposing parents.[29]

The depth of their connection was evident as well in Miriam's sadness when Ralph finally achieved his independence from her. In 1941, as Americans contemplated entry into the European war, Ralph talked with Miriam about his resolve to find a job as a psychologist in the defense effort. Then thirty-six years old, he felt as if he had spent his life in prison, and it was time to leave. Ralph enlisted in the army and spent four years at what he recalled as a "terrific" job as a "classification expert," conducting psychological tests. He left the army as a second lieutenant and formed a consulting office in Boston with one of his fellow officers, then set up his own psychological testing practice. In 1945, as Miriam wept over the destruction of war, she knew that her tears also released "the sorrow I should feel should Ralph and Bert leave me." By then the couple had a small daughter, were expecting another child, and wanted a home of their own. "To have him leave Framingham is surgery," Miriam wrote, expecting a long period of suffering "until I understand the Holy Spirit—and how you keep what goes from you in the flesh."[30]

Even after Ralph established his consulting practice and later built his own house next to Hill Top, the sibling bond remained close. Miriam hired her brother to conduct Rorschach tests at Framingham, and they continued to share family dinners and outings. Ralph sometimes ran errands or escorted her as she grew older, and her idealization persisted. In 1952, for example, Miriam had to attend a party in Boston filled with political opponents. Ralph arrived at 11 P.M. to take her home. "Never was I gladder to see his tall, smiling, faintly ironic, ever-courteous, competent self," she wrote. "We traverse alleys of Skid Row, see sights, such as homosexuals in open solicitation. Home after midnight . . ." The sense of safety she felt in the hands of her brother, contrasted with the dangers of alien social worlds, spoke of his enduring comfort for her.[31]

By the time her brother established his independence, Miriam Van Waters was preoccupied with even more pressing familial responsibilities concerning her daughter, Sarah. In her journal, she sometimes wrote of Ralph and Sarah in the same tone, taking a similar approach to ordering each of their lives. In 1934, for instance, when Ralph was twenty-nine and Sarah twelve, she commented that "Ralph and Sarah are obviously well, and the process must be extended: an encouragement to their activities." Contemplating her own "failures," Miriam listed in one passage her inability to make Sarah happy and her inability to live with Ralph's rare intellectual companionship.[32]

Even though she assumed maternal responsibility for both of them, her relationship with Sarah was unique. Van Waters was raising an adolescent daughter, confronting the very struggles over control and autonomy that she had discussed in her books about youth in conflict. In many ways, the move to Framingham in 1932 had helped resolve some of the problems she had been facing as a mother. For one, her new extended household surrounded her daughter with attentive adults while Miriam worked or traveled. In addition, establishing residency in Massachusetts enabled her to adopt Sarah legally. With Felix Frankfurter providing a reference, the adoption went through "without a hitch." "You will rejoice with me to know that last month very quietly Sarah and I were formally adopted in the Cambridge Probate Court," Miriam wrote to Alma Holzschuh in May 1932. "You will know how relieved I am, because the same issue could not have happened in California without headlines." Becoming Sarah's legal parent gave Miriam "the same feeling of relief as if I had been previously 'living in a state of sin' and had now been blessed by a Justice of the Peace!"[33]

Once settled in Framingham, combining career and parenting continued to require innovative solutions. From 1932 through 1936, while Sarah lived at Framingham and attended the progressive Shady Hill School in Cambridge, Miriam frequently relied on household members to take charge of her daughter. Since Elizabeth Bode had joined the reformatory staff after serving as an intern, Sarah was no longer her primary responsibility. Yet Bode or Anne Gladding often took over when Miriam traveled to address prison or social work conferences, speak on college campuses, meet annually with other women superintendents, or take vacations with Geraldine Thompson. On at least one occasion Miriam boarded Sarah with a family in the country while she was away, and during her first summers in the East she sent Sarah to camp in California, where Alma Holzschuh and Bess Woods continued to stay in touch with her. When salary cuts for Massachusetts state employees strained Van Waters' finances, she relied on family resources instead of camp during summer vacations. One year her sister Ruth took Sarah and other Van Waters nieces and nephews to a family camp in Vermont, and Miriam had her young relatives stay at the superintendent's house for several weeks.[34]

During these years Miriam acted as both teacher and disciplinarian for Sarah. At home, she read to her daughter, talked to her about her schoolwork, offered "She-Talk" on sex when Sarah was eleven, and marked her maturity into young womanhood. Sometimes they went horseback riding together. Miriam took Sarah shopping for her first party dresses, glowed at her accomplishments at Shady Hill, and wrote proudly in her journal of her good days: "Sarah—an angel all day"; "Sarah very sweetly and happily to bed"; "Two lovely letters came from Sarah, one of real literary merit, and both sweet and full of imagination and love."[35]

Miriam continued her pattern of withdrawing affection, rather than reprimanding Sarah, as a form of punishment. As she once explained to her parents, "Sarah is no model, but in her case, I have found that the fewer words the more action. I don't suppose we ever have excited or 'unpleasant' words." As an example she reported that she had been "mad" at Sarah one night for failing to do her chores, clean her room, and return on time from school, "But nothing was said. We had a lovely dinner hour. Then the poor child found on her pillow written notice that 'Your Reader is Out for the Evening.' . . . This morning a new, radiant Sarah got up at 7 and did everything perfectly!"[36]

Like other mothers of daughters, Miriam struggled to mold Sarah into the kind of woman she wanted to be herself. At times she looked at Sarah and saw a self-reflection. Watching her daughter sort through her belongings, she recalled a moment from her own childhood, "Xmas: scene in attic—8—a little Miriam." As her daughter entered adolescence, Miriam began to keep careful track of Sarah's weight, just as she had of her own at that age. Miriam still wanted Sarah to become a "powerful leader" who would follow in her mother's footsteps in the field of social service. At age twelve Sarah declared that she wanted to become a social worker, like Bode and her mother. As a teenager she spent a summer working as an intern at the reformatory and at the Lincoln Settlement House in Boston.[37]

This identification with Sarah may account in part for Miriam's insistence on imposing on her daughter the same discipline and order she demanded of herself. The routine was not without benefit. "Sarah in her own home (with a fixed time and place for everything, and plenty of sleep, and discipline, and not too much to eat, and good books, and a great deal of love and tenderness) is a happy and considerate host," Miriam wrote with pride to her mother. On another occasion, when Sarah acted impulsively, Miriam invoked her father's legacy, commenting that he would have understood her concern with order and structure. "I am so constituted," she concluded, "that search for order is my first law. It may be I seek it too much in 'details' of household and institution."[38]

It is hard to know how much Miriam's recurrent concerns about Sarah's lack of discipline reflected her own internal conflicts as opposed to her daughter's behavior problems. Miriam was struggling to complete her long overdue Harvard Crime Survey, unable to muster the discipline to work on it. "A good day with Sarah and Framingham but nothing done for Harvard," she noted. Sarah's procrastination resonated deeply for Miriam, and she knew that it spoke to her own vulnerability. Yet Sarah did have serious episodes of uncontrolled behavior, or what Miriam once referred to as "a throw back to her defensive-aggressive" childhood behavior, a "wanton, impulsive, 'getting even,'" side.[39] At times the mother-daughter conflicts resulted from a tension between Miriam's need for order and Sarah's childlike spontaneity. Miriam captured the essence of their struggle in recording an incident in 1935. "I commit a discourtesy. I open a package of Sarah's," she wrote. "Now you have opened your birthday present," Sarah said. Only after a "long silence" did her daughter add, "I hope you like it." Miriam cited the causes of this friction: "desire to tidy up: too impulsive in motion: too interfering." In sum, she placed the blame on her self: "Tomorrow I'll be 48: sans discipline, sans good sense."[40]

What is most striking about Van Waters' accounts of her maternal role is the recurrent self-blame, so consistent with her other writings about herself. If Sarah did not meet her expectations, then Miriam was as surely to blame for the failures as she was for Ralph's prolonged unemployment. In her books she had explored the familial origins of delinquency. In her own life, she assumed responsibility for each wayward step. In this interpretation, Sarah could do no wrong, but Miriam could fail to lead her daughter in the proper path, toward her ideal of womanhood. "I have failed with Sarah—and this because of my writing, my afternoon rest—my lack of will and self discipline," she confessed. She considered her chief fault to be insufficient discipline, not only in scheduling Sarah's life but in controlling her own emotions in response to a child's shortcomings. "I am fretful and irritated with Sarah: I am a poor parent," she wrote. "Sarah I wound by nervous impatient attempts to 'get her' to follow her schedule—go to bed on time, conquer her inertia, knowing full well the most important thing for her is happiness and peace and loving support." In dreams reminiscent of her childhood fantasies of saving Maud, Miriam now battled contemporary mobs—"half American legion, half revolutionary workers"—to protect her daughter. As in her own childhood, however, neither love nor heroic action succeeded in these nightmares.[41]

As Sarah prepared to graduate from Shady Hill and leave home for boarding school, Miriam tried to accept that she could not necessarily determine her daughter's future. She still harbored a fantasy that Sarah could someday direct Framingham, as if the job carried royal privilege of succession. Sarah, articulating a newfound independence, said that she was not interested, especially if she got the job because of her mother's connections. Miriam began to leave the choice to her daughter: "Sarah will find her marriage or her career," Miriam wrote, "or she may leave (for a time) the structure which holds the intelligentsia . . . but Sarah has to plant her feet and govern her actions in one world first."[42]

Sarah did begin to seek her own worlds. Miriam favored a more traditional boarding school, but her daughter decided to attend the experimental Putney School in Vermont. She seemed to thrive there, perhaps because of the lack of pressure to achieve academically. Miriam initially had high hopes for the experience, but she soon complained that the school indulged Sarah's interests in the same "trivial" popular amusements that she had opposed in her books. But Sarah was gaining new perspectives on her life, questioning the values of elite education and recognizing that she knew little about the way the majority of Americans lived and thought. She declared another measure of independence when she chose to attend Swarthmore rather than Smith, the school her mother had long favored. Once again Miriam accepted the decision, but she continued to frown on Sarah's adolescent social life, questioning her own daughter's insatiable quest for "nights out — to movies — for Amusement Parks — for Lip Stick?"[43]

It was during this transition period in their relationship that Van Waters recorded a prophetic nightmare. Set amid the great flood that had engulfed Portland during her childhood, the dream placed Miriam and Sarah in a car, trying to drive across a broken bridge, beset by snow, ice, wind, and icebergs. Although Miriam felt confident and tried to comfort Sarah, their car started to slide, and then it "took a nose dive into deep, deep, calm black water." Sarah whispered "O dear, O dear," and Miriam "knew we were drowning — I felt no fear. I felt regret for Sarah. I told her now we must open doors & jump for it. I 'knew' the pressure of water was too strong to escape from car: I 'knew' Ralph had turned back home, would be late in finding us — and *would* find us and rescue us (perhaps — 'in some other world.')"[44] Like other dreams, this one ended with a reference to the possibility of resurrection, but it originated in Miriam's fear that Sarah's life was on a collision course toward disaster.

In fact, Sarah was soon miserable at Swarthmore, her low grades matched by equally low self-esteem. She missed the comfortable atmosphere at Putney, and she wrote home of the troubles she had with overeating and overspending her budget. The next year she transferred to the University of New Hampshire, but her problems escalated. Miriam must have felt tested when Sarah ran up excessive charges on her department store account, forged her mother's name to a weekend permission slip, was placed on social probation, and threw tantrums during a visit home in an effort, she explained, "to make the family take me seriously."

Sarah's frequent admonitions that her mother should stop working so hard, take a rest, or sleep late suggest a rebellion against the self-discipline Miriam had tried so hard to impose on them both. In one letter home, though, Sarah best captured the dynamic that seemed to undermine her confidence. During her visits, she explained, she felt an undercurrent of irritation and disappointment from her mother. "Of course I know I am a failure," Sarah wrote, "but I can't seem to pin down the reasons why so *if* you can I wish you'd tell me when I come home." Was it her own selfishness, she asked, or their one-sided relationship, in which Miriam was "giving and giving and me only taking[?]" She seemed to be saying that it was not easy being the daughter of a saint, and she seemed to cry out for the unconditional love her mother promised to so many. On Miriam's part, it was equally difficult to be a saintly, and unappreciated, mother. In response to the stress, Anne Gladding accurately predicted that "someday Sarah will understand the meaning of her mother's love that has surrounded her life like a benediction so that she was not aware of it."[45]

Unsure of whether to remain in college, Sarah, like other women of her generation, chose another course. In December 1940, she had brought home a twenty-four-year-old engineering student, Richard Hildebrandt. They began to spend weekends together, and by June 1941, they had eloped. Expecting their first child later that year, Sarah and Dick left school and set up a household in Cambridge.[46] However tolerant she may have been of the pregnancies of reformatory women, Miriam grieved over Sarah's behavior. For the most part, she kept her feelings to herself, although she confided her dismay to Howard Kellett, a young prison minister who had become her informal confessor. He expressed his confidence in Miriam's ability to meet the challenge but reminded her, as her close friends had been saying for years, that "the best of us are not sufficient unto ourselves." Van Waters maintained her composure, but in her journal she worried about Sarah, recording a symbolic "fear of new car, speed, skidding" and her sadness that "those brief days of her childhood" had been "ended by short cuts." In retrospect, and very much in character, Miriam blamed herself for failing to teach Sarah responsibility as a child.[47]

Troubled by her daughter's marriage to a Catholic, Miriam talked with Sarah about the importance of birth control. Sarah seemed receptive to the information, but she nonetheless bore three sons between 1941 and 1945. "Sarah has cast herself a hard adult part," Miriam concluded. Although she embraced her son-in-law as part of the family, she viewed him as stubborn, undisciplined, and irresponsible. To make their lives more comfortable, she provided an allowance for Sarah, a student maid on indenture from Framingham, and, as an Easter gift, a baby carriage. Fearful that Sarah would resent the present as an intrusion on her independence, Miriam wrote a deferential note suggesting that if Sarah was very mad at her she could return the carriage for use by the reformatory babies. Sarah clearly took pride in maintaining her own household. For the first time in her life, she explained, "I have anything to offer you. We have a real home now and I think that I can offer not only peace in this house but peace in my mind for the first time in a long while."[48]

Sarah's peace of mind did not endure. Not surprisingly, the young couple had financial worries, as well as conflicts over whether Sarah should go to work. Turning to her mother for a loan, she insisted that their troubles were not due to drinking, but others told Van Waters that Dick drank to escape from his problems. In subsequent letters Sarah wrote of her husband's hard work to get them out of debt. She seemed determined that they would survive on their own. "All I ever seem to do is thank you for all the wonderful things you do," Sarah wrote in 1942, echoing her earlier feelings about being only on the receiving end of her mother's largesse.

When Miriam Van Waters tried to relinquish control, as friends and the staff psychiatrist counseled, she had conflicting emotions. Convinced that Sarah neglected baby George, she felt compelled to intervene. Sarah did not change his diapers frequently enough, or salve his ulcerated sores, while Dick never held or comforted the infant, who seemed, to Miriam, emotionally scarred already. Visiting Sarah's home, she found fault with the unwashed dishes, haphazard housekeeping, and the liquor bottles that evidenced Dick's profligacy. When the couple moved without telling her how to contact them; when Dick periodically abandoned the family, allegedly in search of work; when the couple visited and spent half the day in bed; when they suddenly arrived to claim the children Miriam had been caring for; when they separated periodically and then reappeared together, Miriam's spirits threatened to collapse. Once she felt "so greatly agitated that my 'heart gave out' — a stiffening at the back of my neck — a vertigo, a severe pain," but, she added, "of course, all the surface was calm." [49]

Inside, however, was turmoil. Instead of sleeping, Miriam struggled with the "tragic problem" of Sarah and Dick. She awoke from nightmares calling her daughter's name or imagining her grandson's muffled cry or tortured body. Doubtful of Sarah's ability to keep her life on course, she dreamed of her driving recklessly, escaping tragedy by a hairbreadth. During the day she practiced the prayer of renunciation "which Sarah's marriage has taught me." At the symphony she half listened as she pondered her daughter's marriage. Addressing the Framingham Junior Women's Club, she felt a pang watching the "well scrubbed . . . well dressed" presiding officer, who was Sarah's age but "alight with ideas — instead of the life she leads."

Eventually Miriam confided the depth of her agony to Howard Kellett, and for a night she slept well, having renewed her vows: "for Sarah I must express only love, confidence, buoyancy. For George — I must say prayers — and seek the wisdom of his Guardian Angels. And Visit George & Sarah where *they* live, on *their* terms." Only in this way — by truly giving unconditional love — would Sarah find her own strength to order her life differently. Prayer, she learned, allowed her to surrender control over her daughter and her grandson, so that Sarah could begin to feel secure as a mother. She even wrote to Dick acknowledging and accepting that "you want to solve your own problems and make your own difficult decision[s]." Internally she accepted at last that her daughter would not necessarily embrace her own goals. "My task is not to help Sarah be a career woman," she admitted, "but to have reverence for human relationships." [50]

Gradually, Sarah did begin to recognize the problems in her marriage, confide in her mother, and to turn to her for help. Miriam cared for her grandsons for long periods over the next few years, while she sustained Sarah during periodic separations from her husband. After Dick joined the army, Sarah took a full-time job at the reformatory. When he returned, Miriam hired her son-in-law as a laborer, and the entire family lived in the superintendent's house until he returned to school in New Hampshire. Then she sent a student on indenture to take care of her three grandsons while Sarah worked as a waitress and in a factory.[51]

Over the years, Miriam determined to "deal with the problem of Sarah and Dick—by cheerful service." The more she came in conflict over their social life and child-rearing methods, the more she prayed. "Again—I pray not to be ashamed of my cross—but to 'glory in it.'" When she wanted to intervene with her grandchildren, to protest that she supported and tended them but had no say in their rearing, she held her tongue and prayed to God "to let me be thankful for the opportunity of a humble service. I am so weary and heavy laden. Yet I do not quite take the yoke of Jesus upon me which would make it light. May God deal with me as I deal with Dick and Sarah! This is what I must pray and must expect."[52]

Although she opposed divorce, Miriam's doubts about her daughter's marriage festered, even as she continued to blame her own inadequacies for Sarah's plight. "If my love had been strengthened by Unselfishness (not trying to write at my desk—or employ my leisure to read—even to take naps!) had I not left Sarah's education in the hands of Progressive Educators—had I been bolder, smarter, wiser more challenging—Sarah would not have married Dick," she reasoned. "But this is blasphemy," she quickly added, "for she loves him." Gradually, though, Miriam determined that even Sarah's love could not save Dick. Ralph considered him psychopathic, a popular diagnosis for troubled men at the time, and Miriam concluded that he was an alcoholic. She wondered if the children would not be better off in her own care. By the end of the 1940s, after many reconciliations, Sarah did divorce her husband and took charge of raising her children. Miriam never stopped feeling responsible, but she had learned to pray rather than to intervene, "lest my own fear of 'interruption,' my own sense of frustration—be a stumbling block *again* to Sarah."[53]

In her personal accounts of family relationships, Miriam Van Waters variously represented herself as a teacher of "disciples," as the passionate student Heloise, and as a classic sinner, "thoroughly wicked" and dependent on God. But the strongest of her identities had been captured by Reverend George Van Waters in a letter he wrote in 1932, for his daughter's forty-fifth birthday. "Of course we are greatly blessed in our children—and paradox as it is—you are the mother of us all, for we all look to you instinctively." In her family, as in her work on behalf of imprisoned women, she offered self-sacrificing, maternal love as she assumed responsibility for the welfare, if not the salvation, of others. Hearing in a sermon that "The purpose of Sacrifice is Service, not suffering," she disagreed; "I think it needs greater and more selfless emphasis."[54] This conviction that her suffering, like Christ's, could save others revealed Miriam Van Waters' identification with powerful martyrs. In dreams she not only continued to rescue sinners, as she had in childhood, but she even imagined dying on a wooden tower. In her life, the suffering of a mother was a special cross she had to bear.

Maternalism, though—whether personal or social—had its perils, among them the expectation that sacrifice would be rewarded by gratitude or by the creation of an idealized version of oneself. It also carried a false sense of omnipotence in the belief that trying harder can solve problems that often remain beyond individual control. Many women reformers had adopted similarly unattainable goals of reshaping their clients in their own image.[55] As a public figure, Van Waters more easily distanced herself from those she tried to save. In her family, however, she relinquished fantasies of power slowly and painfully, clinging to a pattern of sacrifice often unrewarded. As she grew older, she used prayer to counteract her tendencies to overwhelm her loved ones with care. By the late 1940s, she had surrendered her hold on her brother Ralph and her daughter Sarah, allowing them to make their own mistakes, and to call on her in their own time.[56]

Guardian Angel

Miriam Van Waters rarely depicted herself as the recipient of comfort from others. Yet carrying the weight of responsibility for so many, and harboring such intense feelings of inadequacy, she deeply needed external support. "The problem," as she once articulated it, was "to establish a vital relationship which feeds and is fed." The love and gratitude of her students constantly revitalized her commitment to them, and the simple pleasures she derived from her domestic life and Hill Top provided some relief from daily stress. But above and beneath all of these was the love of Geraldine Thompson. Unlike either her students, or her "disciples" on the staff, or her relatives, Thompson was "like a guardian angel."[1] She provided what Van Waters would accept from no one else: love, adoration, material comforts, a respite from the cares of work and family, as well as a colleague in her reform efforts.

The relationship between Miriam Van Waters and Geraldine Thompson allowed two highly active women to pool their resources for social activism and to escape from daily cares through a mutually supportive and spiritually refreshing partnership. As they passed through middle age, they seemed to challenge each other toward continual spiritual growth and political survival. "Geraldine at 60," Miriam wrote in 1936, "is fresh, alert, strong, attractive, erect, spontaneous, balanced, no gray hair." In her eyes "the spark of life is as brightly burning" as it was in the young interns at Framingham. Despite rare moments of conflict—when Miriam felt she had burdened or discouraged her beloved, or when she withdrew momentarily if Geraldine became irritated by "trifles"—the two women maintained an intense, compatible, and largely clandestine partnership.[2]

Before she moved to Massachusetts, Van Waters had embraced Virginia Woolf's goal of "a room of one's own," adding that she also hoped to remain in love. She succeeded in balancing independence and connection, in part because she remained in Framingham, while Thompson was based at Brookdale. Living apart, Miriam did not feel the overwhelming sense of responsibility elicited by living near her close family relations. Nor did she require the self-protective aloofness that characterized her public relationships with colleagues. Each of these tendencies—toward merger or distance—kept her from being nurtured by others. The long-distance arrangement, however, avoided the daily possibilities for dependency and merger that both women had feared during their "courtship." In addition to giving each of them enormous autonomy, their separate households helped keep the relationship above reproach from those who might find its romantic underpinnings suspect.

Despite their geographical distance, and in large part because of Thompson's wealth, the two friends were able to maintain frequent contact through regular visits, letters, and telephone calls. They met in person almost monthly, either when Geraldine came to stay at the superintendent's house or at Hill Top, or when Miriam spent weekends at Brookdale. They traveled to conferences around the country, and when Miriam went to New York for meetings of the American League to Abolish Capital Punishment or the annual gatherings of women superintendents, she usually stayed with Geraldine in Manhattan or at Brookdale. Each year the couple took an extended vacation together. Before Lewis Thompson's death in 1936, Miriam would spend a few weeks each winter with Geraldine at Sunny Hill, the plantation in Florida where her husband resided. After 1936, they took late summer vacations, first at Wood's Lake, Colorado, and after 1940 at Clear Lake, in the Adirondacks of New York State. In 1938, they traveled to Europe. When they were apart, Geraldine always called to say good night to Miriam. "I don't want another blank evening—without your goodnight blessing of love," she wrote once when she could not get a phone line. The two friends corresponded regularly, and Geraldine's letters, Miriam wrote in her journal, "carry me through" even the most painful days.[3]

The destruction of most of their correspondence makes it difficult to reconstruct fully this complex friendship. Van Waters' journal entries provide sufficient information to appreciate how important Thompson was to her well-being, while her somewhat cryptic comments about the relationship hint at deeper conflicts it may have raised. Above all, the surviving evidence about their relationship provides an important record of the persistence of female bonding and mutual support in the history of reform in modern America. Like other intimate female friends, whether in the settlement houses, higher education, the women's networks within the New Deal, or the international women's movement, these middle-class women reformers turned to each other to provide emotional sustenance for their political careers. More than most people realized at the time, Geraldine Thompson's love and benevolence made possible Miriam Van Waters' innovations, and assured her longevity, at Framingham.[4]

At first glance, Geraldine Thompson appears to have played the role of bountiful matron whose wealth permitted Miriam Van Waters to enact the exceptionally progressive program she envisioned. Their collaboration as reformers was in fact a central bond in this friendship. Like Ethel Dummer before her, Thompson provided financial support for Van Waters' projects. She made possible staff positions for psychiatric and social welfare workers, created intern stipends, and offered funds for released prisoners to draw on in emergencies. She suggested the expanded use of indenture that became so central to the goal of reintegration into the community. By the 1940s, she contributed over two thousand dollars a year to the Thompson Fund, administered by the Friends of Prisoners. The money supported interns or temporary staff members in the nursery and education departments, paid for the indenture of students onto staff duty, and hired a former Hull House worker to help paroled or indentured mothers. As Miriam once wrote to her mother, "She is so generous and steady in her giving. I don't know what I would do without her. We would make no progress."[5]

Van Waters considered Thompson an important colleague at Framingham, in part because of her financial support, and in part because of the advice she freely gave on institutional matters. In a "half dream—half imagery," in which an old woman with a face like Jane Addams stood serenely watching the dawn, Miriam envisioned Geraldine as "my fellow pilgrim," a coworker who joined in her "quest of the High Gods." During visits to Framingham, Thompson usually addressed either a student assembly or a staff meeting, providing inspiration for the superintendent as well as her charges. "Geraldine tells staff that in defending one's honour one cannot let dishonour touch one's opponent," Miriam wrote on one such occasion. "She gave a close knit talk without a note before her. Never can I forget her image." When Thompson told the student assembly about "politics and airplanes," Van Waters recorded that "the students were enchanted." At age sixty-nine she spoke to the Senior Club, impressing them with her "athletic" looks and erect posture. Thompson sometimes sat in on student case conferences, advising Van Waters on staff problems and counseling her "wisely" on how to respond to conflicts.

Apart from appreciating these talks during routine visits, Miriam could count on Geraldine to fly up to Boston when political storms

threatened. Her influential friend just happened to be visiting, for example, when the dreaded parole board came for lunch. Thompson's
presence added a political as well as moral force to the superintendent's reform efforts. Even when she attended national Republican
Party meetings, Thompson took time to talk up the Framingham cause
with the politicians she met. When critics attacked Van Waters' indenture system or her leniency toward students, the politically influential
Thompson quickly took action. A few months after noting in her journal that "Geraldine telns [telephones] & writes re her plans for Rescu-
ing Framingham," Van Waters recorded a dream typical in its threats
of attack and torture, but unique in that the rescuer was Geraldine,
not Miriam.[6]

Thompson's funds not only provided generous support for the reformatory; they also made Van Waters' life easier. A three-hundred-
dollar check helped her work on her Harvard Crime Survey report,
which she presented orally in 1935.[7] Thompson sent money so that
Van Waters could fly from Boston to Newark to visit her for weekends,
an unusual reliance on air travel at this time. A generous gift to Sarah
Van Waters in 1938 contributed to a trip to Europe, while Christmas
checks went into a "Hill Top Account" to help maintain the rustic retreat. Thompson may also have contributed directly to Van Waters'
New Jersey bank account. Aside from financial gifts, each Christmas
she sent generous presents—a Philco radio one year; "3 silk & woolen
stockings grape fruit pecans $100.00 check sweater coat" another. She
also gave Miriam silver tableware, the kind of gift that mothers often
pass on to daughters.[8]

The relationship was by no means one-sided, however. Although
Thompson had superior material resources, and she insisted on taking
care of Van Waters rather than being cared for, mutual emotional nurturing characterized their friendship. The two women confided about
their family cares, particularly their anxieties about their children, who
faced health and personal crises even as adults. The shared experience
of tuberculosis created another intense personal bond. Although each
had recovered as a young woman, during the 1930s the disease contributed to the ill health of Geraldine's husband and debilitated her daughter Geraldine, known as "Puss," who died in 1949. Miriam provided
understanding when Geraldine worried about her daughter's health
and consolation when Lewis Thompson died. Mutual grief had already
brought the two women closer together, when, just after Miriam's father died in 1934, Geraldine lost both her mother and her sister, Ruth
Morgan. A journal entry captured Miriam's investment in their mutual

recovery: "Geraldine has cried out—at the strangeness of living when Ruth is dead and Mama is dead. She is the fountain head of life for her family. She must live. So must I."[9]

For Thompson, the relationship with Van Waters provided opportunities both to employ her boundless political energies and to enjoy the personal meaning provided by intimacy. "You help more than anyone to make life brave and beautiful to me," Geraldine wrote to Miriam. "You make me eager to have a Merry heart or a gracious manner of living." Describing a diary-like record she kept in 1937, Geraldine explained that "It is full of you. All grateful loving expressions of what you are and have done." Perhaps Thompson's relatives best captured the pleasure the relationship brought when they nicknamed Van Waters "Granny Thompson's yum-yum."[10]

Friends and colleagues also recognized Van Waters' importance in Thompson's life. They noted the differences between the two women, whose public styles complemented each other. Thompson was outspoken, often imperious in executing her commands, and known for her energy and public generosity. Van Waters was more tactful, persuasive rather than direct, but as energetic and committed as her companion. To close friends in Massachusetts and New Jersey, they constituted a reform team. In 1934, for example, Miriam received a confidential letter expressing concern that Thompson was "doing altogether too much," and with too much attention to detail, at the county social service organization she had founded. "I know that Mrs. Thompson confides in you and values your opinion," the executive director wrote to Miriam. "I feel she needs help just now." Always highly commanding while conducting business, Geraldine's nerves may have been especially raw during this period of grief. Miriam knew her friend well enough, though, to respond that "Mrs. Thompson's welfare and morale depend on keeping actively in touch" with county work. She recommended more, rather than less, engagement in the agency. "She needs to feel needed," Miriam explained.[11]

In a sense, Miriam Van Waters filled that requirement for Geraldine Thompson. While the superintendent took care of others, she permitted only her guardian angel to know how much care she needed herself. "Geraldine is so very good to me," Miriam wrote her mother from Brookdale, "[she] sent me the money to come and now insists that I rest." Even though she felt "selfish" about taking time to relax on their vacations, they did her a "world of good," she admitted. Just a few hours with her friend brought renewed strength to the weary superintendent, while Geraldine's letters carried her through her most painful

As superintendent of the Massachusetts Reformatory for Women at Framingham from 1932 until 1957, Miriam Van Waters combined spirituality, social service, and maternal love in an effort to redeem incarcerated women. Below she leads a Bible class for students in the Magdalen Chapel at the reformatory. At left she works at her desk during the 1930s. *(Below, photo by Sheldon A. Glew, courtesy Margaret van Wagenen and Anne Gladding; left, courtesy Mary Q. Hawkes)*

Van Waters typically took a vigorous early
morning ride on her horse, Lady, before
beginning one of her long days at the
reformatory. *(Courtesy Richard J.
Hildebrandt)*

Margaret van Wagenen was one of dozens of college-educated young women who served as interns at the Framingham reformatory during the Depression and then stayed to become staff members. In this picture van Wagenen holds the child of an inmate outside Wilson Cottage, where mothers lived with their babies. *(Courtesy Margaret van Wagenen)*

The superintendent's house, seen in the lower right corner of this nineteenth-century print, is connected to the Massachusetts Reformatory for Women by an overpass. Here Miriam Van Waters made her home from 1932 until 1957, surrounded by family members, staff residents, and inmate servants.

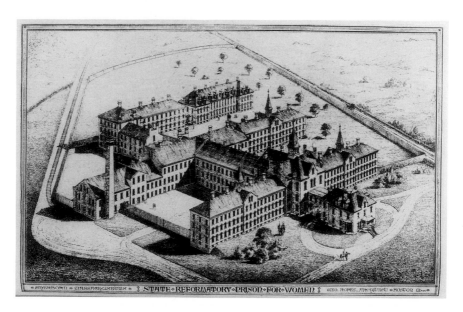

Eleanor Roosevelt, a friend of Geraldine Thompson's, often timed her visits to Framingham to provide maximum political support for Van Waters' reform efforts. Pictured in 1945 *(right)*, just a month after her husband's death, Roosevelt met with Van Waters during a period of growing criticism of Van Waters' administration of the reformatory. *(Courtesy The Schlesinger Library, Radcliffe College)* A visit in 1954 *(below)* brought together Roosevelt, Thompson, and Van Waters. At the far left is Dorothy Wilson, president of the Friends of Framingham, a volunteer group that supported Van Waters' reforms. *(Courtesy Margaret van Wagenen and Anne Gladding)*

BOSTON AMERICAN

8 STAR RACING SPORTS

THE RECORD-AMERICAN HAS THE GREATEST CIRCULATION IN NEW ENGLAND

Vol. XLV—No. 200 72 Pages   Boston, Friday, November 12, 1948   Price 5 Cents

DWYER REPORT ACCUSES DR. VAN WATERS

Her Sherborn Regime Mocks Courts; Laws, Rules Violated; Revels Held
State Dept. of Correction Charges

In the late 1940s, Boston newspapers helped publicize sensational charges against Van Waters' liberal administration of the Framingham reformatory. One of the Hearst papers, the *Boston American*, sided with Commissioner McDowell and Deputy Commissioner Dwyer against Van Waters. Even the more sympathetic *Boston Globe (below)* headlined charges of lax morals and sexual perversion among staff and inmates. *(Left, reprinted with permission of The Boston Herald; courtesy The Schlesinger Library, Radcliffe College; below, reprinted courtesy The Boston Globe; courtesy The Schlesinger Library, Radcliffe College)*

CHARGES VAN WATERS LAX IN PRISON MORALS

27 Reasons for Dismissal Given Out by Her Counsel

Letter Asserts She Employed as Officers Women with Records for Sex Perversion and Use of Drugs

ATTY. CROSS CALLS ACCUSATIONS BASELESS

Dr. Miriam Van Waters, removed head of the Women's Reformatory, Framingham, is charged with employing as reformatory officers women who served time in correctional institutions for offenses ranging from sex practices to drunkenness.

CHARGES REVEALED—Dr. Miriam Van Waters, with her counsel, Claude B. Cross, left, who revealed today 27 reasons for her dismissal as head of the Women's Reformatory by Correction Commissioner Elliott E. McDowell, right.

After Commissioner of Corrections McDowell dismissed her from office in January, 1949, Van Waters insisted on a public hearing to defend her administration. This panoramic view of Gardner Auditorium at the Massachusetts State House shows Van Waters, at the far left, standing like a prisoner in the dock while Deputy Commissioner Frank Dwyer questions her. A packed audience listened intently. *(Reprinted with permission of The Boston Herald; courtesy Boston Public Library, Print Department)*

When the hearings moved to the reformatory, spectators unable to fit into the smaller room watched from outside in the January chill. *(Reprinted with permission of The Boston Herald; courtesy Boston Public Library, Print Department)*

Two women spectators, one of whom travelled to Boston from New York, brought their knitting to the State House hearing room. *(Photo by Anthony Cabral, reprinted with permission of The Boston Herald; courtesy Boston Public Library, Print Department)*

Several of Van Waters' protegees testified at
the hearings, including Elizabeth Bode *(left)*,
who came from California with Van Waters
and later worked at the reformatory; Margaret
O'Keefe *(center)*, who served as an intern and
rose to the position of assistant superintendent;
and Anne Gladding *(right)*, another former
intern, who became child placement officer
in the 1940s and a member of Van Waters'
household. *(Photo by Ernest Hill, reprinted
with permission of The Boston Herald;
courtesy The Schlesinger Library, Radcliffe
College)*

A photographer captured Geraldine Thompson watching anxiously during the hearings over Van Waters' dismissal. *(Courtesy Richard J. Hildebrandt)*

While the panel appointed by Governor Dever deliberated after a second round of hearings, Van Waters and Thompson spent the day outdoors at Hilltop awaiting the governor's decision. *(Photo by George Dixon, reprinted with permission of The Boston Herald; courtesy Boston Public Library, Print Department)*

On March 11, 1949, after learning of her reinstatement, Miriam Van Waters triumphantly returned to the reformatory, where she was greeted by loyal staff members *(above)*. An inmate made the welcome home sign held by Van Waters and her lawyer, Claude Cross. Inside the reformatory *(right)*, Van Waters and Cross raised their hands in triumph in front of a student assembly. *(Photos by Leslie Jones, reprinted with permission of The Boston Herald; courtesy Boston Public Library, Print Department)*

Van Waters and her daughter, Sarah Van Waters Hildebrandt, in the living room of the superintendent's house, adjacent to the reformatory *(above)*, and sharing a laugh during a break in the hearings *(left)*. *(Courtesy Richard J. Hildebrandt)*

Seated at her desk at the reformatory,
shortly before her retirement in 1957,
Van Waters was surrounded by pictures of
her grandchildren, her friends, and the
reformatory she had run for twenty-five
years. *(Photo by Gordon N. Converse,
© The Christian Science Monitor; courtesy
Margaret van Wagenen and Anne Gladding)*

In later life, Van Waters continued to enjoy the friendships of former colleagues and staff. In the 1950s she and her longtime friend Bess Woods held a reunion *(above)*. In the 1960s and 1970s, Anne Gladding *(left)* continued to be a spiritual companion and loyal friend to Van Waters. *(Courtesy Margaret van Wagenen)*

In her retirement, living on Clark Street in
Framingham with two former students, Miriam
Van Waters worked on her memoirs and provided
a lifeline to current and former inmates. *(Photo
by Calvin Campbell, reprinted with permission
of The Boston Herald; courtesy Boston Public
Library, Print Department)*

days. After one "heavenly visit" she wrote that "I had not known how tired I was until the load was taken off my shoulders at Hill Top in the hours of walking, of apple tree pruning and talk by firelight." [12]

Even when she worried about Geraldine's health and spirits, in this unique relationship Miriam only rarely played a maternal role. It was worth noting in her journal the one occasion, when her guest was ill during a visit to Hill Top, that Geraldine "lets me take care of her." When Geraldine required surgery, it was her daughter who alerted Miriam in advance, insisting she join the family at Brookdale before the operation and relaying information about her mother's condition. After the surgery, Miriam spent the night in New York City, standing vigil at the head of Geraldine's hospital bed, accepted by all as a primary friend. Although more typically it was Geraldine who nurtured Miriam, each of them clearly found great satisfaction in caring for the other. [13]

Above all, Geraldine's visits to Framingham provided Miriam with both "stimulus and peace" in the midst of her hectic administrative life. Once, for instance, the day after Geraldine flew up from New Jersey, Miriam wrote that "This lovely fresh morning I am seeking the way with renewed courage, and some sense of life." Meeting her visitor at the airport "in the late golden afternoon" on another trip, Van Waters was "flooded with an unusual happiness." During these visits, the two women took long walks and horseback rides together, appreciating the changing of the seasons in the countryside. They also planted together in the garden; in her friend's absence, Miriam would watch for "Geraldine's" white lilacs to bloom. On Sundays they attended church, often with Maud Van Waters and other family members. During one "perfect visit," the couple walked through Boston's North End, retracing the steps of Miriam's early social work career; another weekend they walked around Walden Pond. It was not unusual for them to take "a five mile tramp" during an afternoon, often talking of life and death, "authority and transubstantiation," or "faith, hope, chastity, the power of Prayer." Their conversations, Van Waters once wrote, "prepare souls for immortal bridges and structures—when 'life' is done." [14]

Anticipating Geraldine's visits kept Miriam's spirits up during their separations. "I must start the day—and prepare my life for the blessing of Geraldine's visit," she wrote. On the rare occasions when Geraldine had to cancel or delay a trip, Miriam felt unnerved and emotionally numb. "This morning I am shaken. Geraldine tells she is not coming." At the end of their time together Miriam felt "stillness and a new category of mysteries and hope and life and blessedness." She also found it hard to see Geraldine go, and sometimes the parting left her feeling "bereft." As her friend flew back to New Jersey, Miriam planned for their reunion. After an August 1935, visit, for example, she wrote, "I must begin earning a holiday for September." Geraldine also felt the partings. "Dearest, dearest love," she wrote after their return from Europe in 1939, "when I look down on the port of New York & its entry through the Narrows, I think of Us, putting forth to sea—& again coming back together after that far flung journeying—And I am happy & thankful, full of renewed courage and joy." [15]

When Miriam escaped to Brookdale, she also found respite from her cares and an inspiration for her work. "The night is soft and windy," she wrote after her arrival. "I am deeply at peace, cherished and blessed beyond words by Geraldine's love and care: and now in bed by lamp light—I ponder the nature of imprisoned Man." There, too, the couple took long walks in the woods, consulted on professional projects, and spent time with family members. Miriam tried to get some writing done, as well. The two women made trips into New York City for dinner, meetings, the theater, or lunch at the Colony Club. These visits clearly combined business and pleasure. As Geraldine once wrote, "Dearest Lamb, couldn't you arrange to spend some days here at Brookdale when you come in for the Nov. Prison Conf. Each time I go into your room I make some little change: & place your nest nearer to my heart & desire." [16]

Brookdale was a stopover en route to conferences, such as meetings of the American Youth Commission, a research project of the American Council on Education for which Van Waters served as executive secretary. Sometimes Thompson accompanied her to the meetings in Washington, D.C. On a few trips the two women stayed at the White House to visit Geraldine's friends, the Roosevelts. In 1939, for example, Van Waters met with FDR in his study, answering his questions about prisons and the parole system. She felt "privileged to make suggestions" to the president, and she found it remarkable to wander about the White House as if it were her own home. The next year, she had tea with Eleanor Roosevelt, and later she and Geraldine dined with Franklin and Eleanor. To mark the significance of the event, Miriam wrote to her mother, "You have made possible all I have and do." In practical terms, of course, it was Geraldine Thompson who made these visits possible. [17]

In addition to their weekend trips, Van Waters and Thompson had more extended visits. From 1934 to 1941, Miriam spent several weeks each summer living at Brookdale while she taught a course at Columbia University's Teachers College. The estate's chauffeur would drive her to the city for her class each day, and she would fly back to Framingham for the weekends. At Brookdale Miriam swam in the mornings and evenings, prepared for her lectures, and enjoyed Geraldine's company. At the end of the summer course, the two women went to Colorado, where they hiked, rode, fished for trout, and spent time with members of Thompson's family. In a birthday letter, Geraldine once imagined stepping across their Colorado cabin "from my room to yours—past the big, grey fire-place, not yet lighted in preparation for breakfast— and feel the warmth of your soft covers and your morning benediction." On other trips, they shared one bed in a rustic, lakeside cabin in upstate New York.[18]

Van Waters' friends knew how important these vacations were for her well-being. As Orfa Shontz once wrote to her, "you have been carrying too heavy a load—Did Geraldine come over the week end—wish she would carry you off on another little vacation." Miriam knew the value of these escapes, as well. Writing to Anne Gladding from upstate New York, she described taking a plunge in a lake on a frosty morning, following the deer runs in the forest, and attending church. "I am resting in my fashion," she explained. "Talks, in the evening and at meals, wonderful talks, full of imagination—and faint and zest: complete silence in the woods, watching, listening for deer—and at night, by the fire, reading Wind in the Willows, and your Bible—are some of the joys I share with Mrs. Thompson."[19]

Geraldine and Miriam had begun the pattern of taking an annual vacation in 1933, spending several weeks each winter at Sunny Hill plantation in northern Florida. Although the South sometimes felt like an alien world to her, she found Sunny Hill enormously refreshing. She felt grateful for the cordial welcome from "Colonel" Thompson, or "The Boss," as Geraldine's husband was called. Miriam and Lew formed a warm attachment. They often sent greetings to each other through Geraldine, and at Sunny Hill they played cards, dined, and conversed with distinguished guests, such as former secretary of war Newton Baker. Miriam even adapted to the racial mores of the region. Describing the local population, she wrote home that the "the darkies are gay and happy," sounding more like a native than a northern critic. She also came to appreciate the hunting trips that gave Geraldine so much pleasure, learning how to shoot from horseback as they stalked wild turkey. Above all, though, she relished the nature walks and philosophical talks with Geraldine. "The moon has made magics," Miriam wrote in her journal in 1935. "On the 10th she was at the full, spreading silver over Sunny Hill: on the 11th Armistice Day, she was witness and mover to an experience that will last my life long." That experience went un-recorded, although the page ended "Geraldine and I struggle with concepts. The night is fragrant with roses and jasmine."[20]

Miriam Van Waters frequently alluded to such discussions of "concepts" when she was with Geraldine Thompson. Often they spoke of philosophical or religious matters, but sometimes they returned to the interpretation of their relationship first broached in the courtship letters of 1930. Writing of love or desire, Van Waters always remained discrete about her subject, but she clearly remained enamored. "Geraldine, Sarah and Ralph dwell in my house of life," she wrote. After accounting for Ralph and Sarah, Miriam continued that "Falling in love—all over again—is an experience only the mature know. One's expression is more concrete: how add to the feeling with life abundant in one's Beloved." Such clues, scattered throughout her journals and letters, reveal how Van Waters came to terms with her love for another woman.[21]

A first turning point appeared following the deaths of Van Waters' father and Thompson's sister, when mutual grief brought the two women closer. After Geraldine visited that spring of 1934, Miriam wrote another enigmatic but suggestive journal entry: "For reasons which need not be gone into, I am in the position of a person whose feet are on a newly discovered road." At Easter that year Geraldine gave Miriam a ring, which for years provided her with "a special message and blessing." The next year, soon after Lewis Thompson had another heart attack, Miriam and Geraldine "talked of plans and death." Walking through the pastures on Miriam's forty-eighth birthday, they spoke "of first loyalties and how one assimilates new experiences demanding new loyalties. Should one's action be such that its principle can be explained to all men?" Anticipating Lew's death may have raised the possibility of explaining to the world the "first loyalties" they had pledged to each other. From the silences in the historical record, they seemed to have decided, consciously or not, to remain discrete about the depth of their love.[22]

Just a month after this conversation, Miriam had an experience that highlighted the conflicts between her private and public representations of their relationship. She was traveling by train to Sunny Hill; Geraldine joined her at Trenton, New Jersey. In the drawing car Miriam met Ruth Shafer, a social worker she once knew who was going to Miami to provide hurricane relief through the Red Cross. Shafer, Miriam noted, "lives with Marjorie Bell in New York," a comment that characterized her as a member of a Boston marriage. Noticing the ring that

Van Waters wore on her left hand—the gift from Geraldine—Shafer asked if she had married. "Like a fool. Called to attention—I said—No," she recorded in her journal. When Shafer persisted by commenting on the ring, Miriam became furious. "Damned insolence," she wrote in a rare use of profanity. "I should have said—not recently—." Shafer's question may have been about conventional marriage, but simply explaining that she was single would not necessarily have been so annoying to Miriam. More likely, Shafer knew that Van Waters was single and traveling, as she often did, with Geraldine Thompson. Her insolence was in alluding publicly to a status that Van Waters preferred to keep private. Even if Shafer and her partner were comfortable about being known as a couple, Miriam Van Waters clearly did not want to be categorized with them.[23]

Miriam did not record whether she told Geraldine about the interchange; perhaps she kept the insult to herself. In any case, it did not interfere with her visit to Sunny Hill. A few days later Miriam described a night that was "enchanted like a Mexican night, caressing, seducing and treacherous." Having employed such erotic terms, she immediately questioned herself: "Why do we use these words to describe an atmosphere?" she asked. "Because they deal with our thoughts as a person does."[24] It was during this visit that Geraldine and Miriam struggled with concepts amid the roses and jasmine.

Lewis Thompson's death both strained and then strengthened Geraldine and Miriam's relationship. During his final illness, Geraldine had to cancel a trip to Framingham. "My grief is muffled in this fog," Miriam wrote. "I built my house of life, and the one in whose presence I seem to touch the force of goodness, and to feel renewed in me the zest of life, did not come." Though numbed by pain, Miriam made sure to leave her door ajar, lest her household members think that she was "suffering too remotely, too acutely," which she was. Geraldine wrote from the train station as she left for Florida, affirming that she loved Miriam with all her heart and pledging to bring her joy and peace. She also sent detailed letters of her days at Sunny Hill, including her vigil at her ailing husband's bedside. Still, Miriam feared that Lew's death would shatter their equilibrium.[25]

Van Waters' dramatic account of her arrival at Brookdale after Lewis Thompson's death in March 1936 bears repeating, for it shows how vulnerable she felt at this time. "In the greatest spiritual lonliness [*sic*] and agony I have known since 'youth.'" she wrote in her journal, "I tried to come to terms with the night. . . . All that has gone before is distilled into a single cup of bitter waters." Drawing on Proust's use of the word *little,* she explored the "very small" moment of great consequence, "the single error which causes us agony and humiliation." Moving from the abstract to the personal crisis, she explained the minute source of her crisis:

> I missed the train. My soul was an agony of apprehension.
> When I attempted to reestablish the line of communication
> with Geraldine the road was blocked not so much by grief
> nor by the fact that Puss came into her room for the bicar-
> bonate of soda but because the interruption broke the thread
> and Geraldine doubted the validity of the relationship.[26]

As she so often did within her family, Miriam felt inadequate, fearful that one mistake—a missed train—at a time when Geraldine needed her could undermine her beloved's trust.

Van Waters' clearly exaggerated her own impact, for within a week, she and Geraldine were walking around Walden Pond during a visit of such "vitality" that it affected her inner world "in feeling and in concept and action." Geraldine felt no break during her mourning. Back at Brookdale, even as she tried to hold on to memories of Lew, she reread Miriam's letters, kissing the pages as she held "your dear wisdom in tender loving hands." Still, Miriam remained insecure, fretting over the "extra hours" Geraldine gave her, and for making her friend cry. But when Geraldine sent "a priceless letter indicating all is well," her equilibrium returned.[27]

Although the death of Lewis Thompson strained their connection temporarily, it also provided a kind of catharsis for Van Waters, as illustrated by a dream she recorded in detail, set at Colonel Thompson's funeral. When Miriam arrived with her mother, Geraldine, "in deep mourning," greeted her, looking "tired, spent, full of mystery, yet somehow gay, whimsical, kind, sensitive, absorbed, tender, good." She had arranged an entertainment, a kind of wake that Miriam compared to an Easter play that had been performed at the reformatory. Indeed, the theme of resurrection recurred in the dream, which involved "a troupe of actors, in pantomime, strange figures, relatives of the Hamiltons, Morgans & Livingstons, relatives too of the Boss," dressed in historical costumes, along with dwarfs and children. As Miriam and her mother watched the pantomime, Harry Emerson Fosdick—the popular liberal Protestant clergyman whose church Geraldine attended—preached "a clear message" about the resurrection.

The theme of eternal love ran through Miriam's consciousness in this dream. After the pantomime, Colonel Thompson "was carried in" and placed on a bed with colorful quilts that Geraldine adjusted. "She seemed to lie down herself," Miriam recalled of her dream, "yet I did not think she was there. I looked for her everywhere: a manager woman seemed to help search. I felt panic: *where* is Geraldine: She died last night, they told me. I rushed up the stairs." Children and an old woman were also going to their deaths, yet Miriam could feel the woman's pulse racing. Was this death, or life? Then Miriam met Geraldine, "walking along as usual," to her death. "Don't go," she said, but Geraldine insisted on departing. Miriam took her hands, feeling "instantly they were alive and capable of giving back a response." She prayed to her, "Come back," and Geraldine replied, "Yes I shall always come back," but still she "proceeded up the stairs on her strange incomprehensible errand."

At this point, Miriam "awoke without fear." Interpreting her dream, she thought of her father, the church, and the "spiritual world." She made no mention of her fear of losing Geraldine. For Miriam, the important element was that she "seemed to have understood some strange glimpse of a way of spiritual life, half theater, half church," a world her father had understood but that had frightened her in the past. Perhaps the dream allowed her to comprehend the meaning of resurrection in a personal way. At the same time, it revealed Miriam's sense of being an observer and outsider among the Morgans and Thompsons, and her inability to stop Geraldine from following her husband to the grave. "I shall always come back," however, was the phrase after which Miriam closed the scene and awoke "without fear," her security restored.[28]

Over the next few years, the theme of resurrection recurred in dreams in which Van Waters tried to come to terms with her sexuality. One of these dreams, she believed, revealed her "life pattern." In it she wandered through the slum of a large city that was "part Oriental," a placement Miriam attributed to "distressful" events in China but which encoded Western cultural stereotypes of both "Shanghaied" girls sold into prostitution and Oriental potentates who demanded sexual service. A pompous little military ruler had Miriam captured and taken to a "House of Pleasure," where "girls and madames" from "all countries" painted her face and dressed her. Miriam protested that she was "too old—too worn out" and asked one of the prostitutes if there was any way to escape the ruler who demanded her services. "She was kind—

said yes—in the evening I was to ask to go to the bathroom, jump through the dirty window to the wall." When Miriam asked, "Would the jump be fatal?" the prostitute replied, "You are as good as already dead."

As the dream continued, longing for spiritual redemption merged with erotic images reminiscent of Van Waters' earlier poetry. Looking out of the brothel window seemed "like the view from an air plane," a sight she observed during her flights to visit Geraldine. She jumped from this window "without hesitation, or fear. There was a symbolic impact—I was dead." Then, however, the dream shifted from terror to release as she "returned to the room," alive, led down "the beautiful rock ledges of a great waterfall." Although the descent was frightening, at the base "great smooth waves rolled." To "consummate the burial," Miriam was "pitched into the water." She swam up to spongy marshes and then felt "free." On dry land, in another "slum village" she was "rearrested: without terror—made to go back—not to the House of Pleasure—but to—life." [29]

For the keeper of a women's prison to dream of being incarcerated in a brothel suggests in part an identification with the women in her care. The images of falling, swimming, and pitching in waves, however, evoke more personal feelings. They could stand for rebirth, or, as they did in her early poetry, for erotic desire. If Miriam feared a loss of sexual innocence, the dream seemed to comfort her, implying her ability to maintain control and to survive. Swimming, a great physical joy of her childhood, saved Miriam in this dream, in contrast to nightmares in which water had the power to drown her and those she loved.

The images of descent—looking down from an airplane, jumping from a window, falling through a waterfall—had appeared in earlier dreams, as well. Once, while visiting Brookdale, she dreamed that "the spirit lay on the high ledge betwixt waking and sleeping conscious of the strata on which she rested poised between earth and sky near the tree tops, alert to soar or to sink downward." Her journal soon turned to a commentary on an inmate committed for a sexual offense. What could sex mean to this woman, Miriam wondered, in a revealing stream of associations: "Is it power—security—adventure—pleasure—sacrifice, giving, increase of the sense of one's value, anodyne to pain or weariness—having a child: receiving a sacrament; a moment of beauty. a flash of red poppies in a field of wheat. falling into an abyss; climbing to a ledge and floating off into space?" [30] Her comment professed a greater interest in the symbolic meaning of sex than the act itself, but in dreams she allowed herself to explore the physical, as well as spiritual, transcendence that the erotic could provide.

Soon after the brothel escape dream, Van Waters recorded her interpretation of another powerful dream with implications for her sexuality. "The details of my dream have dropped out of consciousness," she
wrote, but what is most significant is the meaning she attached to a
feeling of "Understanding" in the dream. It came, she explained, from
time spent with Geraldine that summer and, most importantly, from
"the recent Rorshak [*sic*] and integration." The reference to the Rorschach test is extremely intriguing. In this procedure, psychologists interpret responses to ink blots in terms of the images that subjects project onto the forms. Criminologists had come to rely on the device as a
measure of psychological disorder, and particularly as a test for "innate
homosexuality." The classification conference reports at Framingham
often cited the Rorschach to prove or disprove homosexuality among
inmates. Shortly before the dream about the brothel, her old friend
Bess Woods was visiting, and Miriam asked her to administer the test.
"Bess gives me Rorshak test and opens a new world," Miriam confided
in her journal, seemingly relieved by the results. "The Rorshak is symbol of integration. Bess' recognition of it and my discovery give solidity
and confidence. The Harvard Survey should do this for Felix, Judge
Cabot & Hans." The next line was crossed out heavily in pencil, especially the name. She continued, "Geraldine and I shall learn together."[31]

What had the test revealed? Comparing the results with the completion of the Harvard survey implied that a great weight had been
lifted from Van Waters' shoulders. Just as fulfilling her professional obligations would gain the approval of her colleagues, the Rorschach
brought self-confidence. After the dream, both she and Geraldine felt
"optimistic." But about what? Had there been renewed doubts about
the propriety of their intimacy, or a concern about their sexual identities? Given Van Waters' associations of lesbianism and psychopathology, if the Rorschach reassured her that she was not homosexual, both
women must have been relieved. Ironically, however, by freeing them
of the label of deviance, the test results may have granted Miriam and
Geraldine permission to express the full extent of their love, either
without fear of sexual consequences, or without fear that sexual expression would necessarily label them as homosexuals.

What is most significant, however, is not so much their behavior
as the ability of these middle- and upper-class women to engage in so
loving a same-sex relationship while avoiding the stigma of homosexuality. A generation earlier, Miriam Van Waters might have had no qualms
about expressing her love more publicly, so new was the concept of
homosexuality at the turn of the century and so immune were women

of her class from the label. A generation later, Miriam and Geraldine would probably have been labeled lesbians in need of psychiatric redemption. They lived, though, at an early moment in the emergence of public consciousness of homosexuality among women. Their reticence suggests that they continued to view knowledge of their love as risky. Because stereotypes of middle- and upper-class women of their generation still assumed lack of sexual passion, their age and class positions helped them avoid stigma. Convinced that they were not abnormal, they proceeded to offer devoted love to one another, secure, for the moment, that no public scandal would result.

In her relationship with Geraldine Thompson, Miriam Van Waters came to terms with two related sets of inner needs. She allowed Geraldine to become her guardian angel, the one person who could provide material support and maternal love to the adult Miriam. Without risk of losing her cherished independence, she also enjoyed the material and emotional security that she had so longed for since childhood. At the same time, Van Waters accepted her desires for a mature, sensual love, even as she insisted that those needs did not signify abnormality. In dreams, and perhaps in the letters to Geraldine that have not survived, she allowed herself to elaborate on her subconscious desires for love everlasting. While Miriam Van Waters tried to provide salvation to her students and close relatives, in her most private relationship, Geraldine Thompson offered not only the earthly comforts of respite and companionship, but also the vision of a transcendent, eternal bond of love.

Storm Center in Framingham

iriam Van Waters needed all the emotional and political support she could get during her years as superintendent of the Massachusetts Reformatory for Women. Although she earned the loyalty of most staff and the adulation of many of the students in her charge, she operated within a larger political universe that was not always sympathetic to her style of prison administration. In Los Angeles she had learned painful lessons about the way local politics could impinge on reform efforts, especially when conservative members dominated the boards of control that supervised public institutions. She knew that electoral politics influenced the appointments to those boards, and she lived with a measure of fear that a hostile political climate could make Massachusetts as uncomfortable as Los Angeles had become.

Although she did not contribute behind-the-scenes aid in election campaigns, as she had done in Los Angeles, Van Waters remained quite conscious of the political battles around her. She realized that as an appointed official in the Commonwealth of Massachusetts, she could affiliate with one party only, the Democrats. During the 1920s, Massachusetts state politics had been transformed from the domain of elite, Yankee Republicans to the control of urban, ethnic Democrats. Politicians such as David Walsh and James Michael Curley—the populist urban boss often compared to Louisiana's demagogic Huey Long—had mobilized urban voters, many of them Catholics. They galvanized opposition to Yankee Republicans, whose support for Prohibition and immigration restriction had alienated ethnic voters. As the depression deepened in the 1930s, economic grievances contributed to Democratic victories. Former governor Walsh was elected to the U.S. Senate, and despite recurrent exposes of Curley's involvement in graft and fraud, and a short jail term early in his career, he was elected mayor of Boston and then governor of Massachusetts. Curley also served in Congress in the 1940s before being sentenced to federal prison for his misdeeds.[1]

In the 1930s, the Democrats held tight control of the state that employed Miriam Van Waters. The superintendent had been a lifelong Republican, with the exception of her support for Al Smith in 1928. A former Hoover appointee, she had marked the election of Franklin Roosevelt in 1932 as a "day of gloom" and remained skeptical about him throughout his first term. She did, however, recognize the political realities around her. As she wrote to her brother George in 1932, "I am in the unique position of being a democrat in State politics, and something else in the National field." Only gradually did she become a supporter of FDR and the New Deal.[2]

Aside from keeping in good standing with Democratic state officials, Van Waters faced a complicated structure of authority in her job as superintendent. Her immediate supervisor was the commissioner of corrections, who was appointed by the governor. As long as she had the commissioner's strong support, her work could flourish with relative immunity from interference. Van Waters had been hired during the administration of a "Yankee Democrat" governor, Joseph Ely. The commissioner who appointed her, Warren Stearns, was a psychiatrist she had known during her first job at Boston Children's Aid. Stearns shared Van Waters' view of crime as a disease that required treatment rather than punishment. His successor, Francis Sayre (the son-in-law of Woodrow Wilson), continued to approve of her methods, but when Sayre joined the New Deal State Department, Van Waters expressed concern that a new appointee might prove politically meddlesome. Her fears were not realized. Commissioner Arthur Lyman held office from 1934 to 1945, surviving newly elected Governor Curley's 1934 threat to oust him. Lyman respected Van Waters' methods and gave her a relatively free hand. Only after 1945 would a commissioner who emphasized prison discipline replace these advocates of rehabilitation.[3]

Though protected by sympathetic commissioners, Van Waters also had to deal with an independent state parole board, appointed by the governor. No matter what educational or therapeutic programs she devised, the parole board had the ultimate authority to determine when inmates could leave the institution. The use of parole had spread throughout the country in the early twentieth century. In conjunction with the indeterminate, rather than fixed, sentence, parole rewarded good behavior in prison with the chance for supervised, early release. In the 1920s and 1930s, however, popular concerns about gangsters, crime waves, and recidivism among parolees fueled public demands to tighten requirements for release. Many states shifted authority for parole from prison superintendents to new state bureaucracies. The members of these parole boards were often political appointees, and they tended to assume the role of strict gatekeepers. In Massachusetts, for example, they based their decisions about early release on past criminal records, not on progress toward rehabilitation. Thus, depending on the personnel on the board, its mission could be in direct conflict with Van Waters' goals of reintegrating students into the community. Like the administrative structure in Los Angeles, where the probation committee oversaw El Retiro, the stage was set for political conflict.[4]

The delicacy of her position as an administrator who served under political appointees became apparent early in Van Waters' career in Massachusetts. A few months after she arrived at Framingham, she characterized the chairman of the parole board in terms that revealed her class and gender biases: "He used to be a truck driver—was appointed 30 years ago by some Gov. of Mass[.]—got more trucks, made more money. . . . Some day we may have women on the Board!" Van Waters failed to recall that women appointees could be as conservative as men, but she would later rediscover this political reality. Meanwhile, distaste for working-class parvenus and political hacks recurred as she encountered other Massachusetts politicians. "The gentlemen of the Senate Ways and means Committee, 18 strong, strong too in alcoholic fumes descended on Framingham," she wrote in 1935. "In the nursery they found the babies sleeping and left them howling." According to her confidant Howard Kellett, Van Waters hated meeting with these politicians, and "many a time she burst out to me her feelings on this matter, but she would handle them with all the graciousness of the lady that she was, conceding them nothing, and let them leave frustrated and bewildered. I suspect it was a new experience for them," Kellett recalled.[5]

Conflict between Yankee Brahmin Republicans and Irish Catholic Democrats had characterized Massachusetts politics since the late nineteenth century. Miriam Van Waters aligned herself squarely in the former camp, yet during the late 1930s she had to work under the latter. In 1935, Governor Curley began to fill state offices with political workers and to turn the parole system into a kind of indulgence sale, rewarding the highest bidders with early release. Commissioner Lyman threatened to resign over the infusion of political patronage into the prison system, and Van Waters feared that she would be fired to make way for a Curley appointee. In fact, her job remained secure, but Curley did place political supporters on the reformatory staff. Although he expressed disapproval of women's reform activism (one of his colleagues advised the League of Women Voters that their members would do better to diaper babies than join organizations), he sent a female relative of the state auditor to interview for a job at Framingham. "I feel my Protestantism keenly," Van Waters wrote after the encounter. More typically however, she felt class prejudice toward certain upstart Catholic politicians with conservative views, for she retained deep respect for most priests and their devout followers.[6]

Under Curley and his successor, Governor Charles Hurley, advocates of punishment rather than rehabilitation dominated state correctional institutions, including the Massachusetts State Prison at Charlestown and the Norfolk Prison Colony for Men. Superintendent Maurice Winslow of Norfolk, for example, imposed strict discipline on the inmates in his charge and disliked the laxity he perceived at Framingham. Winslow also tried to purge his institution of "suspected homosexuals" by transferring these men to other state institutions. Other conservative state officials had more impact on Framingham. Parole board appointees, such as P. Emmett Gavin, regularly ignored Van Waters' recommendations for early release and criticized the indenture system.[7]

In some cases, the political appointees who opposed Van Waters represented a social conservatism that had dominated organized Catholicism since the early twentieth century. Under the leadership of Cardinal William Henry O'Connell, the church took strong stands against progressive measures, including the amendment banning child labor and efforts to liberalize the availability of contraceptives. Even when Catholic politicians, such as James Michael Curley, supported progressive legislation to help workers and immigrants, they followed the church in condemning immorality and employing state censorship. A long list of modern arts were banned in Boston under Mayor Curley. Given the traditional association of the Framingham reformatory with "fallen women," it is not surprising that conservative Catholics took a hard line on the women inmates who had usually committed offenses against public morals.[8]

While Miriam Van Waters emphasized the minor nature of offenses like illegitimacy, adultery, and alcoholism, others considered these acts to be serious offenses. Katharine Sullivan, a conservative Catholic and former Curley appointee who joined the parole board in 1946, wrote that almost all women offenders were prostitutes, and that alcoholics were not to be pitied because they tended to commit more serious crimes.[9] Ironically, the majority of the alcoholic women at Framingham were Catholic, a figure that reflected the predominance of Catholics in the surrounding region. Local parish priests went to great lengths to try to restore many of these inmates to their families and communities.

At the level of state politics, however, these older, alcoholic women had few friends. Perhaps they represented a dark underside of Catholic culture, one that did not conform with Cardinal O'Connell's public vision of religious pride and moral force. If so, locking them away at Framingham, and maintaining a punitive approach toward moral offenders, may have made sense to Sullivan and her predecessors on the parole board.

With these kinds of attitudes surrounding her, it is not surprising that Miriam Van Waters privately lamented her fate. Even before Curley took office, she felt the pinch of an inadequate budget and a salary that barely covered her expenses. She also protested characteristically, though privately, about the difficulty of running an institution over which she did not have complete authority. "I do not see how I can accomplish anything permanent unless I have (a) an adequate professional staff—(b) some control over destinies of paroled women," she wrote. Parole board meetings were an agony for her. For one, she never felt comfortable sharing power, and in this case, a majority of the members disagreed with her recommendations. "Some cases I pleaded for like a barrister, some like a mother, for some I was silent." Van Waters depicted the board members as petty, power mongering, suspicious of her work, and destructive of the "faith we build into the students." Only rarely could she claim a moral victory, such as the day a male board member was affected by the story of wife beating that precipitated a woman's crime. More often, she felt frustrated that, despite her extraordinary efforts to uplift her students, their fates could be determined by a handful of political appointees to whom she felt morally superior.[10]

Over the years, Van Waters tried various methods to circumvent the power of the parole board. In 1934 she managed to place independent parole agents under supervision from Framingham rather than from the Department of Corrections at the statehouse. By placing a liberal interpretation on the nineteenth-century indenture law, she devised a way to return women to the community for "daywork" without consulting the parole board. Independent funding, largely from Geraldine Thompson, supported this plan. Van Waters also tried to educate board members about the unique needs of women in order to justify exceptions to the strict rules that parolees could not associate with one another.[11] She even went directly to the statehouse to meet with Governor Curley, a less than pleasant experience for a woman who preferred to associate with the Brahmin class. She shuddered at the scene:

gangsters, ex prize fighters, S. Boston boys, little runts in big clothes, mothers of criminals, glossy [?] ladies, trim young girls seeking a career, great contractors, silly little fat Irish boys—politicians in black overcoats w/ velvet collars, state police in blue uniform were milling around: not one Brahmin of Boston, not one of the old order was present. I was the only lady, a mulatto clerk to the Lieut. Gov. the only gentleman.

A subsequent meeting, at which Curley's henchman, Councilman Coakley, attacked her programs, proved to be "more of an ordeal" than she had expected, leaving the superintendent "shaken with nervous fatigue." [12]

Van Waters' comments reveal a great deal about her political worldview during the 1930s. A reformer of the old school, she identified with Republican progressives who wanted to uplift the masses, bring enlightenment to immigrants, and provide a paternalistic—or in her case maternalistic—form of social justice. Highly disdainful of machine politicians and convinced of the superiority of her views, she cast her opponents as monstrous villains. "How evil and sinister they looked," she wrote of parole board members who opposed her. Few elements of Van Waters' youthful romanticization of the working class survived. Now her solutions to the nation's problems required a kind of noblesse oblige. In family discussions, she aligned more with Geraldine Thompson's brand of charitable reform than with the radicalism then espoused by her brother Ralph. "Our capitalists are the most untamed in the world," she acknowledged, but she then proposed that what "we most need is a conservative, enlightened, educated *class* in America." Curley might satirize the Brahmins of Beacon Hill, but she had observed him "clinging to Mr. Lyman, and glancing at him with pride." [13]

By 1936, Van Waters decided that Franklin Roosevelt represented the better sort of politician in whose hands she trusted the governance of the nation. Perhaps FDR fared well in comparison to Curley, whom the president disliked intensely. Common enemies, or common class alliances, eventually made Van Waters a supporter of FDR's New Deal. The availability of Works Project Administration funds to help build Wilson and Hodder cottages, and to hire artists who painted murals at the reformatory, may have influenced her shift. More important, though, was her personal connection to Eleanor Roosevelt, a result of her friendship with Geraldine Thompson. Once again the ubiquitous First Lady fostered her liberal goals through networks of women reformers. Superintendent Van Waters felt grateful that Roosevelt helped secure the WPA funds for the reformatory, and she was delighted to learn that the First Lady shared her opposition to capital punishment. By the late 1930s, she could count on Eleanor Roosevelt as a political supporter at the national level and a gracious visitor at Framingham.[14]

In the meantime, however, Van Waters had her first taste of political battle in Massachusetts. Early in 1936 the parole board began an investigation of her indenture system, with then–social worker Katharine Sullivan representing Governor Curley. "It seems incredible that the storm center will move in on this peaceful Framingham," Van Waters complained. Commissioner Lyman stood by her, supporting the daywork plan, but new attacks from the statehouse surfaced almost daily. The superintendent was criticized for employing staff and interns from out of state, a key feature of her plan to bring highly educated workers to Framingham. "I must hide the internes under the featherbeds when visitors come," she half joked, revealing her intent to continue their employment. The visitors soon arrived, in the form of an investigative committee from the Department of Justice. Hiding the interns might have been a good idea on several counts, for the superintendent recorded a "curious incident" during the visit. "I glanced at the floor and found a condom. Miss K & Mrs. Watson had no cleu [*sic*] to the mystery. The Roxbury Ladies Choir was here: Our girls sang beautifully. But no one else was about." A few days later she concluded that the "unpleasant swarthy fellow" from the Department of Justice "must be the one who dropped the condom." She left unstated what the act of bringing a condom into a women's reformatory implied—general lack of morals or an intent to exploit her charges sexually.[15]

It was during the attacks from the statehouse and the investigations of her administration that Van Waters began to have the vivid dreams in which mobs of working-class men attacked her institution. "Hordes of investigators" gutted Framingham in one nightmare; "men with blackened faces and angry eyes" sought her "as victim to be trampled" in another. The stress of her political battles began to take a personal toll. "Yesterday the burden was too great for brain or body or nerves," she wrote, "only the will carried it." At the same time, Miriam's personal sources of support were at low ebb. Geraldine Thompson remained with her husband during his final illness, although she continued to send her "dearest love" in letters from Sunny Hill. Then, in August 1936, Hans Weiss died in an automobile accident, removing a soul mate in reform. "I knew grief such as I did not believe possible," Miriam later wrote to Ethel Dummer.[16]

Renewed critiques of the reformatory generated constant thorns in the superintendent's side. The parole board continued to attack the indenture policy, claiming that it allowed inmates to earn spending money for forbidden luxuries, such as movies and manicures off the prison grounds. In 1937 a "high state official" told a Boston newspaper that the system smacked of favoritism and engendered resentment among prisoners who did not partake in day work. The official's main point, however, was that indenture permitted Van Waters to have authority intended for the parole board, whose members had no knowledge of where women worked and how they spent their money. When two indentured students escaped, the superintendent thought that her official report had shrewdly "outwitted the newspapers . . . and allayed the Commissioner's panic," but she knew that critics continued to ask, "What does Dr. Van Waters think she is running?" In her nightmares, the old Framingham of locked cells returned.

Van Waters did survive this round of attack, defeating a legislative bill in 1938 that threatened to limit the indenture system and increase the power of the parole board. Commissioner Lyman opposed the measure, and Geraldine Thompson timed a visit to add her political weight. To keep local political bosses from interfering, Van Waters "made concessions about patronage." Although she won temporarily, she knew that the issue was not going to disappear. That autumn she hoped for the election of Republican gubernatorial candidate Leverett Saltonstall, who might appoint a more friendly board. If Curley won, she would consider resigning. For the time being, Saltonstall's victory in November 1938, removed much of her political aggravation.[17]

Machine politics aside, at the heart of the reformatory's political crisis lay the indenture system. Although it affected only a few dozen women in the state each year, daywork for women prisoners clearly struck a deep nerve in depression-era Massachusetts. At a time when as many as one out of four male workers faced unemployment—and a slightly smaller proportion of women workers—any public policy concerning hiring could cause controversy. The labor movement had already succeeded in closing most prison industries, with the exception of the "state use" system.[18] But anxieties about working women persisted. Some commentators blamed female wage earners for the economic slump; others argued that removing women from the labor force would end the depression. As in other states, Massachusetts considered a bill to limit the employment of married women in state service as a measure to secure jobs for men. Because it would have deprived her of many qualified workers, Van Waters lobbied against the bill. Privately, she welcomed the expansion of economic opportunities for women. "A woman was stewardess on the dining car," she noted that summer on her return from vacation with Geraldine. "What would Virginia Woolf think to add to her evidence in Three Guineas?" [19]

When she eventually took the offensive by going to the press about indenture, Van Waters emphasized the need to make women self-supporting, rather than economically dependent. In 1938 she told a reporter that Massachusetts discriminated against women, since most of her students would not be in prison in other states, where crimes like adultery and fornication were misdemeanors rather than felonies. Furthermore, men but not women could earn money for prison labor in Massachusetts, and only men received state funds upon release. Commissioner Lyman had agreed to give women release money, but only three dollars, compared to men's eight to ten dollars. The woman of today, Van Waters stressed, was a wage earner and should be treated as such. [20]

For a time it seemed that her views would prevail. Governor Saltonstall remained in office for several terms, assuring her of sympathetic parole board members. In 1939 she took pleasure in the overwhelming defeat in legislative committee of another bill to limit indenture. Building her political capital, Van Waters made a point of talking about parole when she met with President Roosevelt. Back home she enlisted the aid of women reformers such as Dorothy Kirchwey Brown, who helped initiate a League of Women Voters investigation of women's parole. In 1940 Commissioner Lyman released to the press his very positive report on the results of the indenture system at Framingham. [21]

Van Water's triumph over the threats to her authority seemed relatively secure in the early 1940s. The appointment of Reuben Lurie as chairman of the parole board at the end of 1940 especially pleased her. Lurie, who had been a good friend of Hans Weiss, stood for the idealistic, patrician reform tradition that she so admired. In addition, the first women appointed to the board—Ruth O'Keefe in 1941 and Isabel Winsper in 1945—worked "in harmony" with the superintendent's goals. [22] The appointment of her protégé Elizabeth Bode as the new supervisor of women's parole insured the continuation of Van Waters' more lenient policies. Some of the new parole board members acknowledged the lesser severity of women's offenses and their need for social services. Community groups steeped in the tradition of women's charitable reform began to cooperate. Both the Catholic Charities and women's clubs in several factory towns provided funds to help parolees get started in industrial jobs abandoned by men during wartime. In addition, a Thompson Fund intern worked with paroled and indentured mothers to help them make the transition from prison to community. Despite these gains, Miriam Van Waters knew that only eternal vigilance could preserve her regime at Framingham.[23]

The lull in political attacks on Van Waters during the Republican Saltonstall administration coincided with the years of World War II, which profoundly affected Van Waters' life and work. During World War I she had been critical of U.S. military involvement and disturbed by the anti-German hysteria of the era. A strong pacifist, her continuing efforts to abolish the death penalty evolved from her belief in the sanctity of all life. In the late 1930s, however, Van Waters began to recognize the threat of German fascism and the horrors of anti-Semitism. At times she struggled to maintain her pacifist views and to understand the sources of fascism. "This day is horrible," she wrote of *kristallnacht* in November 1938, when Germans unleashed violent attacks on Jews and their property. Entertaining a German dinner guest that evening, she could not bring herself to ask the questions on her mind: "What do you see in this America and in Fr[amingham] to warn us or guide us lest we commit these cruelties?" This fear that fascism lurked at home as well as abroad would recur in her journals after the war was over. In the meantime, she sponsored several refugees, including a disciple of Freud who came to work in her household, while she was careful not to invite political accusations that she harbored communists.[24]

After the United States entered the war, Van Waters continued to struggle with her pacifist views. She assured her daughter that conscientious objectors deserved to be treated well in prison. Gradually, she accepted the need for military intervention to combat the evils of Nazism, but doing so made her feel guilty for betraying her father's principle of "Brotherly Love." She prayed that he would understand her "childish" belief in the necessity of this war. In later years, she would still question whether she had been justified in suspending her pacifism.[25]

Meanwhile, mobilization for World War II transformed economic and social life throughout the society. Millions of men and some women entered the armed services, while government propaganda campaigns urged women to take jobs in war industries to replace the departing laborers. Some housewives did become patriotic Rosie the Riveters, working in defense plants or shipyards. More extensive, however, were new opportunities for women who were already earning wages in low-paid jobs in the sexually segregated female labor market.

Waitresses and domestic workers, for example, could now find higher paid jobs previously held by men, earn enough to be self-supporting, and envision a life that included occupational mobility. Along with increased workforce participation and greater job opportunities, new attitudes toward women emerged. On the one hand, public-relations campaigns praised the sacrifices made by wives and mothers who sent their menfolk overseas, worked the swing shift, or purchased war bonds. On the other hand, more menacing imagery appeared, much of it focused on the dangers of female sexuality. Wartime propaganda posters depicted seductive women who lured soldiers into revealing military secrets. As during World War I, young, sexually active women—now termed "Victory Girls," because of their willingness to support the troops through sexual favors—became special targets of moral censorship.[26]

During wartime, women did congregate around training camps and army bases, just as camp followers have throughout military history. In 1918, the U.S. government had launched a campaign to incarcerate potential prostitutes to protect soldiers from venereal disease. Similarly, during World War II some states, such as New York, converted former Civilian Conservation Corps camps into special detention facilities for women. Although Massachusetts did not do so, arrests of women for morals offenses soared. Local authorities periodically conducted raids on lodging houses where casual prostitution flourished; these young, temporary prostitutes often wound up in Framingham. In addition, the state public-health service sent several hundred prostitutes to Framingham for short-term medical treatment for venereal disease before returning them to local jails.[27]

As a result of both these crackdowns and an increase in commitments of alcoholics, Framingham became severely overcrowded. At full capacity the institution could accommodate under 400 women, but 430 had been sentenced there by mid–1942, and almost 500 by 1944, causing some students to double up in their rooms. Moreover, the lure of higher paying jobs had depleted the institution's staff. Women who had been willing, if not desperate, to work there during the depression could now find better jobs in factories or offices. Interns had once worked for room and board only; now the Thompson Fund provided monthly stipends as well. Commissioner Lyman expressed fears that the pool of volunteers who had been so essential to Framingham's unique programs would disappear. These deficits may have encouraged greater hiring of inmates as staff members. In any case, the combination of inmate overcrowding and staff shortages threatened to undermine reformatory programs and institutional control. By the end of the war, for example, several groups of women had managed to escape, a problem that had been held to a minimum in the past.[28]

To alleviate the pressures on Framingham, Commissioner Lyman authorized the opening of a rural annex to the reformatory at a former jail in the western Massachusetts town of Greenfield. In 1942, fifty women transferred from Framingham to the new location. Located on a forty-acre farm, eighty miles west of the reformatory, Greenfield seemed to offer an opportunity to recreate some of the "freedom and zest" of El Retiro. Van Waters did not want the farm to resemble the New York detention centers, which she referred to as "concentration camps for girls." But the new institution consisted of traditional barred cells, with few amenities. Students worked as domestics in local homes and made Red Cross supplies for the war. Van Waters did arrange access to the YWCA swimming pool and, with help from the Thompson Fund, she sent teachers to hold classes for the Greenfield inmates. The superintendent visited regularly herself but assigned an administrator to run the annex.[29]

Van Waters had several good reasons for remaining at Framingham, including her history in Los Angeles, where she lost control of El Retiro while traveling, and the demands of caring for both her aging mother and her grandsons. Above all she worried about possible threats to her authority. A male business agent appointed by the state in 1942 seemed to be undermining her control of the institution. Without her knowledge, she charged, he had been issuing orders and hiring staff, including men she claimed to be drunk at work. Behind him stood a local political boss who sought control of patronage jobs at the reformatory. Boss Murphy threatened an investigation of the institution if Van Waters did not cooperate with him. In nightmares, she imagined him as a soft, fat bull who was "nudging me and manipulating me into Mud."[30]

In a strongly worded, and possibly exaggerated, complaint to Commissioner of Corrections Arthur Lyman, Van Waters wrote that she was "hampered so seriously that I can no longer be said to have the authority to administer the work efficiently." She implored Lyman to restore her complete control, warning that otherwise a collapse of staff and student morale would follow. "In short," Van Waters concluded, "this is a small institution and a woman's institution. . . . [W]e seem to be in some crisis." When Lyman affirmed her command, she felt that she had won a victory of sorts over these "political troubles." Although she had suffered "loneliness, isolation and anxiety," she took pride in the fact that "I did outsmart them." The incident revealed once again Van Waters' desire for total control of Framingham, and it may have contributed to her reputation among correctional officials as a particularly demanding administrator. She certainly made few political friends by standing up to the machine.[31]

Soon after reclaiming her authority, the war began to bring significant changes to Framingham, laying the seeds for later political conflicts. For one, federal contracts encouraged new industrial jobs to support the war effort, including the manufacture of clothing for soldiers. In 1943, the reformatory earned a certificate of merit from the War Production Board for the greatest per capita production of any institution in the country. In addition, because of the departure of male employees for military service, students took over jobs formerly held by men. They worked in the boiler room, shoveled coal, worked on the farm, and did "everything but run the tractors." The indenture system also expanded to include new kinds of jobs. Framingham inmates now labored outside the reformatory in local laundries, a restaurant, a shoe factory, and at the town's hospital; they went to local farms to help harvest crops; and some women entered the defense plants in the area as dayworkers.[32]

Finally, wartime overcrowding, as well as the increased incarceration of prostitutes, may have contributed to greater awareness of homosexual relationships between female inmates. Historians have credited World War II as a turning point in the formation of a homosexual subculture in America. The congregation of young men in the military and of self-supporting young women in the workforce provided new opportunities for same-sex relations to form. In major cities, gay bars flourished in the 1940s. For working-class lesbians, some of whom were casual prostitutes, these bars provided a social world and a place to meet sexual and romantic partners. Despite police surveillance and periodic vice raids, public attitudes toward homosexuality remained relatively tolerant during the war. Even in the military, the necessity of utilizing all personnel led many officials to ignore evidence of homosexuality. After the war, however, a reversal in policy would fuel antigay witch-hunts, in both the military and the society at large.[33]

The prison had long been known as a site of male homosexual activity, but in the 1940s the association of lesbianism and crime began to surface within the professional literature on criminology.[34] At Framingham, Superintendent Van Waters first learned about relationships between students just after her arrival in 1932, when a staff member passed on to her inmate gossip about the "doll" situation—the slang for lesbians—and "the fuss the white girls make over the colored girls."

Observers had long noted the attractions between black and white women prisoners, suggesting that race substituted for gender roles within women's institutions. Even when Van Waters noted no "overt white-white" relationships, she identified several interracial couples and tried to prevent these liaisons by channeling black students into dramatics and music. During the 1930s homosexual relations also surfaced when a student appearing before the parole board submitted love letters between inmates, arguing that fear of sexual advances justified her early release. Officers did occasionally discover two women in bed together, perhaps more frequently during the overcrowding of wartime. For the most part, the staff psychiatrists relied on the Rorschach test to elicit "positive evidence regarding homosexuality," and like Van Waters they recommended recreation to divert women from romantic attachments.[35]

Whatever the extent of homosexual relationships at Framingham, during World War II the subject was more commonly discussed. Some students continued to mention the practice to authorities, as did an escapee who justified her flight by claiming that the "doll business" at the reformatory had been repulsive to her. Attractions between black and white women also continued, according to institutional records. Although the staff accepted close friendships, they drew the line at blatant pairing off. Thus assistant superintendent Peg O'Keefe cautioned one white student not to be so obvious about her close attachment to a black student. Annoyed that the staff assigned them to separate living quarters, the inmate seemed to feel betrayed: "True, I was carrying on an affair," she wrote to O'Keefe, "but I certainly wasn't loud about it."[36]

The psychiatric records at Framingham reveal that the staff tried to avoid "any punitive attitudes" toward homosexual behavior, especially if the Rorschach test did not provide "positive evidence." Nonetheless, some women had their parole revoked and others faced criminal charges of "lewd behavior" when they engaged in homosexual relationships after release. In one well-documented case, for example, a paroled student allegedly had "been engaged in homosexual activities to such an extent that she is unable to adjust in employment." Returned to the reformatory, she later asked to be released in order to marry a man she had managed to meet in a local jail. Officials seemed pleased at this outcome, but on parole she continued to pursue homosexual relationships. The entire case record, and especially the reformatory's willingness to allow a known homosexual to remain on parole, would later be used to accuse Van Waters of tolerating homosexuality at Framingham.[37]

Van Waters' approach, however, was not necessarily unique. Other superintendents, such as Edna Mahan at Clinton Farms, tried to minimize same-sex relationships rather than punish them. When the superintendents of institutions for women and girls invited Margaret Mead to speak at their annual conference, they asked her "how much we should worry about homosexuality." Mead argued that female homosexuality was much less socially dangerous than male homosexuality, in part because women tended toward permanent, rather than "exploitive and promiscuous," relationships. Like Van Waters, the noted anthropologist recommended programs to channel attractions into other forms of self-expression. Mead, who had relationships with both men and women herself, believed that female institutional homosexuality was a temporary substitute for heterosexual relations. In the postwar period, however, she predicted that "For the first time in our lives, we are going to face [a] society that has more women than men in this generation, and female homo-sexuality will be a problem, not alone in the institutions but in society at large."[38] As Miriam Van Waters sat in this meeting, she could not have known how prophetic Margaret Mead's words would be for her own career. The postwar world would not only identify female homosexuality as a problem, but it would target Framingham as a dangerous source of lesbian relationships.

The end of the war brought both new hope and new fear to the reformatory. The dramatic announcement of victory in Europe was made by no less than Boston's Catholic bishop, Richard Cushing, who arrived with full police escort, swept into the chapel in colorful robes, and impressed Van Waters and her students with his message that "Perfection is attainable." A few months later, after the United States had destroyed Hiroshima and Nagasaki, the superintendent felt less sanguine. Weeping about the atomic bombings, she recalled the pacifism that underlay her opposition to war, capital punishment, and vengeance toward prisoners. In the face of such display of military might, she renewed her faith that only "the Love of our neighbors" could protect the world.[39]

The postwar social and political climate, however, did not favor such compassion. In American society in general, reconversion from war to a peacetime economy occurred under the shadow of a number of fears: of return to the prewar economic depression; of the awful power of the atomic bomb, especially in the hands of the Soviet Union; of internal subversion by communist sympathizers; and of external defeat in the cold war, in which capitalist and Communist states competed for the political and economic allegiance of the world's developing countries. Cultural images of women abandoning the workforce to return to marriage, suburban homes, and child rearing helped soothe the nation's fears of a return of male unemployment. At the same time, anticommunism became a powerful force in domestic politics.[40]

Against this backdrop, Miriam Van Waters faced new political dangers in Massachusetts. Former Boston mayor Maurice Tobin, a onetime Curley protégé who now rivaled his former mentor, had been elected governor in 1944. Although he proved to be fairly liberal, soon after taking office Tobin dismissed long-standing commissioner of corrections Arthur Lyman, replacing him with Paul Doyle. This turnover worried Van Waters' supporters, who feared for her job. Tobin also appointed to the parole board Katharine Sullivan, whose conservative views challenged the liberal board members allied with Van Waters.[41]

Politics looked bleak enough that in February 1945, Geraldine Thompson called on Eleanor Roosevelt to help buoy Miriam Van Waters' political clout in Massachusetts. "I may be over-anxious," Thompson wrote, "but now I am concerned with the possibility of Governor Tobin's removal of Doctor Van Waters." Unlike Thompson's own "middle of the road philosophy," she told Roosevelt, Miriam was "not only a liberal, but a radical, and a fighting radical, at that. She gets her current news (and this is probably a well known fact) from 'The Nation', the 'New Republic', and 'P.M.' She is, and has always been, an ardent supporter of yours and Franklin." If Eleanor had any plans of coming to Massachusetts, Thompson asked pointedly, she might write the Democratic governor, "adding a few lines saying that if you came you would like to visit Framingham (as you have done in the past) and expressing to him your knowledge and appreciation of the type of philosophy and administration which has made Framingham the outstanding Women's Reformatory in this country." Roosevelt agreed, and with characteristic authority, Thompson instructed her friend to approach the governor "on a friendly basis; his power for good might be recognized, perhaps combined with a warning." She also told Miriam to invite Roosevelt to speak at a regional social work conference, so that the First Lady could send a note to the governor "saying how sorry you were not to be able to accept Miriam's invitation." Tobin responded with a letter assuring the First Lady of his "high regard" for the superintendent, and Van Waters enjoyed his support during his two-year term.[42]

Despite Roosevelt's efforts to insure the governor's political loyalty, Commissioner Doyle went on the offensive. He published "destructive attacks" on state institutions, including Framingham, where he charged that "savagery, danger, and dirt" were rampant. Van Waters was disturbed enough to go to Doyle's office and demand a public apology. She felt vindicated when the commissioner retreated. Explaining the latest developments to Eleanor Roosevelt, Geraldine Thompson breathed a sigh of relief that, at least for the moment, "the danger signal seems to be down." She added, however, the importance of "building up more constructive knowledge" about Framingham, "so that if a second attack is launched, public opinion will be better informed to defend it."[43] Her prediction would soon come true.

That spring, Thompson arrived on the weekend before Commissioner Doyle visited Framingham. She and Miriam stayed at Hill Top, away from the institution and from Miriam's worries about her mother's failing health, Sarah and Dick's failing marriage, and the care of her grandchildren. The two friends talked late into the night and slept to the warmth of "an all night burning Pine Log." But Miriam's sleep was troubled by dreams of swastikas and of refugees whom she was powerless to save, of broken bridges and blocked escape routes. In the morning she "burst out" to Geraldine, who understood and comforted her. At a time when she had reason to contemplate images of racial prejudice and anti-Semitism, her dream had expressed identification with outsiders. Similarly, in an unusually explicit expression of gender consciousness, she wrote that "I too am an individual of a minority—an isolated female Penologist." And yet, she did have loyal backers. An array of local women's groups, including the League of Women Voters, supported her work; her old friend Bess Woods came to visit from Los Angeles; Geraldine made several trips to Framingham and she kept Miriam's room ready for her at Brookdale, imploring her to visit.[44]

Although Commissioner Doyle continued to monitor Framingham, he did not attack the reformatory. In cooperation with Van Waters, he created an indenture board, composed of Van Waters, her deputies, a physician, and several social workers. Instead of signing blank indenture slips, as his predecessors did, Doyle approved placements on the recommendation of the indenture board. These included daywork in factories, and, in one case, he signed an indenture contract to allow an inmate to attend secretarial school. In the course of sharing authority with Van Waters, Doyle came to believe that she was a "good woman and a religious woman," and he felt proud to be associated with her.[45]

In the meantime, Geraldine Thompson realized that Miriam needed continued support. In the fall of 1945, Eleanor Roosevelt visited the institution. Still dressed in black, six months after her husband's death, she provided ample photo opportunities for Van Waters, the commissioner, and other state politicians. Roosevelt's account of the trip in her newspaper column praised Van Waters for instilling in her charges the "faith and hope, which are rooted in her own soul." Thompson also brought Van Waters and Doyle together at a luncheon during the 1945 American Prison Congress in New York, and she invited Miriam to lunch with Eleanor on her next trip to the city. For the time being, Framingham seemed secure, but early in 1946, the storm clouds threatened once again. Conflict broke out on the parole board, with the result that Van Waters' supporter Ruth O'Keefe resigned. Without her presence, Katharine Sullivan's voice carried more weight in women's cases, and in Van Waters' view she was "the most damaging."[46]

According to Ruth O'Keefe, Sullivan was ignorant, arrogant, and cruel. She seemed to "take pleasure in humiliating the women who appeared before her." Sullivan distrusted experts and "was quite unwilling to suffer any interference from the reformatory staff on the question of *violation of parole*." She thus disapproved of Van Waters' tolerance of minor parole infractions and correspondence between students and parolees. Moreover, Sullivan believed that most reformatory women had such low mental capacity that they could not comply with the terms of early release.[47] Ralph Van Waters advised his sister to steer clear of the parole board dispute; when Miriam told him that she had "smashed the other Board," he cautioned her not to brag of it. But the inveterate crusader, convinced of her righteousness, organized to defend her cause. When one of Boston's tabloid newspapers ran bold headlines decrying abuses in the parole system, Van Waters took her "Parole sorrows" to the Episcopal archbishop, who promised to back her if necessary. With continued newspaper probes of the indenture system, along with reports of rioting at the men's prison at Charlestown, Van Waters felt deluged by "the practical Parole situation and the Press and the Politics." Suffering "intensely" from negative publicity, she even contemplated losing. "*I conceive concept I am expendable*," she admitted in March 1946. Soon she began to look for a potential successor for her work. Entering her sixtieth year, she hoped for five more years as superintendent before turning the reformatory over to a yet unchosen protégé.[48]

Given the threats to her job, and the simultaneous crisis in her daughter's marriage and her mother's fragile health, it is not surprising that Miriam Van Waters felt defeated. She had weathered storms before, but this time the combination of family problems and work pressures seemed to break down her usual public repose and self-reliance. More frequently than in the past, she turned to others for help. Geraldine continued to write, call, and visit. Van Waters also consulted one of the reformatory psychiatrists. When he asked why she didn't devote her energy to a different kind of work, suggesting that she could thrive as a college president, she responded by telling him of her "Conviction, my joyous labor for a Christian Penology." When torturous nightmares and feelings of despair overwhelmed her, she continued to invoke her prayer of renunciation, hoping to be of humble service to others.[49]

Miriam Van Waters sensed that Framingham faced a turning point when she devised an elaborate five-year plan at the beginning of 1947. She hoped that involving the chaplains further in her work might ensure support for reform, and she predicted future political struggles to protect nearby lands, which she wanted to preserve as a nature sanctuary, against encroaching developers. But first, Van Waters had to secure her cherished programs, and her authority. Once again she took the offensive in the battle over indenture. House Bill 1739—"my bill," as she called it—proposed to add the phrase "and other" to the traditional domestic service permitted as a form of work release. This way she could legitimate the nontraditional jobs to which women had been sent during and after the war. Van Waters won Archbishop Cushing's support for the bill, but she faced the vocal opposition of Katharine Sullivan. Her nemesis had been "collecting cases" about Framingham and introduced a new attack, this time criticizing the way that babies had been placed in foster families. By spring 1947, Van Waters found herself "gearing up for battle" again.[50]

Battle lines had indeed been drawn in the state legislature over allowing reformatory inmates to work at nontraditional wage labor outside the institution. Parole board chair Matthew Bullock denounced Van Waters' bill as a form of illegal prison labor, while the reformatory chaplains rallied to the support of broadened indenture. In an editorial, the *Boston Herald Traveler* recognized an important underlying tension in the debate. Because Van Waters "now wants the privilege of indenturing her charges into hospitals, laundries and factories as well as into homes," the newspaper explained, state boards felt that she was encroaching on their authority. The editors acknowledged that Van Waters could be trusted with this power, but they did not necessarily favor its extension to other superintendents. The issue, then, was whether Miriam Van Waters could formally retain the exceptional administrative authority she already exercised without legal sanction.[51]

Other issues converged in the debate. When State Auditor Thomas Buckley charged that indentured Framingham inmates worked for lower wages than prevailed in the open labor market, publicity turned to the issue of women's "illegal" labor. Van Waters countered that her students received the prevailing rates, and she called Buckley's charges "political." Her claim referred to the conflicts between the parole board and her administration, but it could easily have been applied to the broader social debate on postwar women's roles. Only within the context of a national call for women workers to return to their homes could the press raise the specter that a few dozen women prisoners, most of them still working in domestic service, could undercut the free labor market.[52]

Although the organized women's movement did not appear to be strong in the years immediately after World War II, the public attack on Miriam Van Waters' administration elicited an immediate response from several local women's groups. For years the superintendent had worked with women volunteers and local women's clubs, speaking frequently to church and other voluntary organizations. Now these women identified with Van Waters' position and offered their support. In May 1947, for example, Mrs. Hazel Rabbitt, a member of the Altrusa Club of Boston, wrote to Auditor Buckley. Her organization consisted of fifty-four "prominent businesswomen" who had helped raise money to hire additional women workers at the reformatory. Rabbitt protested the unequal treatment of women in prison, stating bluntly, "Massachusetts legislation in this matter—to be vulgar—stinks."[53]

In addition, former parole board member Ruth O'Keefe issued a timely report from the Massachusetts League of Women Voters on injustice to women offenders. She cited the long sentences for cohabitation and adultery that the courts meted out to women but not to men. Echoing the language of nineteenth-century reformers, O'Keefe condemned the incarceration of casual prostitutes, often the victims of men, as if they were serious criminals. "Only poor women," many of them "foreign speaking," she claimed, were prosecuted for morals offenses that would not be considered crimes if committed by men. Although she called for the decriminalization of most sexual offenses, her position was not likely to attract sympathetic public response in the moralistic climate of the postwar years. O'Keefe's report and Rabbitt's letter do suggest, however, that local women's groups were poised to defend Van Waters' work at Framingham as an issue of equal rights for women.[54]

While women's groups tried to shift the terms of the debate to issues of gender and justice, politicians continued to target the indenture program. Most damaging, a Republican member of the state legislature, Leslie Cutler, introduced a bill to abolish indenture entirely, allegedly at the request of parole board member Katharine Sullivan. Auditor Buckley and parole board chair Bullock backed her measure, claiming that it represented an "abolition" movement to end "slavery" at the women's prison. Their rhetoric belied the motive to keep women working in unpaid state industries rather than for wages outside the institution.[55]

In her defense of indenture, Van Waters had the support of an even more powerful network than the women's club movement, namely, the Episcopal clergy of Massachusetts. She turned to the Reverend William Appleton Lawrence, bishop of the western Massachusetts diocese, a former conservative who had embraced more liberal politics during the New Deal. The bishop's daughter, Nancy Lawrence, had been working at the reformatory, and Van Waters imagined that she might someday take over her work as superintendent. With the bishop's support, church leaders worked to defeat House Bill 1544. Reverend Howard Kellett wrote to clergy throughout the state from his office in the diocesan Department of Social Service, urging them to write letters to their legislators opposing the bill. Kellett also suggested to them that "This is a tangible piece of social action that you can interest the women of your parish in doing something about." Some churches added regular prayers "For all prisoners and those who work for prison reform." Petitions in support of prison reform appeared in church lobbies. While the liberal Episcopal clergy had long supported social-justice issues, the debate over women's work at Framingham also attracted support from more conservative religious leaders. Catholic archbishop Cushing assured Van Waters that he would send Catholic chaplains to testify against the bill that would abolish indenture.[56]

As she battled the Cutler bill, Miriam Van Waters faced an even greater challenge to her authority at Framingham. A new commissioner of corrections, Elliot McDowell, took office in February 1948. An engineer and World War I hero, McDowell had directed prison industries at the

Norfolk Prison Colony for fourteen years. Once a promising reform institution for men, under the direction of Maurice Winslow the Norfolk prison had become punitive and custodial, including extensive surveillance of prison homosexuality. Winslow had been asked to serve as commissioner of corrections by newly elected Republican governor Robert Bradford, who succeeded Maurice Tobin. Winslow declined, but he recommended McDowell, who took the job. Although Van Waters had thought highly of Winslow when she met him in the 1930s, he apparently disliked the laxness of her administration. At a meeting with the governor, Winslow allegedly advised McDowell to "clean up" Framingham. According to several commentators at the time, Winslow continued to direct McDowell's efforts in relation to Framingham.[57]

Soon after McDowell took office, Miriam Van Waters tested him. She called on the commissioner at the statehouse to request his permission to hire a former inmate in the reformatory nursery. Her description of their meeting did not bode well for the future. "Commissioner McDowell said he did not like it that almost the first day he was in office his deputy called his attention to the fact that I was trying to employ ex-prisoners," she wrote. "I was greatly surprised at his tone which seemed to imply that I was 'slipping something over.'" McDowell told Van Waters that "it certainly would not work at Norfolk to have an ex-prisoner over inmates." In response she tried to explain "the differences between a woman's and a man's institution." In a letter to McDowell, she argued that the hiring of rehabilitated inmates was good for student morale, citing the precedent of hiring former patients to work in tuberculosis hospitals. She thought that the "Commissioner's attitude of hostility seemed ameliorated" by her comments. The next week, however, when McDowell visited Framingham with his deputy commissioner, former state policeman Frank Dwyer, the visit turned out to be unnerving. As Van Waters explained, "Mr. Dwyer's attitude to me was so belligerently hostile and scornful I could not present my problems to the Commissioner effectively in his presence." Dwyer would continue to haunt the reformatory, and Van Waters, for the next year.[58]

Commissioner McDowell himself proved to be fairly hostile to Van Waters. In contrast to her previous superiors, who routinely approved indenture, hiring, and new programs, McDowell overruled the superintendent at every possible turn. For one, he vetoed the staff appointment she had requested for a former inmate, provoking a private comment on the double standard of justice. Since even the city of Boston was willing to reelect Mayor Curley, a rehabilitated felon, Van Waters wondered disingenuously, "Cannot the Commonwealth of Mass. accept the rehabilitation of its humbler women offenders?" McDowell also refused requests to transfer paroled students to new locations. He overruled individual decisions concerning punishment and loss of good time and denied Van Waters any authority to supervise the indenture system, which effectively ceased. All records of daywork were removed from the reformatory and taken to the commissioner's office for inspection. As Van Waters wrote in 1948, "The impossibility of maintaining discipline when my authority was so undermined became evident in March." A long-term battle of wills had begun.[59]

Adding fuel to the attack, State Auditor Buckley released to the press his report blasting the use of indenture at the reformatory. In addition to charges of substandard wages for the women and their employment in nondomestic jobs, Buckley argued that by allowing inmates to work outside the reformatory, the state was being robbed of their prison labor. If these women had been producing goods for state use in the institution, rather than working in private industry, he reasoned, other state institutions and municipalities would have saved money.[60]

In the face of these critiques, Miriam Van Waters' sense of being under siege intensified, as did her resolve to fight. She felt convinced of the justice of her cause, which she identified as the liberal reform tradition, and not simply the maintenance of her authority. "It has been a matter of intense surprise to me," she wrote, "that the liberalism built from 1879 in Framingham fostered by me for 16 years could be so menaced in a matter of days." She had no doubts about who had right on their side, her supporters or the McDowell-Dwyer-Buckley team. "Mr. Dwyer dwells within the Legal Code," she wrote in her journal. "I try to dwell within the Law of the Kingdom of God on earth—and laws of health, medicine, psychology and social work." Although she contemplated the biblical injunction to render unto Caesar the things that are Caesar's, it seemed unlikely that she would bow to the lesser power of the state when she so strongly believed that she had God on her side. Besides, the injustice of the charges against her seemed clear: "How strange is this spectacle!" she wrote in her journal. "Mayor Curley of Boston a convict released from Federal Prison holds his office and rules the democratic party . . . at the other humble end of the scale—Margaret Stone freed from Prison, is not allowed her appointment as Student-Officer."[61]

Van Waters did begin to realize that her strategies would have to change. She could no longer assume that her personal reputation or charismatic appeal would on their own command authority. Rather, she needed a legal structure that permitted the kinds of programs she had long been allowed to administer in the spirit, rather than the letter, of the law. She would need to educate the public to override McDowell's belief in the custodial goals of the institution. First she determined to gather the support of leading citizens—settlement house workers, former parole board members, clergy, and state legislators who approved of her methods. Through an organization they could help revise the penal code for women offenders. "Important as the work for individuals is," she wrote, "I know now it can be destroyed—unless the frame work of Law is made structurally different."[62]

The hearings on Cutler's bill to abolish indenture provided a testing ground for Van Waters' coalition. While Representative Cutler argued that women sentenced to the reformatory were hopeless cases, the superintendent's forces called for rehabilitation. She was greatly pleased by their efforts. "Mr. Lurie was magnificent," Van Waters wrote. Chaplains Harigan, Kellett, and Wiltenburg also spoke, as did Ruth O'Keefe and settlement house worker Grace Wills. "Any penologist in the world would have been pleased to see the Bar, Church, Psychiatrists and Sociologists Uniting in a programme of treatment for offenders." Behind the scenes, Geraldine Thompson offered political advice on how to utilize past commissioners on Van Waters' behalf. Eleanor Roosevelt initiated a correspondence about prisons with the superintendent, probably at Thompson's suggestion.[63]

Miriam Van Waters may have won this round in her battle with her political enemies, but a worse ordeal soon appeared in the form of Deputy Commissioner Frank Dwyer, who initiated an investigation of the reformatory in May 1948. The inquiry was allegedly inspired by the suicide of Terry Destafano, an Italian American inmate who died the previous fall. State Representative Michael LoPresti, from the young woman's district, charged that she had in fact been beaten to death as the result of homosexual jealousies at the reformatory, a story that originated with a former inmate who claimed to have witnessed the beating. In an effort to substantiate the charge and further discredit Van Waters, Dwyer began to interrogate reformatory staff and students. Suddenly the issue of homosexuality became the focus of public attacks on Framingham, as Dwyer prodded for evidence of sexual perversion and eventually leaked his inquiry to the local tabloid press.[64]

For the remainder of 1948, Framingham was under intense surveillance. Miriam Van Waters had begun to lay the groundwork for the defense of indenture and the hiring of former inmates, but she was not prepared for exposés of sexual immorality. Shifting the grounds of the attack was in one sense a politically astute maneuver on the part of her opponents. In New York City, for example, reform politicians of the 1930s had successfully used exposes of men's prison homosexuality to turn public opinion against the political machine.[65] In the late 1940s, and for some time thereafter, homosexuality carried such a strong stigma that accusations could be used to discredit both public officials and private citizens. On the other hand, the charge that homosexuality had been condoned at Framingham, leveled against so respectable a public figure as Miriam Van Waters, threatened to unleash a powerful backlash against the politicians who sought to discredit her. What had begun as a conflict over administrative authority between the commissioner of corrections and one of his institutional superintendents had escalated into a debate on the nature of women's work and now burgeoned into a public discourse on the extent and meaning of homosexuality among women. The stage was set for Miriam Van Waters' greatest personal ordeal.

The Van Waters Case

For over fifteen years, Miriam Van Waters had succeeded in conducting her Framingham symphony with only a modicum of public criticism. She had circumvented the legal technicalities of indenture, challenged the parole board, and stretched the letter of the law to create an educational as much as a correctional institution. Cooperative supervisors and influential friends, as well as her own impressive personal bearing, had protected her during earlier political attacks. From the time that Elliot McDowell took over the Department of Corrections in 1948, however, her job was no longer secure. Especially after Frank Dwyer began his investigation that spring, a political battle over the future of the reformatory for women at Framingham waged both in the press and at the statehouse. As in her nightmares, Miriam Van Waters had to defend her institution, her family, and her charges against assault from hordes of well-armed opponents. And as in her dreams, for Van Waters and her supporters the battle took the form of a holy war, a struggle to sustain the Kingdom of God at Framingham against the attacks of infidel politicians.

The charges leveled against Superintendent Van Waters—the misuse of indenture for nondomestic jobs, the employment of former inmates, the existence of homosexual relationships among students—could have been made a decade earlier. Indeed, hostile parole board members had tried to discredit her at that time, but she had defeated their efforts without damaging her public reputation. Now, however, renewed charges about the superintendent's excessive authority, fueled by sensationalized publicity concerning homosexual relations at the reformatory, galvanized political opponents and fascinated the public. By the end of 1948, Boston newspapers announced in daily, front-page headlines the latest twists in the controversy: "Sherborn Probe," "Immorality Charged at Reformatory," "The Van Waters Muddle," and, in a full-page, inch-and-a-quarter banner, "Van Waters Denies Charges."

Why had the women's reformatory and Miriam Van Waters herself become so vulnerable to political attack in the late 1940s? In part, conditions at Framingham had changed over the past decade, especially in response to the exigencies of war. Temporarily protected by sympathetic state officials, Van Waters had been able to extend the use of indenture and the hiring of inmates because of the shortage of both male and female workers during wartime. But the political climate in the years just following World War II became more hospitable to critiques of her policies. After the death of FDR, conservatives in both political parties launched attacks on New Deal liberals, which escalated with the cold-war claims that liberalism had spawned communist subversion. In the 1946 national elections, for example, both Joseph McCarthy in Wisconsin and Richard Nixon in California won election to Congress by attacking their opponents for being soft on communism. Although the charges originated in a strategy to discredit the New Deal by associating its supporters with communism, by 1948 both Democrats and Republicans employed anticommunist rhetoric to win election. Soon state and national governments created employee loyalty programs that helped fuel investigations of potential subversives, laying the groundwork for the McCarthy era. Just as they attempted to purge the nation of subversives, the anticommunists also called for the dismissal of suspected homosexuals from government jobs. In the words of one powerful U.S. senator, it was time to "Get rid of the alien-minded radicals and moral perverts in this administration."[1]

At the same time, social critics now called for women's return to the home from the workplace. The postwar backlash targeted both working women and independent female authority. Called upon to give up their wartime jobs for returning veterans, many middle-class women transferred their aspirations from careers to domesticity. Although most working-class women remained in the labor force, a majority of postwar college women chose marriage over professional lives. In this context, Miriam Van Waters' unusual social experiments at Framingham took on larger symbolic meanings. For conservatives who favored what one historian has termed "domestic containment," Van Waters' policies became the target for attacks on women who engaged in nontraditional roles, whether economic, political, or sexual.[2]

Aside from these wartime and postwar roots of the Van Waters case, long-term conflicts fed into the controversy. Throughout her career, and especially since she arrived at Framingham, Miriam Van Waters had pressed the boundaries of her authority. The same spirit that allowed her to defy press censorship at the University of Oregon and stand up to G. Stanley Hall at Clark University had long propelled the crusading superintendent to hold fast to her positions. In Massachusetts, she usually enjoyed adequate political support to protect her unique approach to prison administration. At the same time, however, she represented a solitary, charismatic leader working outside of the political mainstream. To the local machine, her hiring of educated social service personnel represented resistance to patronage. To state bureaucrats, her insistence on running Framingham her own way frustrated efforts to centralize authority within the Department of Corrections. Van Waters had a reputation for "having a mind of her own," one official later recalled. "She did not enjoy criticism," nor did she tolerate disloyalty. Whether or not these arguments would have been applied to a similar male administrator, they made Miriam Van Waters vulnerable to charges that she stood above the law.[3]

Even sympathetic observers, however, criticized Van Waters' singular management style. One staunch supporter confessed that she had "a certain disregard of regulations." A young researcher found that while "flexibility" was the chief virtue at Framingham, "lack of organization is its outstanding fault," exposing the administration to the dangers of "looseness, inefficiency and special privilege." The superintendent's personalized, charismatic appeal also provoked strong reactions. A staff member who worked in several women's institutions contrasted Van Waters, who literally sat on a "throne" when she directed assemblies, with a superintendent who preferred to take a "back seat." A hostile public official was more pointed, calling Van Waters "a little Queen in her own parlor." Although the comment that she was "the Governor's 'favorite' lawbreaker" delighted Van Waters herself, it no doubt fostered resentment in others who distrusted her exceptional authority.[4]

However vulnerable her individual style made Van Waters, the shift in political winds after 1945 undoubtedly contributed to the crisis she now faced. In contrast to his predecessors, Commissioner McDowell expected to exert control over the administration of Framingham. From his first meeting with the superintendent, he knew that she was not interested in taking orders from him. In the past, her influence among a coalition of liberals in both political parties had made her relatively immune from criticism. If it had not been for the ardent mudslinging provided by Frank Dwyer and publicized by the local link in the Hearst newspaper chain, she might have enjoyed continued protection. In the climate of postwar conservatism, a vocal adversary and a sensational press combined to allow Commissioner McDowell to build an extensive case against Van Waters.

Frank Dwyer, the key investigator in the case, represented the kind of self-made, local political appointee whom Miriam Van Waters disdained. A former state trooper, during the 1930s he served as a bodyguard for Governor Charles Hurley. Before leaving office in 1939, the governor appointed Dwyer as deputy commissioner in the Department of Corrections. While he studied law at night, Dwyer worked in the classification division and eventually became a legal counsel for the department. According to one journalist, Dwyer "boasted of his own horror of homosexuals" and of administering a beating to one. During World War II he had clashed with Van Waters over the administration of the Greenfield Annex. At the time Dwyer called for the abolition of the indenture system, and during the legislative hearings on indenture he testified in strong terms. Some observers felt that Dwyer had an axe to grind because Commissioner Paul Doyle had not reappointed him as deputy commissioner. In March 1948, however, Commissioner Elliot McDowell restored Dwyer to this post. He also delegated to his deputy the investigation of the women's reformatory.[5]

In May 1948, Frank Dwyer began to interview current and former inmates in order to expose laxity in the Van Waters administration. The impetus for his investigation was the November 1947 suicide of Terry Destafano, who had been serving a term as a "stubborn child." Although an investigation under the previous commissioner ruled that the death had indeed been a suicide, State Senator Michael LoPresti and the *Boston American* flamed rumors that Destafano had been murdered. McDowell reopened the investigation by sending Dwyer to Framingham, where he set up an office in which to interview inmates. He was particularly interested in finding evidence that the suicide might be related to the "doll racket," or homosexuality.[6]

Dwyer's tactics appeared strong-arm, at worst, and intrusive, at best. He grilled students who had worked with Destafano in the barn, and when they failed to provide evidence of a doll racket connection, he sought confirmation elsewhere. Dwyer's investigators visited a former Framingham student in her cell at a local jail to ask her to testify against the reformatory. Just after she was released, two men invited the woman for a drink to repeat the request; when she refused to testify, policemen arrived to arrest her. Dwyer had better luck with former inmates at the state hospital. One woman claimed that Destafano had been beaten to death, another that reformatory officers were in love with each other. Although Dwyer concluded that suicide, not murder, accounted for her death, McDowell authorized an expansion of the inquiry because of the new charges Dwyer had uncovered.[7]

When Dwyer returned to Framingham in June he questioned Van Waters for over five hours and probed into staff members' personal as well as professional lives. "I could not begin to describe to you the humiliation I have been subjected to in two days interview with Mr. Dwyer," Deputy Superintendent Peg O'Keefe wrote to the superintendent. To document charges that Van Waters hired former convicts, Dwyer had read the court records of staff members. Over twenty years earlier, he learned, O'Keefe had been sentenced to a reformatory on the charge of "manifest danger of falling into vice." Dwyer's list also included students who had been hired as interns at Framingham. Indignant about his effort to ferret out former criminals employed at the reformatory, Peg O'Keefe pointed out that "He omitted one, Mrs. Hodder's appointment," for the respected former superintendent had borne a child (who was now a state representative) in a common-law marriage. O'Keefe's comment highlighted the contrast between the Framingham tradition of overlooking women's "social" offenses and the deputy's depiction of these women as dangerous criminals.[8]

Dwyer's probe expanded beyond the criminal records of staff members to inquire into their sexuality. In an interview with a former inmate who had complained about homosexual advances at the reformatory, Dwyer's assistant asked, "Did you think that anyone on the reformatory staff had homosexual tendencies?" The woman named Peg O'Keefe. To support her claim, she cited the deputy superintendent's style of dress — "going to Church in a shirt and tie, wearing flat shoes and being very mannish." Clearly fishing for any signs of deviant behavior, Dwyer interrogated a student about whether a former intern was a "stud" or a "Queen," introducing slang terms then used among male homosexuals.[9] He also questioned the nature of friendships between staff and students, implying that the close ties Van Waters fostered between officers and inmates indicated homosexuality. Complaining about the interrogations in a letter to the governor, the reformatory librarian described the experience as full of "insult, humiliation, inuendo [*sic*] and attacks" upon staff. She condemned the "malicious gossip" generated by the inquiry, claiming that "the most innocent make the best targets for the slanderer."[10]

Although neither Dwyer nor the newspapers ever publicly accused Miriam Van Waters of homosexuality, the rumor circulated quietly. The relationship between Miriam and Geraldine, some of Thompson's relatives assumed, fueled the political attacks. Others also linked the public charges to Van Waters' private life. In a letter to Ethel Sturges Dummer, Van Waters explained that the "evil Hearst newspapers began this attack and have hinted that I was 'run out of California' because of personal immorality. They call it the 'doll racket.' They mean homosexuality." Van Waters offered no comment on the charge, so sure was she that Dummer and others who knew her would find it unbelievable. Though most politicians avoided making direct accusations against such powerful targets, Frank Dwyer clearly tried to implicate the superintendent in a homosexual scandal during his investigation. A former student wrote to inform Van Waters that a man was "going around to all of us girls that did time years ago." He asked if she had "seen anything queer going on" when she worked in Van Waters' home. Although this woman refused to answer, she feared that someone else might lie "to get even for being kept" at Framingham.[11]

Van Waters must have confided Dwyer's "grilling" to Thompson, who then tried to rally a defense against the probes into homosexuality. Her strategy associated the accusers with depravity, in contrast to women like Van Waters and her staff, who appeared beyond moral reproach. Thus Thompson wrote to another friend of Eleanor Roosevelt, Lois Rantoul, a Republican ally active in the Women's Trade Union League. Because Rantoul's granddaughter, Nancy Lawrence, was an intern at Framingham, Thompson posed a hypothetical question: "Would Bishop Lawrence want his daughter to work in an institution where a Mr. Dwyer might accuse her of homo-sexual practices in the language of the gutter[?]" If her own daughter's character had been assailed, Thompson continued, "I know I would have engaged the most outstanding lawyer." Geraldine had already assured Miriam that she would "gladly pay the fees of such lawyer in Mass[.] to protect Miss O'Keefe" and anyone else charged by Dwyer. Meanwhile, she urged Rantoul to pressure Republican governor Robert Bradford to investigate Dwyer's charges, to keep in close touch with Miriam, and to let the "Governor know you are doing this." Whether political pressure effectively silenced the rumors about Van Waters or not, they remained underground.[12]

The significance of Dwyer's insinuations about homosexuality among reformatory staff lies less in whether any of the allegations were "true" than in the power of deviant labels to discredit women reformers. At a time when the popular meaning of homosexuality remained in flux, Dwyer and others tried to apply its most negative connotations—as coercive, predatory sexuality—in order to stigmatize a wide range of women's behaviors. They targeted not simply love, or even erotic desire, between women, but also any nontraditional female choices, including mannish dress, political authority, and economic mobility. By associating these patterns with the category of aggressive psychopathic homosexuality, Dwyer tried to undermine the legitimacy and moral credibility of Van Waters and her staff. Although his methods were crude, he was not alone in using sexual charges to undermine independent women in politics. In 1948, for example, federal judges blocked the reappointment of their colleague Marion Harron because of "unprovable charges of an ethical nature." The fact that Harron had written love letters to Lorena Hickok, Eleanor Roosevelt's special friend, cost the judge her job. In other cases, as well, threats of revealing lesbianism prevented the appointment of women to public office in the late 1940s. Even within the small feminist movement, charges of lesbianism could discredit women activists in the eyes of their peers.[13]

Van Waters' understanding of homosexuality differed markedly from that of Frank Dwyer. She distinguished between, on the one hand, woman-centered relationships and institutions, in which women nurtured each other through spiritual love, and, on the other hand, homosexual perversions, in which women harmed each other through obsessive and aggressive pursuits. Some medical experts shared this opinion, accepting the former pattern but labeling the latter dangerous. To some extent, but not always, these categories were class based, exempting middle-class romantic friends from the label applied to working-class sexual partners. Yet Van Waters did not necessarily conflate class and sexual deviance. As early as her doctoral dissertation she insisted that a woman vagrant who dressed as a man in order to earn money was not a "homosexual type," and at Framingham she relied on the Rorschach test to detect true homosexuals, whatever their background.[14] Personally convinced that her love for Geraldine Thompson did not make her a "true" homosexual, Van Waters did not necessarily assume that Dwyer's charges applied to her. Whatever personal peace she may have made about the erotic nature of their love, denying lesbian identity seemed essential for her political survival as a public figure. When Miriam Van Waters refuted charges of homosexuality at Framingham, however, she was not necessarily being hypocritical; rather, she based her defense on the distinctions she made between two very different cultural categories. She reserved the term homosexual for a small minority of women who pathologically pursued other women for sex, and she did not necessarily apply it to women who loved women or defied gender conventions.

Given these beliefs, Van Waters firmly denied the charges Frank Dwyer made in his report to McDowell in June 1948, over half of which implied homosexual misconduct. Four of the items concerned special privileges held by inmates, including access to keys and visits off the grounds, and one read explicitly "that many of the inmates receiving special favors are 'known' homosexuals or dangerous psychopaths," suggesting that staff favoritism arose from homosexual relations. Van Waters invoked scientific authority to counteract these claims, inserting a clinical note that would recur throughout her defense. "[T]here are no 'known' homosexuals or dangerous psychopaths receiving special favors," she insisted. "These are medical classifications and can be diagnosed only by competent authority." Resisting Dwyer's labeling of incurable homosexuals, Van Waters concluded that "Medical examination is needed *now* because these states may not be permanent in any event."[15]

Although she publicly denied all charges of homosexuality, privately Van Waters recognized the power of these accusations to sabotage her career. "In the hands of malevolence, the character assassin, has turned gossip into guilt," she wrote, mourning that "all the pleasant kindly innocent ways of Framingham" had been "turned into weapons against our policy." So many of her methods for empowering dispossessed women—the fraternization of staff and inmates, the hiring of former students, the trips for movies and ice cream—now carried the taint of homosexuality.

Van Waters recognized, too, that not only her reforms but also her private life could never seem innocent again. Soon after Dwyer's "inquisition" she took steps to protect her reputation. Her journal entry for June 22, 1948, recorded a painful, momentous decision: "The Burning of Letters continues. One can have no personal 'life' in this battle, so I have destroyed many letters of over 22 years." Miriam had met Geraldine Thompson twenty-two years earlier, and the daily letters that have not survived—all except those from the year of their "courtship"—went up in flames that day. "They might have been inspiration, history, joy, style—to me in 'old age,'" she thought as she destroyed them. Instead, she would keep their message within herself. "The letters are bone and sinew now in my carnage. Doubtless my character has been formed by them."[16]

In response to the Dwyer report, Commissioner McDowell seized the opportunity to rein in Framingham, setting off a heated public debate on the Van Waters administration. On June 7, 1948, he issued twelve "directives" governing the administration of the reformatory, effectively undercutting the superintendent's authority over hiring, indenture, and child placement. McDowell further asserted his authority by calling Anne Gladding to his office, claiming that she had neither the legal authority nor the training to direct child placement for women released on parole.

Underlying McDowell's criticism was the prevailing view that convicted women were not fit to raise their children, who should be put up for adoption rather than placed in foster homes until their mothers could claim them. The parole board, for example, had begun to refuse early release to mothers who would not give their children up for adoption. Gladding's placement efforts seemed to critics like another special privilege. "Why should the reformatory mothers be given something that is denied to lawabiding, good mothers?" McDowell asked Gladding. His contrast between good mothers and reformatory inmates placed him at complete odds with Gladding and Van Waters, for whom rehabilitative maternal justice required the reunion of mothers and babies. To Van Waters, McDowell's actions meant that "We are just another jail."[17]

As the accusations against the reformatory spread through the press, the state legislature established a special committee to investigate the commissioner's charges. Governor Bradford appointed three members who were sympathetic to Van Waters, while the eight legislative members represented both sides of the controversy. Their hearings, however, would not take place until after the November 1948, elections.[18] A period of stalemate ensued, providing each side time to entrench and to gather political ammunition for the coming encounter. To Van Waters, the conflict boiled down to a simple difference in correctional philosophy. McDowell had written to her in July that "the backbone of the penal institution is custody and punishment." In contrast, Van Waters frequently reiterated her belief in "special treatment" for juvenile and women offenders.[19]

To the public, however, the controversy represented much more than a conflict between conservative and progressive penology. Politicians and concerned citizens drew on powerful historical metaphors to interpret the ongoing Van Waters case. State Senator Michael LoPresti, borrowing a popular strategy from national politicians, invoked the threat of communist subversion. He compared the superintendent's administration at Framingham to the communist regimes that had become America's enemy in the recently declared cold war. "She has not only set up an iron curtain but she has ruled with an iron hand," he told the press. LoPresti also accused Van Waters of being "contemptuous of constructive criticism," and, in a rhetorical flourish, he charged her "with malfeasance, misfeasance and nonfeasance in the administration of the State Reformatory."[20]

Like other cold warriors, LoPresti and Dwyer associated communism with sexual perversion, conflating the two as forms of corruption that threatened internal security and the innocence of American youth. Like federal officials, who soon outlawed the employment of homosexuals on the grounds that they spread corruption in the government, Massachusetts politicians claimed that homosexuals corrupted the young women of the state. Charges of immorality at the reformatory, widely publicized in local newspapers, claimed that a "'doll racket' involving evil sex practices" corrupted young girls, who were "innocent of these matters." Instead of prostitution, which had so disturbed an earlier generation of Americans, homosexuality now represented the great destroyer of young women's virtue. As LoPresti told the press, "Supt. Van Waters' administration of the Women's Reformatory has been more damaging to the morals and mental health of young girls than has the operation of White Slavery in all New England over the same period of time." In addition, information about "the sex tendencies of women prisoners," LoPresti claimed, had been "kept secret" from the parole board, suggesting a conspiratorial sexual underground at Framingham.[21]

Incensed by these charges, a former inmate introduced an alternative use of contemporary political imagery. Bettie Cane compared LoPresti and Dwyer to some of their predecessors in Massachusetts: "This is on a par with Salem's Witchcraft and I'm not fooling," she wrote to Van Waters. Not to cede the powerful anticommunist rhetoric to the opposition, Cane also wrote to her local newspaper suggesting there was communism at work in the statehouse and complaining that Van Waters was being tortured as the "red inquisitors tortured Cardinal Mindszenty's associates" in Eastern Europe. She also called Dwyer a "Gestapo-like inquisitor." For similar reasons, a veteran resigned from the American Legion because the group endorsed McDowell's handling of the case. The dissident veteran compared McDowell to Stalin and explained that the American Legion should not be supporting communistic behaviors.[22]

While the political rhetoric flew, behind the scenes organizing proceeded. Geraldine Thompson had contacted Governor Bradford during the Dwyer investigation, pleading with him to save the reformatory and urging her political allies to do the same. She also devised the plan of a citizen's group to represent Van Waters' interests, urging the cooperation of former parole board member Francis Goodale and reformer Lois Rantoul, to provide a "very strong influence for the Kingdom of God as it operates at Framingham." Meanwhile, Van Waters contacted allies such as Ethel Sturges Dummer, who offered official testimonials and financial support. When former commissioner Paul Doyle offered to testify on her behalf, the superintendent employed feminist rhetoric, as well, stating that she "would be awfully proud to see you there speaking up for the rights of women."[23]

The defense committee that formed in the fall, the Friends of the Framingham Reformatory (FOF), had an impressive membership list drawn from local professionals, clergy, and liberal reformers. The group resembled what has been called the "informal third force in Boston politics," a bipartisan coalition of liberal citizens that had in the past included Felix Frankfurter, Lois Rantoul, and Harvard-trained lawyer LaRue Brown, who now became the chairman of FOF.[24] An undergraduate classmate of FDR, Brown had served in the Wilson administration and had worked to defend Sacco and Vanzetti in the 1920s. He married Dorothy Kirchwey, a former president of the state League of Women Voters, whose father, prison reformer George Kirchwey, had known Van Waters for years. Brown's sister-in-law, Freda Kirchwey, edited the *Nation,* the liberal journal that later published a sympathetic account of the case. Other executive committee members included treasurer Francis Goodale, settlement worker Grace Wills, former parole board member Ruth O'Keefe and her husband Dr. Edward Scott O'Keefe, Lois Rantoul, and the Reverend Howard Kellett.[25] The FOF circulated a fundraising letter to help pay legal counsel for Van Waters and her staff. The chief counsel, Harvard-trained Claude Cross, had a background in corporate law and a great love of legal detail. He would later defend accused communist Alger Hiss, but he always ranked the Van Waters case as his favorite. Assisting him was Franklin Flaschner, a young Jewish lawyer who would later become active in FOF.[26]

In the summer and fall of 1948, before the investigative commission held its hearings, Van Waters and her supporters articulated their account of the conflict. In tune with the social climate around them, they portrayed the reformatory as a conservator of, rather than a threat to, traditional gender and class roles. Concentrating on indenture, they praised daywork for exposing inmates to "Mrs. Average American absorbed in the task of home making," and for teaching black students about "New England standards of living." Van Waters emphasized the threatened "separation of mothers and babies."[27] In contrast, the local press continued to publicize accusations of sexual scandal at Framingham. Daily articles in the newspapers quoted liberally from State Senator LoPresti, who claimed that the doll racket at Framingham was "so sordid and revolting that it scandalized the investigators." Although Van Waters had yet to receive a copy of the Dwyer report, the newspaper published excerpts that titillated readers with charges of "shocking sex perversion" and "Immoral Practices." Calling for the dismissal of Superintendent Van Waters, LoPresti claimed that "When sex maniacs are allowed to carry keys to every lock in a prison and have their names placed on a payroll—no matter whether it is a state payroll or one set up by some well-meaning individual [the Thompson Fund]—then it is time to clean house."[28]

Amid this publicity, the legislative commission finally met at the end of November 1948, a lame-duck entity in the closing months of Governor Bradford's administration. After a visit to the reformatory, the commission held one hearing at the statehouse that provided a dress rehearsal for the political drama to come. A mix of friendly and unfriendly commission members questioned Van Waters about the alleged privileges extended to inmates, the charges of homosexuality among inmates and staff, the indenture system, and the hiring of former students. State Representative Michael Batal claimed that the decorated cells of "lifers" gave him the impression that "crime pays," while LoPresti bombarded Van Waters with questions about keys, rooms, and privileges to go outside the reformatory. On each count the superintendent defended her administration. When asked who supplied inmate radios, she calmly explained that Archbishop Cushing had donated some, friends and relatives others. Didn't she allow inmates to go to restaurants, movies, and dances? "I don't know about dances," Van Waters responded, but since "these women got into present trouble by poor use of leisure time," they "needed training in wholesome leisure time activities."[29]

To deflect questions about the hiring of students and about homosexuality, Van Waters repeatedly invoked the disease model of delinquency. Since old methods of cure had not worked, she tried new ones, such as indenture onto the staff. Hiring officers who had criminal records or "homosexual tendencies" had medical precedents: "It is practice to employ recovered patients in TB hospitals, it is practice to employ recovered alcoholics to work for AA. Such persons are sometimes better employees for their history of illness." Besides, she insisted, charges of sexual abnormality could only be answered by a trained psychiatrist. LoPresti began to dig more personally, questioning Van Waters on how many family members she maintained at the superintendent's house and whether she had ever employed her brother and her son-in-law. He also pointed out that her daughter had been adopted, as if to suggest that her family was not quite "natural." He did not, however, raise the specter of homosexuality at the superintendent's house.[30]

The brief hearing did little to resolve the conflict between Commissioner McDowell and Superintendent Van Waters, but it did foreshadow the kind of public response that the case would soon attract. As the press described the scene, "Benches, aisles and the back of the hearing room were jammed with spectators, most of them women, whose partisanship for Dr. Van Waters became eloquent when they applauded the end of her initial statement at such length and with such vehemence that Chairman J. Elmer Callahan of the commission threatened to stop the hearing." Through it all, the "diminutive and white haired" Van Waters sat flanked by attorneys Claude Cross, Franklin Flaschner, and La Rue Brown. "Clad in an electric blue dress, and with a small black toque over her white hair," she valiantly, and elegantly, responded to questions.[31]

As confident as she appeared in public, Miriam Van Waters suffered greatly in private. Aside from the ordeal of the hearings, her beloved mother Maud had died in September 1948, at the age of eighty-two. Her daughter Sarah continued to struggle in her faltering marriage. In dreams Van Waters merged her domestic and political trials. Carrying the young Sarah to a cruel performance, not unlike the hearings, she met a rector's wife who was working for her defense. Realizing that Sarah was missing, she learned that her daughter was being tortured for a confession as an "important witness." After the hearings, as she anticipated her dismissal, Van Waters drew on her positive memories of her father to sustain her spirits. "I am going on a journey—Father pulls from his coat pocket, spilling things, a rail way ticket and gives me a hearty God-speed." She would need his blessings for the journey ahead.[32]

In December 1948, Commissioner McDowell made public his determination to dismiss Van Waters from her job as soon as Governor Bradford left office the next month. In response, Claude Cross announced his client's determination to fight "to a finish." If McDowell did act, Van Waters had the right to appeal his decision, to request a public hearing, and to offer evidence in her defense. The sympathetic press, including the Republican-oriented *Boston Traveler,* editorialized that Van Waters deserved an impartial hearing, as opposed to McDowell's "farcical" investigation. Her supporters hoped she would demand one.[33]

In preparation for her dismissal, the superintendent's supporters escalated their publicity. A petition backing Van Waters, measuring over twenty feet long, made headlines in the *Christian Science Monitor.* Letters to the editor flowed into the press, calling the probable dismissal a "disgrace" and extolling Van Waters as the only "expert" in the Department of Corrections. When Eleanor Roosevelt wrote a letter to Claude Cross urging the retention of Van Waters, the story made headlines throughout New England, proclaiming, for example, "Van Waters Defense Aided by Mrs. FDR." Roosevelt also wrote privately to Truman's secretary of labor, Maurice Tobin, to ask the former Massachusetts governor to support Van Waters. Meanwhile, endorsement letters poured in from a variety of forums, ranging from the more conservative Massachusetts Association of Social Hygiene and the New England Watch and Ward Society to the liberal Americans for Democratic Action. Former commissioners of corrections, local judges, and the Boston Civic League also lined up behind her. Religious organizations endorsing Van Waters included the Rabbinical Association of Greater Boston, the Massachusetts Council of Churches, and the Universalist Church. The Van Waters case became a rallying point for social workers, club women, and Brahmin liberals to defend their reform tradition. A coalition including the American Association of Social Workers, the United Settlements of Greater Boston, the Boston Council of Jewish Women, the Women's City Club of Boston, and the Boston YWCA came out in support of Van Waters' "modern, progressive" program, rather than the "reactionary and unenlightened" McDowell.[34]

By contrast, opponents of Van Waters rarely declared their position in public. Individual Catholic antagonists may have influenced the church hierarchy to withhold its endorsement, despite support from local priests. Some former colleagues, most notably Harvard criminologists Sheldon and Eleanor Glueck, offered behind-the-scenes backing for McDowell.[35] Whispering campaigns and anonymous letters circulated privately. The draft of Eleanor Roosevelt's letter in support of Van Waters alluded to these rumors, in a passage that Claude Cross deleted from the final version he released to the press. "It will be a tragedy," Roosevelt had written, "if the old accusations now whispered about are brought up against Dr. Van Waters." Roosevelt knew about these charges because she had received several "vile" letters that were so disturbing that she destroyed most of them. The reference was clearly to homosexuality, for the one letter she saved mentioned the "seriousness of sex perversions among the Reformatory inmates." Similarly the Friends of Framingham received a postcard that articulated the underground rumors about Van Waters. The writer categorized the appeal letter as written "in behalf of Dr. Miriam Van Waters, supt. (or Chief Pervert) of Sherborn R for W (They may be received as women yet seldom leave as women) after being violated by her stooges." His comments echoed LoPresti's accusations that innocent young women were sexually corrupted by Van Waters and homosexual staff members. Although neither her political accusers nor the press ever made public these charges about Van Waters, they represented a silent subtext that haunted the proceedings.[36]

On January 7, 1949, the day after Democratic governor Paul Dever took office, the dismissal anticipated by Van Waters' supporters and opponents finally took place. "I am fired," she recorded in her journal. "Mr. Holland (with liquor reeking) serves me at 9 A.M. with notice of dismissal." The deputy commissioner had brought an eight-page letter of removal from Commissioner McDowell notifying the superintendent that her tenure in office would end at midnight, January 11. He charged her with failure to comply with departmental rules, listing twenty-seven specific charges that had been raised over the past year.

Among other things, McDowell accused Van Waters of allowing inmates to attend movies, eat in restaurants, attend secretarial school, and visit the institution after release; to retain their rings and watches; to work in restaurants, farms, laundries, and other industries; and to work at the institution as auto mechanics and truck drivers under male supervision. Van Waters, he stated, had "permitted former inmates, inmates on parole, former inmates with a history of homosexual tendencies, to visit at dances and other social functions" held at the reformatory. He listed the names of twelve officers or interns whom Van Waters had employed despite their criminal records, which were largely for charges of drunkenness and drug addiction. Five students convicted of lewdness or lewd and lascivious cohabitation, he stated, had been indentured to Van Waters, without his approval, through the Thompson Fund. The most sensational charge read:

> That you have known of and failed to prevent the continuance of, or failed to know and recognize that an unwholesome relationship has existed between inmates of the Reformatory for Women which is called the "doll racket" by inmates and some officer personnel; the terms "stud" and "queen" are used with implied meanings, and such association has resulted in "crushes", "courtships", and homosexual practises [*sic*] among the inmates in the Reformatory and has been a cause for:

a. fights among inmates

b. being allowed on parole, they desire to return to the R. for W. to renew such association

c. When released on parole or discharged, to renew such relationships with former inmates of the R. for W.[37]

Van Waters clearly expected the dismissal, and she was prepared to fight it. On her first day out of office, she wrote to McDowell formally challenging each of his twenty-seven allegations. She requested, and he granted, the hearing due to her by statute, which was set to begin on January 13, 1949. She also called to inform Geraldine Thompson, who wrote to Eleanor Roosevelt before leaving the next day for Framingham. As Van Waters prepared for her public defense, Thompson worked behind the scenes to garner political support. She asked the former First Lady to speak to newly elected congressman Jack Kennedy and his sister Eunice, who had visited Framingham on several occasions. Dorothy Kirchwey Brown felt that the Kennedy influence on Governor Dever could be important. Thompson herself wrote to Dever, as well, mentioning that she knew that Mrs. Roosevelt was looking for leadership in the Democratic Party and suggesting that federal subsidies for state mental hospitals might be forthcoming. At stake in the Van Waters case, she told the governor, was the uplift of the "*sinner.*" The sinner in question, of course, was not Miriam Van Waters but the reformatory student who would lose the guiding spirit of the superintendent.[38]

During her appeal, Van Waters could remain in the superintendent's house, at her own expense, but she could not enter the adjacent reformatory. Before her departure, she made a dramatic exit from the institution. On the day of her dismissal, she noted, "I get 3 new dresses—two to be fired in, one for assembly of students." Suitably attired, she gathered the inmates into the chapel, where they presented a signed "Pledge of Allegiance" to "our dear and most kind superintendent." Each woman had promised that "During her absence, I shall do all in my power to carry on as she would have me. I shall pray nightly that God will endow her with the necessary courage and grace to meet all adversities. My daily request of God shall be that her days of stress will be short and her return to Framingham speedy." Although she appreciated the student's "mature" response and good humor— "After all," she wrote to Sarah, "they are used to injustice"—her spirits plunged after a round of farewells at each department. Seeing the mothers and babies, Van Waters broke into sobs. "[N]ot 'till the breath comes out do I feel intolerable pain," she wrote in her journal.[39]

The support of students, workers, and friends heartened Van Waters after her dismissal. Although she suspected disloyalty among a few potential staff informants, her inner circle poured out their affectionate faith in her. Typical was a note Peg O'Keefe wrote to her "Dear Boss," in which she alluded to the youthful criminal record that had become an issue in the case:

> I was never in more "manifest danger" than I am at the present moment—But I am only a small part of a great project that is being threatened with wreckage: And tho your labors will stand in glory it will take the Department of Correction about half a century to reorganize & establish any kind of a system after the shattering blow they have dealt themselves.[40]

Van Waters herself tried to find a bright side to her ordeal. On the day after her dismissal, she wrote to Sarah that she expected to "get as much fun out of this situation as possible. I've never been fired before so it is an absorbing experience and adjustment. I have so much to learn." The personal reliance on religious faith that had deepened during her years at Framingham served Van Waters well during her ordeal. To Geraldine Thompson she admitted, "I do so hate this latest attack," but she then turned the proverbial other cheek. Since she could not attend chapel with her students, Miriam explained, "I have had to read and study the Bible more. . . . [T]hanks to Mr. Dwyer and the commissioner I am discovering new glories, and . . . I can 'give' them to the students." In public, as well, Van Waters emanated a calm, professional demeanor. Reporters frequently commented on her matter-of-fact responses to the most sensational charges, her stylish appearance, her poise and sense of confidence.[41] In many ways, the pending hearings would afford Miriam Van Waters her finest hours. For the next two months, her shining performance in the greatest drama of her life would keep Boston audiences and newspaper readers, along with liberal reformers throughout the country, riveted to the daily unfolding of the Van Waters case.

In the Matter of the Removal of
Dr. Miriam Van Waters

etween January 13 and March 11, 1949, the hearings on her removal made Miriam Van Waters a cause célèbre in national liberal circles and a household name in the greater Boston area. The press had already begun to exploit the shock value of the investigation of the reformatory, but public interest peaked when Van Waters defended her administration before Commissioner McDowell. While local reporters emphasized the dramatic elements of the administrative showdown, other writers tried to explain how such an exemplary reformer could have been removed from office. Former superintendent Van Waters welcomed the publicity surrounding the hearings, as "grinding" as they were. "Who would have supposed that the drama of Framingham building all these years would have been played out to that vast audience—all our strivings and secrets made known," she wrote privately after one session. "It was beautiful."[1]

The political reactions to the Van Waters case provide an important context for the drama that was unfolding. Opponents of the superintendent believed that she had overstepped her authority and coddled inmates. Supporters portrayed her as a victim of political forces, citing either rivalries within the Department of Corrections or the symbolic nature of the case as a battle for the survival of liberal reform in postwar America. Several friends of Van Waters felt that by refusing to accept unqualified employees sent by the new administration, she had alienated McDowell. At least one newspaper speculated that parole board member Katharine Sullivan sought the position of superintendent, and Van Waters herself wondered if the commissioner had been motivated by a desire to put his own appointee in power. Conspiracy theories continued to circulate to explain Van Waters' dismissal. One writer accused members of the Boston underworld and the Hearst newspapers of combining to create the scandalous accusations about sexual perversion. A former inmate with close Mafia ties, he suggested, provided informants for both Dwyer and the Hearst reporters. Others pointed to Maurice Winslow's clandestine role in fueling the attacks on Van Waters.[2]

More typically commentators placed the Van Waters case within the larger historical context of antiprogressive and anticommunist trials. The *Nation* linked it with the defense of progressive underdogs in a story that began: "Not since the Sacco-Vanzetti affair has the collective stability of Massachusetts been jolted so violently as by the current Van Waters episode." Some newspapers compared the hearings to the Scopes trial, in which Clarence Darrow had defended the theory of evolution against fundamentalist critics. Beckie Van Waters Bartholomew, then living in Georgia, likened the hearings to the attacks on black civil rights in the South and the "witch hunts" going on throughout the country. Indeed, in the same issue in which *Newsweek* ran a sympathetic story on Van Waters, it also reported on the New York City trial of Eugene Dennis and other American communists charged with conspiracy to advocate the overthrow of the government. According to the *Progressive,* the Van Waters hearings were part of a "national epidemic of investigation," referring to the anticommunist hysteria that would target liberals as well as communists for many years.[3] Although Van Waters would not be accused of communist sympathies, elements of the discourse on subversion reverberated throughout the hearings, especially when critics expressed fears of "softness" toward criminals, "anarchism" in prison, and tolerance of homosexuality.

The unusual courtroom drama that unfolded in Boston in 1949 helps explain how Miriam Van Waters could counteract so forcefully the powerful conservative currents that had influenced her dismissal. For three weeks in January and February, during the first round of hearings before McDowell, she starred in a command performance, employing her individual charm and her widespread public support to state her case. Although they knew that the commissioner would reaffirm the dismissal, Van Waters' supporters hoped to use the first round of hearings "to arouse and excite public opinion" in her favor.[4] Their strategy proved highly effective. Thousands of local citizens flocked to Beacon Hill to witness firsthand the compelling events being daily reported in the press and on the radio. On the opening day, so many spectators arrived at the Massachusetts State House that the hearing moved to the six-hundred-seat Gardner Auditorium. The public spectacle that so intrigued the audience was indeed one of the best shows in town. It had all the trappings of a Broadway or Hollywood courtroom drama, as well as elements of a sporting event in which spectators avidly rooted for their favored players.

The center of attention, sixty-one-year-old Miriam Van Waters, remained quietly in her seat until questioned. Then she insisted on standing, like a prisoner in the dock, throughout hours of interrogation. Usually calm and composed, only rarely did she show an uncharacteristic "outburst of emotion," as when she demanded that inmate names be suppressed at the hearings. "Sir, in my opinion, it is very cruel and unnecessary that this woman, completely rehabilitated, should have this incident brought up here," she asserted to a round of cheers from the audience. Another time, when Dwyer introduced evidence from inmate records, Van Waters visibly "wept in her chair." Even those who knew her well expressed surprise at her ability to withstand day after day of hostile questioning, returning each evening to preside elegantly over her dinner table in Framingham. Van Waters, however, excelled in the use of public ritual, so the hearings provided a welcome forum. The audience, witnesses, and press coverage served to reinforce her convictions and strengthen her political clout. As she wrote in her journal on February 3, "Largest crowd yet. It is a day to lift the heart. Sarah is beside me."[5]

The "small valiant, composed" Van Waters impressed the public immensely. "She has all the answers never misses an opportunity to strengthen her case, never side steps a question, gives a practically awesome impression of the strictest honesty and integrity," wrote a friend. "She was so Helen Hayes like," a staff member later recalled. To strike the right image, Van Waters adopted the habit of wearing a different hat each day of the hearings. Reporters, especially Sara White of the sympathetic *Boston Traveler,* frequently described the stylish outfits. "The penologist today was daintily clad in a plum-colored corded silk suit, a frilly white blouse, a black sailor hat with perky feather, and a handsome amethyst intaglio pendant on a black ribbon," read a typical report. Wardrobe, as any actor knows, is not frivolous, for the impact on an audience can be powerful. A resident of nearby Milton, Massachusetts, who regularly brought her seven-year-old daughter to the hearings, wrote to Van Waters that "I keep thinking, as I see you day by day, in those pretty and becoming clothes . . . of Chesterton's paraphrase . . . 'Thy Eternal summer shall not fade' — you always look so nice."[6]

Next to the stylishly attired Van Waters sat attorney Claude Cross. A "grandfatherly" middle-aged man "with a cherubic face and a short, stocky figure," he combined a sharp mind with slow, deliberate speech, reflecting his Mississippi origins. Cross' courtroom maneuvering provided a dramatic complement to his client's quiet reserve. A quickwitted and vigilant watchdog, Cross played the role of defense attorney.

He constantly interrupted Commissioner McDowell to raise wide-ranging procedural objections to the department's presentation of its case against the superintendent. In the opening moments of the hearings, Cross protested Frank Dwyer's habit of pacing up and down as he asked questions; later he tried to restrict McDowell's line of inquiry and prevent the introduction of damaging evidence. Throughout the hearings Cross called into question undefined terms, such as *perversion,* and he waged vocal counterattacks on the Department of Corrections for having removed inmate records from the reformatory.[7]

At times Cross ran verbal circles around the commissioner, entertaining the spectators in the process. Interjecting his own question while McDowell interrogated a witness, he frustrated the commissioner, who complained "Mr. Cross, I hardly had a chance to mention any facts." Cross immediately took the advantage. "I am going to try to straighten you out, sir," he replied, as the audience applauded. McDowell fell further into the trap by explaining that he was about to ask the very question Cross introduced. "I am always just a block ahead of you," Van Waters' lawyer responded. According to reporter White, this "battling between Cross and the commissioner and his deputy . . . has enlivened the hearings to the great relish of the spectators."[8]

Acting as both judge and inquisitor, Commissioner McDowell presided over the appeal hearings from a raised dais, facing Van Waters and Cross. Just below him—and about fifteen feet across from her—sat Assistant Attorney General George Rowell and Deputy Commissioner Frank Dwyer, both of whom questioned the subpoenaed witnesses. As one woman described the scene, "the stony faced commissioner sprawled in his seat at a sort of judge's bench above her." To most observers, the accusers were clearly the villains in the piece. As a supporter wrote to Van Waters, "Every time Mephistopheles came out on the stage in Faust last week, all I could see were Dwyer and McDowell." The commissioner and his deputy took the brunt of audience reactions, as well. On one occasion when McDowell abruptly adjourned the hearings during one of Cross' objections, the commissioner and Dwyer left the proceedings "amid a chorus of catcalls and boos."[9]

The audience so often took an active role in the hearings that McDowell threatened to clear the auditorium if they did not cease their laughter, applause, or derisive sounds. Housewives, off-duty reformatory staff members, college students, workers on their lunch breaks, and friends filled the auditorium each day; those who could not gain entrance weathered the winter cold as they gathered around the windows and doorways to catch a glimpse of the proceedings. When the hearings moved to the reformatory for a day, state police had to control the "overflow crowd" that had traveled thirty-five miles to Framingham only to encounter a much smaller hearing room. Fifty would-be spectators circulated a petition protesting their exclusion. On some days, when Gardner Auditorium would not accommodate the crowd, the hearings moved across the street to the larger Suffolk Law School auditorium.

A special connection formed between Van Waters and the responsive gatherings at the hearings, reminiscent of the emotional bond that commanded loyalty from students and staff. As one spectator described the scene, "Her audience, of an unbelievable variety of types just rise right up and take her to their hearts." They also responded to attorney Cross as if on cue, laughing when he prodded McDowell and vocally censuring the introduction of lurid testimony concerning homosexuality. A reporter described one installment as "a full blown uproar" with "lawyers shouting at each other and the audience howling its own views," including charges of "Frame Up" and "Kangaroo Court." In a quieter expression of support, Geraldine Thompson "smiled broadly from her seat in the audience," a reporter observed. As she explained to the press, she was attending "as a friend and supporter of Dr. Van Waters, and donor of the 'Thompson fund' money." [10]

The presence of Thompson and other friends cheered the former superintendent as she withstood days of interrogation by Frank Dwyer, with occasional inquiries from Commissioner McDowell and Assistant Attorney General Rowell. Dwyer introduced over a hundred exhibits based on evidence acquired during his investigation. His examination continued for days, while Van Waters stood throughout her questioning and Claude Cross interrupted to engage in sometimes lengthy procedural entanglements. "It is now an endurance contest," Van Waters wrote to Ethel Dummer after twelve days of grueling questioning. For another two days, Dwyer and McDowell called witnesses who were hostile or damaging to Van Waters, including State Auditor Thomas Buckley, acting superintendent Inga Johnson, several parole board members, state employees involved in child placement services, former staff, and at least one inmate whom Dwyer had interviewed. According to a newspaper account, the former inmate "gave such lurid testimony"—about homosexuality—that McDowell ordered the auditorium cleared of minors. "No one was removed," the reporter explained, while "McDowell's edict served only to attract more spectators." [11]

At one point Claude Cross was able to cross-examine his client, providing an opportunity for Van Waters to tell her life story, defend her record, and accuse McDowell of setting "the clock back a quarter of a century" when he restricted the indenture system. Then, during the final week of the hearing, Cross took the lead. First, during an eighty-minute oration that enraged McDowell and delighted the audience, he refuted each piece of the recent testimony against Van Waters. Then he moved that McDowell promptly reinstate the superintendent. Predictably, the commissioner denied the motion, and the crowd of 800 "rose to their feet . . . and booed, hissed and howled at the decision." [12]

Cross next called a series of witnesses to attest to Van Waters' character and the good works she had done at Framingham. The parade of supporters included Catholic and Protestant clergy who had worked at the reformatory; loyal longtime staff members; prison physicians and psychiatrists; former commissioners of corrections Stearns, Lyman, and Doyle; prison reformer Austin H. MacCormick; the president of Framingham State College; the director of the Salvation Army; and several rehabilitated inmates. These grateful former students, some of whom had served as interns, offered moving testimonials to Van Waters' healing powers. One woman, whose family Van Waters had helped to reunite, explained that she "begged" for the opportunity to testify. Another woman summed up the tone of these witnesses when she explained:

> Dr. Van Waters has been my life saver. She has given me a
> new life. I was all finished, I thought, when I first came to
> the Reformatory, and only that she believed in me, I think I'd
> be dead now. She felt that I could make it, as they say. Her
> confidence in me gave me confidence in myself, and hence
> I am happy today, working, happy and a different person.

Similarly, devoted staff members sang Van Waters' praises. As reformatory librarian Lena Watson told an appreciative audience, "I believe her to be a great spiritual leader and a living example of Christian charity as I understand it." [13]

After eighteen days of hearings, Commissioner McDowell adjourned to consider the evidence that had been introduced by Dwyer and the rebuttals and character statements presented by Cross. The decision to affirm or retract his dismissal revolved around four key areas: staff employment practices, student indenture, child placement, and homosexual relations. For the most part, the hearings had reintroduced information previously mentioned in the press or at the November legislative hearing. But the two thousand pages of testimony, transcribed as "In the Matter of the Removal of Dr. Miriam Van Waters," had added moving, sometimes shocking, detail. Meanwhile the audience and press response had indicated overwhelming public support for Van Waters. Even though they had little impact on McDowell, who would undoubtedly affirm his dismissal of Van Waters, the hearings provided a receptive public forum for Miriam Van Waters' unique theories of penology.

Throughout the hearings, the Department of Corrections presented ample evidence that Miriam Van Waters had exceeded her legal authority as superintendent, supporting the charges raised in McDowell's dismissal letter. In response, however, Van Waters and the witnesses called by attorney Cross used the hearings to gain public support for the alternative, quasi-legal forms of maternal justice that had characterized her administration for over sixteen years. By responding to charges of hiring former convicts, for example, Van Waters was able to elaborate on her principles of rehabilitation and self-help. On the first day, when Frank Dwyer asked about Peg O'Keefe's prior reformatory sentence, Van Waters explained that she had not known of it when she first hired her, but that she had learned about it by the time she promoted O'Keefe to assistant superintendent in 1939. According to the press, "Vehemently, her cheeks red with anger but her words calculating and slow, Dr. Van Waters protested that her assistant, Margaret O'Keefe, was of the highest character, that her adult life had been exemplary. . . . [T]he petty offense had been wiped out by study and devotion of herself to the duties of her position." In an effort to place greater responsibility on the commissioner's office, Van Waters further explained that she had never been ordered to fire O'Keefe, and Claude Cross called former commissioner Arthur Lyman to testify that he would have approved of O'Keefe's appointment even if he had known of her juvenile offense.[14]

Van Waters and her witnesses reiterated these themes when they argued that the hiring of former students had been a form of rehabilitation. Cross' first witness, Father Frederick Mulrey, testified to the "complete rehabilitation" of a former student who had been indentured to him and then joined the reformatory staff. Although Dwyer introduced stories of other student interns to discredit the superintendent, the testimony often backfired because of the heartwarming outcomes. A convicted larcenist, for example, had served her five-year sentence and, on the day after her discharge, became the choir director at the reformatory, paid through the Thompson Fund. Another former inmate worked for five years at various state institutions before returning to Framingham as a custodial officer, where she had been working for five years. Of Miriam Van Waters, she testified: "She gave me a chance. I felt that I didn't have a friend in the world. I was way down low when I came there. I was sick, and she encouraged me and told me I could do it." Similarly, McDowell's critique that Caroline Cook was still employed as an intern, although the eighty-year-old former doctor was now bedridden, elicited sympathy, rather than scorn. As Reverend Howard Kellett testified, Cook provided "a marvelous example in the care of the aged." [15]

In addition to the complaints about hiring inmates on the staff, McDowell had charged Van Waters with misuse of the indenture system. At the hearings, he and Dwyer documented the employment of women from the reformatory in nondomestic work, making much of wartime jobs in a shoe factory, a laundry, and a local restaurant. He also presented the case of a student sent to secretarial school on indenture to show how Van Waters had defied the law. While in part these charges echoed postwar concerns about women competing with returning male workers, many of the jobs these inmates held would not have been acceptable to men. Opposition to inmates' paid work may have rested upon a general desire for women to return to the home, but in this case the critique had as much to do with the commissioner's desire to retain authority as it did with the nature of women's work. The critical fact was that Superintendent Van Waters had permitted these nondomestic placements, circumventing the parole board and often the commissioner as well. [16]

One of Dwyer's best-documented points was that Van Waters had routinely placed women on indenture without acquiring the necessary approval for individual cases from the commissioner of corrections. Over the years, she had clearly relied on preauthorized indenture slips. Long-term commissioner Arthur Lyman had signed batches of these forms, to be filled in with student names and work assignments at the time of indenture. Thus Van Waters had been able to usurp the commissioner's authority, but with his cooperation. As Lyman testified at the hearing, the system "seemed to work surprisingly satisfactorily." Paul Doyle, who had replaced Lyman, also testified about the efficacy of indenture under the revised procedures he instituted. When McDowell showed his predecessor the folder of the inmate who had been indentured to attend secretarial school, Doyle recalled his approval in the case. "Would you say that contract was granted for domestic work?" McDowell asked. "If it was a violation of the statute, I am responsible for it," Doyle explained, "I knew that she was going to a secretarial school." As Dwyer and McDowell continued to explore this breach of the indenture law, Paul Doyle seemed to be on trial. Although he had once distrusted Van Waters, he now defended her record. "It doesn't follow the letter of the law, but I think it does the spirit of the law," Doyle explained. Although most prisons did not rehabilitate, he added, "I think Framingham is an exception to that and they do a good job." Expressing his great faith in Van Waters, he left the witness chair to loud applause.[17]

When former students testified about the benevolent effects of indenture, they also undercut McDowell's critiques. One woman named in the commissioner's dismissal letter had lived at the staff home while she performed clerical jobs at the reformatory, her indenture paid through the Thompson Fund. "It was the happiest nine months of my life," she told McDowell as a witness. Because the commissioner questioned her freedom to leave the grounds to attend AA meetings in Boston, Cross read into the record a letter the woman had written about her experiences. Three years before her commitment, "an eminent psychiatrist" had concluded "that *I was a hopeless alcoholic.* Dr. Van Waters doesn't know the meaning of the word hopeless and I have never heard it used in this institution." Van Waters had allowed this student to start an AA group at Framingham and had provided the setting in which she finally became "ready" to accept this rehabilitative program. Once again, the human testimony introduced by Cross overwhelmed the evidence about Van Waters' violation of administrative procedures.[18]

On the subject of child placement, as well, when Dwyer and McDowell provided evidence of irregular procedures, reformatory staff explained the human concerns behind their actions. Legally, children could remain with their mothers up to the age of two, when the state welfare department had responsibility for placing them. The reformatory, however, had established its own child placement services for women on indenture and parole, once again circumventing a state agency. Aside from the jurisdictional conflict, two different approaches to child placement emerged in the hearings. The state welfare department agents sought adoptive homes for the children of Framingham inmates; the reformatory staff favored temporary homes with the goal of reuniting inmate mothers and their children.[19] Witnesses from the Division of Child Guardianship offered a variety of complaints about these placements. They considered some homes below the standards required by the board of health, or they objected to the match with foster parents. In one instance, the reformatory staff placed an illegitimate child with a "very intelligent couple." Because the welfare department considered the inmate mother and several relatives "mentally weak," the agency predicted that the child "could not measure up to the standards of the home." [20]

Rather than challenge the concept of mentality that underlay these objections, attorney Cross placed responsibility for these placements upon the commissioner, from whom Van Waters had asked advice. He introduced into the record a letter the superintendent had sent McDowell asking for recommendations on a list of child placement cases, to which she had received no reply. He also documented child placement officer Anne Gladding's efforts to cooperate with the welfare department and the commissioner. The clearest statement of the reformatory's approach emerged when Cross called Gladding as a witness and read into the record her report to McDowell. Gladding had argued forcefully that Framingham inmates deserved to be mothers. Many were "criminals" only by virtue of their pregnancies; they "might never have come to the Reformatory if they had had financial resources to provide for themselves and for their infants." Even those convicted of neglect, she argued, might never again neglect another child. For the good of the child, Gladding believed, mothers should be encouraged to create homes for their children. Once mothers left the reformatory and completed parole, "our answer to them should not be, 'No, we won't let you try because it might be too much for you,' but, 'Yes, it will be difficult, and we'll try to get outside help for you.'" Only when mothers failed did Gladding wish to call in the Division of Child Guardianship. [21]

Although the strongest evidence of Van Waters' defiance of state regulations involved employment, indenture, and child placement, the charges that attracted the most attention at the hearings and in the press concerned homosexuality. McDowell's reasons for dismissing Van Waters included hiring staff who had homosexual tendencies, showing favoritism toward homosexual inmates, and failing to suppress homosexuality at the reformatory. In contrast to the other grounds for dismissal, no specific state regulations had been violated. Rather, issues of judgment and character were at stake. Did Van Waters knowingly tolerate homosexuality among staff and students? If not, had she been unable to recognize homosexual tendencies, with the result that a pernicious doll racket had flourished at the reformatory? If she could not recognize homosexuality, Van Waters was vulnerable to charges of bad judgment; if she acknowledged its existence, but had not suppressed it, she was vulnerable to charges of poor management. Underlying both claims, of course, was the view that homosexuality had to be eliminated to maintain proper prison discipline.

Van Waters clearly walked a thin line in response to these charges. She could deny the existence of homosexuality and appear naive in the face of contrary evidence; she could claim to have successfully suppressed it and face refutation from Dwyer's investigation; or she could deny that it was as serious a problem as her accusers claimed and risk being seen as "soft" on deviance, perhaps, as the whispering campaign hinted, because of her own personal inclinations. In a sense, Van Waters' response combined elements of all three strategies: She created the impression that the problem was minimal, that it was well under control, and that it was not always what it seemed to be. In tone her testimony often suggested that the entire discourse was beneath her, or more precisely, that it was a matter for psychiatrists, not administrators, to discuss.

During his investigations, Dwyer had gained access to the reformatory's psychiatric records, which identified several women who had acknowledged their homosexual desires. One had been hired as an intern through the Thompson Fund, but she resigned after fighting with another inmate and then getting drunk in town. Dwyer questioned Van Waters about the incident, trying to imply her tolerance of such behavior:

"Does the institution record show that ——— had homosexual tendencies?" asked Dwyer.

"I'd have to see the records," said Dr. Van Waters.

"Do you know, as a result of conferences, that she had homosexual tendencies?"

"Yes."

"Would the inmate body have reason to believe that such homosexual tendencies were condoned by you and rewarded?"

"Certainly not!" snapped Dr. Van Waters to a wave of applause.[22]

To further document the existence of homosexuality at the reformatory, Dwyer introduced material from nine inmate records. Much of the evidence was circumstantial, including the insinuation that by returning to the institution to visit friends, former students continued homosexual attachments. Claude Cross pounced upon these cases, urging McDowell to "spare innocent women" from these charges and forcing the commissioner to admit, "I don't know if these women have homosexual tendencies or not." In other cases, however, the evidence was clearer. As one of the psychiatrists testified, one inmate who reportedly dressed "mannishly" had grabbed another woman, "threw her back, kissed her, had said 'I am like a man and get what I want.'" In some of the most riveting testimony, staff members described instances when they discovered two women in bed together, and Dwyer's star witness, a former inmate, described finding two inmates on a cot engaged "in some acts that were disgraceful to any citizen." Even a staff witness for Van Waters acknowledged having seen Terry Destafano partaking in "an unnatural act" in bed with another student.[23]

For days, Van Waters' listened to such testimony and answered Dwyer's questions about it. She acknowledged that inmates had "crushes" on one another, and that the term *doll racket* had been used even before she became superintendent. Reporter Sara White captured well Van Waters' superior tone—and her dramatic presence—in her account of an exchange on day nine of the hearings. "Dr. Van Waters, as superintendent[,] in the past three years were you aware of inmates being in bed together?" Dwyer asked. "The little penologist, clad in plum cord suit with lacy blouse and a veiled and feather little toque, stood on the high platform, and replied with composure: 'Mr. Dwyer, the answer to that is yes, but it is not a matter of three years. It's a matter extending over a considerable time.'" Van Waters then painstakingly explained that over the years psychiatrists, psychologists, chaplains, and physicians had all contributed to treating those women who had shown homosexual tendencies. She insisted, however, on distinguishing between women's friendships and "unwholesome" relationships. Thus when Dwyer asked whether a psychiatric examination had been made of a woman who had become fond of another inmate, Van Waters replied, "No. None was needed. The incident to which you refer hasn't the slightest reference to any sexual deviation whatsoever."[24]

The testimony at the Van Waters hearings reflected the ambiguity about the meaning of homosexuality then shared by penologists, physicians, and psychiatrists. Did mannish attire or close female bonding necessarily evidence "perversion?" Was there such a thing as a homosexual type, independent of whether one engaged in sexual relations with another woman? The psychiatric category of "the homosexual" had emerged as recently as the late nineteenth century, gradually replacing an earlier Western cultural tradition in which even an individual who acted on same-sex desires did not necessarily acquire a lifetime identity as a homosexual. In defending her policies, Miriam Van Waters leaned toward the older interpretation, arguing that no single act or behavioral characteristic should brand a woman as a homosexual. That label she reserved for those with a deeply rooted and rare psychiatric condition, akin to the male sexual psychopath, whose uncontrollable desires led to compulsive sexual aggression.[25] Very few of the women at Framingham deserved this label, according to Van Waters.

In keeping with these views, when asked by Dwyer if perversion included "homosexual acts" and "acts done because of homosexual tendencies?" Van Waters replied:

> That, sir, is so distinctly a medical and technical question that I would not presume to answer it. One of the first things we are taught is that a homosexual tendency must be distinguished from a homosexual act. A homosexual tendency may be completely repressed and turned into a variety of other expressions, including a great aversion to emotion.

Similarly, when asked if she segregated "inmates who have known homosexual tendencies," Van Waters replied, "Sir, you would have to bring me the records of the person, and demonstrate to me by an authority I can respect—a medical or psychiatric or psychological authority—before I can answer your question." Just as she relied on engineers to maintain a safe physical plant, she explained, "so I depend on the medical, psychiatric, and religious experts to tell me when a certain individual is in need of a given kind of treatment."[26]

The institutional records revealed that in most cases, psychiatrists had not been judgmental but rather had tried to divert women's interest from sexual intrigue to recreation and work activities. Reliance on the Rorschach test to reveal true homosexuality allowed the medical staff to avoid labeling women as homosexuals, despite evidence of strong homosexual desire. As in their practice at the reformatory, during the hearings these experts emphasized benevolent treatment rather than punishment for those who displayed homosexual tendencies. One doctor, who feared that discipline would only encourage rebellion, had recommended that "walks, barn [work], dancing, athletics," as well as the "care of animals might help take care of her need to demonstrate affection."[27]

By invoking the power of psychiatry during her testimony, Van Waters recognized how the meaning of homosexuality had shifted from a criminal act to a mental state. At the same time, she tried to avoid a labeling process that would mark close friends, mannish women, and those who had crushes on other inmates as confirmed homosexuals. When Dwyer presented individual inmate folders, Van Waters pointed out the fact that "no overt sexual act" had been observed by officers. She explained a woman's mannish dress and preference for men's jobs as a result of early childhood neglect, not homosexual desire. Or, as Claude Cross put it, the term *perversion* might "mean one thing to Mr. Dwyer and another to Dr. Van Waters."[28]

Aside from the efforts to defuse the label of perversion, Cross defended Van Waters by asking his witnesses how well she had handled homosexuality at Framingham. Each one—including chaplains, physicians, psychiatrists, staff officers, and former commissioners—minimized the problem and extolled her treatment strategies. There was more rumor than perversion, several clergymen maintained; only since Dwyer's investigation had women been mentioning homosexuality, the chaplain stated. The discoveries of women in bed together, staff explained, were very rare and immediately reported to higher officers. Former commissioner Warren Stearns, who had hired Van Waters in 1932, pointed out that all prisons dealt with homosexuality, but that it occurred more frequently in men's institutions. Stearns could not recall much of a problem at the women's reformatory, but, as he admitted, to knowing laughter from the audience, "Homosexuality wasn't as popular a subject" when he entered the field as it had become by 1949.[29]

Whether consciously or not, Miriam Van Waters' defense represented a form of resistance to the use of homosexual accusations to discredit nonconforming women and to the growing association of female crime and sexual perversion. Rather than sacrifice some "mannish" women or close female friends by calling them either homosexuals, latent homosexuals, or women with homosexual tendencies, Van Waters had drawn a firm line against labeling. At the same time, like other psychologists of the period, she did so by accepting a definition of true homosexuality as a pathology. Both Van Waters and Cross also resisted the labeling process when they criticized Dwyer's introduction of the terms *stud* and *queen* into the reformatory during his investigation. By the time of the hearings, however, the popularization of these terms had already begun, and by repeating them, they probably further reinforced public associations of women prisoners with homosexual roles.

Along with the influence of her professional training, Van Waters may have had personal motives for her position. Just as she had refused to label her own love for a woman as a form of homosexuality, so too she hesitated to assume that other women who appeared to fit the definition really were homosexuals. In doing so she ignored the growing acceptance of lesbian identity among working-class women, including some of those sent to Framingham. Yet the strategy of downplaying women's sexual desires appealed to the middle-class liberals who supported Van Waters. As a New Bedford club woman wrote to the newspaper, "Many of us are genuinely alarmed lest the emphasis on sexual perversion at Framingham destroy the progressive principles of rehabilitation that Dr. Van Waters has introduced there." Even more pointedly, a former staff member at the reformatory wrote to the *Christian Science Monitor* in an effort to divert attention from women by targeting male homosexuals: "As for the homosexuality which has been so overexploited and which has made such a (calculated) bad impression on an uninformed public, it is actually a minor problem, there are few actual overt homosexual activities among women." She continued by recommending that "If some of the zeal directed against them could be turned upon the omnipresent MALE perverts who are preying upon youths and boys it would be better employed."[30] Thus, just as some writers defended Van Waters from red-baiting by calling McDowell a communist, so others defended her from charges of condoning female homosexuality by invoking the fear of male homosexuality that seemed to pervade postwar American society.

Within this climate of moral panic over sexual and social deviance, Frank Dwyer had deftly introduced homosexual scandal into his investigation of Framingham. By doing so he had captured media attention and mobilized official opposition to Van Waters' unorthodox administrative procedures. His strategy persuaded at least a few opponents of Van Waters. Hostile letters to the Friends of Framingham condemned Van Waters for acting "above the law" and coddling criminals. One local housewife, furious about the support for the superintendent, claimed that her maid, who had served at Framingham, reported "much talk about sex perversions—but mainly what a terrible person Dr. V. W. is." One of the few public critics was Marion Clarke Nichols, a well-known Beacon Hill socialite and civil service reformer, who considered the superintendent fully liable to McDowell's charges. Opposition, like support, for Van Waters clearly crossed lines of gender.[31]

During the hearings, however, Dwyer's attack often produced as much sympathy for the superintendent as it did antipathy. When Dwyer named inmates he suspected of homosexual tendencies, he aroused fury not only from Van Waters but also from many citizens who disliked the smear tactics. When the superintendent wept to hear names called in association with charges of perversion, or when she insisted that a woman once accused of homosexuality had been leading a good Christian life in her community before Dwyer's exposure, she deepened the public dislike for Dwyer and McDowell. Their names, rather than hers, became synonymous with the mud they had been slinging. They spoke gutter language, she invoked medical experts. Aside from the fact that she had broken no rules in her treatment of homosexuality, Van Waters' superior tone and the testimony from such respectable supporters as former commissioners made her less vulnerable to either explicit or implicit charges of homosexuality.

In fact, by the time the McDowell hearings closed on February 8, 1949, Miriam Van Waters seemed to her followers more like a saint than ever. The crowds had cheered her on the stand, while the press spread her glory, much to her delight. "Inaugural of President Harry Truman, and deposition of Chiang and Van Waters cases side by side," she observed of one newspaper. Although she did not expect the commissioner to restore her to office, Van Waters knew that the hearings had enhanced her reputation, which would serve her well when she appealed to the governor. After the last day of the hearings, exhausted from weeks of testimony, she retreated to Hill Top with Geraldine Thompson to await the predictable outcome and to begin answering "the dozens of letters from known & unknown friends."[32]

On February 11, when Commissioner McDowell issued his thirty-six-page decision, he sustained almost all of his charges. Although he recognized his philosophical differences with Van Waters, he emphasized that a conflict of authority lay at the core of the dismissal. "The main issue," he wrote, was "whether a superintendent who persistently disregards the laws of the commonwealth and disregards instructions of the Commissioner of Correction should remain in office." Whatever she had contributed toward rehabilitation, Van Waters had stepped beyond the boundaries of her authority. "There is not one law for great penologists and another for everyone else," McDowell pronounced. When Van Waters disregarded the rules "as old and outmoded," she risked "anarchism." Accusations of her laxity, leniency, and disrespect for the law recurred throughout the decision, which portrayed her as coddling criminals rather than obeying orders. Despite Van Waters' reliance on psychiatric diagnosis, for example, McDowell believed that "the real issue" was "whether or not adequate steps were taken in all cases to control homosexuality," and he ruled that she had not. In sum, his order to remove her remained in effect.[33]

The Van Waters case was far from over, however, for all of the players knew that an appeal would follow. During the hearings and after Mc-Dowell affirmed his decision, support poured in for her continuing battle. The Friends of Framingham had circulated ten thousand copies of their letter, which helped raise funds to publicize Van Waters' story. Women's networks also mobilized on her behalf, as did religious groups sympathetic to her faith in redemption. Both the Massachusetts Federation of Women's Clubs and the Connecticut chapter of the American Association of University Women endorsed her, while individual club members pledged their help. A local woman who had attended the hearings wrote to Van Waters as she waited for McDowell's decision. "You do not know me," she began, "I am a member of the Boston Wheelock Club, the Florence Crittendon League, the Women's Charity Club, the Bright & Helmstone Women's Club, and the Women's Association of the Brighton Congregational Church. So you see I would be able to obtain a great many signatures in your behalf." Women's church auxiliaries throughout the country wrote in support. In addition, through the Massachusetts Council of Churches, two thousand Protestant congregations pledged their aid in her fight for reinstatement, while the Massachusetts Council of Arts, Sciences and Professionals declared Commissioner McDowell unfit for office.[34]

Meanwhile, personal outpourings of faith and admiration arrived daily—in handwritten notes from former inmates, on engraved stationery from the wives of prominent men, and in typed letters from professional women. Former secretary of labor Frances Perkins sent sympathy, concern, and gratitude for Van Waters' work. Eleanor Roosevelt sent her sympathies and admiration; she also wrote about the case in her newspaper column and missed hearing President Truman's inauguration on the radio because she was giving a talk to the New York University Woman's Club deploring the ouster of Miriam Van Waters. Male colleagues also sent their good wishes, including forty faculty members at Clark University, a Boston patrolman, and a number of prison wardens around the country. Among the prominent signers of a letter to the *Boston Herald* were psychiatrist Helene Deutsch and sociologist Talcott Parsons. Such letters cheered Van Waters. When the Methodist women's society endorsed her, she wrote to Ethel Dummer, "Think of it! Fourteen thousand New England Methodist women talking like this . . . something like a vast personal uprising is taking place."[35]

Confident of her cause and buoyed by her supporters, Miriam Van Waters immediately exercised her right to appeal McDowell's decision to Governor Paul Dever, thus setting in motion another round of hearings. The governor appointed a three-member panel to decide the case. The final arbiters would be Mrs. Caroline Putnam, a Catholic charities worker whose husband had been the mayor of Springfield, Massachusetts; Robert Clark, a county assistant district attorney; and Erwin Griswold, the dean of the Harvard Law School, who would later denounce McCarthyism and then serve as U.S. solicitor general.[36] The political mix included both Catholics and Protestants, but with a hint of pro–Van Waters bias. Perhaps Geraldine Thompson and Eleanor Roosevelt had impressed on the governor the importance of these appointments.

Claude Cross insisted on a public hearing, which began at the statehouse and then moved to the Court Room at Harvard Law School's Langdell Hall. Among the five hundred daily spectators were Harvard students who followed the events closely and ran front-page stories in the campus newspaper. Because the commission had decided to hear the case de novo, rather than relying on the two thousand pages of earlier testimony, the hearings would not be brief. From February 15 through March 4, 1949, the panel and audience listened to both sides in the conflict repeat the charges and defenses. This time, however, Van Waters' supporters purposely avoided the vocal demonstrations that had characterized the earlier hearings.[37]

In what must have felt like a replay of the main event, Frank Dwyer once again presented McDowell's case, grilling Van Waters on the witness stand for four days, one of them devoted to questions about homosexuality. Staff members repeated their stories of finding women in bed together and taking appropriate action to prevent further occurrences. In this round of hearings, however, Dwyer refrained from calling former students to testify. Claude Cross reexamined the former commissioners of corrections and other sympathetic witnesses to testify to the efficacy of Van Waters' methods. He also elaborated on his earlier charges that McDowell was at fault for failing to respond to Van Waters' request for directions from his office. Under cross-examination by Cross, McDowell acknowledged that when Van Waters first visited him after he took office, he had told her "that loyalty was not due to a Commissioner but to the Reformatory in accordance with her oath of office." That statement provided strong evidence for her defense. McDowell's case also suffered from a weak closing argument by Henry F. Fielding, the elderly counsel appointed by the state attorney general to represent the commissioner. By drawing a biblical parallel of Mary Magdalene defending Christ, Fielding probably contributed to Van Waters' sanctification rather than her crucifixion.[38]

Whether from the strength of Cross' arguments, his continued courtroom antics, or an embarrassing conflict that broke out when McDowell practically assaulted attorney Fielding while Dwyer physically restrained the commissioner, the balance seemed to be shifting toward Van Waters' side. On the final day of the hearings, the audience surged around Van Waters, offering her flowers, homemade bread, and candy. A middle-aged woman told the superintendent that "You have changed me by inspiration. At my age I did not think it possible—but I am changed." Faithful supporter La Rue Brown said little, Van Waters recalled, but "he kissed my hand." After the hearings adjourned, Geraldine Thompson arrived on the late train to await the verdict. She also made a point of meeting with Governor Dever's secretary during her visit.[39]

The panel's decision would be handed down on Friday, March 11, 1949. "Long trying day of waiting for Commission Report," Van Waters noted on Thursday, as she and Geraldine Thompson rested at Hilltop. Whatever the outcome, she wrote to Cross, he had been a "truly great lawyer" and provided her the "sheer enjoyment of watching your mind at work." Cross expected to be disappointed by the decision, but he thanked Van Waters for having made his life "fuller and richer." Attorney and client met in his office that Friday, joined by Geraldine Thompson, LaRue and Dorothy Brown, Ruth O'Keefe, and other "staunch supporters." Commission chair Erwin Griswold called to let them know that he was reporting to the governor, and at noon the decision reached them. The governor's commission ruled unanimously that there had been no just cause for the removal of Dr. Miriam Van Waters, thus reversing McDowell's dismissal. In their deliberations, they concluded that "an irregularity in administration or error in judgement, made in good faith" did not constitute a proper basis for removal.[40]

The Dever commission's published opinion included a point-by-point refutation of McDowell's charges against the now reinstated superintendent. The fact that prior commissioners of corrections had approved many of the procedures to which McDowell objected weighed heavily in their decision. They praised indenture and child placement practices and concluded briefly that no means of dealing with homosexuality had been neglected. Although Van Waters had not complied fully with McDowell's directives, she still operated within her administrative authority and could not be removed from office for doing so. To Putnam, Clark, and Griswold, "the enforcement of the rules necessarily involves some discretion." The superintendent may have stretched the meaning of indenture beyond domestic service, but the commission argued that "no institution can be static," and that progress often occurred because "practices get ahead of the law."[41]

Back in the hearing room, Frank Dwyer was furious when he heard the decision. He turned to Henry Fielding and accused him of spoiling the case. Perhaps the appointment of the aging lawyer had undermined McDowell's position. Perhaps the governor's selection of the three-member panel had tipped the balance toward Van Waters. Behind-the-scenes political influence, or surging popular support, may also have counterbalanced McDowell's case. For all of these reasons, the hearings had gone Van Waters' way. As Eleanor Roosevelt described it, in a masterfully concise understatement, "I think the hearing was most satisfactory as far as Dr. Van Waters is concerned but perhaps not quite so satisfactory from the point of view of the Commissioner who, I think comes off rather badly."[42]

Van Waters' supporters were jubilant. Claude Cross immediately called Peg O'Keefe at the reformatory to tell her that Dr. Van Waters was "on her way back to take over." The deputy superintendent was elated. "I began to live again when I heard your voice over the phone," she told Cross. As they approached the reformatory by car, Van Waters, Thompson, and her other escorts heard "a furious din" made by horns, sirens, the chapel bell, and assorted pots and pans. "We never had so many things banging outside the institution, waiting for her to come in," a staff member recalled. Amid the noise, the superintendent stepped out of the car, into the embrace of her sister-in-law, Bertha Green Van Waters. They walked triumphantly into the reformatory, past a hand painted Welcome Home sign and the cheering staff, who had gathered at the main entrance.

Inside, a student assembly greeted the superintendent with "wild cheering." Flowers sent by admirers filled the chapel, where the chaplain offered a prayer of thanksgiving and the student choir began singing the Te Deum under Anne Gladding's direction. A song of praise to God, the words of the hymn called on Christ to "help your people, bought with the price of your own blood, and bring us with your saints to glory everlasting." The message deepened Van Waters' symbolic status as a Christlike savior, as did the request by the student body president for the assembly to kneel and "thank God for sending us back our angel." After speeches by La Rue and Dorothy Brown and Geraldine Thompson, Superintendent Van Waters herself concluded the assembly. "It is a wonderful home coming," she wrote afterward. According to Howard Kellett, the reunion was "glorious," for "Miriam was everything to these prisoners."[43]

After her victory, the superintendent could resume at least a semblance of her normal life. Conducting morning prayer in the little chapel for the first time in two months gave her great satisfaction, as did a retreat with Geraldine at Hill Top. Having forgone their annual vacation because it did not feel "safe" to leave, Miriam now took the time to recuperate at Brookdale. "As to vacation," she wrote to Anne Gladding, "I sleep at least 9 hours, or 10, a day; I walk in the woods, innumerable treasures I've found—a shrew, many foxes, . . . new flowers in marshes."[44]

Van Waters' reinstatement elicited a deluge of congratulatory stories, letters, and telegrams. The *Boston Traveler*, which had provided the most sympathetic coverage, issued a special edition of the newspaper bearing a three-inch banner headline: VAN WATERS WINS. From California, Miriam's oldest friend, Bess Woods, wired her, "JUST GOT NEWS NO WORDS ADEQUATE TO EXPRESS JOY." Former staff members, county sheriffs, a Connecticut state policewoman, prison reformers, Van Waters' protégé Edna Mahan, and "a perfect stranger" were among the dozens of writers who poured out their feelings of relief in triumphant terms: "I told you so," "victory is yours," "justice has prevailed," a "vindication of your principles," "there is justice." From the U.S. Supreme Court, Felix Frankfurter expressed relief that Van Waters had been formally vindicated through a democratic airing of the issues. Similarly, a *New York Times* editorial on the denouement of this "cause celebre in the annals of prison reform" proudly portrayed "justice once again triumphing in its own unmistakable fashion." But a short handwritten note from Peg O'Keefe best summarized the commission's decision: "Dear Boss—*enuff said!* The spirit & not the letter!—MK."[45]

The deep impact that the Van Waters' victory had on the public emerges in these letters, many from people who had followed the case in the newspapers or on the radio but had never met the now legendary superintendent. The lesson they derived, that good could triumph over evil, seemed to reassure a citizenry primed by the cold war to view the world in these embattled terms. To them, McDowell, not Van Waters, represented totalitarian state rule; she stood for humane and spiritual values. As one letter writer put it, "You are specializing in trying to save souls for God." The religious base of her support was clear in other comments on her victory, as well. "Halleluiah, For the Lord God Omnipotent reigneth, Halleluiah Amen," read one. During the hearings a large segment of the public had come to endorse Miriam Van Waters' approach to prison administration. As one housewife wrote, "I have two sons and I only wish that if by unforeseen future circumstances they are ever incarcerated that it will be their good fortune to be placed under the supervision of a person with your courage, understanding of human frailty and great intelligence. . . . My husband feels the same as I." One admirer even believed that "Now that McDowell was shown up by you . . . you should replace him."[46]

The Van Waters' victory felt especially sweet to the local women who had proved to be her staunchest supporters. Housewives and clubwomen looked to her as a model of respectability, perseverance, and dignity. As one Cambridge resident wrote to Van Waters, "What a victory has been won . . . I am writing especially to tell you what you have done for women in general. Your courage, your complete mastery of your feelings, which must have been almost overpowering at times, your spiritual strength, have given us so clearly an indication of what self-mastery really means." As a result of the case, another woman decided to join the League of Women Voters in order to work for better penal legislation. Others inspired by the case would join Friends of Framingham or the Friendly Visitors at the reformatory over the next years, sustaining the long tradition of women's voluntarism.[47]

The impression that good had triumphed over evil, and that the hearings had won converts to the cause of prison reform, heartened Van Waters and her supporters. Ethel Dummer expressed the view in a letter to her "Blessed Miriam": "your spiritual courage throughout the crucifixion of your dismissal and trial have spread your gospel far and wide." But like the early Christians whom Van Waters had emulated since childhood, the superintendent remained vulnerable to powerful opponents. She returned to her job of directing Framingham, but Elliott McDowell continued to serve as commissioner of corrections; his directives limiting her authority over indenture remained in effect. Moreover, Van Waters' enemies did not take the commission's decision calmly. State Senator Michael LoPresti called it a "vicious miscarriage of justice" and promised not only to continue his legislative probe of the reformatory but also to expand his inquiries into how Van Waters had funded her legal defense. The superintendent knew that unless the state legislature revised the laws that she had been ignoring for so long, McDowell could continue to undermine her work. As the Friends of Framingham geared up for a renewed crusade, Miriam Van Waters dreamed of climbing an unscalable wall, then slipping to the ground with "a feeling of having struggled to the utmost (on the climb) and been defeated." As she wrote knowingly to her daughter Sarah, "We won the battle, but the war is not over yet."[48]

PART IV

1949–1974

16

End of an Era

After her triumphant return to the reformatory, Miriam Van Waters faced one of the greatest challenges of her career: restoring her kingdom of God at Framingham in the face of persistent, sometimes vicious, political scrutiny. On the one hand, her victory over Commissioner McDowell, along with the publicity surrounding her case, had strengthened Van Waters' influence. On the other hand, her opponents were more determined than ever to reduce the superintendent's authority. Between her reinstatement in March 1949 and her retirement in October 1957, Miriam Van Waters tread a thin line, bounded by both public acclaim and political vulnerability. The tensions she faced were reminiscent of her Los Angeles years, when she achieved national prominence while local work conditions deteriorated. Once again, just as she reached a pinnacle in her career, many of her cherished reforms threatened to slip from her control.

A dream she recorded in 1951 captured in rich visual imagery the dilemma Van Waters faced. Alone in a "big public house"—not unlike the reformatory or the superintendent's house—she grew dizzy as she carefully descended an irregular staircase. At the bottom, she had to choose between two paths. To the left, along an athletic track, invisible figures batted a "small white ball . . . swift as gun fire;" to the right, a narrow walkway was bordered by "deadish Juniper" at eye level, so that she could not "see where I am going but bow my head." She chose the latter route, with confidence that "I can make it—my destination."[1] In the dream, she avoided the political bullets that awaited her, but even the safer, garden path evoked the threat of decay and of the unknown. Professionally she would travel both courses simultaneously, fighting politicians who were armed with anticommunist and antihomosexual rhetoric, while partially protected by her reputation and her stalwart supporters. Personally, she would traverse even more difficult paths, marked in part by tragic losses, until she finally stepped down as superintendent.

In the immediate aftermath of her reinstatement, Miriam Van Waters rode a wave of public approval, even acclaim, that exceeded all earlier recognition. Just weeks after her victory, the Friends of Framingham held a mass meeting in her honor at Boston's Jordan Hall, and members of the Woman's City Club exclaimed "Van Waters for Governor." Both Portia Law School—the only law school for women—and Western College in Ohio granted her honorary degrees. "*Herald* says I am Woman of the Year in New England," Van Waters boasted in her journal in January 1950. When the Boston Chamber of Commerce held its first "Assembly of American Women of Achievement," among twenty-five honorees they included Miriam Van Waters, along with former labor secretary Frances Perkins, photographer Margaret Bourke-White, author Cornelia Otis Skinner, and film star Ethel Waters.[2]

Speaking engagements also intensified. In the weeks after her victory she addressed local reformers in the League of Women Voters, the Massachusetts Temperance League, and the Society for the Prevention of Cruelty to Children, among dozens of other groups. In addition to talks at local universities and Boston's prestigious Ford Hall Forum, in 1951 she began to offer a weekly lecture course on criminology at Boston University.[3] She appeared on television with the director of the Federal Bureau of Prisons, and for a year in the mid–1950s she offered a regular Sunday morning radio program, *Dr. Van Waters Speaks.* Even Hollywood sought to project Van Waters' charismatic image. In 1950, Warner Brothers released the classic women's prison film *Caged,* which had been inspired by her case. In it, actress Agnes Moorehead created a remarkable facsimile of the high-minded superintendent, battling both corrupt politicians and the mob. Like the sensationalized women's prison movies that followed in its wake, *Caged* emphasized women's sexual vulnerability in prison, rather than the rehabilitation that Van Waters championed.[4]

This flurry of honors and media exposure did not simply console Van Waters for her recent tribulations; it also strengthened her hand by consolidating community backing for her programs. In an historical period when neither prison reform nor the rights of women commanded national support, Miriam Van Waters kept alive an interest in the needs of prisoners and the special concerns of incarcerated women. Inspired by her case, the Episcopal Diocese of Massachusetts mobilized for changes in the "present archaic laws" governing women offenders; the state League of Women Voters issued a report calling for a similar overhaul of the legal code and began an evaluation of county jail conditions. As letters poured in from women in neighboring towns who were "anxious to offer some service" to the reformatory, Van Waters helped organized the Friendly Visitors. An offshoot of the Friends of Framingham, the Visitors revived the Quaker tradition of befriending individual inmates. In addition, the Friends of Prisoners formed to improve conditions for the men incarcerated at Walpole State Prison. Nationally, as well, former interns and students from Framingham organized visitors groups.[5]

Van Waters also used her public platforms to champion causes that had long been important to her: the treatment of male prisoners and the abolition of capital punishment. For years she had corresponded with individual men in prison, offering the kind of personal lifeline that she held out to her own former students. After almost twenty years of promoting the case of Russell McWilliams, an Illinois prisoner whose death sentence had been commuted to life, Van Waters finally succeeded in her campaign to have him pardoned for a youthful crime. With behind-the-scenes support from Geraldine Thompson and Eleanor Roosevelt, and during the peak of Van Waters' public acclaim, model prisoner McWilliams won release in 1950. Van Waters helped him find a job, and he eventually married a former Framingham staff member.[6] Back in Massachusetts, she frequently preached at the Charlestown men's prison, where her friend Howard Kellett ministered, inspiring several prison artists and writers who remained in touch with her about their work.[7]

Closely related to Van Waters' concerns about male inmates was her long-standing commitment to abolishing the death penalty. During the 1920s she had been a founding member of the American League to Abolish Capital Punishment (ALACP) and in 1939 she succeeded Clarence Darrow as it president. The small, beleaguered national organization appealed for clemency for prisoners sentenced to death and lobbied states to abolish capital-punishment laws or permit juries to grant clemency. Concerned that the league was not strong enough to oppose death for treason, she kept private her opposition to the executions of Julius and Ethel Rosenberg, while concentrating organizationally on the disproportionate executions of immigrant, black, and mentally handicapped prisoners. Van Waters also convinced the conference of superintendents of institutions for women and girls to oppose capital punishment.[8]

The most important political outgrowth of the Van Waters case was the Friends of Framingham. Originally designed as a support committee during the dismissal hearings, in the 1950s the Friends included over eight hundred members who lobbied the state legislature for legal reforms affecting women inmates. Immediately after Van Waters' reinstatement, the Friends drafted legislation that would legitimate the controversial indenture system for Framingham students. Now, instead of facing her hostile commissioner of corrections alone, the superintendent had a citizen's group behind her. Under the leadership of LaRue Brown, Dorothy Kirchwey Brown, and Franklin Flaschner, the Friends waged a letter-writing campaign in favor of work release for women inmates. They gathered over fifty thousand signatures on a petition supporting their legislation. As they had learned to do in the Van Waters' case, the group packed hearing rooms with supporters and offered expert testimony. Eventually they won minor concessions from the legislature to permit daywork by inmates. The Friends also lobbied successfully to reduce long reformatory sentences for petty crimes and they continued to raise money to support Van Waters' projects at the reformatory. In the 1960s, Friends of Framingham established a halfway house in Boston for women released from the reformatory.[9]

Although the afterglow of her victory may have contributed to these triumphs, Van Waters was well aware of her enduring vulnerability. As she wrote to her daughter in 1950, the growing sentiment in her favor made the "Enemy more eager and unscrupulous." Here she referred to Commissioner McDowell as the enemy, but broader conservative forces constrained Van Waters as well, for her case had been only a prelude to a political war against liberalism during the 1950s. Skepticism about reform, and the association of liberalism with the threat of communist subversion, undermined her efforts. Capital punishment enjoyed wide public support, while anticommunists continued to portray opponents of the death penalty as "pink radicals."[10] In the wake of the horrors of World War II, even liberal Christianity seemed more resigned to the existence of sin in the world. And, despite critical steps toward racial justice in the South, in the northern states the renewed migration of African Americans during World War II, combined with persistent economic and social discrimination against them, initiated a shift in the racial composition of the prison population. Even though few black women served at Framingham before the 1960s, the growing proportion of black prisoners in the North, along with racial stereotypes of Blacks as less moral than Whites, weakened support for prison reform, as did an outbreak of prison riots in the mid-1950s. In Massachusetts and nationally, politicians called for tighter administration of correctional institutions.[11]

Against this backdrop, Miriam Van Waters faced determined opposition from old enemies. Accusations of lenience and of homosexuality recurred, along with new charges of rampant drug use at Framingham. The parole board repeatedly opposed Van Waters' personalized approach, arguing that contact between students and women on parole, for instance, violated the tenets of "good social work." Although Van Waters won a partial victory on this point, parole board hearings remained "dreadful" experiences for her, while Katharine Sullivan's reappointment insured "another period of Hell" on the board. The former state auditor, Thomas Buckley, continued to question Van Waters' care for the aging Dr. Caroline Cook, who remained at the reformatory until her death 1952. Above all, the indenture system suffered. Commissioner McDowell turned down requests for non-domestic-service indentures and limited the system to daywork, rather than long-term jobs that had allowed some women to reside outside the reformatory. In response, the Friends of Framingham prepared legislation to establish an expanded "conditional placement" program.[12]

During the slow legislative consideration of this bill, the philosophical differences between McDowell and Van Waters reemerged. Like the parole board, the commissioner preferred an ideal of formal, professional, and bureaucratic prison administration, and he too criticized the Framingham staff as amateurs who coddled women criminals. His opinion reflected broader professional developments. Just as social work had been professionalized at the expense of personalized social services, so too the field of penology now rejected the last stronghold of an earlier, romanticized vision of individual rehabilitation. The conflict resurfaced in gender-specific terms during the legislative hearings on expanding indenture. McDowell testified that women should not be treated "the same as men," explaining straightforwardly that "we think of women differently. We set women up on a pedestal and we don't like it when they fall."[13] His reference to the pedestal echoed those nineteenth-century prison administrators who justified harsh treatment of minor female offenders by invoking the theory of woman's greater fall. Historically, women's prison reformers sought to refute this view, substituting faith in redemption through specialized, maternal justice, a legacy Miriam Van Waters had carried into the twentieth century.

The problem, however, lay much deeper than McDowell's individual vision of fallen women, for the ideological underpinnings for separate women's prison reform had diminished by the mid–twentieth century. An ideology of female uniqueness had been replaced by a more egalitarian gender system, one in which women could, theoretically, compete with men as equals. At the same time, however, older views about the social threat of female sexual immorality, as well as postwar concerns about domestic stability, undermined such egalitarian claims. Thus the debate on women prisoners was symptomatic of a larger tension in American gender relations. In the long run, the contradiction between an ideal of gender equality and the reality of economic and social discrimination against women would spark a revival of the feminist movement. In the short run, however, women suffered from contradictory forms of gender discrimination within the criminal justice system. First, by committing crimes, they lost any claims to special treatment as women, as if they had been desexed by the act of being imprisoned. Second, prisons nonetheless treated them differently than men by imposing long sentences for morals offenses and then refusing to women the right to earn wages while imprisoned.

Commissioner McDowell's decision to retire in 1951 only partially relieved these tensions. Because a new commissioner could make Van Waters' life either easier or much harder, she followed the political appointment closely. As in the past, her guardian angel, Geraldine Thompson, kept an eye on Massachusetts politics, meeting personally with Governor Paul Dever and telling him "with emotion" how she "felt about Dr. Van Waters." When the governor's 1950 message to the legislature called for greater responsibility for the Framingham superintendent, Eleanor Roosevelt congratulated Dever in her newspaper column. Thompson once again engaged her influential friend when "the wicked Commissioner of Prisons," McDowell, resigned. If "Gov. Dever could know that *you* care for 'the whole wide world,'" she suggested to Roosevelt, "it would strengthen his better self."[14] Although Thompson and Van Waters approved of the governor's ultimate choice, Maxwell Grossman, the superintendent still chafed under the legacy of McDowell's legal restrictions. Indenture remained limited, students could not leave the institution to visit family or attend church or concerts, and the counseling services Van Waters so cherished could be practiced "only in defiance" of the law. "We bootleg our rehabilitation," she lamented.[15]

Commissioner Grossman's most important decision was to allow Miriam Van Waters to delay her retirement. In September 1952, just weeks before she would have been forced to leave office on her sixty-fifth birthday, Grossman drew on his War Emergency Powers to reappoint her as superintendent. At the request of Governor Dever, a state appeals board soon ruled that Van Waters could remain in office until age seventy. Reluctant to retire until she had restored the rehabilitative mission of the reformatory and handpicked a successor, the superintendent agreed to serve through 1957. The reappointment proved to be quite timely, for a few months later, both Dever and Grossman would be out of office. In response to the political turnover, Van Waters began to have her classic nightmares, including one that she called a "warning dream of frightfulness." Commenting on the dream, she claimed, "I am not in terror but sad. . . . I had dreams like this before the attack on Framingham but now I am closer to God. I believe Prayer can avert danger or teach Us to deliver the helpless." [16]

As usual, Miriam Van Waters relied on Geraldine Thompson as well as on prayer. Shortly after this dream, Thompson arrived to meet with newly elected Republican governor Christian Herter. On later occasions, she timed visits with the governor to coincide with her meetings with leading Republican women, offering a subtle reminder that well-connected members of his party took a keen interest in his continued good will toward the reformatory superintendent. When Geraldine visited, Miriam invited the governor to dinner at her home. Nor did they neglect bipartisan support. "Miriam is rejoiced beyond words that she can count on your coming to Framingham," Geraldine wrote to Eleanor Roosevelt in 1954, adding tips on "where you could say a few words of blessing and hope to the 'prisoners.'" [17]

As she struggled to maintain control of Framingham in the years after her reinstatement, Miriam Van Waters also faced tragic losses within her family. Wrapped up in the defense of her administration, she had little chance to mourn the death of her mother. Although Maud Van Waters had been "slipping" for several years, the loss of the woman whose love meant so much to her, and whose life she had tried to save for so many years, brought more pain than she could express. [18] Miriam lost other central members of her household when Ralph and Bert, along with their two children, gradually moved into the house her brother constructed on land next to Hill Top. The family still enjoyed weekends together, and Miriam sometimes vacationed with Ralph and Bert, but the older constellation had shifted. "Beginning new era," she noted when her brother's family spent their first night at the new house. In 1955 Bert Green Van Waters resigned from Framingham, where she had been a highly competent and compassionate director of children's nursing and one of Van Waters' most important colleagues. [19]

More wrenching for Miriam Van Waters was the crisis in her daughter Sarah's life. In 1950, only twenty-eight years old, divorced, and with three children under age eight, Sarah Van Waters Hildebrandt struggled to support her sons, with little help from their father. Her mother provided some money and bought her a new Chevrolet, while Geraldine

Thompson created a scholarship fund to send the boys to boarding school. When they visited on weekends, George, Ricky, and Peter Hildebrandt raced through the corridors of the reformatory, went on nature walks with the Rangers, and spent Saturday nights at Hill Top with Miriam, Sarah, Peg O'Keefe, Ralph, Bert, and their two children. They listened to their grandmother tell stories and lead songs, then returned to the institution to sleep, never realizing until they were older that they had been in a prison. Meanwhile, Sarah began to take college classes, earn high grades, and build a social life. While working at Hodder Cottage, she came to appreciate more fully the world in which she had grown up. One day, with tears in her eyes, she embraced her mother and explained warmly, "I had no idea till now after [my] return how much you have builded."[20]

Despite this appreciation, Van Waters continued to worry about her daughter's behavior. She wept when Sarah didn't return from a trip to New Hampshire, then felt relieved when Sarah telephoned to explain that the car had broken down. "It is irrational," Miriam wrote, "but Sarah worries me." Another time, when Sarah and Byron, a man she had been dating, drove to New Hampshire, Miriam prayed as "images of disaster recede, then return." For years she had recorded nightmares in which she had to protect Sarah from attack; in one she had to save her daughter from drowning after their car skidded on icy roads into a river. In waking life, too, she worried when Sarah traveled, especially by car.[21]

On February 5, 1953, a week after these "images of disaster," Sarah and Byron gathered with Bert and Ralph, Miriam's nephew and his fiancé, and several reformatory staff members for dinner at a country home near Framingham. On the return trip, Sarah was driving the Chevy down an icy country road when her car swerved and struck a tree. An ambulance brought Sarah and Byron to the local hospital. At 1 A.M. a nurse telephoned, waking Van Waters from sleep to ask that she come immediately to the hospital. A few minutes later, as she was dressing, a doctor called to say that Sarah was dead. Miriam Van Waters' worst nightmare had come to pass.[22]

In the early morning hours Miriam brought Sarah's body to the funeral home, ordered a casket, and planned a service. She then gathered her three grandsons, fetched from boarding school, to tell them of their mother's death. Ralph Van Waters fielded telephone calls as family and friends arrived for the funeral—brother George from Seattle, Claude Cross and his wife from Boston, staff members from Framingham. When Richard Hildebrandt learned of the accident, he reappeared after more than a year's absence. Miriam could not speak when she saw him. "I was numb," she wrote of that moment, though she could have been describing the entire evening.[23]

Van Waters never recorded the magnitude of her grief. After the funeral she consulted with relatives, Dick, and lawyers about her grandsons' support. Then she left for New York City to attend the annual meeting of women superintendents, see Geraldine, and dine with Eleanor Roosevelt. She rested at Brookdale before returning home to hundreds of messages about Sarah. At Framingham, she took up her daily tasks. She taught her literary class, cooked a birthday dinner for her nephew and grandsons, attended church, and began to answer the condolence notes. Eventually she decided to memorialize Sarah by commissioning a stained-glass window depicting Joan of Arc for the reformatory library. For years, close friends, inmates, or her grandchildren would accompany Miriam on her visits to Sarah's grave, where she planted flowers.[24]

Immediately after Sarah's death, Van Waters remained preoccupied with questions of how to raise her grandsons—as Protestants or, as her daughter had agreed, as Catholics—and how to relate to their father. Miriam cared for the boys on the weekends, and Dick Hildebrandt sent some money for them. "God assuredly plans best," she wrote of their father's belated sense of responsibility for them. In April 1953, a few months after the funeral, Hildebrandt arrived at Framingham while his sons were staying at Hill Top. He told them to gather their belongings, and, afraid that their grandmother might try to stop him, he abruptly moved the children to Maryland, where he worked. "The ache is solemn and inexorable," Van Waters wrote of this additional loss. Within a few years, Hildebrandt had established a stable home for his sons. He then brought them back to Massachusetts to visit their grandmother, and the Hildebrandt children maintained contact throughout her life.[25]

How could Miriam Van Waters comprehend the loss of her daughter? She gave few external signs of her feelings. "I don't know how she coped," Margaret van Wagenen commented, "But certainly, on the surface, she coped." Returning from a particularly hard day to find an unexpected dinner guest, a cry of distress escaped her, but only for half a moment. After the superintendent secluded herself for twenty minutes, she returned dressed for a dinner party at which she was "scintillating." Those close to her assumed that Van Waters kept her grief to herself and that her belief that the spirit, like love, was eternal, eased her loss. As always, her secretary recalled, she kept busy "being strong for other people."[26]

Yet her unresolved pain had lasting costs. Helen Bryan, a new friend who was privy to Van Waters' mourning, observed on the first anniversary of Sarah's death, "It is still for you 'violent' her departure, it is still a tearing, rending separation." Knowing how the superintendent channeled her grief, Bryan captured well Van Waters' personal struggle: "To tell you that you have lived your life gloriously during this past year—to tell you that you have transmuted the pain of her leaving into a greater love for those about you—to tell you that you have transformed losing her into helping others to find Life—is, I know, not what will comfort—not what will still the agony that is yours." [27]

Miriam Van Waters lived silently with many agonies. The daughter she had consciously chosen to raise, in whom she had delighted as a child and supported faithfully as an adult, was gone. So too were any lingering dreams that her daughter would in some way become her successor, as a reformer or as a writer. Miriam had adopted Sarah twenty-four years earlier in part to prove that even the most neglected child, raised in a nurturing environment and surrounded by mother love, could become a great leader. She had not been able to make her case, but she had tried to give Sarah every advantage. Always haunted by fears that she had not done enough to save others, Sarah's death may have confirmed her own sense of inadequacy. It might also have suggested to her that no amount of human salvation could compete with the force of God's will.

A few nights before Sarah's accident, Miriam Van Waters had begun to read Helen Bryan's memoir, *Inside,* which passionately described the author's three months as an inmate at the federal women's prison in Alderson, West Virginia. The daughter of a Presbyterian minister, Bryan had graduated from Wellesley College in 1917 and worked for many years with the Quaker-affiliated Institute of Race Relations at Swarthmore College. During the 1940s she had served as executive secretary of the Joint Anti-Fascist Refugee Committee (JAFRC), a national organization that raised money to relocate republican refugees who fled after General Franco's victory in the Spanish civil war. After World War II, the House Un-American Activities Committee (HUAC), which was dedicated to investigating communist infiltration of American life, asked Bryan for lists of JAFRC members and the refugees they aided. Because she refused to hand over the records to HUAC, Bryan was cited for contempt of Congress and sentenced to Alderson. [28]

Reviewing Bryan's memoir for the *Nation,* Van Waters claimed that the "impact of this book is out of all proportion to its content." Although her comment referred to the book's literary and psychological merits, it also characterized well the personal impact that Bryan's story would have on her. Just a few days after Sarah's funeral, as Van Waters recuperated at Brookdale, she met Helen Bryan. The two women soon began a correspondence and then a friendship that quickly reached rare levels of intimacy. "Beloved of my Life," and "Sweet, my Dear," Helen addressed Miriam in letters, using the same terms of endearment so often written by Geraldine Thompson. Like many students and staff members before her, Bryan found herself deeply attracted to Miriam Van Waters' "creativity, compassion and love." A new romantic friendship was forming.[29]

Miriam Van Waters found in Helen Bryan a kindred spirit, a woman whose courage and whose personal experience of prison life uniquely qualified her for understanding the principles upon which she ran Framingham. At the same time, the recent loss of Sarah had left her longing and vulnerable, while her approaching retirement made her highly conscious of potential disciples. Helen Bryan could not fill Sarah's place, nor did Van Waters ever think of her in those terms. The timing and intensity of their friendship suggested, however, that it both distracted her from some measure of grief over her daughter's death and raised the hope of finding a new protégé. Helen Bryan was a former prisoner in need of friends, and Miriam Van Waters was a friend to all prisoners. Within a few weeks after they began to correspond, Miriam invited Helen to address the students at Framingham. That night the two women dined together by candlelight. They began spending time together, attending church, and talking about the rehabilitation of prisoners.[30]

The new friendship with Helen Bryan did not necessarily compete with Van Waters' relationship with Geraldine Thompson, who had introduced the women. Bryan did, however, prove disruptive to Van Waters' professional life, for she soon became another source of political conflict. Shortly after their friendship began, the superintendent invited Bryan to join the staff at Framingham. Van Waters had long insisted that former inmates best understood the needs of her students. Helen Bryan was not only a former prisoner but also a highly articulate and caring woman who needed a job. Commissioner of Corrections Reuben Lurie agreed to a temporary appointment, and Bryan accepted the job in June 1953. The hiring, along with the conversations they had about the qualities of a superintendent, suggested that Van Waters was considering Bryan as a potential successor.[31]

Within weeks of her arrival, however, Bryan's appointment created a scandal. She was not only a former prisoner but a suspected communist. Governor Herter, responding to criticisms from his executive committee and the press, called the hiring "unfortunate." He summoned Lurie, Van Waters, and Bryan to a meeting, after which the commissioner requested that the controversial officer resign "for reasons of health." Bryan did, in fact, have a weak heart, and Van Waters had been concerned about the stress of reformatory life on her. Politics, however, was clearly the reason for her resignation, which came only a month after her appointment. Anticommunists had begun a "Red Probe" of Lurie and the reformatory. "You know that I have never in my life been a member of the Communist party," Helen assured Miriam. Nonetheless, the taint of communism, in this red-baiting era, made it difficult to retain her. The superintendent appealed to "civil liberties men," but it was "hopeless." When Bryan left the reformatory, the "girls cried softly," Van Waters wrote. She felt the loss deeply, as well.[32]

A prison record, combined with the anticommunist atmosphere of the early 1950s, made it hard for Bryan to find work. Van Waters made inquiries that were reminiscent of her earlier job-seeking campaigns for her brother Ralph, and Geraldine Thompson offered money to help find a position. In the meantime the episode served to weaken Van Waters' own base of support. The Friends of Framingham had to issue a statement to reassure its members that Bryan was not in fact a communist; the organization even maintained that she had turned over the mailing list for the Anti-Fascist Refugee Committee to the proper government authorities.

Even more clearly than her own dismissal, the Bryan incident brought home to Van Waters the terrors of anticommunism during the McCarthy era. Although the press had accused her of "subversive activity" in 1949, anticommunism had been only a minor motif in her case. Now she witnessed the process of red-baiting and knew that not only communists, but liberals like herself, were suffering the impact. As she wrote to another woman penologist after Bryan left, "If we don't take steps what has happened to her will happen not only to ex-convicts everywhere but to progressive leaders in the field of delinquency."[33] The charge of subversion, however, had already become a powerful strategy for discrediting civil rights activists and liberal reformers, and Van Waters' efforts to forestall the effects had little chance of success.[34]

After her resignation, Helen Bryan moved to New York City, but she continued to play an important role in Miriam Van Waters' life. Bryan sent romantic letters that recalled memories of Framingham and encouraged the superintendent's work for prisoners. To maintain the privacy of their relationship, Van Waters rented a post office box in downtown Framingham, and each day at noon she secretly went into town alone to post a letter to Helen and receive one from her admirer. A local informant reported Van Waters' behavior to the Federal Bureau of Investigation, which was keeping close tabs on Bryan. Most likely a postal employee, the informant "had opportunity to observe the contents of the letters" between the two women, and he was shocked by their "unusual" nature. As he told the FBI, the correspondence contained "numerous repeated terms of endearment and other statements," leading him to "the definite opinion that Dr. VAN WATERS and BRYAN are Lesbians."[35] The FBI did not investigate further the allegation of Van Waters' sexual deviance. The comment, however, evidenced not only the intensity of Van Waters' relationship with Bryan but also the growing inclination to label such friendships as lesbian and to associate them with subversion.

For Miriam Van Waters, this new relationship represented the last in a series of intensely romantic attachments with women. The depth of Bryan's affection for Van Waters emerged when she wrote gratefully after receiving "quite the loveliest pictures of my Love I have ever seen." Miriam's beauty, she added, stayed "close with me and brings my life deep joy." Even more than earlier protégés, she pledged to live her life in close identification Van Waters, "attempting to undergo and incorporate your pain into myself—attempting to give to you so limitless, so pure, so selfless a love that it will serve as a kind of background for your day." As had Orfa Jean Shontz and Geraldine Thompson, Helen Bryan also tried to watch over Miriam Van Waters, expressing concerns over her friend's health and adoring her accomplishments. After a "shattering" Saturday evening phone call, when Van Waters seemed in a "befogged state" after several martinis, Bryan warned her friend to think of the impact her drinking might have both on the institution and the children in her household. Since Van Waters had never been much of a drinker, the incident may have reflected either her stress in the year after Sarah's death or her despair over Bryan's resignation. For Bryan, the painful talk with her "Darling" left her "grieving" but still "loving you with my whole heart—with pain and with joy—and with longing."[36]

Miriam Van Waters seemed to return the passion. She championed Bryan's writing, marked the anniversary of her going to Alderson, talked with her regularly on the telephone, and for years visited her, first in New York and later in Vermont. Some close observers noted Helen Bryan's importance and puzzled over the apparent waning of the friendship with Geraldine Thompson. For several years, however, Geraldine and Helen coexisted as Miriam Van Waters' intimates, soothing the great loss of her daughter and sustaining her in the face of renewed, and ultimately successful, political attacks.[37]

Besides the furor over her hiring of Helen Bryan, in the years after her reinstatement, Superintendent Van Waters confronted new problems of morale among employees and students. As in the past, a few staff members quietly opposed her. In addition, the increasingly bureaucratized regulations required by the Department of Corrections seemed to undermine the personal mission embraced by older staff members.[38] Morale problems may also have reflected shifts in the reformatory population. For the first time in its history, the proportion of first offenders fell below one-half. Increasing numbers of women served time for crimes against property and the person, rather than against public order. Although the majority of women had committed minor offenses, those involving narcotics increased. A few, well-publicized cases—including a suburban housewife who had planned the vicious murder of her husband in order to run off with her lover—created an impression that the reformatory housed serious, highly immoral, women offenders.[39]

Miriam Van Waters had to acknowledge that alongside those students who cherished the spiritual refuge she constructed, another subculture recreated the criminal underworld outside the reformatory. A small number of inmates operated a trade in contraband items, including narcotics. The superintendent was concerned enough to go to unusual lengths to uncover the workings of this underground. She asked a friend who taught criminology at Smith College to send her one of his students, whom she would introduce as a reformatory inmate in order to discover the source of the narcotics traffic. A nineteen-year-old Smith student, Katherine Gabel, accepted the assignment. After briefing by Van Waters, she infiltrated the population, passing as an inmate for ten days.[40]

Gabel's reminiscences provide an exceptional view of the reformatory in the final years of Van Waters' administration. Inmates welcomed the young woman into their ranks, thinking that she had just survived the rough isolation period. "You just kind of came into the population," she recalled, where "there was a lot of four-letter words and that sort of thing, but not a lot of meaningful communication in terms of language." It was "immediately evident" to her that "four to five women were assigned to me, to follow me." Out of the total population of about four hundred, Gabel felt that around twenty-five "ran the place." The inmates "had their own social structure and all the things you read in the books about the make believe families and the power structures— they were all there." She referred to classic sociological studies of post-war women's prisons that depicted how incarcerated women formed fictive kinship groups centered on husband-wife couples. Family members both owed allegiance and earned protection.[41]

Gabel's experience resembled not only these academic accounts but also the sensationalized version of women's prison life represented in the film *Caged,* in which the innocent new arrival, played by Eleanor Parker, had to fend off the sexual advances of a hardened inmate. As Gabel recalled, some women watched her closely while others "began to run protection" for her. When a tough woman called "Fang" began to approach her, "another young woman, much more feminine kind of woman, stepped in and told her off, and told her to get away from me. And it became a very, sort of volatile interaction between those two. And I just stood there, not having a clue what was going on." At night, in her unlocked room, Gabel couldn't rest for fear of physical or sexual assault. After making contact with Van Waters, she began to sleep in the superintendent's house, which she reached late at night through a secret underground passage, returning to her cell by 5:00 A.M. each morning.

The "most dramatic" thing that happened during Gabel's stay evidenced the dangerous side of the homosexual underground long suspected by Van Waters' critics. A local band had been hired to play music during a Saturday night dance in the reformatory gymnasium. In retrospect, Gabel found the entire enterprise rather "stunning," given "all these liaisons going between all these women and all these jealousies and everything." Putting the women "into this kind of setting," she explained, "you just really push the button for every kind of acting out." Pushing and shoving broke out between inmates who competed for a particular dance partner, and a group of women formed a circle around the fight. One woman stabbed her adversary several times in the back. The crowd threw the injured inmate behind some chairs, and only after the dance ended did they take her to the hospital. The crowd had been "clapping and making a lot of noise, so that the fight that was going on in the center couldn't be heard. And the matrons were all playing cards somewhere else in another room down the hall."

According to Gabel, Superintendent Van Waters never learned of the stabbing incident. She also never found out exactly how narcotics entered the reformatory. Gabel succeeded in discovering their source—in the necks of ketchup bottles delivered to the kitchen—but she had already decided not to reveal any findings to the superintendent. Having grown friendly with a number of inmates, she refused to become a stool pigeon. Van Waters fully accepted her decision and remained in contact with Gabel long after they had each left Framingham.

The inmate subculture that Katherine Gabel uncovered flourished alongside Miriam Van Waters' programs for education and spiritual uplift. Some of the same inmates who attended her chapel services on Sundays had been at the dance. "It was clear that the women liked her very much and respected her," Gabel recalled. "They went up to her; they wanted to talk to her; they wanted interaction; they spoke very well of her. But she was one person; she was not around in these work environments or anything. She was sort of the special occasion."

As a charismatic leader, Miriam Van Waters was, by definition, a singular person. She could bring momentary relief from the sense of injustice and tedium that characterized prison life, but she could not fully control the behavior of inmates any more than she could influence the actions of the parole board. Nonetheless, Van Waters never gave up trying to win over both kinds of sinners, although she had more faith in her students. As she once summarized the lessons of her career in a television interview, "There never was a hopeless case, only a few hopeless politicians."

More than any other issue, female homosexuality provided these politicians with a powerful weapon for exhausting Van Waters' formidable defenses. Since the superintendent's reinstatement, Senator Joseph McCarthy had targeted not only communists but also "sexual perverts" as dangerous threats to American security. In 1950 a senate committee authorized an investigation into the employment of homosexuals in the U.S. government, and over the next few years, discharges of suspected homosexuals from the civil service and armed forces escalated sharply. In some cities, police stepped up their raids on the lesbian and gay bars that had flourished in the 1940s. As a result, increasing numbers of homosexual men appeared in local courts and jails, reinforcing their image as sexual criminals.[42]

Rumors about homosexuality at Framingham had never receded after the publicity surrounding Van Waters' dismissal. According to Deputy Superintendent Peg O'Keefe, state officials immediately began harassing inmates. "Sinclair Lewis once wrote 'It Can't Happen Here,'" O'Keefe prefaced her description of a meeting she attended. "Well it did last Thursday when the Parole Board met" and members asked an inmate "if you could be remade and have your choice what would it be—a man or a woman?" One board member detailed the possibilities of the newly developed transsexual operation to the point that O'Keefe sensed that "surgery was almost felt to be the solution." Officials referred to the inmate's "boyish swagger," deep voice, and masculine forearms, fired "morbid questions and suggestions" at the woman. They behaved "like animals that has [*sic*] lain in wait for their prey sparring in a most unashamed and barbarous manner," O'Keefe told Van Waters. To the deputy superintendent it felt "as though this might have been a Gestapo guinea pig arena." Such interrogations recurred outside the reformatory. A local police sergeant offered to open the jail door for a former Framingham inmate if she would tell him about the "Lesbians" at the reformatory, and Peg O'Keefe suspected that Frank Dwyer's police contacts tried to blackmail other prisoners into revealing homosexual gossip.[43]

In the climate of antihomosexual campaigns, when both government and private-sector employees were being summarily dismissed upon accusations of homosexuality, few critics spoke out against the stigmatization of lesbians. Because she had long worked with women who were labeled sexual offenders, and given her personal resistance to sexual labels, Miriam Van Waters did argue for tolerance. She tried to use the public discussion of homosexuality to further her long-term goal of winning greater sympathy for imprisoned women. In light of the attacks on sexual perversion at the reformatory, she felt that it was important to clear up superstitions and stave off the witch-hunting tendencies that had surfaced during her case. Thus in response to the Kinsey report on male sexuality—which in 1948 documented extensive premarital, extramarital, and homosexual relationships—Van Waters argued for more lenience toward women accused of fornication, adultery, prostitution, and homosexuality.[44] In her lectures she argued that homosexuality could be "found in all levels of society"; rarely did it manifest in any "abnormal" characteristics, such as the masculine appearance targeted by the parole board; and once revealed through the Rorschach test, homosexual tendencies could be treated by psychiatrists. Even women who indulged in prison homosexuality, she insisted, could "shed it as soon as the conditions change."[45]

The opposite position—that female homosexuality constituted a permanent condition and posed a serious moral threat—had a strong advocate in Massachusetts parole board member Katharine Sullivan. In her book, *Girls on Parole,* Sullivan argued that "the number of confirmed female homosexuals has increased to a marked degree." Women introduced to "perversion" in prison did not necessarily return to normal life after release. "A normal girl can become addicted to homosexuality very quickly," Sullivan warned. Elaborating on the horrors of homosexuality, she depicted lesbians as almost subhuman, writing of homosexual pairs who spent "hungry days and sleepless nights haunted by jealousy, fear, and fantasy" and who engaged in "hand-to-hand fights or even free-for-alls." If separated, she warned, the surviving partner "may suffer an acute attack of homosexual panic, with violent screaming and frothing at the mouth, followed by a period of wan anxiety." The abandoned woman then took another partner. "Many a young girl can and has been saved from a life of degrading sorrow," Sullivan moralized, but "it is not an easy task, for progress is slow." [46]

Sullivan's views held much greater weight in the world of Massachusetts correctional policy than did those of Miriam Van Waters. The image of the corrupt lesbian who preyed upon young innocents in prison had been broadcast during the Van Waters' hearings, through the Hollywood film *Caged,* as well as in Sullivan's book. In Massachusetts, the "aggressive homosexual" became the focus of greater surveillance during the 1950s, in part because of a growing homosexual subculture, but also in response to social fears about the dangers of uncontrolled female sexuality. The image, and the political pressures, ultimately influenced even Superintendent Van Waters' policies at Framingham. [47]

Despite her public repudiation of a homosexual problem, and her ignorance of the rumble in the gym, Miriam Van Waters was not totally unaware of the institutional and political dangers posed by lesbian relationships in prison. In response to inmate behaviors and renewed surveillance, she reluctantly adapted her policies. Instead of the treatment that she believed could channel homosexual impulses toward more appropriate objects, in the 1950s she allowed women who had sexual relationships in prison to be labeled "hard core." In order to maintain the reformatory as an educational, rather than punitive, institution, Van Waters' staff requested that both drug traffickers and "aggressive homosexuals" be transferred from Framingham to the county jails. As a social worker explained in her request to transfer an inmate convicted of assault and battery, "She is also a homosexual and while on parole she made a connection with a married woman with the result that the woman left her husband." Homosexuality was the most frequent justification for transfer requests in the effort to weed out "hard core" offenders. [48]

The decision to remove troublesome inmates intended to avoid not only further political attacks but also the kinds of internal conflicts that had begun to plague American prisons. Thirty serious prison riots occurred across the country in the early 1950s, including outbreaks at the Massachusetts State Prison at Charlestown and the Concord Reformatory for Men. During a three-day siege in 1955, for example, Charlestown inmates held five guards hostage. Throughout the correctional system, discipline tightened. A new maximum-security prison opened at Norfolk to replace the outdated Charlestown, which closed down. Riots and hunger strikes continued to plague the Massachusetts prison system, placing more liberal administrators on the defensive.[49]

Although Framingham remained relatively calm, in 1953 Van Waters had averted a near riot between "Negroes and White" inmates. Using her traditional approach to volatile situations, she spoke directly with inmates, calming them with her forceful yet loving presence. In 1954, the superintendent held a series of talks with inmates about the problems of homosexuality, stealing, and drugs. At the same time, she initiated the first of her efforts to discover the operations of the drug ring and sought to transfer intransigent inmates to county jails. Even with these combined efforts, inmate morale seemed to be fragile. The number of women who ran away from the institution provides some measure of discontent. In the early 1950s, escapes had decreased to an average of ten per year, in part because limitations on daywork created fewer opportunities for running away. Between 1953 and 1955, however, the average rose to thirty-one escapes per year and remained high, at twenty per year, for the rest of Van Waters' administration.[50]

Although almost all women who escaped were returned to Framingham, usually within days, they always drew the attention of correctional department officials and the press. In August 1955, a newspaper account of one escape labeled as a "riot" the noisy demonstration inmates used to try to conceal the attempt. The next day, an actual riot did take place, when several black inmates armed themselves with sticks. During the outbreak both inmates and staff suffered injuries. Van Waters asked the commissioner of corrections to launch a state investigation into the disturbance, instituted tear gas training for her staff, and transferred three students from Framingham. In her journal, she called their departure "the necessary torturing sacrifice of a principle." For someone so steeped in the Social Gospel, so convinced that every person is a redeemable child of God, the policy shift was indeed a torture.[51]

In 1956, as the tensions at Framingham escalated and her sixty-ninth birthday approached, Miriam Van Waters frequently thought about finding a successor. On several occasions she noted in her journal when a prospect looked hopeful, or when she had eliminated a candidate from consideration. Although she remained active in community and professional affairs, Van Waters was also getting tired. Brief journal entries recorded periodic bouts with viral pneumonia, pleurisy, and heart pains. In January 1956, a fall left her bruised in the head and chest, although she remained well enough to record with pride when she split a log with a wedge for the first time. On November 17, however, Van Waters' life changed abruptly. While working at her beloved Hill Top, she felt "a frantic pain" in her neck. She had been lifting heavy bags of seed and corn, and at first she thought she had broken her neck. Determined "*not* to have a shock," Miriam hunched herself next door "to Bert's front steps." Doctors at the local hospital diagnosed a brain hemorrhage.[52]

For two weeks Van Waters lay unconscious in Framingham Union Hospital. When she was stable enough to be transferred to Boston by ambulance, she underwent surgery to repair the aneurysm, or ruptured artery, in her brain. After the operation, working from her bed in New England Baptist Hospital, she optimistically made plans for Christmas at Framingham. By mid-December she did return to Hill Top, weighing a mere ninety pounds but "so happy" to be home and nursed by her sister-in-law, Bert Green Van Waters. As soon as she returned, she wrote a brief account of her ordeal, requesting that a copy be sent to Geraldine Thompson. Her handwriting had changed markedly from before the aneurysm, and though it would improve over time, she never recovered either her firm scrawl or the facility with language that had characterized her writing since adolescence.[53]

A week after she returned to Hill Top, Van Waters recorded her ability to sit up for twenty minutes. By February 1957, she was able to walk in the woods. In the meantime, friends and family had reached out to help her. Helen Bryan visited, as did Van Waters' brother George and his wife Helen. Anne Gladding, Miriam wrote, became "the courier between the institution and the town and the forest home at Hill Top." As in the past, Van Waters' own will to survive defied medical probabilities. Her doctor called the recovery "a Miracle," but she still did not want her patient to return to Framingham to complete the final months of her administration. A new commissioner of corrections allowed Van Waters to work half-time, but occasionally the superintendent still found herself reeling and confined to bed under Bert's care. In her absence, Peg O'Keefe served as acting superintendent.[54]

By the first day of spring 1957, Van Waters felt distinctly better. She began to plan her return to Framingham, invited Eleanor Roosevelt for a visit, and taught her literary group. In May she and Anne Gladding spent a week visiting Helen Bryan in Vermont, where Miriam read and slept soundly. On her return she still needed assistance, and "spasms" she experienced may have been minor strokes. Too ill to travel to New Jersey for the celebration honoring Geraldine Thompson's retirement from the State Board of Control, she sent Anne Gladding and Margaret van Wagenen as her representatives. Geraldine, now eighty-five years old, visited in June, accompanied by her daughter and a granddaughter. They coordinated their trip to coincide with Eleanor Roosevelt's talk to the student assembly. By August, Miriam was able to visit Brookdale, with the help of a former student.[55]

While Van Waters recuperated, she followed closely the final act in the ongoing political drama over the women's reformatory. In July 1957, Louisiana authorities located a Framingham inmate who had escaped the previous spring. The woman tried to fight her extradition on the grounds that "low moral standards," including alcohol, drugs, and homosexuality, made her afraid to return to Framingham. Headlines reminiscent of the 1948 attack soon appeared in the press, especially after conservative politicians joined in the melee. State Senator Leslie Cutler, long a critic of the reformatory, initiated a new investigation. Another state senator charged that there was "an utter lack of discipline, the industrial program was a farce, and there was documentary information that there is a disgraceful situation at the institution."[56]

Newspapers colorfully publicized the renewed assault, emphasizing sexual scandal. "Charge Sex Fiends, Boozers Run Wild in Women's Prison" and "Girl Inmates 'Wed' in Mock Prison Rites," read the headlines. Once again homosexuality served as a wedge for a more general attack upon the reformatory. According to State Senator Francis X. McCann, Framingham was a disgrace because the workday was broken up by events such as choir and band practice, French lessons, and typing classes. Between the charges of sexual immorality and those of educational frivolity, the institution was once again represented as too lenient, inefficient, and undisciplined. The timing of the charges, while Van Waters recuperated and just months before her successor would be named, pointed toward a political effort to appoint someone "with less liberal views on penology," as one reporter put it.[57]

Largely confined to her sickbed, Miriam Van Waters had few forums in which to defend her administration.[58] Given her residual political clout, ill health, and near retirement, she was unlikely to be dismissed again, but neither could she command the widespread support of the past. Even Arthur Lyman, an old ally who was reappointed as commissioner of corrections, promised that after Van Waters retired "there will be a very radical change." Newly elected governor Foster John Furcolo, a Democrat, vowed that he would keep his hands off the reformatory until Van Waters retired at the end of October 1957; the special legislative subcommittee waited until that date to begin to investigate charges against the reformatory.[59] Behind the scenes, friends of Van Waters scrambled to find a suitable successor for the ailing administrator. But as her retirement approached, no candidate had emerged.[60]

As she prepared to leave office, Miriam Van Waters had good reason to worry about the future of the institution she had nurtured for so long. As soon as she retired, her political enemies descended upon Framingham. Despite opposition by the Friends of Framingham, a legislative commission led by a former FBI agent and several state police officers, including the head of state policewomen, launched into the reformatory. As a result of their investigation, several staff members resigned or were dismissed, largely because of charges that they had fraternized with inmates. In a confidential report to Commissioner Lyman, made public in May 1958, State Senator Cutler's committee presented fourteen recommendations for changes in the administration of Framingham. Most of them called for tighter security, including greater involvement of the state police in controlling the institution.[61]

The grounds for change listed in the Cutler committee report revealed how the modern recognition of women's sexuality created new vulnerabilities for the female reform tradition. Many of the charges echoed the Dwyer and McDowell critiques of a decade earlier, beginning with the claim that "Homosexuality had been allowed to exist at Framingham uncontrolled mainly because of the open-door policy in effect there." Discipline had to be tightened, allegedly to prevent "belligerents and non-conformists" from becoming an "increasingly dominant force."[62] By transferring authority to state police, instituting a maximum-security program, and segregating "aggressive homosexuals and belligerent non-conformists," they recommended, Framingham could return to the disciplinary norms of the state correctional system. The Cutler report did not reject all of the reformatory's rehabilitative features, but it dismissed Miriam Van Waters' most cherished methods. In place of the child-centered institution, a "more enlightened procedure" required "the placing of the child as soon as possible, in a family group." Within a year after her retirement, the programs to keep mothers with their children had been dismantled. The traditional "fraternization of the officers and staff" would be forbidden, along with gifts or favors for students.

At the heart of many of these recommendations lay the pervasive fear that homosexual contagion spread throughout the reformatory. References to "open door policy" and "inmate fraternization" were often codes for opportunities for female intimacy. Complaints about contraband implied homosexual favoritism. Aside from legitimate concerns about physical assaults and sexual coercion, the Cutler committee, echoing Katharine Sullivan, pointedly condemned even consensual homosexuality outside of prison, especially among "girls who had not been acquainted with homosexual activities previously in their career" but who "later participated and persisted in such activities." In short, the subtext of the report identified female homosexuality as the chief ill of the reformatory, even though the committee admitted that homosexuality "is not rampant" at the institution. Tolerance of even a few homosexual practices, however, had to be wiped out. The "real factor to be considered here," the report explained, "is not the extent but the fact that it appears to have been overlooked." As evidence, they pointed out that "there have been mock marriages; there have been unnatural acts witnessed and reported by members of the staff, and there have been numerous indications of parolees carrying this type of activity outside the institution in association with others who had never participated in such actions before."[63]

Although no one ever accused Van Waters of being a lesbian, the old insinuations may well have fueled the emphasis on homosexuality in the investigation. Recurrent rumors about Van Waters' protégé and deputy, Peg O'Keefe—whose working-class background, youthful reformatory sentence, and lack of feminine style had made her vulnerable—may have kept this loyal disciple of Van Waters from continuing in her job. After twenty-five years at Framingham, O'Keefe resigned "in the best interest of the institution." Geraldine Thompson hired her as a "helper and guide" in her projects with juvenile offenders and parolees in New Jersey, and Peg O'Keefe moved to Brookdale.[64]

When Miriam Van Waters celebrated her retirement, the sure knowledge of the attack to follow must have made the event terribly bitter-
sweet. As much as she appreciated the accolades, she knew that her
life's work could not possibly be sustained after her departure. For one,
she had cultivated no disciple who could succeed her. The women she
recommended either could not serve or were not acceptable to the
commissioner of corrections. In addition, whoever did succeed her
would face severe political pressures to tighten discipline and defer to
departmental authority. Above all, her successor could never be Miriam
Van Waters, the unique, charismatic, maternal figure who had guided
the institution with her vision of Christian penology since 1932.

As retirement approached, honors flowed into Hill Top—letters
from friends and students, a citation from Vassar College on her seventi-
eth birthday, telegrams from Eleanor Roosevelt and Senator John F. Kennedy on her retirement. The central celebration took place at the Harvard Club on October 15, 1957, when five hundred people attended a
testimonial dinner for Van Waters. She listed the speakers in her journal—Francis Sayre, Erwin Griswold, Claude Cross, La Rue Brown—all
influential men who had stood up for her during her career. Even more
meaningful to her were the forty-seven women who rose at their dinner
tables when Arthur Lyman asked if any former students wished to stand
up. "No one could have told the ex-prisoners from the non-prisoners,"
Van Waters recalled proudly of these "self-reliant, self-supporting ex-
students." Along with the seventy Friendly Visitors who attended, these
women represented her legacy. As the dinner program put it, "the most
eloquent testimonial to her greatness is the long roll of women who
have been lifted from the slough of despond and have found, under her
guidance, the way to places of respect in the community."[65]

In March, Commissioner Lyman announced that Mrs. Betty Cole
Smith would take over as superintendent. The daughter of a Methodist
minister, and the married mother of two teenagers, Betty Cole Smith
had a strong background in social work administration. In the 1940s
she had conducted a study of women alcoholics at Framingham, and
she was sympathetic to Van Waters' methods. Friends of Framingham
supported the appointment, and the retiring superintendent offered
implicit support when she wrote to Anne Gladding, "I hope you and
Van remain there for many more years" as loyal employees. But Smith
was not one of the inner circle of disciples, and in 1957 she inherited
the job of implementing the tighter rules called for by Senator Cutler
and supported by Commissioner Lyman.[66]

An era had ended at Framingham. Although Miriam Van Waters had already retired, the naming of a replacement and the publication of the Cutler committee report in spring 1958 reiterated the fact that the reformatory would move in a new direction. So, too, would Miriam Van Waters during the remaining sixteen years of her life. Although she would continue to work for prison reform, an entirely new domestic and social world replaced the public office she had directed for over twenty-five years. The conductor of the Framingham symphony had stepped down.

Lifeline

When Miriam Van Waters retired as the superintendent of the women's reformatory, she chose to remain in Framingham, the community in which she had resided since 1932. The area abounded with memories and personal connections. Her church, St. Andrew's, was there, while spiritual comrades such as Howard Kellett worked nearby in Boston. Loyal friends, including Anne Gladding and Margaret van Wagenen, continued on the staff at the reformatory. Her closest kin, Ralph and Bert Van Waters and their children, had settled next to Hill Top. Knowing how hard-won his independent family life had been, Miriam did not join her brother's household. Nor did she consider following Peg O'Keefe to Brookdale, which had for so long provided a refuge. Just as she had once chosen to settle in Massachusetts rather than New Jersey, she now continued to maintain her separate residence.

The unusual household Van Waters established when she left the superintendent's house fit well with her life's work. She moved in with two former inmates, Alice May and Irene Jenner, who had previously served on the reformatory staff. They located a semidetached, three-bedroom house on Clarke Street, near downtown Framingham, which Van Waters rented for one hundred dollars a month. There the three women—"Doctor," Alice, and Irene—along with Miriam's dog, Tricky, established a household together. Jenner was a former alcoholic who credited Van Waters with her recovery. A vigorous grandmother, she kept house, shoveled snow from the walk in winter, and nursed Miriam when necessary. May, who worked at a local dry cleaners, was a "paying guest" who boarded at the house. In addition to this income, Van Waters had some money from her pension and from a trust fund Geraldine Thompson established. The Clarke Street household, however, operated on a limited budget. Meals continued to be served formally, as they had at the superintendent's house, but there were no extravagances.[1]

Removed from the intense public scrutiny that typified her controversial career, and more physically limited than in the past, Miriam Van

Waters maintained quiet routines at her new home. She rose early, took her own breakfast, then stayed in her room, where she wrote, worked on her memoirs, and read books. At about 11:00 A.M. each morning, she and Irene Jenner would take a walk downtown to check her postal box. Along the way she enjoyed talking with people, whether she knew them or not. She was "very friendly that way," Jenner recalled. After lunch, Van Waters read her letters and immediately began to answer them. She usually ate dinner at home, and occasionally she hosted a meeting of the county Muscular Dystrophy Association, of which she was president. As a former staff member reported to Geraldine Thompson in 1959, the retired reformer seemed "*very well* and still indomitably using the last ounce of her strength—this time at a meeting of the Muscular Dystrophy."[2]

Van Waters continued to visit Hill Top, Ralph's family, and nearby towns. Every Saturday evening Ralph brought his sister to Hill Top or his home for dinner. Sometimes friends joined them there; Anne Gladding and Margaret van Wagenen might arrive to play bridge, entertain Ralph and Bert's children, or celebrate "Doctor's" birthday. Miriam also visited Anne and Van in the home they now shared in nearby Ashland. On Sundays Ralph took Miriam to St. Andrew's for services. According to Alice May and Irene Jenner, Van Waters continued to worship Ralph, who treated her affectionately, as if she were his mother. Together they mourned the death of Bert Van Waters in 1960, and four years later they celebrated Ralph's remarriage to Elizabeth Bode, one of his sister's early protégés.[3]

During the 1950s Miriam Van Waters and Geraldine Thompson continued to visit. For five summers they had attended Audubon camps in New England, often accompanied by Anne Gladding or other staff members, who were awarded Audubon "scholarships" by Thompson. Before Van Waters' retirement, the two friends walked in the woods, attended church, and talked of family and work at Hill Top or Brookdale. Once they had traveled to Hyde Park for lunch at Eleanor Roosevelt's Val-Kill cottage, stopping to see Geraldine's future grave site, next to her husband Lew, at Hyde Park. As she entered her eighties, Thompson's concern for Van Waters and her pleasure in her company had not diminished. Anticipating a ten-day visit at the Cosmopolitan Club in New York, Geraldine had sent her "own Dearest Dearest and soon arriving love" a message of "love, welcome and deep rejoicing over your coming." Soon after Van Waters' retirement, Thompson visited again, spending New Year, 1958, at Hill Top and accompanying her friend when she spoke to the Fellowship of Reconciliation in Cambridge.

Aging, however, was beginning to take its toll. Thompson's increasing deafness, for instance, gave her a somewhat comic reputation for repeatedly shouting "Miriam, speak up!" when the two friends were together. Although Geraldine flew up for Audubon Camp as late as 1962, Miriam rarely made the trip to Brookdale anymore.[4]

Other friends remained important to Van Waters in her later years. She had stayed in touch with her old Colony housemates, visiting Orfa Jean Shontz, Bess Woods, and Caroline "Pole" Fisher in Los Angeles in 1952. Bess came to visit at Framingham again, cementing a relationship begun over forty years earlier at the University of Oregon. Orfa, whom Miriam helped support in a nursing home, died in 1954, the year of Ethel Sturges Dummer's death. Close friends nearer to home continued to nurture Van Waters after these losses. Anne Gladding became an important spiritual partner; for her constant service to others, Van Waters dubbed her "St. Anne of Framingham." Gladding brought flowers and useful gifts to the retired superintendent. "You have been a comfort to me, Anna, in these days of adjustment to a new variety of mental pain," Van Waters wrote in 1963, revealing how difficult the transition from an active professional life to relative seclusion could feel.[5]

Van Waters formed another new spiritual relationship in the 1950s when she applied for membership in the Society of the Companions of the Holy Cross (SCHC), a select group of Episcopalian women who were committed to social justice and class reconciliation. The SCHC had been founded in 1884 by wealthy Episcopalian women involved in settlement houses and other services for working-class women. In the Boston area, 150 members of the group met at annual retreats, offering intercessionary prayers for God's help in their good works and discussing social issues. Van Waters had learned about the Companions through Vida Scudder, a Wellesley professor and settlement house leader, who was approaching her ninetieth birthday when she and Van Waters began to visit and correspond. "Your friendship," Scudder wrote, "is one of the most exciting events of my old age." Van Waters felt a kinship with both Scudder and the Companions, who, she felt, offered a means for "changing public attitudes towards prisoners." She spoke at retreats and drew members into the ranks of friendly visitors and opponents of the death penalty. Van Waters also sponsored former Framingham staff and inmates as members. In her later years, the Companions brought together Van Waters' lifelong grounding in the Episcopal Church with her commitments to social reform and women's institutions.[6]

At Clarke Street, Miriam Van Waters enjoyed visits from former students, staff, and relatives who lived nearby. Margaret van Wagenen stopped by after her weekly marketing, and Cynthia Thomas, Van Waters' secretary, regularly helped answer the mail. Because there were no rooms to accommodate overnight guests, the residence lacked the bustle of the superintendent's house. Out of town friends did travel to Framingham to see Van Waters, though. Russell McWilliams and his wife Lois visited, as did Katherine Gabel, the Smith student who had once infiltrated the reformatory and now studied criminal justice. Peg O'Keefe brought Geraldine Thompson, and Geraldine's daughter, Betty Babcock, came with her mother as well. Sometimes Van Waters traveled within New England to visit former staff members, especially Helen Bryan, who now lived in Vermont.[7]

Van Waters' grandsons—George, Richard, and Peter Hildebrandt— wrote letters and continued to visit as they grew up. Richard fondly recalled both the gracious meals at Clarke Street and that "miserable animal," Tricky, whom his grandmother loved so dearly, despite the dog's habit of biting people. When her grandchildren asked about their mother, Miriam would tell stories of Sarah's childhood. As they grew older, she sometimes discussed her social ideas. They learned of her beliefs in the rehabilitation of prisoners and racial equality, and of her opposition to the death penalty. When the young men expressed more conservative views, she never argued or condescended; rather, she answered kindly in a way that seemed to say "whatever you want to do, go ahead." Each one established a family, and in 1971, Peter wrote to tell his grandmother of the birth of a daughter named Sarah.[8]

Although a familiar social world surrounded her, a visible, physical change had occurred in Van Waters' life. "If she had just retired from the job," Margaret van Wagenen speculated, "I think she would have gone on to something else." Her aneurysm, though, had made her "quite a different person after the surgery," as though "the spark . . . the spontaneity had gone." Previously, Van Waters had been able to express herself fully. She loved to choose the perfect words to make her points, and she could radiate compassion, holding an assembly full of students in awe. Now she had to work harder to communicate. She could no longer be the charismatic leader who touched others deeply through voice, words, and looks.[9]

Despite these limitations, Van Waters found ways to continue the reforms that had been central to her for forty years. As she wrote to Howard Kellett, "My own work now is to restore the lost confidence of . . . ex-students of the reformatory and perhaps to do away with public apathy and indifference as to the fate of those in captivity."[10] Without an institutional base or public platform, and given her physical limitations, she found new avenues for her efforts. Van Waters concentrated on creating a personal lifeline from her home in Framingham, with the help of a private secretary funded by Geraldine Thompson.[11] Largely through her voluminous correspondence, she remained in touch with those she had served for years—Framingham students, former El Retiro students, and male prisoners. She also expanded her concerns to others who suffered social injustice. To a limited extent she continued to speak publicly and take leadership in voluntary organizations. But especially as her health deteriorated in the 1960s, personal, written outreach to those in need represented the core of her working life.

Even after she left her job, Miriam Van Waters remained deeply interested in the Framingham reformatory. She contributed articles to the student newspaper and worried about the political fate of the babies and the farm. She gladly accepted Superintendent Smith's invitation to address the student assembly on the Memorial Day after her retirement, when she spoke about the black children of Little Rock, Arkansas, who "stood so bravely" in the face of hostile mobs as they integrated the public schools, and of Martin Luther King Jr., whose picture she had hanging in her home.[12] She also offered personal assistance to Framingham students, serving in the role of a Friendly Visitor, though usually through correspondence rather than in person. At times she did appear in court to support inmates, but more often she provided encouragement to those trying to make a new life. Hundreds of grateful inmates wrote to thank her for her efforts. A poem she had sent "really made me feel it is worthwhile to go and try just a little bit harder," wrote a student who was halfway through her reformatory sentence. Van Waters let paroled inmates know that she would always be interested in hearing from them. One former student addressed her letters to "Dearest Ma," a reminder of Van Waters' maternal role.[13]

In their correspondence, women on parole spoke of their difficulties finding jobs, paying medical and dental bills, and resisting the temptations of drugs and alcohol. Van Waters' continued faith and her encouraging words helped many of them succeed. Sometimes she simply kept them aware of her message of unconditional love. As one woman who jumped parole a week after release commented on her return to Framingham, "I guess I hurt Dr. Van Waters by doing this." The women who finished parole with good jobs and a sense of independence wrote to tell Van Waters about the pleasures of going bowling, driving a car, and having a family life. One inmate proudly wrote that she had just sold her prison writings to the *Saturday Evening Post*.[14]

In addition to letter writing, Van Waters offered small gifts and checks to former students and their children. When a former Framingham student had a new child or grandchild, she continued to send engraved silver cups to commemorate the births. She also sent birthday cards enclosing small checks to the children of students and staff members. Many wrote back to "Aunt Miriam" to thank her and to keep her informed of their lives. Van Waters explained her reason for this policy: "I wish to get as many people as possible interested in what I believe to be the best ways to deal with the problems of the offender." Spreading the word through good works drew on her Social Gospel heritage and fit well with her belief in a personalized, Christian penology.

Because she was known to send small financial gifts to help women in transition, some former students did not hesitate to take advantage of Van Waters' generosity. "It got so that sometimes the girls would come out to the house, you know, and I knew what they were after," Irene Jenner recalled. "And I told them that Doctor was in no condition to be talking to anyone, which was the truth." As Margaret van Wagenen observed, "If anybody wrote to her for money, I know they got a check in the return mail." Not responding immediately, she explained, felt to Van Waters like sending a message of rejection, for "they had written to her out of need and to reject would be an act of uncaring—as a destructive act to them." And so, true to her principles of renunciation, Van Waters spread her limited resources around. "She'd write out a check even if she had nothing. Oh, God!" Jenner recalled, in a tone of both humor and despair.[15]

Van Waters also maintained a large correspondence with male inmates, many of whom sent her examples of their prison writings. Some men had met her when she spoke at the Charlestown prison in the 1950s; others got her address from those who had heard her speak. She always answered with encouraging notes. Van Waters also continued to write to men whose cases she had championed, including southern black prisoners for whom she sought legal aid, and both black and white death row inmates in whose innocence she believed. In the 1960s, she advised a local branch of the ex-offender self-help movement, which opened a halfway house for released prisoners. In the 1970s she was still corresponding with several Massachusetts prisoners who had filed a suit against the state for preventing them from communicating with their lawyers while in solitary confinement. Her old friend and attorney, Claude Cross, argued successfully to change this policy.[16]

Along with her outreach to former inmates, Van Waters continued to write about penology. For some time she had been working on a memoir of her career, tentatively called *The Prison Must Go.* In the early 1950s she had interested publishers in the project, which she worked on during vacations at Audubon Camp. After her retirement she continued to write, recasting her book as *Redemption in Prison.* Although she never completed her memoirs, in 1962, one of Sarah's former teachers, Burton Rowles, published a popular biography of Van Waters. Titled *The Lady at Box 99,* after the post office box for the reformatory, the book offered an upbeat journalistic account of the dramatic moments in Van Waters' life. For the most part, Van Waters' own writing appeared locally, in letters to the editor of the *Framingham News* or in the *Witness,* an Episcopalian magazine.[17]

As new social movements transformed American politics in the 1950s and 1960s, Miriam Van Waters kept abreast and offered commentaries. She wrote on the occasion of the closing of Alcatraz prison, "the symbol of hopelessness," and after the violent confrontations between police and protesters at the 1968 Democratic National Convention in Chicago. Quite lucidly she recalled greater moments in Chicago's history, such as the founding of Hull House and of the juvenile court.[18] She followed closely the civil rights movement in the South, praying when racial tensions erupted and trying to help in her personal ways. Working with a local Catholic priest, she helped raise money for the United Negro College Fund and sent small personal contributions to southern black schools. She also persuaded Geraldine Thompson to send a contribution to the fund to enable a former Framingham student to attend college.[19]

Van Waters was not alone in her continuing involvement in voluntary reform movements. Throughout the country, women who had spent their careers in the field of social service now devoted their retirement years to local efforts to help others. Van Waters' oldest friend, Bess Woods, wrote from Los Angeles in 1959 about her involvement in the American Civil Liberties Union, the National Association for the Advancement of Colored People, the Urban League, and the American Association for Indian Affairs. Another former L.A. colleague, Ruth Baker, had worked as a hospital volunteer after retirement from the juvenile court. She continued to be active in the Women's Club of Hollywood and the Episcopal Church. Hebe Mac Robinson, an African American social worker at the juvenile court, now helped senior citizens through the L.A. branch of the National Council of Jewish Women and served as president of her church women's group. Another juvenile court worker, Lucille Smith, wrote from Dallas, where she served on the advisory board to a campus YWCA. Her voluntary efforts included the American Cancer Society, the Heart Association, and the Community Chest; her husband worked on Latin American tuberculosis clinics; and they both supported an Interracial Committee and the anti–capital punishment movement. These women and members of their families helped sustain community-based social services throughout the conservative 1950s and brought home within local communities the message of the civil rights movement. Their services, like Van Waters', provided historical continuity between women's nineteenth-century charitable work, Progressive Era reforms, and the new social movements of the mid–twentieth century.[20]

In September 1964, while she was walking downtown with Irene Jenner, Miriam Van Waters stumbled and fell on the sidewalk. Despite her characteristic insistence that she could walk home, Jenner called an ambulance. Van Waters had broken her hip, and she spent the next several months in the hospital recuperating. The change in her level of engagement after the fall made Jenner wonder if Doctor had suffered a stroke at the same time. After she returned home at Christmastime, she stopped going out very much. Now seventy-seven years old, she no longer took her daily walks downtown, and she remained "pretty much housebound." She also spent less time with guests, excusing herself to go upstairs to her room after only short visits.[21]

Although she rarely traveled now, Van Waters did sometimes visit close friends. Anne Gladding would pick her up and drive her to Ashland for the day. A note of gratitude after one visit contained sparks of her old style. Apologizing for her bad handwriting, she assured Gladding that she had "clear thoughts" to offer: "When you touched a few chords on your new piano it awakened in me all the chapel services and the assemblies and the students and I have shared. All this is happy and living memory without regret." Gladding also drove her to Vermont, and her secretary, Cynthia Thomas, took her on longer drives, such as a visit to Worcester to see a former male prisoner, for whom she had helped secure a job at her alma mater, Clark University.[22]

After she recovered from her fall, Van Waters also made a final trip to Brookdale. Despite distance and aging, she had kept in touch with Geraldine Thompson, who remained active into her nineties. On the occasions of Thompson's birthdays, local newspapers recounted the lifetime of dedicated service by the "Grand Lady of Brookdale." Until her friend Eleanor's death in 1962, Thompson and Roosevelt had continued to cooperate, writing to each other about requests to aid prisoners and the poor. When the two friends lunched together in 1960, Roosevelt wrote, they talked fondly of Miriam.[23]

By August 1965, when Miriam visited Brookdale, ninety-three-year-old Geraldine was not always her "usual dynamic self." She had lapses of memory and very poor hearing and vision. Yet mentally, Van Waters wrote to Edna Mahan, "she can be as keen as ever." Geraldine rose to the occasion when guests arrived, and during Miriam's visit they had a fine reunion. The two women had always loved to walk or ride around the countryside. Now, with the aid of nurses and a driver, Miriam and Geraldine enjoyed "four good drives around the country together." Miriam seemed to delight in Geraldine's continued joy in nature. "[S]he loves to walk the short distance to feed the ducks," she wrote Edna. "I think she enjoys life and I am happy that she is so well physically."[24]

Because of Geraldine's deafness, the regular telephone calls that had kept the friends in close touch had nearly ceased. Miriam sometimes wrote to Edna to check on Geraldine. "Now and then I send her a letter," Miriam explained, but one of Thompson's daughters, rather than Geraldine, usually responded. Although lines of communication had diminished, Miriam never stopped caring about Geraldine's well-being. Friends wrote to let her know that "Mrs. Thompson is contented and comfortable," and Van Waters wrote to inquire whether new household staff were providing proper care. When Geraldine died in September 1967, she had lived for ninety-five extraordinarily full years, almost half of them as Miriam Van Waters' "Dearest Love" and protector. As a small, final tribute, Van Waters wrote an obituary for Thompson in the *Framingham News.*[25]

In the remaining years of her own life, Miriam Van Waters became decreasingly active in the world and increasingly dependent on Irene Jenner for physical care. Even in her final years, however, the lifeline to former prisoners continued. She also began to sort through her past, conscious of her historical significance. In 1971 Van Waters donated her books to the University of Oregon Library. She went through her voluminous papers, scrawling comments about her correspondents on envelopes and then depositing the letters and her professional files at the women's history archive at Radcliffe. In late 1972, she had a slight stroke that caused some concern among those who were in touch with her. Although she celebrated her eighty-seventh birthday in October 1973, her health was clearly failing, and Jenner did not expect her to live long. On Thursday, January 17, 1974, Miriam Van Waters died at her Clarke Street home in Framingham.[26]

"This week St. Andrew's most famous parishioner entered the larger life of God's paradise," Reverend Mason Wilson told the congregation that assembled for a Memorial Eucharist on Sunday, January 20, 1974. Miriam Van Waters "was the most charismatic woman that I have ever known," he declared, explaining that the word charismatic meant "gifts of the spirit," and Van Waters "was extraordinarily endowed with spiritual gifts." She would no doubt have agreed with Reverend Wilson's interpretation of her life: "The holy spirit gave Miriam Van Waters a vision of how prisoners should be treated, and she spent her life trying to see that her vision was implemented and fulfilled." Years earlier, as a theological student, Wilson had visited the women's reformatory in Framingham. "I'll never forget as long as I live hearing her speak on that great text from the parable of the last judgement, 'I was in prison and ye visited me.' Or that other text which she spoke on so movingly about the woman who was taken in adultery." Before the crowd could throw stones, the superintendent had reminded the students, Jesus had said, "He who is without sin let him cast the first stone." And Jesus had refused to condemn her, or the crowd. Wilson's memories provided a fitting tribute to Miriam Van Waters, who had lived so fully with "a concept of forgiveness," and who had been, in her own way, a preacher of the gospel.[27]

It was easy to apply the language of Christianity to Van Waters' life. As Reverend Wilson recalled the horror of her dismissal in 1949, he pictured Van Waters at the hearings, dressed in black with a silver cross around her neck, looking like a "Christian martyr." When she returned to the reformatory, he claimed, preacher after preacher felt that her victory was like "moving from Good Friday to Easter." The singing of the Te Deum by her loyal students had celebrated her resurrection. Like the prayer on that day of triumph, this service, too, ended by praising God for her works, and "for making her an instrument of thy holy spirit."

Half of the congregation that Sunday morning did not know Miriam Van Waters, and even those who had heard of her did not know her well. It had been years since she could attend church regularly, and her legendary administration at the Framingham reformatory no longer captured the attention of the media. So many friends and colleagues had predeceased her—Hans Weiss in 1936, Sarah Van Waters Hildebrandt in 1953, Bert Van Waters in 1960, Peg O'Keefe in 1962, Geraldine Thompson and LaRue Brown in 1969. None of Miriam's sisters were still living, but Ralph Van Waters and Elizabeth Bode Van Waters attended the service, as did Anne Gladding, Margaret van Wagenen, Irene Jenner, Alice May, Cynthia Thomas, and a handful of surviving former students. In honor of her long career in prison reform, the ushers that day included Massachusetts Superior Court justice Reuben Lurie, a former parole board chair and commissioner of corrections, and Franklin Flaschner, then chief justice of Massachusetts District Courts, who had assisted Claude Cross during the hearings on Van Waters' dismissal and later chaired the Friends of Framingham. The Reverend Howard Kellett, Van Waters' confidant and informal confessor since the 1930s, preached at the burial office, attended by over two hundred admirers.[28]

Many of those who had been touched by Miriam Van Waters could not have attended the services at St. Andrews that day. Some remained in prison; many correspondents lived scattered throughout the country. They had already expressed their testimonials during Van Waters' lifetime, not only in public accolades but also in private letters that recalled her inspiration. Their words suggest how profoundly Van Waters' memory, and her legacy, affected those who knew her.

Within her own family, Miriam Van Waters had kept alive her father's commitment to the Social Gospel, and she passed on their mutual concerns about social service to a younger generation. Although her own daughter had not survived, her nieces and nephews let Aunt Miriam know how much she had affected their lives. Her sister Beckie's daughter, Ann Bartholomew, who served as an intern at Framingham in the 1950s, considered her aunt a saint. Before marrying and having children, she worked in a family service agency in Georgia, and when she moved to Texas, she became the only white woman teaching in a "neglected" black school, developing reading materials that reflected the culture of her students. Beckie's son, Richard, who reminded Miriam of her father, became an Episcopal minister. Another niece, George Van Waters' daughter Barbara, had lived at the superintendent's house for a year and attended the Shady Hill School with Sarah. Her own family held quite conservative values, but Barbara had been touched by another vision of activism. As she once wrote to Aunt Miriam, "It is hard to say to you the things I think of you and much harder to write. You have influenced my life though I am just a housewife and mother. I love what I am doing more than anything in the world but I look up to you and admire you so."[29]

Outside of her family circle, Van Waters' legacy survived in the careers of younger women for whom she had been a mentor. Alma Holzschuh went on to direct the California women's prison at Tehachapi; Edna Mahan became superintendent of the New Jersey women's reformatory at Clinton Farms; Elizabeth Bode directed the Lancaster School for Girls in Massachusetts; Katherine Gabel directed reformatories for girls in Georgia and Arizona before becoming dean of the Smith College School of Social Work and then president of Pacific Oaks College. One of the young men Van Waters took under her wing, Howard Kellett, devoted his life to prison ministry.

Former interns and even casual visitors to the reformatory let Miriam Van Waters know how the personal faith she showed in prisoners had inspired them to emulate her model. Even a passing contact with Doctor could have an enormous impact, as numerous letters attested. Miriam Pollock wrote to Van Waters in 1965 that "Unbeknownst to you, I have been an ardent admirer of yours for thirty years," since her student days at the Harvard School of Education, when she spent two days at the reformatory. Pollock still recalled the superintendent's lectures and "how impressed we all were with the awesome fact that you had so much faith in the women under your care." She had left "with a personal commitment to rehabilitative services. You kindled a spark in all of us which is still burning greatly."[30] Similarly, high-school guidance counselor Charles Cummings wrote of her effect. In his first job after Harvard, as an apprentice probation officer in Boston Juvenile Court, Hans Weiss had told him how much he admired Miriam Van Waters. As a teacher Cummings brought groups of students to Framingham. The superintendent "helped these young people (and me) to see themselves through the eyes of others, and I think they learned a little humility and honesty." He wrote that "I am deeply grateful," and, reminded of Shakespeare, asked rhetorically "How far that little candle throws his beams?. . . how far we cannot tell."[31]

A comment in one of the many letters of gratitude she received raised intriguing questions about Miriam Van Waters' place in history. Helen Gray, who provided legal aid to inmates in the 1950s, wrote of the retired superintendent: "I put her in the same category with those other great women I have been privileged to meet, Jane Addams, Carrie Chapman Catt and Margaret Sanger."[32] Unlike Addams, Catt, and Sanger, however, Miriam Van Waters did not become a nationally recognized figure in women's history. Despite her popularity as a writer in the 1920s and her notoriety during her dismissal in the 1940s, she has remained historically significant largely to those who knew her personally. Perhaps her choice of penology, a small and marginal arena even within reform circles, kept Van Waters from gaining the kind of reputation afforded leaders of the settlement house, suffrage, and birth control movements. Perhaps the publication of her memoirs would have drawn greater attention to her reform efforts. Even more important in explaining her historical reputation, however, is the fact that Miriam Van Waters' unique contribution consisted not in the leadership of a social movement but rather in her exceptional ability to touch individuals deeply. Although she campaigned nationally for her beloved causes—improved treatment of juvenile delinquents, the abolition of capital punishment, the rehabilitation and the rights of women inmates—it was her personal charisma, her spiritual power to heal lost souls, that most impressed others. Thus it has been in individual memory, not in political history, that her legacy has endured.

Despite this historical silence, Miriam Van Waters' life provides rich lessons for women's history. Each stage in her dramatic career illuminates the contours of women's reform in America, from her early decision to work for juvenile justice, to her efforts to transform Framingham into a social service institution, to her struggle after World War II to defend her reforms. Although her spiritual moorings and her unique personality strongly influenced Van Waters' choices, she operated within a modern female reform tradition, one that bridged voluntarist and professional worlds for over a generation.

Van Waters and her colleagues kept alive an older tradition of personalized service, even as they embraced the new social science and the professional world of social work. For these women—whether in prison reform, the Children's Bureau, the Women's Bureau, or local service agencies—continuity as much as change marked the period after women's suffrage. Even as they pressed for equality with men in politics, the workplace, or the criminal-justice system, reformers like Van Waters still believed in the unique qualities of women, based on their roles as mothers. For them, the Social Gospel, maternalism, and professionalism coexisted naturally.

When local politics threatened to undermine the work of these reformers, more traditional female voluntary associations often came to their aid. That Miriam Van Waters could bring such an array of women's community-based organizations into a prison from the 1930s through the 1950s reveals the rich yet still largely untapped history of middle-class women's voluntary associations in the twentieth century. Many middle-class women in these organizations, both black and white, joined neither the expanding female paid labor force nor the small feminist movement. Their support, however, helped sustain social service at a time when the power of women reformers had been reduced from its height during the Progressive Era.[33]

Over the course of Van Waters' career, maternalist authority came under increasing political scrutiny. The mood of social crisis of the 1930s may have allowed an alternative institution like Framingham to survive periodic attacks from fiscal and moral conservatives. During the cold war, however, opposition to liberal reform strengthened, while motherhood became a powerful rhetorical tool for confining women to the home, rather than expanding their public roles. At the same time, the conformist atmosphere encouraged sharper penalties for those who defied gender roles. Unwed mothers, juvenile delinquents, and homosexuals, who now symbolized moral weakness, evoked condemnation rather than compassion.[34]

Throughout her career, but especially in her final battles, Miriam Van Waters confronted the power of deviant labels to control women's lives. Within the juvenile court, she participated in the labeling of youthful sexual offenses as crimes that justified state intervention in family life. At Framingham, however, Van Waters recognized more fully the injustice of imposing criminal penalties on unwed mothers, adulteresses, alcoholics, and other "morals" offenders. With the support of liberal clergy and women's groups, she determined to circumvent the incarceration of such women and to restore them to full lives within their communities. Conservatives opposed her extralegal authority and accused her of coddling criminals and failing to extract the penalties deserved by women who defied their social roles.

When critics could find no other way to undermine popular support for her child-centered institution, they employed a more powerful charge of deviance, lesbianism. Their success suggests that Van Waters had good reason to fear the labeling of homosexuality that was occurring during her lifetime. The association of same-sex love with criminal or pathological states effectively suppressed lesbian identity formation among women who, like Van Waters, sought public authority. Although never targeted publicly herself, the exaggerated charges of rampant, aggressive homosexuality at Framingham helped undermine her liberal programs. Van Waters may have been particularly vulnerable to this political strategy, given her personal stake in minimizing the existence of lesbianism. Yet for others as well, the threat that even tolerance of homosexuality could weaken a reformer's credentials contributed to the long national silence about lesbianism.

Of all the ways that Van Waters' life illustrates the history of female reform, however, one stands out most clearly. For her, and for other modern women, motherhood remained a powerful component of both personal and public identities. In her youth, Van Waters had longed for connection with her own beloved mother; in response she assumed a maternal role in her family. Convinced that her health prevented her from bearing children, she recommitted her life to child saving. As L. A. juvenile court referee, founder and guiding light of El Retiro, and mother superior at Framingham, she created ample opportunities for achieving her goal of redeeming even the most outcast women. Van Waters also raised an adopted daughter as a single mother, learning painfully the limitations on her ability to save others. At the same time, she forged intensely maternal ties with her protégés and staff and celebrated the motherhood of imprisoned women.

Miriam Van Waters' reform career had originated in her Social Gospel faith in the goodness of all children of God. To this she later added the investigative methods of social science and the interventionist techniques of social work, each of which proved inadequate to the task of reform. Increasingly, Christian faith and mother love dominated her unique brand of social service. Like her reform allies, she believed that equality could not be accomplished without securing the rights of motherhood for all women, and she argued fiercely for a compassionate form of justice rooted in mother-child relations. Miriam Van Waters' vision of maternal justice insisted on an equality that acknowledged gender difference, rejected deviant labels, and placed great faith in redemption through love. This vision remains her most powerful legacy.

EPILOGUE
The Superintendent's House

In October 1992, just as I was beginning to draft this biography of Miriam Van Waters, I returned to Framingham to attend a reception to honor women who had worked at the reformatory during the 1930s, 1940s, and 1950s. Former staff members who lived in New England were coming to this event, to be held in the house where Van Waters had lived for twenty-five years. On that crisp, autumn Sunday I arrived eager to hear the memories of women who had known and worked for Van Waters and to walk through the spaces she had once occupied. What I saw both disturbed and inspired me.

As I approached the "superintendent's house," still attached by overpass to the original prison entrance, the building seemed neglected, rundown, barren. No superintendent had lived here since Betty Cole Smith, Van Waters' successor, retired in the early 1970s. The house had been converted for office use, but now heavy padlocks barred the outer doors, as well as many of the interior rooms. After a mammoth state policeman appeared to unlock the back entrance, I entered and slowly walked around the ground floor rooms, now stripped of furnishings. The house felt institutional rather than domestic. Correctional officers who had used the living room for violence control training had left large, orange padded mats lined up against one of the walls. The kitchen had no supplies, and its sink no longer worked. In the conservatory, weeds flourished rather than flowers.

A double staircase led to the two upper floors, where I searched out the rooms in which the superintendent, her mother, her daughter Sarah, her brother Ralph and his wife Bert, inmate house servants, interns, and assorted guests had once lived. Now these rooms were in disarray. Old police jackets and pants lay scattered in a former bedroom that had been used, for a time, to distribute uniforms; the place looked as if it had been ransacked. Down the hall, in an unlocked makeshift office, a 1985 calendar lay on a large wood desk, surrounded by scattered papers and uncollected trash. The dozen or more locked upstairs rooms seemed to be used for storage.

Seeing the superintendent's house in this condition saddened me.

355

I had spent the previous days reading Van Waters' animated descriptions of life in this house during the 1930s. One year Sarah had shared the second-floor sleeping porch with various Van Waters nieces and nephews during their summer vacations. The Blue Room, next to Van Waters' bedroom, had housed Geraldine Thompson on her frequent visits. In the downstairs dining room Van Waters had entertained reformers and politicians, including Eleanor Roosevelt. The superintendent always believed that a good luncheon well served by the students put parole board members in a better frame of mind for their hearings, so even her enemies had dined here. The house had not been fancy, but at one time it had been full of life, and now it felt deserted.

I had been invited here by a graduate student in criminal justice, Nancy Rubackin, who organized the reception for former staff. Through a nonprofit group called Remember the Ladies she sought the historic preservation of the Framingham superintendent's house, where Clara Barton, Eliza Mosher, Jessie Hodder, and Miriam Van Waters each lived when they directed the reformatory. The group was trying to turn the now abandoned house into an archive, visitor center, and exhibition space on the history of women's prisons. Rubackin and I tried to make the living room seem inviting for the event. We added plants and flowers and placed a signed photograph of Van Waters on the wooden mantel. She displayed scrapbooks and cartons full of old pictures and other reformatory memorabilia, while I set up a tape recorder to play excerpts from the 1954 radio program, *Dr. Van Waters Speaks.*

Gradually former staff members began to arrive. Their ages ranged from seventy-five to ninety-seven, and they had worked at the reformatory for anywhere from five to thirty-five years. Harriet Gunning, Lois McWilliams, Nan Neilsen, Pauline Orsi, Margery Osburg, and Margaret van Wagenen would be honored with commendations from Governor William Weld, presented by Framingham's representative to the state legislature, Barbara Gray. One woman came to accept a citation on behalf of her mother, Ida Rice, who had been a Friendly Visitor and a member of the Friends of Framingham.

In the audience were friends and relatives of the women being honored, along with community members whose lives had intersected with the history of Framingham. Charlie Ayer, a newspaper reporter whose first big story was Van Waters' dismissal and subsequent reinstatement in 1949, came with his aunt and cousin, who were each being honored. Reverend William Wiltenburg, the former Protestant chaplain, joined longtime community activists. A local architect described his volunteer efforts to restore the house to its original state.

Before the ceremony began, the current superintendent, Kathleen Dennehy, offered to take me for a ride along the periphery of the institution grounds. Dennehy was young, cordial, and very interested in the history of the women who preceded her at Framingham. She had agreed to host the reception, despite the skepticism of her superiors. In the course of her work Dennehy had found archival treasures stored away in the institution, including a huge clipping book kept by Van Waters and extensive transcripts of the 1949 dismissal hearings. Reading old staff conference notes, she had been thinking about Van Waters' management style. Her own background was in administration, not social work, the field that attracted most of the staff members in Van Waters' heyday. Yet the young superintendent felt a kinship with Van Waters' habit of walking the institution and getting to know the inmates.

The population Dennehy superintended, however, differed greatly from the one Van Waters knew. Drug addicts had largely replaced the alcoholics, and alongside women who had killed their batterers were women who had sexually abused their children. The institution, once intentionally called a reformatory rather than a prison, had also changed. Mothers could no longer keep their infants at the institution's nursery, as they did until 1958. Security concerns had replaced many of the open, rehabilitative features of the past. A tall, razor-wire fence surrounded much of the institution. It would surround more of it except for the location of the superintendent's house, which was, in part, why we were there that day. Preserving this house as a part of women's history would also prevent that fence from being completed. I thought that Miriam Van Waters would have appreciated this effort to circumvent excessive security in the name of historical memory.

Kathy Dennehy took me down the country road that borders the institution to visit a clearing marked by a neat, carved wood sign reading: "Clara Barton Cemetary, [*sic*] Commonwealth of Massachusetts." When babies born at the reformatory died, they were buried here. We got out of the car and entered a fairly barren area. At first I could not see any graves. But at our feet, covered by autumn leaves and old pine needles, we disclosed a dozen or more headstones. Most were marked simply "Baby Jones" or "Baby Smith." Some, however, had full names and were larger. These graves held women inmates who had died in prison with no family or funds to provide for their burial.

Across the road we saw another clearing, where we located stand-ing tombstones, each bearing the name of several infants who had died in a given year. Inmate graves lay here, too, and one stopped me short. The name on the headstone was familiar, for I had read the handwritten autobiography this woman doctor prepared while she served one of several prison terms for having performed abortions. In my writing I had disguised the actual names of women who served at Framingham, but at that moment of recognition, standing at Dr. "Caroline Cook's" grave, I wanted others to know who she was and where she is buried. I wished that I had brought flowers to pay my respects.

As we stood there I told Dr. Cook's story to Kathy Dennehy. I ex-plained how, when she was finally released, the doctor was too old and ill to support herself outside, so Miriam Van Waters kept her on as an intern. Student work assignments included nursing Dr. Cook. Allowing the aging doctor to remain, and permitting former students to visit her, had been included in charges justifying Van Waters' dismissal. When I finished this story, the superintendent looked at me and said, in all seriousness, "There is no justice in this world." I told her that she, of all people, would know.

We returned to the superintendent's house, which had filled with almost thirty guests. Older staffers were reminiscing together, and I walked around with my tape recorder, learning what had brought them to Framingham to work in a women's reformatory and why so many stayed on as staff members, as did Margaret van Wagenen, who worked in the mothers' cottage, and Harriet Gunning, who worked in the nurs-ery. These women felt they had a mission, that they were part of a progressive movement to help forgotten inmates, many of whom were poor, unwed mothers, alcoholics, or otherwise in need of social ser-vices. Staff and students idolized Miriam Van Waters, who seemed to me that day a bit too much like "Saint Miriam." I thought that I had more perspective, having learned how much vulnerability her public masks had hidden, and how much her own need for authority had helped create her battles. Yet that day, when I looked out the window at the prison as it is now — with its razor-wire fence and high-tech secu-rity systems — and then remembered Van Waters' simple, secure faith in the redemption of all women, I could appreciate the staying power of her charisma.

I had been asked to introduce the ceremonies, so I talked about the historical contribution of the women who had worked at the refor-matory. Representative Gray then gave each honored guest a commen-dation from the governor and asked the women to reminisce about their work. We presented a long-stemmed red rose to each of them, and I offered signed copies of my earlier book on the origins of women's prison reform, if anyone wanted one. To my surprise, everyone did. Just like the older women whom the students in my college classes interview for oral history assignments, these former staffers seemed surprised and deeply moved to be considered part of history. As ninety-seven-year-old Nan Neilsen put it, "This is the best day of my life." Finally someone had stopped to notice their contribution.

There were not many younger people in the room, and I wondered whether the historical moment when women in prison could attract sympathetic community attention had long passed. Aside from efforts by some contemporary feminists to reach out to "sisters inside" state and federal prisons, most Americans have been content to lock away female, as well as male, offenders and forget about the increasingly harsh conditions under which they live. An occasional exposé, such as recent indictments of Georgia prison officers for sexually abusing women inmates, reminds us briefly of the daily injustices suffered by inmates. But the reform movement of the late nineteenth and early twentieth centuries seems to have disappeared, and a new vengeance toward prisoners now pervades much of our culture.

Toward the end of her career, Miriam Van Waters regretted that she had not found a true successor, a disciple who could carry on her unique approach. Was her crusade a lost one, then, because it had not survived her strong personal appeal? Walking around the house, recording the reminiscences of several older women, I noticed Nancy Rubackin, who has spearheaded the campaign to preserve this house, with a young friend of hers, who had just begun working in a state institution. They were listening intently to the stories of the past. Earlier that week I had met a theology graduate student from Harvard pouring over Van Waters' diaries in the library as research for a master's thesis on Christian penology. This woman coordinates volunteers at Project Connect for Women in New York City, helping women released from prison make the transition into the community. Perhaps these younger women were now making the kind of commitment that the older women just honored had made almost sixty years ago. During Kathy Dennehy's superintendency, two hundred volunteers worked at Framingham, far more than at any other state institution. In this sense, Van Waters' tradition of bringing the community into the prison had survived.

On this day, at least, the work of women who once chose to go inside a prison to serve others had been recognized. I left Framingham with the hope that the movement to restore the superintendent's house might help revive consciousness about the plight of imprisoned women, both in the past and in the present.

The morning after the reception, Kathy Dennehy made a point of stopping by Miriam Van Waters' grave. On it she left the red rose we had given to her at the reception. "Somehow," she wrote to me later, "it seemed to belong there."

NOTES

PROLOGUE

1. Two journalistic accounts of Van Waters' life have been published: Burton J. Rowles, *The Lady at Box 99* (Greenwich, Conn.: Seabury Press, 1962), and a chapter in Adela Rogers St. Johns, *Some Are Born Great* (New York: New American Library, 1974). Several doctoral dissertations have discussed episodes in Van Waters' career: Mary Bularzik, "Sex, Crime, and Justice: Women in the Criminal Justice System of Massachusetts, 1900–1950" (Ph.D. diss., Brandeis University, 1982) and Mary Odem, "Delinquent Daughters: The Sexual Regulation of Female Minors in the United States, 1880–1920" (Ph.D. diss., University of California, Berkeley, 1989).

2. I first developed this theme in "Separatism Revisited: Women's Institutions, Social Reform, and the Career of Miriam Van Waters," in Linda Kerber, Alice Kessler-Harris, and Kathryn Kish Sklar, eds., *U.S. History as Women's History: New Feminist Essays* (Chapel Hill: University of North Carolina Press, 1995), 170–88.

3. On women's public culture and the relationship of maternalism and social welfare policy, see Paula Baker, "The Domestication of Politics: Women and American Political Society, 1780–1920," *American Historical Review* 89 (June 1984): 620–47; Seth Koven and Sonya Michel, eds., *Mothers of a New World: Maternalist Politics and the Origins of Welfare States* (New York: Routledge, 1993); "International Trends: Maternalism as a Paradigm," *Journal of Women's History* 5:2 (fall 1993), 95–131, esp. Molly Ladd-Taylor, "Toward Defining Maternalism in U.S. History," 110–13; and Kathryn Kish Sklar, *Florence Kelley and the Nation's Work: The Rise of Women's Political Culture, 1830–1900* (New Haven: Yale University Press, 1995). On maternalism outside the white, Protestant majority, see, e.g., Linda Gordon, *Pitied but Not Entitled: Single Mothers and the History of Welfare, 1890–1935* (New York: Free Press, 1994), chap. 5; Faith Rogow, *Gone to Another Meeting: The National Council of Jewish Women, 1893–1993* (Tuscaloosa: University of Alabama Press, 1993); Kathleen D. McCarthy, ed., *Lady Bountiful Revisited: Women, Philanthropy, and Power* (New Brunswick, N.J.: Rutgers University Press, 1990). An alternative language of class appeared within the socialist Left, in which women participated, but men dominated. See Mari Jo Buhle, *Women and American Socialism, 1870–1920* (Urbana: University of Illinois Press, 1981).

4. See Joan W. Scott, "Deconstructing Equality-versus-Difference; or, The Uses of Poststructuralist Theory for Feminism," *Feminist Studies* 14 (spring 1988): 33–50.

5. Charles K. Cummings to Miriam Van Waters (hereafter MVW), 22 Nov. 1959, file 151, in Miriam Van Waters Papers, Schlesinger Library, Radcliffe College, Cambridge, Mass. (all subsequent citations to manuscript sources refer to this collection, unless otherwise noted); Miriam Pollock to MVW, 17 Dec. 1965, file 153; anonymous letter from inmate to "Dearest Mom," 30 May 1948, file 350; Commissioner of Corrections E. E. McDowell, memorandum, 19 March 1949, file 252; MVW journal, vol. 8, 5 March 1948. MVW's journals are divided between two collections at the Schlesinger Library: the MVW Papers and the Anna Gladding-Miriam Van Waters Papers. Unless otherwise noted, MVW journals and volume numbers refer to those in the MVW Papers.

CHAPTER ONE

1. MVW to parents, 26 March 1926, file 54, and ms. memoir, file 510; Miriam Van Waters, *Parents on Probation* (New York: New Republic, 1927). MVW's letters home were usually addressed either to her parents jointly or to her mother (sometimes called "Mumsie"); occasionally she would address a letter to her father. As she explained to him, the letters to her mother were meant for both of them, and she expected her mother to tell him all her news. Because the addressee is often unclear, I use "MVW to parents" for all letters to her mother and/or father.

2. MVW journal, vol. 3, precedes entry for 30 July 1935 (see also vol. 1, 25 Jan. 1933 on childhood suffering); vol. 2, 9 March 1935 and 11 April 1935.

3. MVW journal, vol. 4, 16 May 1936.

4. Handwritten genealogy of Robinson family prepared by Aunt Mary Robinson, n.d., file 23; DAR acceptance letter to Mrs. Maud O. Van Waters, n.d., file 28.

5. Certificate of Baptism, Maud Ophelia Vosburg, 18 Sept. 1867 (gives birth as 29 June 1866), and "Biographical Sketch of the Rev. George Browne Van Waters for the University of Oregon Library Memorial," George Browne Van Waters Papers, box 1, Special Collections, University of Oregon Library, Eugene, Oregon (hereafter GBVW Papers); MVW journal, 14 Jan. 1932, file 211, in Anna Gladding-Miriam Van Waters Papers (all further references to this collection will cite the Gladding-VW Papers); Maud Van Waters (hereafter Maud VW) to GBVW, 2 Nov. 1883, box 2, GBVW Papers; newspaper clipping, 15 July 1884, file 30; Lewis Cass Aldrich, ed., *History of Clearfield County, Pa.* (Syracuse, N.Y.: D. Mason, 1887), 394, 406; *Commemorative Biographical Record of Central Pennsylvania* (Chicago: J. A. Beers Co., 1898), H. A. Vosburg entry, 759–60. Maud's brothers were George, who eventually directed the Wheeler Lumber Company in Portland; J. Lawrence (Lonnie), who also settled in Oregon; E. Fred, who managed Vosburg Drug Company in DuBois; Harry A., who ran a general store in DuBois; and Ralph, who died in DuBois 1888 *(Commemorative Biographical Record).*

6. The "Biographical Sketch of the Rev. George Browne Van Waters"

claims that Sarah Anne Browne Van Waters was a "scholar in Latin and Greek." Other errors in this source, for example, that GBVW received a doctor of divinity degree from Harvard Divinity School, raise doubts about its accuracy. Sarah may have been the daughter of J. W. Browne, postmaster and general merchant in Rensselaer Falls. The occupation of Cornelius is not evident; an 1873 business directory lists him as "retired," but he was only forty-six years old at the time (Hamilton Child, *Gazetteer and Business Directory of St. Lawrence County, NY* [Syracuse, N.Y., 1873], 190, 201). MVW believed that her father's mother descended from Sir Thomas Browne, the seventeenth-century British physician who wrote *Religio Medici* (MVW journal, 3 Feb. 1938, file 213, Gladding-VW Papers).

7. Charles left Ohio in 1873, but George remained at Oberlin for four years (Oberlin College Catalogs, 1871–75, box 7, College General Archives, and George Browne Van Waters Alumni Records, Student Files, Series B, box 340, Oberlin College Archives, Oberlin College, Oberlin, Ohio). Charles C. Van Waters also attended St. Lawrence University but did not graduate. He received a medical degree from the College of the City of New York in 1879 (*Laurentian,* vol. 37, Oct. 1934, 235).

8. John Barnard, *From Evangelicalism to Progressivism at Oberlin College, 1866–1917* (Columbus: Ohio State University Press, 1969), 4–10, 25, 30. Oberlin remained tied to the Congregational Church.

9. Richard M. Spielman, *Bexley Hall: 150 Years: A Brief History* (Colgate Rochester Divinity School/Bexley Hall/Crozer Theological Seminary, 1974), 7, 25, 35; Sydney Ahlstrom, *A Religious History of the American People* (New Haven: Yale University Press, 1972), 624. "Broad term churchman" is the phrase used by Reverend Van Waters' son (interview with Ralph Van Waters, 10–11 Sept. 1989, Cochituate, Mass.; hereafter RVW interview).

10. RVW interview. Rev. Van Waters was ordained deacon in 1883 and ordained priest in 1884. In 1901 Western University awarded him an honorary doctor of divinity degree. (Information supplied by the Archives of the Diocese of Oregon, the Episcopal Church in Western Oregon, Lake Oswego, Oregon.)

11. GBVW to Maud VW, 7 Aug. 1895, box 1, GBVW Papers.

12. Maud VW to GBVW, 2 Nov. 1883, box 2, GBVW Papers.

13. Maud VW to family, 18 Sept. 1887, box 2, GBVW Papers; memorial card, n.d., file 111; RVW interview; MVW journal, 19 Nov. 1944, file 219v, Gladding-VW Papers; GBVW to Father, 5 Oct. 1887, file 198, Gladding-VW Papers.

14. MVW journal, vol. 5, 28 Sept. 1938; GBVW to MVW, 30 Sept. 1933, file 25.

15. Maud VW to GBVW, 5 March 1888, box 2, GBVW Papers; MVW to Ethel Sturges Dummer, 1 June 1923, file 820, Ethel Sturges Dummer Papers, Schlesinger Library, Radcliffe College, Cambridge, Mass. (hereafter Dummer Papers); Dr. Miriam Van Waters interviewed by Miss Anne Gladding, tape transcription, 1 May 1969, Gladding-VW Papers.

16. Maud's father and brothers transferred several properties to her at the turn of the century, and she purchased some from them at low fees. Deeds and transfer documents are in GBVW Papers.

17. Maud VW to parents, undated 1892, box 2, GBVW Papers; MVW to "my dear papa," n.d. (c. 1894), file 32; MVW, "Portland, Oregon," 29 Jan. 1952, file 489; E. Kimbark MacColl, *The Shaping of a City: Business and Politics in Portland, Oregon, 1885–1915* (Portland, Oreg.: Georgian Press, 1976), 112, 168-72, 174-78, 215-17, and MacColl, with Harry H. Stein, *Merchants, Money, and Power: The Portland Establishment, 1843–1913* (Portland, Oreg.: Georgian Press, 1988), 304.

18. Maud VW to family, c. 1892, box 2, GBVW Papers.

19. Maud VW to family, 23 Jan. 1893, box 2, GBVW Papers.

20. Maud recounted her fear of miscarriage during the "quickening" period to GBVW, 14 July 1895 and 5 Aug. 1895, box 2; also GBVW to Maud VW, 7 Aug. 1895, box 1, all in GBVW Papers. On neurasthenia, see Ann Douglas Wood, "'The Fashionable Diseases': Women's Complaints and Their Treatment in Nineteenth-Century America," in Mary Hartman and Lois W. Banner, eds., *Clio's Consciousness Raised: New Perspectives on the History of Women* (New York: Harper and Row, 1974), 1–23, and Barbara Sicherman, "The Uses of a Diagnosis: Doctors, Patients, and Neurasthenia," *Journal of the History of Medicine and Allied Sciences* 32 (1977): 33-54.

21. MVW journal, 6 March 1930, file 209v, Gladding-VW Papers. Maud had also lost her youngest brother, Ralph, in 1888, a year after her daughter Rachel died. The deaths of her brother and mother are listed in *Commemorative Biographical Record,* H. A. Vosburg entry, 759-60. It is possible that postpartum depression merged with her mourning during these years to make Maud VW "nervous."

22. GBVW to Maud VW, 15 July 1895, box 1, GBVW Papers; Bertha Hallam, "The First One Hundred Years" [of St. David's Parish], ts., Diocese of Oregon Archives; GBVW to Maud VW, 21 Oct. 1898, box 1, GBVW Papers. GBVW wrote frequently of his concerns about expenses, sometimes enclosing money he raised while traveling (e.g., 14 Oct. 1895, 7 Aug. 1895, 12 Aug. 1895 all in GBVW Papers). He sought financial help from his mother and sold some properties Maud inherited from her father. In an effort to ease her parish responsibilities, he took charge of the Ladies Auxiliary Maud had founded at St. David's, an unusual act for a rector. (MVW to parents, 9 May 1902, file 32; GBVW to Maud VW, 2 Oct. 1904, file 24; Oregon Branch of the Woman's Auxiliary, 1895 Report, in Diocese of Oregon Archives, and letter to the author from Rev. Chandler C. Jackson, Diocesan Archivist, 8 Sept. 1992.)

23. Maud VW to GBVW, 14 July, 1895, box 2, GBVW Papers; GBVW to MVW, 2 Oct. 1932, file 25; MVW journal, 6 March 1930, file 209v, Gladding-VW Papers.

24. MVW to parents, 21 April 1896, file 31.

25. MVW to parents, 12 July 1898, file 31; 13 April 1902, 26 April 1902, 4 May 1902, file 32; MVW journal, 21 June 1938, file 213, Gladding-VW Papers.

26. Maud VW to GBVW, 2 July 1901, file 31 and 11 Aug. 1901, file 26.

27. MVW to parents, undated 1902, file 32; GBVW to Maud VW, 14 March 1902, box 1, GBVW Papers. Miriam left school that term in order to care for the household.

28. MVW to parents, 20 March 1902, file 31; 23 March, 18 April, and undated April 1902, file 32.

29. MVW to parents, 23 March 1902, file 31, 26 April 1902 and 17 June 1902, file 32. On mother-daughter ties and female romantic friendships, see Carroll Smith-Rosenberg, "The Female World of Love and Ritual: Relations between Women in Nineteenth-Century America," *Signs* 1 (autumn 1975): 1–29.

30. MVW to parents, 2 May and 7 May 1902, file 32; MVW journal, 26 Aug. 1936, file 213, Gladding-VW Papers.

31. MVW to parents, 3 June 1902, file 32.

32. MVW, ms. memoir, file 510.

33. MVW to parents, 26 March 1926, file 54; MVW journal, vol. 3, 2 Sept. 1935, vol. 4, 28 May 1936, vol. 7, 11 Nov. 1945; typed memoir, file 508, n.d., fragment 6, 2–3; MVW journal, 4 Dec. 1937, 24 June 1936, 21 Sept. 1936, file 213, Gladding-VW Papers.

34. William R. Hutchison, *The Modernist Impulse in American Protestantism* (New York: Oxford University Press, 1976), 3–9, 80, 113; Paul Carter, *Decline and Revival of the Social Gospel: Social and Political Liberalism in American Protestant Churches, 1920-1940* (Ithaca, N.Y.: Cornell University Press, 1954), 10–11, 14; Henry F. May, *Protestant Churches and Industrial America* (New York: Harper and Row, 1967), 182–86.

35. Robert T. Handy, *A Christian America: Protestant Hope and Historical Realities* (New York: Oxford University Press, 1971), 157, 164, 187; Donald K. Gorrell, *The Age of Social Responsibility: The Social Gospel in the Progressive Era, 1900-1920* (Macon, Ga.: Mercer University Press, 1988), 17, 29; Ronald C. White Jr. and C. Howard Hopkins, *The Social Gospel: Religion and Reform in Changing America* (Philadelphia: Temple University Press, 1976), 149; Mary Sudman Donovan, *A Different Call: Women's Ministries in the Episcopal Church, 1850-1920* (Wilton, Conn.: Morehouse-Barlow, 1986), 150. Other Episcopal settlement women included Mary Simkhovitch and Mary Van Kleek. On the Society of the Companions of the Holy Cross, see below, chap. 16.

36. Reverend Van Waters' mother belonged to a Methodist church, and his brother was a Congregationalist who prided himself on his freethinking. In a letter praising a new congregational minister, Charles Van Waters wrote his brother that he was pleased that the minister was as liberal as "you or I" (8 Dec. 1921, file 111). On GBVW's interest in world religion see MVW to GBVW, 2 Aug. 1915, file 42; and newsclipping, Baker, Oreg., 7 Feb. 1921, GBVW Papers.

37. Miscellaneous Newspaper Clippings file, GBVW Papers, e.g. Klamath Falls, Oreg., 28 Jan. 1921, *Klamath Daily Record,* 29 Jan. 1921, Baker, Oreg., 7 Feb. 1921, Dale, Oreg., 5 March 1921; "Some Sidelights on the Work in Eastern Oregon," n.d. (by Rector of St. Stephens, Baker, Oreg.) and

GBVW, "The Church for a Changing World," n.d., box 4, GBVW Papers; Charles Van Waters to GBVW, 25 Jan. 1909, file 111; honorary doctor of divinity degree, 8 May 1901, Western University (chartered in Illinois and Tennessee), in GBVW Papers.

38. GBVW, undated sermon, c. 1920, box 4, GBVW Papers; MVW to Ethel Sturges Dummer, 1 July 1925, file 821, Dummer Papers.

39. GBVW, sermon ms., 1920, box 4, GBVW Papers. In addition to supporting woman suffrage, Reverend Van Waters supported women's right to divorce and to use birth control, positions that were then highly controversial within his church. On divorce, see John Steven McGoarty, ed., *History of Los Angeles County* (Chicago: American Historical Society, 1923), 2:137. Van Waters' unpopular positions, such as defending Margaret Sanger during a visit to Portland in 1916, may have kept him from rising in the church hierarchy. When Van Waters' close friend and political ally, Bishop Robert Paddock, suffered a nervous breakdown and resigned in 1922, the movement to have GBVW appointed bishop was defeated, in part because of Van Waters' social views. See file on "The Paddock Case Documents," GBVW Papers. (Support for GBVW's nomination as bishop appears in *Baker (Oreg.) Morning Democrat,* 5 Sept. 1922, GBVW Papers.)

40. MVW, ts. memoir, fragment 6, file 508; ms. notes for memoir, file 510; MVW journal, vol. 5, 25 Feb. 1939.

41. Rt. Rev. Benjamin Wistar Morris, "St. David's Mission Work," in "The Bishop's Annual Address at the Diocesan Convention, 1899," *Journal of the Proceedings of the 11th Annual Convention and the 46th Annual Report of the Church in the Diocese of Oregon* (Portland, Oreg.: Diocese of Oregon, 1899), 15–16.

42. Interview with MVW by "RPM," 6 Aug. 1963, file 497; interview with MVW, 1 May 1969, Gladding-VW Papers; letter to the author from Rev. Chandler C. Jackson, 8 Sept. 1992. On the Protestant urban-mission movement, see Paul Boyer, *Urban Masses and Moral Order in America, 1820–1920* (Cambridge: Harvard University Press, 1978), 134–38.

43. Interview with MVW [RPM], file 497; MVW to parents, c. 16 March 1902, file 31.

44. MVW journal, 12 July 1949, file 220, Gladding-VW Papers. See also MVW journal, 21 Sept. 1928, file 208v; MVW journal, vol. 2, 9 March 1935, vol. 4, 18 Jan. 1936, and vol. 7, 8 Jan. 1946. Throughout this study I use Van Waters' accounts of her dreams primarily as clues to her feeling states, rather than to interpret symbols according to psychoanalytic method. At times, however, Van Waters, who had read Freud critically, did try to interpret her own dreams, providing further insight into her self-understanding.

45. MVW to parents, 12 July 1898, file 31; MVW to parents, 12 Jan. 1922, box 2, GBVW Papers. The classic works on nineteenth-century middle-class women's networks are Smith-Rosenberg, "The Female World of Love and Ritual," and Nancy Cott, *The Bonds of Womanhood: Woman's Sphere in New England, 1780–1835* (New Haven: Yale University Press, 1977). On new female images see Lois W. Banner, *American Beauty* (Chicago: University of Chicago Press, 1983).

46. MVW to parents, 7 Oct. 1934, file 68; ms. memoir, file 510; MVW to mother, 31 July 1902, file 32. The town of Vosburg (later Wheeler) housed the Wheeler Lumber Company, which was directed by Maud's brother George Vosburg after he moved to Oregon. (Lewis A. McArthur, *Oregon Geographic Names* [Portland, Oreg.: Press of the Oregon Historical Society, 1982], 764.)

47. MVW to parents, 12 July 1898, file 31; 7 Oct. 1934, file 68; 29 July 1900, file 31.

48. MVW to parents, undated Aug. 1901, file 31; 8 June, undated Aug., and 17 June 1902, file 32.

49. MVW, ms. memoir, file 510.

50. MVW, ms. memoir, file 510; Donovan, *A Different Call,* 61, 71; Sally Reed Stout, *St. Helen's Hall, the First Century, 1869-1969* (n.p.: Portland, Oreg., 1969), 7, 16, 20. The school had been founded by Oregon's Episcopal bishop, Wistar Morris, who was the only male teacher at the school. Morris had brought Reverend Van Waters to Portland, and MVW's father served on St. Helen's board. Tuition in the early twentieth century was $330 a year, or $40 a term for day students. Reverend Van Waters is listed as a board member in Joseph Gaston, *Portland, Oregon: Its History and Builders* (Chicago: S. J. Clarke, 1911), 395.

51. Catalog of Saint Helen's Hall, *Twenty-Eighth Year, 1896-1897* (Portland, 1897); advertisement for St. Helens Hall, *Polk's Portland City Directory* (Portland, Oreg.: R. L. Polk and Co, 1914), 30; Stout, *St. Helen's Hall,* 20, 53-54. At about the time MVW graduated, in 1904, the charge of the school was taken over by the Sisters of St. John the Baptist (Stout, 21).

52. MVW, untitled speech, 29 Jan. 1952, file 489.

53. Ibid.; Stout, *St. Helen's Hall,* 19-20.

54. Luella Clay Carson Papers, Special Collections, University of Oregon, Eugene, Oregon; her graduation is listed in the *Tenth Annual Catalogue of St. Helen's Hall* (Portland, 1879), 10.

55. MVW to parents, undated 1894, file 31; report cards in box 2, GBVW Papers. MVW's brother and her grandson, in separate interviews, each spoke about the Van Waters' family emphasis on education. RVW interview; interview with Richard J. Hildebrandt, 18 Aug. 1989, San Pedro, Calif.

56. Photocopy of letter from Lonnie Vosburg, n.d., box 3, GBVW Papers; MVW to parents, June 1902, file 32.

57. For example, at age thirteen Miriam wrote to her parents about a particular piece of clothing that made her look "ten times fatter" and told her mother that "I weigh only 106 now. Indeed I feel quite exalted" (MVW to parents, undated Aug. 1901 and 16 July 1901, file 31).

58. MVW to parents, 26 Oct. 1929, file 58 and 7 Oct. 1934, file 68.

CHAPTER TWO

1. On the controversy over Dr. E. H. Clarke's *Sex in Education* (1873), which claimed that educated women destroyed their reproductive capacity, see Rosalind Rosenberg, *Beyond Separate Spheres: Intellectual Roots*

of Modern Feminism (New Haven: Yale University Press, 1982), chap. 1. Coeducation is discussed in Helen Lefkowitz Horowitz, *Campus Life: Undergraduate Cultures from the End of the Eighteenth Century to the Present* (New York: Alfred A. Knopf, 1987) and Barbara Miller Solomon, *In the Company of Educated Women: A History of Women and Higher Education in America* (New Haven: Yale University Press, 1985), esp. 127.

2. Lynn D. Gordon, *Gender and Higher Education in the Progressive Era* (New Haven: Yale University Press, 1990), 5.

3. Between 1880 and 1900, one-half of female college graduates did not marry, compared to 10 percent of all American women. After 1900 more coeds did marry, and by the 1940s, three-quarters of women college graduates wed (Horowitz, *Campus Life,* 198–99). Marriage rates for alumnae of both coed and single-sex schools rose (Solomon, *Company of Educated Women,* table 4, 120).

4. For national trends, see Gordon, *Gender and Higher Education,* 6, 40, and Solomon, *Company of Educated Women,* 89, 103. On Oregon, see Henry D. Sheldon, *History of the University of Oregon* (Portland, Oreg.: Binfords and Mort, 1940), 153, 176, 181, and the *1907 Bulletin,* University of Oregon, 38–39. Statistics on gender composition of the classes of 1904 through 1908 were provided by Keith Richards, archivist, University of Oregon Special Collections.

5. Luella Clay Carson, "Young Women and the State," *1907 Bulletin,* University of Oregon, 38–39.

6. MVW to parents, n.d. and undated Nov. 1905, file 33.

7. MVW to parents, 5 Dec. 1905, file 33.

8. MVW, ms. memoir, file 510; MVW to parents, 12 Aug. and 2 Nov. 1907, file 35; undated Jan. 1909, file 37 and undated Nov. 1908 (before 17 Nov. 1908), file 36; GBVW to Maud VW, 19 Nov. 1908, box 1, GBVW Papers; John E. DuBois to Maud VW, 24 May 1906, file 28.

9. MVW to father, 11 Oct. 1908, box 2, GBVW Papers.

10. MVW to parents, 29 Sept. and 5 Dec. 1907, file 35.

11. MVW to parents, undated June 1908 and undated Nov. 1906, file 36; 3 Nov. 1906, file 34; MVW to parents, undated 1906, and 6 June 1906, file 34.

12. MVW to parents, 8 Oct. 1905, file 33; 15 Oct. 1906, file 34; 8 Jan. 1907, file 35; 15 Oct. 1906; n.d. 1906; and undated March 1906, file 34. Cf. MVW to mother (n.d., box 2, GBVW Papers).

13. MVW to parents, undated 1906, file 34; 2 Nov. 1907, file 35; undated Nov. 1906 and undated 1908, file 36.

14. On college women's romantic friendships and the literature they read, see Carroll Smith-Rosenberg, "The Female World of Love and Ritual: Relations between Women in Nineteenth-Century America," *Signs* 1 (autumn 1975): 1–29; and Sherrie A. Inness, "Mashes, Smashes, Crushes, and Raves: Woman-to-Woman Relationships in Popular Women's College Fiction, 1895–1915," *NWSA Journal* 6:1 (spring 1994): 48–68.

15. On "college" versus "outsider" campus cultures, see Horowitz, *Campus Life,* esp. chap. 3.

16. Barbara Gelb, *So Short a Time: A Biography of John Reed and Louise Bryant* (New York: W. W. Norton, 1973), 39; Virginia Gardner, *"Friend and Lover": The Life of Louise Bryant* (New York: Horizon Press, 1982), 24–25; newspaper clipping from *Oregonian,* 28 Feb. 1908, file 36. The grades for Bryant and Van Waters appear in Registrar's Office, University of Oregon, Graduates by Classes, Special Collections, University of Oregon.

17. MVW to parents, 6 Oct. 1905, file 33; 3 Nov. 1906, file 34; 2 Nov. 1907, file 35; 15 Oct. 1906, file 34.

18. MVW to parents, 5 Dec. 1905, file 33; 26 Jan. 1906, file 34; 12 Jan. 1908, file 36.

19. MVW to parents, undated 1906, file 34.

20. MVW to parents, undated 1908 and before 17 Nov. 1908, file 36; 25 Jan. 1909, file 37.

21. MVW to parents, 21 June and 7 Oct. 1907, file 35.

22. MVW to parents, 5 Jan. 1906, undated 1906, and c. 15 Oct. 1906, file 34. On censorship, see 7 Dec. 1930, file 59.

23. MVW to parents, 5 Dec. 1907, file 35. On Oregon suffrage, see Abigail Scott Duniway, *Path Breaking* (New York: Schocken Books, 1971), 124–26; G. Thomas Edwards, *Sowing Good Seeds: The Northwest Suffrage Campaigns of Susan B. Anthony* (Portland, Oreg.: Oregon Historical Society Press, 1990), 196, 212; Lauren Kessler, "The Fight for Woman Suffrage and the Oregon Press," in Karen J. Blair, ed., *Women in Pacific Northwest History: An Anthology* (Seattle: University of Washington Press, 1988), 43–58.

24. MVW to parents, undated Jan. 1909, file 37 (her emphasis).

25. MVW to parents, 21 June and undated April 1907, file 35.

26. MVW to parents, undated April 1907 (sometime before 20 April), file 35; *1908 Bulletin,* University of Oregon, 43; MVW to family, 1908, box 8, GBVW Papers; *1909 Beaver* (replaced the *Bulletin*).

27. MVW to parents, undated Jan. 1907, file 35; 25 Feb. 1908, file 36; c. 15 Oct. 1906, file 34.

28. Gordon, *Gender and Higher Education,* 72, 78; *Oregon Monthly,* Jan. 1908, 42.

29. *Oregon Monthly,* March 1908, 33–34 and April 1908, 34. On the emergence of feminism and the tension between individualism and collective politics, see Nancy Cott, *The Grounding of Modern Feminism* (New Haven: Yale University Press, 1987).

30. The historical literature on progressivism is vast; for a review, see Daniel T. Rodgers, "In Search of Progressivism," *Reviews in American History* 10 (December 1982), 113–32.

31. MVW to parents, 7 Oct. and 5 Dec. 1907, file 35; undated Jan. 1909, file 37; undated Oct. 1906, file 34. Oregon instituted the elective system in 1905 at the urging of the younger faculty (Sheldon, *History of the University of Oregon,* 176).

32. Lawrence Veysey, *The Emergence of the American University* (Chicago: University of Chicago Press, 1965).

33. MVW, "The Reign of Law or the Survival of the Unlike, Failing-

Beekman Oration," file 464. In addition to the influence of Darwin on her ideas, Van Waters may have been responding to her reading of Oscar Wilde. She was writing about Wilde, she told her parents, "Because he is misunderstood, and judged conventionally and narrowly. This is a favorite theme of mine so I might write an essay on it" (undated 1908, file 36).

34. MVW to parents, undated Jan. 1907, file 35; Sheldon, *History of University of Oregon,* 153; Gardner, *"Friend and Lover,"* 25; Miriam Van Waters, "The Night Eugene Went Wild with Joy," *Sunday Oregonian,* 14 June 1908, 2; MVW, ms. memoir, file 510.

35. MVW to parents, 5 Dec. 1905, file 33; MVW to Clark University, 19 March 1910, and "Statement of Work at University of Oregon," Miriam Van Waters file, box 46, G. Stanley Hall Papers, Clark University Archives, Worcester, Mass. (hereafter Hall Papers); Records of the Registrar's Office, University of Oregon, Graduates by Classes, University of Oregon Archives; MVW, ms. memoir, file 510.

36. Henry Sheldon to G. Stanley Hall (hereafter GSH), 25 Jan. 1910, Hall Papers; MVW to parents, 23 Oct. 1906, file 34.

37. MVW to parents, 12 Aug. and 29 Sept. 1907, file 35; 25 Jan. 1909, file 37; MVW, ms. memoir, file 510.

38. Dorothy Ross, *G. Stanley Hall: The Psychologist as Prophet* (Chicago: University of Chicago Press, 1972), esp. chap. 11; Thomas K. Fagan, "Compulsory Schooling, Child Study, Clinical Psychology, and Special Education: Origins of School Psychology," *American Psychologist* 47:2 (Feb. 1992): 236–43; William A. Koelsch, *Clark University, 1887–1987: A Narrative History* (Worcester, Mass.: Clark University Press, 1987), chap. 2. MVW later recalled applying to Cornell, where she was admitted, and Columbia, where she was not (ms. memoir, file 510).

39. MVW to GSH, 20 Feb. 1910; GSH to MVW, 28 Feb. 1910; F. G. Young to GSH, 23 March 1910; P. L. Campbell to GSH, 17 March 1910, all in MVW file, box 46, Hall Papers.

40. H. D. Sheldon to GSH, 25 Jan. 1910 and MVW to GSH, 12 May 1910, MVW file, box 46, Hall Papers.

41. Sheldon, *History of University of Oregon,* 177–78.

42. MVW to parents, 10 June 1910, file 38.

CHAPTER THREE

1. MVW to parents, undated Sept. 1910, 14 Sept. 1910, and undated 1910, file 39.

2. GBVW to Maud VW, 24 Sept. 1910, 27 Sept. 1910, box 1, GBVW Papers.

3. Dorothy Ross, *G. Stanley Hall: The Psychologist as Prophet* (Chicago: University of Chicago Press, 1972), 186–92, 219; William A. Koelsch, *Clark University, 1887–1987: A Narrative History* (Worcester, Mass.: Clark University Press, 1987), 29. Professor Arthur Michael resigned in protest over Hall's duplicity in reneging on his promise that Helen Michael could have access to her husband's lab.

4. Patricia Albjerg Graham, "Expansion and Exclusion: A History of

Women in American Higher Education," *Signs* 3 (summer 1978): table 1, 766; Margaret W. Rossiter, "Doctorates for American Women, 1868-1907," *History of Education Quarterly* 22:2 (summer 1982): 164-65.

5. Rosalind Rosenberg, *Beyond Separate Spheres: Intellectual Roots of Modern Feminism* (New Haven: Yale University Press, 1982) esp. 29, 68; Ellen Fitzpatrick, *Endless Crusade: Women Social Scientists and Progressive Reform* (New York: Oxford University Press, 1990), chap. 2; Ross, *G. Stanley Hall*, 301-2, 317; May S. Cheney, "Will Nature Eliminate the College Woman?" *Association of Collegiate Alumnae Magazine*, series 3:10 (Jan. 1905): 3.

6. GSH to Col. George Bullock, 20 Nov. 1909, box 20, folder 3, Hall Papers (GSH's letters of inquiry about women at Johns Hopkins, Harvard, and other schools are also in this folder); Koelsch, *Clark University*, 72-74. On Johns Hopkins see Margaret W. Rossiter, *Women Scientists in America: Struggles and Strategies to 1940* (Baltimore: Johns Hopkins University Press, 1982), 46-47. The collegiate course opened at Clark in 1902.

7. Data compiled from Clark Register, Clark University Archives. Psychology had the most female graduate students. There was one woman each in biology, pedagogy, anthropology, and math. Nationally, women's graduate enrollments and their proportion of college faculty peaked much later; women constituted 28 percent of college faculty in 1940, a proportion that then declined until the 1980s. (Graham, "Expansion and Exclusion," table 1, 766; Rossiter, "Doctorates for American Women, 1868-1907," 164-65; Barbara Miller Solomon, *In the Company of Educated Women: A History of Women and Higher Education in America* [New Haven: Yale University Press, 1985], table 6, 133.)

8. MVW to parents, 22 Sept., 30 Sept., and 12 Dec. 1910, file 39; Koelsch, *Clark University*, 53; Lawrence A. Averill, "Reminiscences of a Psychologist," *Educational Forum* 5:2 (Jan. 1941): 175-76. (Both Koelsch and Averill quote from Lewis Terman's account of the seminar.)

9. MVW to parents, 22 Sept., 5 Nov., and 22 Oct. 1910, file 39. On efforts to control working-class leisure in Worcester see Roy Rosenzweig, *Eight Hours for What We Will: Workers and Leisure in an Industrial City, 1870-1920* (New York: Cambridge University Press, 1983), chaps. 4-6.

10. MVW to parents, 25 Sept. 1910, file 39.

11. MVW to parents, undated Jan. 1911 and 25 Jan. 1911, file 40 and 15 Oct. 1911, file 42; Margaret Jacobson to MVW, 31 Jan. 1925, file 502; Bernard K. Johnpoll, "John Spargo," in Bernard K. Johnpoll and Harvey Klehr, eds., *Biographical Dictionary of the American Left* (New York: Greenwood Press, 1986), 365. On the Portland radical community, see Nancy Krieger, "Queen of the Bolsheviks: The Hidden History of Dr. Marie Equi," *Radical America* 17:5 (Sept.-Oct. 1983): 58-59; and Virginia Gardner, *"Friend and Lover": The Life of Louise Bryant* (New York: Horizon Press, 1982), 25-26.

12. MVW to parents, 22 Sept., 5 Oct., and 11 Oct. 1910, file 39 (cf. 30 Oct. 1910, file 39). MVW stayed in touch with Ellis; she later sent him a sympathy card on the death of Booker T. Washington (11 Jan. 1916, file 44).

On Ellis see *The National Cyclopaedia of American Biography* (New York: James T. White and Co., 1920), 17:400.

13. MVW to parents, undated 1911, file 40; 14 April and 26 April 1911, file 41. On her use of stereotypes, see, e.g., 11 Jan. 1916, file 44, 13 Feb. 1919, file 47; 29 Sept. 1922, 16 Oct. 1922, file 50. Cf. a later comment on politicians: "If you can't educate them . . . you should leave them, as God left the Jews" (MVW to Edna Mahan, 20 Sept. 1928, file 251, Gladding-VW Papers). Royce wrote the introduction for Jessie Sampler's book *The Seekers* (New York: M. Kennerly, 1910).

14. MVW to parents, 11 Oct., 5 Oct., 25 Oct., and 12 Dec. 1910, file 39; 2 Feb., 7 Feb., and 9 Feb. 1911, file 40. After G. Stanley Hall had his wife committed, she was diagnosed as having progressive arteriosclerosis of the brain (Ross, *G. Stanley Hall*, 275).

15. MVW to parents, 30 Sept. and 30 Oct. 1910, file 39; 12 March 1911, file 40.

16. MVW to parents, undated May 1911, file 41. Calkins never did receive a doctorate, but she was the first woman president of both the American Psychological Association and the American Philosophical Association (Rossiter, "Doctorates for American Women," 173). On Theodate Smith—who coauthored Hall's study of college women's fertility—see Elizabeth Scarborough and Laurel Furumoto, *Untold Lives: The First Generation of American Women Psychologists* (New York: Columbia University Press, 1987), 198-99.

17. MVW to parents, undated May 1911, file 41; undated Nov. 1911, file 42.

18. Eleanor Flexner, *Century of Struggle: The Woman's Rights Movement in the United States* (New York: Atheneum, 1970), 253.

19. MVW to parents, 3 Oct. 1910, 12 Dec. 1910, file 39.

20. MVW to parents, 5 Nov. 1910, file 41.

21. MVW to parents, 27 Nov. 1910, 22 Dec. 1910, file 39 and undated May 1911, file 41. On the WEIU see Sarah Deutsch, "Learning to Talk More Like a Man: Boston Women's Class-Bridging Organizations, 1870-1940," *American Historical Review* 97 (April 1992): 370-404; and on the emergence of feminism and the revival of the suffrage campaign, see Nancy Cott, *The Grounding of Modern Feminism* (New Haven: Yale University Press, 1987).

22. MVW to parents, 12 March 1911, file 40; 4 Oct. 1911, file 42.

23. Jane Addams, *The Spirit of Youth and the City Streets,* with introduction by Allen F. Davis (1909; rpt., Urbana: University of Illinois Press, 1972), esp. 4, 6, 34-35, 44-45, 55-57, 69, 91, 124, 154. Davis points out the parallels with Hall in his introduction, xiii.

24. MVW to parents, undated May 1911, file 41; 10 Feb. 1911, file 40; Nov. 1911, file 42.

25. MVW to parents, 18 Oct. 1911, undated Nov. 1911, file 42. On Addams' similar influence on women of Van Waters' generation, see, e.g., Joyce Antler, *Lucy Sprague Mitchell: The Making of a Modern Woman* (New Haven: Yale University Press, 1987), 31, 157.

26. MVW to parents, 30 Sept. and 22 Sept. 1910, file 39; Clark University Register, 1911, 86-95; MVW to parents, 15 Oct. 1911, file 42; 14 April 1911, file 41. The lectures included Hall on comparative and genetic psychology, John Baird on physiological and experimental psychology, William Burnham on pedagogy and school hygiene, and Alexander Chamberlain on anthropological psychology. On Burnham, see Ross, *G. Stanley Hall,* 294-95; on Baird, *National Cyclopaedia of American Biography,* 22:213.

27. MVW to parents, 25 Jan. 1911, file 40; 19 May 1911, file 41.

28. MVW to parents, 2 Feb. 1911, 23 March 1911, file 40, and 31 March 1911, file 41. In a generous justification for his behavior during these meetings, intended no doubt to reassure her mother, MVW wrote, "You see Dr. Hall has taken absolutely *no* vacation for three years—writing and studying constantly, and he is a very old man. So is this year unusually nervous, self-opinionated and—charming. We all love him" (31 March 1911).

29. Ross, *G. Stanley Hall,* 68, 70-73, 261-67.

30. MVW to GSH, 8 June 1911, MVW file, box 46, Hall Papers; MVW to parents, 23 March 1911, file 40. On the emergence of "objective" social science, see Robert C. Bannister, *Sociology and Scientism: The American Quest for Objectivity, 1880-1940* (Chapel Hill: University of North Carolina Press, 1987); Mary O. Furner, *Advocacy and Objectivity* (Lexington: Published for the Organization of American Historians by the University Press of Kentucky, 1975); and Thomas L. Haskell, *The Emergence of Professional Social Science* (Urbana: University of Illinois Press, 1977).

31. MVW to parents, 23 March 1911, file 40. On Hall's views, see Ross, *G. Stanley Hall.*

32. Hall apparently suggested that MVW edit his lectures on the history of ancient philosophy for her thesis. She graciously declined this project, citing as reasons her own weakness in Greek philosophy and the fact that Dr. Theodate Smith had already edited his lectures. MVW clearly did not want to serve as another "memory bureau" for Hall. (MVW to parents, 31 March, 14 April, 15 April, and 11 May 1911, file 41). Terman is quoted in Ross, *G. Stanley Hall,* 425-26. Like other students who came to study with Hall, Terman switched advisers to complete his degree under another professor's tutelage (Koelsch, *Clark University,* 51, 54).

33. On Hall's reputation and the effect of his administrative style on the faculty, see Koelsch, *Clark University,* 39-40, 53, 78-80; and Lawrence Veysey, *The Emergence of the American University* (Chicago: University of Chicago Press, 1965), 165-70.

34. MVW to parents, 17 Sept., 26 Sept., and 4 Oct. 1911, file 42.

35. MVW to parents, 10 Oct., 15 Oct., and 27 Oct. 1911, file 42; MVW et. al. to GSH, 29 Sept. 1911, box 20, file 3, Hall Papers. Eighteen women, including MVW and Caroline Fisher, signed the petition asking for limited hours of use for women and suitable equipment in a separate room.

36. G. Stanley Hall, *Adolescence: Its Psychology and Its Relations to Physiology, Anthropology, Sociology, Sex, Crime, Religions, and Education,* vol. 1 (1904; rpt., New York: D. Appleton and Co., 1920), 325-34, 407.

37. MVW to parents, undated 1911, file 41. The work of female social scientists is described in Estelle B. Freedman, *Their Sisters' Keepers: Women's Prison Reform in America, 1830-1930* (Ann Arbor: University of Michigan Press, 1981), chap. 6.

38. MVW to parents, 10 Oct. 1911, file 42 (misdated, probably 9 Oct. 1911); MVW, "Topical Syllabus" No. 44 (A) and No. 44 (B) [for teachers], "Psychology of Adolescence," Clark University, Worcester, Mass., 15 Nov. 1911, box 48, Hall Papers; GSH to MVW, 10 Nov. 1911, box 46, MVW file, Hall Papers. On Hall's methods, see Ross, *G. Stanley Hall*, 290–91; and on the use of "topical Syllabi" by Hall's students, see Koelsch, *Clark University*, 58.

39. MVW to parents, undated May 1912, file 42. She struggled with Hall one last time over the level of her fellowship for the following year (MVW to GSH, 7 Oct. 1912, MVW file, box 46, Hall Papers).

40. MVW to parents, 2 Feb., 10 Feb., and 28 March 1911, file 40.

41. "In Memoriam: Alexander Francis Chamberlain," *American Anthropologist* 16:2 (April–June 1914): 34; Alexander Francis Chamberlain, *The Child: A Study in the Evolution of Man* (1900; rpt., New York: C. Scribner's Sons, 1911), 457–58, 462–63; Ross, *G. Stanley Hall*, 221–27; Koelsch, *Clark University*, 56–57; George W. Stocking Jr., ed., *The Shaping of American Anthropology, 1883-1911: A Franz Boas Reader* (New York: Basic Books, 1974), 58. Chamberlain's *The Child* went through over ten editions between 1900 and 1917 (National Union Catalog, vol. 102). Along with his other interests, Chamberlain studied the concept of "women's languages" among primitive peoples (Alexander Francis Chamberlain, "Women's Languages," *American Anthropologist*, n. s. 14:3 [July–Sept. 1912]: 570–81).

42. Clippings from *Worcester Telegram*, 18 Oct., 11 Nov., 2 Dec., 1912; 8 Jan., 13 Jan., 1913; and 9 April 1914 (obituary) clippings book, Clark University Archives; MVW to parents, 9 Oct. 1911, file 42. On the temperance conflicts in Worcester, see Rosenzweig, *Eight Hours for What We Will.*

43. MVW to parents, 28 March 1911, file 40; 9 April 1911, file 41; undated Nov. 1911, file 42; Roy M. Cushman, "Harvey Humphrey Baker: Man and Judge," in Judge Baker Guidance Center, *Harvey Humphrey Baker: Upbuilder of the Juvenile Court* (Boston: Judge Baker Foundation, 1920), 1–10.

44. MVW to parents, undated Nov. 1911, file 42. MVW's view of monopolies appeared in a letter contrasting American and Japanese society, in which she reported that "they sacrifice individual welfare to the group" (9 Oct. 1911, file 42).

45. MVW to parents, undated 1911, file 41; undated May 1912, file 42.

46. MVW to parents, 10 Feb. 1913, file 42; Miriam Van Waters, "The Adolescent Girl among Primitive People," *Journal of Religious Psychology* 6:4 (Oct. 1913): 375–421 and 7:1 (Jan.–May 1914): 75–120.

47. On Boas and fieldwork, see George W. Stocking Jr., "The Ethnographer's Magic: Fieldwork in British Anthropology from Tylor to Malinowski,"

in Stocking, ed., *Observers Observed: Essays on Ethnographic Fieldwork* (Madison: University of Wisconsin Press, 1983), 70–120.

48. Van Waters, "Adolescent Girl," esp. part 1, 377–78; part 2, 102–5.

49. She spoke positively of sterilization in a letter of Nov. 1911, file 42.

50. Van Waters, "Adolescent Girl," esp. part 2, 108–12.

51. MVW to parents, 23 Oct. 1912, file 42; Ross, *G. Stanley Hall,* 399–400; Margaret Mead to MVW, undated 1944, file 587; William Healy, *The Individual Delinquent* (1915; rpt, Montclair, N.J.: Patterson Smith, 1969).

52. MVW journal, 14 June 1930, file 209v, Gladding-VW Papers; "Record of Candidacy," and "Examination of Miss Miriam Van Waters" in MVW file, box 46, Hall Papers; MVW journal, vol. 2, 13 June 1935 (in Van Waters' memory, the exam lasted until 7:00 P.M., an hour longer than the record indicates). Her degree was one of only two doctorates awarded in anthropology at Clark (Koelsch, *Clark University,* 57).

53. MVW to parents, 19 May 1913, file 42. Her close friends, Bess Woods and Caroline Fisher, each completed their doctorates as well, having written more conventional dissertations on the psychology of perception.

54. MVW to parents, 10 Feb. 1913, file 42.

CHAPTER FOUR

1. Lori D. Ginzberg, *Women and the Work of Benevolence: Morality, Politics, and Class in the Nineteenth-Century United States* (New Haven: Yale University Press, 1990); Paula Baker, "The Domestication of Politics: Women and American Political Society, 1780–1920," *American Historical Review* 89 (June 1984): 620–47; Kathryn Kish Sklar, "The Historical Foundations of Women's Power in the Creation of the American Welfare State, 1830–1930," in Seth Koven and Sonya Michel, eds., *Mothers of a New World: Maternalist Politics and the Origins of Welfare States* (New York: Routledge, 1993), 43–93; Koven and Michel, "Womanly Duties: Maternalist Politics and the Origins of Welfare States in France, Germany, Great Britain, and the United States, 1880–1920," *American Historical Review* 95 (Oct. 1990): 1076–1108; Ellen Fitzpatrick, *Endless Crusade: Women Social Scientists and Progressive Reform* (New York: Oxford University Press, 1990); Lynn D. Gordon, *Gender and Higher Education in the Progressive Era* (New Haven: Yale University Press, 1990); Susan Ware, *Partner and I: Molly Dewson, Feminism, and New Deal Politics* (New Haven: Yale University Press, 1987); Linda Gordon, "The New Feminist Scholarship on the Welfare State," in Gordon, ed., *Women, the State, and Welfare* (Madison: University of Wisconsin Press, 1990), 9–35; Ann Firor Scott, *Natural Allies: Women's Associations in American History* (Urbana: University of Illinois, 1993). On women's entry into social work, see Nancy Cott, *The Grounding Of Modern Feminism* (New Haven: Yale University Press, 1987), table 7.1, 219; and Daniel J. Walkowitz, "The Making of a Feminine Professional Identity," *American Historical Review* 95 (Oct. 1990): 1051–75.

2. Robert Mennel, *Thorns and Thistles: Juvenile Delinquents in the*

United States, 1825–1940 (Hanover, N.H.: University Press of New England, 1973), esp. 132; Ellen Ryerson, *The Best-Laid Plans: America's Juvenile Court Experiment* (New York: Hill and Wang, 1978), 45; David J. Rothman, *Conscience and Convenience: The Asylum and Its Alternatives in Progressive America* (Boston: Little, Brown, 1980), chap. 6; Eric C. Schneider, *In the Web of Class: Delinquents and Reformers in Boston, 1810s–1930s* (New York: New York University Press, 1992), chap. 8.

3. In its first five years, for example, the Boston Juvenile Court recommended probation in over half of its cases (Judge Baker Guidance Center, *Harvey Humphrey Baker: Upbuilder of the Juvenile Court* [Boston: Judge Baker Foundation, 1920], 39). On probation, see Rothman, *Conscience and Convenience,* 218–19.

4. Mennel, *Thorns and Thistles,* 43–44; *Harvey Humphrey Baker,* 17, 21, 66, 99, 106 (based on data from the first ten years of the court, 1906–16); MVW, ts. memoir, c. 1950, file 508; *Forty-Ninth Annual Report of the Boston Children's Aid Society, 1863–1913* (Boston: Children's Aid Society, 1914), 5, lists MVW as a "visitor."

5. MVW, ts. and ms. memoir, undated, file 508, 1–2, and ms. memoir, July 1957, file 510; *Fiftieth Annual Report of the Boston Children's Aid Society, 1863–1914* (Boston: Children's Aid Society, 1915), 37.

6. Anthony Platt, *The Child Savers: The Invention of Delinquency* (Chicago: University of Chicago, 1969); Rothman, *Conscience and Convenience,* part 3; Steven Schlossman, *Love and the American Delinquent: The Theory and Practice of "Progressive" Juvenile Justice, 1825–1920* (Chicago: University of Chicago Press, 1977); Mennel, *Thorns and Thistles;* Ryerson, *The Best-Laid Plans;* Schneider, *Web of Class,* chap. 6; Linda Gordon, *Heroes of Their Own Lives: The Politics and History of Family Violence* (New York: Viking, 1988), esp. 293–99.

7. Notes for "A Social Worker's Estimate of Social Workers," written in 1913, appear on pages used for her 1916 writing journal, MVW journal, dated 15 Nov. 1913, file 204, Gladding-VW Papers; "In Memoriam: Alexander Francis Chamberlain," *American Anthropologist* 16:2 (April–June 1914): 34.

8. On taxes, e.g., MVW to parents, 15 July 1915, file 42. The 1912 *Portland City Directory* listed GBVW as vice president of the Oregon Brass Works. Financial documents, mortgages, deed copies, and correspondence with banks are in GBVW Papers, addendum.

9. City of Portland, Oregon, *Mayor's Message and Annual Reports for the Fiscal Year Ending November 30, 1914,* (Portland, 1915), 7; Allan East, "The Genesis and Early Development of a Juvenile Court: A Study of Community Responsibility in Multnomah County, Oregon, for the Period 1841–1920" (M.A. thesis, University of Oregon, 1939), 47–48; MVW to GSH, 13 Aug. 1913, MVW file, box 46, Hall Papers. On the establishment of Bedford Hills and other reformatories during the vice crusades of the Progressive Era, see Estelle B. Freedman, *Their Sisters' Keepers: Women's Prison Reform in America, 1830–1930* (Ann Arbor: University of Michigan Press, 1981), chaps. 6–7. The Portland campaign is discussed in E. Kimbark Mac-

Coll, *Merchants, Money, and Power: The Portland Establishment 1843-1913* (Portland, Oreg.: Georgian Press, 1988), 435-36.

10. MVW to GSH, 19 Aug. 1913, GSH to Governor West, 20 Aug. 1913 and to MVW, 20 Aug. 1913, and MVW to GSH, 8 Sept. 1913, box 46, MVW file, Hall Papers (MVW's letter to Hall also feigned praise for Hall's son, who was then in Portland, and withdrew an old complaint over the amount of her graduate fellowship in 1912).

11. Joseph Gaston, *Portland, Oregon: Its History and Builders* (Chicago: S. J. Clarke Co., 1911), 471-73; Allan East, *A History of Community Interest in a Juvenile Court: Positive and Negative Manifestation during the Period 1885-1942 in Multnomah County, Oregon* (Portland, Oreg.: Oregon Probation Association, 1943), 5; and East, "Genesis and Early Development," 81-82. East, *History of Community Interest,* notes that Mrs. Millie Trumbull, the moving force in promoting the juvenile court idea in Portland, had moved there from Chicago, where she helped pass the Illinois juvenile court law. The movement to place juveniles in detention homes rather than city jails is described in Mary Odem, "Delinquent Daughters: The Sexual Regulation of Female Minors in the United States, 1880-1920" (Ph.D. diss., University of California, Berkeley, 1989), 178. Odem states that by 1910, at least fifteen states had passed legislation allowing for juvenile detention homes.

12. East, "Genesis and Early Development," 85-86 and East, *History of Community Interest,* 8-10; MacColl, *Merchants, Money, and Power,* 443-44; Nancy Krieger, "Queen of the Bolsheviks: The Hidden History of Dr. Marie Equi," *Radical America* 17:5 (Sept.-Oct. 1983): 58-59; Rothman, *Conscience and Convenience,* 208.

13. East, "Genesis and Early Development," 86-87; MVW, ts. memoir, fragment 6, file 508.

14. East, "Genesis and Early Development"; MVW, ts. memoir, fragment 6, file 508; MVW to parents, 1 Dec. 1930, file 60.

15. MVW, ts. memoir, fragment 6, file 508, and MVW to GSH, 6 Oct. 1914, MVW file, box 46, Hall Papers.

16. Copy of GBVW to Harry Vosburg, 5 Dec. 1914, box 3, GBVW Papers; MVW to father, Feb. 1915, file 42.

17. East, "Genesis and Early Development," 87-88 and East, *History of Community Interest,* 10.

18. Barbara Bates, *Bargaining for Life: A Social History of Tuberculosis, 1876-1938* (Philadelphia: University of Pennsylvania Press, 1992), 1, 8, 17; Sheila M. Rothman, *Living in the Shadow of Death: Tuberculosis and the Social Experience of Illness in American History* (New York: Basic Books, 1994); Michael E. Teller, *The Tuberculosis Movement: A Public Health Campaign in the Progressive Era* (New York: Greenwood Press, 1988), 3; Mark Caldwell, *The Last Crusade: The War on Consumption, 1862-1954* (New York: Athenaeum, 1988), 5-10; Mortimer Spiegelman and Carl L. Erhardt, "Mortality in the United States by Cause," in Carl L. Erhardt and Joyce E. Berlin, eds., *Mortality and Morbidity in the United States* (Cambridge: Harvard University Press, 1974), 21-22; Frank Ryan,

The Forgotten Plague: How the Battle against Tuberculosis Was Won—and Lost (Boston: Little, Brown, 1992), esp. chap. 2.

19. Copy of GBVW to Harry Vosburg, 5 Dec. 1912, box 3, GBVW Papers; Dr. Miriam MacLachlan to MVW, card dated 1916, file 112; "Good Samaritan Hospital," *Polk's Portland City Directory* (Portland, Oreg.: R. L. Polk and Co., 1914), 40. A fragment of a letter to her father dated 12 Aug. 1915 is written on the back of a letter from a drug company concerning Miriam's overdue account (file 42).

20. MVW to parents, undated June, 15 July, 28 July, 2 Aug., and 9 Aug. 1915, file 42; Abby [Whiteside] to Maud VW, 12 Aug. 1915, file 28.

21. MVW to parents, 15 July and 12 Aug. 1915, file 42; Abby to Maud VW, 12 Aug. 1915, file 28.

22. MVW to parents, 26 Dec. 1912 and 12 Aug., 16 Aug., 20 Aug., and 8 Sept. 1915, file 42.

23. MVW to parents, 8 Sept. 1915, file 42. On GBVW appointments, "Grace Memorial Episcopal Church, How It Began and Grew," [no author, n.d., 2] Western Oregon Episcopal Archives, and Rev. Chandler C. Jackson, letter to author, 8 Aug. 1992.

24. Bates, *Bargaining for Life*, 259, also 26–27; Rothman, *Living in the Shadow of Death*, esp. 197–98, 207, 230, 238; Francis Marion Pottenger, *The Fight against Tuberculosis: An Autobiography* (New York: Henry Schuman, 1952), 119, 123, 131; MVW journal, vol. 3, 11 Nov. 1935.

25. MVW to parents, 16 Aug. 1915, 6 Nov. 1915, file 42; "Conversation," MVW journal, 24 Jan. 1916, file 204, Gladding-VW Papers.

26. MVW to parents, 10 Jan., 11 Jan., and 20 Feb. 1916, file 44.

27. MVW to parents, 5 May 1902, file 32; "A Box of Jade," 1909 *Beaver*, University of Oregon, n.p.; "Eagle Hearted," *Oregon Monthly*, 1907–8, 31–35. On college women's fiction, see Lynn D. Gordon, *Gender and Higher Education in the Progressive Era* (New Haven: Yale University Press, 1990), 109, 153–55. The settings of her works resembled the Klondike and Oriental tales by the popular western writer Joaquin Miller, a former Eugene editor whose home MVW had rented during college. (See Martin Severin Peterson, *Joaquin Miller: Literary Frontiersman* [Stanford: Stanford University Press, 1937]).

28. "In Memoriam: Alexander Francis Chamberlain," 34.

29. "Playmates," 7 Jan. 1916, "Earth Kiss," 16 Jan. 1917, "Death, the Sand Dunes," 16 Oct. 1916, "A California Love Song," 5 Jan. 1916, "Nature Love Song, Sea and Mountains," 14 Oct. 1916, "Sea-Fog," 15 March 1916, all in MVW journal, file 204, Gladding-VW Papers. On cultural representations of tuberculosis and sexuality, see Susan Sontag, *Illness as Metaphor* (New York: Farrar, Straus and Giroux, 1978), esp. 20–22.

30. Mss. of both poems appear in file 464. "Illness" is dated Los Angeles 11 Jan. 1916; "Art Is Born" is dated 1 April 1916. "Notes for a Verse: Illness," 11 Jan. 1916, MVW journal, file 204, Gladding-VW Papers.

31. MVW to parents, 7 April, 27 April, 10 Jan., and 20 Feb. 1916, file 44; "Conversation," MVW journal, 24 Jan. 1916, file 204, Gladding-VW Papers.

32. On Anderson and *The Little Review,* see W. G. Rogers, *Ladies Bountiful* (London: Victor Gollancz, 1968), 29, 149-53, and Mathilda M. Hills, "Margaret Anderson," in Barbara Sicherman and Carol Hurd Green, eds., *Notable American Women: The Modern Period* (Cambridge: Harvard University Press, Belknap Press, 1980), 21-23.

33. MVW to parents, 7 May 1917, 9 May 1917, and undated 1917, file 45; "The Verse Libre Contest," *Little Review,* April 1917, 11-23.

34. "Abortion," MVW journal, 7 April 1916, file 204, Gladding-VW Papers. In this fragment, written around the time that the *New Republic* rejected her article but before the *Little Review* published her poem, MVW condemned those who crushed and choked her art more strongly than she would condemn an abortionist. Later in her life, however, she referred to abortion as the destruction of life and thus a sin (MVW journal, 20 Nov. 1944, file 219v, Gladding-VW Papers).

35. MVW to Ralph Van Waters (hereafter RVW), 6 March 1916, box 2, GBVW Papers; MVW to parents, 9 May, 27 July, and 15 Sept. 1916, file 44.

36. "Wood Ashes," MVW journal, 1 Sept. 1916, file 204, Gladding-VW Papers; MVW to parents, 24 Sept. 1916, undated Sept. 1916, file 44. Originally MVW invited Ralph to join her at the beach for tutoring; she seemed reluctant to add George, but the letter of 24 Sept. 1916 suggests that Maud wished to include him as well, despite the difficulties MVW had in handling George.

37. MVW to parents, 2 Aug. 1915, 6 Nov. 1915, 20 Feb. 1916, 3 July 1916, 4 July 1916, 7 Oct. 1916, file 44. Both of them condemned the Portland police for arresting Sanger when she demonstrated in support of three men charged with distributing her pamphlet, *Family Limitation.* On the Sanger incident, see Krieger, "Queen of the Bolsheviks," 62-63. After meeting Sanger, MVW sent her a copy of her thesis.

38. GBVW to Maud VW, 8 Sept. 1919; "Zealous and Able Church Worker," *Oregon Morning Democrat,* 5 Sept. 1922; Bishop Robert Paddock to GBVW, telegram 22 Sept. 1922, box 4; Rector, St. Stephen, Baker, Oreg., "Some Sidelights on the Work in Eastern Oregon," and miscellaneous clippings and documents in the Paddock Case Documents file, all in GBVW Papers. One hostile letter in this file, to GBVW from a Reverend Lockwood of Pendleton, Oregon, suggests that Van Waters may have been forced out of his current position as archdeacon, as well, because of his support for Paddock. See also the obituaries for Paddock in *New York Times,* 19 May 1939 and *Radical Religion* (fall 1939): 5-6, and "Robert Lewis Paddock," in *The National Cyclopaedia of American Biography* (New York: James White Co., 1941), 29:394-95. In retirement Paddock worked with the Church League for Industrial Democracy and the American Civil Liberties Union; he championed the Loyalists in Spain during the Civil War and helped fund the journal *Radical Religion,* published by the Fellowship of Socialist Christians in the late 1930s.

39. MVW to parents, 9 May, 14 May, and 21 May 1917, file 45.

40. MVW to parents, 30 July, undated July, and 12 Aug. 1917, file 45.

CHAPTER FIVE

1. The term was used by Ethel Sturges Dummer in letters to MVW, e.g., 10 Sept. 1921, file 819, Dummer Papers.

2. On Los Angeles, see Robert Fogelson, *The Fragmented Metropolis: Los Angeles, 1850–1930* (Cambridge: Harvard University Press, 1967), esp. chap. 10; Elaine Tyler May, *Great Expectations: Marriage and Divorce in Post-Victorian America* (Chicago: University of Chicago Press, 1980), esp. 25–26, 52–56; Franklin Hichborn, "Anti-vice Movement in California," *Journal of Social Hygiene* (March 1920) 6: 213, 219; George Mowry, *The California Progressives* (Berkeley and Los Angeles: University of California Press, 1951), 289–90; Kevin Starr, *Material Dreams: Southern California through the 1920s* (New York: Oxford University Press, 1990), 170–71.

3. Louis S. Lyons, ed., *Who's Who among the Women of California* (San Francisco: Security Publishing Company, 1922), esp. 4, 49, 55; Judith Raftery, "Los Angeles Clubwomen and Progressive Reform," and Mary Odem, "City Mothers and Delinquent Daughters: Female Juvenile Justice Reform in Early Twentieth-Century Los Angeles," in William Deverell and Tom Sitton, eds., *California Progressivism Revisited* (Berkeley and Los Angeles: University of California Press, 1994), 144–74, 175–99. See also Odem, "Delinquent Daughters: The Sexual Regulation of Female Minors in the United States, 1880–1920" (Ph.D. diss., University of California, Berkeley, 1989) and Janis Marie Appier, "Gender and Justice: Women Police in America, 1910–1946" (Ph.D. diss., University of California, Riverside, 1993).

4. Mary Odem, "City Mothers," chap. 4.

5. Odem, "Delinquent Daughters," table 1, 300. Odem used the juvenile court cases for 1920 to calculate charges against juveniles (table 5, 301) and sentences at initial court hearings for all girls and a sample of boys' cases (table 10, 304); she uses a 1920 county probation report for family backgrounds (table 1, 300; and 229). Five percent of the juveniles brought to court were black, which reflected the African American population of Los Angeles. Immigrants comprised about 20 percent of the total Los Angeles population at the time; thus all immigrant families were overrepresented in court. The high percentage of Catholic children at juvenile hall— 28 percent of the boys and 29 percent of the girls in 1922—was probably due to this overrepresentation of Mexicans and Italians. (*Annual Report of the Bureau of Catholic Charities, Diocese of Monterey and L.A.,* 1 Jan. 1921–1 Jan. 1922, file 465.) Figures for the Mexican American population appear in Albert Camarillo, *Chicanos in a Changing Society: From Mexican Pueblos to American Barrios in Santa Barbara and Southern California, 1848–1930* (Cambridge: Harvard University Press, 1979), table 21, 200.

6. Mary Odem shows that in juvenile courts throughout the country, girls remained institutionalized more often than boys (Odem, "Delinquent Daughters," 183–85; table 10, 304). During the 1920s, approximately 20 percent of the girls brought to L.A. juvenile court had venereal disease

(Cynthia Eckert, "The Price of Rebellion: Female Sex Delinquents in the 1920s" [paper presented at the annual meeting of the Pacific Coast Branch of the American Historical Association, 12 Aug. 1993, Los Angeles], 9).

7. On changing sexual mores see John D'Emilio and Estelle B. Freedman, *Intimate Matters: A History of Sexuality in America* (New York: Harper and Row, 1988). On youth rebellion in L.A., see Eckert, "Price of Rebellion." At times, sexual rebellion could correlate with political protest, as with the southern workers discussed in Jacquelyn Dowd Hall, "Disorderly Women: Gender and Labor Militancy in the Appalachian South," *Journal of American History* 73 (Sept. 1986): 354-82.

8. Starr, *Material Dreams,* 135; Barbara Ann Dreyer, "The Influence of the Social Hygiene Movement on the Education of Children during the Early Decades of the Twentieth Century in America" (Ph.D. diss., Johns Hopkins University, 1972), 180; Mary Odem, "Single Mothers, Delinquent Daughters, and the Juvenile Court in Early Twentieth-Century Los Angeles," *Journal of Social History* 25:1 (fall 1991): 27-43; May, *Great Expectations,* 26, 53.

9. MVW to parents, 12 Aug., 15 Sept., and 6 Oct. 1917, file 45; Odem, "Delinquent Daughters," 181.

10. MVW to parents, 12 Aug. 1917, 15 Sept. 1917, and undated 1917, file 45; undated Jan. 1918, file 46; 23 Feb. 1919, undated April 1919, file 47; 8 Feb. 1920, file 48; 3 April 1922, file 50; Los Angeles County Juvenile Hall, Staff as of 28 Nov. 1924, box 5, Georgia Bullock Papers, Special Collections, University of California at Los Angeles.

11. MVW to parents, 15 Sept., 5 Oct., and undated Oct. 1917, file 45.

12. MVW to parents, 5 Oct. 1917, and undated 1917, file 45; 20 Jan., 14 Feb., and 29 Nov. 1918, file 46; 23 Feb. 1919, 31 May 1919, file 47; MVW to parents, 9 June 1918, box 2, GBVW Papers; Anne Shannon Monroe, "When Women Sit in Judgement," *Good Housekeeping,* April 1920, 150.

13. MVW to parents, 15 Sept. 1917, and undated 1917, file 45; undated Jan. 1918, 26 April 1918, file 46; 23 Feb. 1919 and 24 May 1919, file 47.

14. MVW journal, 23 Aug. 1936, file 213, Gladding-VW Papers; MVW to parents, 14 Feb. 1918, file 46; *Los Angeles Sunday Times,* 3 Feb. 1918, 14; Monroe, "When Women Sit in Judgement," 157.

15. Odem, "Delinquent Daughters," 259-61.

16. MVW to parents, 31 Jan. 1919, 19 April 1919, file 47.

17. MVW to Friday Morning Club, 12 Oct. 1920, quoted in John Steven McGoarty, ed., *History of Los Angeles County* (Chicago: American Historical Society, 1923), 136-37; MVW to parents, 23 Feb. 1919, file 47.

18. MVW to parents, 13 March 1918, file 46; Maud VW to Rebekah Van Waters (hereafter Beckie), 15 Dec. 1919, 17 Dec. 1919, box 2, GBVW Papers.

19. MVW to parents, 26 Sept. 1917, file 45; "Woman's Day at City Hall," *Los Angeles Daily Times,* 23 Dec. 1920, II, 5; Monroe, "When Women Sit in Judgement," 149; Clara Spalding Ellis, "Interesting Westerners," *Sunset,*

May 1921, 50; Obituary, *Los Angeles Times,* 7 May 1954, 2. Among other associations, Shontz was a charter member of the Women Lawyers' Club of L.A. On the court see Francis H. Hiller, *The Juvenile Court of Los Angeles County California* (Los Angeles: LA Lithograph Co., for Rotary Club, 1928), 20; Miriam Van Waters, "The Socialization of Juvenile Court Procedure," in Ernest Bryant Hoag and Edward H. Williams, eds., *Crime, Abnormal Minds, and the Law* (Indianapolis: Bobbs-Merrill, 1923), 158–67; *Women Lawyers Journal* 6:4 (Jan. 1917): 30; Odem, "Delinquent Daughters," 175–76.

20. MVW to parents, undated Oct. 1917, and undated 1917, c. Oct., file 45; 28 July 1918, file 46; Ellis, "Interesting Westerners," 49; "Aspires to Be Our First Woman Judge," *Los Angeles Sunday Times,* 14 July 1918, III, 16.

21. "Wing Missive with a Swat," *Los Angeles Times,* 30 Dec. 1920, II, 8; "Give Tea Just to Prove Solidarity," *Los Angeles Times,* 7 Feb. 1921, II, 1; "Woman's Day at City Hall." Shontz never achieved her goal of joining the bench as a justice of the California Superior Court, but in 1934 she won election to the State Bureau of Equalization on Upton Sinclair's End Poverty in California (EPIC) ticket, creating controversy, and a recall threat, for her determination to end liquor sales to minors. Between 1935 and 1947, she served as a municipal court judge. (*Los Angeles Times,* 1 April 1935, II, 2 and 7 June 1935, II, 3; Dummer to MVW, 15 July 1927, file 822, Dummer Papers.)

22. MVW to parents, 13 March 1918, file 46; 19 Aug., 29 Aug., and 14 May 1920, file 48; MVW to Dummer, 9 May 1921, file 819, Dummer Papers. Judge Jackson had a grudge against Reeve and an unseemly reputation for having been picked up out of the gutter and bailed out during a police raid on a brothel (MVW to parents, 19 Aug. 1920, file 48).

23. McGoarty, *History of Los Angeles County,* 137–38; Miriam Van Waters, "The Juvenile Court as a Social Laboratory," *Journal of Applied Sociology* 7:6 (July–Aug. 1923): 318–24; Van Waters, "The Socialization of Juvenile Court Procedure," chap. 14; Odem, "Delinquent Daughters," 290–91.

24. MVW to parents, 16 Oct. 1922, file 50; MVW to Dummer, 19 Oct. 1922, file 819, Dummer Papers; MVW to Dummer, 8 Aug. and 28 Oct. 1923, file 820; and 1 Sept. 1936, file 823, Dummer Papers.

25. Kathy Peiss, *Cheap Amusements: Working Women and Leisure in Turn-of-the-Century New York* (Philadelphia: Temple University Press, 1986); Elizabeth Lunbeck, *The Psychiatric Persuasion: Knowledge, Gender, and Power in Modern America* (Princeton: Princeton University Press, 1994), 189–99. On the response to prostitution, see Estelle B. Freedman, *Their Sisters' Keepers: Women's Prison Reform in America, 1830–1930* (Ann Arbor: University of Michigan Press, 1981) and Ruth Rosen, *The Lost Sisterhood: Prostitution in America, 1900–1918* (Baltimore: Johns Hopkins University Press, 1982). On the girl problem, see Ruth M. Alexander, *The "Girl Problem": Female Sexual Delinquency in New York, 1900–1930* (Ithaca, N.Y.: Cornell University Press, 1995). On new sexual values among immigrant and working-class women, see also Odem, "Delinquent Daughters," 184–85, and Eckert, "Price of Rebellion."

26. MVW, Boston University lectures, 4, 17 Oct. 1951, copy in possession of author (hereafter BU lectures). I am grateful to Katherine Gabel for making these lectures available to me.

27. Odem, "Delinquent Daughters," chap. 4: of 220 cases of girls brought to court in 1920, most of whom would have been seen by Van Waters, two-thirds came from single-parent families (table 2, 300); 80 percent were charged with sexual or moral offenses (234). Only 8 percent of all initial hearings led to detention in a public or private institution, but when institutions were used, the Catholic House of Good Shepherd and El Retiro received over half of the girls sentenced (table 10, 304, and table 12, 305). On pregnancies and the greater stigma attached to rebellion than to sexual relations themselves, see Eckert, "The Price of Rebellion," esp. 9. On maternity homes, see Regina Kunzel, *Fallen Women, Problem Girls: Unmarried Mothers and the Professionalization of Social Work, 1890–1945* (New Haven: Yale University Press, 1993).

28. Los Angeles County Juvenile Court Cases 17153 (1920), 25406 (1924), and 18448 (1921) 16936 (1920), 35596 (1927), 35574 (1927), and 38739 (1927), quoted in Cynthia Eckert, "Juvenile Court Records," unpublished ms. (all further references to L.A. Juvenile Court Case numbers refer to this source). See also Odem, "Delinquent Daughters," 266, 270–73.

29. L.A. Juvenile Court Cases 24768 (1924), 16889 (1920).

30. Odem, "Delinquent Daughters," table 7, 302, 341–45; L.A. Juvenile Court Case 16364 (1920); Miriam Van Waters, "When Children Sit in Judgment: The Juvenile Court as Its Own Wards See It," *Survey,* 1 June 1925, 293–95; father of El Retiro girl to Miss Smith, Juvenile Hall, 9 Sept. 1927, file 159; cf. L.A. Juvenile Court Case 24769 (1924).

31. L.A. Juvenile Court Cases 24769 (1924), 26877 (1924), and 17015 (1920); Odem, "Delinquent Daughters," 272, 279, 287, 289; 18 Jan. 1921, file 48; 25 Jan. 1929, file 57. In her study of girls' cases at the L.A. juvenile court during the 1920s, Cynthia Eckert found that 14 percent of the girls accused their parents of physical abuse, while 16 percent accused some family member of incest (Eckert, "The Price of Rebellion," 4).

32. L.A. Juvenile Court Cases 16889, 19331; Odem, "Delinquent Daughters," 253, 287; Los Angeles Business Girls Club Conference, 27 June 1928, file 161; MVW to parents, undated Sept. 1922, file 50. On interpretations of the juvenile courts, see Steven Schlossman and Stephanie Wallach, "The Crime of Precocious Sexuality: Female Juvenile Delinquency in the Progressive Era," *Harvard Educational Review* 48:1 (Feb. 1978): 65–94; Ellen Ryerson, *The Best-Laid Plans: America's Juvenile Court Experiment* (New York: Hill and Wang, 1978); Anthony M. Platt, *The Child Savers: The Invention of Delinquency,* rev. ed. (Chicago: University of Chicago Press, 1977); Steven L. Schlossman, *Love and the American Delinquent: The Theory and Practice of "Progressive" Juvenile Justice, 1825–1920* (Chicago: University of Chicago Press, 1977).

33. Miriam Van Waters, "Future Growth of the Juvenile Court," paper delivered at Chicago, Twenty-fifth Anniversary of Founding of First Juvenile Court, 2 Jan. 1925, file 467; Van Waters, "The Juvenile Court as a Social

Laboratory," and Van Waters, *Youth in Conflict* (New York: Republic Publishing, 1925) (see below, chap. 7, on her ideas). On sexual liberalism, see D'Emilio and Freedman, *Intimate Matters,* part 4.

34. MVW journal, 4 July 1928, file 206v, and 14 Oct. 1936, file 213v, Gladding-VW Papers.

35. Miriam Van Waters, "El Retiro: The New School for Girls," *California State Board of Health Monthly Bulletin* 15:8 (Feb. 1920): 255-61; MVW to Ruth Askin and Hilda Vincent, 23 March 1940, file 159; Miriam Van Waters, "Where Girls Go Right: Some Dynamic Aspects of State Correctional Schools for Girls and Young Women," *Survey,* 27 May 1922, 361-76; *Los Angeles Times,* 9 Nov. 1918, 18 March 1919, 1 April 1919, 2 July 1919; Margaret Reeves, *Training Schools for Girls* (New York: Russell Sage, 1929), 142, 150, 256, 267, 389, and table 7, 417-19. On precedents for self-government, see Jack M. Holl, *Juvenile Reform in the Progressive Era: William R. George and the Junior Republic Movement* (Ithaca, N.Y.: Cornell University Press, 1971).

36. Beckie to Maud VW, undated 1919, and Maud VW to GBVW, 15 Dec. 1919, both in box 2, GBVW Papers; MVW to Ruth Askin and Hilda Vincent, 23 March 1940, undated 1940, file 159; and Van Waters, "El Retiro: The New School for Girls"; Monroe, "When Women Sit in Judgement," 160-61.

37. MVW to parents, undated July 1920, file 48; MVW to Dummer, 22 Nov. 1925, file 821, Dummer Papers; Van Waters, "The Socialization of Juvenile Court Procedure," chap. 14.

38. Maud VW to GBVW, 15 Dec. 1919, box 2, GBVW Papers; Van Waters, "Where Girls Go Right," 361-76.

39. MVW to Dummer, 10 March 1921, file 819, Dummer Papers.

40. Van Waters, "El Retiro: The New School for Girls"; John Monlux (Deputy Superintendent of Los Angeles City Schools) to California Congress of Parents and Teachers, 19 Aug. 1927, file 159; Monroe, "When Women Sit in Judgement," 158; MVW to parents, 9 March 1920, file 48; Ruth Askin and Hilda Vincent to MVW, 23 March 1940, file 159; Rita Harrison, talk given at Riverside University, 1928, file 160; MVW to parents, undated 1919, file 47; undated April 1920, file 48; 4 Oct. 1922, file 50.

41. Rita Harrison, talk, 1928, file 160; MVW to parents, 30 Aug. 1920, file 48; 17 Feb. 1920, file 48; 19 Aug. 1927, file 159; John Monlux to California Congress of Parents and Teachers, 19 Aug. 1927, file 159; MVW to Ruth Askin and Hilda Vincent, 23 March 1940, file 159; *Los Angeles Times,* 11 Sept. and 17 Sept. 1920. El Retiro accepted black students only if more than one attended at the same time; it is not clear if the rationale for this rule was to avoid integrated roommates or to insure companionship (Dorothy Willy Lawrence, "Some Problems Arising in the Treatment of Adolescent Negro Girls Appearing before the Los Angeles Juvenile Court," [M.S.W. thesis, Graduate School of Social Work, University of Southern California, 1941], 84-85). I thank Janis Appier for bringing this source to my attention.

42. MVW to parents, undated 1922, file 50. On Healy, see Robert M. Mennel, *Thorns and Thistles: Juvenile Delinquents in the United States,*

1825-1940 (Hanover, N.H.: University Press of New England, 1973), 161-65.

43. El Retiro Conference Reports, 24 Feb. 1926 and 17 Nov. 1926, file 161. All inmate names have been changed.

44. El Retiro Conference Reports, 17 Nov. 1926 and 22 June 1927, file 161. The persistence of Van Waters' cultural pluralism during the 1920s contrasted with other progressive reformers, who then stressed assimilation. On changing liberal views of ethnicity, see Gary Gerstle, "The Protean Character of American Liberalism," *American Historical Review* 99 (Oct. 1994), 1043-73.

45. MVW, "The Delinquent Attitude — a Study of Juvenile Delinquency from the Standpoint of Human Relationship," in *Proceedings of the National Conference on Social Work* (Chicago: University of Chicago Press, 1924), 160-65. On social work, see, e.g., John Ehrenreich, *The Altruistic Imagination: A History of Social Work and Social Policy in the United States* (Ithaca, N.Y.: Cornell University Press, 1985); Clarke A. Chambers, "Women in the Creation of the Profession of Social Work," *Social Service Review* (March 1986) 60:1, 1-33; and Kunzel, *Fallen Women, Problem Girls.*

46. El Retiro Conference Report, 8 Dec. 1926, file 161.

47. Letters from students to MVW, 23 April 1926, file 165.

48. Ibid.

49. On the companionate family, see Steven Mintz and Susan Kellogg, *Domestic Revolutions: A Social History of American Family Life* (New York: Free Press, 1988), chap. 6. On conflicts between reformers and families, see Linda Gordon, *Heroes of Their Own Lives: The Politics and History of Family Violence* (New York: Viking 1988), and Odem, "Delinquent Daughters."

50. Freedman, *Their Sisters' Keepers,* and "Mary Bartelme," in Barbara Sicherman and Carol Hurd Green, eds., *Notable American Women: The Modern Period* (Cambridge: Harvard University Press, Belknap Press, 1980), 60-61; MVW to parents, 10 Feb. 1921, file 48; MVW to Dummer, 17 July 1921, file 819, Dummer Papers. The Clubhouse was located at 176 So. Bonnie Brae St. On the girls club movement as prevention for delinquency, see Alexander, *The "Girl Problem."*

51. L.A. Juvenile Court Case 17015 (1920); Los Angeles Business Girls Club, Student conference, 27 June 1928, file 161; MVW to Dummer, 17 July 1921, file 819, Dummer Papers; Agnes Scott Donaldson, "The Business Girls Club, Los Angeles, from October 15, 1926 to January 1, 1929," Report to the Board of Managers, file 172. Van Waters also planned a second camp for "psychopathic girls."

52. Donaldson, "Business Girls Club."

53. Asst. Probation Officer to MVW, 23 Sept. 1927, file 159; 16 Oct. 1922, file 50; "The Business Girl," 1:1 (14 March 1927), file 172; Donaldson, "Business Girls Club." Statistics from 1926 to 1929 showed that 27 percent of the residents had married, while 29 percent lived either in apartments with two or three other women or at their workplace. Most of the remain-

der had returned to their parents' homes. Sixteen percent went to other institutions, and 6 percent had "whereabouts unknown" (Donaldson, 4).

54. MVW to parents, undated April 1922 (before 11 April), file 50; 3 April 1922, file 50; 22 June 1927, file 161; El Retiro Conference Report, 22 June 1927, file 161; Donaldson, "Business Girls Club."

55. MVW journal, 4 July 1928, file 206, 23 Aug. 1936, file 213, Gladding-VW Papers; student to MVW, 1 July 1970, file 165.

CHAPTER SIX

1. MVW to Dummer, undated Nov. 1924, file 820, Dummer Papers.

2. For reviews of women in the 1920s, see Estelle B. Freedman, "The New Woman: Changing Views of Women in the 1920s," *Journal of American History* 71 (Sept. 1974): 372-93; "Separatism as Strategy: Female Institution Building and American Feminism, 1870-1930," *Feminist Studies* 5:3 (fall 1979): 512-29; and "Separatism Revisited: Women's Institutions, Social Reform, and the Career of Miriam Van Waters," in Linda Kerber, Alice Kessler-Harris, and Kathryn Kish Sklar, eds., *American History as Women's History: New Feminist Essays* (Chapel Hill: University of North Carolina Press, 1995), 170-88.

3. On the postsuffrage outlook for women's political and professional lives, see Nancy Cott, *The Grounding of Modern Feminism* (New Haven: Yale University Press, 1987), chaps. 3, 6, 7; Robin Muncy, *Creating a Female Dominion in American Reform, 1890-1935* (New York: Oxford University Press, 1991); and Felice Gordon, *After Winning: The Legacy of the New Jersey Suffragists, 1920-1947* (New Brunswick, N.J.: Rutgers University Press, 1986).

4. On black women's activism, see Elsa Barkley Brown, "Womanist Consciousness: Maggie Lena Walker and the Independent Order of Saint Luke," *Signs* 14 (spring 1989): 610-33; Darlene Clark Hine, "'We Specialize in the Wholly Impossible': The Philanthropic Work of Black Women," in Kathleen D. McCarthy, ed., *Lady Bountiful Revisited: Women, Philanthropy, and Power* (New Brunswick, N.J.: Rutgers University Press, 1990), 70-95; Jacqueline Anne Rouse, *Lugenia Burns Hope: Black Southern Reformer* (Athens: University of Georgia Press, 1989); Evelyn Brooks Higginbotham, "In Politics to Stay: Black Women Leaders and Party Politics in the 1920s," in Louise Tilly and Patricia Gurin, eds., *Women, Politics, and Change* (New York: Russell Sage Foundation, 1990), 199-220; Anne Firor Scott, "Most Invisible of All: Black Women's Voluntary Associations," *Journal of Southern History* 56 (February 1990): 3-22; Linda Gordon, "Black and White Visions of Welfare: Women's Welfare Activism, 1890-1945," *Journal of American History* 78 (Sept. 1991): 559-90; Debra Gray White, "The Cost of Club Work, the Price of Black Feminism," in Nancy Hewitt and Suzanne Lebsock, eds., *Visible Women* (Urbana: University of Illinois Press, 1993), 247-70. On white women's networks, see Blanche Wiesen Cook, "Female Support Networks and Political Activism: Lillian Wald, Crystal Eastman, Emma Goldman," in Nancy F. Cott and Elizabeth H. Pleck, eds., *A Heritage*

of Her Own: Toward a New Social History of American Women (New York: Simon and Schuster, 1979), 412–44. On continuity between progressivism and the New Deal, see J. Stanley Lemons, *The Woman Citizen: Social Feminism in the 1920s* (Urbana: University of Illinois Press, 1973), and Clarke Chambers, *Seedtime for Reform: American Social Service and Social Action, 1918–1933* (Minneapolis: University of Minnesota Press, 1963).

5. MVW to parents, 2 Sept. 1917, file 45; undated 1918, file 47; 23 March 1919, 1 April 1919, file 47; undated Dec. 1925, file 53; 23 Jan. 1928, 28 Dec. 1928, file 56. On interracial cooperation, see Jacquelyn Dowd Hall, *Revolt against Chivalry: Jessie Daniel Ames and the Women's Campaign against Lynching* (New York: Columbia University Press, 1979); and Susan Lynn, *Progressive Women in Conservative Times: Racial Justice, Peace, and Feminism, 1945 to the 1960s* (New Brunswick, N.J.: Rutgers University Press, 1992).

6. MVW to parents, undated Jan., 24 Feb., and 22 April 1918, file 46; 20 June 1919, file 47; 23 Jan. 1928, file 56; 21 June 1929, file 57; *Los Angeles Herald*, 15 May 1922; *Los Angeles Evening Herald*, 21 June, 23 June, 25 June, 28 June, 30 June, 2 July, all 1921; clipping, 20 June 1921, file 465. MVW also wrote for the *Los Angeles Examiner*, e.g., on the evils of amusement places and hotels, 26 May 1921, file 465.

7. MVW to parents, c. 26 May 1917, file 45.

8. Robert M. Fogelson, *Fragmented Metropolis: Los Angeles, 1850–1930* (Cambridge: Harvard University Press, 1967), chap. 10; Kevin Starr, *Material Dreams: Southern California through the 1920s* (New York: Oxford University Press, 1990), chaps. 6–7.

9. Friday Morning Club clipping book, vols. 6, 10, and Mrs. Henry Christian Crowther, *High Lights: The Friday Morning Club of L.A., 1891–1938* (Los Angeles, 1938), 38–40, Friday Morning Club, Ephemera Collection, Huntington Library, San Marino, Calif.; MVW to parents, 9 Feb., 8 April, and undated Sept. 1925, file 53. MVW became the state chairman of the Juvenile Court Division of the State Federation of Women's Clubs.

10. MVW to parents, 23 Jan. 1928, file 56; Louis Lyons, ed., *Who's Who among the Women of California* (San Francisco: Security Publishing, 1922), 44–45; Friday Morning Club clipping book, vol. 6; Margaret to MVW, 28 May 1970, file 165.

11. MVW to parents, 14 May 1917 and undated Oct. 1917, file 45.

12. The Colony was at 324–28 East Avenue 60 in Los Angeles. In 1917 Miriam paid $8.50 a month as one-third of rent. Fisher remained when Reynolds left sometime after 1923. Shontz and Woods joined later, and by 1927 Fisher had moved closer to UCLA (L.A. City Directories, 1920, 1923, 1925, 1927; 14 Feb. 1918, file 46; 4 Sept. 1919, file 47). On Woods, see Barbara Ann Dreyer, "The Influence of the Social Hygiene Movement on the Education of Children during the Early Decades of the Twentieth Century in America," (Ph.D. diss., Johns Hopkins University, 1972), 36.

13. MVW to parents, 19 Nov. 1922, file 50; 28 Dec. 1928, file 56. When

Shontz's cat, Viking, died, Miriam asked her mother to send a sympathy note because "Viking was not a cat to us, he was one of our best friends" (10 Feb. 1921, file 48).

14. MVW to parents, 24 July 1926, file 54; 16 Oct. 1922, file 50; 14 April 1919, file 47.

15. Dummer to MVW, 4 Dec. 1921, file 819, and MVW to Dummer, 1 July 1925, file 821, Dummer Papers; MVW to parents, 19 Sept. 1926, file 54, 3 April 1922, file 50.

16. MVW to Dummer, 21 Aug. 1921, file 819, Dummer Papers; 19 July 1925, file 53; MVW to parents, 24 March 1918, file 46; MVW to mother, 12 Jan. 1922, box 2, GBVW Papers.

17. MVW to Geraldine Thompson (hereafter GT), 31 July 1927, and MVW to Edna Mahan, 7 July 1927, file 115; MVW to Dummer, 22 July 1927, 9 Sept. 1927, file 822, Dummer Papers. Stone House was at 1833 Verdugo Vista Rd., Glendale.

18. Anne Shannon Monroe, "When Women Sit in Judgement," *Good Housekeeping,* April 1920, 149, photo 144; Clara Spalding Ellis, "Interesting Westerners," *Sunset,* May 1921, 49, 50; obituary, *Los Angeles Times,* 7 May 1954; MVW to parents, 26 Sept. 1917, undated Oct. 1917, and undated 1917, c. Oct., file 45. Shontz was a charter member of the Women's Lawyers' Club of Los Angeles.

19. MVW to parents, 3 April 1919, file 47; Mary Odem, "Delinquent Daughters: The Sexual Regulation of Female Minors in the United States, 1880–1920" (Ph.D. diss., University of California, Berkeley, 1989), 23; MVW to Edna Mahan, 22 Aug. 1928, file 251, Gladding-VW Papers; MVW journal, 15 Sept. 1928, file 208, Gladding-VW Papers.

20. Maud VW to Beckie, 17 Dec. 1919, box 2, GBVW Papers; MVW to parents, 6 July 1920, undated Aug. 1920, file 48; Dorothy M. Brown, *Mabel Walker Willebrandt: A Study of Power, Loyalty, and Law* (Knoxville: University of Tennessee Press, 1984), 39, 41, 46. Journalist Adela Rogers St. Johns describes the "ladies table" at the Pig n' Whistle restaurant in downtown L.A. in *Some Are Born Great* (New York: New American Library, 1974), 222–26.

21. Shontz to MVW, 17 Oct. 1930, file 117; Shontz to MVW, 10 April 1934, 24 Feb. 1937, Shontz file, and GT to MVW, 11 Nov. 1930, GT file, Gladding-VW Papers; on second mother, RVW interview; MVW journal, 28 Sept. 1928, file 208, 20 Aug. 1931, file 211, 3 Oct. 1944 (on Orfa and Eve), file 219, all in Gladding-VW Papers. Linda Gordon estimates that at least one-fourth of the women reformers she studied had female life partners (*Pitied but Not Entitled: Single Mothers and the History of Welfare, 1890–1935* [New York: Free Press, 1994], 78–79).

22. Studies of American women's intimate relationships include Carroll Smith-Rosenberg, "The Female World of Love and Ritual: Relations between Women in Nineteenth-Century America," *Signs* 1 (autumn 1975): 1–29; Nancy Sahli, "Smashing: Women's Relationships before the Fall," *Chrysalis* (summer 1979): 17–27; Lillian Faderman, *Surpassing the Love of Men: Romantic Friendship and Love between Women from the Renais-*

sance to the Present (New York: William Morrow, 1981) and *Odd Girls and Twilight Lovers: A History of Lesbian Life in Twentieth-Century America* (New York: Columbia University Press, 1991); Vern Bullough and Bonnie Bullough, "Lesbianism in the 1920s and 1930s: A Newfound Study," *Signs* 2 (summer 1977): 895–904; Leila J. Rupp, "Imagine My Surprise: Women's Relationships in Historical Perspective," *Frontiers* (fall 1980): 61–70; Blanche Wiesen Cook, *Eleanor Roosevelt: Volume 1, 1884-1933* (New York: Viking, 1992), 295–99, 319–26; Helen Lefkowitz Horowitz, *The Power and Passion of M. Carey Thomas* (New York: Alfred A. Knopf, 1994), esp. 87, 290.

23. MVW journal, 30 March 1929, file 208, Gladding-VW Papers. MVW's phrasing suggests an ambivalence about the value of motherhood: Gordon, she wrote, might have been "anything—everything in fact but a stupid wife and mother—Wife she co[uld] have been and mother too." In her study of the educator M. Carey Thomas, historian Helen Lefkowitz Horowitz stresses the importance of fiction reading in women's formation of sexual identity among the generation of educated women that preceded Van Waters; by the turn of the twentieth century, however, for women like Van Waters social science literature may have played a more important role in constructing notions of deviant homosexuality. See Horowitz, "'Nous Autres': Reading, Passion, and the Creation of M. Carey Thomas," *Journal of American History* 79 (June 1992): 68–95.

24. Shontz to Dummer, 27 July 1920, 30 July 1926, file 750, Dummer Papers; Ethel S. Dummer, *Why I Think So: The Autobiography of an Hypothesis* (Chicago: Clarke-McElroy Publishing Co., 1937), 13, 60; Robert Mennel, "Ethel Sturges Dummer," in Barbara Sicherman and Carol Hurd Green, eds. *Notable American Women: The Modern Period* (Cambridge: Harvard University Press, Belknap Press, 1980), 208–9, and Mennel, *Thorns and Thistles: Juvenile Delinquents in the United States, 1825-1940* (Hanover, N.H.: University Press of New England, 1973), 173–76; Margo Horn, *Before It's Too Late: The Child Guidance Movement in the United States, 1922-1945* (Philadelphia: Temple University Press, 1989), 13–15. Another of Dummer's early teachers was Theodate Smith, who went on to earn her doctorate in psychology at Clark, where MVW knew her (Dummer, *Why I Think So,* 17).

25. Dummer, *Why I Think So,* 100, 109–12; Dummer to MVW, 4 Dec. 1921, file 819, Dummer Papers; MVW speech, Memorial Service for Mrs. Ethel Dummer, Institute of Juvenile Research, Chicago, 6 March 1954, file 402. Dummer spent winters from 1917 to 1927 at Coronado in southern California, near her daughter, who was a school principal in San Diego (Dummer, *Why I Think So,* 152). On the Children's Bureau, see Muncy, *Creating a Female Dominion in American Reform.*

26. Shontz to Dummer, 30 June 1920, file 750, Dummer Papers.

27. Dummer to Shontz, 27 July 1920, and Shontz to Dummer, 7 Jan. 1921, file 750, Dummer Papers; 29 Aug. 1920, file 48; undated Nov. 1920; see also Dreyer, "The Influence of the Social Hygiene Movement," 82, 186.

28. MVW to Dummer, 30 Dec. 1920, 6 Jan. 1921, 12 Jan. 1921, file 819,

Dummer Papers; undated Nov. 1920, file 48. On theories of juvenile delinquency proposed by Meyer, Healy, and Taft, see Mennel, *Thorns and Thistles,* esp. 158–71. On Janie Porter Barrett, see Dolores Nicholson entry in Jessie Carney Smith, ed., *Notable Black American Women* (Detroit: Gale Research, 1992), 56–59.

29. MVW to parents, 26 Dec. 1920, 30 Dec. 1920, 24 Jan. 1921, 10 Feb. 1921, file 48; MVW to Dummer, 6 Jan. 1921, 12 Jan. 1921, 10 Feb. 1921, file 819, Dummer Papers; Miriam Van Waters, "Where Girls Go Right: Some Dynamic Aspects of State Correctional Schools for Girls and Young Women," *Survey,* 27 May 1922, 361–76.

30. MVW to Dummer, 6 Jan. 1921, 12 Jan. 1921, file 819, Dummer Papers.

31. MVW to Dummer, 6 Jan., 12 Jan., 22 Jan., and 6 March 1921, file 819, Dummer Papers; 15 March 1921, file 48. Reformatory commitments increased from 25,251 in 1923 to 30,496 in 1923, or from 22.8 to 24.4 per 100,000 population (David J. Rothman, *Conscience and Convenience: The Asylum and Its Alternatives in Progressive America* [Boston: Little, Brown, 1980], 258).

32. MVW to Dummer, 12 Jan. 1921 and Dummer to MVW, 7 Feb. 1921, 10 Feb. 1921, 19 May 1922, file 819, Dummer Papers; 10 Feb. 1921, file 48. For a critique of progressive reforms see Rothman, *Conscience and Convenience;* and Ellen Ryerson, *The Best-Laid Plans: America's Juvenile Court Experiment* (New York: Hill and Wang, 1978). On gender, cf. Dummer to MVW, just after discussing the work of W. I. Thomas: "How differently men and women write! You and Jessie Taft can, with a sentence, illuminate a principle and by the search-light of your understanding educate thousands of folk never touched by the contributions of academic type" (25 June 1925, file 821, Dummer Papers).

33. Dummer to MVW, 5 Aug. 1921, undated Sept. 1921, file 819, Dummer Papers. In her original letter instigating the leave for MVW, Orfa Shontz had explicitly asked that there be no requirement of a particular product. She may have known how hard it was for MVW to work under pressure of a deadline or meeting external standards (Shontz to Dummer, 30 June 1920, file 750, Dummer Papers).

34. MVW to Dummer, 26 Aug. 1921, file 819, Dummer Papers.

35. MVW to Dummer, 31 Oct. 1921, 11 Dec. 1921, file 819, Dummer Papers; MVW to parents, 8 Jan. 1922, 11 April 1922, file 50.

36. Maud VW to GBVW, misdated Dec. 1916, box 2, GBVW Papers; Van Waters, "Where Girls Go Right," 362. A copy of the unpublished report, "Some Dynamic Aspects of State Correctional Schools for Girls and Young Women," appears in file 465.

37. Van Waters, "Where Girls Go Right."

38. MVW to Dummer, 13 Sept. 1922, Dummer to MVW, 28 Oct. 1922, 2 Dec. 1922, file 819, and Dummer to MVW, 10 June 1923, 16 June 1923, file 820, Dummer Papers.

39. Dummer, *Why I Think So,* 101; MVW to Dummer, 25 June 1923, file 820, Dummer Papers. Dummer discussed psychoanalysis, e.g., in a letter to

MVW, 9 June 1924, file 820. MVW also wrote about the role of transference in social workers' approach to delinquent girls (in "How They Make Good," *Survey,* 1 Oct. 1924, 40–41).

40. MVW to parents, 19 Feb. 1919, 4 Sept. 1919, file 47; Maud VW to Beckie, 6 Nov. 1919, box 2, GBVW Papers; MVW to Dummer, 1 June 1923, file 820, Dummer Papers; MVW to parents, 1 Oct. 1922, file 50, 6 Nov. 1925, file 53; 26 May 1929, file 57; 24 July 1926, file 54; Maud Van Waters, "Talks to Friday Club by Maud Vosburg," n.d., after 1923, file 29.

41. Dummer to Shontz, 20 May 1924, file 650, Dummer Papers.

42. E.g. Shontz to MVW, 22 Feb. 1934, file 259, Gladding-VW Papers; Abby to MVW, 24 Feb. 1934, file 306, Gladding-VW Papers; Clara Maria to MVW, 18 Sept. 1928, file 116.

43. MVW to Dummer, 28 Oct. 1923, file 820, Dummer Papers; MVW to Felix Frankfurter, 1 Nov. 1931, Harvard Crime Survey Correspondence, Miriam Van Waters Folder, container 140, Felix Frankfurter Papers, microfilm n.s. 3967, reel 87.

44. M. A. DeWolfe Howe, *The Children's Judge: Frederick Pickering Cabot* (Boston: Houghton Mifflin, 1932), 81–82; Declaration of Intention No. 160525 (District of Massachusetts) and Certificate of Arrival No. 527679 (Ellis Island, N.Y.), U.S. Naturalization Service, Department of Labor, National Archives, Boston, Mass.; MVW journal, 10 Oct. 1928, file 208, Gladding-VW Papers; Hans Weiss (hereafter HW) to MVW, 6 Jan. 1929, 19 Jan. 1929, file 276 and 4 Aug. 1930, file 280, Gladding-VW Papers; HW to Felix Frankfurter, 21 Aug. 1927, file no. 002274, General Correspondence, container 109, reel 66, Felix Frankfurter Papers. No photographs of HW survive, but his coloring and weight are listed in the naturalization file.

45. Howe, *The Children's Judge,* 81–82; Burton Rowles to MVW, undated 1962, file 645; HW to MVW, 24 July 1928, file 274, Gladding-VW Papers; MVW to Dummer, 1 Sept. 1936, file 823, Dummer Papers; HW to MVW, 16 March 1929, file 277, Gladding-VW Papers. For HW's views on juvenile reform, see his essay "The Social Worker's Technique and Probation," in Sheldon Glueck, ed., *Probation and Criminal Justice: Essays in Honor of Herbert C. Parsons* (New York: Macmillan, 1933), 165–96.

46. HW to MVW, 1 July 1928, 24 July 1928, file 274, and 4 Oct. 1927, file 271, Gladding-VW Papers.

47. HW to MVW, 16 Nov. 1924, file 271, Gladding-VW Papers.

48. HW to MVW, 1 July 1928, file 274, 16 Nov. 1924, file 275, 17 Nov. 1924, file 271, and 8 Aug. 1927, file 272, Gladding-VW Papers.

49. MVW journal, 28 June 1928, file 206, Gladding-VW Papers; cf. HW's sweet memory of "what you did for me when you had the tremendous courage of giving yourself to me" (HW to MVW, 24 July 1930, file 279, Gladding-VW Papers).

50. MVW journal, 19 Feb. 1928, 14 June 1928, file 206, and 23 Nov. 1928, file 208; HW to MVW, 7 Aug. 1930, file 280, all in Gladding-VW Papers.

51. HW to MVW, 19 Jan. 1929, file 276, Gladding-VW Papers. In a letter MVW gave HW before leaving Cambridge, which he kept on his desk, she

explained that she could have given her life to him if he had been able to convince her that in doing so she was "also serving humanity." He wrote to her that the comment hurt him deeply because he did not consider himself to be a man of high enough caliber to measure up to this standard. On the dilemmas of marriage and career for twentieth-century reformers, see Nancy F. Cott, *The Grounding of Modern Feminism* (New Haven: Yale University Press, 1987) chap. 3; and Joyce Antler, *Lucy Sprague Mitchell: The Making of a Modern Woman* (New Haven: Yale University Press, 1987), 345–72.

52. HW to MVW, 13 Nov. 1927, 29 Nov. 1927, 9 Dec. 1927, 20 Dec. 1927, file 272, and 31 March 1928, 18 May 1928, file 273, Gladding-VW Papers.

53. HW to MVW, 1 July, 4 July, 9 July, 20 July, 24 July, and 20 Aug. 1928, file 274, Gladding-VW Papers. Although he did not draw a connection between his efforts to find a wife and his status as an alien resident of the United States, HW did face problems with the immigration service during 1928. Both MVW and Orfa Shontz testified at his naturalization hearings that fall. (HW to MVW, 25 Aug. and 5 Sept. 1928, file 274, and MVW to Edna Mahan, 20 Sept. 1928, file 251, Gladding-VW Papers.)

CHAPTER SEVEN

1. Joan M. Jensen, "All Pink Sisters: The War Department and the Feminist Movement in the 1920s," in Lois Scharf and Joan M. Jensen, eds., *Decades of Discontent: The Women's Movement, 1920–1940* (Westport, Conn.: Greenwood Press, 1983), 199–222; Paula Baker, "The Domestication of Politics: Women and American Political Society, 1780–1920," *American Historical Review* 89 (June 1984): 620–47. On the professionalization of social work, see Roy Lubove, *The Professional Altruist: The Emergence of Social Work as a Career, 1880–1930* (Cambridge: Harvard University Press, 1965); and on women's roles, Clarke A. Chambers, "Women in the Creation of the Profession of Social Work," *Social Service Review* 60:1 (March 1986): 1–33, and Linda Gordon, *Heroes of Their Own Lives: The Politics and History of Family Violence, Boston, 1880–1960* (New York: Viking, 1988) and Gordon, *Pitied but Not Entitled: Single Mothers and the History of Welfare, 1890–1935* (New York: Free Press, 1994), chap. 4.

2. MVW to parents, 12 Nov. 1922, box 2, GBVW Papers; Mary Odem, "Delinquent Daughters: The Sexual Regulation of Female Minors in the United States, 1880–1920" (Ph.D. diss., University of California, Berkeley, 1989); Los Angeles Probation Committee, *Report* [1929–35] (Los Angeles, 1936), 31.

3. MVW to parents, undated April 1920, 13 Aug. 1920, 18 Jan. 1921, file 48; 7 July 1922 and undated Sept. 1922, file 50; MVW to Dummer, 22 Aug. 1922, and MVW to Dummer, 13 Sept. 1922, file 819, Dummer Papers; MVW to parents, 12 Nov. 1922, box 2, GBVW Papers.

4. MVW to parents, 12 Jan. 1922, box 2, GBVW papers; 19 Nov. 1922, file 50; MVW to Dummer, 29 Dec. 1922, file 820, Dummer Papers.

5. MVW to Dummer, undated Nov. 1924, file 820, Dummer Papers; MVW to parents, 15 Nov. 1925, file 53; 28 Dec. 1928, file 56.

6. MVW to Dummer, 19 June 1923, file 819 and 28 Oct. 1923, file 820, Dummer Papers. While Densmore was away, Van Waters had instituted a protégé at El Retiro, who reported the use of blows.

7. MVW to Dummer, 7 Nov. 1923, file 820, Dummer Papers.

8. MVW to Dummer, 27 June 1923, 12 Dec. 1923 and Dummer to MVW, 4 July 1923, file 820, Dummer Papers.

9. MVW to Dummer 28 Oct. 1923, 7 Nov. 1923, 12 Feb. 1924, 9 June 1924, file 820, Dummer Papers; Margo Horn, *Before It's Too Late: The Child Guidance Movement in the United States, 1922-1945* (Philadelphia: Temple University Press, 1989), 5.

10. Dummer to MVW, 16 Nov. 1923 and 17 Dec. 1924, and MVW to Dummer, 20 Nov. 1923, 15 Jan. 1924, 16 Feb. 1924, file 820, Dummer Papers.

11. MVW to Dummer, 27 March 1924, file 820, Dummer Papers; Daniel Mebane to MVW, 6 Aug. 1924, and MVW to Mebane, 13 Aug. 1924, file 502; Miriam Van Waters, *Youth in Conflict* (New York: Republic Publishing, 1925).

12. Van Waters, *Youth in Conflict*, vi, 17-18. For example, see her romanticization of Russian immigrant men as "ruddy, honest giants of fathers" descended from peasants; "apart from beating their wives and children from tradition, they were the gentlest of men." See William I. Thomas, *The Unadjusted Girl* (Boston: Little, Brown, 1924) and William I. Thomas and Florian Znaniecki, *The Polish Peasant in Europe and America* (New York: Alfred A. Knopf, 1927).

13. Elizabeth Lunbeck, *The Psychiatric Persuasion: Knowledge, Gender, and Power in Modern America* (Princeton: Princeton University Press, 1994), 189-99; Ruth M. Alexander, *The "Girl Problem": Female Sexual Delinquency in New York, 1900-1930* (Ithaca, N.Y.: Cornell University Press, 1995).

14. Van Waters, *Youth in Conflict*, 46, 113, 117-22.

15. Ibid., 136-40 ff.

16. For examples of the continuing popularity of hereditarianism in general, and feeblemindedness in particular, as explanations for female sexual delinquency, see Julia Mathews, "A Survey of 341 Delinquent Girls in California," *Journal of Delinquency* 7:3-4 (May-July 1923): 196-231; Walter L. Treadway, L. O. Weldon, and Alice Hill, "Psychiatric Studies of Delinquents," *U.S. Public Health Reports* 34:21-27 (21 May, 28 May, 25 June, 2 July, 1920): 1195-1221, 1247-69, 1501-37, 1575-96.

17. Van Waters, *Youth in Conflict*, 284ff.

18. W. A. White to Dummer, 16 Jan. 1925, file 502; Ira S. Wile in *Progressive Education*, file 501 and clipping of *Journal of Social Hygiene* review, file 501; Katherine Bement Davis in *New York Evening Sun*, 14 March 1925. Other contemporary books on youth included Thomas, *The Unadjusted Girl*; Ben B. Lindsey, *The Revolt of Modern Youth* (New York:

Boni and Liveright, 1925); and Phyllis Blanchard, *The Adolescent Girl* (New York: Moffat, Yard, 1920).

19. Ellis, "My Mail Bag," *New York American,* 20 Feb. 1933, newsclipping, file 504; Dan Mebane to MVW, 23 Feb. 1926, file 504; MVW to Dan Mebane and Dummer, 14 March 1925, and MVW to HW, 2 Sept. 1925, file 503; 14 April 1929, file 57; MVW to Roxanne Ilhany and Dr. Najee Saeed, 13 April 1928, file 504; Dan Mebane to MVW, 14 Oct. 1946, file 504; MVW to Dummer, 23 March 1925, undated Oct. 1925, file 821, Dummer Papers. Approximately two thousand of the fifteen thousand copies printed sold in the first year.

20. *Bulletin* of the Social Workers Association of Oregon, 11:27 (11 March 1925); MVW to parents, 5 Sept. 1925, undated Nov. 1925, file 53; MVW to Mebane and Dummer, 14 March 1925, file 503.

21. MVW to parents, 3 Oct. 1926, file 54; MVW to Dummer, 9 July 1926 and Dummer to MVW, 14 Oct. 1926, file 821, Dummer Papers. Cf. Dummer's response when MVW asked advice on resigning from the California Juvenile Delinquency Commission: "Save your valuable time and brains, for more profitable channels than the political" (26 Feb. 1928, file 822, Dummer Papers).

22. MVW to Dummer, 7 Nov. 1926, file 821, Dummer Papers.

23. Michael Gordon, "The Social Survey Movement and Sociology in the United States," *Social Problems* 21:2 (fall 1973): 284–98; Robert M. Mennel, *Thorns and Thistles: Juvenile Delinquents in the United States, 1825–1940* (Hanover, N.H.: University Press of New England, 1973), 152–53; Felix Frankfurter, intro. to Sheldon Glueck and Eleanor T. Glueck, *One Thousand Juvenile Delinquents: Their Treatment by Court and Clinic* (Cambridge: Harvard University Press, 1934), x.

24. "Discussion of Harvard Law School Survey," 3 March 1927, box 24-10, Sheldon Glueck Papers, Harvard Law School, Cambridge, Mass. Glueck was willing to manipulate the presentation of cases in order to gain public support; in addition to including typical cases, for example, he sought those with "a certain degree of dramatic and sensational interest to the public," and "that indicate also such characteristics as homosexuality, or other features which may be infectious, even if they do not exist in the majority of cases" (3). His approach culminated in *One Thousand Juvenile Delinquents.* In its introduction, however, Frankfurter claimed that the survey was "undertaken not as an agency for reform but as a contribution to knowledge" (xii).

25. Shontz to Dummer, 30 July 1926, file 750, and MVW to Dummer, 6 Jan. 1927, file 822, Dummer Papers.

26. MVW to parents, 3 Feb. 1926, file 54.

27. *Los Angeles Times,* 1 April 1919, 2 July 1919; MVW to Dummer, 21 Oct. 1924, file 820, Dummer Papers.

28. Letters to Elizabeth McManus from Addie M. Graff, F. Ione Fulmer, Susan Allen Paisley, and Margaret H. Jaynes, 30 July 1924, box 5, Georgia Bullock Papers, UCLA Special Collections, Los Angeles, California (hereaf-

ter Bullock Papers); letters to Elizabeth McManus from Margaret More-wood, Mrs. Sibley, and Anna Holt, 30 July 1924, box 5, Bullock Papers.

29. MVW, "For the Nation," ts., undated 1927, file 163; El Retiro Super-intendent's Reports, Miss Holzschuh, Oct.–Dec. 1924, box 5, Bullock Papers.

30. El Retiro Monthly Report, Feb. 1915 and March 1925, box 5, Bullock Papers.

31. MVW to Dummer, 22 Nov. 1925, file 821, Dummer Papers; MVW "For the Nation"; Harry Archbald to Board of Supervisors, 23 Oct. 1924 and Board of Supervisors to Efficiency Committee, 6 Nov. 1924, OD2362J, Box 10.4810.209, Juvenile Hall and Juvenile Court File, Los Angeles County Board of Supervisors Records, Los Angeles County Archives, Los Angeles, California; MVW to parents, 9 Dec. 1925, file 53.

32. MVW to Dummer, 19 Feb. 1927, file 822, Dummer Papers; MVW to parents, 2 Nov. 1928, file 56; Mary Q. Hawkes, *Excellent Effect: The Edna Mahan Story* (Arlington, Va.: American Correctional Association, 1994).

33. C. D. Lusby, acting chairman, Los Angeles County Probation Com-mittee, to Alma Holzschuh, 16 Aug. 1927, file 163; MVW, "For the Nation"; *Los Angeles Times,* 18 Aug., 23 Aug., 26 Aug., and 27 Aug. 1927; MVW to Mary Ross, 6 March 1928, file 159.

34. MVW used the phrase "sacking" in "For the Nation"; MVW to Dum-mer, 21 Aug. 1927, file 822, Dummer Papers; HW to MVW, 11 July 1927, 18 July 1927, file 271, Gladding-VW Papers.

35. MVW to Dummer, 16 Sept. 1927, file 822, Dummer Papers.

36. MVW to Dummer, 16 Sept. 1927, file 822; MVW, "For the Nation"; MVW to Mary Ross, 6 March 1928, file 159.

37. MVW to Mary Ross, 6 March 1928, file 159; MVW to parents, 23 Jan. 1928, file 56; MVW to Dummer, 11 June 1928 and 5 Aug. 1928, file 822, Dummer Papers; MVW to parents, 14 Jan. 1929, file 57.

38. MVW to Dummer, 16 Sept. 1927, file 822, Dummer Papers; MVW to Judge Harry Archbald, 17 Aug. 1927, file 163; MVW, "For the Nation"; MVW to Ruth Askin and Hilda Vincent, 23 March 1940, file 159.

39. Student testimony on walkout, L.A. Juvenile Court, Orfa Jean Shontz Acting Referee, 15 Aug. 1927, file 164.

40. Rita Harrison, talk given at Riverside University, 1928, file 160; Shontz quoted in *Los Angeles Times,* 17 Aug. 1927; MVW journal, 4 July 1928, file 206, Gladding-VW Papers.

41. MVW to GT, 31 July 1927, file 261, Gladding-VW Papers; MVW jour-nal, 27 Sept. 1927, file 206, Gladding-VW Papers; Marjorie Mansfield, re-view in *New York Herald Tribune,* 13 May 1928, file 505. For critical com-ments about MVW's lack of sympathy to parents, see Tess Schlesinger's review in the *New York Post,* 25 Feb. 1928. By 1930, over forty-four hun-dred copies of *Parents on Probation* had been sold.

42. Miriam Van Waters, *Parents on Probation* (New York: New Repub-lic, 1927), 113–15; Dan Mebane to MVW, 30 July 1930, file 117.

43. MVW journal, 13 Jan. 1929, 8 Oct. 1928, 10 Oct. 1928, file 208,

Gladding-VW Papers; MVW to parents, 10 Sept. 1928, file 56; MVW to Mahan, 8 Oct. 1928, 2 Nov. 1928, file 251, Gladding-VW Papers; HW to MVW, 18 Nov. 1927, file 272, Gladding-VW Papers; Miriam Van Waters, "Why Hickman Hangs," *Survey,* 1 Oct. 1928, 20–23.

44. MVW to Mahan, 9 May 1928, 20 Sept. 1928, file 251 and HW to MVW, 6 Dec. 1928, file 275, Gladding-VW Papers.

45. HW to MVW, 23 Dec. 1928, file 275; 19 Jan. 1929, 17 Feb. 1929, file 276; 25 May 1929, 10 July 1929, 11 Aug. 1929, file 278, all in Gladding-VW Papers.

46. MVW to parents, 21 Oct. 1928, file 56; MVW to Dummer, 8 Oct. 1928, file 822, Dummer Papers; MVW journal, 4 Oct., 5 Oct., 6 Oct., and 7 Oct. 1928, file 208, Gladding-VW Papers.

47. MVW to parents, 2 Nov. 1928, 26 Oct. 1928, file 56.

48. MVW to parents, 28 May 1928, 2 Nov. 1928, 28 Dec. 1928, file 56 and 27 Nov. 1929, file 58; HW to MVW, 27 Jan. 1929, file 276, Gladding-VW Papers; MVW to Edna Mahan, 13 May 1928, file 251, Gladding-VW Papers; HW to MVW, 5 Sept. 1927, file 272; 18 July 1927, file 271; 18 Sept. 1927, file 272; 29 Feb. 1928, file 273, Gladding-VW Papers; medical report from Drs. Lissner and Rosenfelt, Aug. 1927, file 178. On Davis, see Bruce Henstell, *Sunshine and Wealth: Los Angeles in the Twenties and Thirties* (San Francisco: Chronicle Books, 1984), 20–21, 49–50.

49. MVW to parents, 17 Feb. 1929, file 57; MVW journal, 21 Feb. 1928, file 206, Gladding-VW Papers.

50. MVW to parents, 20 May 1928, file 56; 17 March 1929, file 57.

51. HW to MVW, 25 Feb. 1929, file 276; 20 March 1929, 24 March 1929, 31 March 1929, file 277, Gladding-VW Papers. HW had determined to return home to Switzerland, and he looked forward to this "sacred pilgrimage" as his final visit with her in California.

52. MVW to parents, 12 June, 21 June 1929, file 57; program for National Conference of Social Work, June 26–July 3, 1929, San Francisco, file 581. MVW ran against C. M. Bookman of Cincinnati (*Los Angeles Times,* 29 June 1929).

53. MVW to parents, 21 June 1929, 5 July 1929, file 57; MVW, "The New Morality of the Social Worker," ms., file 472, and reprinted in *Opportunity* (Sept. 1929), file 174.

54. NCSW, *Conference Bulletin* 33:2 (Feb. 1930): 10–11 and 33:4 (Aug. 1930): 2, file 582; *Opportunity,* Sept. 1929, in file 174; Bess to Maud VW, 12 July 1924, file 28; MVW to parents, 18 July 1929, file 57.

55. MVW to parents, 8 May 1929, file 57; letters to Jack MacFarland in file 173, and GT to Mrs. MacFarland, 21 June 1928, file 173; MVW to parents, 9 March 1929, file 57; 6 Dec. 1930, file 59.

56. On the Children's Bureau, see Robin Muncy, *Creating a Female Dominion in American Reform: 1890–1935* (New York: Oxford University Press, 1991).

57. MVW to parents, 18 Sept. 1929, file 58; HW to MVW, 2 Oct. 1929, file 278, Gladding-VW Papers.

58. MVW to parents, 9 June 1929, file 57; 22 Oct. 1929, 26 Oct. 1929

and 1 Nov. 1929, file 58; MVW to Dummer, 23 Nov. 1929, file 822, Dummer Papers. The other members of the commission were Henry Anderson, Newton Baker, Ada Comstock, William Grubb, William Kenyon, Monte Lemann, Frank Loesch, Kenneth Mackintosh, Paul McCormick, and Roscoe Pound (National Commission on Law Observance and Enforcement, *Report on the Child Offender in the Federal System of Justice*, no. 6, 28 May 1931 [Washington: Government Printing Office, 1931], 6).

59. MVW journal, 5 May 1929, file 208, Gladding-VW Papers; MVW to parents, 23 Nov. 1929, 27 Nov. 1929, file 58; Dummer to MVW, 27 Nov. 1929, file 822, Dummer Papers; *Los Angeles Times*, 27 Nov. 1929, 14 Dec. 1929.

60. MVW to parents, 11 Dec. 1929, file 58.

61. MVW to parents, 29 Nov. 1929, file 58; *Los Angeles Times*, 21 Jan. 1928. Ethel Sturges Dummer also expressed disillusionment with the juvenile court (Dummer to MVW, 20 Nov. 1933, file 823, Dummer Papers).

62. Miriam Van Waters, "Philosophical Trends in Social Work," in *Proceedings of the National Conference of Social Work* (Chicago: University of Chicago Press, 1930), 3–19, quote p. 19.

63. MVW's board and committee memberships for 1930–31 appear in file 528.

CHAPTER EIGHT

1. MVW to Dummer, 25 Feb. 1929, file 822, Dummer Papers. The term "house of life," which recurs in MVW's journals after 1934, may come from a sonnet sequence of that title by nineteenth-century British poet Dante Gabriel Rossetti. The poems emphasize the notion of soul partnership that became increasingly important to Van Waters at midlife. "The House of Life" appears in *The Works of Dante Gabriel Rossetti* (London: Ellis, 1911), 74–108. On the appeal of Rossetti's poetry for American women, see Helen Lefkowitz Horowitz, "'Nous Autres': Reading, Passion, and the Creation of M. Carey Thomas," *Journal of American History* 79 (June 1992): 68–95.

2. MVW to parents, 1 Oct. 1922, file 50; 4 Feb. 1925, 19 July 1925, file 53; 18 April 1926, file 54.

3. MVW to parents, 1 Oct. 1922, file 50; 6 Nov. 1925, file 53; 27 Sept. 1930, file 59; 8 Feb. 1931, file 26; 8 Feb. 1931, file 26; George Van Waters (hereafter GVW) to MVW, 20 Nov. 1930, file 105.

4. Ruth, the second child, seemed to be the most independent. She and her husband, Norman Burton, an accountant, settled outside of Chicago in 1918 and moved with their children (George, Bobby, and Peggy) to Buffalo, New York, in the late 1920s. MVW maintained warm relations with the Burton family, sending the children presents and visiting when possible, but she had only a long-distance influence on their lives.

5. GVW to MVW, 19 Jan. 1920, file 105; MVW to GVW, 25 Jan. 1920, file 80; MVW to parents, 14 Feb. 1920, file 48; newsclipping on Van Waters and Rogers, 1926, file 103. George had been attending the University of Oregon before the war. He and his wife, Helen, later had three daughters—Barbara, Nancy, and Miriam, the youngest named after his sister.

6. MVW to parents, undated 1920, file 79; MVW to Dummer, 29 April 1924, and Dummer to MVW, 30 April 1924, file 820, Dummer Papers; MVW to parents, 22 March 1922, file 50. Beckie married Lee Bartholomew, who entered the lumber industry in Seattle. They lived in Buffalo, Cleveland, and Savannah with their three children, Richard, Ann, and Jack.

7. Maud VW to Beckie, 8 Oct. 1919, box 2, and GBVW to Maud VW, 2 Feb. 1921, box 1, GBVW Papers.

8. MVW to parents, 22 March 1922, file 50; RVW interview, 11 Sept 1989.

9. RVW interview, 11 Sept. 1989; RVW to parents, 13 Jan. 1926, file 106.

10. RVW to parents, 6 May 1927, 2 Nov. 1927, file 106.

11. MVW to parents, 18 Nov. 1928, file 56; 24 July 1929, file 57; 17 Nov. 1929, file 58; 30 Jan. 1930, 4 March 1930, file 59; 6 Dec. 1931, 24 June 1930, file 62.

12. MVW to parents, 6 Dec. 1931, file 62; 15 Aug. 1930, file 59; undated March 1931, file 106; MVW journal, 25 Aug. 1936, file 213, Gladding-VW Papers; RVW to parents, 25 Aug. 1930, file 106. Professionally Bert used her family name, usually written as Green rather than the original Groen.

13. MVW to parents, 24 June 1931, 22 Sept. 1931, file 62.

14. MVW journal, 6 Aug. 1929, file 208, Gladding-VW Papers; MVW to parents, 21 June 1929, file 57; 11 Aug. 1929, file 58; MVW to Edna Mahan, 21 June 1929, file 252, Gladding-VW Papers.

15. MVW to parents, 21 June 1929, 21 July 1929, file 57; 11 Aug. 1929, file 58; MVW journal, 8 June 1929, 20 July 1929, file 208, Gladding-VW Papers.

16. See June Axinn, "Jessie Taft," and Dorothy M. Brown, "Mabel Walker Willebrandt," in Barbara Sicherman and Carol Hurd Green, eds., *Notable American Women: The Modern Period* (Cambridge: Harvard University Press, Belknap Press, 1980), 674, 736.

17. MVW to parents, 21 July 1929, file 57; MVW to Alma Holzschuh, 18 May 1932, file 119; guardianship papers in possession of Richard J. Hildebrandt (Van Waters' grandson). The California adoption statutes, which allowed adoption by "any adult person," appear in California State Library, *California Laws Relating to Women and Children* (Sacramento: California State Library, 1926), 31, 131. I am grateful to historian Barbara Melosh for clarifying state adoption law during this period.

18. MVW to Edna Mahan, undated Aug. 1929, file 252, Gladding-VW Papers; MVW to parents, 21 July 1929, file 57; MVW to Edna Mahan, 21 June 1929, file 252, Gladding-VW Papers; State of Ohio, Bureau of Vital Statistics, Certificate of Birth, in possession of author. MVW later wrote in her journal that Sarah's mother had died in childbirth (vol. 6, 27 Aug. 1941), but the mother was still living two weeks after the birth, when the certificate was filed.

19. MVW journal, 8 June 1929, 20 July 1929, 1 Aug. 1929, file 208, 14 Sept. 1929, file 209, 5 March 1930, file 209, and 24 Oct. 1943, file 219, all in Gladding-VW Papers.

20. MVW to parents, 21 July 1929, file 57; 11 Aug. 1929, file 58.

21. MVW to parents, 11 Aug. 1929, 18 Aug. 1929, file 58; MVW journal, 20 July 1929, file 209, Gladding-VW Papers.

22. MVW to parents, 21 July 1929, file 57; 1 Aug. 1929, 11 Aug. 1929, 18 Aug. 1929, file 58.

23. MVW to parents, 11 Aug. 1929, file 58; MVW to Mahan, 1 Aug. 1929, file 209, Gladding-VW Papers; MVW to parents, 25 Aug. 1929, file 58.

24. MVW to parents, 21 July 1929, file 57; 18 Aug. 1929, file 58.

25. MVW to parents, 18 Aug. 1929, 10 Sept. 1929, file 58; 23 Feb. 1930, file 59.

26. MVW to parents, 5 Sept. 1929, undated Sept. 1929, file 58; Elizabeth Woods to GBVW, 9 Feb. 1931, box 3, GBVW Papers; MVW journal, 25 Aug. and 27 Aug. 1929, file 209, Gladding-VW Papers.

27. MVW to parents, 17 Sept. 1929, 18 Sept. 1929, file 58; MVW journal, 16 Oct. 1944, file 219, 4 Aug. 1929, file 208, 18 Aug. 1929, file 209, Gladding-VW Papers.

28. MVW journal, 4 Aug. 1929, file 208, 18 Aug. 1929, 15 Sept. 1929, file 209, Gladding-VW Papers; MVW to parents, 18 Sept. 1929, file 58.

29. MVW to parents, 14 Nov. 1929, 16 Nov. 1929, file 58. For insight into the reproduction of maternal longing, see Alice Miller, *Prisoners of Childhood: The Drama of the Gifted Child and the Search for the True Self* (New York: Basic Books, 1981). Miller's analysis could easily apply to MVW: "A mother such as we once urgently needed—empathic and open, understanding and understandable, available and usable, transparent, clear, without unintelligible contradictions—such a mother was never ours, indeed she could not exist; for every mother carries with her a bit of her 'unmastered past,' which she unconsciously hands on to her child. Each mother can only react empathically to the extent that she has become free of her own childhood, and she is forced to react without empathy to the extent that, by denying the vicissitudes of her early life, she wears invisible chains" (28).

30. MVW journal, 5 March 1930, file 209, Gladding-VW Papers, MVW to Edna Mahan, 17 Nov. 1929, file 252, Gladding-VW Papers; MVW to parents, 22 Nov. 1929, 26 Nov. 1929, file 58; Bess Woods to Van Waters family, 1 Jan. 1930, file 28, referring to MVW as "Bob" and "Bobbie"; MVW to parents, 26 June 1930, file 62; Elizabeth Bode to MVW, e.g., undated April 1930, 30 June 1930, file 247, Gladding-VW Papers.

31. MVW to parents, 22 Sept. 1931, 14 Sept. 1931, 9 Oct. 1931, file 62; Maud VW to GBVW, undated 1931, box 2, GBVW Papers; MVW to Dummer, 8 Nov. 1931, file 822, Dummer Papers.

32. MVW to Edna Mahan, 29 Oct. 1929, file 252, Gladding-VW Papers.

CHAPTER NINE

1. MVW to parents, 31 Oct. 1930, file 59; GT to MVW, 31 Oct. 1930, file 261, and 4 Nov. 1930, file 262, Gladding-VW Papers. On courtship letters, see Karen Lystra, *Searching the Heart: Women, Men, and Romantic*

Love in Nineteenth-Century America (New York: Oxford University Press, 1989), esp. chap. 1.

2. Northern Monmouth County Branch of the American Association of University Women, *A Triangle of Land: A History of the Site and the Founding of Brookdale Community College* (Lincroft, N.J.: Brookdale Community College, 1978), 189–90 (hereafter AAUW, *Triangle*).

3. This account of the early lives of GT and Lewis Steenrod Thompson draws from "Profile: Mrs. Thompson of Brookdale Farm," *Welfare Reporter* (New Jersey Dept. of Institutions and Agencies), 5:1 (May 1950): 6, 10; "Friends Pay Farewell Tribute to Mrs. Geraldine L. Thompson," *Welfare Reporter* (April 1957): 3–4; "Grand Lady of Brookdale Turns 95," *Red Bank (N.J.) Daily Register,* 3 March 1967, 1; "Shore Pioneers," *Asbury (N.J.) Park Sunday Press,* 13 April 1967; and the *New York Times* obituaries for Lewis S. Thompson (26 March 1936) and GT (10 Sept. 1967). Information on the Thompsons is compiled in AAUW, *Triangle.* GT also had a brother, Gerald Morgan.

4. AAUW, *Triangle,* 38; Elisabeth Thompson Babcock to Leigh Cook, 28–31 March 1974, Geraldine Thompson File, New Jersey Collection, Learning Resources Center, Brookdale Community College, Red Bank, New Jersey (hereafter GT File, BCC); Geraldine Boone to author, 6 March 1995. Shortly after their marriage the couple adopted Anne Thompson, a twelve-year-old orphaned cousin of Lewis Thompson. GT then bore her first child, William Payne Thompson III. When her sister-in-law died, she took in the four Preston children (William, Jerome, Evelyn, and Lewis). Subsequently GT bore Elisabeth (Betty), Geraldine (Puss), and Lewis Jr. (AAUW, *Triangle,* 38–39).

5. Elisabeth T[hompson] Babcock to Dr. Ervin Harlacher (President, Brookdale Community College), 8 Dec. 1971, and to Mrs. Leigh Cook (Asbury Park Press), 17 July 1974, both in GT File, BCC; AAUW, *Triangle,* 53–54. While some of her children and grandchildren respected Thompson, others found her domineering, manipulative, and selfish. She clearly evoked strong feelings in those whose lives she touched (Geraldine Boone to author, 6 March 1995).

6. "Grand Lady of Brookdale," *Daily Register,* 3 March 1967; obituary, *Asbury Park Press,* 10 Sept. 1967, 1; Rhoda Southall (Deputy Director, Monmouth County Welfare Board) to Mrs. Rowan Boone (GT's daughter "Puss"), 5 June 1946, Monmouth County Organization for Social Services file (MCOSS), GT File, BCC; League of Women Voters of Monmouth County, *Monmouth County New Jersey : A Citizen's Guide* (Tinton Falls, N.J.: Park Avenue Printer, 1986), 59; AAUW, *Triangle,* 76.

7. Felice D. Gordon, *After Winning: The Legacy of the New Jersey Suffragists, 1920–1947* (New Brunswick, N.J.: Rutgers University Press, 1986), 54–56; obituary, *New York Times,* 10 Sept. 1967; GT to Republican National Committee, 12 Oct. 1927, file 115; GT quoted in AAUW, *Triangle,* 83. On Ruth Morgan, obituary, *New York Times,* 14 March 1934.

8. AAUW, *Triangle,* 83–85. On their lasting collaboration, see, e.g., GT to Eleanor Roosevelt, 21 Feb. 1956, and Eleanor Roosevelt to GT, 6 Dec.

1961, General Correspondence, Joseph Lash Papers, the Franklin D. Roosevelt Library, Hyde Park, New York (hereafter FDR Library).

9. AAUW, *Triangle,* 78–82; interview with Mary Q. Hawkes, 12 Sept. 1989; MVW to Dummer, 5 Aug. 1928, file 822, Dummer Papers.

10. MVW to GT, 31 July 1927, GT to MVW, 4 Nov. 1927, file 261, and HW to MVW, 9 Dec. 1927, file 272, all in Gladding-VW Papers.

11. GT to MVW, 14 Jan. 1928, file 261, Gladding-VW Papers; Medical report from Drs. Lissner and Rosenfelt, Aug. 1927, file 178.

12. MVW to parents, 17 Dec. 1928, file 56; 22 July 1930, file 59.

13. Helen Lefkowitz Horowitz, *The Power and Passion of M. Carey Thomas* (New York: Alfred A. Knopf, 1994), esp. 278–79, 287; Leila J. Rupp, "Sexuality and Separatism: The International Women's Movement in the Early 20th Century," ts.; and Susan Ware, *Partner and I: Molly Dewson, Feminism, and New Deal Politics* (New Haven: Yale University Press, 1987).

14. GT to MVW, 4 Nov. 1930, file 262, Gladding-VW Papers and GT to MVW, 28 Oct. 1939, file 129; GT to MVW, 22 Sept. 1945, file 136; GT to MVW, 30 June 1946, file 137; MVW to GT, 4 July 1946, file 137; MVW journal, vol. 2, 11 May 1934. GT probably destroyed MVW's letters. One of GT's adult grandchildren recalled that her grandmother kept a large number of letters from MVW under her bed, but no family members located these letters after GT's death (Geraldine Boone to author, undated 1989; Ann Bristow to author, undated 1989; telephone interview with Geraldine Boone from Princeton, N. J., 17 Feb. 1995).

15. MVW journal, 4 Oct. 1928, 11 Dec. 1928, file 208, Gladding-VW Papers; MVW to parents, 22 Oct. 1929, file 58; GT to MVW, 3 March 1929, file 261, Gladding-VW Papers.

16. GT to MVW, 3 March 1929, undated June 1929, file 261, Gladding-VW Papers.

17. GT to MVW, 3 March 1929, file 158 and undated 1929, file 261, Gladding-VW Papers; MVW to parents, 16 March, 21 March, and 25 March 1930, file 59; MVW journal, 25 March 1930, file 209, Gladding-VW Papers. The visit may have been limited in time because Dummer was due to arrive (MVW to parents, 25 March 1930, file 59). The shift in MVW's relationship with Dummer appears also in letters of 19 Sept. 1930 and 3 Oct. 1930 (file 822, Dummer Papers) in which MVW clarified why she did not stay with Dummer in Chicago but instead sought solitude at Hull House.

18. MVW to Edna Mahan, 30 Sept. 1930, file 253, Gladding-VW Papers; MVW to parents, 27 Sept. 1930, file 59; GT to MVW, 31 Oct. 1930, file 261, and 4 Nov. 1930, file 262, Gladding-VW Papers; GT to MVW, 31 Oct. 1930, file 261 (referring to her earlier explanations of church bells and justice of the peace during the summer); MVW journal, 27 Sept. 1930, file 209v, Gladding-VW Papers. Van Waters used the phrase "hills of life" to represent an elevated spiritual state that she and Geraldine aspired to, above the "foothills" of mere mortals, where angels experienced eternal love. The phrase comes from a poem, "Thoughts in Separation," by the nineteenth-century British writer Alice Meynell. (*The Poems of Alice Meynell: Com-*

plete Edition [London: Burns, Oates and Washbourne, 1923]). Van Waters quoted the poem in her journal for 10 Jan. 1934 (vol. 2); here and in a later entry she combined it with Rossetti's phrase "house of life" to represent "what contributes most to enjoyment, and courage: to concepts and to understanding—and grasp of essences" (MVW journal, vol. 2, 13 Jan 1934).

19. GT to MVW, 14 Aug. 1930, file 261, Gladding-VW Papers; MVW to parents, 15 Aug. 1930, 16 Oct. 1930, 31 Oct. 1930, file 59; 25 Aug. 1930, file 60; GT to Maud VW, before 27 Oct. 1930, box 2, GBVW Papers; AAUW, *Triangle,* 65.

20. GT to MVW, 28 Oct. 1930, file 261, and 7 Nov. 1930, file 262, Gladding-VW Papers.

21. GT to MVW, 21 Nov. 1930, file 263, 24 Nov. 1930, file 264, 1 Dec. and 3 Dec. 1930, file 265, 12 Dec. and 18 Dec. 1930, file 266, Gladding-VW Papers. GT also did not like to write to MVW when someone else was present. "Sweetheart I've been caught by Lew's secretary," explained an interruption in one letter (6 Dec. 1930, file 265, Gladding-VW Papers).

22. GT to MVW, 24 Nov. 1930, file 264, 1 Dec., 7 Dec., and 9 Dec. 1930, file 265, 14 Dec. and 20 Dec. 1930, file 266, all in Gladding-VW Papers.

23. GT to MVW, 4 Nov. 1930, file 262, 31 Oct. 1930, file 261, 29 Nov. 1930, file 264, all in Gladding-VW Papers.

24. GT to MVW, 31 Oct. 1930, file 261, 10 Nov. and 6 Nov. 1930, file 262, all in Gladding-VW Papers; MVW journal, 27 Sept. 1930, 11 June 1931, file 211, Gladding-VW Papers. On self-discipline in women's erotic relationships, see Martha Vicinus, "Distance and Desire: English Boarding-School Friendships," *Signs* 9 (summer 1984): 600–622.

25. GT to MVW, 6 Nov. 1930, file 262, Gladding-VW Papers. The marriage may have accommodated other relationships; relatives rumored that Lew may have had women lovers, and that Geraldine had fallen in love with a woman before she met Miriam (telephone interview with Geraldine Boone, 17 Feb. 1995).

26. GT to MVW, 6 Nov. 1930, file 262, 13 Dec. 1930, file 266, and 11 Nov. 1930, file 262, all in Gladding-VW Papers.

27. MVW to Edna Mahan, 26 May 1931, file 254, Gladding-VW Papers; GT to MVW, 26 Nov. 1930, file 264, Gladding-VW Papers (citing a letter from MVW and adding parenthetically "not an accurate quotation").

28. GT to MVW, 11 Nov. 1930, file 262, Gladding-VW Papers.

29. Ibid. On Lew see, e.g., GT to MVW, 4 Nov. 1930, file 262, 31 Oct. 1930, file 261, 11 Nov. 1930, file 262, and included in a letter to MVW, a letter from Lewis S. Thompson to GT, 13 June (1924 or 1934 unclear), expressing their love, Gladding-VW Papers.

30. Enclosed with GT to MVW, 11 Nov. 1930, file 262, Gladding-VW Papers.

31. HW had been unsuccessful in his search for a mate, and he still harbored hopes about Miriam. In 1930, for example, he wrote "Miriam— I am not begging for love. If it doesn't mean to you what it used to—if you no longer need me—I'll go my way in silence. But—if you still care for me

that way—totally—just as I am—body and soul—let's be together once more—if it can be done without endangering Sarah's security." (HW to MVW, 24 July 1930, file 279, 17 Nov. 1930, file 280, Gladding-VW Papers).

32. GT to MVW, 29 Nov. 1930 (Sat. 9 A.M.), file 264, Gladding-VW Papers. MVW eventually sent HW's letter, for it appeared in GT's correspondence.

33. HW to MVW, 14 Aug. 1931, file 280, Gladding-VW Papers. MVW acknowledgment of receipt of letters from GT suggests a comfortable resolution of the triangle (GT to MVW, 12 Nov. 1930, file 263, Gladding-VW Papers). HW married twenty-three-year-old Margaret Steidle (MVW to parents, undated Sept. 1931, file 62).

34. GT to MVW, 11 Nov., 13 Nov. 1930, 21 Dec. 1930, file 266, Gladding-VW Papers, quoting MVW.

35. GT to MVW, 26 Nov. 1930, file 264, 12 Nov. and 14 Nov. 1930, file 263, Gladding-VW Papers.

36. GT to MVW, 12 Nov. and 14 Nov. 1930, file 263, Gladding-VW Papers.

37. GT to MVW, 21 Nov. 1930, file 263, 24 Nov. and 26 Nov. 1930, file 264, Gladding-VW Papers.

38. MVW journal, 11 June 1931, file 211, Gladding-VW Papers.

39. MVW journal, 19 May 1931, file 211, Gladding-VW Papers.

40. On women's intimate relationships, see n. 22, chap. 6, and Ware, *Partner and I,* esp. 57. Bode to MVW, 8 Sept. 1935, file 125, tells of Miss Shontz and Evie.

41. On gender roles and lesbianism, see Esther Newton, "The Mythic Mannish Lesbian: Radclyffe Hall and the New Women," *Signs* 9 (summer 1984): 557–75; Carroll Smith-Rosenberg, "The New Woman as Androgyne: Social Disorder and Gender Crisis, 1870–1936," in *Disorderly Conduct: Visions of Gender in Victorian America* (New York: Alfred A. Knopf, 1985), 245–96; George Chauncey Jr., "From Sexual Inversion to Homosexuality: Medicine and the Changing Conceptualization of Female Deviance," *Salamagundi* (fall–winter 1983): 114–46; and Estelle B. Freedman, "The Prison Lesbian and the Construction of the 'Aggressive Female Homosexual,' 1913–1960" (paper presented at the annual meeting of the American Historical Association, San Francisco, 8 Jan. 1994).

42. MVW to Edna Mahan, 20 July 1930, file 253, Gladding-VW Papers; Katherine B. Davis, *Factors in the Sex Life of Twenty-two Hundred Women* (New York: Harper and Row, 1929), 312, 295, 280. The data showed that 28 percent of the women's college graduates and 20 percent of those from coeducational schools recognized sexual components in their relations; in addition, almost equal numbers had enjoyed intense emotional attachments that involved kissing and hugging.

43. MVW to parents, 6 Dec. 1930, file 59; 3 May 1931, file 61; 14 June 1931 and 2 Aug. 1931, file 62.

44. *Los Angeles Times,* 9 July 1931; Sanford Bates to MVW, 10 July 1931, file 62; letters to Wickersham from Adolf Meyer (20 April 1931), William A. White (18 April 1931), and Grace Abbott (21 April 1931), all in file 822,

Dummer Papers; National Commission on Law Observance and Enforcement, *Report on the Child Offender in the Federal System of Justice*, no. 6, 28 May 1931 (Washington: Government Printing Office, 1931), esp. 154–57.

45. MVW to parents, 17 Jan. 1931, file 61; 9 July 1931, 16 July 1931, file 62. MVW also turned down an offer to write a syndicated column about juvenile delinquents for the Hearst newspaper chain, in part because the reputation of the Hearst papers as sensationalistic might keep her from getting a government job. "One has to walk a tightrope between the fate of Judge [Ben] Lindsey and a 'respectable' career," she explained to her parents (13 July 1931, file 62). She did apply for a position as chief probation officer for a Los Angeles social work organization, an act that startled GT, who could not see why she would want the job (MVW to parents, 6 Dec. 1930, file 59, and GT to MVW, 8 Dec. 1930, file 265, Gladding-VW Papers). To her parents she contended that she wanted to be offered a job in California, but her friends there did not have the political power to arrange one (4 July 1931, file 62).

46. MVW to Dummer, 14 May 1931, file 822, Dummer Papers; MVW to parents, 13 Nov. and 14 Nov. 1931, file 62; HW to MVW, 3 Dec. 1931, file 119.

47. HW to MVW, 14 Aug. 1931, file 280, Gladding-VW Papers; HW to MVW, 3 Dec. 1931, file 119; 26 Dec. 1923, file 122 (significantly, she deposited these letters with her papers, although she kept all of his earlier correspondence in her possession). MVW seemed skeptical about HW's remorse. "As to Hans," she wrote in her journal six months later, "the price you mention, the price you say you were unwilling to pay. You were not unwilling: you were blind to the necessity of the process" (21 June 1932, file 211, Gladding-VW Papers).

48. MVW to Dummer, 12 Jan. 1921, file 819, Dummer Papers; MVW journal, 24 Dec. 1931, file 211, Gladding-VW Papers.

49. MVW to parents, 14 Nov., 24 Nov., and 27 Nov. 1931, file 62; MVW to Warren Stearns, 12 Dec. 1931, Harvard Crime Survey Correspondence, Felix Frankfurter Papers, container 140, microfilm n. s. 3967, reel 87; MVW, "Introduction," ts. memoir, file 508.

CHAPTER TEN

1. MVW journal, vol. 2, 18 April 1934, and 5 Oct. 1936, file 213, Gladding-VW Papers.

2. Estelle B. Freedman, *Their Sisters' Keepers: Women's Prison Reform in America, 1830–1930* (Ann Arbor: University of Michigan Press, 1981), 67–74, 134–36; Mary Bularzik, "Sex, Crime, and Justice: Women in the Criminal Justice System of Massachusetts, 1900–1950" (Ph.D. diss., Brandeis University, 1982), 165.

3. On the nineteenth-century inmates, see Freedman, *Their Sisters' Keepers,* 80–81; Sheldon Glueck and Eleanor T. Glueck, *Five Hundred Delinquent Women* (1934; rpt., New York: Kraus, 1965), 301; Harvard Survey of Criminal Justice—Penal Section, "Reformatory for Women Population

Study of Women in the Institution on January 1, 1928," Sheldon Glueck Papers, Harvard Law School, Manuscript Division, Cambridge, Mass. (hereafter "Reformatory for Women, 1928"). Only 4 percent had committed crimes against the person, and 16 percent served for crimes against property, mostly larceny.

4. Bularzik, "Sex, Crime, and Justice," 173, 281–92; Glueck, *Delinquent Women* (based on the 1925 data); "Reformatory for Women, 1928." Data on the 1930s (see tables 1 and 2) was compiled from Mass. Dept. of Corrections, *Annual Reports* and *Statistical Reports,* 1934 (table 10, 50–51, table 23, 70–71, and table 13, 54–55) and 1936 (table 11, 66–67, table 25, 88–89, and table 15, 72–73):

Table 1 Population of Framingham Reformatory, by Type of Offense

	Person (%)	Property (%)	Public Order (%)
		Offense Against	
1934	0.4	5.7	93.9
1936	2.0	6.7	91.3

Table 2 Population of Massachusetts Reformatories Serving First Term

	Framingham (%)	Men's Reformatory (%)
1934	62.7	35.6
1936	54.5	32.7

On the increase in prostitution during the depression, see Bascom Johnson and Paul M. Kinsie, "Prostitution in the United States," *Journal of Social Hygiene* 19 (Dec. 1933): 467–91.

5. David J. Rothman, *Conscience and Convenience: The Asylum and Its Alternatives in Progressive America* (Boston: Little, Brown, 1980), 407 and chap. 11 for detailed treatment of Norfolk; Larry E. Sullivan, *The Prison Reform Movement: Forlorn Hope* (Boston: Twayne, 1990), 37–40, 58; Nicole Hahn Rafter, *Partial Justice: Women in State Prisons, 1800–1935* (Boston: Northeastern University Press, 1985), esp. chaps. 4, 6. On New Deal politics, see Susan Ware, *Women and the New Deal* and Steve Fraser and Gary Gerstle, eds., *The Rise and Fall of the New Deal Order, 1930–1980* (Princeton: Princeton University Press, 1989).

6. Louis Lyons in *Boston Globe,* 28 Dec. 1931, file 406; MVW to parents, 21 March 1932, file 63; MVW journal, 23 Jan. 1932, file 211, Gladding-VW Papers. The Gluecks remained loyal to Jessie Hodder, who had cooperated with their research and who had not been impressed by Van Waters.

7. MVW, ts. memoir, file 508, fragment 15; MVW to parents, 16 Jan. 1932, file 63; MVW journal, 24 Dec. 1931, 26 Jan. 1932, 20 March 1932, 21 March 1932, all in file 211, Gladding-VW Papers.

8. Nancy Newell to Sanford Bates, 1 July 1935, file 181. When MVW took over, she visited the Norfolk Prison Colony for Men and declared that

its worst quarters were superior to Framingham's best (MVW to Martha Falconer, 5 Feb. 1932, file 177).

9. "Preamble of Ten Year Events, 1932–1942," file 245; Edith Stedman, "Dog's Body at Sherborn Prison: Four Years behind Bars," *Radcliffe Quarterly* 73:4 (Dec. 1987): 9; interviews with Harriet Gunning and Margaret van Wagenen, 18 Oct. 1992, Framingham, Mass.

10. MVW, ts. memoir, 14–18, file 508.

11. MVW, ts. memoir, fragment 15, file 508; Joseph Fulling Fishman, "Madam Warden," *Today,* 25 May 1935, 21.

12. Miriam Van Waters, "Delinquency on the Distaff Side," in Marjorie Bell, ed., *Probation and Parole Progress: Yearbook* (New York: National Probation Assoc., 1941), 118–23; Anne Gladding to MVW, 23 Feb. 1938, file 330.

13. MVW journal, 8 July 1936, 20 July 1936, 23 July 1936, file 213, 24 Nov. 1944, file 219, Gladding-VW Papers.

14. MVW, ts. memoir, c. 1957, file 508, 11–13. The staff did not always absorb Van Waters' lessons. Many continued to call the inmates "girls," taking care never to call staff by that name (interview with Harriet Gunning, 26 March 1993, Ashland, Mass.).

15. MVW journal, vol. 4, 1 June 1936.

16. MVW journal, 30 Nov. 1937, file 213, Gladding-VW Papers; Mrs. Mary Lena Watson, quoted in MVW, ts. memoir, fragment 15, file 508.

17. MVW journal, 27 March 1932, file 211, Gladding-VW Papers; "Preamble of Ten Year Events, 1932–1942," file 245; MVW, intern-staff meeting notes, 7 Oct. 1936, file 238; MVW journal, 22 March 1932, file 211, and 8 Nov. 1948, file 220, Gladding-VW Papers.

18. Elizabeth Borton, "Inmates Get Students' Status at Framingham Reformatory," *Boston Herald,* 23 Oct. 1932; Anne Gladding, "Impressions of the Reformatory, n.d. (c. Aug. 1932), file 235; "Impressions of the Reformatory," 30 Sept. 1932, file 235.

19. MVW journal, vol. 1, 5 Oct. and 8 Oct. 1932.

20. MVW journal, vol. 2, 1 Aug. and 3 Aug. 1934; *Boston Herald Traveler,* 4 Aug. 1934. She faced another food riot in Aug. 1936, the source of a nightmare in which she faced death and survived by refusing to panic (MVW journal, 1 Aug. 1936, file 213, Gladding-VW Papers).

21. The descriptions in the preceding paragraphs are taken from interviews with Margaret van Wagenen, 31 July 1989, Ashland, Mass., and van Wagenen and Harriet Gunning, 18 Oct. 1992, Framingham, Mass., and from various MVW journals. On windows: Connick to MVW, 10 April 1934, and MVW to Francis Sayre, 15 Sept. 1934, file 179.

22. Historian's report, Student Assembly, 2 June 1932, file 357; *Framingham News,* 28 Oct. 1940, file 186; Public Document No. 115, the Commonwealth of Massachusetts, *Annual Report of the Commissioner of Corrections for the Year Ending 30 Nov. 1933* (Boston: Wright and Potter, 1933); Friends of Prisoners, 22 July 1940, file 243; MVW to Dummer, 20 Feb. 1940, file 823, Dummer Papers; MVW reminiscence of Frost visit in newsclipping, *Framingham News,* 11 Feb. 1963, Gladding-VW Papers. GT

probably contributed the money to the Friends of Prisoners, which in turn funded the psychiatrist (MVW to GT, 24 Jan. 1945, file 191).

23. MVW to parents, 23 Aug. 1932, file 64; Denison House worker to MVW, 21 June 1936, file 181; MVW journal, vol. 4, 15 March 1936; "General Plan for Women's Parole as Tentatively Adopted by Present Parole Board," 1 May 1942, file 188; Mrs. Hazel Rabbitt to Thomas Buckley, 21 May 1947, file 193.

24. MVW to GT, 3 Nov. 1942, file 188; MVW journal, vol. 2, 8 May 1934; Fishman, "Madam Warden," 20; description of intern program, c. 1936, file 238; MVW to parents, 8 Feb. 1933, file 65.

25. Margaret van Wagenen to Anne Gladding, 16 June 1936, file 181; Marjorie Nield to MVW, 13 May 1932, file 177; Margaret van Wagenen interview, 31 July 1989; interview with Lois Rice McWilliams, 18 Oct. 1992, Framingham, Mass.; various letters to MVW, file 181.

26. Anne Scott to MVW, 12 March 1938, file 184; interview with Pauline Orsi, 18 Oct. 1992, Framingham, Mass. In 1934 a male doctor served an internship at Framingham through the Rockefeller Institute and Harvard/ Children's Hospital (MVW to mother, 30 Sept. 1934, file 68), and in 1939 Van Waters sponsored a Czech refugee as an intern (MVW to Dummer, 2 July 1939, file 823, Dummer Papers). At the end of World War II, a former staff member who then worked for the American Friends Service Committee arranged internships at Framingham for pacifist students from Haverford College (Rachel Pickett to MVW, 14 April 1944, file 190).

27. MVW to Peg O'Keefe, 22 Feb. 1934, file 180; interview with "Irene Jenner," 15 Sept. 1989, Framingham, Mass. (all inmate names have been changed).

28. Harriet Gunning interview, 26 March 1993.

29. MVW to parents, 14 Aug. 1932, file 64; Hilda Hinkley, "Cell-Block into Greenroom," *Theatre Arts Monthly* 21:10 (Oct. 1938): 805–11; MVW journal, vol. 1, 1 Oct. 1932; 1 Oct. 1933, file 66; MVW journal, vol. 2, 29 Jan. 1934 and 17 April 1934; Catharine Bancroft Beatley, "Radcliffe Women at State's Prison," *Radcliffe Quarterly* (April 1935): 86–91, file 406; MVW to Helen Van Dyke, 20 Feb. 1933, file 122; Helen Dennison Smith, "Music in a Reformatory," *Radcliffe Quarterly* (April 1935): 90–91, file 406; Mrs. John Sloan to Amy Row, 17 May 1934, file 180. Beatley counted fourteen Radcliffe alumnae from the classes of 1905 through 1934 who worked at Framingham as interns or staff members. Several interns lived at the superintendent's house, and several members of her household served as interns, including Elizabeth Bode, who then became a staff member, and Sarah Van Waters, who was an intern during the summer of 1937.

30. Felix Frankfurter to MVW, 14 Dec. 1931, file 119; MVW to Elizabeth Thatcher, 16 Sept. 1935, file 181; "Notes on Staff Meeting," 13 Aug. 1934, file 237; MVW, "Problems concerning the Mental Health of Framingham— an Outline for Dr. Marianna Taylor," ms., 11 April 1938, file 241; interview with Rev. William Wiltenburg, 26 March 1993, Ashland, Mass.

31. MVW journal, vol. 1, 11 Oct. 1932; Jane [M.] Stetson to MVW, undated 1950, file 229.

32. Bode to MVW, 13 May 1934, file 248, MVW to Edna Mahan, 25 Sept. 1934, 22 Oct. 1934, file 254, Anne Gladding to MVW, undated 1933, file 6, staff member to "Dear Doctor," undated, and MVW journal, 5 March 1943, file 217, Gladding-VW Papers; and Helen Schnefel to MVW, 4 Oct. 1932, inmate to MVW, 6 Sept. 1932, file 177; MVW journal, vol. 2, 4 Jan. 1935, vol. 3, 5 Oct. 1935.

33. "Preamble of Ten Year Events, 1932–1942," file 245; student publications and writings, files 361, 369, 397; Thornton Wilder to MVW, 3 April 1939, file 185; MVW journal, 27 April 1943, 24 June 1943, file 217, and 1 July 1943, file 219, Gladding-VW Papers.

34. In 1940, for example, 232 of 369 inmates were in classes (*Annual Report of the Commissioner of Corrections,* Public Document No. 115, the Commonwealth of Massachusetts [1940], 38); inmate writings, file 365; MVW to Dummer, 11 May 1937, file 823, Dummer Papers; Dottie Green, obit., *New York Times,* 28 Oct. 1992; Sarah Ann Van Waters, "State Reformatory for Women: Framingham, Mass.," Jan. 1937, ts. in possession of Richard J. Hildebrandt; MVW to GT, 3 Nov. 1942, file 188; *Boston Herald Traveler,* 24 July 1935; *Harmony News,* July 1957.

35. Former inmate to MVW, April 1941, file 292 and 14 January 1944, file 293; MVW journal, vol. 7, 19 August 1945; Ruth F. Weinberg to MVW, 10 March 1947, file 193.

36. Austin MacCormick, quoted in newspaper clipping, 1949, file 407; Miriam Van Waters, "Progress at the Reformatory for Women," *Church Militant,* April 1952, 1–5; "Doctor Van Waters Speaks—Babies," WKOX radio script, 3 Oct. 1954, file 493; Mrs. Nancy Newell to Sanford Bates, 1 July 1935, file 181; 16 Jan. 1932, file 63.

37. MVW journal, 25 Dec. 1943, file 219, Gladding-VW Papers; *Annual Report,* 1934, 37; "Preamble of Ten Year Events, 1932–1942," file 245; *Boston Herald Traveler,* 6 March 1935, clipping in Framingham file, *Boston Herald Traveler* Newspaper Library Collection at Boston University, School of Public Communication (all further references to newsclippings from this collection are cited as BU SPC); MVW, "The Treatment of Sex Offenders," Ford Hall Forum speech, 20 Oct. 1957, file 495. On social workers' efforts to have white single mothers give up their babies for adoption, see Regina G. Kunzel, *Fallen Women, Problem Girls: Unmarried Mothers and the Professionalization of Social Work, 1890–1945* (New Haven: Yale University Press, 1993), chaps. 3 and 6.

38. MVW journal, 24 March 1931, file 211, Gladding-VW Papers; Superintendent, Reformatory for Women, *Annual Report* in Department of Correction *Annual Report of the Commissioner of Correction for the Year Ending Nov. 30, 1932* (Boston: Mass. Dept. of Correction, 1932), 36; MVW journal, vol. 2, 23 July 1934, and vol. 4, 13 Feb. 1936.

39. MVW to GT, 3 Nov. 1942, file 188; M. Kemper, "Life of the Mothers and Babies at the Massachusetts Reformatory for Women," 16 June 1936, file 238. The nursery also provided an informal laboratory for child study, e.g., Sibylle K. Escalona, "Feeding Disturbances in Very Young Children," *American Journal of Orthopsychiatry* (Jan. 1945): 76–80.

40. "A Convict Speaks," undated 1957, file 280; interview with Margaret van Wagenen, 31 July 1989.

41. "Notes on Public Hearing at State House, Room 433, before the Appointed Legislative Commission on Conditions at the Reformatory for Women, Framingham, Senator J. Elmer Callahan, Chairman," ts., 22 Nov. 1948, file 250; Elizabeth Borton, *Boston Herald,* 23 Oct. 1932; child of former student to "Aunt Miriam," 28 May 1971, file 350, with MVW handwritten explanation of practice on envelope; interview with Margaret van Wagenen, 31 July 1989. On child-centered institutions outside the United States, see Jennifer M. Pearson, "Centro Femenil: A Women's Prison in Mexico," *Social Justice* 20:3–4 (fall–winter 1993): 85–127.

42. Fishman, "Madam Warden," 21; MVW to parents, 15 Dec. 1937, file 73; MVW note, 11 April 1938, file 241.

43. Student to sister, 21 May 1933, file 271 (in letter from Nancy Newell to MVW).

44. "The Tapering Off Process from Institution to Community Living," ts. of speech, 12 Oct. 1950, file 487; *Boston American,* 30 Dec. 1932, file 406; student writings, file 357; interview with Rev. Wiltenburg, Pauline Orsi, and Harriet Gunning, March 26, 1993. Ashland, Mass.

45. "Reformatory for Women, 1928"; MVW journal, vol. 3, 8 Oct. 1935.

46. "Notes on Meeting of Research Group," 22 March 1933, file 236.

47. Glueck and Glueck, *Five Hundred Delinquent Women,* 120, 138.

48. "Reformatory for Women, 1928"; *Boston Herald Traveler,* 12 Nov. 1937, BU SPC; "Madam Warden," 20; MVW to parents, 7 Aug. 1932, file 64; MVW journal, 3 April 1945, file 219v, Gladding-VW Papers.

49. Elizabeth Bode, "Meeting with Work Girls," 23 Sept. 1934, file 237; MVW journal, vol. 5, 16 Feb. 1939, 17 Feb. 1939; *Boston Herald Traveler,* 24 March 1940, BU SPC.

50. MVW, Report on "favoritism," undated Nov. 1948, file 248; "Text of Van Waters' Reply," *Boston Sunday Globe,* 9 Jan 1949, file 408; MVW, book proposal, chap. 7, file 508.

51. The doctor's story is detailed in several documents in file 283, including a handwritten autobiography dated 12 Dec. 1946; MVW to "Dr. Cook," 2 Feb. 1933, and 8 May 1939, file 283; MVW journal, 18 July 1936, file 213v, 3 Oct. 1944, file 219, Gladding-VW Papers.

52. McDowell, 7 Jan. 1949, file 201; report, Nov. 1948, file 248; "In the Matter," 1901; letters from former student, April 1941, files 292–93; MVW journal, vol. 6, 27 Sept. 1941.

53. Interview with "Irene Jenner," 15 Sept. 1989.

54. Interview with Rev. William Wiltenburg, 26 March 1993.

55. Interview with "Irene Jenner," 15 Sept. 1989; interview with Margaret van Wagenen, 31 July 1989; Joan Sakalas, "Toward Fellow Sinners: An Ethical and Historical Exploration of the Penology of Miriam Van Waters" (M.A. thesis, Episcopal Divinity School, Cambridge, Mass., April 16, 1993), esp. 60; MVW journal, 10 Jan. 1944, file 219, Gladding-VW Papers.

56. On clinical trends, see e.g. Kunzel, *Fallen Women.*

57. 29 Sept. 1932, file 357.

58. Inmate writings, file 369; 25 Sept. 1931, file 64.

59. Inmate to MVW, 14 Jan. 1944, file 293; inmate writings, file 189; Anne Gladding to MVW, 17 March 1944, file 189; inmate to MVW, 5 June 1952, file 282.

60. Inmate to MVW, 30 May 1948, file 350; inmate's father to MVW, 19 July 1948, file 195; inmate to MVW, 9 June 1946, 17 Sept. 1946, file 283; inmate to MVW, 5 June 1952, file 282; inmate to MVW, 17 March 1946, file 288.

61. E.g., Amy Rowe, the art intern whom MVW privately termed "helpless" for losing several students on an outing, later turned against the superintendent; Mary Curran hated the term *students* and the respect afforded these "bums" who stole or drank; MVW suspended an officer who told a black inmate that she was not fit to live with white girls. (MVW journal, 11 July 1937, 9 Jan. 1938, 8 March 1938, file 213, Gladding-VW Papers, Amy Rowe to Sheldon Glueck, 2 January 1949 and 20 Feb 1949, box 111, file 8, Sheldon Glueck Papers, Harvard Law School, Cambridge, Mass.)

62. Interview with "Alice May," 15 Sept. 1989; MVW journal, 18 April 1937, 11 July 1937, file 213, Gladding-VW Papers.

63. Jack Black to MVW, undated 1932, and clipping from Carmel, Calif. newspaper, file 595; MVW journal, 14 Oct. 1936, 28 Jan. 1938, 24 June 1938, file 213, Gladding-VW Papers.

CHAPTER ELEVEN

1. Interview with Margaret van Wagenen, 31 July, 1989; MVW journal, vol. 2, 17 May 1934.

2. For an example of her schedule, see MVW journal, vol. 3, 26 Oct. 1935. In Jan. 1933, MVW suffered a fractured skull after her horse, Lady, slipped on the ice and threw her; she was riding again by June (MVW journal, vol. 1, 20 June 1933).

3. Priscilla Reed to MVW, 10 March 1955, file 225; enclosure in Helen Gray to MVW, 19 July 1971, file 228; interview with Margaret van Wagenen, 31 July 1989. Another observer compared her "purposeful, kind of controlled compassion" to Eleanor Roosevelt (Lawrence H. Fuchs, letter to author, 5 Sept. 1992).

4. MVW journal, 5 Feb. 1932, 211v, Gladding-VW Papers; MVW journal, vol. 2, 21 June 1934, vol. 1, 14 Feb. 1933.

5. MVW journal, vol. 2, before 30 June 1934 and 29 Sept. 1934, vol. 3, 29 July 1935., vol. 4, 16 May 1936.

6. MVW journal, 12 Sept. 1942, 3 Feb. 1943, file 217v, Gladding-VW Papers; MVW journal, vol. 4, 20 Feb. 1936; vol. 1, 4 Sept. 1933.

7. MVW journal, vol. 2, 16 Oct. 1933 and 17 June 1934. The idea for "Vital Conduct" was first mentioned in MVW to Dummer, 6 July 1931 (file 822, Dummer Papers); MVW journal, vol. 2, 4 May 1934, 25 June 1934; vol. 4, 13 June 1936.

8. MVW journal, vol. 5, 5 Nov. 1939. She once wrote: "When you— Richard, or Sarah—read this—I shall be 'dead'—but my vital—self—*is*

with you" (vol. 5, 18 Aug. 1938). Her nephew, Richard Bartholomew, sister Beckie's son, was a child at the time; he later became an Episcopal minister.

9. GBVW to MVW, 7 June 1933, 29 July 1933, 12 Feb. 1932, file 230, Gladding-VW Papers; Maud VW to MVW, 22 Jan. 1932, and cf. 28 Jan. 1932, Gladding-VW Papers.

10. MVW journal, vol. 2, 24 Aug. 1934 and 2 Dec. 1934. MVW commissioned a stained-glass window of St. Martin of Tours for the reformatory library in his memory (MVW to Sayre, 15 Sept. 1934, file 179). His appearance in her dreams always signaled comfort and acceptance, e.g., MVW journal, 12 April 1937, 1 Nov. 1937, file 213v, and 14 June 1942 and 10 April 1943, file 217v, Gladding-VW Papers.

11. MVW journal, vol. 2, 3 Sept. 1934, 6 April 1934, 23 April 1934, 6 May 1934, 11 May 1935; interview with "Irene Jenner," 15 Sept. 1989.

12. MVW journal, vol. 2, 11 April 1935, 16 May 1934, 15 July 1934, 17 Sept. 1934; MVW to mother, 7 Oct. 1934, file 68; MVW journal, vol. 3, 13 Sept. 1935.

13. MVW to mother, 10 June 1934, file 67; MVW journal, vol. 2, 9 March 1935, vol. 5, 28 June 1939. Other nightmares portrayed the rectory besieged by the unemployed (vol. 4, 18 Jan. 1936) and cronelike women (MVW journal, 12 Sept. 1942, file 217v, Gladding-VW Papers).

14. MVW journal, vol. 4, 19 March 1936, 12 April 1936; MVW to mother, 21 Sept. 1938, file 74; MVW journal, 27 Oct. 1943, file 219v, Gladding-VW Papers.

15. MVW to mother, 15 Aug. 1940, file 78; MVW journal, vol. 6, 11 Nov. 1941; interview with Harriet Gunning, 18 Oct. 1992; interview with Richard J. Hildebrandt, 18 Aug. 1989.

16. MVW journal, 21 Jan. 1945, 10 April 1945, 11 Sept. 1944, file 219v, Gladding-VW Papers.

17. However insecure Ralph's future, MVW clearly considered him her closest sibling. In a codicil to her will, written after her skull fracture in 1933, she instructed executor Orfa Jean Shontz that in the event of her death Sarah should be sent to Ralph and Bert. (MVW journal, vol. 1, 1 Oct. 1932; RVW to MVW, 4 Oct. 1932, file 108; original will 9 April 1933 in file 122; MVW to Ruth Van Waters Burton, 29 June 1932, file 80.) In 1938 Van Waters made Ralph her sole beneficiary (MVW to mother, 3 June 1938, file 128), as she did in her final will (Commonwealth of Mass., "Last Will and Testament of Miriam Van Waters," 31 Oct. 1957, Probate of Wills, County Courthouse, Cambridge, Mass.).

18. MVW journal, vol. 1, 1 Aug. 1933; MVW to parents, 2 Aug., 6 Aug., and 10 Sept. 1933, file 66; MVW to HW, 30 June 1933, file 122. MVW claimed that Ralph had been invited to come to Mass. by Sayre to work for the Department of Corrections; Ralph continued to believe that he had been offered a job that did not come through. (MVW to Dummer, 25 Aug. 1933, file 823, Dummer Papers; RVW interview.) MVW hoped that Ralph could get a job in the parole department, but he was unable to do so because of civil service obstacles (MVW to Harvey Carr, 20 Feb. 1934, file 123).

19. MVW journal, vol. 2, 16 Oct. 1932; MVW to parents, 20 Aug. 1933, file 66; MVW journal, vol. 2, 30 April 1934; MVW to mother, 26 Oct. 1938, file 75; GT to RVW, 22 June 1938, file 128; RVW to GT, 5 July 1938, file 128.

20. MVW journal, vol. 2, 19 Jan. 1934, 18 July 1934; interview with RVW, 10 Sept. 1989. Still looking for a job, Ralph asked his brother George for a position in his company (MVW journal, vol. 5, 21 Oct. 1939).

21. MVW journal, vol. 3, 5 Oct. 1935, vol. 6, 17 Aug. 1941; MVW to mother, 13 Aug. 1933, file 66, 27 Apr. 1934, 20 Sept. 1934, file 68, 24 Jan. 1938, file 74; MVW journal, vol. 2, 11 Sept. 1934; vol. 2, 18 July 1934; vol. 3, 18 June 1935.

22. MVW journal, vol. 2, 22 April 1934.

23. MVW journal, vol. 3, 18 July 1935, vol. 4, 24 Feb. 1936; MVW journal, 21 June 1936, 23 Aug. 1936, 26 Aug. 1936, file 213v, Gladding-VW Papers. MVW believed that Bert's depression stemmed from her lack of a home of her own; she credited Ralph's faithful attendance on his wife as the source of her cure. The depression, however, returned years later.

24. 20 Aug. 1933, file 66; MVW journal, vol. 2, 28 Jan. 1934, 18 April 1934. In part she may have been trying to substitute Ralph for her father (a hard job to fill), for she often noted his resemblance to their father (MVW journal, 4 Dec. 1937, 3 Feb. 1938, file 213v, Gladding-VW Papers).

25. The novel depicted the carnal lust between Abelard and Heloise, the birth of their child, and the nun's constant love for her former teacher (George Moore, *Heloise and Abelard*, 2 vols. [New York: Boni and Liveright, 1925]). Van Waters' spiritualization of the story in her journals parallels her insistence on sublimating the admittedly erotic elements in her correspondence with both HW and GT.

26. MVW journal, vol. 3, 6 July 1935, contains first reference to the story, also vol. 3, 18 July 1935, 5 Oct. 1935; vol. 4, 16 Nov. 1935, 19 Dec. 1935; vol. 5, 24 May 1939, 16 Nov. 1939.

27. RVW to MVW, 12 Aug. 1942 and 31 March 1932, file 238; MVW journal, 15 July 1942, file 217v; 1 June 1948, 21 Nov. 1948, file 220v; all in Gladding-VW Papers.

28. MVW journal, vol. 3, 6 Oct. and 4 Nov. 1935; vol. 4, 28 May 1936; vol. 5, 12 July 1938; vol. 3, 23 Aug. 1935; Sarah to MVW, 27 Feb. 1938, file 88. Sarah preferred the approach of MVW and GT.

29. E.g., MVW to mother, 2 May 1935, file 69, 25 April 1936, file 70; MVW journal, vol. 3, 6 Oct. 1935; vol. 4, 24 Feb. 1936, 28 May 1936, 15 June 1936; vol. 5, 27 Jan. 1939.

30. MVW journal, vol. 6, 17 Aug. 1941; MVW to Dummer, 27 Nov. 1942, file 823, Dummer Papers; interview with RVW, 10 Sept. 1989; MVW journal, vol. 7, 11 Nov. 1945. Wartime destruction, and especially the atomic bomb, triggered strong feelings for MVW, leading her to think of her father's pacifism and the uselessness of war (29 March 1946; MVW journal, vol. 7, 18 Aug. 1945, 6 Jan. 1946, 29 March 1946).

31. MVW journal, vol. 8, 26 April 1947; vol. 9, 17 Jan. 1952. In 1952 Miriam helped Bert and Ralph get a mortgage to build the house by signing

a joint deed for the Hill Top land her mother had left to her; by 1955 Ralph, Bert, and their children, Susan and Ralph Jr., had completely moved from the reformatory; in 1964 Miriam deeded the entire property to him (vol. 9, 13 Sept. 1952; vol. 10, 10 Dec. 1955; quit claim deed thanks to Susan Girgenti of Sherborn, Mass.).

32. MVW journal, vol. 2, 13 Jan. 1934; vol. 5, 13 Nov. 1938.

33. MVW to parents, 30 April 1932, file 63; MVW to Alma Holzschuh, 18 May 1932, file 119.

34. MVW to Jack Black, 9 Feb. 1933, file 595; MVW to Mrs. Henry Lissner, 13 June 1932, file 120; MVW to parents, 15 Aug. 1932, file 64, 4 April 1933, file 65, and 2 Aug. 1933, file 66; MVW to Dummer, 24 June 1933, file 823, Dummer Papers. MVW's finances were strapped during the depression. She had lost her savings from book royalties in a bank failure, and she was paying tuition for Sarah at Shady Hill (MVW to mother, 15 Jan. 1938, file 74).

35. MVW journal, vol. 1, 5 Aug. 1933; vol. 2, 19 Jan. 1934; vol. 4, 19 Dec. 1935; vol. 3, 23 Sept. 1935; vol. 2, 22 April 1934, 24 April 1934; MVW to Mother, 3 Dec. 1934, file 68.

36. MVW to parents, 10 Feb. 1932, file 63.

37. MVW journal, vol. 2, 12 June 1933, 10 May 1934, undated, back page, 1935; MVW to parents, 3 May 1932, file 63; vol. 3, 11 Sept. 1935; MVW to mother, 6 July and 12 July 1937, file 72.

38. MVW to parents, 13 Aug. 1933, file 66; MVW journal, vol. 3, 2 Sept. 1935.

39. MVW journal, vol. 3, 2 Sept. 1935; MVW journal, 27 Feb. 1932, file 211v, and 29 July 1936, file 213v, Gladding-VW Papers.

40. MVW journal, vol. 3, 3 Oct. 1935.

41. MVW journal, 2 Aug. 1936, file 213v, Gladding-VW Papers; MVW journal, vol. 3, 6 Oct. 1935; vol. 4, 3 Jan. 1936, 19 March 1936; 20 Feb. 1936.

42. MVW journal, vol. 4, 28 May 1936; MVW journal, 14 July 1936, file 213v, Gladding-VW Papers.

43. On the Putney School, see Susan McIntosh Lloyd, *The Putney School: A Progressive Experiment* (New Haven: Yale University Press, 1987); MVW to Edna Mahan, 30 Oct. 1936, file 255, Anne Gladding to MVW, 13 April 1939, file 9, and MVW to Austin MacCormick, 13 Feb. 1937, all in Gladding-Van Waters Papers; Sarah to MVW, 13 June 1938, file 88; 16 Oct. 1938, file 75; 26 June 1939, file 77; MVW journal, vol. 5, 15 July 1939, 4 Nov. 1938.

44. MVW journal, vol. 5, 27 Jan. 1939.

45. Sarah to MVW, 21 Nov. 1939, file 87; Filene's to MVW, 13 March 1941, file 130; Sarah to MVW, 15 March 1941, file 89; MVW to Sarah, 16 March 1941, file 84; MVW to Sarah, 22 April 1940, file 84; Sarah to MVW, 22 Oct. 1940, 3 Jan. 1941, 14 Nov. 1940, file 89; Anne Gladding to MVW, 13 June 1941, file 10, Gladding-VW Papers.

46. Sarah to MVW, 3 Jan. 1941, 23 June 1941, file 89. In announcing

their marriage to her friends, Van Waters backdated the event to Jan. 1941, claiming that they postponed the announcement until June (MVW to Dummer, 28 July 1941, file 823, Dummer Papers).

47. Howard Kellett to MVW, 27 June 1941, file 130; MVW journal, vol. 6, 24 Aug. 1941; vol. 6, 27 Dec. 1941; telephone interview with Howard Kellett, 14 Sept. 1989, from Kennebunkport, Me.

48. MVW journal, vol. 6, 21 Dec. 1941, 10 Sept. 1941; MVW to Sarah, 24 March 1942, file 85; Sarah to MVW, 10 Feb. 1943, file 89.

49. MVW journal, 12 Feb., 15 April, 1 July, 6 Sept., 22 Sept., and 29 Nov. 1942; 9 Jan., 11 March, and 31 March 1943, file 217v, Gladding-VW Papers.

50. MVW journal, 30 Sept. and 7 Nov. 1942, 8 March, 22 March, 23 March, 28 March, and 12 April 1943, file 217v; 26 July 1943, 3 Oct. 1944, file 219v, Gladding-VW Papers; MVW to Richard Hildebrandt, 4 Oct. 1943, file 85.

51. Sarah to MVW, 12 Jan. 1942, 15 Oct. 1943, file 89; 24 April 1944, file 87; MVW journal, vol. 7, 15 May 1945, 9 Nov. 1945, 6 May 1946, 14 Nov. 1946; MVW to Dummer, 8 Nov. 1947, file 825, Dummer Papers; Sarah to MVW, 12 Nov. 1948, file 89; Jeannette Estes to MVW, 7 May 1942, file 308, Gladding-VW Papers.

52. MVW journal, vol. 7, 1 Oct. and 11 Nov. 1945, 6 Jan., 24 Feb., and 1 July 1946.

53. MVW journal, vol. 7, 6 April 1947; MVW to Sarah, 27 Aug. 1949, file 86; MVW journal, 2 Oct. 1943, 24 Oct. 1943, 20 Aug. 1944, 14 Oct. 1944, file 219v, and 3 July 1949, file 220v, Gladding-VW Papers.

54. GBVW to MVW, 2 Oct. 1932, file 25; MVW journal, vol. 7, 23 Sept. 1945. The label *codependent,* drawn from the model of coalcoholism developed by AA and popularized in mass psychology literature during the 1980s, would seem to apply to MVW's behavior. Many of the qualities associated with codependency, however, parallel the behaviors to which women have been socialized in western culture. On female narcissism and extension of the self through children, see Alice Miller, *Prisoners of Childhood: The Drama of the Gifted Child and the Search for the True Self* (New York: Basic Books, 1981).

55. For an excellent analysis of the interaction of reformers and clients, see Peggy Pascoe, *Relations of Rescue: The Search for Female Moral Authority in the American West, 1874–1939* (New York: Oxford University Press, 1990); on clients' use of reform agendas, see Linda Gordon, *Heroes of Their Own Lives: The Politics and History of Family Violence* (New York: Viking, 1988), Ruth M. Alexander, *The "Girl Problem": Female Sexual Delinquency in New York, 1900–1930* (Ithaca, N.Y.: Cornell University Press, 1995), and Regina Kunzel, *Fallen Women, Problem Girls: Unmarried Mothers and the Professionalization of Social Work, 1890–1945* (New Haven: Yale University Press, 1993).

56. MVW journal, 24 Aug. 1943, 28 June 1944, file 219v, Gladding-VW Papers.

CHAPTER TWELVE

1. MVW journal, vol. 4, 3 June 1936; vol. 1, 9 Feb. 1933.

2. MVW journal, 17 June 1936, file 213v, 26 Oct. 1948, file 220v, Gladding-VW Papers; GT to MVW, 3 Oct. 1939, file 267, Gladding-VW Papers.

3. GT to MVW, 3 July 1946, file 130; MVW journal, vol. 5, 20 Aug. 1938 (citing letters from both Sarah and GT that sustained her on painful days).

4. On relationships among women reformers, see above, chap. 6, n. 22.

5. 26 Oct. 1938, file 75; MVW to GT, 3 Nov. 1942, file 188 and 24 Jan. 1945, file 191; GT to Eleanor Roosevelt (hereafter ER), 10 Feb. 1945, file 191. GT also provided funds at the Clinton Farms Reformatory for Women in New Jersey, which named a building for her in the late 1940s (interview with Mary Q. Hawkes, 12 Sept. 1989, Newton, Mass.).

6. MVW journal, 7 Nov. 1936, 8 July 1936, and 26 Feb 1938, file 213v; 15 June 1942 and 12 Sept. 1942, file 217v, Gladding-VW Papers; MVW journal, vol. 3, 3 Aug. 1935, 5 Oct. 1935; vol. 2, 15 Jan. 1934 (misdated 15 Dec.); vol. 6, 29 Aug. 1941; vol. 7, 10 April 1947.

7. MVW journal, vol. 4, 13 Nov. 1935. For years MVW was "plagued" by the unfinished written version, of which there is no record in her papers. In a footnote to *One Thousand Delinquent Girls: Their Treatment by Court and Clinic* (Cambridge: Harvard University Press, 1934), Sheldon and Eleanor Glueck claimed that a volume on juvenile institutions by Van Waters would be forthcoming (5 n. 4). It was never published, and the Gluecks continued to be hostile to Van Waters throughout her career. See also Felix Frankfurter to MVW, 19 Feb. 1934 and 28 Oct. 1938, box 27, file 11, Miriam Van Waters Papers, Harvard Law School Library, Cambridge, Mass.

8. MVW to Sarah, 16 Aug. 1938, file 84; bank officer to GT, 23 Sept. 1938, file 128; Harry Reynolds to GT, 3 Sept. 1938, file 128; MVW journal, vol. 2, 5 Jan. 1935, vol. 4, 20 Feb. 1936.

9. MVW journal, vol. 5, 29 Nov. 1938; vol. 2, 17 May 1934. Puss sought cures for tuberculosis in sanatoriums during the 1930s; she died in 1949.

10. MVW journal, 3 Oct. 1939, file 215v, Gladding-VW Papers; GT to MVW, 22 Sept. 1945, file 136; telephone interview with Geraldine Boone, 17 Feb. 1995.

11. Interview with "Irene Jenner," 15 Sept. 1989; interview with Mary Q. Hawkes, 12 Sept. 1989; Evelyn Walker to MVW, 26 July 1934, file 124; MVW to Walker, 1 Aug. 1934, file 124.

12. 12 May 1934, file 67; 16 Sept. 1936, file 71; MVW journal, vol. 5, 18 Aug. 1938, 20 Aug. 1938; MVW journal, 10 Oct. 1942, file 217v, Gladding-VW Papers.

13. MVW journal, vol. 6, 2 Sept. 1941; MVW journal, 21 Feb. to 11 March 1944, file 219v, Gladding-VW Papers.

14. 14 Jan. 1938, file 74; MVW journal, vol. 2, 12 July 1934, 11 May 1935; vol. 3, 25 Aug. 1935; MVW journal, 16 June 1938, 14 Dec. 1936, 5 Feb. 1937, 14 Jan. 1938, 6 Dec. 1943, 8 Sept. 1937, file 213v, Gladding-VW Papers.

15. MVW journal, vol. 2, 11 Oct. 1934; vol. 5, 25 Nov. 1938, 3 Nov. 1939, 20 Oct. 1938; vol. 2, 22 Feb. 1935; vol. 3, 26 Aug. 1935; GT to MVW, 28 Nov. 1939, file 129.

16. MVW journal, vol. 2, 11 May 1934; vol. 3, 18 June 1935; MVW to mother, 8 May 1937, file 71; vol. 5, 13 Aug. 1938, vol. 6, 25 Nov. 1941, 19 Dec. 1941; GT to MVW, 22 Sept. 1945, file 136; also MVW journal, 11 July 1936, file 213v, and 17 Nov. 1943, file 219v, Gladding-VW Papers.

17. MVW journal, vol. 5, 20 April 1939; MVW to mother, 21 April 1939, file 76; MVW to mother, 16 April 1940, file 78.

18. 16 Sept. 1936, file 71; 29 Aug. 1938, file 74; MVW journal, vol. 5, 26 Aug. 1939; GT to MVW, 3 Oct. 1939, and MVW journal, 30 Aug. 1937, 3 Sept. 1937, file 213v, Gladding-VW Papers; telephone interview with Geraldine Boone, 17 Feb. 1995.

19. Shontz to MVW, 10 April 1934, 14 May 1934, file 259, 13 Dec. 1938, file 260, and MVW to Anne Gladding, 3 Sept. 1946, file 18, Gladding-MVW Papers.

20. GT to MVW, 21 Feb. 1936, file 267, Gladding-VW Papers; MVW journal, vol. 1, 14 Feb. 1933; 7 Nov. 1935, file 69; MVW journal, vol. 2, 3 Dec. 1934; MVW to mother, 2 Dec. 1934, file 68; MVW to mother, 7 Dec. 1934, file 68; MVW journal, vol. 4, 11 Nov. and 13 Nov. 1935.

21. MVW journal, vol. 2, 13 Jan. 1934 [misdated 13 Dec., but follows 10 Jan.], 15 Jan 1934.

22. MVW journal, vol. 2, 14 April 1934, also 9 April 1934; vol. 4, 13 April 1936; vol. 2, 16 July 1934; vol. 2, 22 Feb. 1935; vol. 3, 5 Oct. 1935.

23. MVW journal, vol. 3, 8 Nov. 1935.

24. MVW journal, vol. 3, 12 Nov. 1935.

25. MVW journal, vol. 4, 7 Dec. 1935, 11 March 1936, 10 March 1936; GT to MVW, 2 Feb. 1936, 21 Feb. 1936, 17 March 1936, file 267, Gladding-MVW Papers.

26. MVW journal, vol. 4, 29 March 1936.

27. MVW journal, vol. 4, 7 April 1936, 28 May 1936; GT to MVW, 10 April 1936, file 267, Gladding-MVW Papers.

28. MVW journal, vol. 4, 15 June 1936.

29. MVW journal, vol. 5, 9 July 1938.

30. MVW journal, vol. 3, 17 July 1935.

31. On Rorschach, e.g., inmate record, 21 Feb. 1949, file 251; MVW journal, 11 June 1938, file 213v, Gladding-VW Papers; MVW journal, vol. 5, 26 June 1938.

CHAPTER THIRTEEN

1. J. J. Huthmacher, *Massachusetts: People and Politics, 1919-1933* (Cambridge: Harvard University Press, Belknap Press, 1959); Charles H. Trout, *Boston, the Great Depression, and the New Deal* (New York: Oxford University Press, 1977), 102, 281; Jack Beatty, *The Rascal King: The Life and Times of James Michael Curley, 1874-1958* (Reading, Mass.: Addison-Wesley, 1992). Edwin O'Connor based his fictional portrait of the

decline of the urban boss, *The Last Hurrah* (Boston: Little, Brown, 1956), on Curley.

2. MVW journal, vol. 1, 9 Nov. 1932; MVW to GVW, 23 Sept. 1932, file 80. At the same time that she feared FDR's election, Van Waters endorsed Upton Sinclair's radical End Poverty in California (EPIC) campaign, which elected Orfa Jean Shontz to state office (Shontz to MVW, 20 June 1934, file 259, Gladding-VW papers).

3. MVW to Dummer, 4 Dec. 1933, file 823, Dummer Papers; Transcript of "Public Hearing in the Matter of the Removal of Dr. Miriam Van Waters as Superintendent of the Reformatory for Women. Before Elliott E. McDowell, Commissioner of Correction. Jan. 13-Feb. 8, 1949," 1760, 1771ff. (ts. located at the Office of the Superintendent, MCI-Framingham, Framingham, Mass; hereafter "In the Matter"); Beatty, *Rascal King,* 257.

4. David J. Rothman, *Conscience and Convenience: The Asylum and Its Alternatives in Progressive America* (Boston: Little, Brown, 1980), 159-63, 404.

5. 24 May 1932, file 63; MVW journal, vol. 4, 20 Dec. 1935.

6. Beatty, *Rascal King,* 357-58, 432; Trout, *Boston,* 271; MVW journal, vol. 2, 8 April 1935; vol. 4, 17 Jan. 1936.

7. On Winslow, see Thomas Eliot, "The Van Waters Case," The Inter-University Case Program, Cases in Public Administration and Policy Formation (Swarthmore, Pa.: Swarthmore College, 1953), [later published by University of Alabama Press, 1954, 1960], 6-9, and Arthur W. Hepner, "Ordeal in Massachusetts: The Vindication of Dr. Van Waters," *Harpers,* June 1949, 81-89; Winslow to Arthur Lyman, 17 Aug. 1939, "Administrative Correspondence" file, Human Services, Corrections, Reference Files, Series 1137x, Commonwealth of Massachusetts Archives, Boston, Mass.; *A Manual for the Use of the General Court* (Boston, 1935-40) gives annual parole board members; MVW journal, vol. 4, 15 Jan. 1936.

8. On Catholic conservatism, see Beatty, *Rascal King,* 103-5, 175-77.

9. Katharine Sullivan, *Girls on Parole* (Boston: Houghton Mifflin, 1956), 97.

10. MVW journal, vol. 1, 13 Oct. 1932; MVW journal, 9 Oct. 1936, file 213v., Gladding-VW Papers; MVW, "Notes on Parole Board Meeting," 6 Dec. 1932, file 235; MVW journal, vol. 2, 12 Nov. 1934, vol. 3, 8 Oct. 1935. Catholics outnumbered Protestants and Jews by over 2:1 in Boston (Trout, *Boston,* 143). Van Waters felt more sympathy for Irish Catholic women, admiring both those who entered the professions and those who remained wives and mothers (e.g., MVW journal, 19 Jan. 1938, file 213v, Gladding-VW Papers).

11. MVW, "General Staff Meeting," 8 Feb. 1934, file 257; Elizabeth Bode, "Meeting with Work Girls," 23 Sept. 1934, file 237; MVW to Richard Olney, Chair of Board of Parole, 27 Nov. 1935, file 181.

12. MVW journal, vol. 4, 6 Dec. 1935, 4 Jan. and 5 Jan. 1936.

13. MVW journal, 19 Jan. 1938, file 213v, Gladding-VW Papers; MVW journal, vol. 4, 5 Jan. 1936. Charles H. Trout's analysis of Curley as a classic Weberian charismatic personality could apply equally to Van Waters' ap-

peal and her assumption of power (Trout, "Curley of Boston: The Search for Irish Legitimacy," in Ronald P. Formisano and Constance K. Burns, eds., *Boston, 1700–1980: The Evolution of Urban Politics* [Westport, Conn.: Greenwood Press, 1984], 189).

14. MVW journal, vol. 4, 9 Jan. 1936; Trout, "Curley of Boston," 186; MVW journal, vol. 1, 1 March 1933; MVW to editor, *Framingham News*, 7 Nov. 1962, file 495, and 28 Oct. 1940, file 186.

15. MVW journal, vol. 4, 14 Jan., undated Jan., 6 March, 13 March, 15 March, and 19 March 1936.

16. MVW journal, vol. 3, 22 Sept. 1935, vol. 4, 18 Jan. 1936, 31 March 1936; MVW to Dummer, 7 Aug. 1938, file 823, Dummer Papers. MVW met with HW's widow and child in Washington several months after his death (MVW journal, 11 Jan. 1937, 15 May 1937, file 213v, Gladding-VW Papers).

17. *Boston Herald Traveler*, 12 Nov. 1937, BU SPC; MVW to parents, 6 Feb. 1938, file 74, 4 Nov. 1938, file 75; MVW journal, vol. 5, 8 Nov. 1938; MVW journal, 10 April 1937, 24 June 1938, file 213v, Gladding-VW Papers. A former parole board chair later claimed that MVW had blocked his investigation of the reformatory in 1937 (*Boston Herald Traveler*, 19 May 1948, BU SPC).

18. The federal Hawes-Cooper Bill of 1929 outlawed prison-made goods from interstate commerce, effective in 1934; during the 1930s and 1940s, the state use system allowed prisoners to manufacture goods for sale to state institutions (Larry Sullivan, *The Prison Reform Movement: Forlorn Hope* [Boston: Twayne, 1990], 37).

19. 3 March 1938, file 76; MVW journal, vol. 5, 20 Sept. 1938. On married women's work bills, see Lois Scharf, *To Work and to Wed: Female Employment, Feminism, and the Great Depression* (Westport, Conn.: Greenwood Press, 1980).

20. MVW notes on staff problems, 26 Oct. 1937, file 240; Ruth Berns, *Boston Herald Traveler*, 26 June 1938, BU SPC. Van Waters' emphasis on wage earning contrasted with other liberal reformers whose social policies made motherhood central. See Linda Gordon, *Pitied but Not Entitled: Single Mothers and the History of Welfare, 1890–1935* (New York: Free Press, 1994), esp. chaps. 3 and 7.

21. MVW journal, vol. 5, 17 Feb., 20 April, and 26 May 1939; League of Women Voters (LWV) report, 26 July 1939, file 242; *Boston Herald Traveler*, 24 March 1940, BU SPC.

22. 13 Dec. 1940, file 78; MVW to Bishop Lawrence, 12 Feb. 1948, file 194.

23. MVW journal, vol. 6, 5 Nov. 1941; MVW, "General Plan for Women's Parole as Tentatively Adopted by Present Parole Board," speech dated 1 May 1942, file 188; MVW to GT, 24 Jan. 1945, file 191, includes the financial statement for the Thompson Fund.

24. 26 April 1918, file 46; MVW journal, vol. 5, 12 Nov. 1938 and vol. 8, 8 Feb. 1947; MVW to Dummer, 2 July 1939, file 823, Dummer Papers; 5 March 1938, file 76; Marietta [?] Kampe [?] to MVW, undated April 1939, file 129.

25. MVW journal, vol. 7, 29 March 1946.

26. Leila J. Rupp, *Mobilizing Women for War* (Princeton, N.J.: Princeton University Press, 1978); Karen Anderson, *Wartime Women: Sex Roles, Family Relations, and the Status of Women during World War II* (Westport, Conn.: Greenwood Press, 1981); D'Ann Campbell, *Women at War with America: Private Lives in a Patriotic Era* (Cambridge: Harvard University Press, 1984).

27. Minutes of the Conference of Superintendents of Institutions for Girls and Women, 1944, file 587 (hereafter Conference of Superintendents), and Ruth O'Keefe letter on LWV stationery, 20 June 1947, file 247. On the "girl problem" during wartime and calls for greater police surveillance, see [Survey Committee], "A Study of Protective Measures in the City of Boston," *Journal of Social Hygiene* 28 (Oct. 1942): 403–18 and [American Social Hygiene Association], "Sex Delinquency among Girls," *Journal of Social Hygiene* 29 (Nov. 1943): 492–501. On national increases in runaway girls and prostitution, see Walter C. Reckless, "The Impact of War on Crime, Delinquency, and Prostitution," *American Journal of Sociology* 48 (1942–43): 378–86.

28. *Boston Herald Traveler,* 22 May 1942, 29 July 1942, undated Feb. 1944, 17 March 1944, BU SPC; Conference of Superintendents, 1944, 8, file 587; MVW to GT, 3 Nov. 1942, file 188; MVW testimony, "Notes on Public Hearing at State House, Room 433, before the Appointed Legislative Commission on Conditions at the Reformatory for Women, Framingham Senator J. Elmer Callahan, Chairman," 22 Nov. 1948, file 250, 17–19 (hereafter Callahan Hearings); Comments from Annual Reports of the Commissioners of Corrections, 1940, file 243.

29. MVW to Dummer, 27 Nov. 1942, 19 March 1943, 26 Jan. 1946, file 823, Dummer Papers; Margaret van Wagenen to MVW, 20 Sept. 1943, file 189; testimony of Arthur Lyman, "In the Matter," 1778; Hepner, "Ordeal in Massachusetts," 85.

30. MVW journal, 11 June 1942, file 217v, Gladding-VW Papers.

31. MVW, "Memo for Discussion with Commissioner Arthur Lyman," 14 July 1942, file 245; MVW to Sarah Van Waters Hildebrandt (hereafter SVWH), 17 July 1942, file 84. On resentments by other officials, see below and Eliot, "Van Waters Case."

32. Report to the Friends of Prisoners, 5 Dec. 1945, file 246; MVW testimony, Callahan Hearings, 17–19, file 250; testimonies of Arthur Lyman and J. Paul Doyle, "In the Matter," 1776–1800.

33. Allan Berube, *Coming Out under Fire: The History of Gay Men and Women in World War Two* (New York: Free Press, 1990); Leisa D. Meyer, "Creating G. I. Jane: The Regulation of Sexuality and Sexual Behavior in the Women's Army Corps during World War II," *Feminist Studies* 18:3 (fall 1992): 581–602; Allan Berube and John D'Emilio, "The Military and Lesbians during the McCarthy Years: Archives," *Signs* 9 (summer 1984): 759–75; Madeline Davis and Elizabeth Lapovsky Kennedy, *Boots of Leather, Slippers of Gold: The History of a Lesbian Community* (New York: Routledge, 1993).

34. Two earlier studies did explore lesbianism in women's institutions: Margaret Otis, "A Perversion Not Commonly Noted," *Journal of Abnormal Psychology* 7 (June–July 1913): 112–16, and Charles A. Ford, "Homosexual Practices of Institutionalized Females," *Journal of Abnormal Psychology* 23:4 (Jan.–March 1929): 442–48. Studies in the 1940s include Theodora M. Abel, "Dominant Behavior of Institutionalized Subnormal Negro Girls: An Experimental Study," *American Journal of Mental Deficiency* 47:4 (April 1943): 429–36; John Holland Cassity, "Socio-Psychiatric Aspects of Female Felons," *Journal of Criminal Psychopathology* 3 (April 1942): 597–604 (on lesbian homicides); and "Female Homosexuality in Correctional Institutions," in file 420 and listed as presentation at the 1942 Conference of Superintendents, file 247. See also Estelle B. Freedman, "The Prison Lesbian and the Construction of the 'Aggressive Female Homosexual'" (paper presented at the annual meeting of the American Historical Association, San Francisco, 8 Jan. 1994).

35. Helen Schnefel to MVW, 4 Oct. 1932, file 177; MVW handwritten notes, 11 April 1938, file 241; interview by Mr. Swanson, 19 Jan. 1949, file 251; Dr. Pavenstedt, report on student 16590, 1943–47, and 18572, 30 March 1948, in McDowell Exhibits, 126 and 126A (20 Feb. 1949, 21 Feb. 1949), file 251.

36. McDowell Exhibits 128 (14 March 1944), 126 and 126A (20 Feb. 1949, 21 Feb. 1949), 129 (29 Feb. 1944), file 251 (with the reformatory file for this student from 1943 to 1947, including psychiatric reports).

37. McDowell Exhibits 126 and 126A, and case 18572, file 251.

38. Minutes of the 15th Conference of Superintendents of Correctional Institutions for Women and Girls, New York, 14–16 Feb. 1944, 21 (reporting Mead's comments), file 587.

39. MVW journal, vol. 7, 7 May 1945, 11 Nov. 1945.

40. On domestic effects of the cold war, see esp. Elaine Tyler May, *Homeward Bound: American Families in the Cold War Era* (New York: Basic Books, 1988).

41. On Tobin, see *Current Biography Yearbook* (New York: H. W. Wilson, 1946), 600–603, and Trout, *Boston,* 145.

42. GT to ER, 10 Feb. 1945, file 191; GT to ER, 17 Feb. 1945, file 191; Maurice Tobin to ER, 12 March 1945, file 136; MVW journal, vol. 7, 27 Dec. 1946.

43. GT to ER, 3 March 1945, file 191.

44. MVW journal, vol. 7, 2 May, 3 May, 12 June, and 1 Aug. 1945; GT to MVW, 22 Sept. 1945, file 136. Anti-Semitism among the members of GVW's family is described at length in Beckie Van Waters to MVW, 19 Feb. 1945, file 241, Gladding-VW Papers, and is recorded in MVW journal, vol. 7, 23 July 1945. Maud Van Waters had both suffered a heart attack and broken her hip in Nov. 1944. Her health deteriorated gradually over the next few years (MVW journal, 30 Nov. 1944, 219v, Gladding-VW Papers).

45. MVW testimony, "In the Matter," 145 and J. Paul Doyle testimony, 1792–95.

46. MVW journal, vol. 7, undated Oct. 1945; Eleanor Roosevelt, "New

England Visit," *New York World Telegraph,* 1 Nov. 1945, file 191; MVW journal, vol. 7, 15 Nov. 1945, 9 Jan. 1946, 13 Feb. 1946.

47. O'Keefe comments in file 266, n.d.; Sullivan, *Girls on Parole,* 70ff, 92–93.

48. MVW journal, vol. 7, 18 Jan., 19 Jan., 3 Feb., and 4 Feb. 1946, 12 Feb., 13 Feb., 24 Feb., 1 March, 3 March, and 11 March 1946; 20 June 1946; 24 Jan. 1947; MVW journal, vol. 8, 5 Feb. 1947; MVW journal, 8 July 1947, 23 July 1947, 29 Oct. 1947, file 220v, Gladding-VW Papers.

49. GT to MVW, 3 July 1946, file 137; MVW journal, vol. 7, 27 May, 20 June, 27 June, and 1 July 1946, 1 Jan. 1947.

50. MVW journal, vol. 8, 5 Feb., 8 Feb. 1947; vol. 7, 28 Feb., 5 March, 20 March, and 2 April 1947. MVW was correct about threats to the land; against her wishes, Commissioner McDowell sold several acres of reformatory land to a subsidiary of General Motors, to build a manufacturing plant (Eliot, "Van Waters Case," marginal note on ts., file 259).

51. MVW journal, vol. 7, 8 April 1947; *Boston Herald Traveler,* 10 May 1947, BU SPC. MVW tried to elicit support from labor leaders, but there is no evidence that organized labor took a stand on either side.

52. *Boston Herald Traveler,* 18 May 1947, BU SPC.

53. Copy of letter from Rabbitt to Buckley, 21 May 1947, file 193.

54. Ruth O'Keefe, Report to League of Women Voters, 20 June 1947, file 247. In light of the report the LWV began a prison-visiting program at the reformatory (Agnes Cook of Andover LWV to MVW, 22 Nov. 1947, file 193).

55. MVW journal, 9 Jan. 1948, file 220v, Gladding-VW Papers; Business Agent to MVW, 2 July 1947, file 193; MVW journal, vol. 8, 7 July 1947, 8 March 1948; *Boston Herald Traveler,* 24 Feb. 1948, BU SPC.

56. Rev. W. Appleton Lawrence to MVW, 17 Jan. 1948, file 194, as well as other correspondence in this file; Howard Kellett and Joseph Fletcher, to the Clergy, 10 Feb. 1948, file 194; Church of the Advent, *Weekly Message,* 22 Feb. 1948, 1, 3, file 248; MVW to Bishop Lawrence, 12 Feb. 1948, file 194. Bishop Lawrence's mother-in-law, Lois Rantoul, had been a Republican reformer active in the Women's Trade Union League and a friend of ER (Trout, *Boston,* 133–34, 161).

57. Eliot, "Van Waters Case," 6–9 of mimeo draft, file 259; MVW journal, vol. 4, 31 March 1936. On views of Winslow's roles, see Hepner, "Ordeal in Massachusetts"; Daisy to Katharine C., undated Jan. 1949, file 202; and transcript of interview with LaRue Brown, box 14, folder 4, LaRue Brown Papers, Harvard Law School Library.

58. MVW, "Contacts with Commissioner McDowell" (1948), file 250; MVW to McDowell, 24 Feb. 1948, file 194.

59. MVW journal, vol. 8, 5 March and 12 March 1948; MVW, "Contacts with Commissioner McDowell," file 250; McDowell to MVW, e.g., 19 March 1948, file 194; Eliot, "Van Waters Case," 11–12.

60. *Boston Herald Traveler,* 5 March 1948, BU SPC; MVW journal, vol. 8, 5 March 1948.

61. MVW journal, vol. 8, 16 March 1948 and n.d., 10–11.

62. MVW journal, vol. 8, 8 March and 12 March 1948.

63. MVW journal, vol. 8, 9 March 1948; GT to MVW, 25 March 1948, file 194; ER to MVW, 2 May 1948, file 139.

64. *Boston Herald Traveler,* 9 May 1948, BU SPC; "Belle" to MVW, 20 May 1948, file 280 (claiming that the informant was motivated by a desire for money from the deceased student's family).

65. George Chauncey, *Gay New York: Gender, Urban Culture, and the Making of the Gay Male World, 1890-1940* (New York: Basic Books, 1994), 92-95.

CHAPTER FOURTEEN

1. David Caute, *The Great Fear: The Anti-Communist Purge under Truman and Eisenhower* (New York: Simon and Schuster, 1978), 26-27, 36, 339.

2. On reactions to women's roles during World War II and changing cultural models of womanhood, see Susan M. Hartmann, *American Women in the 1940s: The Home Front and Beyond* (Boston: Twayne Publishers, 1982), and Elaine Tyler May, *Homeward Bound: American Families in the Cold War Era* (New York: Basic Books, 1988), esp. 79.

3. Interview with Raymond Gilbert, 13 Oct. 1990, Newton, Mass.; telephone interview with Cynthia Thomas, 18 Jan. 1994. MVW complained of machine pressures about hiring throughout the 1930s. She also noted that Commissioner McDowell asked her to take on a male employee from Norfolk, a possible test of her loyalty to the larger correctional system (MVW journal, 23 June 1948, file 220v, Gladding-VW Papers).

4. Transcript of interview with LaRue Brown, n.d., 34, box 16, file 4, LaRue Brown Papers, Harvard Law School Library; Janis Howe, "Framingham Report," ts., 21 Sept. 1946, file 247, 1-2; Mary Q. Hawkes, *Excellent Effect: The Edna Mahan Story* (Arlington, Va.: American Correctional Association, 1994), 127; *Boston Evening American,* 6 Jan. 1949, 18; MVW journal, 7 Jan. 1948, file 220v, Gladding-VW Papers. Commissioner of Corrections Arthur Lyman thought that ER's intervention with Governor Tobin had given MVW too much freedom from authority, leaving her more vulnerable in the long run (MVW journal, 29 Feb. 1948, file 220v, Gladding-VW Papers).

5. Sara White, "Says McDowell," *Boston Herald Traveler,* 27 Jan. 1949; Charles Currier, "Bradford Seen on Spot in Reformatory Probe," *Boston Telegram,* 10 Dec. 1948, 44; Edwin Lukas, "Bridewell Revisited," *Nation,* 12 Feb. 1949, 178-81; Arthur W. Hepner, "Ordeal in Massachusetts: The Vindication of Dr. Van Waters," *Harpers,* June 1949, 81-89; interview with Raymond Gilbert, 13 Oct. 1990; "Interview between Miss Anne Gladding and Mr. McDowell in his office," 8 Sept. 1948, file 248.

6. Thomas Eliot, "The Van Waters Case," The Inter-University Case Program, Cases in Public Administration and Policy Formation (Swarthmore, Pa: Swarthmore College, 1953) 18-20 of mimeo draft [later published by University of Alabama Press, 1954, 1960]; Callahan Hearings, 10-11.

7. *Boston Herald Traveler,* 9 May 1948, BU SPC; MVW journal, 14 Sept. 1948 and 29 Dec. 1948, file 220v, Gladding-VW Papers.

8. *Boston Traveler,* 27 Jan. 1949, BU SPC; Peg O'Keefe to MVW, 30 Nov. 1948, file 198 and 25 May 1948, file 194. On Hodder, see Mary Bularzik, "Sex, Crime, and Justice: Women in the Criminal Justice System of Massachusetts, 1900-1950" (Ph.D. diss., Brandeis University, 1982), 159-64.

9. Although medical texts used the term *lesbian,* neither Dwyer nor the reformatory staff did so in the 1940s.

10. Interview with former inmate by Mr. Swanson, file 251; Miss "Z" to MVW, 12 July 1948, file 196; Lena Mary Watson to Gov. Robert Bradford, 29 May 1948, file 197.

11. Telephone interview with Geraldine Boone, 17 Feb. 1995; MVW to Dummer, 26 Sept. 1948, file 825, Dummer Papers; former student to MVW, 1 June 1948, file 195; Harry R. Archbald to MVW, 7 Feb. 1949, file 203. In response to the rumors about California, Dummer sought written evidence that Van Waters had left voluntarily; she also contacted noted penologists to attest to Van Waters' integrity.

12. MVW to Dummer, 26 Sept. 1948, file 825, Dummer Papers; GT to Lois Rantoul, 2 June 1948, file 194 (Rantoul was Bishop Lawrence's mother-in-law).

13. Leila Rupp, "'Imagine My Surprise': Women's Relationships in Mid-Twentieth Century America," in Martin Bauml Duberman, Martha Vicinus, and George Chauncey Jr., eds., *Hidden from History: Reclaiming the Gay and Lesbian Past* (New York: New American Library, 1989), 407, and Rupp, "Feminism and the Sexual Revolution in the Early Twentieth Century: The Case of Doris Stevens," *Feminist Studies* 15:2 (summer 1989): 289-309.

14. Miriam Van Waters, "The Adolescent Girl among Primitive People," 108-9; Albertine Winner, "Homosexuality in Women," *Medical Problems* 218 (Jul.-Dec. 1947): 219-20. Rupp cites other middle-class female couples who did not identify as lesbians during the era in which lesbian identity emerged, arguing that "the choice to reject that identification has a meaning of its own" (Rupp, "Imagine My Surprise," 410). On the emergence of working-class lesbian culture, see Madeline Davis and Elizabeth Lapovsky Kennedy, *Boots of Leather, Slippers of Gold: The History of a Lesbian Community* (New York: Routledge, 1993).

15. Dwyer complaints, 1 June 1948, file 248; "Superintendent's Answers," 1 June 1948, file 248.

16. MVW journal, 16 June, 19 June, and 22 June 1948, file 220v, Gladding-VW Papers.

17. MVW to McDowell, 7 June 1948, file 195; "Interview between Miss Anne Gladding and Mr. McDowell in his office," 8 Sept. 1948, file 248; MVW to Austin MacCormick, 8 June 1948, file 194. McDowell's report to the governor, based on Dwyer's investigation, was not made public at this time (*Boston Herald Traveler,* 7 July 1948, BU SPC).

18. Claude Cross to MVW, 9 July 1948, file 194; *Boston Herald Traveler,* 9 July 1948, BU SPC.

19. MVW, "Contacts with Commissioner McDowell," 28 July 1948, file 250; "Superintendent's Answers" to "Complaints or Charges from the Dwyer Report," 1 June 1948, file 248.

20. LoPresti quoted in "Sherborn Probe," *Boston Herald Traveler,* 9 June 1948, BU SPC.

21. Elliot E. McDowell (hereafter EEM) to MVW, 28 July 1948, file 250; MVW, "Superintendent's Answers," 1 June 1948, file 248; LoPresti quoted in "Sherborn Probe," *Boston Herald Traveler,* 9 June 1948, BU SPC; "Immorality Charged at Reformatory," *Boston Herald Traveler,* 13 Sept. and 15 Sept. 1948, BU SPC; *Boston Evening American,* 10 Nov. 1948. On the cultural context for associating homosexuality with communism, see John D'Emilio, *Sexual Politics, Sexual Communities: The Making of a Homosexual Minority in the United States, 1940-1970* (Chicago: University of Chicago Press, 1983) and Elaine Tyler May, *Homeward Bound: American Families in the Cold War* (New York: Basic Books, 1988). Massachusetts enacted laws against the employment of communists in the 1950s (Caute, *Great Fear,* 550).

22. "Bettie Cane" to MVW, 2 July 1948 and Cane to Claude Cross, 7 Feb. 1949, file 280.

23. GT to Gov. Bradford, 31 May 1948, file 194; GT to Rantoul, 26 June 1948, file 194; transcript of Thompson-Goodale meeting, 2 Sept. 1948, file 197; Dummer to MVW, 6 Aug. 1948, file 139; MVW to Dummer, 8 Feb. 1949, file 825, Dummer Papers.

24. Charles H. Trout, *Boston, the Great Depression, and the New Deal* (New York: Oxford University Press, 1977), 137, 101, 134.

25. The "Sponsoring Committee" of FOF included over one hundred names, including former commissioner of corrections Warren Stearns, the Rt. Rev. William Appleton Lawrence, Dr. Samuel A. Eliot, and several local rabbis, ministers, judges, and physicians.

26. *Harvard Law School Record,* 15 Nov. 1950, file 142; John C. Smith, *Alger Hiss: The True Story* (New York: Holt, Rinehart and Winston, 1976), 400–401. The original lawyer was dropped because he was the partner of Gov. Dever, who was expected to rule on appeal (Eliot, "The Van Waters Case," 36).

27. Staff memos to MVW, 8 Sept. and 10 Sept. 1948, file 197; MVW to Dorothy Canfield Fisher, 1 Aug. 1948, file 196.

28. *Boston Herald Traveler,* 13 Sept., 14 Sept., 15 Sept., and 24 Sept. 1948; *Boston Evening American,* 10 Nov. 1948; *Boston Sunday Advertiser,* 14 Nov. 1948. Although some staff members at the *Christian Science Monitor* felt sympathetic to Van Waters, they had to fight "tooth and nail" to keep the paper from supporting her dismissal. Former Norfolk colony superintendent Maurice Winslow had spoken to the editors at length off the record, convincing them of Van Waters' guilt (copy of letter from Saville Davis to Katherine [?], Jan. 1949, file 202).

29. "Notes on Public Hearing at State House, Room 433, before the Appointed Legislative Commission on Conditions at the Reformatory for

Women, Framingham, Senator J. Elmer Callahan, Chairman," 22 Nov. 1948, esp. 10, file 250 (hereafter Callahan Hearings).

30. Callahan Hearings, 24–25, 27–29.

31. *Boston Herald Traveler,* 18 Nov. 1948, and "Says Former Chiefs Backed Techniques," *Herald Traveler,* November 1948, BU SPC.

32. MVW journal, 14 Oct. 1948, 220v, Gladding-VW Papers.

33. *Boston Herald,* 17 Dec. 1948, and editorial in support 13 Dec. 1948, and *Boston Traveler,* 28 Dec. 1948, file 408; *Christian Science Monitor,* 27 Dec. 1948, 28 Dec. 1948, file 408.

34. *Boston Herald,* 13 Dec., 14 Dec., and 16 Dec. 1948, file 408; *Christian Science Monitor,* 31 Dec. 1948; *Boston Herald,* 17 Dec., 18 Dec., and 19 Dec. 1948; ER to *Daily News* 29 Dec. 1948; *Boston Traveler, Boston Globe,* 29 Dec. 1948 and 6 Jan. 1949; *Boston Record, Boston Herald, Providence Journal,* all 30 Dec. 1948; other clippings from New England newspapers in file 408; copy of letter from Dorothy Kirchwey Brown to GT, n.d., c. 5 Jan. 1949, General Correspondence, Eleanor Roosevelt Papers, FDR Library (hereafter ER Papers); endorsement letters in files 198-99; *Boston Post,* 3 Jan. 1949, file 408. MVW also received private endorsements, e.g., from former commissioner of corrections Francis Sayre, who offered any help and the confidential information that Supreme Court justice Felix Frankfurter "feels the same way as I do" (Sayre to MVW, 28 Dec. 1948, enclosed with letter from GT to ER, 7 Jan. 1949, General Correspondence, ER Papers).

35. GT to ER, 15 Jan. 1949, file 201; MVW journal, 10 Dec. 1948, file 220v, Gladding-VW Papers. Although Sheldon Glueck later denied that he advised EEM directly, his papers contain materials that suggest that he drafted some of the commissioner's attacks. The Gluecks considered Van Waters to be autocratic, and they harbored resentment because she had never produced a book based on her work for the Harvard Crime Survey. (Sheldon Glueck to LaRue Brown, 27 Jan. 1949, Amy Row to Sheldon Glueck, 2 Jan. 1949 and 20 Feb. 1949, and Sheldon Glueck to Thomas Eliot, 7 Dec. 1953 box 111, file 8, Sheldon Glueck Papers, Harvard Law School Library, Cambridge, Mass.)

36. ER letter, 19 Dec. 1948, file 200; GT to Dorothy Kirchwey Brown, 4 Jan. 1949, file 201; ER to GT, n.d., in response to an enclosed letter from GT dated 5 Jan. 1949, General Correspondence, ER Papers; ER to GT, 13 Jan. 1949, file 8, Friends of Framingham Papers, Schlesinger Library, Cambridge, Mass. (hereafter FOF Papers); Miriam Clark Nichols to ER, 18 Jan. 1949, file 8, FOF Papers (the letter was reprinted in *The Civil Service Reporter* in Feb. 1949); Geo. Hooper to FOF, 1 Jan. 1949, file 8, FOF Papers. Nichols was a well-known "character" at the statehouse, according to the *Boston Herald* (26 Feb. 1949).

37. EEM to MVW, 7 Jan. 1949, file 201.

38. GT to Dorothy Brown, 4 Jan. 1949, file 201; Dorothy Brown to GT, enclosed with GT to ER, 5 Jan. 1949, General Correspondence, ER Papers; GT to Dever, 14 Jan. 1949, file 201.

39. GT to ER, 7 Jan. 1949, General Correspondence, ER Papers; 8 Jan. 1949, file 351; MVW journal, 7 Jan. 1949, file 220v, Gladding-VW Papers; 8 Jan. or 9 Jan. 1949, *Boston Traveler* BU SPC; MVW to SVWH, 8 Jan. 1949, file 86; MVW journal, 11 Jan. 1949, file 220v, Gladding-VW Papers.

40. MVW to SVWH, 8 Jan. 1949, file 86; Peg O'Keefe to MVW, 9 Jan. 1949, file 201;

41. MVW to GT, 20 Oct. 1948, file 139; MVW to SVWH, 8 Jan. 1949, file 86; e.g., *Boston Globe,* 10 Jan. 1949, and unmarked clipping, Nov. 1948.

CHAPTER FIFTEEN

1. MVW journal, 27 Jan. and 4 Feb. 1949, file 220v, Gladding-VW Papers.

2. Dorothy Canfield Fisher to David [?], 17 Jan. 1949, file 201; interview with Cynthia Thomas, 18 Jan. 1994; MVW to SVWH, 8 Jan. 1949, file 86; Edwin Lukas, "Bridewell Revisited," *Nation,* 12 Feb. 1949, 178–81; "Canton Woman Mentioned for Van Waters Post," undated newspaper clipping, file 408; Arthur W. Hepner, "Ordeal in Massachusetts: The Vindication of Dr. Van Waters," *Harpers,* June 1949, 81–89; On Winslow's role see also S. Daisy to Catharine C., Jan. 1949, file 202; Thomas Eliot, "The Van Waters Case," The Inter-University Case Program, Cases in Public Administration and Policy Formation (Swarthmore, Pa.: Swarthmore College, 1953), 9–11, file 259 [later published by University of Alabama Press, 1954, 1960]; LaRue Brown interview, 35, box 14, folder 4, LaRue Brown Papers, Harvard Law School Library.

3. Lukas, "Bridewell," 178; MVW to Dummer, 27 Jan. 1949, file 825, Dummer Papers; Beckie Van Waters Bartholomew to MVW, 28 Jan. 1949, file 100; "Mass: The Big House Lady," *Newsweek,* 31 Jan. 1949, 22; Charles Milligan, "A Probe with a Happy Ending," *Progressive* 13:5 (May 1949): 23. A state representative called the hearing "a Salem witch hunt," ignoring the fact that Van Waters had called for the opportunity to defend herself (Laura Haddock, "Dr. Van Waters Presents Her Side of Controversy," *Christian Science Monitor,* 21 Jan. 1949, 2).

4. LaRue Brown interview, 36.

5. MVW journal, 21 Jan. 1949, 3 Feb. 1949, file 220v, Gladding-VW Papers; Sara White, "McDowell Produces Records," 13 Jan. 1949, and "Van Waters," 17 Jan. 1949, *Boston Traveler;* Laura Haddock, "McDowell Offers to Hear Dr. Van Waters in Private," *Christian Science Monitor,* 20 Jan. 1949, 2; interview with Margaret van Wagenen, 31 July 1989.

6. Alice Crane Baldwin to Elizabeth Woods, 4 Feb. 1949, file 203; interview with Harriet Gunning, 26 March 1993, Ashland, Mass.; Sara White, "McDowell Produces Records," *Boston Traveler,* 13 Jan., 24 Jan., and 25 Jan. 1949; Deborah Webster to MVW, 3 Feb. 1949, file 203. Several staff members recalled in interviews the care Van Waters took in dressing for the hearings. According to Margaret van Wagenen, Claude Cross advised her to wear short sleeves in order to dispel rumors that her long sleeves hid needle marks that indicated drug use (interview, 31 July 1989).

7. Telephone interview with Cynthia Thomas, 8 Jan. 1994; John C. Smith, *Alger Hiss: The True Story* (New York: Holt, Rinehart and Winston, 1976), 400; transcript of "Public Hearing in the Matter of the Removal of Dr. Miriam Van Waters as Superintendent of the Reformatory for Women. Before Elliott E. McDowell, Commissioner of Correction. Jan. 13–Feb. 8, 1949," e.g., 145, 346 (located at the Office of the Superintendent, MCI-Framingham, Framingham, Mass.; hereafter "In the Matter").

8. "In the Matter," 3–4, 341, 346, 1808–10; Sara White, *Boston Traveler,* 19 Jan. 1949, BU SPC.

9. Hepner, "Ordeal in Massachusetts"; Mrs. Willa Brown to MVW, 10 Feb. 1949, file 203; Alice Crane Baldwin to Elizabeth Woods, 4 Feb. 1949, file 203. John O'Connor, "Hearing Breaks Up in Angry Outburst," *Boston Herald,* 3 Feb. 1949.

10. Alice Crane Baldwin to Elizabeth Woods, 4 Feb. 1949, file 203; Sara White, *Boston Traveler,* 15 Jan. 1949; John O'Connor, *Boston Herald,* 29 Jan. 1949 and "Van Waters Counsel Says File Altered," undated clipping, Feb. 1949, BU SPC; MVW to Dummer, 27 Jan. 1949, file 825, Dummer Papers; "The Big House Lady," *Newsweek,* 31 Jan. 1949, 22; Sara White, "McDowell Produces Records against Aides," *Boston Traveler,* 13 Jan. 1949.

11. "In the Matter," 3–9, 145–60, 341, 846; MVW to Dummer, 27 Jan. 1949, file 825, Dummer Papers; John O'Connor, *Boston Herald,* 29 Jan. 1949.

12. John O'Connor, "McDowell Refuses to Restore Job," 26 Jan. 1949, and "Abrupt Edict on Indenture Upset Regime," *Boston Herald,* 27 Jan. 1949.

13. "In the Matter," 1730–2206, esp. 1836, 1897, 2003.

14. Ibid., 5–6, 1785–86; Sara White, *Boston Traveler,* 19 Jan. 1949. In her journal, Van Waters noted that Lyman had been angry with her for not informing him of O'Keefe's juvenile record (MVW journal, 2 June 1949, file 220v, Gladding-VW Papers).

15. "In the Matter," 1734, 110, 1903, 109, 1750.

16. Ibid., 145–55, 341; Sara White, *Boston Traveler,* 19 Jan. 1949; John O'Connor, "McDowell Would Listen but Not Cross," *Boston Herald,* 20 Jan. 1949.

17. "In the Matter," 1775, 1793–95, 1806–15.

18. Ibid., 1932–40.

19. Ibid., 1629–89. MVW explained to a reporter that when the state placed babies in boarding homes, mothers could only visit once a month; the Framingham staff had encouraged more frequent contact (Sara White, *Boston Traveler,* 11 Jan. 1949, clipping in file 408).

20. "In the Matter," 1669, 1672, also 1676.

21. Ibid., 1652, 2027–39.

22. Sara White, "McDowell Produces Record against Aides," *Boston Traveler,* 13 Jan. 1949; John O'Connor, "Insists Cases Approved by Other Chiefs," *Boston Herald,* 14 Jan. 1949.

23. John O'Connor, "Counsel Says McDowell Ruining Lives," *Boston*

Herald, 21 Jan. 1949, O'Connor, *Boston Herald,* 29 Jan. 1949, Sara White, *Boston Traveler,* 25 Jan. 1949, BU SPC; "Van Waters Probe Ends until Monday," *Christian Science Monitor,* 29 Jan. 1949, 2; "In the Matter," 1611.

24. John O'Connor, "Van Waters Rejects Inmate Sex Charge," *Boston Herald,* 25 Jan. 1949, Sara White, *Boston Traveler,* 25 Jan. 1949, BU SPC.

25. Mary McIntosh, "The Homosexual Role," *Social Problems* 16:2 (fall 1968), 182–92; Estelle B. Freedman, "'Uncontrolled Desires': The Response to the Sexual Psychopath, 1920–1960," *Journal of American History* 74 (June 1987), 83–106.

26. John O'Connor, "Van Waters Rejects Inmate Sex Charge," 25 Jan. 1949, BU SPC.

27. McDowell Exhibits 126, 126A, 129 and 129A, and case 18572, file 251; "In the Matter," e.g., 1815, 1947–51, 1884.

28. O'Connor, "Van Waters Rejects Inmate Sex Charge," 25 Jan. 1949, and "McDowell Refuses to Restore Job," 26 Jan. 1949, BU SPC.

29. "In the Matter," e.g., 1738, 1753, 1614–18, 1989, 1775, 1764, 1885.

30. Virginia R. Hatch [Pres., New Bedford Women's Club], 23 Jan. 1949, *Boston Herald,* BU SPC; Nancy Newell to editor, *Christian Science Monitor,* 25 Feb. 1949. For other favorable letters to the *CSM,* see 22 Jan. 1949, 20.

31. P. W. Linscott to LaRue Brown, 2 March 1949, and Helen [?] to Dorothy [?], undated Feb. 1949, file 8, FOF Papers; "Flays Regime of Dr. Van Waters," press clipping, file 408; "Clash on Data Marks Van Waters Hearing," *New York Times,* 26 Feb. 1949, 30.

32. MVW journal, 2 Jan. 1949, 9 Feb. 1949, file 220v, Gladding-VW Papers.

33. McDowell decision, 11 Feb. 1949, file 203; Eliot, ts. 59–63.

34. *Survey,* 21 Jan. 1949, 3; John O'Connor, *Boston Herald,* 19 Jan. 1949; Mrs. Willa W. Brown, 10 Feb. 1949, file 203 and various letters in files 202, 203, 204, including Congregational Church Boston Woman's Guild, Massachusetts Episcopal Church Service League Women's Division, and Lincoln Settlement House (Frederick B. Taylor to Gov. Dever, 19 Jan. 1949, file 202).

35. Letters and clippings in files 202, 203, 204, 210; Perkins to MVW, 2 March 1949, file 205; ER newsclip, 22 Jan. 1949 and ER to MVW, 31 Jan. 1949, file 202; MVW to Dummer, 2 Feb. and 8 Feb. 1949, file 825, Dummer Papers.

36. Eliot, "Van Waters Case," 64. Griswold served as solicitor general under Presidents Lyndon Johnson and Richard Nixon (obituary, *New York Times,* 21 Nov. 1994).

37. "The Decision of the Impartial Commission," in *The Van Waters Case,* pamphlet published by the Friends of Framingham, 1949, 4 (hereafter *Van Waters Case*); Eliot, "Van Waters Case," 64–66; *New York Times,* 5 March 1949, Harvard *Crimson,* 16 Feb. 1949, file 104, Gladding-MVW Papers; LaRue Brown interview, 38. The commission also met once at the reformatory.

38. *Van Waters Case,* 6; Eliot, "Van Waters Case," 66–69; *New York*

Times, 5 March 1949; MVW journal, 4 March 1949, file 220v, Gladding-VW Papers. Attorney General Francis Kelly had originally appointed Bernard Killion to represent EEM, but he replaced him with Fielding (Eliot, "Van Waters Case," 64–65, 70).

39. MVW journal, 4 March, 5 March, and 6 March 1949, file 220v, Gladding-VW Papers.

40. At the end of his summation, EEM leaped up and shouted, "This is a case for justifiable homicide!" (Eliot, "Van Waters Case," 66–69; "Van Waters Hearing Ends on Sharp Note," *New York Times,* 5 March 1949); MVW to Cross, 6 March 1949, and Cross to MVW, 8 March 1949, file 205; Hepner, "Ordeal in Massachusetts"; Claude B. Cross, Memorial to LaRue Brown, 10–11, box 8, Dorothy Kirchwey Brown Papers, Schlesinger Library, Cambridge, Mass.

41. *Van Waters Case,* 7–15.

42. ER to GT, 19 March 1949, General Correspondence, ER Papers.

43. Interview with Pauline Orsi, 26 March 1993, Ashland, Mass.; O'Keefe to Cross, 18 March 1949, file 209; Bill Dorman, "Rousing Welcome for Van Waters," *Boston Traveler,* n.d. (11 or 12 March 1949), BU SPC; Cross to inmate, 12 March 1949, file 210; letter to editor, *New York Times,* 21 March 1949; telephone interview with Howard Kellett, 14 Sept. 1989; MVW journal, 11 March 1949, file 220v, Gladding-VW Papers.

44. MVW journal, 13 March 1949 and MVW to AG, 11 July 1949, file 220v, Gladding-VW Papers.

45. *Boston Traveler,* 11 March 1949; letter and telegrams in file 206, 208; O'Keefe to MVW and Felix Frankfurter to MVW, 12 March 1949, file 207; *New York Times,* 21 March 1949, 22. Other congratulatory messages came from ACLU founder Roger Baldwin, the president of Vassar College, a successful small businessman with a reform school past, women's club members, and relatives (all in file 208). The theme of justice triumphant recurred in editorials in the *Progressive, Newsweek,* and the *Boston Herald.*

46. All letters to MVW, March 1949, in file 208.

47. Maybelle Blake to MVW, undated March 1949, file 309, Gladding-MVW Papers; Nancy Newell to MVW, undated March 1949, file 208.

48. Dummer to MVW, 6 Oct. 1950, file 142; Eliot, "Van Waters Case," 71–72; "LoPresti Hits Decision as 'Vicious,'" undated newsclipping, BU SPC; MVW journal, 4 Aug. 1949, file 220v, Gladding-VW Papers; MVW to SVWH, 22 March 1949, file 86.

CHAPTER SIXTEEN
1. MVW journal, vol. 9, 4 Aug. 1951. The superintendent's house had two divergent stairways leading up from the front hall and the back hall. The back staircase faced toward the reformatory, the front faced toward the lawn.

2. Circular for mass meeting, 30 March 1949, file 407; Portia Law School to MVW, 23 May 1949, file 527, and Commencement, 18 June 1949, in Gladding-VW Papers; Western College (Oxford, Ohio) honorary doctorate

recorded in MVW journal, vol. 10, 30 May 1955; MVW journal, 14 Nov. 1949, 1 Jan. 1950, file 220v, Gladding-VW Papers; clippings on American Women of Achievement, 15 May 1951, file 527.

3. Speaking engagements in files 462, 484; Public Relations Clippings, 1 Oct. 1953, Clark University Archives; MVW journal, vol. 10, 17 April 1955; "Juvenile Delinquency," *Encyclopedia Britannica,* 1950, file 484; Miriam Van Waters, "Christian Social Reform," in J. Richard Spann, ed., *Fruits of Faith* (New York: Abingdon-Cokesbury Press, 1950); Marynia Farnham to MVW, 13 Oct. 1950, file 142; "Dr. Van Waters Asks Public to Curb Sex Crimes," *Boston Herald Traveler,* 24 Sept. 1950; MVW journal, 16 Aug. 1949, 20 June 1951, file 220v, Gladding-VW Papers. MVW was also asked to testify at the U.S. Senate subcommittee hearings on juvenile delinquency. Whenever she received fees for her talks, she deposited them in the reformatory student fund.

4. Transcript of 2 March 1952 program, file 489; transcript of *Dr. Van Waters Speaks,* file 493 and tape recordings, file T-35; correspondence concerning *Caged,* file 218. Other television appearances include WBZ-TV, 30 Sept. 1953 and WGBH (MVW journal, vol. 10, 12 Aug. 1957).

5. "Resolution" of Protestant Episcopal Church, Diocese of Massachusetts, 4 May and 5 May 1949, file 214; League of Women Voters, 27 June 1949, file 407; MVW to Mrs. Taylor, 3 Jan. 1952, file 22; Friends of Framingham Report, April 1952, and correspondence to MVW, file 222; Mrs. Freeman to MVW, 7 Nov. 1955, file 225 (and other Friendly Visitors to MVW in this file); Training Course for Friendly Visitors, file 256; Virginia Rae on Friendly Visitors, 1 Nov. 1956, file 226; MVW lecture to Friendly Visitors, Jan. 1956, file 261; Miriam Van Waters, "Progress at the Reformatory for Women," *Church Militant* 45:4 (April 1952): 1–5; MVW, ts. memoir, fragment, file 508; Ann Bartholomew to MVW, undated 1954, file 100.

6. MVW first visited McWilliams on death row at Joliet penitentiary in 1931, when he was seventeen years old (MVW to parents, 6 Dec. 1931, file 62). His sentence—for the shooting of a motorman during a gas station robbery—was commuted to ninety-nine years. MVW recounted the case in "Social Responsibility of School and Court," *Educational Record* 18:3 (July 1937): 3–11, file 478. She later explained that Julia Lathrop had left a small legacy to pursue McWilliams' appeal (MVW to Mrs. Cheek, 3 Sept. 1969, file 627). See also: GT to ER, 23 Dec. 1949, General Correspondence, Lash Papers, FDR Library; MVW to Dummer, 11 Dec. 1950, file 825, Dummer Papers; Adlai Stevenson to GT, 15 Feb. 1951, and MVW to Stevenson, 26 Feb. 1951, file 627.

7. MVW, notes for state prison talk, 18 Dec. 1949, file 484; letters from male prisoners in file 596; Howard Kellett, ts. reminiscence of MVW, read at the Parson's Club, n.d., 1960s (in possession of author).

8. Vivian Pierce to members, ALACP, 15 May 1947, file 530; ALACP correspondence, file 531; Massachusetts Council, file 580; Miriam Van Waters, intro. to Wenzell Brown, *Women Who Died in the Chair: The Dramatic True Stories of Six Women Who Committed the Deadliest Sin* (1958; rpt., New York: Collier, 1963); "Women Prison Heads Oppose Death Penalty,"

New York Herald Tribune, 8 Feb. 1951, file 587. ALACP membership lists contain about five hundred names; other sponsors included, in 1941: ACLU founder Roger Baldwin; Hull House resident Jessie F. Binford; psychiatrists A. A. Brill, Karl Menninger, and Winfred Overholser; social reformers Fannia M. Cohn, Dorothy Canfield Fisher, Arthur Garfield Hays, and Paul Kellogg; and criminologists Thorsten Sellin, Frank Tannenbaum, Negley K. Teeters, and Warden Lewis E. Lawes (file 529). The League had been run single-handedly for years by a devoted crusader, Vivian Pierce. On the obstacles to reform, see her annual reports, e.g., 1945, 1946, file 529.

9. *Dr. Van Waters Speaks,* program 2, reel 8, file T-35; Franklin Flaschner to Austin MacCormick, 18 Nov. 1949, and various correspondence, file 1 and file 6, Friends of Framingham Papers, Schlesinger Library (hereafter FOF Papers); Dorothy Kirchwey Brown to Ethel Sturges Dummer, n.d. [1949], file 825, Dummer Papers; former inmate-MVW correspondence, e.g., 5 June 1952, file 282; Franklin Flaschner, "Address in memory of LaRue Brown at the Friends of Framingham Annual Meeting," 8 May 1969, "LaRue Brown," memorial pamphlet, 23, file 8, box 205, Dorothy Kirchwey Brown Papers, Schlesinger Library, Cambridge, Mass.

10. MVW to SVWH, 4 Feb. 1950, file 86; *Better American Federation Bulletin,* 7 March 1930, cited in ALACP FBI file, in author's possession. Although legislators in Connecticut, New Jersey, Ohio, and Massachusetts introduced bills to abolish capital punishment in the 1950s, they did not pass. Hawaii eliminated the death penalty in 1957 (*New York Times,* 4 June 1955, 7 July 1957, 7 April 1959, 15 July 1959).

11. Larry Sullivan, *The Prison Reform Movement: Forlorn Hope* (Boston: Twayne, 1990), chap. 3.

12. Bullock to MVW, 28 June 1949, file 215; MVW to Kellett, 13 Jan. 1950 (copy provided by Kellett, in possession of author); MVW journal, vol. 10, 10 March and 9 June 1955; MVW to EEM, 3 May 1949 and EEM to MVW, 29 June 1949, file 215; "Van Waters Regime to Get Freer Hand," unmarked newsclipping, 6 July 1949, file 408; Frederick H. Guildry, "Van Waters Case: Five Years Bare Hollow Victory," *Christian Science Monitor,* 10 Aug. 1954.

13. Guildry, "Van Waters Case"; MVW, "Situation to Date," 22 Sept. 1949, file 253; testimony of Commissioner McDowell, 2 Nov. 1949, transcript in file 253.

14. Erwin Griswold to MVW, 18 Jan. 1951, file 221; ER to GT with clipping, 12 Jan. 1950, file 142; GT to Dever, 1 Dec. 1950 and GT to ER, 22 Jan. 1951, General Correspondence, ER Papers.

15. GT to ER, 22 Jan. 1951, General Correspondence, ER Papers; MVW journal, vol. 9, 12 July 1951; transcript, 2 March 1952, file 489; FOF report, April 1952, file 222, FOF Papers; Miriam Van Waters, "Progress at the Reformatory for Women," 1–3; MVW journal, vol. 9, 8 Oct. 1951, 25 Sept. 1951; Guildry, "Van Waters Case."

16. MVW journal, vol. 9, 30 Sept. 1952, 15 Dec. 1952; FOF report, Dec. 1952, file 222. MVW had hoped that Nancy Lawrence, an intern who was the daughter of Episcopal bishop William A. Lawrence, would become her

successor. When Lawrence decided to marry and leave the reformatory, MVW began to pray for someone else to appear (MVW to Bishop Lawrence, 13 Aug. 1949, file 215). Republican congressman Christian A. Herter—who would later serve as U.S. secretary of state—defeated Dever in the 1952 gubernatorial election. In the meantime, Grossman came under attack because of riots and scandals in the state prison system.

17. MVW journal, vol. 9, 14 Dec. and 27 Dec. 1952, 9 Jan., 27 Jan., and 13 Aug. 1953; vol. 10, 5 Oct. 1954; GT to ER, 24 Feb. 1954, General Correspondence, Lash Papers, FDR Library. GT added: "Forgive me for making suggestions to one of the great speech-makers of the U.S.A., but I care more and more about the necessity to create a person-to-person atmosphere."

18. MVW journal, 13 April 1945, file 219v, Gladding-VW Papers; MVW to SVWH, 11 Oct. 1948, file 86.

19. MVW journal, vol. 9, 21 July and 13 Sept. 1952 on sharing deed to Hilltop land; vol. 10, 10 Dec. 1955; interview with Margaret van Wagenen, 31 July 1989.

20. MVW to SVWH, 19 Feb. 1950, file 86; MVW journal, vol. 9, 12 July 1951; interview with Richard J. Hildebrandt, 18 Aug. 1989; MVW journal, vol. 9, 2 June 1952, 16 July 1951; MVW journal, 2 Oct., 4 Oct., and 6 July 1951, file 220v, Gladding-MVW Papers.

21. MVW journal, vol. 9, 2 Oct. 1951, 30 Jan. 1953.

22. MVW journal, vol. 9, 5 Feb., 6 Feb., 7 Feb., and 31 March 1953.

23. MVW journal, vol. 9, 6 Feb., 7 Feb. 1953.

24. MVW journal, vol. 9, 8 Feb., 9 Feb., 10 Feb., 12 Feb., 13 Feb., 14 Feb., and 21 Feb. 1953.

25. MVW journal, vol. 9, 22 Feb., 31 March, 12 May, 20 Dec. 1953, 30 Jan. 1954, 25 Dec. 1955; vol. 9, 9 April 1953; interview with Richard J. Hildebrandt, 18 Aug. 1989.

26. Interview with Margaret van Wagenen, 31 July 1989; telephone interview with Cynthia Thomas, 18 Jan. 1994.

27. MVW journal, vol. 9, 9 March 1953; Helen Bryan to MVW, n.d. [1954], file 224.

28. Helen Bryan, *Inside* (New York: Houghton Mifflin, 1953); MVW journal, vol. 10, 11 Feb. 1953; Netty Radvanyi, *Anna Seghers [and] Constancia de la Mora Tell the Story of the Joint Anti-Fascist Refugee Committee* (n.p.: New York, 1944), n.p.; David Caute, *The Great Fear: The Anti-Communist Purge under Truman and Eisenhower* (New York: Simon and Schuster, 1978), esp. 170, 177–78; *New York Times,* obituary, 11 Sept. 1976. Both liberals and leftists served on the JAFRC board, which included several CIO officials, actor-activist Paul Robeson, former Mt. Holyoke president Mary Woolley, and, coincidentally, Dr. Francis M. Pottenger, in whose tuberculosis sanatorium MVW once resided.

29. "On Doing Time," *Nation,* 2 May 1953, 379–80; Bryan to MVW, 28 Jan. and 5 Feb. 1954, file 224.

30. Bryan to MVW, 17 March 1953, file 223; MVW journal, vol. 10, 30 March 1953.

31. MVW journal, vol. 10, 2 April, 1 May, 31 May, 1 June, and 6 June 1953; Lurie to MVW, 24 June 1953, file 223.

32. *Boston Herald,* 20 June, 26 June, 30 June, and 21 July 1953 and *Boston Traveler,* 15 July and 21 Aug. 1953, BU SPC; MVW journal, vol. 9, 25 June 1953, 2 July 1953; MVW to AG, 26 June and 2 July 1953, file 21, Gladding-VW Papers.

33. Bryan to MVW, 1 July and 15 July 1953, file 223. MVW to Austin MacCormick, 7 Aug. 1953 and to Henry Cadbury (American Friends Service Committee), 8 Aug. 1953, file 223; Katharine Driscoll to FOF members, 10 Aug. 1953, file 223; Bishop Lawrence to editor, *Springfield Union,* 19 Oct. 1949 (re: charge of subversive activity in a 8 Oct. 1949 article on MVW); MVW to Dr. Dorothy Banton, 30 Oct. 1953, file 532.

34. Van Waters' FBI file, released under the Freedom of Information/ Privacy Acts, included documentation of her participation, since the 1920s, in organizations such as the American Civil Liberties Union, the Mary Ware Dennett Defense Committee, the Los Angeles Anti-Narcotic League, the American Youth Commission of the National Council on Education, the Massachusetts Minute Women for Peace, and the American League to Abolish Capital Punishment.

35. SAC, Boston (100–15782) to Director, FBI (100–206852), "Office Memorandum" re: Helen Reid Bryan, 20 Jan. 1954, FBI file (emphasis in original).

36. Bryan to MVW, 28 Jan. 1954 n.d. [1954], file 224; MVW journal, vol. 10, 13 Nov. 1953 and 7 Jan. 1957; Bryan to MVW, undated 1954, and 28 Jan. 1954, file 224. There are two versions of the latter letter, one for Van Waters' eyes and one, with fewer intimate endearments, for the Friends of Framingham.

37. MVW journal, vol. 10, 6 June 1955, 7 Jan. 1957; MVW to Dr. Richard Coswell Smith, 23 Jan. 1956, file 226; 6 March 1954, 6 May 1954.

38. Ann Bartholomew to MVW, undated 1954, file 100; MVW staff notes, 19 Jan. 1950, file 254.

39. Data compiled from the Massachusetts Department of Corrections, *Annual Reports* and *Statistical Reports* evidence the shift:

Table 3 First-Time Offenders in Framingham Reformatory and
Type of Offense Committed

	First-Time Offenders (%)	Offense Against		
		Person (%)	Property (%)	Public Order (%)
1934	62.7	0.4	5.7	93.9
1946	50.0	2.0	9.3	88.7
1950	43.7	3.7	9.5	86.8
1953	51.2	7.4	11.1	81.5
1956	34.4	4.9	7.7	87.4

40. Interview with Katherine Gabel, 1 Feb. 1991, Pasadena, Calif.

41. See David A. Ward and Gene G. Kassebaum, *Women's Prison: Sex and Social Structure* (Chicago: Aldine, 1965) and Rose Giallombardo, *Society of Women: A Study of a Women's Prison* (New York: John Wiley, 1966).

42. John D'Emilio, *Sexual Politics, Sexual Communities: The Making of a Homosexual Minority in the United States, 1940–1970* (Chicago: University of Chicago Press, 1983), 41–53.

43. Margaret O'Keefe to MVW, 15 June 1949, file 215; MVW journal, vol. 9, 20 Sept. 1951.

44. MVW to Mrs. Dorothy Miller, 16 June 1949, and Dr. Augustus S. Rose to Miller, 20 July 1949, file 68, Papers of the Mass. Society for Social Hygiene, Schlesinger Library, Cambridge, Mass.; MVW, 24 Oct. 1951, BU lectures.

45. MVW, BU lectures, 24 Oct. 1951. MVW also stressed the need to "distinguish between homosexual activity which is commercial and homosexual activity which is not predatory and not promiscuous." Homosexual prostitution, she argued, was as exploitative as heterosexual prostitution. Her belief in the redemption of lesbians was consistent with her evangelical Protestant belief in salvation.

46. Katharine Sullivan, *Girls on Parole* (Boston: Houghton Mifflin/Riverside Press, 1956), 111–19.

47. On the fears of unleashed female sexuality, see Elaine Tyler May, *Homeward Bound: American Families in the Cold War Era* (New York: Basic Books, 1988), chap 4.

48. A. Perry Holt, Jr., Deputy Commissioner, to Commissioner Reuben L. Lurie, 21 May 1954, in "Escapes," Framingham file, Mass. Archives, Human Services, Corrections, Reference Files, Series 1137x (hereafter Framingham file, Mass. Archives).

49. *Boston Globe*, editorial, 22 May 1954, file 410; news clipping Jan. 1955, file 416[v]; *New York Times*, 19 Jan., 4 June, 29 Aug. 1955.

50. MVW journal, vol. 9, 17 Aug. 1953; vol. 10, 18 June, 28 July, and 1 Aug. 1954. Before MVW came to Framingham, only one or two women ran away each year. With the expansion of indenture, escapes rose to approximately 17 per year, with a return rate of 72 percent. Between 1950 and 1952, when outside employment was limited, the average was 10 per year, all of whom returned. The return rate for 1956–57 was 90 percent. (Figures derived from Matthew W. Bullock to Commissioner of Corrections, 2 Oct. 1937, "Analysis of Statistics of Escape from RW: 1907 to 1 June 1937," and Margaret O'Keefe to Arthur Lyman, 23 Aug. 1957, in "Escapes," Framingham file, Mass. Archives.)

51. *Boston Evening American*, 18 Aug. 1955, file 408; MVW journal, vol. 10, 18 Aug., 22 Aug., 24 Aug., 28 Aug., 1 Sept., and 2 Sept. 1955. Eight inmates were indicted by a grand jury after the investigation (*Boston Herald Traveler*, 13 Sept. 1955, BU SPC). As a result of a series of prison disturbances, Commissioner Spurr soon left office and was replaced by Russell Oswald, a liberal from Wisconsin.

52. E.g. MVW journal, vol. 10, 17 Jan., 1 June, and 19 June 1956; vol.

10, 8 Jan., 12 March, 21 April, 6 May, and 10 June 1956; MVW to GT, 2 July 1956, file 267, Gladding-VW Papers; MVW journal, vol. 10, 17 Nov. 1956 and 18 Nov. 1956.

53. MVW journal, vol. 10, 18 Nov., 20 Nov., 22 Nov., and 13 Dec. 1956; 19 Dec. 1956, MVW to *The Intercession Paper,* 14 Dec. 1956, file 585; telephone interview with Cynthia Thomas, 18 Jan. 1994.

54. MVW journal, vol. 10, 7 Jan., 18 Jan., and 25 Jan. 1957; MVW to AG, 17 Jan. 1957, file 23, Gladding-VW Papers; MVW journal vol. 10, 14 Feb., 18 Feb., 28 Feb., and 3 March 1957.

55. MVW journal, vol. 10, 21 March, 19 April, 25 April, 16 May, 15 June, 10 July, and 19 Aug. 1957.

56. MVW journal, vol. 10, 12 March 1957; *Christian Science Monitor,* 29 July 1957, file 418[v]; Leslie Cutler, et al., "Report of the Special Committee Authorized to Study the Reorganization of the Correctional System," Commonwealth of Mass. House Document No. 3015 (Boston, May 1958), 6–7 (hereafter Cutler Report).

57. *Christian Science Monitor,* 27 July, 1 Aug., and 2 Aug. 1957 (reporter James Nelson Goodsell made the suggestion); *Boston Herald Traveler,* 29 July and 31 July 1957, BU SPC.

58. A few supportive articles did appear, e.g., "Miss Van Waters Answers Reformatory Charges," and "Van Waters Defends Her Prison System," *Boston Herald,* undated 1957, BU SPC; *Harmony News,* July 1957, file 397; *Boston American,* 3 Sept. 1957, file 418v; *Christian Science Monitor,* 1 Aug. 1957, in file 6, FOF Papers.

59. *Boston Herald Traveler,* undated July 1957, BU SPC; "Legislative Information" Bulletin No. 20, Mass. Community Organization Service, "Correctional System of Massachusetts: Report of Special Legislative Committee Re: Women's Massachusetts Correctional Institution at Framingham," 12 May 1958, file 70, Papers of the Mass. Society for Social Hygiene, Schlesinger Library, Cambridge, Mass.

60. One of her supporters, Dean Erwin Griswold of the Harvard Law School, who had in 1949 chaired the commission that exonerated MVW, drew on elite male networks to help find a successor. Griswold wrote to his friend Eugene Rostow, then dean of Yale Law School, in the hopes that Rostow could influence his former classmate, Governor Furcolo, to appoint someone acceptable to MVW (Griswold to LaRue Brown, 20 Sept. 1957, file 6, and Rostow to Furcolo, 17 Sept. 1957, file 5, FOF Papers).

61. LaRue Brown, "Politics, Publicity, and Prisons," Jan. 1958, file 6, FOF Papers; Cutler Report, 6–7.

62. Cutler Report, 12–13.

63. Ibid., 56–59, 60.

64. GT to Peg O'Keefe, 31 Oct. 1957, file 227; O'Keefe to MVW, undated Oct. 1957, file 262; MVW notes, Jan. 1962, file 228. In 1955, Peg O'Keefe resigned temporarily but returned to the institution after three months (MVW journal, vol. 10, 17 Feb. 1955, 6 April 1955).

65. MVW journal, vol. 10, 15 Oct. 1957; John F. Kennedy to MVW, 18

Oct. 1957, file 227; "Forty-Seven Stood Up," ts. memoir chap., file 508; Program, Dinner to Honor Dr. Miriam Van Waters, Harvard Club, 15 Oct. 1957, file 335, Gladding-VW Papers.

66. Betty Cole Smith to MVW, "Report," 8 Dec. 1947, file 247; 1971 Retirement Banquet Program, in Framingham file, Mass. Archives; "Prison Chronicle," *New Yorker,* 12 June 1965, 47, 56. Before Smith's appointment, Elizabeth Bode served as acting superintendent.

CHAPTER SEVENTEEN

1. MVW journal, vol. 10, 7 Oct. 1957, 1 Nov. 1958; interviews with Margaret Van Wagenen, 31 July 1989, and with "Irene Jenner" and "Alice May," 15 Sept. 1989.

2. MVW journal, vol. 12, undated 1958 and 22 April 1959; Mrs. Watson to GT, 15 Oct. 1959, file 151. Unless otherwise noted, the following paragraphs derive from interviews with Margaret van Wagenen, Richard J. Hildebrandt, "Irene Jenner," "Alice May," and Cynthia Thomas.

3. MVW to AG, 2 Oct. 1961, file 24, Gladding-VW Papers; MVW journal, vol. 12, 1 Jan. 1958, undated April 1958, 1 Nov. 1958, 16 Dec. 1959. Ralph and MVW remained close through a series of family tragedies. In 1960, Bert Van Waters committed suicide after a recurrence of the depression that had plagued her in the 1930s. Her son, Ralph, Jr., who was then a teenager, also took his life. RVW survived until 1989; Elizabeth Bode Van Waters, who had long been incapacitated by a stroke, died in 1992.

4. MVW to SVWH, 27 June 1948, file 86; MVW to Dummer, 26 Sept. 1950, file 825, Dummer Papers; MVW to AG, 11 July 1949, file 19, Gladding-VW Papers; MVW journal, vol. 9, 25 July 1953, vol. 10, 2 Aug., 1 Aug., and 28 July 1956; MVW to GT, 2 July 1956, file 267, Gladding-VW Papers; MVW to AG, 3 March 1953, file 21; 9 Aug. 1955, file 22; 3 July 1951, file 20, all in Gladding-VW Papers; MVW journal, vol. 9, 23 Nov. 1951, vol. 10, 5 May 1953, 15 June 1953, 26 Jan. 1954, 3 Oct. 1954, 12 Nov. 1954, 2 Jan. 1955, 21 April 1956; GT to MVW, 11 Jan. 1950, file 142; GT to MVW, 3 Nov. 1952, file 144; MVW journal, 26 May 1951, file 220v, Gladding-VW Papers; MVW to AG, 21 July 1962, file 24, Gladding-VW Papers; MVW to AG, 2 Oct. 1961, 5 July 1962, 26 Aug. 1963, all in file 24, Gladding-VW Papers. Van Waters also started an Audubon Club at Framingham.

5. MVW journal, vol. 9, 2 March 1952, 25 July 1953; MVW-AG correspondence, files 20–25 (esp. MVW to AG, 26 Aug. 1963) file 24, Gladding-VW Papers.

6. At the time Scudder wrote, in the 1930s, there were between 400 and 500 members of the SCHC throughout the country. Each August the Companions held a two week retreat in Massachusetts. See Vida Scudder, *On Journey* (New York: E. P. Dutton and Co., 1937), 377–431; Mary Sudman Donovan, *A Different Call: Women's Ministries in the Episcopal Church, 1850–1920* (Wilton, Conn.: Morehouse-Barlow, 1986), 148–52; MVW journal, vol. 9, 11 Oct. 1951, 11 Jan. 1952; Scudder to MVW, 13 May, 19 Sept.,

and 14 Nov. 1952, file 585. MVW to SCHC, 16 June 1952, file 586; Scudder to MVW, 4 April 1953, file 585; MVW to SCHC, 3 Feb. 1956, file 585.

7. MVW journal, vol. 12, 23 July 1958, 13 April 1959, 3 May 1959, 16 Dec. 1959, undated 1959.

8. Interview with Katherine Gabel, 1 Feb. 1991; MVW journal, vol. 12, 3 May 1959, 6 Dec. 1959, 23 Dec. 1959; Peter Hildebrandt to MVW, undated 1971, file 92.

9. Interview with Margaret van Wagenen, 31 July, 1989; Bess Woods to MVW, 12 March 1959, file 151.

10. MVW to Kellett, 3 March 1959, file 151.

11. Telephone interview with Cynthia Thomas, 18 Jan. 1994.

12. MVW to Anne Gladding, 26 Aug. 1963, file 24, Gladding-VW Papers; MVW, notes for speech, 30 May 1958, file 264; cf. MVW journal, vol. 10, 28 March 1956.

13. Inmate to MVW, 12 Nov. 1970, box 9, Gladding-VW Papers.

14. Ibid.; e.g. inmate to "Dear Ma," undated Dec. 1957, file 334; correspondence with inmate, 1958–59, file 334 (e.g., 12 March 1959, 21 Aug. 1959); correspondence with inmate, file 396.

15. E.g., 28 May 1971, file 350, 22 Aug. 1971, file 157; MVW note on letter to Rebecca Yankauer, undated 1971, file 157; interviews with "Irene Jenner" and "Alice May," 15 Sept. 1989, and Margaret van Wagenen, 31 July 1989.

16. Various letters in file 591; MVW to inmate, 11 Sept. 1969, file 156; see also files 264, 154, and 590, and former inmate to MVW, 27 Oct. 1971, file 157; Claude Cross to MVW, 11 Jan. 1971, Gladding-VW Papers. Cf. GT's letters to ER to aid a Puerto Rican prisoner, 3 July 1958, General Correspondence, ER Papers.

17. MVW to SVWH, 4 Feb. 1950, file 86; MVW journal, vol. 10, 8 Feb. 1954; MVW to publishers, undated 1963, in file 152; Burton J. Rowles, *The Lady at Box 99* (Greenwich, Conn.: Seabury Press, 1962).

18. *Framingham News,* 7 Nov. 1962, file 495, 25 Mar. 1963, file 497; *Framingham News,* 19 Sept. 1968, box 2, folder 18, Crime, Criminals, and Prisons, Sophia Smith Collection, Smith College, Northampton, Mass.; Rebecca Low to MVW, 22 Oct. 1965, file 153.

19. Catharine O'Brien to ER, 24 Oct. 1960, General Correspondence, ER Papers, encloses MVW to GT, 20 Oct. 1960; MVW to AG, 8 June 1962, file 24, Gladding-VW Papers; Piney Woods Country Life School to MVW, undated 1970, file 157; clipping on Msgr. Callahan, *Framingham News,* 2 Nov. 1961, file 496.

20. Bess to MVW, 12 March 1959, file 151; Ruth Baker to MVW, 23 July 1965, file 153; Mrs. Richard Smith to MVW, 5 Aug. 1965, file 153; Hebe Robinson to MVW, 16 Nov. 1965, file 153; Mary Robinson to MVW, 7 July 1971, file 157. Cf. Susan Lynn, *Progressive Women in Conservative Times: Racial Justice, Peace, and Feminism, 1945 to the 1960s* (New Brunswick, N.J.: Rutgers University Press, 1992).

21. MVW to Mahan, 23 Aug. 1965, file 255, Gladding-VW Papers; inter-

view with "Irene Jenner" and "Alice May," 15 Sept. 1989; interview with Margaret van Wagenen, 31 July 1989.

22. MVW to AG, 13 May 1961, file 24; 12 July 1965, 21 July 1966, 18 July 1967, file 25, Gladding-VW Papers.

23. "Mrs. Thompson is 94 Tomorrow," *Red Bank Daily Register,* 1 March 1966, 3 March 1967, GT File, BCC; ER to MVW, 8 Jan. 1960, file 152; ER to GT, 6 Dec. 1961, General Correspondence, ER Papers.

24. MVW to Mahan, 6 Sept 1965, file 255, Gladding-VW Papers.

25. MVW to Mahan, 7 Feb. 1967, file 255, Gladding-VW Papers; *New York Times,* obit., 10 Sept. 1967; *Framingham News,* 20 Sept. 1967.

26. Commonwealth of Massachusetts, Certificate of Death lists cause of death as "chronic obstructive pulmonary disease."

27. Sermon by the Rev. Mason Wilson, Rector, "Memorial Eucharist for Miriam Van Waters," 20 Jan. 1974, St. Andrews Church, Framingham, tape recording, file 203at, Gladding-VW Papers.

28. Program of service in file 199, Gladding-VW Papers; *Boston Globe* 20 Jan. and 21 Jan. 1974; *New York Times,* 19 Jan. 1974.

29. Ann Bartholomew, "Through the Keyhole," c. 1955, file 102; Ann Bartholomew [Mrs. D. L.] Harrison to MVW, 16 Jan. 1955, 13 April 1956, 5 June 1967, file 100; Barbara Van Waters [Strom] to MVW, 4 Feb. 1956, file 105.

30. Pollock to MVW, 17 Dec. 1965, file 153.

31. Charles K. Cummings to MVW, 22 Nov. 1959, file 151.

32. Gray to MVW, 19 July 1971, file 228.

33. Until recently, historians of women's reform have concentrated largely on the century between the second great awakening, in the 1820s, and the New Deal, in the 1930s. On the twentieth century, see Jacquelyn Dowd Hall, *Revolt against Chivalry: Jessie Daniel Ames and the Women's Campaign against Lynching* (New York: Columbia University Press, 1979); Lynn, *Progressive Women;* David J. Garrow, ed., *The Montgomery Bus Boycott and the Women Who Started It: The Memoir of Jo Ann Gibson Robinson* (Knoxville: University of Tennessee Press, 1987); Ann Firor Scott, *Natural Allies: Women's Associations in American History* (Urbana: University of Illinois Press, 1993); Amy Swerdlow, *Women Strike for Peace: Traditional Motherhood and Radical Politics in the 1960s* (Chicago: University of Chicago Press, 1993); Harriet Hyman Alonso, "Mayhem and Moderation: Women Peace Activists during the McCarthy Era," 128–50, and Margaret Rose, "Gender and Civic Activism in Mexican American Barrios in California," 177–200, in Joanne Meyerowitz, ed., *Not June Cleaver: Women and Gender in Postwar America, 1945–1960* (Philadelphia: Temple University Press, 1994); and Linda Gordon, *Pitied but Not Entitled: Single Mothers and the History of Welfare, 1890–1935* (New York: Free Press, 1994).

34. Elaine Tyler May, *Homeward Bound: American Families in the Cold War Era* (New York: Basic Books, 1988); Lynn, *Progressive Women;*

Swerdlow, *Women Strike for Peace;* Ricki Solinger, *Wake Up Little Susie: Single Pregnancy and Race before Roe v. Wade* (New York: Routledge, 1992); Donna Penn, "The Sexualized Woman: The Lesbian, the Prostitute, and the Containment of Female Sexuality in Postwar America," 358–81 in Meyerowitz, *Not June Cleaver.*

INDEX

Note: The abbreviation MVW is used for Miriam Van Waters.